Great Britain. Royal Commission Taxation.

Local government and taxation of towns : Ireland: part II; Belfast, Trim and Wicklow

Great Britain. Royal Commission Taxation.

Local government and taxation of towns : Ireland: part II; Belfast, Trim and Wicklow

ISBN/EAN: 9783741104558

Manufactured in Europe, USA, Canada, Australia, Japa

Cover: Foto ©ninafisch / pixelio.de

Manufactured and distributed by brebook publishing software (www.brebook.com)

Great Britain. Royal Commission Taxation.

Local government and taxation of towns : Ireland: part II; Belfast, Trim and Wicklow

LOCAL GOVERNMENT

AND

TAXATION OF TOWNS INQUIRY COMMISSION (IRELAND).

PART II.

REPORT AND EVIDENCE,

WITH

APPENDICES.

BELFAST, TRIM, AND WICKLOW.

Presented to both Houses of Parliament by Command of Her Majesty.

DUBLIN:
PRINTED BY ALEXANDER THOM, 87 & 88, ABBEY-STREET,
PRINTER TO THE QUEEN'S MOST EXCELLENT MAJESTY.
FOR HER MAJESTY'S STATIONERY OFFICE.

CONTENTS.

LIST OF WITNESSES.

BELFAST.

TRIM.

WICKLOW.

LOCAL GOVERNMENT AND TAXATION OF TOWNS INQUIRY COMMISSION (IRELAND).

SPECIAL GENERAL REPORTS

ON

BELFAST, TRIM, AND WICKLOW.

BELFAST.

The municipal borough of Belfast, which is one of those included in Schedule A of the 3 & 4 Vict., cap. 108, is governed by a Corporation consisting of ten aldermen and thirty councillors. The Mayor is elected by the Council from the general body.

The town is partly in the county of Antrim and partly in Down, and is divided into five wards, of which the names, valuation, and number of burgesses in each are as follows:—

Name of Ward	Valuation £	s.	d.	Number of Burgesses
No. 1. Dock Ward,	86,034	13	0	921
No. 2. St. Anne's Ward,	[illegible]	5	0	1,136
No. 3. Smithfield „	72,312	0	0	460
No. 4. St. George's „	106,520	15	0	875
No. 5. Cromac „	157,981	0	0	1,398
	£508,610	15	0	[illegible]

The population, which by the census of 1861 was 121,602, had risen in 1871 to 174,412, and is now approximately estimated at 210,000. The valuation of the borough was, on the 1st of July, 1862, £278,807, and has now risen to £508,670, thus showing an increase of nearly £230,000 in fifteen years, during which time, we were told by the borough surveyor, the building of new houses had been proceeding at the rate of about 1,000 per annum.

The Corporation of Belfast was not at the time of the report of the Irish Municipal Commissioners in 1835 possessed of any property.

Their real property consists of the cemetery, and of two public parks, known as "the Ormeau" and "the Falls" parks—the latter of which was formed out of a portion of the ground originally purchased for the cemetery; of the Town Hall, and the public markets; and of the gas works and premises acquired by the Corporation under the Local Act in 1874.

The rapid growth of trade and manufactures, and the increase of property and population since 1840, have, from time to time, rendered special legislation necessary in Belfast; and we proceed to notice briefly the principal local Acts now in force.

By the Act of 8 & 9 Vict., cap. 142, entitled "an Act for the Improvement of the Borough of Belfast," the Corporation were authorized to borrow sums not exceeding £150,000 upon the security of the rates, with powers for re-borrowing. Of this £150,000, £100,000 was to be applied to the making of new and the widening of old streets, and the remaining £50,000 for other purposes, including the purchase of markets.

By section 220 the Corporation were empowered to appoint a borough police force, but this provision was repealed by the 28 & 29 Vict., cap. 70, "the Constabulary (Ireland) Amendment Act, 1865."

The 248th section fixed the rate which the Corporation were empowered to levy for the purposes of the Improvement Act, at 1s. 6d. in the pound upon tenements of which the annual value should not exceed £20; at 3s. in the pound upon those above £20 and not exceeding £80; and at 4s. 6d. in the pound above £80. This rate, though really an improvement rate, is known, and hereinafter referred to, as the police rate.

By a subsequent Act (the Belfast Borough Extension Act of 1853) hereinafter referred to, the 4s. 6d. rate was repealed, and a 3s. rate substituted as the maximum.

We do not consider it necessary to refer further in detail to the provisions of this statute, which contains 191 sections, and which conferred on the Corporation very ample powers for the general government and improvement of the town, the purchasing of property, the making of streets, and providing markets. But many of its provisions relating to the construction of drains and sewers, and the building clauses generally, have been subsequently amended or repealed by the "County Antrim and Belfast Borough Act" of 1865, or by the "Provisional Order Act" of 1878.

In 1846, in addition to the borrowing powers conferred by the Act of 1845, the Corporation obtained power under the 9 & 10 Vict., cap. 294, to borrow a further £30,000 for gas purposes, upon the security of the rates authorized by the Act of 1845, and of the rents to be received for gas, which by this Act (9 & 10 Vict., cap. 291) they were empowered to manufacture and to supply to private consumers.

The Corporation did borrow, as will be seen hereafter, this £30,000 upon the security of the rates, but did not apply any part of it to the purposes authorized by the Act, and they did not acquire gas works until many years after.

In 1847 an Act "for the further improvement of the Borough of Belfast," the 10 & 11 Vict., cap. 254, was passed.

This Act contains a recital that—

"The drainage of the borough would be considerably improved, and it would be a benefit to the inhabitants of the said borough, if a certain stream or watercourse called the Blackstaff river, which passes through the borough, were straightened, widened, deepened, embanked, and otherwise altered and improved; if certain weirs* on the said stream were lowered or removed, if the bridges and sewers over the same were enlarged; and if all other obstructions affecting the same were removed, and also if a new cut or watercourse (therein described) were made."

Full powers were accordingly given to the Corporation by this Act (sections 15–25) for these purposes, and to purchase a certain mill called "the Cromac paper mill," then supplied from the Blackstaff river, and all mill-dams and weirs causing obstructions to drainage, the cost of such purchases to be defrayed out of moneys raised under the Act of 1845.

By the 25th section the Corporation were empowered to order lands, yards, and other premises to be drained at the expense of the owners, who were made liable to a penalty of £1 a day for every day such necessary works were left undone after expiration of the time specified in the order.

By the 27th section the purchase by the Corporation of certain markets and market rights under the Act of 1845, was confirmed, and the Act contained other provisions, to which we do not deem it here necessary to refer.

The required improvements of the Blackstaff river not having been made, further legislation was considered necessary, and three years afterwards "the Belfast Improvement Act, 1850," 13 & 14 Vict., cap. 103, was passed. This Act recites that—

"It is necessary that provision should be made for the speedy removal of certain nuisances, and for the prevention of contagious and epidemic diseases within the borough, and it is expedient that provision should be made for the removal of the Blackstaff nuisance within two years from the passing of this Act, and for such purpose that power should be granted to the Council of the borough to borrow a sum not exceeding £15,000, to be exclusively applied to the abatement of the said nuisance in the manner provided by the said third recited Act"—

(the Act of 1847); and after reciting in the 3rd section the provisions of the Act of 1847 in relation to the Blackstaff river, the Council are required, subject to the provisions of the Lands Clauses Consolidation Acts, to enter upon certain houses and lands specified in schedule B of the Act of 1847, and if necessary to purchase the same, or any of them that might be required for the purposes of that Act, in the manner thereby required, so that the same shall be completed within two years from the passing of this Act, provided that the consent of the owners, lessees, and occupiers be first obtained.

The 6th section directs that arrangements shall be made under the joint direction of the surveyor of the borough, and the engineer of the port and harbour, subject if necessary to reference to the engineer of the Admiralty, or some other competent engineer, for the removal of the deposit at the Blackstaff weir; and by the 7th and follow-

* Not fishing weirs, but weirs to accumulate the water for the use of the mills on this stream.

ing sections the Town Council are empowered, for the more speedy removal of any nuisance arising from the stream or watercourse called the "Pound Burn,"* upon receipt of a notice complaining of it as a nuisance, to cause examination to be made of the same, and if it appear that the nuisance exists, to summon the owner before two justices who are empowered to order abatement of the nuisance, and to impose a penalty for neglect, and if the order be not complied with the Council shall remedy the nuisance at the expense of the owners.

Summary powers for the abatement of other nuisances, and to make and enforce by-laws, are given to the Corporation by other sections of this Act.

By section 26 the Corporation are empowered to borrow £15,000 upon security of the rates, rents, and other moneys authorised to be levied under the preceding Acts, and by section 27 it is enacted that the £15,000 shall be exclusively applicable to the abatement of the Blackstaff nuisance, and that a separate account shall be kept of it, under the name of the "Blackstaff Improvement Fund."

This £15,000 has never been raised nor set apart for this purpose, the reasons assigned by the town solicitor, Mr. Black, being, that it was wholly insufficient for the purposes contemplated by this and the preceding Act of 1847, and that the consent of the owners, lessees, and occupiers, to the purchases required for the contemplated improvements could not be obtained as required by the Act.

In 1853 "the Belfast Borough Extension Act" (16 & 17 Vict., cap. 114), was passed, by which the borough boundaries were extended to their present limits, and the 4s. 6d. scale of rating under the Act of 1845 was abolished, and a limit of 8s. substituted, as already noticed.

The Corporation, in the exercise of the powers conferred on them by the Acts of 1845 and 1846, borrowed on mortgages authorised in those Acts, in all £200,000, of which £50,000 borrowed under the Act of 1846 was applicable to the purchase of gas works only.

In consequence, however, of the Corporation not having applied this £50,000 to the purpose for which it was so limited, but having expended it, with other moneys exceeding £84,000, in the purchase of premises for public markets, and otherwise improving the town, a Chancery suit was instituted in 1855 against the Corporation, at the instance of Mr. John Rea, an attorney in Belfast, and protracted litigation ensued. In 1858 a Royal Commission, appointed to inquire into the several matters in dispute, recommended an arrangement to be come to, in pursuance of which, on the 13th June, 1860, all matters in difference between the parties were referred to the arbitration of Messrs. William Bryden and Richard Henry Wyatt, parliamentary agents, subject to the approval of the Right Honorable Edward Cardwell as umpire. This arbitration resulted in an award, dated 5th December, 1863, which was confirmed and carried out by the "Belfast Award Act, 1864" (27 and 28 Vict., cap. 198). By this Act it was declared that the said sum of £200,000, and also the sum of £84,640 0s. 11d. therein mentioned, should be deemed to have been applicable to all or any of the purposes of the Acts of 1845–47, and the application of these moneys and all purchases by the Corporation were thereby confirmed. It also conferred powers to borrow and pay off existing mortgages, and mortgages created under this Act, and contained provisions regulating the priority of such mortgages. It authorised the Corporation to sell their surplus lands within ten years, with the consent of the Lords of the Treasury, and to apply the net proceeds in payment or reduction of certain mortgages therein specified, and after that in aid of the sinking fund required by the Act of 1845; and in a subsequent section (the 15th) it directed a sinking fund to be provided out of the rates directed to be raised under the authority of this Act and the Acts of 1845 and 1853, which by the preceding section (the 14th), were fixed at 1s. 8d. in the pound upon premises the annual value of which should not exceed £20, and at 3s. 4d. in the pound upon premises of the annual value of £20 and upwards. The remaining clauses direct that no moneys of the Corporation shall be applied in payment of the costs of the Relator (Mr. John Rea), or the special Respondents in the Chancery suit, that the pending Chancery suit be stayed, and that the costs of the said arbitration and umpirage be paid, and a sum not exceeding £2,000 in respect of the expenses of this Act.

It will be seen that by the 14th section just referred to, the incidence of taxation under the previous Acts of 1845 and 1853 is altered, the rate to which property not exceeding £20 annual value is liable being raised thereby from 1s. 6d. to 1s. 8d. in the pound, and this is still felt as a great grievance by the poorer class of ratepayers, and was one of the grounds of opposition to the Bill which resulted in this Act, and which

* "The Pound Burn" is a stream or watercourse running into the Blackstaff river, respecting which, and the pollution arising therefrom, a great deal of evidence was given, and still more sought to be given, before us in the course of the inquiry.

was the subject of a very bitter contest before a Select Committee of the House of Commons, of which the late Mr. Milnes Gaskell was chairman, in the session of 1864. Mr. A. J. M'Kenna, Mr. J. F. Ferguson, Mr. H. Nelson Smith, and Mr. John Rea, were heard as petitioners against the Bill; and upon the occasion of our inquiry at Belfast, the Blue Book containing the minutes of evidence taken before the Select Committee was tendered and received by us in evidence.

It appears from these minutes that attempts were made while the Bill was before the Select Committee to bring about an arrangement by which it should be allowed to pass; and we here deem it sufficient to refer to the letter of Mr. Baker, parliamentary agent for Mr. Ferguson, one of the petitioners against the Bill, of 9th May, 1864, and the answer of Mr. Dyson, the agent for the promoters, of 12th May, 1864, which were read before the Committee, and which summarize the grounds of objection to the Award Bill, and the remedies suggested.

At the meeting of the Select Committee on the 13th May it was—

"Resolved, That the Committee is unanimously of opinion that a public Bill is necessary to regulate the municipal affairs of Belfast, and they would be glad to know whether such a proposal would meet with general concurrence."

Counsel for the promoters stated that they would entirely accede to the principles of a public Bill, provided it did not interfere with the integrity of Mr. Cardwell's award.

After some discussion between the parties and their advisers, the Chairman of the Committee announced that—

"The Committee have unanimously resolved that the preamble of the Bill is proved."

They determined further to intimate—

"That they understood that the parties on both sides had agreed to refer the provisions of a public Bill to arbitration."

The Chairman further stated that—

"The Committee were aware that a distinct understanding existed that a public Bill should be introduced during the present session. If no such Bill were introduced the petitioners would have a very strong ground of opposition before the other House."

At a meeting of the Select Committee on the 26th May, 1864, the names of referees to whom the provisions of a public Bill were to be referred were mentioned by counsel for the promoters as agreed upon.

Notwithstanding the agreement arrived at before the Select Committee, no public Bill was brought in to remedy the evils complained of.

The Act of 1865 (28 & 29 Vict., cap. 133) entitled the "County Antrim and Belfast Borough Act," separated the portion of the borough in the county Antrim from that county for fiscal purposes, abolished the county cess within that portion of the borough, and transferred the duty of repairing streets, roadways, and footpaths therein, to the Corporation.

But the 6th section of this Act continues the liability of the borough to contribute to the payment of certain general county purposes, the subjects of which are enumerated in that section, and it is provided by subsequent sections that the amount of contribution shall be settled periodically by Commissioners appointed under the Act for the purpose.

By sect. 25 the Corporation are empowered to entertain applications for compensation for malicious injuries to persons or property, and to award compensation out of the general purposes rate and the malicious injuries rate, thereby authorized to be levied; and secs. 51 and 52 authorize the levying of a general purposes rate not exceeding 2s. in the pound within the lighted and watched districts, and 1s. 6d. in the pound upon all other rateable property within the borough.

The Act then provides for the application of such rates; and the subsequent provisions (following the 57th section) extend to the entire borough, including that part which is in the county of Down.

These relate chiefly to the drainage, sewerage, and improvement of the town, and confer powers to form and alter separate drainage districts, to levy special sewer rates, and to close streets not properly formed or completed, to order the widening, sewering, paving, &c., of streets either wholly or in part by owners, and to insist on general building regulations to the satisfaction of the borough surveyor; and by sections 100 and 101, new street expenses and other required works are made recoverable from owners.

The next Act was "The Belfast Burial Ground Act (1866)," by which the Corporation were empowered to purchase by contract, or compulsorily, ground for a public cemetery, and to levy a borough rate, and to borrow upon the security thereof sums not exceeding £25,000, to be paid off by annual instalments. This has been done, and the amount now outstanding is reduced to £9,200.

Then followed in 1868 the "Belfast Borough Act" (31 & 32 Vict., cap. 117), by which the powers of the Grand Jury of the county of Down to levy county cess within the limits of the borough were determined, and the duties of repairing the streets, roads, bridges, &c., were transferred to the Corporation; but (as in the Act of 1865) the borough was not exempted from contribution towards certain "general county purposes" which are defined in sections 6, 9, and 10. By section 15 that portion of the borough situate in the county of Down may be included in any general purposes rate under the "County Antrim and Belfast Borough Act (1865)," and the provisions of the last named Act as to compensation for malicious injuries are by sections 17 and 18 extended and made applicable to the entire borough. By section 20 it is provided that the Recorder and magistrates shall commit all persons to the County Antrim Gaol, and by section 21 all appeals from the Recorder are directed to be brought before the Judge of Assize for the county of Antrim, and not for the county of Down.

Certain sections of the Act of 1865 are then amended by this Act, and by section 33 the Corporation are to put in force in the portions of the borough in the county of Down the sewerage provisions of the former Act; and by section 29 the sum of £6,000 is to be applied within three years from the passing of the Act, either as a contribution towards the expenses of widening, improving, sewering, and completing the streets and roads in the townlands of Ballymacarrett and Ballynafeigh under the 78th section of the Act of 1865, or, at the discretion of the Corporation, in the permanent paving of such streets and roads.

By section 30 the Corporation are empowered, upon certain terms, to close a certain foot passage between Donegall-street and North-street at the rear of the Belfast Bank, and section 31 provides that all the borough rates which the Corporation are empowered under any Act to levy shall be henceforth imposed and collected as one rate.

In 1873 the Corporation took advantage of the Local Government (Ireland) Acts of 1871 and 1872, and obtained a provisional order (confirmed in that session of Parliament by the 36 & 37 Vict., cap. 199), under which they obtained compulsory powers of purchasing certain property for street improvements, the purchase-money to be repaid out of the police rate; to borrow on security of the general purposes rate £25,000 for paving of streets, and £15,000 for district drainage; to apply surplus lands at the cemetery for the purpose of a public park outside the borough, under the provisions of the Public Parks (Ireland) Acts, 1869 and 1872; and to apply the sum of £5,000, to be raised under the provisions of such last mentioned Acts, in part payment of £19,000 which had been up to that time raised under the Burial Grounds Acts. The provisional order also contained several amendments of the Act of 1845, and the amending Acts of 1850, 1865, and 1866.

The street improvements authorized under this order and the said "Provisional Order (Belfast) Confirmation Act, 1873," have been partly effected; several leading streets have been paved, and district sewers made and in progress, and the Falls Park has been formed out of the surplus grounds at the cemetery. Two loans of £3,500 each have been obtained from the Board of Works, at three and a half per cent. for district sewers.

In 1874 the "Belfast Corporation Gas Act" (37 & 38 Vict., cap. 125) was passed, by which the Corporation were empowered to purchase the Belfast Gas Works, then the property of the Belfast Gas Company, at the price of £386,550, and by sections 4 and 20 the entire property and assets of the company, with their debts and liabilities, were transferred to and vested in the Corporation.

Up to the 30th June, 1876, interest was to be paid on any portion of the purchase-money remaining unpaid, at four and a half per cent., and after that date at five per cent., and by section 9 the purchase-money and interest was made to be a charge upon the undertaking, and also upon the police rates; but as to the police rates, subject to the priority of existing mortgages.

The 24th section empowered the Corporation to borrow for any of the purposes of the Act sums not exceeding £500,000, to be secured by mortgages of the gas undertaking and revenue, and of the police rates, but the interest upon all moneys borrowed is made primarily payable out of the gas revenue (section 33), and all payments out of the police rate for the purpose of making good any temporary deficiency are by section 34 to be recouped from the gas revenue.

By section 47 the Corporation are directed to form, after two years, out of the gas revenue, and so far as may be needful out of the police rates, a sinking fund, at the rate of £1 per cent. upon the outstanding debt, for its gradual liquidation.

The 49th section gives power to charge the police rates, and credit the gas account yearly, with such sums as the Corporation shall think reasonable for the lighting of the town, the price of gas for this purpose to be fixed as near as can be at the same sum per

Provisional Order (Belfast) Confirmation Act, 1873.

The Belfast Corporation Gas Act, 1874.

1,000 cubic feet as the lowest price charged for the time to private consumers, together with the cost of lighting and maintaining the lamps.

A committee was to be appointed, *vide* section 31, to execute the purposes of the Act, and it is provided by section 39 that in any year in which the average price charged for gas shall not exceed 3s. 9*d*. per 1,000 cubic feet, the surplus profits may be applied by the Corporation to public purposes.

The Corporation went into possession of the gasworks on the 30th June, 1874, and have ever since manufactured gas for the public lighting of the town and the supply of private consumers. They have borrowed under the powers of the Act £468,754 on debentures, and £3,245 14s. 11*d*. on annuities, of which £459,989 11s. 4*d*., bearing interest principally at four and a half per cent., remains unpaid. The abstracts of the gasworks' accounts for the year ending the 30th June, 1876, audited by the Local Government Auditor, will be found printed in the Appendix (No. 3).

The cost of the gas for lighting the public lamps for the year ending the 30th June, 1875, was £7,044 2s. 5*d*.

The net profit on that year's working, according to the chairman's (Sir John Savage's) report of 26th August, 1875, confirmed by that of the Local Government Auditor in October, 1875, amounted to £11,671 6s. 1*d*., and the net profit of the following twelve months, ended the 30th of June last, was £7,949 9s. 2*d*., as certified by the Local Government Auditor; but it should be remarked that no rest fund appears to have been set apart for depreciation of plant and renewal of mains, and other necessary works not usually charged to revenue account.

By the 220th section of the Belfast Improvement Act, 1845, the Corporation of Belfast were, as we have already seen, empowered to appoint a local municipal police force. Such a force was appointed, but party feeling, which has always run high in Belfast, led to party fights and riots between lower classes of the Orange or Protestant party on the one side, and the Catholic party on the other, which became of annual and often more frequent occurrence, and the police appointed by the Corporation having been found insufficient for the preservation of the peace of the town, in November, 1864, Commissioners were appointed under the warrant of the Lords Justices of Ireland to hold an inquiry at Belfast, and to report upon "the existing local arrangements for the preservation of the peace of that borough, the magisterial jurisdiction exercised within it, and the amount, constitution, and efficiency of the police force usually available there, and other matters relating thereto." The Commissioners made their report on the 8th March, 1865, and in that session of Parliament "the Constabulary (Ireland) Amendment Act, 1865" (28 & 29 Vic., c. 70), was passed. This Act, after reciting the above mentioned commission, &c., and that "it is expedient to provide for the more effectual preservation of the peace of the borough, and to alter the distribution of the constabulary force in Ireland," enacts that the then police force in Belfast shall cease to exist, and that all their powers and duties shall devolve upon and be discharged by the constabulary, the number of whom for Belfast is fixed at not less than 130 constables and sub-constables.

By section 4 the Lord Lieutenant is authorised to add to this constabulary force allotted to Belfast any number of men not exceeding 320, on payment of one half of the cost out of the town rates, and such additional number of men, together with the 130 before mentioned, are to constitute the ordinary constabulary force of the town.

Section 5 provides for the levying of the necessary rate for the purpose. Section 6 enacts that the officers of the constabulary force of Belfast shall consist of one inspector and two or more sub-inspectors. The inspector to be paid £400 a year out of the rates by the Town Council.

Section 9 enacts that the Inspector-General of Constabulary shall fix the number of men, not exceeding 150, who are to act as a night watch, for each of whom there shall be charged 6*d*. per day, to be paid by the Town Council of Belfast out of the rates.

At the time of our inquiry the police force, including extra police, in Belfast consisted of 640 men, instead of 450, the Inspector-General, upon a memorial from some of the magistrates, having thought it necessary some time before to send down an additional force, but none of these extra men are free of charge upon the local rates, and it was represented to us as a hardship that they were now paying one moiety of the cost upon a larger proportion of the whole force than was contemplated by the Act of 1865. A representation to that effect had been made to the Lord Lieutenant, with a request that the proportion free of charge should be increased, when the Corporation were informed that the time for revising the distribution of the constabulary force (which can, it seems, only be done under the existing Acts once in five years) would not arrive until the 1st of July next, when their claim would be considered.

For the year ending the 31st March, 1876, the entire cost of the constabulary charged upon the town rates amounted to no less than £16,281 14s. 2*d*., of which

£15,160 15s. 11d. was paid out of the police fund, and £1,082 18s. 3d. out of the general purposes fund. Belfast.

The principle upon which the cost was thus apportioned between these two funds was explained by Mr. Samuel Black, the town solicitor, who, throughout, rendered us most valuable assistance during the inquiry, and indeed we feel it only due to Mr. Woods, and the other officers of the Corporation, to remark upon the admirably clear and accurate manner in which the whole of the voluminous accounts of this Corporation are kept, and were, to the minutest detail, presented for our examination. Mr. S. Black, Ev. 145, 667.

The finances of the Corporation are in a satisfactory state. The sinking funds prescribed by the various Acts under which loans have been effected have been regularly set apart, and from this source, and the proceeds of sales of ground rents and surplus lands, a reduction of nearly one-half (amounting to £194,687 14s. 8d.) has been effected upon the total capital debt, viz. £392,116 5s. 8d. (exclusive of that for the gasworks), which has been borrowed from time to time during the last thirty years. Thus the primary mortgages contracted under the Act of 1845, which, as we have already seen in noticing the Award Act of 1864, amounted to £200,000, have been reduced to £112,245, and the secondary mortgages which, with the addition of the capitalized interest under the said Act of 1864, amounted to £119,081 12s. 8d., are now reduced to £33,000, no less than £68,753 4s. 7d. having been applied to the extinction of the latter debt from the sales of ground rents and surplus lands. There was, moreover, at the time of our inquiry a sum of about £4,000 set aside to partly meet this remaining debt, which had been invested in the funds until some of the remaining mortgages should come to maturity. Mr. J. Charters, Ev. 744, 833. Ev. 563, 843.

The capital debt upon the police rate, upon which these mortgages are all charged, has been thus reduced to £145,245. A statement at the foot of the list of mortgages (Appendix 4) shows the application of the loans borrowed upon the security of this rate.

The original loan of £21,000 under the Burial Act of 1866, has been reduced to £13,200, of which £9,200 only remains charged to the burial fund, £4,000 having been transferred to the public parks account upon security of the borough and parks rate under the Public Parks Act of 1869. Ev. 291-2.

Upwards of £26,000 has been borrowed for district sewers, which is charged on the general purposes rate, and on the several district sewers rates in the proportion set out in the list of the several loans (Appendix 4), and a further sum of £17,600, borrowed for permanent paving of the streets, is also a charge on the general purposes rate under the Provisional Order Confirmation Act of 1878, which (*vide* section 3) empowered the Corporation to borrow £25,000 for this purpose on the security of that rate. Ev. 704-821. Ev. 290.

Of these last named recent loans, amounting together to £43,679, £4,694 9s. has been already paid off, leaving £38,983 11s. still due, of which £27,670 15s. 6d. is a charge upon the general purposes rate, and £11,312 15s. 6d. upon the several district sewers rates. The whole outstanding mortgage debt, exclusive of the gasworks, has been, it will be seen, reduced to £197,428 11s. Ev. 303.

The annual accounts are made up under four principal heads—the Police Fund, the General Purposes Fund, the Borough Fund, and the Burial Fund—and a separate account is kept for the gas, which has been already sufficiently noticed when treating of the Act under which the Corporation gasworks were acquired; but it may be convenient here to note that there remained in the hands of the treasurer to the credit of this account, when the accounts were closed for the last audit on the 30th of June last, a balance of £21,639 12s., and that out of a gas rental of £79,929 10s. 2d., only £799 1s. 7d. then remained in arrear, which amount had been further reduced to £515 15s. 8d. at the date of the audit in September last. The price of gas, which was last year reduced from 4s. 6d. to 4s. 2d. per 1,000 cubic feet, has been since further reduced to 3s. 11d. Mr. H. Mc. Woods, Ev. 387-393.

The abstracts of the four first-named accounts for the year last audited will be found in the Appendix (Appendix 5), and show the following balances due to and from the Treasurer upon the respective accounts in the Belfast Bank:— Mr. Woods, Ev. 648, 662.

Balances against the Corporation, including Cheques issued but not presented.	£	s.	d.	*Balances in favour of the Corporation.*	£	s.	d.
Police Fund,	2,086	11	9	Borough Fund,	4,748	13	8
General Purposes Fund,	4,329	8	6	Burial Fund,	1,211	19	9
	6,416	0	3	Malicious Injuries Account (on General Purposes Fund),	936	7	11
Net balance in favour of the Corporation,	475	19	11				
	6,892	0	2		6,892	0	2

Thus, notwithstanding the large overdrafts, to which attention was called by us, upon the General Purposes and Police Fund Accounts, there was a small net balance to the credit of the Corporation, and the balance in the cashier's hands for current expenses, wages, &c., further amounted at the same time to £112 1s. 8d.

The "Malicious Injuries" Account requires a brief explanation. Upon that fund, which arises under the provisions of the Act of 1865 (the County Antrim and Belfast Borough Act), there is an increasing balance in hand, owing to the calls upon it having been less during the last few years than the bank interest upon the balance remaining in hand from the rate laid to meet the heavy claims after the Belfast riots in 1872. These claims amounted to about £14,000, but were reduced to £8,577 11s. 8d. To meet this the Corporation had, for the first time, to strike a special rate of 2d. in the pound, being only allowed under the Act of 1865 to set apart £1,000 out of the general purposes rate for this object.

We have already commented on the largest item of charge upon the police rate, viz., that for the Constabulary. The heaviest charge on the general purposes rate is that for County Antrim Grand Jury on general purposes account, viz., £16,817 13s., and this likewise is deserving of some attention.

The contributions to the County Antrim Grand Jury, which are revised every five years, are determined by arbitration in the manner prescribed by the Act of 1865 (the County Antrim and Belfast Borough Act), and a list of these, from 1865 to 1875, was handed to us by Mr. Black, and will be found set out in the Appendix to this Report (Appendix 6), from which it will be seen that, from the year 1872, when the last award was made under the Act, they have increased at the average rate of about £2,400 per annum. This large increase has been mainly caused by the cost of maintenance of the prisoners in gaol and the payments to industrial schools and reformatories; and it was represented to us as a great grievance that the borough of Belfast should actually pay 82 per cent. of the cost of the prisoners for the entire county, and yet have no voice whatever in the expenditure, the Corporation having no representative either on the Grand Jury or on the Board of Superintendence of the Gaol. The charge is, it seems, based upon the number of committals, quite irrespective of the time for which the prisoner is committed; and we were told that the arbitrators themselves admitted the hardship of the case, but felt they had no power to frame their award otherwise.

The same grievance does not exist in respect of the contributions to the County Down Grand Jury, as, although contributing to its maintenance, no prisoners are sent from the borough to the gaol of the county. But a small portion of the borough is in county Down, and the annual contributions to that Grand Jury for all purposes average only about £700 a year.

A statement prepared and handed in by Mr. Black, showing the particulars of all the rates levied in 1875, the heads of the principal objects to which they were applied, the percentage collected, and the maximum taxing powers under the several local Acts authorizing these rates, will be found in the Appendix (Appendix 13), and is confirmatory of Mr. Black's evidence as to the satisfactory manner in which the rates are collected by the five rate collectors, over 90 per cent. of all rates having been collected in that year; and after allowing the statutable 25 per cent. discount on all ratings of £8 and under for rates paid within one month, and for vacancies, &c., only 1·35 per cent. remained uncollected at the close of 1875.

This is the best practical answer to the suggestions, that to some extent (though not, it is admitted on all hands, to so great an extent as formerly) the system still prevails in Belfast of delaying the collection of the municipal rates with a view to the disfranchisement of voters in the interest of the Conservative majority in the Town Council.

These collectors are required to lodge daily in the bank the amounts collected by them, and their books and counterfoils are carefully checked and compared with the bank book by Mr. Woods, the accountant, every day, and are subsequently examined by the audit and finance committees.

The public markets, which are twelve in number, and which, in round figures, have cost about £100,000, are apparently well managed, and have been a considerable pecuniary success. The net profit upon them for the year 1875 was £5,325 10s., the gross receipts having been £9,223 7s. 5d., and the outgoings, including rent, rates, and taxes, salaries, wages, and some small repairs and alterations, £3,897 17s. 5d., of which the salaries and wages amounted to over £1,800. In reduction, too, of their original cost, considerable sums have been realized from the sale of surplus ground, which, as we have already seen, have been applied to the partial extinction of the mortgages under the Acts of 1846 and 1864.

Net profits have also been realized of £84 16s. 11d. from the weights and measures adjusting account, and of £179 14s. 3d. from the public slaughter-house, after payment of all wages, repairs, alterations, and other outgoings connected therewith.

The fines imposed at petty sessions in 1875 amounted to no less a sum than £2,168 3s. 6d., and with the small sum of £15 2s. arising from fines on carmen, and some arrears of petty sessional fines from the previous year, reached the large total to the credit of the police fund of £2,896 19s. 2d., after deducting £166 17s. 6d. for stamps, summonses, &c.

Licenses to car-drivers and owners of lodging-houses and slaughter-houses, &c., further produced £263 6s. to the credit of the same fund.

The large sum of £8,079 18s. 3d. appears to the credit of the general purposes account as realized from the sale of manure and street and road scrapings; and on the other side of that account it will be seen that the "scavenging" cost £10,504 17s. 3d. Under the heads of street repairs, permanent paving, and special, estimated, and ordered works, there was expended and charged to the general purposes rate in 1875 £24,257 6s. 2d.; but against this there was received from owners and sundry persons in return for such works, and upon deposit account under the head of "permits," &c., £7,279 19s. 4d. This street expenditure is exclusive of the "Ballymacarrett account," which represents the outlay on the portion of the town which lies in county Down, and which amounted to £3,093 3s. 1d. Neither does it include the purchase of materials on store yard account, amounting to £17,137 6s. 3d., nor any portion of the expenditure on sewers, &c., in the several drainage districts of the borough, which make up a further total of nearly £15,000 more.

The only rates levied to the full amount authorized by the Local Acts were the general purposes rate of 2s. in the pound within the lighted and watched district, and 16d. in the pound beyond that limit; and the borough rate of 3d. in the pound; the whole amount of rates levied in the year reaching the total of £96,785 1s. 8d., and £91,234 6s. 1d. being brought into account as received from rates within that period.

Complaint was made of the municipal taxation as excessive in comparison with towns in England and Scotland; but Mr. James Kennedy, one of the gentlemen who raised the objection, had scarcely taken into consideration the great disproportion which exists in Ireland, and notably in Belfast, between the Government valuation and the letting value. Some striking instances of this were given by Mr. Black, the town solicitor, who, before we left Belfast, handed us a paper (Appendix 11), which he requested us to bring under the notice of the Select Committee of the House of Commons, containing illustrations of the discrepancies between the valuation and the letting value of houses and warehouses in some of the principal streets. "In some parts of the town," he said, "houses are not valued at more than one-third of their letting value, and in other parts the valuation is not more than one-third or one-fourth below the letting value," and even houses erected in recent years are, it seems, not unfrequently valued at about 50 per cent. below their letting value. The difficulties attendant upon obtaining a revaluation here were very clearly pointed out by him. Under the Valuation Acts it appears to be necessary not only that the application for a revaluation should come from the Grand Jury, but that a revaluation, if made at all, should be over the entire county, barony, or union. The Grand Jury of county Down on being applied to, refused consequently to make any application, and the reply of the Grand Jury of the county of Antrim rendered them no further assistance, for they said, "We will forward your application, and confine it to that portion of the borough within the county Antrim," and as this forms a portion only of the barony and of the union, they were precluded from obtaining any revaluation.

One class of expenditure in Belfast which struck us in the first instance as unusually large, was the annual charge for salaries and wages, especially in the Surveyor's department, where it amounts to £1,382 5s. 10d., but the work in this department is very great, and it is certainly well done, and no more effective head of such a department could well be found than Mr. Montgomery, the borough surveyor, who well earns his present salary of £650, which is the highest paid to any officer of the Corporation. The total charge for salaries is £6,893 10s., a list of which will be found in the Appendix (Appendix 2), but this includes £500 a year to the Recorder, and £900 a year to the Clerk of the Peace, and the more we saw of the generally efficient manner in which the business of the several departments was transacted, the less we felt disposed to cavil at the expenditure under this head. Indeed Mr. Kennedy himself did not consider the salaries excessive for a town of this magnitude.

The Mayor of Belfast at present receives no salary, nor has he ever done so, except for some six years between 1865 and 1871, when he received £1,000 a year. It was suggested by Mr. Rea—who sought to attribute personal motives to every member of the Council with whom he had been engaged in litigation, and who finally so abused the privilege we had accorded him of putting questions through the Chairman, as to necessitate his removal from the Court—that this salary was first voted in 1865 to *[illegible]* *Mr. Mullan, Ev. [illegible]. Mr. Henderson, Ev. [illegible].*

indemnify the late Mr. Lytle, the then Mayor, and at least two succeeding Mayors for their share in the costs of the Chancery suit in which Mr. Rea was the relator, but this was indignantly denied by Mr. Mullan, the senior Alderman, and by Mr. Henderson, a Town Councillor, and no evidence was adduced to confirm Mr. Rea's insinuation, nor to lead us to doubt the substantial accuracy of the account given by Alderman Mullan of the circumstances under which the salary was first granted and subsequently discontinued.

Comparing the rates levied here for municipal purposes with those at Cork and Limerick, the two largest municipal boroughs upon which we have hitherto reported, it will be found that Belfast contrasts very favourably with both; the "improvement" and "general purposes" rates levied in those towns for the corresponding year (1875), being at the rate of 5s. 6d. in the pound in Cork, and 5s. 11½d. in Limerick, while at Belfast the same rates amounted to but 4s. in the pound on the highest rated houses within the lighted and watched district, and to 3s. only on all below £20 rateable value.

Mr. M'Causland, Ev. [illegible]. Mr. Kennedy, Ev. [illegible].

If the borough and burial rates, and the highest district drainage rate in Belfast that of the Newtownards road district—be added to the above, they do not bring up the total of rates levied by the Town Council to quite 5s. 3d. in the pound in the highest rated portion of the borough; and outside the drainage districts the highest rates do not amount to more than 4s. 4½d., while it must further be taken into consideration that the Corporation of Belfast have not inherited from their predecessors any landed estates or ancient tolls or dues such as conduce largely to swell the revenues of Limerick, Cork, and the majority of old municipal boroughs in Ireland.

Water supply.

The water supply of Belfast is at present under the management of Water Commissioners, incorporated under the Belfast Water Act of 1870, for the purpose of supplying the town with water.

Mr. Black, Ev. [illegible].

Mr. Black, the Town Solicitor, having brought this fact under our notice, and advanced an opinion that some inconvenience, and, to a certain extent, a conflict of authority resulted from the water supply not being under the control of the Corporation, we thought it only fair to receive the explanation of the Water Commissioners on the matter, and the Chairman of the Water Commissioners, Mr. W. J. Scott, and Mr. Luke Macassey, their principal engineer, were consequently examined by us upon the points raised by Mr. Black, which resolved themselves principally into the question of the high price charged by the Commissioners to the Corporation for water for watering the streets, and the occasional deficiency of the water supply in the case of fires breaking out in the town. Mr. Black gave the officers of the Water Commissioners credit for being anxious to meet the views of the officers of the Corporation as far as possible, but he considered the system an inconvenient one, which gave the Commissioners power, without previous notice, to open the streets, and to examine and relay their mains, although by arrangement they pay the Corporation for repairs whenever they have interfered with the streets.

Mr. W. J. Scott, Ev. [illegible]. Mr. L. Macassey, Ev. [illegible].

Mr. Black, Ev. [illegible].

Upon the general question whether the water supply should be under the control of the Water Commissioners or the Corporation, on which Mr. Rea was desirous of being heard as their solicitor, we declined to enter, or to allow him to cross-examine the officers of the Corporation as he was urgently desirous of doing on this and many other points which arose in the course of our inquiry.

Mr. Biggar, Ev. [illegible].

The only other body between whom and the Corporation it was suggested that there could be any conflict of authority is the Harbour Board. Mr. Biggar, M.P., who came forward in the first instance as an old member, both of the Board of Water Commissioners and the Town Council, to give his opinion upon the action of the Water Commissioners, raised the point that a very material conflict had arisen between the Harbour Board and the Town Council with regard to the outlet for the sewage of Belfast; on the other hand Mr. Black, who also referred to this difference between the Corporation and the Harbour Board, stated that although the Corporation were only represented on the Board of Harbour Commissioners, as they are on the Water Board, by the Mayor who is *ex officio* a member of each Board, there was no conflict between the Harbour Board and the Corporation, and little or no inconvenience found to result from the existence of the former as a distinct body.

Mr. Black, Ev. [illegible].

General complaints.

The complaints against the administration of the rates and the municipal affairs by the Town Council were numerous, and occupied much of our time, involving as they did, several of serious nature, which required full explanation from the authorities; while others were of a frivolous and almost contemptible character.

Mr. R. Stewart, Ev. [illegible]. Mr. Dempsey, Ev. [illegible]. Mr. A. Black, Ev. [illegible].

An instance of the latter will be found in the charge brought against the Town Council by Mr. Stewart, and supported by Mr. Dempsey, of permitting Temperance League coffee stands to be erected in the streets to the obstruction of the highway, and to the injury of the publicans and lodging-house keepers. It turned out that there was but one such coffee stand in existence at the time of our inquiry, and as we passed it daily in the Police-square, on our way to the town hall, we are able to say positively that it gave rise to no obstruction.

The principal charges may be arranged under the following heads:—

1st. That a fair proportion of the rates is not expended for the benefit of the Roman Catholic inhabitants.

2nd. That several members of the improvement committee of the Town Council, who are engaged in the timber and building trades, exercise undue influence on that committee, in consequence of which the law is not strictly and uniformly carried out as laid down by the 75th section of the Act of 1865.

3rd. That the pollution of the Blackstaff River, which arises in the first instance from the action of the Corporation in introducing the town sewage into the "Pound Burn" and other tributary streams, is greatly increased by the mill-owners, who further contribute the sewage of their mills, and who, after using the water for condensing purposes, return it to the bed of the stream in a heated and far more offensive condition; and it is alleged that owing to the influence of these mill-owners, the Corporation have hitherto resisted all schemes for the purification of the Blackstaff by the diversion of this contaminated water from its course.

4th. That some of the officers of the Corporation, with the knowledge and approval of at least certain members of that body, interfere actively at the municipal elections in the interest of the Conservative majority of the Town Council.

Mr. Dinnen in making this charge broadly stated it in these terms:—"I believe the Corporation to be a huge political engine worked by the officials of the Corporation who are paid out of the rates of the town."

It will be seen that these charges all arise, more or less, from a feeling of dissatisfaction with the present composition of the Town Council, and although we have hitherto, in the inquiry intrusted to us, invariably refused to receive evidence relating to matters of politics or religion, and have endeavoured to eliminate all such from our consideration, it would be idle here to ignore the fact that these complaints proceeded almost exclusively from the Roman Catholic portion of the community, and from a certain party of Liberals among the Protestants and Presbyterians, who, in consequence of being almost unrepresented on the Town Council, were disposed to attribute to political or religious influences very many of the actions of that body in relation to municipal affairs.

From this point of view these parties were certainly desirous of making common cause before us against the Corporation. Mr. M'Erlean, a solicitor, applied to represent the Catholic party, and Mr. Rea, though applying in the first instance to represent the Water Commissioners, as their solicitor, appeared far more anxious to be heard as the representative of his own personal and political animosities. Mr. Dinnen, another solicitor, who gave evidence at considerable length, was, however, the main exponent of the complaints of the Liberal party. These gentlemen and others were all extremely desirous of going into the question of the franchise, and Mr. Rea also sought to re-open the past history of all the party fights for which Belfast is unhappily so notorious. Upon these matters we steadily and persistently declined to hear them, but we considered that we could not refrain from patiently investigating any matters of complaint which they were desirous of bringing before us bearing on the administration of the rates, and the conduct of the officers intrusted with their collection or expenditure, or those relating to the sanitary condition of the town.

The cemetery question, which falls under the first head of these complaints, has caused a considerable amount of ill-feeling in the minds of the Roman Catholic portion of the inhabitants. Under the Belfast Burial Ground Act of 1866 (29 and 30 Vic., c. 113), the Corporation were authorised to purchase certain lands therein mentioned for the purpose of a public cemetery for the use of the inhabitants of Belfast, and also to dispose of any surplus portion of such lands not required for the purposes of the cemetery. The ground they were so authorised to purchase comprised in all about 103 acres, and the Corporation set apart forty-five acres of this for a cemetery. This was divided into two portions; the larger, consisting of thirty acres, was allotted as a burying-ground for Protestants; and fifteen acres for that of Roman Catholics. A division was made between the two portions of ground, and it was arranged that a mortuary chapel should be erected in each. The Roman Catholic bishop applied to the Corporation to vest in him and his successors the sole and exclusive control over the Roman Catholic portion, and insisted that he should have the right from time to time to regulate and determine who should and who should not be interred in that burying-ground. He submitted certain propositions as to the conditions on which the ground should be set apart for the Roman Catholic inhabitants (vide Appendix 11), but the Corporation refused to accede to them, and when they appeared before the Privy Council to have the rules and regulations of the cemetery approved of, and an order made for the closing of certain

BELFAST. burial-grounds in the borough, the bishop opposed the application of the Corporation, and sought to obtain the sanction of the Privy Council to the rules submitted by himself.

The case before the Privy Council was adjourned in the hope that some arrangement could be come to, and the bishop made further propositions to the Corporation, to which they declined to accede. (See report of cemetery committee of 19th July, 1869, Appendix II.)

Finally, in order to enable the bishop to determine what course he should pursue, the Privy Council decided that the "Friar's Bush" burying-ground (being the place where the Roman Catholic inhabitants had been usually buried up to that time), should not be closed until the 25th November, 1869. In the meantime the bishop, finding that he could not induce the Corporation to agree in his views, purchased about eleven acres of ground for a cemetery for the Roman Catholics, which has been since enclosed and laid out at a cost, including the purchase-money of the land, of about £7,000, the entire of which has been raised by the bishop. The fifteen acres set apart by the Corporation have never been accepted by the bishop and his flock, and they positively decline to avail themselves of it. The Corporation have since built a mortuary chapel on the Protestant portion of the cemetery, and they were willing to do the same for the Roman Catholic portion, had it been occupied by them; but this was not looked upon by the bishop as a matter of much importance. It is, however, felt as a grievance, that in consequence of what has occurred the Roman Catholics are obliged to pay a burial rate exclusively for the benefit of the Protestants of Belfast, while they have had to provide themselves with a cemetery of their own at a cost of £7,000, to which the Protestants do not contribute. The ill-feeling thus arising among the Roman Catholic inhabitants has been aggravated by what has since taken place.

Mr. [illegible] Ev. [illegible] After the allotment of the forty-five acres for the cemetery there remained of the 103 acres so purchased, fifty-eight acres of surplus land, which, under the 10th section of the Burial Ground Act of 1866, the Corporation advertised for sale, but in consequence of a memorial very numerously signed by the inhabitants of that district, they abandoned the intention, and resolved to comply with the wishes of the inhabitants of the Falls-road district by forming a public park there. It was then discovered that the Public Parks Act of 1869 gave no power to make parks outside the borough and an amending Bill (the Public Parks Amendment Act of 1872) was introduced by Messrs. M'Clure and Johnston the members for the borough, and adopted by the Government, which gave power to the Corporation to purchase parks outside the borough boundary, and to sell surplus lands. A further difficulty being then raised as to what constituted a sale within the meaning of the Act, a local inquiry was held by the direction of the Local Government Board, which was followed by the Local Government Board's "Provisional Order (Belfast) Confirmation Act" of 1873, by the 3rd section of which the Corporation were authorized and empowered to apply the lands not required and unappropriated for a cemetery for the purpose of a public park, under the provisions of the Act therein mentioned, and to apply a sum of £3,000, being the estimated value of said lands in manner therein mentioned, and the 10th section of the Act of 1866 was also thereby repealed.

Notwithstanding the obtaining of the Provisional Order and Act at a considerable expense, to enable them to secure this park, the Corporation are now seeking to add thirteen of the fifty-eight acres again to the cemetery, on the ground that the portion allotted to the Protestants is not large enough, having regard to the death-rate of Belfast, although it was alleged, and not denied, before us, that in the inquiry held by

Mr. [illegible] Ev. [illegible] the Local Government Board it had been stated by the borough surveyor that there was then sufficient space in the existing ground for sixty years. The fifteen acres of the burial ground which has been refused by the Bishop lies between the Protestants' burial ground and that which, under the Act of 1873, was to be added to the park, and it was contended, on the part of the Roman Catholics, that if the Corporation wanted more ground they should re-allot the Protestant portion, and avail themselves upon certain

Ev. [illegible] terms of the fifteen acres allotted to the Roman Catholic community, which are lying practically unused, though it was admitted that some few Roman Catholics "outside the

Ev. [illegible] pale of the Church" had been buried there.

The practical result, undoubtedly, is that the Roman Catholics derive no benefit from the cemetery authorized to be formed by the Act of 1866, to the rates for maintaining which they are bound to contribute, while they have had to raise £7,000 among themselves for their own cemetery, in addition to which the Corporation are now seeking to deprive them of what they believe to be a portion of the park formed for the benefit of the locality in which they more particularly reside.

Ev. [illegible] It was also alleged, that about the time the park and cemetery were being formed, a pledge was given by the Corporation that they would flag a portion of the footway of the public road, leading to those places. It was not denied that this promise was made, and it certainly has not been carried out; but it was alleged that a considerable amount of partial work had been done there from time to time, and that the promise was conditional on there being sufficient funds at the disposal of the Corporation for this object. This was answered by saying, that the Corporation had flagged the footways in other parts of the town, which did not require it so much; and although this was again answered by saying, that in those cases the owners have invariably contributed by giving ground or the value of it, there is no doubt whatever, that the minds of the Roman Catholics are strongly impressed with the idea that they have been unfairly treated in this and other matters of a similar character by the Corporation.

In illustration of this another matter was brought up at some length more than once before us, relative to the non-purchase by the Corporation out of the funds at their disposal of a vacant plot of ground at the end of Milford-street, an important thoroughfare, in which one of the principal Roman Catholic Churches in Belfast had been recently built. By the 384th sec. of the Belfast Improvement Act, of 1845, 8 & 9 Vic., cap. 142, the Corporation are empowered to set apart annually a sum of £1,500 for widening, improving, and making such alterations in the streets as they may think necessary, and although they had originally under the advice of the borough surveyor, Mr. Montgomery, refused to pass building plans submitted to them by the owner of the plot of land in question, on the ground that such building would close up the entrance of the street, yet they subsequently granted him permission to build, and declined to avail themselves of his offer to sell them the ground for £140, although pressed to do so by a deputation, including ministers of the Roman Catholic and Presbyterian churches in the neighbourhood, who were desirous of having the street prolonged into Denis-street, and free communication thus preserved for the accommodation of the residents in that locality, and especially those frequenting those churches.

Mr. Colligan, who was in a great measure the representative of the grievances felt by the Roman Catholic community, no doubt expressed the views of his co-religionists when he said, that it was the opinion of all the people in the neighbourhood that the reluctance shown to expend £140 of the funds of the Corporation in purchasing this ground and maintaining it as a public thoroughfare, arose from the fact that it would be a particular accommodation to the Roman Catholic inhabitants attending the services of the Milford-street church; and the fact that in another street (Rosemary-street), the Corporation have laid out a larger sum from this fund of £1,500 a year in purchasing property in order to set back the street and widen it, would seem to give some colour to this suggestion. On the other hand it must be borne in mind that Mr. Black gives other reasons for the withholding of the grant in this instance. He distinctly expresses his disbelief as to the Town Council being in any way influenced by any sectarian motive in reference to their expenditure in this or any other matter. Ultimately, after half the plot of ground at the end of Milford-street had been built on, the other half was purchased for £70, to which the Corporation gave £35, and the remainder was made up by subscription—the then chairman of the improvement committee, Mr. J. Browne, and Alderman Hughes, also a member of that committee, being among the contributors.

The second principal ground of complaint was with respect to the conduct of the improvement committee in not carrying out the 75th section of the Act of 1865, in relation to the occupation of houses in new streets.

By that section of the 28 and 29 Vic., cap. 183, it was provided that—

"Any street or road formed or set out within the borough after the commencement of this Act should not be opened for traffic, nor should any house or other building built after the commencement of the Act abutting thereon or approached thereby, be inhabited, unless and until the roadways and footways thereof have been properly constructed and completed (according to plan therein mentioned) to the satisfaction of the surveyor,"

and the surveyor was thereby empowered to close the street until it was so completed. This section was further extended by the 25th section of the Act of 1868—the 31 & 32 Vict., cap. 117—which imposes a penalty of 20s. a week on the owner of each house which shall be so inhabited for every week it shall continue to be inhabited. Notwithstanding the provisions of these sections, which were manifestly enacted for the sake of the health and comfort of the people likely to inhabit such houses, it is certain that very many new streets have been laid out and opened for traffic without the roadways or footpaths having been formed, and the houses in these streets have been inhabited, wholly regardless of the provisions of the sections above mentioned. Some of these streets, which were described as built on a swamp, and impassable with any degree of comfort from their unpaved, unchannelled, and muddy condition, had been laid out and the houses built by members of the improvement committee, and were afterwards sold by them; while others were, at the time of our inquiry, owned by members of that com-

BELFAST.

mittee. The houses in these were said to have been occupied—some six or twelve months, and others two years.

Mr. O'Neill, Ev. [illegible]

One instance was stated to us by Mr. O'Neill, who had bought a number of houses in streets which had been, he said, unmacadamized for years, and after he had bought them he was required by the Corporation to pave the streets at once, and did so at considerable cost, and upon his objecting on one occasion, he was served with a summons, and was told he would have to pay £3 10s. costs, but he refused to pay a farthing, and has not been asked for it since. Another instance of a similar character, but in which proceedings were taken for a much larger amount for a work alleged to have been done for him by the Corporation, was adduced by the Rev. J. Nelson, a Presbyterian minister.

Rev. J. Nelson, Ev. [illegible] Mr. Biggar, Ev. [illegible]

Mr. Biggar, who spoke of the committee as the "Timber Ring," made a direct charge against four members of it, that they availed themselves of their position as such to benefit themselves or their friends, in their business as timber merchants and building speculators; and although no other witness put the charge in such direct terms, the number of persons on that committee connected with the building and timber trades was more than once referred to, and instances in which they were alleged to be favoured were brought forward. In reply to these imputations, it is only right to refer to the evidence of Mr. Montgomery, the Borough Surveyor, whose character was entirely unimpeached, and to whose fair dealing and impartiality in the discharge of his duty Mr. Biggar paid a just tribute. His whole evidence on this subject (pages 112, 113) deserves a careful perusal, and it will be seen that he says:—

Mr. Montgomery, Ev. [illegible]

"I have been thinking it over carefully. I do not recollect any instance where a member of the committee got concessions or favours shown to him that were not on other occasions given to the very bitterest of their opponents. . . . I do not think that party or religion has anything to do with their actions on the Town Council."

He said more than once that it was impossible to carry out the 73th section of the Act of 1868 in its integrity in a rapidly growing town like Belfast, and that the section of the Act was put in contrary to his advice. With reference to some of the particular instances complained of he says he has—

Ev. [illegible]

"Always advised that the older streets should be taken first."

And that although his recommendations were not always treated as infallible, yet he could positively say this had never been owing to the influence of the members mentioned by Mr. Biggar. And he added:—

Ev. [illegible]

"I think I have been better supported in Belfast than any other town I have been in."

Mr. Carlisle, Ev. [illegible]

Mr. Carlisle who certainly cannot be considered a witness in favour of the Corporation said—

"I believe this talk of the timber ring is incorrect, so far as I could see, for the three years I was on that committee there was no undue influence brought to bear. I had no connexion with any of the timber merchants and I believe that they did their duty to the best of their ability and that they have done so without favour."

Mr. Black having also stated that the 73th section of the Act of 1865 ought never to have been in the Act in consequence of the difficulty in carrying it out, we enquired why, if they had found that to be the case, they had not had the clause repealed by the Act of 1868, instead of asking for the more stringent powers in dealing with the matter which they obtained under the 23th section of that Act. It appeared to us that the Corporation should seek to get rid of these clauses altogether if they find they cannot carry them out fairly, but while they are part of the law of the land they certainly ought to be so carried out as to leave if possible no colour for the suspicions, which are undoubtedly entertained, that strict impartiality is not invariably observed.

SANITARY MATTERS.

THE BLACKSTAFF NUISANCE.

The serious and continually growing nuisance arising from the polluted condition of the Blackstaff river is part of the history of Belfast, and deserves special consideration.

The legislation with a view to the improvement of this river has been already noticed in our review of the Acts of 1874 and 1880, and certain recitals in these Acts with reference to the Blackstaff have been quoted at length. No steps having been taken to improve its condition save some temporary annual cleansing by the removal of the accumulated filth along its banks, it has, as a matter of fact, been getting worse each year from the additional quantity of sewage matter which is discharged into it.

Mr. [illegible], Ev. [illegible] Mr. [illegible], Ev. [illegible] Sir Robert [illegible], Ev. 1720-2.

The Blackstaff is itself a pure stream down to the point where it is joined by the Pound Burn, but this and other small contributory streams from the Falls-road district have become thoroughly impregnated with the sewage of the numerous houses which have been built along their courses, and to such an extent has this been introduced from time to time that the Pound Burn is now practically a common sewer. As each successive mill is reached the water is used for condensing and boiler purposes, and, having usually received in addition the sewage of that mill, it goes on to the next with increased impurity.

When this subject was first brought to our notice we could hardly believe it possible that mill-owners could use such polluted and filthy water for the purposes of their mills, but as the enquiry proceeded it was only too palpable that they not only did so, but were ready to take proceedings against the Corporation when threatened to be deprived of any portion of it; in illustration of which we would refer to Mr. Montgomery's evidence touching his diversion of the Fairywell stream, which he described as "a miniature Pound Burn," into the North-street main sewer by which it is conducted into the river Lagan below the tide-way.

The reason assigned for the use of this contaminated water by more than one witness among the mill-owners was that at present it was a matter of necessity and not of choice; that they would prefer pure water if the Water Commissioners could supply it at a moderate price and in a sufficient quantity all the year round, but that the price charged was practically prohibitory, and thus a large proportion of the manufacturing establishments in Belfast would have to be closed if the use of the water from these polluted streams was discontinued. On the other hand, two mill-owners at least seemed to think a sufficient supply from the Water Commissioners might be obtained, and one of these gentlemen said "We want no compensation but a supply of water, which they" (meaning the Corporation) "could easily give us from the Water Commissioners."

It was not sought to be denied on the part of the mill-owners that the water was returned to the bed of the stream from the boilers of these mills in a highly heated and far more offensive condition, and we were informed that the vapour and steam thus generated contaminated the surrounding atmosphere to an extent which could not fail to be detrimental to the health of the mill hands and their families, and others dwelling in the immediate locality.

It was likewise admitted by the town solicitor (Mr. Black), and by Mr. Montgomery, the borough surveyor, that the Corporation had first contributed to the pollution of these streams by causing the public sewers to run into them, and Mr. Montgomery said he had found the system in existence before he came to Belfast, and that the Fairywell stream had been polluted for twenty years. He reminded us that the same thing prevails in Bradford and other large manufacturing towns, but said he was endeavouring to carry out a main drainage scheme which would prevent any further necessity for this in Belfast, though it is at present, in certain districts, unavoidable. He also told us that the Town Council had already constructed several large intercepting sewers which had diverted from the Blackstaff, and the other streams referred to, a very large quantity of sewage, and that in every case where plans had come in for new streets and buildings, he had objected to any fresh sewage being turned into these streams, and had generally succeeded in preventing it.

Mr. Black, who said that he was "not there on the part of the Corporation to deny that the Blackstaff was a nuisance," contended that "the difficulties hitherto in the way of remedying that nuisance had been so great, that so far they had been unable to overcome them." Referring to a report in October, 1673, by a sub-committee consisting of Messrs. J. Dinnen, R. Carlisle, and Alderman Hughes—of which it was made a matter of serious complaint before us by the two first-named gentlemen that it was shelved and had not been entered on the minutes—he said—

"An effectual remedy does not lie in these petty suggestions made by that sub-committee, but by the construction, as Mr. Montgomery has suggested by his scheme, of a system of main drainage for the town, and this system the Corporation have been prevented from carrying out owing to the differences existing between the Corporation and the Harbour Board as regards the outlet for the sewage, and also the serious expense that would be incurred in constructing the works. When the town is prepared to meet these difficulties the work no doubt will be carried out. No suggestion has ever been made about dealing with the Blackstaff nuisance or any other nuisance, that was not carefully considered."

He further stated that the Corporation had taken the opinion of the late Attorney-General (and present Chief Justice) May, on the subject, and he handed in that opinion (Appendix 15), which was, he said, to the effect that the Corporation of that day having carried their sewers into the Blackstaff and other streams, they could not insist on the mill-owners taking their sewage out of those streams or abstaining from other pollution of them until they, the Corporation, had first diverted the town sewerage. Mr. Black, moreover, himself contended that the Corporation had only acted in exercise of the powers conferred on them by the 90th sect. of the Act of 1846, and the 51st sect. of the Act of 1850.

We have quoted thus at length Mr. Black's observations at this stage, as they sum up the whole case for the Town Council in reply to the charges of supineness and neglect, or of succumbing to the undue influence of the mill-owners in leaving the Blackstaff in its present condition, which were, by various witnesses, advanced against the Corporation. The names of these witnesses are quoted in the margin, but the witness who constituted himself the principal accuser of the Corporation in this matter, and who was, indeed, the only one who alleged in terms that the influence of the mill-owners was directed to the obstruction of the improvement and purification of the Blackstaff, was Mr. Robert Carlisle, who, with Mr. Dinnen, was a member of the Corporation, and of the sub-committee already referred to in 1873, in the November of which year he lost his seat.

Another nuisance which arises from the present condition of the Blackstaff is the flooding, to which several of the streets below its junction with the Pound Burn are subject, and it was to this point principally that the evidence of Dr. Bryce Smith (incidentally corroborated by his friend Dr. Ferguson) was directed.

Mr. Montgomery contends that his scheme, which embraced three principal objects, and a summary of which will be found in the Appendix (Appendix 9), would not only, by means of intercepting sewers, remove all sewage and other impurities from the Blackstaff and other streams flowing through the town into the river Lagan, but would, by impounding the storm waters of the Pound Burn and the Blackstaff in regulating reservoirs on their upper course, both abate the flooding and economise the water for the mill-owners and the public. The cost of the three intercepting sewers and the works in connexion with them, was estimated in Mr. Montgomery's report of 13th of February, 1875, at £200,000, and that of the impounding reservoirs, at £100,000, but Mr. Montgomery very fairly stated that until the remaining portion of his scheme—the disposal and utilisation of the sewage—was decided on, no reliable estimate could be given of the cost of the whole. And it is certain that this question of cost has hitherto constituted the main obstacle to the carrying out of his scheme, which was proposed so long ago as 1866, when it was examined on the spot, and favourably reported on by Sir Joseph (then Mr.) Bazalgette; and Mr. Dinnen and Mr. Gaffikin both stated their objection to it substantially in the same terms, viz., that the Blackstaff would thereby have been made the lever for a grand drainage scheme for the entire town, which would have been a great expense, and "with which," in the opinion of the latter gentleman, "the Town Council had nothing to do."

We do not here propose to enter upon the rival merits of this or any other of the various schemes which their promoters were anxious to bring before us, but as so much stress was laid upon the omission from the minutes of the sub-committee's report of October, 1873, and the absence of any further action upon it beyond referring it to the borough surveyor for his observations and report, we think it only right to draw attention to the evidence in relation to this at pages 87, 91, and 135.

While very decided differences of opinion exist upon this and many other matters in Belfast, there is at least one point upon which we may safely say that all parties and all classes are unanimous, and that is the disgusting nature of the nuisance arising from the present condition of the Blackstaff from its junction with the Pound Burn; and we are bound to add that the prevailing opinion among a large portion of the ratepayers is that the Corporation are, from whatever cause, responsible for the continuance of this monster nuisance.

Numerous other complaints as to imperfect sewage, flooding of streets, &c., were made in the course of our inquiry, which it would occupy too much space to notice at length in this already far too long report. We content ourselves, therefore, with referring in the margin to the names of the witnesses who came forward to speak as to those, almost all of which Mr. Montgomery came forward to answer in detail.

We subjoin in the Appendix (Appendix 7), a report put in by Dr. Samuel Browne, who has been the consulting sanitary officer since the passing of the Public Health Act of 1874, in which he enumerates his duties and the amount of work done in the last year, &c., and at the close of which he offers suggestions for changing the title of "consulting sanitary officer" to that of "superintendent medical officer of health"; of the "sanitary officers" to "district medical officers," and of the "sub-sanitary officers" to "inspectors of nuisances," and of the "executive sanitary officer" to "sanitary inspector." These names would certainly more nearly represent the nature of the duties discharged by each than those by which they are at present distinguished, and would more nearly coincide with those by which the officers holding similar positions are known in England.

Dr. Browne's position here is very much the same as that occupied by the Medical Officer of Health of a large English borough, and we have no hesitation in saying that he appears to devote great attention to his duties, and in his case the title of Consulting Medical Officer is certainly not misapplied, as we have so often found it to be elsewhere. He has been practically conversant with all the sanitary arrangements of Belfast since 1846, is daily kept informed of all the work done by the various officers of the sanitary staff, who take their instructions from him, and all of whose reports pass either through his hands, or those of the executive sanitary officer, with whom he consults daily; and every week he attends the meeting of the sanitary committee, and those of the Town Council as often as he thinks necessary. He also sends in monthly reports, and a general report every three months. Under his advice the Corporation are about to take proceedings under the provisions of the Artisans' Dwellings Act, for the improvement of a portion of the town, the reports relating to which were handed in by him, and will be found in the Appendix. (Appendix No. 6, page 210.) Belfast.

The last charge, in the order in which we have arranged them, relates to the conduct of some of the officers in regard to the municipal elections.

Our first impression was that it would not fall within the scope of our inquiry to take evidence on such a matter, but when it was distinctly charged with respect to one at least of the officials, Mr. De Cobain, the cashier, that his active interference on these occasions was with the knowledge and approval of a majority of the Town Council, and that his salary had been increased from time to time by the Corporation, as a reward for political services, we felt we had no alternative but to investigate the matter. In and previous to the year 1872, a belief existed in the minds of at least some of the Town Council and of several of the ratepayers, that certain officials were in the habit of unduly interfering in municipal and parliamentary elections, and to put a stop to the practice, Mr. John Dinnen gave notice that he would move on the 1st February, 1872, a resolution in the following terms— Mr. Dinnen, Ev. [illegible]

"That it be an instruction to the employés of the Corporation not to take any active part prior to, or at, any municipal or parliamentary elections beyond recording their votes."

Mr. Dinnen moved the resolution on that day, and mentioned instances in which, as he and others alleged, at least one of the officers had so interfered; but notwithstanding this, and without holding an investigation into the matter, the resolution was negatived by seventeen votes to six. On our inquiry why this most reasonable and proper resolution was thus summarily rejected, the reason assigned was, that the injudicious course adopted by some of its supporters led to this result, as the passing of it would have made it appear that there was some foundation in the charges against the officials, which the majority voting against it believed to be untrue. With respect to this, we can only observe that it must be admitted, so far at all events as relates to Mr. De Cobain, that there was ample foundation for the motion. He was for some years before, and in the year 1872, a member of a Conservative association governed by rules which in terms provided that the society's committees of the different wards in Belfast, should have the nomination of candidates for the offices of Town Councillors, Harbour Commissioners, Water Commissioners, and any other public body in the borough. While this or a like rule was in force, Mr. De Cobain was on the committee of the Dock Ward, and at another time of Cromac Ward, and as some members of the Town Council were from time to time members of the association and of its committees, these gentlemen must have known as a matter of fact, that Mr. De Cobain did take an active part in the promotion of the candidature of certain persons for election to the Town Council. Mr. De Cobain, Ev. [illegible]

He admitted himself that he had canvassed for the return of members of the Council, and had actively interfered in such elections, and he justified his right to do so out of office hours and outside the Corporation buildings. He stated that he had not acted thus for about the last three years, but the reason of his not doing so (if it be the fact, seeing that he admitted having taken the chair and spoken at a public meeting last year in Cromac ward) may be probably traced to the circumstances detailed in the evidence of James Larmour in relation to an action brought by him against Mr. De Cobain, as after the publicity given to Mr. De Cobain's proceedings at this trial in November, 1874, it would have been impossible for the Town Council to shut their eyes to such conduct if continued. Mr. De Cobain, Ev. [illegible] Mr. James Larmour, Ev. [illegible]

On the 2nd February, 1876, a proposal was brought before the Town Council to increase the salaries of some of the officers, including Mr. De Cobain, and he admitted that he had spoken to members of the Town Council with reference to an increase of his salary which he desired to have raised to £850. Mr. Thomas Gaffikin, one of the Town Councillors, opposed this resolution to increase the salaries, and speaking of Mr. De Cobain said— Mr. Thomas Gaffikin, Ev. [illegible]

"His qualifications, except in a political and electioneering point of view, did not justify his claim upon the Council."

[illegible] In answer to questions put by us, Mr. Gaffikin stated that he thus referred to Mr. De Cobain's qualifications as being of a political or electioneering character from his knowledge of Mr. De Cobain's- -

Ev. [illegible] "Canvassing in every way in his power, attending Conservative meetings, and making himself as influential as possible with reference to every change that took place in the Town Council."

Ev. 7391-2. He also stated that he had been put out of the Council in November, 1874, and that Mr. De Cobain had interfered adversely to him at that election, and that there was a feeling amongst the officers of the Town Council (from whom he, however, excepted Mr. Black and Mr. Montgomery), that he, Mr. Gaffikin, should not be on the Town Council. Sir John Savage, who had been lately Mayor of Belfast, was also present at the same meeting, and was in the chair. He had succeeded at the election of 1874, though opposed, and previously to going to the meeting he had been informed by Mr. Gaffikin, whom he described as a most respectable member of the Corporation, that Mr. De Cobain had asserted that it was a most ungrateful thing for him, Sir John Savage, to oppose the proposed increase of his salary, because he, Mr. De Cobain, had largely influenced Sir John's return as alderman for St. Anne's ward. At the meeting Sir John Savage alluded to this matter, complained of Mr. De Cobain's conduct in making such an assertion, and said that he believed such a statement had no existence in fact. He further stated that he thought Mr. De Cobain was carrying the matter a little too far in canvassing and endeavouring to influence the members of the Town Council to increase his salary.

Notwithstanding these statements, Sir John Savage voted for a modified increase of Mr. De Cobain's salary to £300, and a vote was passed raising it to that amount without calling on him for any explanation as to the conduct charged against him. It is true that he denied before us having made any such statement to Mr. Gaffikin, and he had also denied it privately to Mr. Black and to Sir John Savage; but Sir John said that he believed Mr. Gaffikin, who had informed him that the statements were so made. Sir John strongly condemned any active interference on the part of the officers in electioneering matters, and stated that complaints on that head had been made against Mr. De Cobain, and that he had told him his mind with regard to any official of the Corporation taking the slightest part, *pro* or *con*, with regard to the return of a member of the Council, or doing anything that might bear a partisan or political character, that such conduct was to be highly disapproved of, and that if he ever attempted such a thing he would lose his (Sir John Savage's) confidence and support.

Mr. De Cobain however entertains very peculiar views with regard to the propriety of his interference in municipal elections, and while admitting that he had canvassed for some members of the Corporation as against others, claims to have two identities, and that the fact of his being a well known officer of the Corporation ought not to override what he terms his "rights of citizenship." It is, however, only fair to add, that looking to his duties as cashier and to the large sums of money which pass annually through his hands, amounting to some £43,000 a year, of which about £19,000 is directly expended by him in the payment of weekly wages, it can scarcely be held that £300 a year is an excessive salary; and although we cannot but regret the rejection by the Town Council of the very reasonable resolution proposed by Mr. Dinnen on the 1st February, 1872, nor doubt that some members of that body were at least partially cognisant of Mr. De Cobain's activity in municipal elections, we do not find it necessary to accept Mr. Dinnen's inference—and this is the question with which our inquiry is more immediately concerned—that the rates were corruptly expended by raising his salary as a reward for political services.

We have already noticed the suggestion that the rate collectors still, to some extent, manipulate the burgess lists in the interests of the predominant party on the Town Council, by not collecting rates in due time, and thus disfranchising voters, and we think it only necessary to add that whatever may have been the case prior to the Award Act of 1864, this charge was, as regards the existing state of things, virtually abandoned. Mr. Dinnen's own evidence affords perhaps the best commentary upon his statement—that "there is an inner circle of the Corporation who manage the entire borough, and the others are but tools in their hands."

Application was made to us by Mr. Michael Andrews on behalf of the "Flax Spinners and Power Loom Linen Manufacturers Association" of Belfast to take evidence with respect to the members of limited liability companies not being entitled to the franchise, though their places of business were within the municipal area, and were among the highest rated establishments in Belfast. He stated that the valuation of concerns of this class, on which municipal rates were paid, amounted to the sum of £24,094, while the owners had no voice in the selection of municipal representatives.

We informed him that we considered we had not power to entertain this question, as it related to an alteration in the franchise; but we think it right to report the fact of this application having been made to us for the information of the Select Committee of the House of Commons.

D. CORBETT, (*Seal*).
R. R. LAWLESS, (*Seal*).
WM. A. EXHAM, (*Seal*).

FOUR COURTS, DUBLIN, 14*th May*, 1877.

H. A. ROBINSON,
Acting as Secretary.

TRIM.

TRIM, the county and assize town of Meath, adopted the Towns Improvement Act of 1854, shortly after it became law, and is now governed by nine Town Commissioners under that Act. Mr. Reilly, Ev. 1–6.

The town was previously governed by thirteen Town Commissioners under the 9th Geo. IV., cap. 82. Ev. 22.

The principal revenues administered by the Corporation are derived from real property known as "The Trim Commons," of which, when the Irish Municipal Commissioners made their report in 1835, 439A. 3R. 37P. Irish plantation measure, equivalent to nearly 750 statute acres, were in the hands of the old Corporation. From that report it appears that these "Commons" were divided, under a by-law of 3rd May, 1705, into "burgess lots" of from ten to twenty acres, and "freemen's lots" of from four to ten acres, which were held for the life of the grantee (and one year additional for his widow), at the nominal rent of 1s. per annum. There were in 1835, fifteen burgess lots, and forty-seven freemen's lots, and the largest lot held by any one person was nineteen acres. Some four or five of these lives are still running, but they all hold small "freemen's lots" of from three to five acres each.

The Town Clerk, Mr. John Reilly, who gave his evidence in a remarkably straightforward fearless manner, describing the mode in which these successive bodies of Commissioners have dealt with the lots which have fallen in since 1840, said, "Nearly every Commissioner got some. As the lives fell in, the parties who purchased the life interest of the grantee were preferred, and the lot was then valued by a committee consisting of the Chairman and two Commissioners. They came to some agreement with the tenants, who generally accepted it. Until within the last three years nearly all the lands were valued by themselves, and, in the majority of cases, there is no doubt they were let to the Commissioners themselves."

No Town Commissioner appears to have resigned on obtaining a lease of the Commons land, and (except in three instances subsequently brought to our notice), no public notice appears to have been ever given of the letting of these lots, nor any tenders invited by advertisement or otherwise, although we were privately told that this was a matter of common complaint among the inhabitants of Trim. One person only, and that not till the third day of our inquiry, came forward to represent this grievance to us.

"Generally," says Mr. Reilly, "the persons managed to get into possession of the lands because they knew the Commissioners would grant the leases; they gave good sums to get in." And instances were brought to light, though not without difficulty, in which both individual Commissioners and the agent himself had thus got into possession.

One of these lots (an old freeman's lot of five acres Irish plantation measure), which the agent alleged had been given up to him by a man named John Allen upon his emigrating, in consideration of a debt of £30 which he said Allen owed him, was afterwards avowedly parted with by the agent to a Mr. G. D. Hipwell for a sum of £30. A lease was then granted to Mr. Hipwell, who was at that time a Town Commissioner, at £5 a year, Duignan having, in the meantime, held the land himself for about three years. Mr. Duignan at first said he paid £5 rent for it, but afterwards, on being pressed as to the payment of rent by himself, he said, "I could not swear that I did unless I had my books here."

Another transaction of a similar character, in which he gave an old woman named Phœbe Corry £10 for her interest in her lease, is, considering the position which he held as agent, equally discreditable to him; and the circumstances in connexion with a lease, which he had induced the Commissioners to grant to one Thomas Fox, of Dogstown, then an emigrant in America, for whom he was acting as agent at the same time that he was agent to the Town Commissioners, appear pregnant with suspicion.

Mr. Duignan also holds another lot of commons (allotted to him by the Town Commissioners of that day) for thirty-one years, from 25th March, 1836, at £7 10s. per annum, which lot is valued to the poor-rate at £13 per annum.

The rental kept by the agent is very defective, and neither shows the quantity of land held by each tenant, nor the yearly rate at which it is let per acre, nor the Government valuation. In short, it simply gives the name of the tenant and the amount of rent and arrears due from each; and it hardly admits of doubt that this man, who has been the Town Commissioners' agent since 1843, has not only, from the commencement, grossly neglected his duties as such, but still wilfully withholds from the present town clerk and the Commissioners, information which they have a right to look for at his hands.

He is, however, supported by Mr. Patrick Malone, and some other Commissioners, who appear to look jealously on the efforts of Mr. Reilly, the present town clerk, to identify and put upon record all the successive dealings with these various lots of commons, from the time when each first lapsed to the Commissioners after the Municipal Corporations Act of 1840. Indeed, some of these gentlemen, and notably the agent himself, were at no pains to conceal their dislike to Mr. Reilly, and their annoyance and irritation at the whole tenor of the evidence given by him on the first day of the inquiry.

Ev. 63, 64.

There are certain houses in the town which Mr. Reilly has no doubt were the property of the old Corporation, of which the rents are now received by other parties, non-resident, and of whom the Commissioners knew nothing; but there appears to be some difficulty in identifying them, as the tenements within the town are not delineated on the Commissioners' map, which, as regards the landed portion of their property, appears to have been carefully and correctly drawn. This map, at the time of our inquiry, was in the hands of Mr. E. Vaughan, a land valuer and civil engineer in Dublin, who in 1873 was called in by the Trim Town Commissioners with reference to making a valuation of their property.

Ev. 62, 63.

In addition to these houses in the town, there are also at least two lots of "Commons;" one a lot of about eight acres, which is shown on the Corporation map as part of the Trim Commons, overheld by a man named Molloy, and another small lot called "the Crickowns," consisting of a cottage and a piece of grass land between the town and the railway, of which the rents are received by a solicitor in Dublin named "Ball," and a Mr. Donovan, and which, as yet, neither the agent nor the Town Commissioners have taken any steps to recover.

The alleged excuse for this apparent apathy on the part of the Commissioners was the great expense incurred by them in recovering before the late Chief Baron Pigot the lot of land already referred to, which the agent (C. P. Duignan) obtained from Allen, and afterwards sold his interest in to Mr. Hipwell. Even of this lot a small portion would have been ultimately lost to them but for the energy of the Town Clerk Mr. Reilly, who recovered this before Judge Flanagan in the Incumbered Estates Court, without putting the Commissioners to any expense, under circumstances which appear to present a remarkable contrast to the conduct of the agent, who is of course primarily responsible for looking after the property which has been for so many years entrusted to his charge.

Indeed it is not too much to say that Mr. Duignan's conduct in respect of some of these leases, and his evasive answers with reference to more than one transaction in the course of the present inquiry, lead to the inference that it is owing to something more than mere neglect on his part that many of these difficulties have arisen.

Molloy, the farmer who has so long overheld the lot of commons above referred to, is brother-in-law to Mr. James Plunkett, one of the Commissioners, but Mr. Reilly was of opinion that this relationship had not in any degree influenced the Commissioners to abstain from taking proceedings to recover the land in question.

With one exception, and that so far back as 1848, no transfers are recorded on the leases, and thus difficulties naturally arise in ascertaining who are the parties entitled. Indeed the Town Clerk told us he knew "several instances of persons paying rent of whom there was no mention on the lease, and no transfer executed to them with the sanction of the Town Commissioners.

Ev. 103.

One instance he mentioned in which a tenant called to know how much land he had, and the Commissioners could not tell him.

In consequence of the attention of the Commissioners having been called to these matters by Mr. Reilly, a resolution was passed on the 2nd September, 1876, calling upon the agent to furnish a list of the present occupiers of the corporate property, with the names of the original occupiers of such holdings from 1840, and to deliver the list to the Town Clerk to be used in the preparation of the new rental and map on which Mr. Vaughan is engaged.

This order the agent did not comply with, and at a subsequent meeting had the impertinence to object to the signing of the minutes. Upon the chairman reminding him that no objection to the signing of the minutes could be entertained unless made by a Town Commissioner, Mr. Patrick Malone then objected to them on the ground that he wished only the present tenants' names to appear on the rental.

The only two instances of which we heard until the third day of the inquiry, in which lots were let by any form of competition were the case of a lot known as "Chambers' lands" which fell in in 1856, and a lot of Samuel Allen's, which, in 1864, was let to a man named Patrick Donovan at £3 16s. In the latter case the rent was subsequently reduced to £3 per acre, and, at the same time, the rent of each of the four lots which had been carved out of Chambers' lands was reduced by 10s. an acre. Thus in both these instances in which the form of inviting tenders by hand-bills was gone through, the rents were subsequently reduced. How far the Commissioners were justified in reducing these rents may be inferred from the fact that on the second day of the inquiry a rate-payer named Henry Duignan (not related to the agent), volunteered the observation that he had offered £3 15s. per acre for the land let to Patrick Donovan, and was still willing to give it.

It was also proved that a Mr. Brennan, who obtained one of Chambers' lots, and who shortly after became a Town Commissioner, disposed afterwards of his lot for a consideration to a man named Kelly, he being at that time one of the Commissioners.

We were told that it was understood the rent would be reduced when he sold his interest in the land to Kelly, but Mr. Brennan denied that there was any understanding between Kelly and himself that he should use his interest as a commissioner to procure the reduction of the rent. He, however, admitted that he got a year's rent from Kelly for surrendering it to him, which year's rent he alleged he had paid in advance, upon the land being allotted to him. Mr. Reilly, on the other hand, told us that it was currently stated and believed that Brennan received £40 from Kelly for surrendering this lot, but we could not ascertain on which side the truth lay as Kelly was not forthcoming, and we experienced, indeed throughout, great difficulty in getting any independent rate-payer to come forward.

We were informed for instance by one of the most respectable residents in Trim, that a Mrs. King, the widow of a man who held under an original grantee, and who would therefore under the ordinary practice have had a prior claim to be accepted as tenant on the death of the original grantee, was passed over in favour of a Mr. Kennedy, then a Town Commissioner (whose son, now a Commissioner, holds this land) although she offered a considerably higher rent than it was let for to Kennedy. The gentleman who gave this information, however, begged that he might not be called as a witness or have his name mentioned in connexion with the matter. We then endeavoured to procure the attendance of Mrs. King, but she declined to come forward, and although Kennedy when questioned on the subject, admitted he had "heard" that Mrs. King had made an offer for the land, we could extract no further confirmation of the communication thus made to us, although from the character of our informant we entertain no doubt of its truth.

This Mr. Kennedy holds two lots of commons, the one first referred to which he inherited from his father upon a thirty-one years' lease at £2 1s. per Irish acre, and another lot of which the quantity was variously stated, but which it finally transpired, was eight and a-half acres, for which he pays £18 a-year, having given £150 or thereabouts for the interest of a man named William Burnell in this lot. How difficult it was to get a straightforward answer from this witness will be seen on reference to his evidence passim, but his reluctant admission that he gave something like £150 for Burnell's interest in the lease of these few acres of Corporation lands is at least conclusive testimony to the under-letting of these lands, and disposes we think of all the efforts of Messrs. Malone and Sheridan to depreciate their letting value.

Mr. Sheridan is the witness at whose urgent request we went a third time to Trim, he having pledged himself as an old Town Commissioner for many years, and formerly chairman of that body, to vindicate the character of the Trim Town Commissioners and to refute entirely the statements of the Town Clerk, which he characterised as being "in direct variance with the truth."

How far he succeeded in doing so may be judged from his evidence. He certainly expressed a very decided opinion against the principle of letting Corporation lands by public auction or indeed against letting them by competition in any form; but the only facts elicited from him were that when a certain Captain Mocler, who held some twenty Irish acres of the Corporation lands in the North Commons, died in 1845 or 1846, it was agreed by the then Town Commissioners that his lot should be divided into five portions and let by competition. Subsequently it was agreed that a committee of the Town Commissioners should retire to value the lots, and to select the names of the tenants. This was done when—there being twenty-two applications—it was announced that four out of the five subdivisions of Captain Mocler's lot were allotted to Town Commissioners (whose names are given in the evidence), who were then present and voting.

Mr. Sheridan gave it as his opinion that these lots were thus let very much above their value, at about 40s. per Irish acre, he having been previously sub-lessee of ten acres of the same land under Captain Mocler at £1 7s. 6d. per acre; but it is only reasonable to suppose that the Town Commissioners who selected themselves as tenants at the higher rent, did not take his view of their value. It is but fair to Mr. Sheridan to say, that when he was a Town Commissioner himself, he not only held no land belonging to the Corporation, but was opposed to the principle of letting corporate property to the Commissioners, and in 1863 he moved a resolution to the effect that no Town Commissioner should in future be considered eligible to be proposed for any lot of commons falling in. To this notice an amendment was moved and carried by a majority of one vote "that Mr. Sheridan's notice is out of place."

The statement embodied in the report of Mr. Finlay, the auditor, in 1873, and repeated by him to the Select Committee of the House of Commons in reference to the dealings of the Town Commissioners of Trim with this property, will be thus found fully borne out by the evidence taken before us, but within the last three or four years, since Mr. Reilly has been town clerk, the practice of valuing the Corporation lands, as they have fallen in, by a committee of three of the Town Commissioners has ceased, and Mr. Vaughan, a public valuer in Dublin, as has been already stated, has been called in to survey and value the whole property, since which, with one exception, no lot has been valued for re-letting by the Commissioners themselves, and in that instance, it has been arranged that the tenant shall pay the rent which Mr. Vaughan will put upon it. Nor since 1874 does it appear that any lot has been let to a Town Commissioner, but in that year James Plunkett, then and now a Town Commissioner, and C. M'Keon, who, although not then a Commissioner, had more than once been chairman of the Town Commissioners, have each obtained a small lot upon Mr. Vaughan's valuation. In these instances, no public competition was invited, but there is no reason to suppose that these lands were let below their fair market value.

How great a disparity exists between the actual value and the terms on which the Commissioners' land was let in other instances, will be seen by Mr. Vaughan's statement respecting the lands held by Mr. Thomas Kennedy.

A return showing the holdings which have fallen into the hands of the Town Commissioners since the year 1840, with all particulars respecting the re-letting, is appended to this report (Appendix No. 19, page 117).

No rate has ever been levied by the Town Commissioners, and their only receipts beyond their rental arise from some small tolls for weighing corn, butter, and market produce, and from the dog tax and petty sessions fines.

Last year, for the first time, the Commissioners worked their gasworks at an assumed profit. This, after crediting themselves with the cost of lighting the town lamps and the stock of coals in hand, amounted to £51 13s. 4½d., and was, doubtless, due to improved management, as the preceding year the gasworks showed a loss of £19 5s. 10½d., and the year before of £101 8s. 10d. The price charged to private consumers is 6s. 8d. per 1,000 cubic feet.

There is a fair-green, the property of the Commissioners, and four fairs are held upon it, but there are no tolls collected at these fairs, and monthly fairs for the sale of small stock are held in the streets of the town with, apparently, the general approval of the inhabitants.

The grazing of the fair-green is let for £7 a year, and the Government pay a nominal rent of 1s. per year for the site of the infantry barracks which stand on a portion of this green.

Three good main-sewers were made after the passing of the Public Health Act of 1874, and were said to be sufficient to sewer the principal streets of the town, but more connecting drains with the houses are still wanting—the making of which the Guardians, who are the sanitary authority under the Act of 1874, appear to have thought it was still incumbent upon the Commissioners to enforce.

In other respects the sanitary condition of the town appears to be satisfactory, although no active steps are taken by the rural sanitary authority to look after it.

C. CORBETT. (Seal.)

H. A. Robinson,
Acting as Secretary.

WICKLOW.

Wicklow is governed by twenty-one Town Commissioners, under the 9 George IV., cap. 82.

The municipal area extends inland for about a mile from the town hall, which is at one extremity of the town. No rate has ever been struck, and the principal income of the Town Commissioners is derived from rents of real property and houses in the town. The other sources of income consist of small sums arising from the dog-tax, and the sale of stones and sand, and £10 annually charged to the Dublin, Wicklow, and Wexford Railway Company for the supply of water to their station.

The rental of the property which in the year 1873 was only £1,103 19s. 11d. has, during the three last years, somewhat increased, but the startling disparity between the actual rental and the letting value of the property may be readily judged of, when we find that in May, 1876, Griffith's valuation of the Town property, which is always far below the letting value, was no less than £4,165 11s., while the entire rental for that year was but £1,243 7s. 11d.

The total acreage of the property is 189a. 3r. 2p.

We proceed to cite a few illustrations of the mode in which the Town Commissioners have dealt with the property entrusted to them as leases have fallen in.

A small house in the town had been held by Lord Powerscourt under a lease which expired in 1868, and a man of the name of Newbold was the sub-tenant of the house at the expiration of the lease to Lord Powerscourt, at a rent of £7 a year. In 1870 the Commissioners granted him a new lease for seventy-five years, at £5 a year; and in August, 1874, it was resolved that a new lease be granted to him for seventy-five years, from the 25th March, 1874, of the same premises at £1 10s. a year. No reason was assigned for the reduction of the rent, nor could any defence be set up for this flagrant violation of their trust, beyond the answer given by Mr. Oakes, one of the Commissioners:—"We did it by a resolution. The property is vested in us, and we can deal with it as we think right."

A large and valuable property in the town had been held by Colonel Gun Cunningham, under a lease which expired on the 25th March, 1874, at a rent of £3 13s. 10½d. a year. He had been receiving up to the termination of the lease from the tenants in possession, who mostly held as yearly tenants, £167 12s. a year, and those premises were then valued in Griffith's valuation at £300 10s. 2d. a year. Just prior to the expiration of this lease a resolution was passed by the Commissioners on the 2nd day of March, 1874, that the secretary and agent take possession of the buildings out of lease on the 25th of March next, and that the parties in possession be put in as caretakers at one penny a week until the plots are arranged.

The next meeting with reference to the re-letting of this property was held on the 6th of April, 1874, and between that date and the 22nd May following, all the plots were re-let on lease—under the circumstances set forth in the extracts from the minutes produced by the town clerk at the adjourned inquiry on the 10th of February last—mostly to the old tenants, at rents producing in the aggregate £67 3s. 6d. per annum, being £100 a year less than the rent the same persons had been previously paying to Colonel Gun Cunningham, as yearly tenants.

The particulars of the principal lettings, showing the names of the tenants, the rents paid to Colonel Cunningham, and the new rents fixed by the Commissioners in 1874, are as follows:—

The last named tenant, the agent and rent-collector of the Commissioners, built four small houses on his lot while tenant to Colonel Cunningham, from which he derived a rent of about £15 a year, and these he gave up to the Commissioners, who gave them to Miss Dunne as a portion of the lot given to her at £5 18s. 6d. Griffith's valuation of Chapman's lot in March, 1874, was £40. It will be thus seen that Miss

Dunne's rent was not only reduced from £20 to £3 19s. 6d. a year, but she got in addition the four houses which had been producing Mr. Chapman £15 a year.

Tenants' Names.	Old Rent.			New Rent.			Lease.	Extent.
	£	s.	d.	£	s.	d.		
H. M'Phail (Town Commissioner),	5	0	0	3	1	10	75 years.	House and Buildings.
William M'Phail (Town Commissioner),	5	0	0	3	6	4	75 "	do.
P. Fox (Miss Hamilton),	6	0	0	3	8	9	75 "	do.
Dr. O. Halpin (Town Commissioner),	5	15	0	3	12	0	75 "	do.
Do. do.	0	15	0	1	10	0	Yearly.	Yard.
Joseph Fitzgerald,	1	0	0	3	12	9	75 years.	House and Buildings.
Mrs. Hepenstall,	22	0	0	2	0	0	76 "	do.
J. Sullivan,*	12	0	0	3	0	0	75 "	do.
R. Caldwell (Town Commissioner), late J. Byrne,	17	19	0	7	10	6	75 "	do.
J. Watkins,	6	10	0	3	0	0	Yearly.	do.
J. Newman,	6	10	0	3	0	0	do.	do.
— Maguire, late W. Williams,	6	0	0	3	15	6	75 years.	do.
J. Ellis,	6	0	0	1	5	0	75 "	do.
Miss Dunne,	20	0	0	3	19	6	75 "	do.
J. Chapman (Agent to the Commissioners),	30	0	0	15	0	0	75 "	do.

Ev. [illegible] * A Mrs. Kealy put in a claim to get this house. Sullivan offered to give her £[illegible], and to pay £[illegible] a year rent. Ultimately the Commissioners gave him the lease at £[illegible] a year, on his agreeing to pay Mrs. Kealy £[illegible], which he has done.

We give the above table in order to show at a glance the difference between the rents paid to Colonel Gun Cunningham and those received by the Corporation. Before these new leases were granted the Commissioners memorialized the Lords of the Treasury to sanction them *en masse*, but they refused to do so, stating that each case must be considered on its merits, and that they would require the particulars of each lease before they gave their sanction to it. These particulars were not furnished, and the leases were made without any sanction from the Treasury. (Mr. E. Halpin, Ev. 677, 678.)

On all the property so leased buildings of a more or less substantial character existed, and the tenants had been for many years paying the rent stated to Colonel Cunningham. In most cases the tenants had built or rebuilt the existing houses. The excuse given by the agent to the Commissioners for the almost nominal rents at which they were relet was, that there was an understanding that when Colonel Cunningham's lease fell in, the tenants in possession, who had built, would get their holdings upon something like a ground rent. One Commissioner, Mr. Oakes (already referred to), informed us that a resolution to that effect had been passed several years ago, but neither the agent nor the Town Clerk believed that any such resolution had ever been passed, and nothing of the kind was to be found recorded on the books. (Mr. John Chapman, Ev. 111, 1[illegible]. Ev. 116. Ev. 117.)

At the meeting of the 6th of April, 1876, when the tenders for the new leases of this property came on for consideration, there were present the two Messrs. M'Phail, Mr. Caldwell, and Dr. Halpin, all Town Commissioners, who had been tenants under Colonel Gun Cunningham, and who had sent in applications for new leases; and at that meeting resolutions were passed to grant leases for seventy-five years to the two Messrs. M'Phail and to Dr. Halpin; and at the adjourned meetings of the 7th and 9th April, when the same Commissioners were present, it was resolved to grant two leases for seventy-five years each to Mr. Caldwell, and "that Dr. Halpin get his yard on the South-quay as yearly tenant at the yearly rent of £1 10s." (Mr. E. Halpin, Ev. [illegible]. Ev. [illegible].)

On the 13th April another adjourned meeting was held, at which the same Commissioners, amongst others, attended, and there was also present Mr. Burkitt, solicitor to the Commissioners. It appears they were anxious at the time to be advised whether or not the Commissioners could with safety make leases to members of their own body, and Mr. Burkitt was directed to lay a case before counsel for his opinion thereon. This he did, and afterwards read that opinion to the Town Commissioners then present, including the four gentlemen above named. Counsel advised that leases could only be made to persons who were not Commissioners at the time of the execution of the lease, and further, that the proper course for the Commissioners to adopt, as trustees for the public, was to set up the premises to public competition, and to procure the most favourable terms they could. (Ev. [illegible]. Mr. John Chapman, Ev. [illegible]. Mr. Burrows, Ev. [illegible].)

Shortly after this opinion was communicated to them, the four Town Commissioners referred to sent in their resignations, which were duly accepted, and their vacancies were shortly afterwards filled up by the other Commissioners. On the 25th of April, 1876, (Mr. E. Halpin, Ev. [illegible]. Ev. 110. Ev. [illegible].)

a resolution was passed that advertisements should be inserted in the local papers calling for sealed tenders for the several houses about to be let, the same to be sent in on or before the 11th May then following. Several tenders were sent in, but, with only two or three exceptions, all were from the occupying tenants.

These tenders were subsequently considered on the 18th May, when leases were ordered to be granted to Henry M'Phail, William M'Phail, and Dr. Halpin, and upon the 19th of May to Mr. Caldwell, upon the same terms and substantially upon the same tenders as those sent in by them before their resignations.

Two of these gentlemen, Mr. William M'Phail and Dr. Halpin, were re-elected as Town Commissioners at the next election, and although the other two were not, yet, viewing the entire transaction in its true light, it can hardly be disputed that the resignation of these Commissioners was not *bonâ fide*, but merely for the purpose of evading the difficulty raised by the opinion of counsel above quoted.

It was stated that Mr. Caldwell, who was an excise officer and stamp distributor, resigned in consequence of being required to do so by the Custom House authorities; but his own letter of resignation of the 25th April, 1874, shows the real object of his resignation, and that it was entirely the result of the opinion of counsel communicated by Mr. Burkitt to the Commissioners on the preceding evening.

Another lease appears to have been made in 1869 to a Mr. W. J. Nolan, of premises in the main street, for seventy-five years, at a rent of £15 15s. a year, the valuation of which, at that time, was £45 10s., buildings being then actually on the premises deemed representing that annual valuation.

Instances were brought to our notice in which reductions were made in existing rents. That of Mr. F. Wakefield, a tenant of lands on the Murrough, under a lease made in March, 1858, was reduced from £10 19s. 6d. to £6 19s. 6d. while he was a Town Commissioner, the reason assigned by him for the reduction being that he surrendered a small bit of land included in the lease which he found was of no use to his hotel, but it did not appear that this bit of land was subsequently let to anyone else, so that there was a clear loss of £4 a year to the ratepayers upon this transaction.

On the 25th March, 1855, a lease was granted to Mr. John Hayden, then a Town Commissioner, of a plot of building ground, for seventy-five years, at a rent of £6 10s. a year. Mr. Hayden sold and assigned his interest in this lease to Mrs. Meagher, the Superioress of the Nunnery at Wicklow, and the Commissioners then agreed to give her a new lease at a reduced rent of £2 a year. No new lease has been granted, but the agent was instructed to receive from her the reduced rent, and has done so for the last two years in pursuance of those instructions, notwithstanding that he had been cautioned by Mr. Burkitt, the solicitor to the Town Commissioners, against receiving any rent from Mrs. Meagher, lest a tenancy from year to year might be created, which would prejudice the Commissioners. When this happened Mr. Hayden was a Commissioner, and himself proposed the resolution for the granting of the new lease to Mrs. Meagher on behalf of the nuns, he being then threatened with an ejectment for non-fulfilment of the covenants contained in his lease. On the same occasion Mr. Hayden also proposed to petition the Lords of the Treasury for their sanction to grant her a lease in perpetuity of this ground, but no such petition was ever sent. Another instance of reduction of rents is that of Mr. J. A. Travers, on the North-quay; the rent under his lease was £20 a year, and this was reduced to £15, and no explanation was given as to the circumstances under which this was done.

The property vested in the Town Commissioners is at present subject to large debts under the Act of the 5 and 6 Vict., c. 111, by which the Board of Harbour Commissioners for Wicklow was constituted, and they were empowered to borrow certain sums of money. The Town Commissioners in 1854 lent them, with the consent of the Lords of the Treasury, two sums of £8,000 and £4,000, to bear interest at 4 per cent. and 5 per cent. respectively, on mortgage of the tolls, &c., to be levied under the provisions of that Act. No interest whatever has been paid on these loans. Subsequently the Public Works Loan Commissioners lent the Harbour Commissioners two sums of £3,000 each, on which there is now due the sum of £8,885 for principal and interest. Priority was given by consent to the Government loans for £6,000 over those for £12,000 advanced by the Town Commissioners, and the harbour dues are now received, and are said to be accounted for to the Public Works Loan Commissioners, by Mr. Robert Halpin, as secretary to the late Harbour Commissioners.

The last Board of Harbour Commissioners, consisting of five members, was elected in the year 1867, and they purported to continue in office until the year 1872, since which time no persons have assumed to act in that capacity. Mr. Halpin, Town Clerk, acted as secretary to that Board, and received the moorage and quayage dues payable by vessels frequenting the port and using the quays, but no tolls have ever been received *[illegible] Ev. [illegible]* under the Act of 1851, as the harbour was never sufficiently deepened to entitle them to levy them. These tolls were said to have been estimated at £1,500 a year, which would have sufficed to pay interest and form a sinking fund to redeem the capital debt of £28,696 18s. 6d.

Up to the time that the last Board ceased to act Mr. Halpin used to account to them for the sums received by him. He has continued to receive them, as he states, by the *Ev. [illegible]* authority of the Loan Fund Commissioners, who are the mortgagees, and that authority, he says, was given him by Mr. Barnes, the London solicitor of the Board, in 1874. He *Ev. [illegible]* stated that his accounts were audited by Mr. Wakefield, who had been the Chairman of the last Board of Harbour Commissioners, and who, he represented to us, audited them on the part of the London Board. No authority for such a proceeding or for the collection of the tolls, other than the statement of the Town Clerk, was produced to us. The result is that the funds of the town have to pay interest on the large sums advanced to the Harbour Commissioners on the security of a mortgage of town property, while no account has been taken of the expenditure of this money, nor any supervision exercised in relation thereto. Practically, the money appears utterly lost to the town, as no one now appears to take the slightest interest in carrying out the provisions of the Act of 1851.

There is a strong feeling on the part of several of the inhabitants that there is no real disposition to improve the port, so as to make it navigable for vessels of a large class, *[illegible] Ev. [illegible]* as that would interfere with the trade of the owners of a small class of coasting vessels who monopolise the business of the port.

It appeared to us that our powers did not authorise us to inquire further into the affairs of the late Harbour Board, but it is clearly desirable in the interests of the ratepayers of the town, whose property is so deeply pledged, that a thorough investigation should be made into their proceedings, especially with a view to the ultimate recovery of the £12,000 advanced on mortgage of the harbour tolls by the Town *Ev. [illegible]* Commissioners in 1854, which, if the harbour could be completed and placed under an efficient board of management, might soon become a not impossible contingency.

Mr. Halpin, Ev. [illegible] The two last-mentioned sums of £8,000 and £4,000, with interest due thereon respectively, are the only debts on the corporate property or rates, and the particulars of the interest due thereon are stated in Mr. Halpin's evidence.

Mr. [illegible] Ev. [illegible] Fairs for cattle are held on the fair-green, which is the property of the Commissioners, on the last Tuesday in every month, but no tolls are collected—pig-fairs are held in the street opposite the town hall. The Town Commissioners are not an urban sanitary *Mr. [illegible] Ev. [illegible] Dr. George [illegible] Ev. [illegible]* authority, and complaints were made as to the sanitary condition of the town, which in some respects does not appear to be satisfactory. The sanitary officer of the Board of Guardians pointed out the difficulties the sanitary officers had to contend with in cases of nuisances, from the delay attending on their having to get the authority of the Guardians at Rathdrum, a considerable distance off, before they could take any action. He also stated that the water supply at present was not satisfactory, but steps are being taken to procure a much better supply. Another matter was brought to our notice with respect to the expenditure of the rates by the Commissioners. At a *Mr. John Nolan, Ev. [illegible]* recent election for a Town Commissioner, a so-called "polling-booth" was fitted up in the town hall by the placing across a table at one end of the room a screen, which the Town Clerk brought from his own house, and for the use of which he charged and was paid the sum of £3 17s. Mr. Oakes, one of the Commissioners, also charged and was paid a sum of £3 for his services in presiding at the election. These payments were included in a bulk sum of £10 charged for the expenses of this election, but Mr. Finlay, the auditor, surcharged the above sums against the Commissioners who had *Ev. [illegible]* signed the cheque for their payment, on the ground of illegality. It appears also that two cheques of £10 each were signed by the Town Clerk and given to Mr. Nolan and Mr. Oakes, both Town Commissioners, for their expenses in going to London to oppose a Bill promoted by the Dublin, Wicklow, and Wexford Railway Company, and in which it was stated that the Town Commissioners, as representing the town, were vitally interested. They took the cheques to the houses of some of the Commissioners and got them signed there, and they were not in fact voted or signed at any meeting of the Commissioners. The auditor surcharged the amount of the cheques against the Commissioners who had signed them.

U. CORBETT. (*Seal.*)
W. A. EXHAM. (*Seal.*)

H. A. Robinson,
Acting as Secretary.

MINUTES OF EVIDENCE.

BELFAST.—December 11th, 1876.

(Before Messrs. [illegible], [illegible], Q.C., and [illegible], Q.C.)

[The Chairman read the Commission authorising the inquiry.]

Mr. [illegible] examined.

1. Chairman.—Are you the law adviser to the Corporation?—Yes; I am.

2. How long have you occupied the position, and have held the appointment since April, 1871.

3. I think town solicitor is your proper title?—Yes, that is my proper title.

4. Prior to your appointment were you not a member of the Corporation?—Yes, I was. I was a member of the Corporation from the year 1859.

5. Until the time of your appointment as town solicitor?—Yes.

6. And you are, I presume, a solicitor by profession?—I am.

7. Now I will first proceed to the constitution of the Corporation, and the Acts under which they exercise their powers. The Act under which the municipal authority was incorporated was the Municipal Corporations Act of 1840, was it not?—It was.

8. And the Corporation has been, I think, since governed by that Act, and various Acts passed from that time down to the year 1873?—Yes, several Acts were obtained since that time, and if you wish I will give you particulars of them.

9. The first principal Act was the Act of 1845, I believe?—Yes; it was.

10. Was not that Act of 1845, the 8th and 9th of Victoria, chap. 142?—It was.

11. And it is generally known as the "Belfast Improvement Act"?—Yes.

12. It contained, I believe, general powers for the control and regulation of the town?—It did.

13. And to purchase property, widen streets, and so on?—Yes.

14. And also to purchase markets?—Yes.

15. And it gave you large borrowing powers?—Yes; to the amount of £150,000.

16. Of which £100,000 was for widening streets, and the remaining £50,000 for other purposes?—Yes.

17. Including the purchase of markets?—Yes; for other purposes including the purchase of markets.

18. That Act laid down your rating powers at that time?—Yes; it empowered the Corporation to strike a police rate on different classes of property according to the valuation. Up to £20 of annual value the rate was 1s. 6d. in the pound; from £20 to £50 2s. in the pound; and 2s. 6d. in the pound upon property above that valuation.

19. A differential rate was, I believe, found to be inconvenient and objectionable, and so the 2s. 6d. rate was afterwards abolished?—Yes; it was abolished by the Act of 1853.

20. That Act limited your rate to 2s.?—Yes.

21. By a subsequent Act, has that rate been reduced to 2s.?—Oh no; the rate is only limited to 3s. 6d. and 1s. 6d. It was fixed by the Act of 1864 at 3s. 6d. and 1s. 6d., in place of 2s. and 1s. 6d. Practically, however, we have only found it necessary to strike a rate of 1s. and 2s. in the pound.

22. And is that the rate you now levy under that Act?—Yes; the police rate is now 2s. in the pound on all houses above £20 annual valuation, and 1s. in the pound on all ratings under £20. On property up to £8 annual value, landlords are allowed twenty-five per cent. discount if they pay within a month after the rate is struck.

23. Then the landlord compounds for that rate?—The landlord is liable for that rate; and if he pays it within a month after the rate is struck, he receives a discount of 25 per cent.

24. You call it a police rate, but it is levied for other purposes by the Act I have mentioned?—Yes, it is.

25. Then there was the Act of 1846, the 9th and 10th of Victoria, chap. 334, section 2, which gave you power to borrow £60,000 for the purchase of gasworks, which power was never, I believe, acted upon?—The power never was acted upon, except in so far as that the money was borrowed.

26. Yes, I was coming to that; but it was not applied to the purchase of gasworks?—It was not.

27. It was, in fact, applied to the general purposes of the town?—It was. All the Acts were to be read as one, and the then solicitor to the Corporation of that day, I believe, considered that the £60,000 was applicable to any purpose authorised by the Acts, even other than the purchase of gasworks.

28. Then the next Act was the Act of 1847, the 10th and 11th Victoria, chap. 284?—Yes; that confirmed the purchase of the markets, which had been previously arranged for.

29. But they cost more than £50,000?—Yes; I believe they cost about £101,000.

30. And was it by a subsequent Act that you got power to borrow another £50,000 for the markets?—Oh no; the Act of 1864 confirmed all the borrowings.

31. That Act of 1847 gave you power to purchase lands and a paper mill called the "Cromac Mill"?—Yes; and the Act of 1850 gave us power to borrow £15,000 for the improvement of the Blackstaff. The Act of 1847 gave no power to borrow.

32. It gave you powers to purchase lands specified in a schedule to that Act, and to improve the Blackstaff?—But it gave us no funds to do it with.

33. Were not the council required by that Act to sell any surplus lands within ten years, if not less?—They were.

34. And the Harbour Commissioners were to make a return of the harbour dues?—Yes; those were all provided for by that Act.

35. The next Act (1850), gave you power to borrow £15,000 to improve the Blackstaff river; that was the 13th and 14th Victoria, chap. 108?—Yes; but the Corporation have not exercised that power. The fund was quite insufficient, and the work could be only carried out with the consent of the owners of property, and the owners of property refused their consent.

36. The next Act was the Improvement Act of 1853, the 16th and 17th Victoria, chap. 114. That, I believe, is known as the Belfast Borough Extension Act?—Yes; it extended the municipal boundary to a considerable extent and abolished the 2s. 6d. rate.

37. Then, in consequence of your having overborrowed and applied the money provided for under the Act of 1846 for gas purposes and street improvements and markets, a Chancery suit, I believe, was instituted against the Corporation, which led to the award by the present Lord Cardwell?—Yes; after protracted litigation, it was referred to arbitration, and an award was made by the present Lord Cardwell. The award so made was given effect to by the Act of 1864, known as the Belfast Award Act.

38. By that Act the original £300,000 which you had power to borrow before was treated as primary mortgages?—Yes; section 9 of the Act of 1864 states that.

39. And as to the further sum of £84,840 0s. 11d. which remained unsecured, the application of all those moneys was confirmed by this Act. The priority of the mortgages was settled by that Act under clause 11?—Yes.

40. Then there is the Act of 1865 called the "County Antrim and Belfast Borough Act," the 28th and 29th Victoria, chap. 183. Was not the principal object of that Act to separate so much of the borough as was in the county Antrim from that county for all fiscal purposes?—Yes.

41. It also, I believe, authorised, for payment of expenses, a general purposes rate of 2s in the pound, on the lighting and watching within the district, and of 1s. 6d. outside the district; it abolished the county cess within the borough; it contained provisions for district drainage, and for a portion of the cost of such works to be paid by owners of property within the district?—Yes, by that Act not exceeding one half; but a subsequent Act made it only one third.

42. Under that Act as well as under your original Act of 1845, were not certain building regulations provided?—Yes; both Acts provided building regulations; but now we are principally governed by the Act of 1865 in reference to plans for buildings.

43. The next Act in order is the Act of 1866—the 29th and 30th of Victoria, chap. 113?—That was the Burial Ground Act.

44. Under that Act you were enabled to borrow £25,000 for the purposes of a cemetery?—Yes.

45. That amount was borrowed, I believe?—It was.

46. And a good deal of it has been paid off since?—Yes; the debt has been very much reduced.

47. It has been reduced by £10,000, I think?—Yes; I can give you the exact amount. It is now reduced to £3,300.

48. Then came the Act of 1868, which was in relation to the county Down, to the same effect as that just referred to relating to the county Antrim of 1865—separating that portion of the borough in the county Down for all fiscal purposes, abolishing the Grand Jury cess, and extending the General Purposes Act of 1865 to that portion of the borough within the county Down?—Yes, that is so.

49. That was the 31st and 32nd Victoria, chap. 113—the Belfast Borough Act of 1868?—Yes.

50. In 1873, I believe, after the passing of the Local Government Act, you applied for a provisional order to give you some additional powers?—Yes.

51. What are those powers?—Some amendments to Local Acts, required under the building regulations; also power to borrow on the security of the general purposes rate for district drainage purposes, and power to borrow on loan for the permanent paving of the streets, to the extent of £25,000.

52. That was for power to borrow to the extent of £40,000 in all—£25,000 for the paving of the streets, and for district drainage purposes another £15,000, I believe?—Precisely. It also empowered us to purchase some property for sewer improvements.

53. Well, that provisional order was granted, and in a succeeding session an Act confirming it was passed, called the 36th and 37th Victoria, chap. 109—the Local Government Board *Provisional* Order (Belfast) Confirmation Act?—Yes.

54. Have you borrowed the moneys you were empowered to borrow under the provisions of that Act?—A considerable portion of them. £17,150 has been borrowed for the permanent paving of the streets. For the Newtownards district drainage we borrowed from the Board of Works two loans of £3,119 each, and we estimate we will have to borrow two loans of £3,836 each for the Windsor district drainage. We have already borrowed on account of that £3,500, but the whole amount is not yet borrowed.

55. What did you borrow on the Antrim-road district?—There is still £5,600 due. I cannot tell you the amount we originally borrowed.

56. Did you also borrow for the Crumlin and Oldpark roads district?—Yes, we did; a sum of £1,200 and odd. £1,300 was the exact amount, I find, on the Crumlin-road district.

57. And you don't know the amount on the Antrim-road district?—No.

58. I see in the last year's accounts an item, and I do not know whether it is an error; perhaps you may be familiar with it, and can explain it to us. The entry I refer to is this—at page 34—"Loans received on mortgage of the general purposes rate, £3,000, under the Provisional Order Confirmation Act"—the Act we were speaking of just now—"for one-third of the Newtownards drainage expenses, payable out of said rate"; and there is another £3,000 also for Newtownards drainage works—at page 46—one charged to the general purposes rate, and another to the Newtownards road district rate?—Under the Acts of 1865 and 1868, the district drainage was arranged, and one-third of the cost is paid out of the general purposes rate, one third out of the district sewers rate, and the other third paid by the owners of property, who have houses fronting the streets through which the sewers are made. By the provisional order we got power to borrow on the general purposes rate in respect of the one third we had to pay out of that rate, because we found it totally impossible to take so much out of one year's revenue as would pay for the cost of a large district, and we got power to borrow, and spread the repayment over a number of years.

59. You have had two loans really applicable to the Newtownards road district?—Yes, two; but these are only two-thirds of the expense of executing the works. The one is paid out of the district sewers rate, spread all over the district benefited by the sewers; the other is paid out of the general purposes rate, all over the town; and the third by the owners of property fronting the streets through which the sewers are made. The Act of 1873 gives us power to borrow for drainage works. Previously to the passing of that Act we had no power to borrow on the general purposes rate for the district drainage works.

60. What was the total amount you borrowed for the drainage of the Newtownards road district?—£12,238 has been borrowed for the drainage works of the Newtownards district, of which £6,119 was borrowed upon the security of the general purposes rate, and £6,119 upon the security of the Newtownards district sewer rate.

61. How is it that in the account the two principal sums are down at £3,000 each, and not at £6,130?—That would be the amount borrowed in that year.

62. You had previous advances in the year before?—Yes, as we required the money we borrowed it.

63. Were these loans both contracted with the Commissioners of Public Works?—Yes, they gave us all the money.

64. They are payable of course principal and interest together, in the usual form, by annual instalments?—They are.

65. I see by a paper in my hand that these two loans have been already reduced to £3,830 15s. 6d. each, by the payment of the first instalment and interest?—Yes.

66. Then we now come to the last of the local Acts, the Gas Works Act of 1874—the 37th and 38th of Victoria, chap. 125?—Yes.

67. Known as the Belfast Corporation Gas Act?—Yes.

68. What amount had you power to borrow by that Act?—Up to £500,000.

69. And to what extent did you exercise these powers?—£470,000 or thereabouts.

70. I see the entry—gas loans, debentures, £468,784. Was that the total amount borrowed on debentures?—Yes, that was the total amount of the debentures.

71. Then there are, "Annuities, £3,345 11s. 11d."?—Yes; that is quite correct.

72. That would give you for that item, in round figures, £472,000?—Yes. I may mention that I have already sent forward the money for the first instalment to the Bank of England on their loan.

73. The Constabulary Act is a general Act although it is applicable specially to the town of Belfast?—That was an Act passed in 1865—the 28th and 29th Victoria, chap. 70.

74. That Act limited the number of constables of the Royal Irish Constabulary to be paid for by the Government to 150, did it not?—It did.

BELFAST, Oct. 11, 1876.
Mr. Samuel Black.

75. And it provided that the Lord Lieutenant might add any number not exceeding 320 to the Belfast Constabulary force, on payment of one half of the cost by the borough of Belfast. Is that right?—It is.

76. There is a subsequent clause—the 6th clause—which provides that the Inspector-General of the Royal Irish Constabulary shall fix the number of men, not exceeding 160, to discharge the duties of the night-watch, for each of whom there is to be charged 6d. per diem, to be paid by the borough of Belfast?—The Inspector-General has exercised that power.

77. To the full extent?—I do not know the number. We have a night-watch, but we do not control the police.

78. That 160 are not, I imagine, additional to, but they are taken out of the 320?—I regret to say that the number is not 160, as it was intended it should be, but it is 340. The number in the town is increased very largely. The Inspector-General thought it necessary to send an additional force. Some of the magistrates, in point of fact, memorialised for an additional force, and the force instead of being 450 is now 540.

79. But have you any extra men free of charge?—I regret to say not; but we are entitled to a much larger number. Some time ago an application was sent by the Corporation to the Lord Lieutenant for an additional number of men free of charge, and his Excellency said in reply, that under the general Acts he had only power to revise the distribution of the force every five years, but that the time for revision would not arrive until the 1st of July next. There was a promise, we understood, that the matter would come up for reconsideration then, and I hope then we shall get the full number of free men to which we are entitled.

80. Mr. LAWSON.—Do you consider that the proportion fixed by the Act of 1865 has not been preserved?—Certainly not. There is a much larger police force now.

81. What is the estimated proportion of men for night duty, having regard to the number of men in the town?—I do not know the number of men for night duty.

82. CHAIRMAN.—You mean to say, as I understand you, that you pay one half on a larger proportion of the whole force than was contemplated by the Act of 1865?—Yes; we think we are entitled to upwards of 200 men free.

83. And you have applied to the Lord Lieutenant to have the present number of free men increased, and there has been an intimation made to you that next July your application will be considered?—That is so.

84. The population of Belfast has increased greatly within the last ten years. I find that in 1861 it was 121,602, and according to Thom, it was 174,394 in 1870, and now I suppose it is over 200,000, probably?—It is.

85. The area of your new boundary, which you got under the Act of 1853 is, I gather from Thom, 6,900 acres?—That is correct.

86. That includes the Ballymacarrett suburb. Is not that in the county Down?—Yes; the suburbs of Ballymacarrett and Ballynafeigh are.

87. I see there are special accounts relating to Ballymacarrett?—Yes; the Act of 1846 provided that a certain sum should be expended out of the general purposes rate upon the improvement of the Ballymacarrett streets, so as to bring them up to the standard of the other portions of the town, and that sum has been expended, and considerably more than it, too.

88. The river divides the two counties, does it not?—Yes; the river Lagan divides the two counties.

89. I have got from Thom the rateable value of the property in 1861 and 1871, and I find that in the former year it was £270,830, while in 1871 it had increased to £430,434. Perhaps you will tell me now what it is in 1876. You see it had risen in ten years from £270,000 to £434,000, in round figures?—Yes, that is so. It is now £508,676.

90. Then it has not increased in quite the same proportion within the last five years, compared with the previous period?—It would increase very largely if we had a proper valuation of the borough.

91. Of course your valuation is the same as the rest of Ireland?—Our valuation was made in 1860, and is Griffith's valuation, but the value of property has increased enormously in Belfast since that year, and yet the valuator is unable to alter the valuations unless in a case where some structural changes are carried out. The result is that new property is valued very nearly at its fair value, but adjoining property not touched, remains, perhaps, paying one-third or one-fourth of what its fair proportionate taxation would be. I could give you many instances of that. I know of one case in particular where a house was valued in 1860 at £25 per annum. I subsequently let those premises myself at £85 on a ten years' lease. When seven years of that lease was up, the man who had taken it came to me and surrendered the remaining three years of his lease, and I gave him another lease for ten years at £120 per annum, and yet that man is only paying taxes on £25 a year. In some parts of the town houses are not valued at more than one-third of their letting value, and in other parts the valuation is one-third or one-fourth below the letting value.

92. But houses erected in recent years are valued up to their letting value, are they not?—About fifty per cent. below their letting value. The difficulty we have to contend with in endeavouring to obtain a revaluation is that unfortunately under the General Valuation Acts the Corporation are not recognised in any way in obtaining a revaluation. It is absolutely necessary that the application for a revaluation should come from the Grand Jury. We applied to the Grand Jury of Down to seek a revaluation, but they ignored our request, and refused to make any application, considering that if such were made it would affect their own valuation outside the borough. We also applied to the Grand Jury of the county Antrim, and they said, "We will forward your application and confine it to that portion of the borough within the county Antrim." But another difficulty arose, and it was this—that under the Valuation Acts it was necessary that if a revaluation were made at all, it should be over the entire county, barony, or union. Unfortunately, we only form portion of the union, a portion of the barony, and a portion of the county, so that we could not get any revaluation.

93. What is the extent of the barony of Belfast?—The barony of Belfast extends, I should say, ten miles from the borough; but now I am merely speaking of the county Antrim. In Down it extends fully that.

94. There are two baronies, are there not?—Yes; there are two baronies, the barony of Belfast and the barony of Castlereagh, in the county Down.

95. Is the boundary of the parliamentary borough of Belfast coterminous with the municipal boundary?—Yes.

96. When the area of the borough was extended, it was extended to that of the parliamentary borough?—It was.

97. Mr. EXHAM.—Are there not a great many new buildings outside the borough?—Yes; new buildings are being erected every day, but we have nothing to do with them. The owners take advantage as far as they can of the proximity of such buildings to Belfast without contributing towards the taxation of the town. If they did—and I must say that I think it is to their own disadvantage that they do not—they would have all the benefits that arise from the lighting, watching, paving, cleansing, &c., of the town.

98. CHAIRMAN.—Is not the municipal area divided into five wards?—Yes.

99. And the Corporation, I believe, consists of ten aldermen and thirty town councillors?—Yes.

100. Two aldermen and six councillors for each ward?—Yes.

101. Are these the wards fixed by the Act of 1870, or has there been any alteration or re-distribution of them?—The wards remain known by the same names, but by a subsequent Act they were extended. They are substantially the same.

[The witness here handed in a list of the members of the Municipal Council.]

102. When were these wards last fixed?—I think about 1852.

103. At the time of the extension of the borough boundary?—Yes; there was a local inquiry then, and the boundaries of the wards were then fixed.

104. Beyond taking in the extension, did they remain substantially the same, or was there an entire revision?—They were remodelled altogether.

105. Are these wards tolerably equal in point of rateable valuation and population?—Some of them have increased more than others. They are not equal now.

106. You think on the whole it was a fair division?—I do.

107. The business of the Corporation is transacted chiefly, I suppose, by committees. Would you kindly give me the names of those committees and their duties?—We have the Audit Committee, the Finance Committee, the Improvement Committee, the Police Committee, the Market Committee, the Sanitary Committee, the Law Committee, the Sewerage Committee, the General Purposes Committee, the Gas Committee, and the Public Parks Committee.

108. I suppose that the committees undertake pretty much the duties that their names signify?—Yes.

109. With the exception of the Police Committee, and that has, I believe, much larger duties?—Yes. The Police Committee have charge of the fire department, and the engagement and dismissal of firemen, and the regulation of that department generally. In cases of misconduct they fine or dismiss the men. That committee also has charge of the licensing of cars and drivers, and the enforcement of the hackney car by-laws. They also look after the scavenging department and the manure yards; and they see to the lighting of the town, and to the testing of the quality of the gas.

110. Mr. LAWLESS.—But they have nothing to do with the police?—Nothing, unfortunately, but to pay the money for them.

111. CHAIRMAN.—The scavenging that they attend to I should have thought would form part of the duty of the Improvement Committee?—No, it is not; but the Improvement Committee attend to the improvement of the streets of the town. They have special charge of the superintendence of the surveyor's department, including the approval or disapproval of all plans and specifications submitted for private works and buildings, and of all plans and specifications prepared by the surveyor for public works, and the outlay on streets, roads, and footpaths; also the bridges and sewers of the borough.

112. What are the duties then of the General Purposes Committee?—The principal duty referred to that committee by the Council is the selection of members to serve on the several committees of the Council; and matters requiring special consideration are also referred to them.

113. Most matters are in reason referred to the Police and Improvement Committees. Those are the two committees that practically manage the working of the town?—They are, in reference to the streets.

114. Your Law and Finance Committees are separate, I see?—Yes.

115. Then there is the Audit Committee. What does that committee do?—The members of the Audit Committee meet once a week, and examine all the accounts of the different other committees. They also audit the accounts of the cashier and collectors, and all the payments made by the different committees, and take charge of the cash, and see after the cashier's department.

116. What do the Finance Committee do?—They have special charge of the collection of the rates and other revenue the property of the Council, and the management of the mortgage debt, and the paying off and re-borrowing money. They also examine, fortnightly, the returns of the collectors of the rates.

117. You have a collector for each ward?—Yes.

118. Five collectors in all?—Yes; and the collector in each ward collects all the rates for his own ward.

119. Would you tell me the nature of the check you have on the collectors, and how often they pay moneys into the bank?—They are required to lodge daily in the bank the amount of their collections, if the amounts are anything considerable. Their books are checked by the accountant of the Corporation, Mr. Woods, very frequently, to ascertain that they correspond with the receipts given and the returns made, and if any irregularity were discovered, he would at once report the matter to the Town Clerk, who would summon the Finance Committee at once.

120. Under any circumstances do these accounts come before the Finance Committee every week?—Weekly or fortnightly, because the Finance Committee do not meet regularly every week. As a rule, the Finance Committee meet every fortnight.

121. Do these accounts go first before the Audit Committee or before the Finance Committee?—The abstract of them goes before the Audit Committee weekly.

122. I suppose Mr. Woods gets an account of the sums paid in by the collectors every day from the bank, and he also sees the collectors' books to see what they lodged?—The bank book is taken with the amounts entered in it, and Mr. Woods checks them with the collectors' accounts. The collector makes the lodgment, and there is a special form of lodgment docket, which specifies each rate to the credit of which the money has been lodged, and the bank initial the amounts received.

123. Are the rates collected up satisfactorily, as a rule?—Extremely well.

124. And the collectors give bonds?—Each gives £1,000 security for the due collection, and so on.

125. Who has the custody of those bonds?—The town clerk.

126. What other officers give bonds?—Every officer who receives cash for the Corporation is obliged to give security in the shape of a bond, in order to keep the Corporation safe.

127. Have you a list of the officers?—I have.

128. Mr. LAWLESS.—Are the collectors appointed annually?—Yes; the same men are appointed; but a formal appointment is made every year.

129. And are the securities renewed?—When I became town solicitor, I found that the securities were renewed annually, and I recommended the finance committee of the Corporation to take one bond from each of the officers or collectors to cover all subsequent engagements.

130. Are there sureties for these bonds?—Yes; the collector himself and two or three sureties; and once a year the town clerk is obliged to report to the finance committee upon the solvency and sufficiency of the sureties, and if there were any deaths in the course of the preceding year, he is bound to call the attention of the committee to the fact, so that new bonds may be procured.

131. CHAIRMAN.—Who are the other accounting officers? I suppose the clerk of the markets is an accounting officer?—He is.

132. He receives money and gives a bond?—He does. The cashier receives money also, and he gives a bond.

133. What money passes through the hands of the cashier?—Payments for street expenses and the moneys received from fire insurance companies for the services of the fire brigade. With reference to the receipts on account of street expenses, the council may, under the Acts of 1845 and 1848, order a street to be completed at the expense of the owners of property adjoining the street, and all these sums are received on account of that——

134. These are payments made by owners of property in respect of the paving, repairs, or making of new streets, which they are called upon to pay, and they all pass through his hands?—Yes; and he pays the workmen of the Corporation.

135. And not through the borough surveyor's?—No.

136. Does the borough surveyor receive any money?—No; he does not. He receives no money whatever.

137. Does Mr. Woods, the accountant?—He receives no money.

138. Those we have gone through are apparently the only officers who do receive money?—Some small sums may be received by the street inspector for the removal of manure, but that is a trifling amount very small indeed.

139. You could tell me how many officers give bonds, could you not?—The town clerk gives security; the treasurer, although an honorary officer, also gives security; the cashier gives security; the five collectors give security, and the clerk of the markets and the superintendent of the cemetery also give security.

140. The last-named receives fees for burials; does he not?—Yes, some small fees; and we think it better to have some security from him.

141. I see the total amount of the salaries is £6,972 18s.?—Yes; that is the amount, but that including the Recorder's salary.

142. The Recorder receives £500 per annum, and the clerk of the peace, £200?—Yes.

[The witness here handed in a list of the salaries of the officers of the Corporation. Appendix 2.]

143. There is one Act of Parliament you have availed yourselves of here that we have not referred to, and it is a public Act—the Public Parks Act?—Yes; the Public Parks Act of 1869 authorised Corporations to acquire parks for the recreation of the public. Acting upon those powers, we obtained the ground from Lord Donegall, of Ormeau Park, containing 173 acres, at a rent of £10 per acre. We obtained a grant in fee of that land. We never intended that the entire of the ground should be devoted to a public park, but that 100 acres should be set aside for a public park, and we anticipated that the portion of ground that would remain after doing that would be considerably enhanced in value by the making and laying out of a public park beside it; and that we would be able to let it for building purposes at high rents. We have made arrangements to put a portion of that land into the market, and the sale of it under the Public Parks Amendment Act will take place by public auction on the 11th of January.

144. Is that land within the limits of the borough?—It is. The Public Parks Act of 1872 or 1873 went further, and enabled Corporations to acquire parks outside the borough, if necessary. This Corporation had some ground that it was considered would be suitable for the purposes of a public park, just adjoining the cemetery, outside the borough, and they have since allocated a portion of that ground for the purposes of a public park.

145. Is that called the Falls Park?—Yes, it is.

146. What is the extent of that park?—About forty-five acres.

147. Was that a portion of the ground purchased for the making of the cemetery?—Yes; and not required for the purpose; but as a matter of fact the cemetery committee feel now that they will want some of that land back inasmuch as the ground is being more rapidly filled up, I regret to say, than was anticipated.

148. The new park is not marked out yet, then, is it?—It is, but there is a portion of surplus land connected with the park, which will be available for the cemetery.

149. With the exception of the cemetery, the Ormeau and the Falls Parks, have the Corporation any real property?—None, except the gasworks.

150. With regard to the ground acquired under the Act of 1845, and the Act continuing the purchase of the markets, have the ground rents all been sold?—All of the surplus ground we became possessed of has been sold. We still, however, have rents coming in to the amount of about £3,000 a year from portions of the markets. Portions of the markets are let to brewers, and these portions bring in a rent of about £3,000 a year—they are portions of the premises used for market purposes.

151. I now wish to draw your attention to the Public Parks Acts of 1869 and 1872, which I have in my hand; the first Public Parks Act, by which you acquired Ormeau Park, was the Act of 1869, and the Amendment Act is the 35th of Victoria, chap. 6. That is dated May, 1872, and gave power to the Corporations to purchase parks outside the boundary of the borough, and power to sell surplus lands?—Yes, that is so.

152. At present you do not, I believe, derive any rent from Ormeau Park?—Yes, we do; we let it for grazing purposes.

153. Your expenditure connected with that park amounts I see to a good round sum?—Unfortunately it does.

154. It amounted last year to £2,978 3s. 9d.—over £3,000 in fact, because there is another £100 for the curator?—We have estimated the expenditure on both parks for the coming year at £3,366 15s. 11d.

155. Your receipts from the two parks last year were £234 from the Ormeau Park, including sale of timber, &c., and £26 from the Falls Park for grazing?—Yes; this year we estimate the rents of the Ormeau Park at £250 and the Falls Park at £100.

156. You will be able to let them on much better terms than last year?—Yes, we will; we will be able to realise more out of our park property now than formerly.

157. Mr. Lawlor.—I see in this printed list of salaries, there are entries, some of them for nine months' salaries, and some for twelve months. Then there is an entry—"F. W. Montgomery, apprentice, £10 for the twelve months ending the 31st of July, 1875." Who are these apprentices?—We found it very convenient to get a staff of young lads to come into the different offices of the Corporation—the town clerk's office, the accountant's, the cashier's, and so on, and they are allowed to pass through the different offices, so that they may be ready to take a superior situation in any of the offices in which there is a vacancy. They commence at £20 a year, and increase £10 annually. They are, in fact, assistant clerks. They are bound for five years, unless the Corporation have reason, and wish to dispense with their services, or they wish to retire. The system has been found to work extremely well. We get by this means a great deal of the work done at very low salaries, while these young persons have an opportunity for advancement if they remain in the service of the Corporation.

158. Chairman.—I see you have a car inspector?—Yes, we have two.

159. And I suppose they exercise control over all the public vehicles in the town?—Yes.

160. There is a scale of fares I presume?—Yes; there is a scale fixed by the Corporation and confirmed by the Recorder. There are also by-laws framed under the Act of 1845, for the regulation of cars and car-drivers, and these inspectors go round and assist the police in seeing that these by-laws are enforced. I regret to say that the duty of enforcing these by-laws has fallen almost entirely upon the car inspectors. The police do not seem to think that the duty comes within the scope of their operations as a general rule. They sometimes, it is true, bring forward a case but it is a very rare exception. Our car inspectors are engaged almost day and night, performing this very useful duty. Under the Police Act I think the burden of seeing that these by-laws are properly enforced is thrown on the police to a great extent. Section 1 of the Constabulary Act of 1865, provides that the Constabulary Force of the town of Belfast shall discharge the powers and duties then lawfully had and discharged by the Police Force of the town. Mr. Inspector Bayley, has always recognised that the duty should be done by the police, and he has given orders from time to time that the police should carry out these duties, but we think that the police have not been so active as they should have been in that respect.

161. As a rule are the public conveyances worked satisfactorily in the borough?—I think so. As a rule we have a very good class of cars. We have not been able to introduce flys or cabs to the number that we would have wished; but my impression is that the

BELFAST. Mar. 21, 1876. Mr. Samuel Black.

fares are too low. You see each one take four passengers, whilst Hansom cabs can only take two.

162. What is the staff of the fire brigade?—We have a superintendent of the fire brigade, an assistant superintendent, and a permanent staff of I think four men; besides thirty-two others who are always at hand, should any alarm of fire be given. If an alarm is given a bell is rung and these men are within easy distance as a rule and attend at once.

163. I see you received a pretty good sum from the different fire insurance companies last year as their contributions for fires extinguished?—We have certainly received some contributions, but not as much as we think the fire insurance companies should pay.

164. You received, however, altogether £329 11s. 3d. in various small sums from twenty-two companies and others, under that head?—Under the terms of the Act of 1845, they are obliged to contribute to the entire expense incurred at the extinguishing of fires.

165. Mr. Exham.—Is there a scale regulating the amounts these companies should pay?—There is. Under the Act of 1845 we were empowered to recover the extraordinary expenses of the brigade at fires from the assurance companies; and in order to avoid any question at between the insurance companies and ourselves a scale was fixed.

166. Chairman.—I see that that payment did not cover your extraordinary expenses. The extra expense was £391 1s. 4d. while the receipts were £329 11s. 3d.?—Yes.

167. I see also an entry of which I should like an explanation—"One year's salary to the Water Commissioners' turncock"?—The water supply of the borough is not under the control of the Town Council; there is a separate corporation having the control of the supply of water for the town, and called the Belfast Water Commissioners.

168. Under what Act?—The Belfast Water Act.

169. Do you know the date of that Act?—1840. I think it would be a great improvement if the corporation had the control of the water supply themselves in place of having two separate bodies.

170. Do you find much inconvenience resulting from that state of things?—There is always a conflict of authority, and sometimes we have to complain that there is a deficient water supply, for instance, at the extinguishing of a fire, and then if we complain the Water Commissioners attribute that deficiency to our men, and there are constant little petty unpleasantnesses between the officers of the two Boards on account of that.

171. What arrangement exists with regard to the flushing of the streets?—None at all. We get water from the Commissioners for the watering of the streets, but their charge for it is so excessive, that we could not possibly think of getting water from them for the flushing of the sewers, or the washing of dirty courts. They charge us 4d. a load for all taken from the pipes. Each of the carts holds about 230 gallons. Virtually the charge is 1s. 6d. per thousand gallons. They give water to the general public at 6d. per thousand gallons, but they charge the Corporation 1s. 6d. per thousand. They do that, they say, because we only take the water in the summer months when it is most valuable to the Commissioners. They, however, would give us water at 1d. per load, provided we would take it out of a particular basin which is of no earthly use to them; but it costs us the same to take it from that, in fact, almost more than it would to pay the excessive charge which they make of 1s. 6d. per load.

172. Mr. Exham.—In case of fires what do they do?—They are obliged to give a supply of water in that case.

173. Chairman.—Is this annual salary to the turncock for attending to that?—Yes; that is what the annual salary is for. It is paid for a turncock. In a great portion of the town they have not laid fire-mains, simply service pipes, and put fire-plugs upon these pipes. Then occasionally the water will be turned off, and there will be no supply of water in these pipes at all. It is necessary to turn on the pipes at particular places, and there are constant disputes as to whether our men—the men connected with our brigade—had turned on the right cock or not; so in order to prevent further disputes we agreed to pay a salary of £7 10s. to the Water Commissioners' turncock, and he is expected to attend at fires and turn on the proper cock. As a matter of fact, however, a town like Belfast should have mains specially charged for fire purposes, because it is highly inconvenient to have to depend on service pipes, as very often these pipes have to supply a large number of cisterns, and therefore it is highly desirable if we can always have a sufficient supply for fires.

174. Are the Corporation represented on the Water Commissioners?—The Mayor is entitled ex officio to a seat on the Board; but it is only one out of the fifteen.

175. How many Commissioners do you say there are?—Fifteen, I think.

176. Is there not a certain proportion elected by the Corporation?—Not at all.

177. How are the Commissioners elected?—By the water ratepayers.

178. Are persons excluded from voting for the Water Commissioners?—They are, by the construction given to the Water Act.

179. Mr. Exham.—Did the Corporation ever try to obtain representation on that Board?—No; they did not.

180. Chairman.—It seems to me that there must be a conflict of authority in this way; for instance—in the Commissioners taking up the streets to get at their service pipes or mains?—They frequently require to examine and relay their mains. Of course that leads to a conflict of authority. By an arrangement made some time ago they pay the Corporation, however, for repairing where they have interfered with the streets. Still the whole thing is an inconvenient arrangement, and it is one that should be remedied for the benefit of the town.

181. Mr. Exham.—They have power themselves to open the streets?—Yes, they have power to open the streets. They may open the streets, and only give us notice when the works are in progress. However, I am bound to say that I think the officers of the Water Commissioners are anxious to meet the views of the officers of the Corporation as far as they can; but for all that the system is, in my opinion, a bad one.

182. Chairman.—Is there any other authority that conflicts with the Corporation?—There is another body here—the Harbour Commissioners—but there is no conflict between that body and the Corporation.

183. Are the Corporation represented on the Harbour Commissioners?—The Mayor is, ex officio, a member of that board also.

184. But the Corporation do not elect any of the Harbour Commissioners?—They do not.

185. They are quite a distinct body, and there is, you say, no inconvenience found to arise from their existence as such?—Very little.

186. Do you remember what Act or Acts of Parliament the Belfast Harbour Commissioners are incorporated under?—I can tell you. The Belfast Harbour Act of 1847; the Belfast Port and Harbour Conservancy Act of 1852; and the Belfast Dock Act of 1854. There was an old Act previously in existence, the 1 & 2 William IV., but the Act of 1847 was the first the present Harbour Board obtained.

187. Mr. Exham.—Do the Harbour Commissioners keep the quays in repair here?—They do.

188. Chairman.—Do they light them or do you light them?—They light and pay us for the lamps, and they pay the same price as is paid for the town lamps, £3 per lamp.

189. How many public lamps are lit by the gas company for the town?—2,847 were lighted by the last contract, and that number at £3 each lamp makes the total cost under this head £8,541.

190. The Corporation have only had the gas works since July, 1874. Can you tell me what was the price per thousand feet that the gas company charged the

[illegible] when they were supplying them before the Corporation obtained the control of the gas works?—[illegible] 4s. 6d. per thousand, with discount varying from 2½ per cent. up to 20 per cent. in some cases, according to the amount consumed. We were able last year to reduce the price to 4s. 3d. per thousand with the same discount. This year we have reduced it to 3s. 11d. per thousand, with the same discount, and I have every expectation that we shall be able to reduce it in price still further.

191. And notwithstanding that you cleared a profit last year of something like £[illegible],000?—Since July, 1874, we have netted for the ratepayers of the town upwards of £[illegible],000 profit on the gasworks.

192. Mr. Exham.—Do you supply gas outside the borough?—Yes, for a considerable distance outside—perhaps three miles, I should say, in some places.

193. Mr. Lawless.—The Corporation do not exercise any control over the dock and harbour?—None whatever.

194. And you receive no profit?—No profit; we simply receive rates—the police rate is calculated upon the tonnage of vessels entering the harbour, upon the terms fixed by the Act of 1847.

195. Chairman.—The Act of 1847 provided that the Harbour Commissioners should make an annual return to the Town Council of the tonnage and the amount of rating the tonnage is thereon provided for. I do not remember what was the amount of their contribution?—It was provided by the Act.

196. Is that return furnished by the Harbour Commissioners?—Yes, it is always furnished by the Harbour Commissioners. The general purposes rate is assessed on a different basis.

197. The Act provides, I see, that the toll for police rate shall be 3d. on the registered tonnage on vessels from foreign ports, and 1½d. on vessels discharging goods in the docks of the Commissioners?—Yes.

198. Mr. Exham.—Are there sheds erected on the quays by the Commissioners, the same as at the North Wall, Dublin?—Yes; there are sheds built on the quays.

199. Are they rated?—They are.

200. Chairman.—Do you lay a separate burial rate?—Occasionally we do. For the existing year we have not found it necessary to levy any separate rate. It is levied as a portion of the borough rate.

201. Your borough rate is limited to 3d. in the pound?—Yes; for ordinary borough purposes; but for sanitary purposes and burial purposes, under special and general Acts the limit is not applicable.

202. What is the limit for burial purposes?—I think the rate is limited to 6d. in the pound; but we have never found it necessary to strike that rate in one year. We have had a 2d. rate.

203. What is the sanitary rate limited to?—It is unlimited for sanitary purposes.

204. Practically the amount of the rates you levy is divided as follows:—What you call your police rate—your last rate was 1s. in the pound on valuations up to £20, and 2s. on valuations over that. That is the rate you laid on in 1875?—It is.

205. Your maximum being 2s. 4d. and 1s. 6d.?—Just so.

206. For general purposes you laid the maximum rate of 2s. within and 1s. 6d. outside the lighting and watching district?—Yes.

207. For district sewers you laid a rate of 3d. in the Crumlin and Old Park-road district?—Yes.

208. And 7d. in the Antrim Road district, and 7d. in the Newtownards Road district?—Yes.

209. For a district you mentioned, the Windsor district, you have not levied a rate there yet?—The works are only in progress; but there will be a rate levied of 7d. in the pound next year.

210. You laid a rate of 1½d. for burial purposes in 1875?—Yes, but next year there will be none. I may observe that for the coming year the borough rate will be 3½d., and that for the parks 1½d.

211. You did not lay any special sanitary rate?—We did not; we paid the expenses out of the borough rate under the Public Health Act.

212. Then the total amounts you levied last year were as follows:—£[illegible],7[illegible] 0s. 6d. was the total amount you levied under the police rate; £[illegible],416 13s. 9d. for the general purposes rate, £7,010 4s. 10d. for the three district sewers rates already mentioned, £1,9[illegible] 1s. 6d. burial rate, and £[illegible],[illegible]3 8s. 3d. for the borough rate?—Yes; that is correct.

213. The only two rates up to the maximum were the general purposes and the borough rates?—Yes; they were the only two. I may remark that we are unlimited as regards the levying of district sewers rates; and the police rate was very little more than half of what we could levy.

214. Mr. Exham.—Have the Crown here a local crown solicitor?—They have. The crown solicitor does not prosecute, except in cases of extraordinary emergency. The magistrates found in the prosecutions for street offences and everything of that kind, that it was very inconvenient to be without a public prosecutor, because in almost every case here an attorney appears for the defence, and the fact of having only a sub-constable for the prosecution opposed to a sub-attorney for the defence created great inconvenience, and so the magistrates requested that they should get [illegible].

215. Chairman.—What commission do you pay your collectors?—One and a half per cent. on the amount collected.

216. That does not apply to anything besides the rates?—No; they simply get that commission on the rates collected. They have nothing to collect but the rates; each collects all the rates in his own ward but nothing else.

217. The commission is one and a half per cent. on the amount actually collected?—Yes; and to show you the care taken to prevent unnecessary outlay in this respect, I may mention that when the gas committee got charge of the gasworks, they declined to allow the collector to receive the rates on the gasworks, but simply paid the amount direct over to the cashier's hands by cheque, so as to save the collector's poundage.

218. Is there no collector of the gas rents?—Oh yes; I was referring to the rates payable on the gasworks, and I was saying, that in place of allowing the collector to receive those rates as he would have been entitled to do had the works been the property of the company, the gas committee paid the money direct into the cashier's hands, and by that means saved the collector's poundage.

219. Who collects the gas rents?—The officers of the Corporation. There are separate and regular collectors appointed for the purpose.

[Witness handed in a list of the officers of the gasworks. Appendix No. 8, page 304.]

220. You say you keep the accounts of the gasworks separate?—Yes, by Act of Parliament. The collectors are paid by salary and not on commission. We took over the staff of the gas company, when the premises came into our hands, and carried out the same arrangements as previously existed as far as we could.

221. You charge a less rate per 1,000 cubic feet?—We have reduced the price. In point of fact the company had arrived at that stage of success that they had no object in economising. They were always able to pay their comfortable dividends of seven and ten per cent. on the subscribed capital. They had applied for power, and were going to raise another £100,000 capital, and so we bought them up with the result that I have previously told you. We have every reason to believe that it will be a good speculation for the town.

222. Before the Act of 1874 came into operation, you did, under your Improvement Act of 1845, I suppose, a certain amount of sanitary work?—Yes, always. We had a sanitary inspector always, and I think five assistants, one for each ward. When the Public Health Act came into force we appointed a consulting sanitary officer, Dr. Samuel Brown. Actually his proper name would be the medical officer of health for

BELFAST. Oct. 11, 1876.

Mr. Samuel Black.

the borough. The Local Government Board and myself differed as to his proper name, but as they paid half the salary we did not quarrel with them about the matter. Then we have an executive sanitary officer whose duty it is to see to and carry out all the sanitary improvements required.

223. He is not the town surveyor?—Not at all. He has no other duties except as sanitary officer. He is also a civil engineer by profession. Then we have the assistants, one for each ward.

224. Those are subsanitary officers or inspectors of nuisances?—Yes; with one additional man to do special duty when required, and attend to the office work.

225. Have these men no other work to do?—None, except to attend to sanitary matters.

226. Under the Act all dispensary doctors are sanitary officers. How many are there?—Eight, I think; we do not pay them any salary; they are paid by the Poor Law Union.

227. The reports which the subsanitary officers make go, I suppose, through the consulting sanitary officer to the committee?—Yes; these reports go before the committee, and their orders are made upon them.

228. Has there been much progress made in sanitary reform in Belfast?—A great deal has been done, but I think a great deal remains to be done.

229. I only want to know from you whether the Corporation are earnest in their desire to bring about sanitary reform?—I am decidedly of opinion that they are as far as they possibly can. At the same time I think it right to mention that there has been a scheme of main drainage for a considerable time before the town, which, owing to certain difficulties in the way, we have not been able to carry out. In the first place there is the great cost, which is one considerable difficulty, and secondly, there is some difference between the Corporation and the Harbour Commissioners as to the proper outlet for that drainage; but it is only a question of time.

230. In the meantime you seem to be carrying out district drainage works to a considerable extent?—We have, and we have been making a considerable number of new streets. Since 1866, when we got powers under the Act of 1846, a lengthy litigation had been put an end to, we have paved and sewered upwards of 700 new streets.

231. Is that all within the last ten years?—Yes.

232. Are the streets and lanes generally kept clean?—They are regularly swept and the scavengers are instructed to go to these places if possible every day. Some of these thoroughfares are swept once a day, some oftener than that, and others twice a week according to the nature of the work.

233. Are the scavengers under the control of the town surveyor?—No; they are under the direction of street inspectors, specially appointed for the purpose. There are two assistant street inspectors under them again. The town is divided into two districts. Each inspector has a district, and has an assistant and a certain number of gangers under him to carry out his orders. If the streets are not being properly attended to one of the street inspectors reports to the police committee and receives instructions from them, from time to time, as to what he should do.

234. I suppose the number of men on the gangs varies according to the time of year, and the nature of the reports of the street inspectors. In case of emergency has he unlimited authority to engage men to a sufficient number for the carrying on of the work without waiting for a meeting of the committee?—If any emergency arises he has full power to get as many horses and men as he requires, and report to the committee. He is in no way limited as to the number of horses and carts, but he gives a return daily of the number. The horses are supplied by contract, but we furnish the carts.

235. I see there is an item in the accounts referring to the amount you paid for the removal of the statue of Lord Belfast, and it would seem that you received from Lord Donegal a larger sum than you expended. Can you explain that?—We certainly did not charge a larger sum than it cost us. I take it that the explanation is this—A portion was work done and paid for directly by cheque, and another portion will appear in another account.

236. Lord Donegal seems to have paid you £53 0s. 6d. for the removal of the statue of Lord Belfast, and on the other side of the account it only appears that you expended £71 4s. I asked you the question because I thought you might be familiar with the matter and might be able to explain it to me?—I cannot explain it accurately. All I know is that we only received the exact amount we paid. I suppose other payments will appear in other portions of the account. As an evidence of that I may tell you that I perceive another item of £3 15s. 6d. in another account on the same matter.

237. With regard to your markets—you worked them at a considerable profit, I perceive?—Yes, they are very successful, and a great source of advantage to the public.

238. I see that the net profit on the markets, exclusive of cost of additional buildings, was £6,325 10s.?—Yes; that was the net profit on the working of the markets last year.

239. After paying rent, and some small repairs and alterations, and all the wages and salaries?—Yes.

240. The head of the markets is Mr. Wood, "Clerk of Markets," and under him is there a considerable staff, weighmasters, inspector of provisions, and other officers?—There is a considerable staff.

241. You have, of course, a table of tolls?—Oh, yes; for each market.

242. How many markets are there?—There are twelve markets.

243. The two principal being the Smithfield and the potato and vegetable?—Yes; but the pork market is also a large one.

244. The fines, I see, realized a large amount?—Yes; these were fines levied in the police courts.

245. No less than a sum of £3,048 14s. 6d. received as fines from the petty sessions clerk?—Yes; but we anticipate that next year they will be less.

246. Mr. [illegible].—Do you get all the fines here?—I claimed them all, and succeeded in persuading the law officers of the Crown that we were entitled to them.

247. You have public slaughter-houses here?—Yes, we have.

248. And they realized a net profit of £179 14s. 3d., I perceive?—Yes.

249. After paying the superintendent and other expenses connected with them?—Yes.

250. I see there is a weights and measures adjusting account. Just explain that?—There is an officer appointed for the purpose, and a schedule of fees fixed, which are charged to the public, and he adjusts all weights brought to him, and charges according to the schedule of fees. The office cost something like £70 for the year, and we received about £150.

251. You got, I see, an actual profit on that of £84 18s. 11d.?—Yes; it varies from year to year. We are obliged to have the office, and the police look after the dealers to see that the weights are kept properly adjusted.

252. After paying your car inspectors, you got a net profit of £380 8s. upon the licenses?—Yes; we only charge 2s. 6d. for each license issued. That is a very small charge, and we, in a great measure, allow free trade in licenses. Any man who has a good horse and car can have a license at once if he chooses to apply for it, without having to wait to buy up a number as they do in Dublin.

253. There is an item here—"Amount transferred from burial fund, £3, to police fund." How do you explain that?—It has been some item paid out of the police fund really chargeable to the other fund, and at the end of the year a cheque would be passed from one account to the other for the amount.

254. What is the next item—"House account. From Sub-Inspector H. A. Blake, proceeds sale of forfeited property, &c., &c., £50 15s. 6d."?—When articles are found upon men and are claimed after a certain lapse of time, they are sold after public notice, and the proceeds go to the benefit of the borough.

255. What place are they brought to?—Either to the Constabulary or to the car inspectors.

256. CHAIRMAN.—In the malicious injuries account I see there is always a large and increasing balance in favour of that account. You started with £483 13s. 1d., and then you received in arrear from the special rate £36 18s. 6d., that rate was laid in 1874, and you left off with a balance in the treasurer's hands of £[illegible] 17s. 1d.?—That was increased by interest on the balance in the treasurer's hands. We have an arrangement with the bank by which they allow us interest on all balances in their hands in our favour. There were very large claims upon the Corporation after the riots of 1872—claims which amounted, as well as I recollect, to about £[illegible],000 for malicious injuries to property. These claims were minutely examined, and reduced to £3,500, or thereabouts. We had to strike a special rate, as we were only able to take £1,000 out of the general purposes rate. We accordingly struck a special rate; we could not levy less than 1d. in the pound for the purpose, and that rate left a considerable balance. That balance is carried forward, and is applicable to the liquidation of any claims for malicious injuries that might arise in future years.

257. You only paid for malicious injuries the sum of £26 1s. last year?—Yes, that was; but I regret to say that we have more claims this year, owing to what transpired in the month of August last.

258. Out of the general purposes rate you are enabled to set apart £1,000 for that purpose?—We are; and we only once—in 1873 or 1874—had to strike a special rate for the purpose.

259. Although these accounts are admirably kept, I was surprised to find that you have an overdrawn account on the two principal accounts—the police and the general purposes rate—you have an overdrawn account on each?—We have.

260. Is that exceptional?—It is somewhat exceptional. During the past two years we have bought property at Peter's-hill for street improvements to the amount of £4,000. We have also expended £2,000 in the purchase of other property for the purpose of street improvements; so that that would affect the police rate; and besides that, the expense of the police is really so heavy upon the town, that our funds have been exhausted in great measure.

261. Mr. EXHAM.—Do you pay any interest on the overdrawn accounts at the bank?—Yes; they charge us interest.

262. CHAIRMAN.—There are cross charges for interest on overdrawn accounts, I suppose. They allow and disallow?—Yes; and as a matter of fact, the balance of interest is altogether in favour of the Corporation, on taking the banking transactions as a whole.

263. You had a balance of £4,318 against you on the general purposes fund, and of £2,003 on the police fund?—These balances are rapidly diminishing.

264. The gross balance against you was then £6,321?—Yes.

265. Does not the auditor, Mr. Sharpe, quarrel with that state of things?—No; he does not; so long as the whole account is not against the Corporation. If the whole of the balances were against the Corporation, he would, doubtless, object to that.

266. Do they allow you the same rate of interest on the other side of the account?—They allow us the highest deposit rate of interest for all money in their hands; but they charge us 5 per cent. on all overdrawn accounts.

267. What rate are they at present allowing you?—I think they are allowing us 1½ per cent.

268. In round figures on the borough and burial rate, you have £4,000 in your favour?—Yes, they only, I may mention, charge us 1½ per cent. on a particular overdrawn account; but if the whole of the accounts were overdrawn, then they would charge us 5 per cent.

269. The heaviest overdrawn balance was on the general purposes account, and the amount charged as interest against that account on the year was £3 17s. 7d.?—Yes.

270. While on the police rate, notwithstanding you were overdrawn at the end of the year, there was a sum of £165 17s. 6d. allowed for interest to the credit of the Corporation?—Yes.

271. There are, if I understand you, forty members of the Town Council?—Yes.

272. What number constitutes a quorum?—We must, in order to have a meeting, have one-third of the members present.

273. Is there generally a good attendance?—Generally a good attendance. During my experience I do not recollect a single meeting adjourned for want of a quorum. There may have been one in the last fifteen years.

274. Does the same observation apply to the committees where I suppose a great deal of your work is done?—Yes; there is an admirable attendance at the committee meetings. Three forms a quorum; and at these meetings we always have quorums as a rule.

275. These committees, I suppose meet once a week?—Yes. The audit committee meets every Monday; the cemetery committee meets every fortnight; the improvement committee meets once a week; the parks committee once a week; the police committee once a week; the sanitary committee once a week; the law committee when summoned, if there is anything special to come before them. The general purposes committee, as well as the gas committee, meets once a week.

276. With the exception of the cemetery committee and the law committee, all the committees meet once a week?—Yes.

277. Mr. EXHAM.—I suppose all the costs paid to you as town solicitor are taxed in the regular way?—Yes; I never get payment for a bill of costs unless they were taxed by the taxing officer of the proper court.

278. You receive no salary?—No salary. The Corporation were anxious to fix a salary for the office, and had fixed the salary they intended to pay my predecessor, and he had drawn the first quarter of it as so fixed; but the late Mr. Walsh decided that the Corporation had no power to make a contract of that kind with their solicitor; and he had to return to the old plan of bills of costs. In an increasing town like Belfast, the expenses under this head must be necessarily very considerable; but I think any gentleman who receives merely his taxed costs will run no risk of being over-paid.

[illegible]
Jan. 12, 1876.
Mr. Samuel Black.

Belfast. Jan. 15, 1877. — Mr. [illegible]

285. That is now called the police rate? Yes.

286. The secondary mortgages are under the Act of 1864?—Yes.

287. Which is the Award Act?—Yes.

288. And was not £34,640 0s. 11d. the amount of these secondary mortgages?—£110,091 12s. 6d. is the amount of the secondary mortgages issued with the interest added.

289. £64,640 0s. 11d. was the capital sum named in the 8th section of the Award Act?—Yes; and the interest allowed to be added, under the 9th section of the Act, was capitalized and the whole amounted to £110,091 12s. 6d.

290. And has that been now reduced to £33,000?—Yes, that is what they now stand at, and there is now about £4,000 in the funds to partly meet that which we cannot dispose of until some of the mortgages mature.

291. Under the Burial Act of 1866, you borrowed the sum of £23,000?—Yes.

292. Which is now reduced to £9,200?—Yes, but it is right to explain that £4,000 of that £23,000 has been lately transferred to the parks account under authority. It is £13,200 taking the two together.

293. £13,200 then remains of that—£9,200 stands to the burial fund and £4,000 to the public parks?—Yes.

294. How much did you borrow originally on the district sewage rates?—I have not totted it up. However, there remains due on the Antrim-road sewerage district, £2,702.

295. And £2,400 on the general purposes rate?—Yes.

296. On the Crumlin and Old Park roads district sewers rate there is £520 still outstanding?—Yes; that is all that remains due.

297. You borrowed for this district £1,300 originally?—Yes; that is correct, I believe.

298. And these sums were all borrowed under the Acts of 1865 and 1868?—Yes; we borrowed from the Government £12,000 odd, and it is being paid off by yearly instalments.

299. Under the Act of 1873, were you not enabled to borrow £25,000 for permanent paving?—Yes; we only owe now £17,160, we had power to borrow £25,000, but we only borrowed £17,400.

300. For the permanent paving?—Yes, and we have paid off £450, leaving a balance of £17,160.

301. You also I see owe £3,400 on the Windsor district drainage rate, and £2,800 on the general purposes rate?—Yes; we had power to borrow £7,000 for this drainage district, and we have only borrowed £5,000 so far, and we have a margin of £2,000.

302. And on the Newtownards road district there are two sums still outstanding of £3,580 14s. 6d. each; the one secured on the district sewers rate, and the other on the general purposes rate?—That is quite right.

303. That makes your total outstanding mortgage debt £197,128 11s. exclusive of the gasworks?—Quite right.

304. Then under the Corporation Gas Act in 1874, you raised the amounts here?—We borrowed £446,764 on debentures; and £3,343 14s. 11d. on annuities. There is an instalment paid to the Bank of England of £11,000, which, taken off, would leave a total net debt under that head of £439,107 14s. 11d.

305. Did you borrow all that money from the Bank of England?—£120,000 only from the Bank of England and the rest from the public. A great many shareholders of the old gas company re-lent their money.

306. What were the terms upon which the Bank of England lent the money?—At 4½ per cent.; repayable by twenty yearly instalments.

307. Did you pay 4½ per cent. on the private debentures?—No; I think 4½ is the highest on the private debentures, and some of them less.

308. What are the rates of interest?—£3,250 at 5 per cent.; £78,550 at 4½ per cent.; £348,664 at 4¼ per cent.; and £40,300 at 4½ per cent. If we had money now to borrow we could get the bulk of it at 4 per cent., but at the time this was borrowed it was done on the best terms we could get.

309. Can you tell me the rate of interest paid on the primary and secondary mortgages?—For a long time we paid on the primary mortgages 5 per cent.; and that we reduced from time to time as the mortgages became due according to the state of the money market. We now replace any mortgages being paid off, by borrowing at 4 per cent.

310. Do not the primary mortgages vary from 4 to 4½ per cent.?—Yes.

311. While the secondary mortgages are all at 4½ per cent.?—Yes.

312. What are the checks upon the collectors of the rates?—That is one of the collector's books—it shows the money which he lodges in the bank. (Hands in book.)

313. He keeps an account showing the amount he has lodged?—Yes.

314. What is done with this book?—It is brought to the cashier and entered in his book; and he sees that it corresponds with the bank book. Then the accountant (Mr. Woods) checks the entries with the blocks of the receipts which the collector gives to the parties paying the rates. The collector's lodgments and Mr. Woods' sheet must tally, and both are examined by me, and I certify that they are correct.

315. They are all submitted to you?—Yes.

316. Does the cashier make up the account entirely from the collector's books?—Yes; and Mr. Woods makes a separate account of the returns from the block receipts given by the collectors to the ratepayers. They are further checked by the bank book to see that the amounts correspond. The two statements are made from different sources daily. All are examined by me before being submitted to the finance committee.

317. Are the collectors required to make lodgments daily?—They are authorised to hold small sums up to £5, but every sum over £5 they are required to lodge every day.

318. Have you the custody of the collectors' bonds?—I have.

319. What is the amount of their bonds?—They each give a bond in £1,000.

320. What moneys pass through your hands?—The only moneys that pass through my hands are, that I superintend all the borrowing and paying off of mortgages. If a mortgage is to be paid off a cheque is signed by the finance committee, and I take the cheque and pay the cash, and get away the mortgage. I am a sort of superintendent.

321. You are a medium between the two?—Yes.

322. What is the amount of your bond?—A bond of £2,000; two sureties of £1,000 each.

323. Who is that lodged with?—With the town solicitor, Mr. Black.

324. Will you now give me the burgess roll. There are 6,380 names on this roll?—Yes; that is for the present year.

325. Can you give me the rateable value of each ward separately?—The Dock ward is £94,684 10s. number of burgesses 997. This is the revised roll you have before you now. St. Anne's ward, £105,553 5s., number of burgesses 1,136; Smithfield ward, £72,842, number of burgesses 640; St. George's ward, £106,480 10s., number of burgesses 973; Cromac ward, £137,521, number of burgesses 1,696.

326. I observe you keep a regular account of the sinking fund applicable to each loan?—Invariably; we do not mix them at all.

327. And this is published in your annual statement?—Yes.

328. What assistants have you in your office?—I have an assistant and two juniors. These last are apprentices. Mr. Calwell is my assistant.

329. And does not he also act as registrar of the cemetery?—Yes.

330. Is he empowered to act in your absence as your deputy?—No; that is an omission in the Act that should be remedied. If I was ill or laid aside

for a while, nothing could be done. If I was unable to attend to my duties, I think the mayor should have power to appoint a locum tenens.

331. You think there should be power to appoint a deputy town clerk in case of the illness or temporary absence of the town clerk?—Yes; but I would not wish to have the responsibility of making the appointment myself.

332. What are the borough surveyor's (Mr. Montgomery's) special duties?—He superintends all sewerage matters, the repairs of roads, laying out new streets, and all other matters that a surveyor and engineer is bound to look after in a large town.

333. He sees, I suppose, that the Building Act is properly carried out?—Yes.

334. I think we understood from Mr. Black that the provisions of the Act of 1845 are those that are now acted upon, and not those of 1848?—I think we work by the later Act.

335. Are the provisions of the Act carefully enforced?—Mr. Montgomery is very particular in enforcing them so far as he can.

336. Do you act in any way as clerk to the gas committee, or is there a separate clerk?—I take their minutes and consider myself their secretary, but they have a staff in the office.

337. I see by this list they have two clerks in their office. Mr. Stelfox, the manager, is here described as a clerk?—He is the manager, and it is his brother who is clerk there.

338. I see; and then there is Mr. Gibson, who is another clerk?—Yes.

339. The manager, I see, gets £600 a year?—Yes, and a house.

340. Is he a civil engineer?—He was brought up in these works under his father, who was a civil engineer.

341. And was he assistant to his father who was manager when the gasworks were owned by a public company?—Yes.

342. *Witness.*—I want for a moment to call your attention to the fact that as regards the balance of the secondary mortgages we have £4,075 invested in stock.

343. Ready to pay off as soon as the mortgages mature?—Yes; £4,075 three per cent. stock.

344. Now, to proceed, who pays all these wages?—The cashier. He keeps a book. All the receipts go into his hands under the police fund, the general purposes fund, the borough fund, and the cemetery fund, which is prepared every week and presented every week to the audit committee, and signed by the chairman of the committee.

345. He receives everything, in short, except the rates and the gas revenue?—Yes.

346. He is, of course, one of the officers who gives security?—Yes, £1,000 is his security, I believe. He enters the receipts in this book as they are paid into the bank, and gets an account of them from the bank. The market revenues are lodged in the bank in this way. He lodges everything and pays by cheque. The cheque is given by the committee having charge of the department.

347. How is the manure sold?—By auction.

348. How often?—About once a fortnight.

349. Have you the manure depot placed outside the town?—It is inside the town, unfortunately.

350. Is it surrounded by houses?—It is complained of occasionally.

351. *Witness.*—I ought to say, if I have not already told you, that all payments made are made by cheque. The cheque is signed by three members and the town clerk.

Belfast, Dec. 11, 1874.

Mr. James Guthrie.

Mr. HUGH M'CALMONT WOODS examined.

Mr. Hugh M'Calmont Woods.

352. CHAIRMAN.—You are the accountant?—Yes.

353. How long have you held that office?—Next month I shall be eleven years.

354. All the accounts in this book (the annual statement of receipts and expenditure), I understand from Mr. Black, are kept by you?—They are.

355. Would you just tell me from what sources you make this up. Just tell me the system on which these accounts are made up?—The cashier's book forms the basis.

356. That and the bank book together?—Yes.

357. These accounts are made up, I see, under four different heads—the police fund, the general purposes fund, the borough fund, and the burial fund?—Yes; they are all made up the same way. (See Appendix No. 6, page 307.)

358. And there is a separate account kept for the gas?—Yes.

359. Do you keep that?—No.

360. You have nothing to do with that?—No.

361. Now the police rate, we understand, is levied under the Act of 1845, and the amending Acts?—Yes.

362. You appear to have started that account last year with a balance in hand of £3,415 19s. 4d. in the treasurer's hands?—Yes.

363. And £16 0s. 3d. petty cash in the cashier's hands?—Yes.

364. That gave you £3,431 19s. 7d. to start with?—Yes.

365. I will just go through the receipts and the payments, as I have summarised them. You received on this account, £34,816 2s. 6d. from rates last year?—Yes; that is less the amount refunded—the net amount.

366. Yes; what I want to know from you is, how far that is short of the rate that was laid?—I have got the amount here—"Police rate levied, £36,713 0s. 2d." last year.

367. And you received £34,816 2s. 6d., which included arrears from the preceding rate?—Yes, and included £997 7s. 4d. which we received from the Government in lieu of rates.

368. Is not that carried into those arrears?—It is.

369. What arrears of the preceding rate were carried forward into that last year?—£997 7s. 4d.

370. Then I see those arrears consisted wholly of the Government bounty?—Yes.

371. You only strike one rate in the year?—That is all.

372. Under any of these Acts?—That is all.

373. Is that rate always struck on the 1st January?—Yes.

374. Are all your rates struck at the same time and collected at the same time?—Yes.

375. Now, I find here, amount of arrears brought forward, £3,518s. 9d. Are these all irrecoverable arrears?—No.

376. All collectable arrears?—A small portion of those have been recovered.

377. Does not the collector of the police rate bring forward what is supposed to be collectable arrears distinct from those which he considers cannot be collected?—I presume he, at least, submits the list to you as the accountant, and then to the finance committee or the audit committee, and gets the really irrecoverable arrears allowed by the committee?—Yes.

378. Well, then, after deducting those struck off, I remark that there are arrears brought forward into the last rate of ——?—£344 8s. 9d.

379. That, with the £997 7s. 4d., would give a total amount of £38,254 17s. 4d. to be collected, and, deducting £34,816 2s. 6d., the amount brought in, would leave £3,438 14s. 10d. still outstanding, still to be allowed as irrecoverable or uncollected?—Yes; £3,438 was the actual amount not collected, and of that sum there was for discount 25 per cent. allowed, and payments subsequently received £2,080.

380. Then there would be only between £300 and £400 collectable rates outstanding?—Yes; £344 carried forward into the next rate.

381. After allowing for the discount, &c.?—Yes.

382. The next receipts, after leaving the rates, arise

Belfast. Dec. 11, 1877. Mr. Hugh M'Calmont Woods.

from the markets, and I see that your gross receipts from them amounted to £9,773 7s. 3d.?—Yes.

383. And the expenditure on the other side for rents and salaries, weighmasters, market patrols, rates, and taxes, amounted to £3,487 17s. 6d., leaving a net profit from the markets of £6,325 10s.?—Quite correct.

384. Following the order in this book, we have the weighs and measures, from which you received £154 13s. 3d., and you expended in wages to the adjusters, and sundry small payments, £71 18s. 4d., leaving a net profit of £84 16s. 11d.?—Quite correct.

385. Slaughter-houses come next. From the slaughter-houses you received £528 6s.?—Yes.

386. What are these receipts made up of?—The use of slaughter-houses for slaughtering cattle.

387. This is, of course, confined to the public slaughter-houses?—Yes.

388. How many of them are there?—A whole block of buildings.

389. Are they outside the town?—They are not; they are towards the river Lagan.

390. Are they so large as not to be a nuisance in any way?—As to that I cannot say.

391. Do you know whether there are any complaints of their being a nuisance?—The only complaint that I heard of was from the gas manager.

392. Does he live near them?—He does.

393. Mr. Exham.—Do they charge so much per head for the use of the slaughter-houses?—The clerk of the markets will be able to tell you that.

394. Chairman.—Then as to your expenditure on them, you have, I see, a superintendent?—Yes.

395. Then his wages and those of the people employed under him, and gas, water, taxes, repairs, and alterations, insurance, &c., amount altogether to £348 10s. 9d., leaving a net profit of £179 14s. 3d.?—Yes.

396. Then we come to a large item—the fines accounts. The gross amount of receipts from fines was £3,063 16s. 6d.?—Yes.

397. And the expenditure for summons, checking returns, and summonses was £166 17s. 6d., leaving a net balance of £2,896 19s. 2d.?—Yes.

398. Your next receipt is £831 6s. for licenses?—Yes.

399. Of which £316 16s. is for carriage licenses, and the balance from owners of lodging-houses, and slaughter-houses?—Yes.

400. On the other hand you paid for car inspectors—wages and clothing, £185 18s. 6d.?—Yes.

401. Next comes your rent account. What are these houses for which rent is paid you in Church-street and Chichester-street? Are they houses for markets?—No; they are not in connection with the markets at all.

402. I understand you had no real property except the property for the markets, and the public parks?—I believe that is the only house there is.

403. The only two houses?—That house from which we receive £16 in Chichester-street, is part of the market property.

404. Mr. Lawless.—What is that other house?—It is the only house we have apart from the market property.

405. Do the Corporation use it?—We pay head-rent of £13 6s. 8d. on it.

406. And you receive £26 a year for it?—Yes.

407. Chairman.—Where is this plot land from which you appear to get £8 a year?—It was merely a temporary purchase.

408. Where is it?—At the Lagan; convenient to Ormeau Park.

409. You have also some small weekly tenements?—One small house at the Albert-bridge, and there is another small house at the Linfield-road.

410. How do these small tenements happen to be the property of the Corporation? Have they been recently purchased, or have they belonged to them for a long period?—Before I joined the Corporation they belonged to it. As regards the house at Albert Bridge-road, Albert-bridge was built by a private company, and they have part of the house at the bridge; but eventually the Corporation and the counties of Antrim and Down, bought the rights of the owners in this bridge and threw it open to the public, and the bridge and the whole of the house vested in the Corporation. That is the house referred to. As regards the house on Linfield-road, we had a claim upon the house and the little piece of ground near it, for some work executed at the street in front of it. The property was sold in the Landed Estates Court, and that was put up as a separate lot and would not bring anything, and we thought that if we were to widen the bridge there, we would have the ground for doing it, and the Landed Estates Court handed us over the place, in consideration of the claim we had against them.

411. The net amount you receive on the rent account is £34 10s. 7d.?—Yes.

412. Next comes the fire brigade, which cost you £1,810 17s. 3d. Is that all the expenditure connected with it?—Yes.

413. And you receive, as we already heard in Mr. Black's evidence, £369 11s. 3d.?—Yes.

414. Leaving a net charge against the fire brigade account of £1,451 5s.?—Yes.

415. Income tax, as entered upon the expenditure side of your account, stands thus:—Amount on estimate amount of interest for one year £34 19s. 2d., and the receipts from sundry persons £31 5s. 11d. They do not balance themselves?—We pay the amount of income tax on the interest.

416. But you do not get the full amount, you ought to get what you pay?—It is always a little more than we receive.

417. They ought to balance themselves exactly; however, they do to within a very few shillings. Then next there is your lighting account. You pay for gas for the public lamps £7,084 3s. 6d. for one year, and for lamp columns and other expenses connected with them you pay £211 10s. 7d.?—Yes.

418. And then, deducting from that £36 which you got back from private individuals for moving and re-fixing lamp-posts, shows a net charge against this fund on the gas account of £7,352 13s.?—That is so.

419. You got, I see, from the Belfast Bank £153 16s. 6d. to the credit of this fund, although it is overdrawn at the close as interest on your bank account for the year?—Yes; they started with a balance of £3,000 odd in hand.

420. "House Accounts." Are these the accounts for keeping the courts and the cells for the prisoners?—You might call it the court account.

421. It consists principally, I see, of expenses connected with the police cells, and the coals and gas for the courts and town-hall?—Quite right.

422. That, of course, is an account showing a considerable balance on the wrong side, for after deducting "£30 10s. 6d. from Sub-Inspector Blake, proceeds of the sale of forfeited property, &c.," your expenditure connected with the courts and the police cells shows a balance on the debit side of £840 6s. 6d.?—Yes.

423. Mr. Exham.—Does not the Government pay a portion of the keeping up of the court-house?—We get those fines.

424. Are there not many who are not fined at all?—We have to pay all the expenses connected with prisoners in the gaol, amounting to £6,000 or £7,000 a year.

425. Chairman.—That is a different matter. You pay that under the Antrim and Belfast Borough Act?—Yes, under the Act of 1865. We paid that previously as portion of the county. If they were committed in the county, they would have to pay it in the county.

426. Mr. Exham.—From what fund do you pay it?—It is under the general purposes fund. The Government receive all the money upon summonses and things of that sort, and all they have to pay is the petty sessions clerk's fees.

427. You get all the fines?—Yes; but they get the proceeds of the summonses.

428. Chairman.—The only salaries which appear charged to this fund are Mr. Green's and Mr. Coleman's.

Who is Mr. Green?—He was the superintendent of the borough police court, and he has now retired on his allowance.

429. There are, I see, two other fixtures superannuated—French and Stewart?—Recently retired lately.

430. And the salary of Mr. Colvin, the cashier, is charged partly to this fund and partly to another?—Yes.

431. The salaries on this fund are £875 10s., and superannuation allowances, £209 2s. 6d. Then there is the miscellaneous account, being the large item of £649 10s. 6d., of which, however, very full details appear to be given, and which have been all, of course, submitted to the auditor?—Yes.

432. The law costs which stood in your accounts at £1,123 12s. 6d. would, if the two first items of this miscellaneous account were added, be brought up to £1,165 3s. 1d.?—Yes; if you include the expenses of a deputation to London, amounting to £41 9s. 3d.

433. And if you add to the printing, stationery, &c. from these miscellaneous items, £22 13s. 11d., which properly would seem to belong to that account, you would bring that up to £117 4s. Other items might very well have been classed under the heading of street improvements, but taking the miscellaneous items as they stand at £649 10s. 6d., deducting as per contra the £59 3s. 7d. which you received principally from Lord Donegall for the removal of Lord Belfast's statue, the net charge under this head is reduced to £590 6s. 11d.?—Yes.

434. Then comes the next, and the heaviest charge in this account—constabulary, £15,160 19s. 11d., in addition to which there is apportioned, I find, to the general purposes fund, a further sum of £1,083 16s. 3d., which makes the total expense of the police to the town, £16,243 14s. 9d.?—Yes.

435. How do you apportion these? There is no portion, I think, charged on the borough fund account?—No; there is not.

436. Who makes this apportionment?—I do. (Hands in estimate.)

437. This does not explain the principle upon which you apportion such a small proportion to the general purposes fund. The Act of 1845 gives you instructions how to apportion it. You make the apportionment, and you must know how it is done. You put the largest amount on what I would call the improvement rate?—We put as much as possible on the police rate.

438. You call it the police rate, because you pay so large an amount of the police expenses out of it, but I should call it the improvement rate; it answers to the improvement rate elsewhere?—As far as I remember, we were advised that it would be absolutely necessary to do it.

439. I have no doubt there is some very good reason for it.

440. Your expenditure on public improvements was £2,991 0s. 11d. Were these mainly substantial improvements, irrespective of repairs?—Yes.

441. And on the erection of slaughter-houses you spent, I see, £49 12s. 7d., and on street improvements, £5,835 6s. 3d., against which you got back from private owners, £83 17s. 6d., making your net expenditure under this head, £5,751 11s. 6d., and on municipal buildings, which is all the same class of expenditure, you spent £1,271 12s.?—Yes.

442. That makes up all your expenditure except what was set apart under the Improvement Act of 1845, and the Award Act of 1841, for a sinking fund. There was £3,028 15s. 6d. set apart, I see, for that purpose under the former Act, and under the Award Act you set apart £1,840 16s. 6d., which makes up altogether £4,869 10s. paid to the sinking fund out of the current rates?—Yes.

443. That left you not in nearly so favourable a position on this account, as when you started in the beginning of the year. There was then a balance in hand of £2,431 10s. 7d., and now the account is overdrawn by £2,064 11s. 9d.?—Yes.

444. On the other hand there is a trifling balance, I see, in the cashier's hands of £5 4s. 6d.?—Yes.

Adjourned.

December 12, 1876.

Mr. Black re-examined.

445. Chairman.—I believe you desire to supplement your evidence with regard to the police fund?—Yes; I wish to explain the principle of the apportionment of the police rate upon the two funds—the police fund and the general purposes fund. The first Act relating to the subject is the 25th and 26th Victoria, chap. 70, a public Act that altered the distribution of the constabulary force in Ireland to make better provision for the police force in the borough of Belfast. After fixing the number of constables, and so on, the 5th section goes on to say that one moiety of the expenses of the additional police force shall be paid by the Council by means of the rates to be applotted and levied in the same manner as the moneys theretofore raised and applied, or which might be applicable to the maintenance of a police force in the town of Belfast. That section authorised the payment of the cost of the constabulary out of the police rate. Then came the Local Act of 1865 which was passed immediately after the Constabulary Act, and if you refer to section 64 of that Act, you will perceive that the Council are there authorised to levy a general purposes rate, and the section I refer to empowered the Council to estimate yearly the amount that would be required during the ensuing year, for several purposes, including the following:—To pay such proportion of the cost of maintaining the police force of the borough as the Corporation might declare to be chargeable against the entire borough. Section 54 of the same directed the rate to be applied to the purposes referred to in the section I have just referred you to. Therefore the Corporation are of opinion that they have power to charge any portion that they may think reasonable of the cost of the police force against the general purposes rate; and under the public Act I have referred you to before that, that the remaining portion should be charged to the police rate, so that the expense shall be put partly on the general purposes and partly on the police fund.

446. There is no doubt you have power to apportion the cost of the police force on these two funds, but no principle is laid down on which you shall so apportion it?—No; it is left quite discretionary with the Corporation; and as they could not exceed the limit of taxation in respect of the general purposes fund they were obliged reluctantly to put a large proportion of the cost of the police on the other rate—the police rate—than they would have been disposed to do under other circumstances.

447. Mr. Lawless.—Is there any minute of the Corporation bearing on that?—I have not looked.

448. Chairman.—Who makes the apportionment?—The finance committee. The finance committee yearly make an estimate—the estimate I gave you yesterday—that is brought before the Corporation at a special meeting usually held about the 20th of November—it must be held before the 1st of December—and the Corporation approve of that estimate, or alter or amend it as they think necessary; and sometimes I have known instances in which the estimate was amended by altering the proportions of the cost of the police to be charged upon each fund.

449. Have you then known the estimate to be altered by the Town Council, after the finance committee have made their estimate. The finance committee make their estimate upon an estimate prepared by the officers of the Corporation—usually yourself or the accountant, I presume?—It is usual for the ac-

Sept. 21, 1876. — Mr. Samuel Black.

comment and myself to make up the estimates, and in doing so, we are always guided by the law, as well as by the state of the finances.

450. Mr. Lawson.—There is a balance remaining on the malicious injuries account after the rate was made in 1874, of between £900 and £900. At the beginning of the year it was £963 12s. 1d. in the hands of the treasurer, and then there is a sum of £54 18s. 6d. arrears of the rate struck for malicious injuries in 1874, and brought in to the general purposes account before us. I wish to know whether—you having struck a rate for a sum of above £1,000, which you were empowered to apply out of the general purposes rate for the payment of malicious injuries—the Act does not provide that any balance remaining over should be applied in aid of the rate?—Yes; in aid of the malicious injuries rate.

451. That is the question—whether it is in aid of the malicious injuries rate. Of course it is necessary that you should keep a balance in hand for malicious injuries; but the question is, whether the words of the Act do not apply to the general purposes rate. The section of the Act I refer to is section 48, and that section is to the effect that any balance remaining over in hand for any particular purpose for which a special rate is levied, shall be applied by the Corporation in aid of the rates to be levied for the next following year. It is quite an open question whether that means the malicious injuries rate to be levied in the next following year, or the general purposes rate, inasmuch as you would not levy a malicious injuries rate unless you wanted a sum of over £1,000; and so it occurred to us that it must be the general purposes rate?—Sections 46 and 47, both refer to a special rate; and section 48 provides that any balance remaining over—any balance of a special rate—shall be applied by the Corporation in aid of the rate to be levied in the next following year.

452. But it does not follow that it should be the malicious injuries rate. You will find that the special rate is referred to both in the 46th, 47th, and 48th sections of the Act?—We would have, I may tell you, no desire but to put it in aid of the general purposes rate if we could.

453. That special rate produced £3,577 16s. on the first levy in 1874?—It was a rate of 2d. in the pound in the lighting and watching district, and 1½d. in the pound in the other portions.

454. Chairman.—The compensation had been previously assessed in the year before—1873?—Yes.

455. And it was, of course, paid?—Yes; the actual amount paid was £3,577 11s. 8d.

456. And we understand that claims amounting to £11,000 were reduced to that sum?—Yes; in addition to that £11,000 we had also claims for injuries to the person, but I succeeded in defeating all of those claims.

457. Your special rate was to meet that £3,577 11s. 8d.?—Yes, it was. The reason it was necessary to levy a rate of 2d. was this—because a rate of 1½d. would not have been sufficient; besides, if we attempted to levy a rate of 1½d., we would get into trouble, because we have to keep a certain proportion—a fourth—between the lighted and watched district, and the other properties outside the borough; so that we had to strike a rate of 2d. in the pound in order to do that.

458. In 1874, after satisfying the £3,577 odd, there remained a balance of £963?—Precisely, and any claims for any injuries that have occurred since have been paid out of it.

459. That is kept as a separate account?—Yes.

460. Mr. Exham.—What is the value of the portion to which the 1s. 6d. rate applies, because I thought the lighting extended to the whole borough?—Oh no; but substantially it is the whole borough.

461. Then it must be a very small portion that is under the 1s. 6d. rate?—Yes; it is a very small portion. The total valuation outside the lighting and watching district is £8,333—about one-sixteenth part of the valuation.

462. How is it that all the salaries are charged to the borough fund with the exception of one or two?—The officers of the corporation—the town clerk and all his department we have always looked upon as chargeable against the borough fund. The surveyor's department being connected with the streets and sewers, is charged to the general purposes rate.

463. I can understand that that should be charged to the general purposes fund, but almost all the other salaries are charged to the borough fund?—Yes, that is the rule we adopt.

Mr. Hugh M'Connell Woods.

Examination of Mr. Woods resumed.

464. Chairman.—We will now turn to the general purposes fund—that is your largest fund I believe?—Yes.

465. Last year, the year we have before us, ending December 31st, you had a balance of £53 0s. 10d. in the hands of the cashier?—Quite right.

466. And there was a balance in the hands of the treasurer, under the head of malicious injuries account, of £983 12s. 1d.?—Yes.

467. On the other hand there was a balance due to the treasurer on the general account, of £3,720 2s. 3d. at that moment?—Yes.

468. You struck a rate of 2s.?—Yes; 2s. within the lighted and watched district, and 1s. 6d. outside that district.

469. Practically we may call that a 2s. rate, of which there was collected, with the arrears of former rates, £43,007 12s. 11d.?—Yes, that is so.

470. And you received from the Government in lieu of rates, £997 7s. 4d.?—Yes.

471. The total amount struck of rate was £49,416 12s. 9d.?—Yes.

472. Can you tell me what were the arrears carried into that rate from the preceding one?—£266 5s. 6d.

473. Collectable arrears?—What were supposed to be collectable arrears.

474. That gave you £50,282 18s. 3d. to collect, exclusive of the Government payment in lieu of rates?—Yes, that is so.

475. Of that you collected £46,007 12s. 11d., and that left you exactly £3,275 5s. 4d. to collect at the close of the year?—That is quite correct.

476. Of that £3,275 5s. 4d., how much have you had pronounced as irrecoverable?—£4,715 17s. 6d.

477. That is by reason of void and uninhabited houses, and the allowance of twenty-five per cent. to landlords on houses under £8 a year?—Yes, quite correct. I may mention that the discount allowed would represent 3·67 of the total assessment upon that rate.

478. Can you tell us how much of that £4,715 17s. 6d., the discounts would represent?—I have not got that made out.

479. That left you a recoverable arrear of £559 1s. 11d., and that was I suppose carried into the new rate?—Yes.

480. Mr. Lawson.—By what authority do you allow that discount to landlords?—By the Act of 1843.

481. Is that balance of £559 7s. 11d. now in course of collection with the new rate?—There is a slight difference in that, and it occurs in this way—the Government valuator amends the valuation on appeal and these amounts are sent in about the month of April, and the rate books are amended in accordance with that, and that has increased the amount slightly, making it up to £563 17s. 6d.

482. You refunded I see £16 16s. 2d. That is a rate I suppose that had been paid in error and refunded. How does that arise?—When an occupier leaves a house; if it is at the latter end of the year, the amount is refunded by cheque drawn upon the treasurer.

483. If an occupier pays the rate for the whole year and only occupies the house for part of it, you return the balance; and do you then get it from the incoming tenant?—Yes; if the house is occupied. There is a section in one of our Local Acts of Parliament bearing on the subject. If the tenant enters a fresh quarter he pays the whole quarter.

484. That gave you as the net receipts from the general purposes rates £15,768 1s. 1d.?—Yes; that is quite correct.

485. And then you get that balance we have already alluded to from the sanitary expenses rate of 1871, which amounted to £36 18s. 6d.?—Yes.

486. That cleared up that rate?—Yes; with a trifling sum of £1 13s. 6d., which was carried forward.

487. The 300th section of the Act of 1845, I see, deals with the apportionment of the rates on the occupier quitting the premises, and provides that the Council shall recover the portion of such rate for such portion of time as he shall be in occupation of the premises, provided always that no allowance shall be made for any portion of a quarter of a year?—Yes; that is so.

488. The commission on the amounts the collectors received reached the sum of £663 0s. 1d. at 4½ per cent.?—Yes.

489. And then we get a payment for malicious injury to property amounting to £39 14s. Was that all that accrued due under that head last year?—Yes; that was for all.

490. You had to pay a balance of £3 17s. 7d. to the Belfast Bank for interest, but considering that you owed the bank at one time £6,000, at the time I can hardly understand how it is that the charge for interest is so small?—The large amount of rates got in in the first month of the year and placed to our credit accounts for that.

491. Then you were overdrawn to the extent I have referred to for but a very short time?—Precisely; only a month or two; and then, the time at which the bank make up their interest account is in July, and not in January.

492. And probably in the preceding July you had a balance in hand nearly equal to the balance against you in December, and that is how the two accounts so nearly balance each other?—Yes.

493. The net result at all events is that you were only charged £3 17s. 7d. interest by the bank during the year upon this account?—Yes.

494. I will now proceed to go through the receipt side of the account. The next receipt is one of those loans which we referred to yesterday, of £5,000 on mortgage of the general purposes rate for the Newtownards-road drainage district. You borrowed from the Commissioners of Public Works £5,000 on the general purposes rate?—Yes.

495. Which is entered as credit in that account here?—Yes.

496. And then there is a small cross entry for income tax. On the police rate yesterday, we noticed that they did not pay you quite so much as you were assessed at on your estimate. In this account, on the other hand, you received a little more than your estimate, 16s. 3d.?—We were receiving loans day after day which accounts for that.

497. With regard to this £5,000 that was borrowed on the general purposes rate for one-third of the Newtownards-road district drainage expenses. Was that sum expended on the Newtownards-road district drainage entirely?—It was.

498. Where does the expenditure appear in this account?—It does not appear in that account. The works had been principally completed before the loan was got.

499. Did the expenditure appear on the preceding year's account then?—It does partly appear there.

500. Just refer me to that?—I will.

501. It was all expended on the sewerage and works connected with the sewerage in the Newtownards-road district—was it?—It was.

502. I find that the sum of £13,828 17s. 7d. was expended on the Newtownards-road district last year, and £2,150 had been expended during the year before?—Yes.

Second day. Dec. 12, 1872.

Mr. Hugh M'Cammond. Town

503. Of that £13,828 17s. 7d., £9,839 1s. 10d. was a payment to the contractor on account, and £3,000 was paid to what you call your store yard account for bricks?—Yes, that is quite correct.

504. What are these "permits" which are the next item—"amount refunded to sundry persons, £1,381 10s."?—They are deposits lodged by ratepayers when they choose to erect new premises or alter old ones, and have to put up hoardings—to ensure that they make good the footway when the work is completed, and if that is done to the satisfaction of the Corporation, the money so lodged is refunded. The course adopted is this—A party applies to the Corporation for liberty to erect a hoarding in a particular street, and take up a portion of the flagway in that street for the purpose opposite the building, and in order to secure that that flagway shall be properly restored when the work is done, the surveyor requires that a certain sum, £15 or £20 or £30 as the case may be, shall be deposited with the cashier of the Corporation, who gives a permit for the work to be done in the shape of a receipt for the deposit. At the proper time after the work has been completed the surveyor initials the permit as evidence that the work has been done to his satisfaction, and the flagway properly restored, and the person may then get back on that permit the amount of money lodged as a deposit.

505. And thus then these two cross accounts arise. You received £1,416 for these permits, and you refunded to persons in consequence of their having fulfilled their guarantee, £1,381 10s., which leaves £35 10s. a balance to the credit of this year's account in the end?—Yes.

506. And now come your miscellaneous items. I should have added the stamps to the stationery account, and "the compensation for way leave for sewers," and "the fees in the suit against Mr. M'Teer," as that matter to law costs. In round figures, however, your miscellaneous account shows a balance of £155 3s. 7d. against you?—That is quite correct.

507. Of which part are applicable to law costs, and part to other items, stationery, &c.?—Yes.

508. Then we come to the store yard account, which to my mind is the most complicated account of the whole. The result, however, seems to be this—that you purchased materials for various works in the town to the amount of £17,157 6s. 3d., which were principally paving stones, bricks, flags, curbstones, quarried stones, &c., amounting to the large sum of £17,157 6s. 3d.?—Yes, that is so.

509. These are properly carried into your store yard account as expenditure?—Yes.

510. And sums are set down on the opposite side as receipts from the different works for which these stores, and also other stores, which you had in hand of the same description were used. You actually supplied out of your store-yard materials for repairs, &c., representing the sum of £20,302 8s. 11d., which is entered to the credit of this account?—Yes, that is quite correct.

511. Leaving a balance in favour of that account of £3,145 2s. 8d.?—Yes.

512. Do you give out these materials at about the same price as you buy them?—At about the same price.

513. Mr. Kernan.—Is there any labour applied to these materials in the store-yard before they go out, and if so, how do you arrange for that on the other side of the account?—The material goes out, I may say, at the same price.

514. Chairman.—The labour in connexion with all these works is found at the opposite side of the account charged separately?—Yes.

515. Then in the Ballymacarrett account you get a sum of £7 5s. 6d. from certain persons, their contribution towards making crossings, &c.?—Yes.

516. The whole cost in the Ballymacarrett account for the repairs of streets, watering them, &c.; and constructing the middle-path, street sewer, &c.,

Belfast. Oct. 23, 18[illegible].

Sir Hugh M'Calmont [illegible].

amounts, after deducting the £? 6s. 6d. as repaid, to £3,064 14s. 7d.?—Yes, that is quite correct.

517. Of course you take stock of the stores in your storeyard account from time to time?—Yes; every year.

518. And the estimated value of the stores in hand is submitted to the committee, I presume, or do the committee not take cognisance of it?—The stock is taken at the end of the year by the surveyor, and he supplies an estimate of the value of the stock in hands.

519. Just, I suppose, as they do at the gasworks when they take stock of the coals and other materials on hands?—Yes.

520. Mr. Emerson.—But that does not appear on the account. Have you any account that will show that?—If you look at the account for 1874, you will find that the cost of the material purchased in that year was £10,113 10s. 2d., and the amount transferred £11,036, which would leave a balance of about £2,903.

521. Chairman.—Your scavenging for the year, including what you gave the Belfast Water Commissioners for watering the streets, amounted to £10,304 17s. 3d.?—Yes.

522. Against which you sold manure amounting to £2,879 14s. 3d., leaving a balance of £7,874 19s. against the Corporation on their expenditure for keeping the streets in order?—Yes; that work was all done in the Antrim portion of the borough; that is on this side of the Lagan.

523. I do not see any expenditure under that head in the county Down portion of the borough, unless that is contained in the Ballymacarrett account?—Yes, you will find it in the Ballymacarrett account.

524. Yes, in the Ballymacarrett account there is, I see, a sum of £831 6s. 10d. for scavenging out of the total sum I previously mentioned?—Yes.

525. So that in point of fact £8,716 was the total expenditure on scavenging for the two portions of the borough?—Yes.

526. After setting off the sum of £2,879 14s. 3d. which you realised by the sale of manure?—Yes; but against these receipts you have the expenses of the street inspectors, &c., which are charged to the county Antrim side of the account.

527. The net result is, that after deducting the proceeds of the sales of manure the scavenging cost £8,716 3s. 10d.?—Yes; that is correct.

528. The repairs of streets do not appear to be charged to any special portion of the borough. On the general repairs of streets you expended £12,136 6s. 8d., and you got back from the gas department, the Belfast Water Commissioners, the Cemetery Committee, and other persons for repairs over the report gather £711 11s. 7d., leaving a net charge on the general purposes fund £11,414 5s. 1d.?—That is quite correct. That is for the Antrim portion of the borough.

529. That is for the general repairs of the streets only on this side of the Lagan?—Yes.

530. In what sense are the permanent flagging and paving and making of crossings, &c., on sundry streets described as "special works"?—These are works permanent in the sense that we expect them to last for some time.

531. Are these all for the Antrim portion of the borough?—Yes.

532. You appear to have there expended a sum of £1,252 14s. 5d. for paving and crossings. You got back from private individuals for flagging footways opposite their houses £413 1s. 11d., leaving the expenditure under that head at £840 12s. 6d.?—That is quite right.

533. Why is Town-hall-street a separate item under the head of estimated works. Why should not that be included with the other streets?—It was estimated work to be done, in which the owners were to pay the actual cost when completed.

534. The owners did not do it though?—The Corporation are owners of a considerable portion.

535. Is it the street in which the Townhall is situated?—Yes.

536. You spent on that work £1,079 6s. 7d., and got back from private owners £479 15s. 6d.?—Yes.

537. Leaving the net expenditure under that head £599 7s. 1d.?—Yes.

538. Then you borrowed under the Provisional Order Act of 1873 £9,800 for permanent paving beyond what we have just noticed, and you spent £9,823 11s. 8d. on four streets?—Yes.

539. Which is £23 11s. 8d. more than you borrowed?—Yes.

540. Of that there was no less than £7,754 odd which went back for material supplied to the credit of the store-yard account which we have just passed?—Yes, that is so.

541. Here is a long cross entry for what are described as "ordered works" under the two borough Acts?—The County and Borough Acts, 1865 and 1866.

542. Are these works which would have been paid for out of the Grand Jury cess?—No, they are not. They are new streets that are ordered by the Corporation, where the owners of the property have a month, which is allowed to all per for the purpose of commencing the works themselves. If they take no steps to proceed with the carrying out of the works the Corporation take them in hand themselves, and afterwards recover from the owners of the property the amount of their portion of the cost of such works. If the estimated cost exceeds the actual cost, the difference is refunded to the owners of property, but if, on the other hand, the works cost more than was estimated, they pay the balance to us.

543. That is done as regards the Antrim portion of the borough under the 69th section of the Act of 1865, and there is a corresponding provision in the 23rd section of the Act of 1866 as regards the county Down portion, I presume?—Yes.

544. These "ordered works" occupy two pages of your accounts, but the net result, so far as I can make out, is that you received, in the first instance, £1,761 18s. 9d. from the owners, and refunded £217 8s. 2d. upon over estimation, leaving a net receipt of £1,544 11s. 7d. from the owners?—Yes.

545. While you expended only £977 16s. 8d.?—Yes.

546. So that you have to expend something like £550 more to do the work you have undertaken to do, unless you did it in the preceding year?—They pay upon the estimate, and the works are not yet completed. The works are still going on.

547. You have money in hand from the owners at present, or rather you had at the end of 1875, to the extent of £566 18s. 11d.?—Yes.

548. Now we come to the drainage works in special districts. I see you struck a distinct sewerage rate on the Cromac and Oldpark road district, and the rate you collected amounted to £201 18s. 7d.; was not the the 2d. rate for the district?—Yes.

549. Did you get all of it in?—Yes.

550. And you paid interest on mortgage in respect of that district to the amount of £33 13s., and you repaid on the mortgage account an instalment of £100?—Yes.

551. Making up, with commission to the rate collector, your net expenditure (out of that rate of £201 18s. 7d.) to £165 15s. 6d. on the roads of the Cromac and Oldpark district?—Yes.

552. Were no works then done there last year?—No.

553. The next item is the Antrim roads district, where you struck a rate of 1d. in the pound—what did that rate amount to?—£241 18s. 3d.

554. Of which you got £203 5s. 10d.?—Yes.

555. And you received from sundry persons in that district, as their one-third of the cost of the sewers, £102 18s. 4d.?—Yes.

556. And you expended in paying off instalment of loans and interest on mortgages, and in the final payment of £50 to Thomas Hunt on the contract, £409 2s.?—Yes.

557. Did that complete all your payments in regard of the works of the Antrim road district?—Yes.

558. And left you a balance in hand of £37?—Yes.

559. Now we come to the larger works—those of

the Newtownards road district. We have already had the statement that you borrowed £9,000 on the general purposes rate for that district, and you borrowed another £3,000, which was a special charge on the Newtownards road district sewerage rate—that made a loan of £10,000 altogether, applicable to that drainage district?—Yes.

560. And you got, I see, £2,204 0s. 6d. from private individuals, as their one-third of the estimated cost of the sewers?—Yes.

561. And made a 1½d. rate, which realized how much?—£946 6s.

562. Of which you collected £821 6s. 3d.?—Yes.

563. And that brought up your receipts to £3,520 13s. 1d., exclusive of the £9,000 borrowed on the general purposes rate?—Yes.

564. So that, as a matter of fact, you had a sum of £13,529 13s. 1d., which you received, and which was applicable to the Newtownards road district drainage?—Yes.

565. And you expended £13,828 17s. 7d., so that although on the Antrim road district you had a balance in hand, the Newtownards road district owes you, as nearly as possible, £300?—Yes; I may mention that the total amount of the loans on the Newtownards road district is £1,118, received this year, which completes the loan. Previously we had only got £10,000.

566. Have you got any more to receive from private individuals, as their one-third of the estimated cost of the works?—We have.

567. Then the Newtownards road district will not be in difficulties, and probably has not a deficit by this time?—It has not, or will not have, by the time the money due is collected.

568. The result of all these complicated transactions on the general purposes rate is, that you left off at the end of the year with a balance still against you, but about £4,000 less than it was at the beginning of the year's account. According to the treasurer, the balance against you at the end of 1875 was £4,229 8s. 6d., per contra, you had £99 0s. 6d. cash in the hands of the cashier, and £936 7s. 11d. in the hands of the treasurer to the credit of the malicious injuries account?—That is quite correct.

569. All those particular items have, I presume, been gone through by the auditor, and he has satisfied himself of their correctness?—Yes.

570. I see I omitted to notice page 33 of this account, where I find, besides the salary of the borough surveyor, £375, and his assistants, £436 2s. 6d. There are the salaries charged of two persons named Millar and Munro—who are they?—Millar is the surveyor of roads, and Munro is the book-keeper in the surveyor's office.

571. Are they both in the surveyor's department? —Yes.

572. Then the annual charge directly under the head of salaries for the surveyor's department is £1,393 3s. 10d.?—Yes.

573. Of which Mr. Montgomery receives the largest salary of any person, £375?—Yes; but his salary is now raised to £650 a year.

574. Then I see there is on the same page a sum of £348 5s. 1d. charged for advertising, printing, and stationery?—Yes, that is quite correct.

575. And then you paid in instalments on mortgages £463 7s. 3d., and you also paid interest on mortgages to the amount of £297 3s.?—Yes.

576. We have now noticed everything that appears on the "general purposes" fund account?—Yes.

577. I see in the borough fund account you commenced the year 1875 with a good balance in hand—£6,061 13s. 10d.?—Yes.

578. You struck a three penny rate on the borough fund, and I find that it realized £5,897 16s. 6d., whereas it was only estimated to produce £5,896 8s. 5d. You will perceive that there is a difference of something over £31?—Yes. That is accounted for in this way, by the Government valuator giving us an amended valuation. We adopted that amended valuation, and that raised the amount of the rate a little.

579. Then after the rate was struck was there an amendment in the valuation?—Yes.

580. In consequence of your having a general purposes rate of 2s. your borough rate is limited to three pence, but you can, as I understand, if necessary, lay a separate burial rate. You did so last year, and you laid a penny or three halfpenny burial rate the year before?—Yes, for the present year it is a penny, but next year we will be enabled to do without any rate for burial purposes.

581. You laid your one-thousand rate for the borough fund, and that rate amounted on the amended valuation to £5,897 16s. 6d., I understand?—Yes.

582. And you had a sum of £1,381 3s. 5d.—an outstanding balance from the rate of the preceding year?—Yes.

583. So that you had £7,278 19s. 10d. to collect last year and which you collected £5,919 4s. 3d.?—Yes, quite right.

584. Then I see that £50 11s. 7d. was struck off, I presume by the finance or audit committee as irrecoverable rate?—Yes.

585. And that left you £1,306 1s. 7d. still to be collected?—Yes.

586. The reason the irrecoverable rates represent so much smaller an amount on the borough rates than the others is, I suppose, because you do not allow the twenty-five per cent. to landlords?—Yes; nor do we allow for vacancies in the collection of this rate.

587. What constitutes your irrecoverable rate in that case?—New premises rated at the first year, if not occupied, the town solicitor has advised the Corporation that the rates should be written off these premises as irrecoverable.

588. But houses that have been previously occupied are not allowed for in consequence of vacancies?—Yes, that is correct.

589. But in the case of a new house that has never been occupied, the rate is not charged on that, if I understand you, until it is occupied?—Yes; and then it is charged from the date of occupation.

590. That course is, I may take it, adopted under the provisions of the Act of Parliament?—Yes. I may here observe that the year, in the case of the borough fund account, ends on the 31st of August, 1875, so that the accounts before you does not take in the whole year's collection of the borough rate which ends on the 31st of December.

591. Then the rate was balanced five months before the end of the year. Why was that—why so much earlier than the others?—I do not know upon what principle the plan is resorted to; but the year ends on the 31st of August, by the terms of the Municipal Corporation Act.

592. Mr. Ekman.—I wish to know as a matter of fact whether or not the £300 which remained uncollected of the outstanding rate for 1874, has been since collected?—I can explain that. At the close of the rate books, we got £438 6s. 6d. of the uncollected rate, and at the end of 1875, we brought forward into the next year's account, £365 8s. 7d., arrears still outstanding at the end of last year; and at the end of last year there was written off as irrecoverable a sum of £197 8s. 3d.

593. Chairman.—The borough rate does not appear to be written up so well as the others?—The year ends as I have said before, on the 31st of August, and the year's collection, on the 31st of December. I can only explain any want of clearness in the account by that fact.

594. You don't go to the landlord for the rate on unoccupied houses, you wait until such houses are tenanted?—The collectors call upon them, but they won't pay until the houses are occupied.

595. The rate is payable on the property, but you don't get it from the landlord, but wait until the tenant comes in, and then the tenant pays and deducts it from the landlord?—Yes, precisely.

596. You got for dog licenses, in 1874, £323 12s. 9d., and for corporate seals—what does that mean?—There is a fee of £1 1s., paid when the

BELFAST. Jan. 12, 1877.

Mr. Hugh M'Calmont Weeks.

city and is allowed to any department. Portion of the amount so realised goes to the mayor, and a portion to the town clerk, but the latter pays the sum into the credit of the corporation as he is only paid by salary.

597. Mr. EXHAM.—Have you any appraisers to look after the pawnbrokers?—There are some appraisers appointed by the Town Council.

598. The powers of the grand jury are transferred to you? We have none of those powers.

599. CHAIRMAN.—I see in the miscellaneous expenses another item, £12 10s. fine paid by Alderman Campbell, on the resignation of his office. Is that prescribed by the Act of Parliament?—No; the Act of Parliament prescribes a certain fine, but it is by the by-laws of the council that the amount is fixed. If the councillor has previously served within a prescribed time it is reduced to half. £25 is the amount fixed by the by-laws, and Alderman Campbell paid half—£12 10s.

600. Then the whole of your receipts under the head of miscellaneous—including the amount realised for dog licenses in 1876, £253 17s. 7d., the sum paid by Mr. Guthrie, town clerk, for corporation seals, pawnbrokers' certificates, burgess lists, &c., £17 18s.; and the fine of £12 10s. paid by Alderman Campbell, on his resignation of office—reach a total of £284 6s. 7d.? —Yes.

601. You received as interest from the treasurer on your bank balance, £140 13s.?—Yes.

602. Then there are the receipts from the Ormeau and Falls parks. I see you got £177 10s. for rent from the Ormeau-park for grazing and grass-cutting, and £30 16s. 2d. for the sale of timber and garden produce?—Yes.

603. And from the Falls-park you got for grazing, £25, making a total on both parks, of £233 6s. 2d. of receipts?—Yes.

604. That makes your total receipts on that fund—including the balance with which you commenced the year, of £12,031 1s. 3d.?—Yes.

605. Now, when I turn to the expenditure side of this account I find that your two largest payments are for the public parks and the salaries. Most of the salaries of the officers are charged on this rate? —Yes, most of them are.

606. The salaries and allowances amounted to £2,179 11s. 6d. What are the allowances?—The clothing of the sergeant-at-mace and the hall porters.

607. The collector's commission on the borough rate amounted to £103 8s. 4d.?—Yes.

608. Making a total of £2,533 (?) 9s. for the officers? —Yes.

609. The apprentices who begin with salaries of £20 per annum rise to £40—do they?—They rise to £60.

610. I see one has risen to £30 in the course of the year?—Yes.

611. Your salary was £300 last year, and has now been increased to £350 a year?—Yes.

612. The salary of Mr. Montgomery, the town surveyor, is not charged to this account?—No; it is charged to the general purposes account.

613. Then there is a sum of £145 15s. 5d. in connexion with burgess lists and the elections of Town Councillors, of which a sum of £31 3s. 8d. was for polling booths?—Yes.

614. Were these wooden booths—not such as we heard of at Wicklow?—Yes.

615. Then comes the principal amount, that of the expenditure under the head of public parks, which came to £3,929 10s. 8d. The items are all described in the schedule?—They are.

616. And so are the contingent expenses?—Yes.

617. The great item in the park payments is a sum of £1,735 4s. 8d. to Lord Donegall for rent?—Yes.

618. And £641 1s. 10d. for rangers' and labourers' wages?—Yes.

619. And £839 14s. 7d. for materials supplied from the storeyard, and which are accounted for in the account of the general purposes fund?—Yes.

620. £3,974 3s. 6d. seems to be the total expense incurred on the Ormeau-park, and £155 6s. 8d. on the Falls-park?—Yes.

621. Then there is the salary of Mr. Dickson, the superintendent, of £100. He is the superintendent of both parks, is he not?—Yes.

622. Did you put up a new house for the ranger?—No; we put an old house into a proper state of repair.

623. What is the salary of the ranger of the Falls park?—12s. per week. Mr. Dickson is the superintendent of both parks, and there are two rangers under him.

624. They are both laid out as pleasure and recreation parks, are they not?—Yes.

625. And planted with young trees, shrubs, and flowers?—They are. They are ornamental parks.

626. There is a large miscellaneous charge of £311 2s. 8d., out of which I see, there is no less than £190 for the mayor's chain of office?—Yes, but the chain cost nearly double that.

627. You don't get a new one every year?—No; I may observe that each of the ex-mayors gave a link value £5, and in that way there were twenty-five new links added to the chain.

628. There is a charge of £73 3s. 11d. for the cleansing of the Blackstaff, which it was said was such a big job that you could not attempt to do it with your general powers, so that there was no use in borrowing £1,500 for the purpose?—It would cost £3,000 to do it. That charge is only for dredging the mud out of the river.

629. Mr. EXHAM.—Is that all that was expended on that work?—Yes; all that was expended in that year. In the year before, the sum spent was larger. In the year 1871, it was £127.

630. CHAIRMAN.—Is the *Northern Whig* the only paper you subscribe to?—No; we subscribe to the *News-Letter* too.

631. I presume all your newspaper expenses are for advertising. The *Whig* seems to be the only one newspaper subscribed for?—We subscribe to the *Newsletter* as well as the *Northern Whig*.

632. Then there was the large sum of £213 1s. 5d. for printing and advertising in the different newspapers circulating in the borough?—Yes; that is quite correct.

633. What is the sum of £8 10s. paid to the Inspector-General of Constabulary for?—It is the rent of an office for keeping the weights and measures in, and for the expenditure in connexion with that.

634. In connexion with the Ormeau Park you do not appear to have deducted the poor rate when paying the rent to the Marquess of Donegall. It is specifically put down?—Under the agreement we cannot do so. Half of the poor rate we pay is upon that park.

635. We have noticed all the payments now except those contained in the sanitary portion of this account. There is a separate schedule for that. The expenses, I observe, are not heavy under this head considering the size of the borough?—No; the Act did not come into operation until after the commencement of the current year.

636. Then the amount expended was only for eight months?—Yes.

637. These two officers, Dr. Browne and Mr Scott, were appointed for the first time?—They were.

638. And Dr. Browne has £300 a year as consulting sanitary officer?—Yes.

639. Mr. Scott is the executive sanitary officer, at a salary of £250 a year?—Yes.

640. Sanitary inspector Mr. Norwood, retired on the appointment of Mr. Scott, and you gave him compensation to the amount of £187 10s. What was the authority for that?—It was approved of by the Local Government Board.

641. What salaries do you pay to the sub-sanitary officers?—There are five at 25s. per week each. There is one at £1 also. I may add, that these men get clothes in addition to their wages.

642. You paid £3 7s. 6d. compensation for the destruction of infected clothing?—Yes.

643. Here I find a sum of £3 6s. law costs in the case of "The Corporation against Fisher." Is that sum

action in connection with the carrying out of the sanitary measures?—We got a conviction against the owner of a house that had no water closet or year accommodation of any description. The conviction was appealed against, and on the appeal being heard, the conviction was set aside with £5 5s. costs. The result of that case has crippled our proceedings in sanitary matters very much.

644. The other expenses under the head of "sanitary," amount to £28 4s. 2d.?—Yes.

645. So that on the borough fund account you began with a balance of £4,013 13s. 10d., and wound up the year with a balance in hand of £1,136 10s. 2d.?—Yes; that is quite correct.

646. You commenced the year I find on the burial fund account, with a balance in hand of £1,873 1s. 1d., including £43 16s. cash in hands of the collector?—Yes.

647. You laid on the 1st of January a 1½d. rate. What was the amount that realised?—£2,9[illegible] 16s. 2d. on the essential assessment.

648. And you had outstanding of the rate on the preceding year £375 0s. 10d., making a total to collect of £3,3[illegible] 16s., and of that you collected £3,071 11s. 4d.?—Yes.

649. £21 15s. 7d. was pronounced irrecoverable, and that left you with a balance lying over uncollected of £277 8s.?—Yes.

650. The burial rate is on the same principle as the borough rate?—Yes.

651. There is no allowance to landlords, and no allowance for vacancies, except in the case of new houses?—Yes; quite so.

652. You received £25 from Mr. Burrows for half a year's rent of bowling mill—a mill I presume standing on the land that was bought for cemetery purposes, on the surplus portion which is now set apart as a park. The mill is still standing, but it comes into the park account?—Yes; we get £50 a year for the mill.

653. You got £11 1s. 5d. from the treasurer for interest on the balance you received of £106 5s. from private individuals, for the formation of vaults, and £1,197 3s. 4d. for the purchase of proprietary ground from sundry persons?—Yes.

654. And £411 as fees for the opening of graves?—Yes.

655. And £168 4s. 10d. miscellaneous receipts, of which £20 was for hay, and £42 10s. for grazing on the surplus land, &c. Now, is the surplus land which you let for grazing purposes a portion of the Falls Park?—This was in connection with the cemetery at the time this money was received. We are receiving nothing now from the surplus land of the Falls Park.

656. I think I understand now how it is. Is not this account a year behind the other?—The burial fund account is for the same period as the borough fund account, i.e. to 31st August, 1875; the transfer from the burial ground to the park only occurred last year. In other words these receipts from the burial fund will never come under that head again. They will all go to the parks account.

657. Out of that £168 4s. 10d. was there not a sum of £38 16s. received as the moiety of cost of the formation of the ground set apart as the Jewish burial ground?—Yes.

658. The total receipts of the burial fund amounted to £6,671 6s. 9d., including the balance in hand?—Yes.

659. And if we turn to the expenditure side, I perceive that your expenditure commenced with £44 1s. 10d. paid as commission to the collectors on the rate?—Yes.

660. And then there is a sum of £30 16s. 10d. as rent and rectorial rentcharge, together £30 in round figures for rent alone, and apparently the Marquess of Donegal, Mr. M'Cance, and Mr Montgomery are the three owners of the cemetery. Have you got a lease for ever of the ground?—We have a grant for ever—the fee-simple.

661. On the same terms as Ormeau Park?—No; quite different. Ormeau Park is held in fee-farm subject to an annual rent. The cemetery property is held in fee-simple, not subject to any rent whatever. The rent was taken off the cemetery and put upon the other portions of the ground.

662. It is a charge this year on the cemetery, but for the future it will be, you mean, charged on that part of the ground that is portion of the park?—Yes.

663. So that the cemetery will be eventually free of rent?—Yes; that is done under the Act of 1866.

664. You paid £760 4s. 2d. interest on mortgages for the year?—Yes.

665. You transferred to the sinking fund in the year a sum of £2,116?—Yes; but we paid off £2,700 altogether. We had to sell credit Government stock which realised £253 5s. 3d., and we devoted that also to the sinking fund.

666. But you paid out of income £2,116 14s. 5d.?—Yes, that is so.

667. Advertising, books for registering burials, printing, stationery, and so forth, came to £119 16s. 8d.?—Yes.

668. The formation of vaults cost £190 14s. 1d. for which we saw just now that you had received £106 5s., so that you have not got back the whole amount from the private owners yet?—We have a stock of bricks, flags, and soforth, and we do not charge private parties for making drains in connection with the vaults to the main drains. We have a large stock up at the cemetery.

669. Then a good portion of that £190 14s. 1d. was expended on drainage?—Yes.

670. The shrubberies and road work connected with the cemetery cost £219 10s. 1d., and the drainage £21 16s. 6d.?—Yes.

671. The amount of wages paid for grave-digging was £401 10s. 8d.?—Yes.

672. The salaries amounted to £190 8s. 4d.?—Yes.

673. Are those the salaries that you pay the registrar and superintendent of the cemetery?—Yes; and there is a porter, but he is paid weekly wages.

674. Then there were miscellaneous payments, water-piping, and plumbers' work at the lodge, &c., all that came to £142 15s. 8d., but there appears nothing under that head which requires special notice?—No; that is so.

675. Then there was £13 17s. 6d. paid for county cess and poor rate?—Yes.

676. What is the building for the temporary reception of the dead which cost £832?—That is the mortuary.

677. Was that a sum paid on account of the contract for the building of the mortuary?—Yes.

678. And then there is your balance, which, at the beginning of the year, was £1,839 6s. 1d. in hand, which is reduced to £1,811 19s. 8d. Have you still that balance?—Yes.

679. What is the total amount of the contract for the mortuary do you remember?—£1,040.

680. After realising £253 5s. 3d. by selling out Government stock, and having paid the instalment of the loan of £33,000, have you still any surplus income standing in stock on the burial fund account?—Not on that account. That £253 5s. 3d. was the only sum we had.

681. Your original loan on the cemetery account was £33,000, and I see you paid last year £2,700 of sinking fund. You will not require now so large a sinking fund as that?—£1,850 is all we require. Some of the mortgages had not matured, and then we invested the money, and paid off as much as cleared off our arrear of sinking fund. We have £4,000 invested on the police fund applicable to secondary mortgages, and as soon as a mortgage falls due we would sell out and apply the proceeds of such sale to the payment of the mortgage.

682. As all the accounts pass through your hands, could you not save us a good deal of unnecessary time, and prevent the necessity of calling the different collectors, by giving us shortly the system of checks you exercise over their collections, and the collections from the markets and other moneys that

pass through your hands?—The moneys do not pass through my hands.

683. I should have said the accounts, the moneys go direct to the bank I mean, but the accounts all pass through your hands; and we heard from the town collector yesterday, that there is a check exercised by you upon all these accounts before they go to the finance committee. (Witness hands in form of notice supplied to each collector.)

684. Is that the usual form of notice?—Yes; they give the schedule of each rate, and the amount in the pound.

685. And this is the receipt book?—Yes.

686. It includes every rate and is a very full form I see?—Yes; all the particulars are given.

687. And the counterfoil gives the fullest information?—It does. The counterfoils are handed to me daily.

688. And are they initialed by you after examination?—Yes; by me or by one of my assistants. Each rate is marked—the police rate, the general purposes rate, and so on.

689. There is, I see, a column for each?—Yes; and then we have the total.

690. Is this entered by you or by the collector?—By the collector. The total sum collected in that ward (St. George's ward), is £7,765, and there is a deduction you see, allowed upon that, for discount and irrecoverable rates of £286 5s. 1d. A declaration is made before the magistrates where vacancies in the houses exist, where the rates are not recoverable.

691. Does the collector make that declaration?—He does; the list is always examined by me, and afterwards by the solicitor. If there are any in that amount which we find ought to be recovered we strike them out, and bring them forward.

692. Even after the declaration before the magistrate?—Yes.

693. Are the collectors' rate books examined and compared with these counterfoils to test the correctness of the entries of payment?—Yes; by my assistants or by myself, as the case may be, and they are checked off here, and initialed by me if there is nothing wrong. If the rates are not fully paid, my assistants draw my attention to it, and I inquire and have them made right.

694. And do you test the correctness of the payments to the bank by the bank-book every day?—Yes; every day.

695. Before every meeting of the committee?—Yes; it is done every day.

696. Do all the market accounts pass through your hands?—Not all, all the market accounts pass through my hands—all connected with the weighing.

697. Are the prices of all materials purchased checked when the invoice is brought in, by what you know to be the price current which should be paid for such materials?—Yes.

698. And is every invoice then posted in this book?—Yes. The invoice is checked by me, and the cheque is drawn for the amount.

699. Do you pay the wages?—No; the cashier pays the wages, and gets a cheque for them from each committee by whom the payments should be made.

700. So that these cash balances are always cash balances in the hands of the cashier?—They are.

701. He is the only person who holds a cash balance?—Yes.

Mr. Samuel Black

Mr. Samuel Black re-examined.

702. Mr. Black, the town solicitor, here handed in list of contributions paid by the borough to the county Antrim Grand Jury from 1860 to 1873, inclusive (Appendix No. 6, page 202), and was re-examined thereon.

703. Chairman.—The principal items, I suppose, in respect of which these contributions are made are the County Lunatic Asylum, the County Infirmary, and the Gaol?—Yes; there are some others.

704. Which are set out in sec. 6 of the Act of 1865, but these would be the three principal items?—Yes, and we have here the account showing the percentage that we paid on each item——

705. The last award determining the rate of contributions in pursuance of the provisions of the Act of 1865 was, I believe, made in 1873?—Yes.

706. In that year, 1873, the payment seems to have been £9,689, and last year it was £16,417 16s. I see that from 1873 it has increased, on an average, from £1,000 to £2,000 each year?—Yes.

707. What was the cause of that great increase?—The maintenance of prisoners, and also the payments to the industrial schools and reformatories.

708. Did the lunatics increase very much?—No; not much. We are now getting a contribution from Government. The one thing we feel sore upon is the price we pay for the maintenance of the prisoners in the gaol. We pay 93 per cent. of the entire cost, and we have no voice whatever in the expenditure of that money. We have neither representation on the Grand Jury nor the Board of Superintendence of the gaol. Not a single member of the Corporation is on the Board of Superintendence of the gaol, and we pay 93 per cent. of the entire expenditure.

709. Mr. Exham.—Does the whole county Antrim only pay 8 per cent.?—Yes.

710. Do you not also pay 80 per cent. of the money expended on the lunatic asylum as well as 93 per cent. on the maintenance of the prisoners?—Yes. If the Prisons Bill passed, it would relieve us from the last. The charge is based on the number of committals, without respect to the length of time that the committal is for, so that a committal for twenty-four hours will amount to the same as a committal from the country for two or three months. Those from the country are much longer than those from the borough. The hardship was admitted by both the arbitrators, but they felt they had no alternative but to make the award in the way they did. There is no way to alter it except by Act of Parliament.

711. What are your contributions to the county Down?—It only averages about £700 a year.

712. The contribution to the county Antrim Grand Jury is revised every five years. Is that to the county Down revised in the same way?—No; we send no prisoners to the county Down gaol at all. It principally depends on the valuation of the property in the county Down part of the town.

713. But you do contribute to the county Down—to the lunatic asylum and to the gaol, I presume?—We do. To the maintenance of the county lunatic asylum, to the maintenance and enlargement of the county gaol, and the salaries of its officers, and for the militia accommodation. We have only a small portion of the town in the county Down, and the contribution is very small.

Mr. Edward S. W. De Cobain

Mr. Edward S. W. De Cobain examined.

714. Chairman.—How long have you been in the employment of the Corporation?—Between twelve and thirteen years.

715. As cashier the whole time?—No; between eleven and twelve years as cashier.

716. What are your duties?—To receive all the moneys exclusive of the rates and the gas revenues, and the market tolls, and to make disbursements under the various funds.

717. You do not, I believe, pay the wages in the markets?—No.

718. And you do not pay anyone connected with the gasworks?—No.

719. Do you pay all other wages?—Yes.

720. And make all petty disbursements?—Yes.

721. Are not all above a certain sum made direct by cheque to the individual concerned?—Sums over £5 are paid direct by cheque.

722. To the party to whom it is due?—Yes; they are

723. Among the principal moneys that you receive are the police fines, which amount to a large sum, over £3,000 a year, and such small rents as there are belonging to the Corporation?—Yes.

724. Also incomes, and contributions towards the expenses?—Yes.

725. And I suppose also, all these payments that are made by private owners for the improvement of streets? —Yes; the original cost of the construction of streets.

726. In 1875 there was over £4,840 under the police fund only; and on the general purposes fund you receive nearly £3,000 more from all these summary sales, besides various large sums in respect of parade and street improvements?—Yes.

727. Upon this fund alone your receipts seem to have exceeded £13,000?—Yes.

728. You receive also payments for grazing on the parks; sales of hay, and so on; and in fact everything connected with the surplus lands of the parks, which amounted to £525 12s. 0d.; and the whole of the cemetery receipts also pass through your hands?—Yes; they are lodged with me by the registrar of the cemetery.

729. They are received by him in the first instance, and afterwards lodged by you direct to the bank?—Yes; lodged by me.

730. These amounted to £1,800 10s. last year?—Yes.

731. Something very little, if at all, short of £30,000 passed through your hands?—Yes; in the form of revenue.

732. What is your course of procedure when you receive these sums; are you required to lodge the money as sound them, or when the amount in your hands is more than a certain sum?—I generally lodge when the sum of money is sufficiently large to warrant me.

733. What do you call sufficiently large?—I keep £30 or £40 to meet current expenses.

734. I observe there is generally a small balance in your hands?—Yes, there is.

735. What do the weekly wages amount to?—I should say to £[illegible] a year, or perhaps, to a very little more than that.

736. Is not your account of receipts and disbursements presented every week either to the auditor or to the finance committee?—To the various committees.

737. With which the expenditure agrees?—Yes.

738. And after that it goes to the audit committee? —Yes, and they check the vouchers. I present the accounts of all my receipts and payments in the week to the various committees. These accounts are sent from that committee to the audit committee, by whom they are checked; and they supply me with the means of meeting this expenditure.

739. Do the audit committee know exactly what cheques are drawn on the bank by the various committees?—Yes; there is a statement of necessary expenditure presented to each committee. They go over those accounts and authorise the payment of them, and pass cheques in my favour enabling me to make the payments. These accounts passed by the various committees are entered in the various cheques, and they are submitted to the audit committee at each meeting weekly, and they check them.

740. Are all the sums you lodge lodged to the credit of the various committees?—Yes. With regard to the check upon the lodgments irrespective of the collectors, they lodge in a separate book, and I enter upon the debit side of my account the entries in the respective dates. I send over my books to the bank, and the lodgments are transferred from their books to my books, so that if there is any difference between the two it would appear at once. That enables them to be perfectly checked.

741. And is it a daily check?—Yes.

742. Mr. Exham.—With regard to the whole outgoings of the markets, you get a return I suppose? —Yes; there is a docket lodged with me by the collector of the amount that he lodges in the bank, and the entry is made in the bank pass-book, so that it is checked.

743. You pay wages to the scavengers?—Yes.

744. Who gives you a return of these?—There is a wages book returned to the accountant, which is checked, there is a statement put by him to the committee and he certifies the item, and a cheque is drawn in my favour to enable me to discharge the debt.

745. £30,190 is, I find, the exact amount received by you; your disbursements in small sums under £5, wages, &c., amounted, I believe, to £43,130, so that in point of fact, you got cheques amounting to nearly £13,000, in addition of the £30,000 received by you? —Yes.

746. Cheques pass through your hands to the extent of nearly £13,000 more than you received?—Yes. In point of fact, I get cheques for that full amount.

747. Yes; I mean in excess of your cash receipts. You give only £1,000 weekly?—Yes.

748. But I understand you to say, that as a matter of fact, you never hold more than £30?—From £40 to £50 generally; I retain that amount to meet current expenses.

749. Do your accounts all go through the accountant's hands before they go to the committee?—The accountant certifies to the accuracy of the account itself. I make up a list of payments, which is presented to the committee to show the amount of expenditure for the week. It is also entered in this pass-book, and when the statement is brought before the finance committee fortnightly, they compare the amounts of their returns with the amounts lodged with the bank, and find the amounts to correspond.

Mr. Hugh Crawford examined.

750. Chairman.—How long have you been acting as assistant clerk of markets?—Close on eighteen years.

751. So that you are thoroughly familiar with the practice, as regards the markets?—Yes.

752. How many markets are there?—Twelve markets.

753. "Smithfield market, Park market, Corporation-street market, Potato and Vegetable market, Cattle market, May's market, George's market, Cattle market, and Horse fair, Flax and Fruit market, Fish market, Police square market, and the Hay and Straw market." Your total receipts for last year were £3,323 7s. 5d. Your outgoings, which we found in going through Mr. Woods' accounts, were £2,097 17s. 4d., left a clear profit of £1,225 10s. on the markets?—Yes.

754. Who receives the money, and what is the check upon the receipts, and to whom is it all given? —There is a collector in each market.

755. Is there not more than one in any of these markets?—In some of them there are more than one. In the grain market there are four, but in the hay and straw market only one.

756. Are not these tolls levied principally on weighing?—Yes.

757. There is a weigh-master, I suppose?—Yes, in each market.

758. And all articles going into these markets are weighed by the weigh-master, I presume?—A great deal of the potatoes are not weighed.

759. They are taken in, I suppose, by basket?—They charge for what they have by the cwt., but the dealers take the farmer's word for whatever they state they have?—If they say they have 20 cwt., the dealers will take their word.

760. The tolls on the potatoes are ½d. per cwt. Suppose they are not weighed, are you paid?—It is just the same charge—½d. includes the weighing.

761. The weight is declared, although they are not weighed?—Yes.

762. I suppose the collector receives the whole amount in each market?—Yes.

Belfast. Dec. 13, 1875.

Mr. Edward S. W. [illegible]

Mr. Hugh Crawford.

BELFAST. Jan. 13, 1876. Mr. Hugh Crawford.

763. What does he do then?—He enters it in the book—the name of the party and the commodity, and he gives him a ticket which passes him out of the market, and that is returned to the clerk of the market.

764. How often are those examined by the clerk of the markets?—Once every week.

765. By the clerk of the market, or by you, as assistant?—I and another man: he brings the books that he uses every week.

766. Does he pay the money the same day?—Yes; the day that he receives it he hands it in to the clerk of the markets.

767. Then what does the clerk of the markets do with it?—Lodges it in the bank.

768. Does he lodge daily or weekly?—He lodges it sometimes daily. If there is a small amount, he does not lodge it.

769. What do you call a small amount?—Below £20.

770. Does he lodge all above £20 as he receives it?—Yes.

771. What bond does he give (the clerk of the markets)?—I think it is £400, but I could not say exactly.

772. Do you give security?—No.

773. Does no money pass through your hands?—None, except as assistant of the clerk of the markets.

774. Is the clerk of the markets held responsible for anything that passes through your hands?—Yes.

775. The largest amount received from any of these markets seems to be Smithfield market?—Yes; it consists principally of stalls and booths.

776. What is Smithfield market for?—For selling turf and bricks, and for all sorts of furniture, and so on.

777. It is, in fact, very like a bazaar?—Yes.

778. Are those shops and stalls let out to weekly tenants?—Yes.

779. Then the bulk of the money received from this market, is for stalls?—Yes.

780. Paid weekly, I suppose?—Yes, weekly in advance.

781. Do you know how much the rental of the stalls and shops in Smithfield market is?—I think about £2,000 last year.

782. And the odd £250 would be for tolls on certain produce?—Yes; for small things that might come in.

783. Mr. Exham.—Is turf sold there?—Very few go for turf to Smithfield market, the bulk of it is sold in Police-square.

784. Then the next largest market is the potato and vegetable market—the receipts were I see nearly £1,600 in the year?—Yes.

785. And then the pork market is the next largest?—Yes.

786. That produced £1,331?—Yes.

787. Is the pork market for live stock?—No.

788. Only for pork after it is killed?—Yes.

789. There is one of the markets in which I see the charge upon pigs varies?—That is in the pork market—farmers are charged 2d. each, and dealers who bring in a large quantity are only charged 1d. each.

790. Is that for live pigs?—No; and if they weigh them they are charged the same rate as the farmers, but there are very few of these weighed.

791. Does that charge of 2d. include weighing and inspection?—Yes.

792. Are they examined there?—No; the dealers' pigs are not examined.

793. Are the farmers'?—No.

794. Where do the dealers get these pigs killed?—They come in slaughtered by rail.

795. Chairman.—Is there not any inspection as to whether they are fit for food or not?—If there were any diseased pigs in the lots they would be seized—the inspector would seize them.

796. There is then an inspector?—Yes; there is one in the market—Edward Hamill is the name of the inspector.

797. Mr. Exham.—It takes a great deal of care to ascertain if they have got what is called measles or not?—It would be impossible for him to examine them all.

798. Chairman.—The difficulty seems to me to be with the pigs that are brought in in large lots by the dealers?—Yes; they cannot be examined so closely, but he could see very well if the pigs were diseased as he passed along.

799. It is impossible though to say that there is an examination of every one of these pigs?—Yes.

800. Your butter market is not apparently a very large market?—No; it is a small market.

801. Is there any live stock market?—Yes, the cattle market and horse fair.

802. The receipts of that appear very small for a place like Belfast, £124 10s. 9d. Is there usually a large attendance?—No; on fair days the principal business is done. We have not a large attendance except on fair days.

803. Where is it situated?—In Cromac-street.

804. It is not in a fair field?—No; it is enclosed.

805. Under head of "Borough slaughter house" I see receipts £338 3s., and expenditure £348 10s 2d. What do those receipts arise from—is it so much for each animal slaughtered?—Yes, so much per animal—1s. for cattle and 3d. for sheep; and there is the sale of the manure, and two slaughter places are let to yearly tenants.

806. Under whose charge are the slaughter-houses? Who is responsible for keeping them clean and wholesome?—There is a superintendent there. Arthur Gradiggan is the name of the superintendent.

807. We heard there were complaints made of it by the gas engineer, who lives near it. Are you aware of that?—I never heard anything of it; there might be, but I did not hear of it.

808. Have you ever heard complaints of it from any one else?—No.

809. Is it a thickly populated district of the town?—It is not; it is just at the extreme end of the town in Maysfield-street.

810. Mr. Exham.—Where is the drainage of the slaughter-houses discharged into?—It is discharged into the Lagan.

811. Chairman.—Have you often occasion to inspect it?—No.

812. You do not know, therefore, whether, in fact, it is kept thoroughly clean and washed out?—It is.

813. You cannot know of your own knowledge?—Not to my own knowledge.

814. Where do they get the water for flushing it?—The town supply.

815. We heard yesterday that the charge on water was so great that it is not used for many purposes that it might be used for. Do you know whether there is a constant supply to the slaughter-houses?—Yes; there is a constant supply.

816. Mr. Exham.—Do they slaughter and take away the offal for 1s. per beast?—Yes.

817. Chairman.—£11 4s. was, I see, the cost of the water for the year?—Yes; it is paid by meter.

818. It is not a large amount for public slaughter-houses in a place like Belfast, for they, of course, want continual flushing?—Yes.

819. Mr. Exham.—Where do the butchers take the offal, and how often must they take it away?—They must take it away immediately after the slaughtering of the beast. They do not take away the entrails; that goes into the manure.

820. Chairman.—Is that removed every day?—Yes.

821. Mr. Exham.—Does it go over to the manure depot at Ballymacarrett?—No; the parties have a contract to draw it away daily.

822. Where do they take it to?—To the country.

823. Chairman.—Are you familiar with the adjusting of weights and measures?—Yes.

824. What are the charges for testing weights?—½ cwt., 4d.; ¼ cwt., 3d.; 14 lbs., 2d.; and from 7 lb. to ½ oz., 1d.

825. And for measures?—For a 5 gallon measure, 1s.; 4 gallon measure, 10d.; 3 gallon measure, 8d.; 2 gallon measure, 6d.; 1 gallon measure, 4d.; and ½ a gallon, 3d.; from ½ gallon to ½ a glass, 1d.

826. I see the receipts from that department were £106 13s. 3d., and the expenditure, £71 11s. 4d., leaving a net profit of £35 1s. 11d.?—Yes.

827. Mr. Exham.—Do the police look after the adjustment or do the people bring them to you voluntarily?—The police look after them.

828. Chairman.—Who receives the moneys paid for the adjustment of the weights and measures?—The adjuster receives them in the first place and he hands them over to Mr. Woods, who receives them weekly.

829. In the same way I suppose the superintendent of slaughter-houses hands his receipts over to Mr. Woods?—Yes, just the same way.

830. Mr. Lawless.—Is there any stamp or certificate given with adjustment of the weight?—No.

831. Mr. Exham.—Is the weight stamped?—Yes; the weight is stamped by the police; each weight is stamped with a die, and the measures are stamped in the same way.

832. How many other slaughter-houses are there. Have you anything to say to them?—There are thirty-two licensed slaughter-houses.

833. Are they all inspected?—Yes; but we have nothing to say to them—the sanitary staff look after them.

834. Do the police keep order in your markets?—Yes.

835. The local police I suppose?—Yes.

836. Chairman.—Have you a number of constables on duty there?—Yes; but there are not a sufficient number to keep order.

837. I see the principal outgoings are the cost of the staff. Your yearly salary is £120, and Mr. Woods' £224, and the inspector of provisions £104. Is he personally responsible for the condition of the meat, fish, &c., exposed for sale?—Yes.

838. £1,343 1s. 3d. is paid, I see, in regular weekly wages alone, and £166 11s. 11d. on workmen's wages during repairs?—Yes.

839. Then there is £133 17s. 7d. rates and taxes, £226 17s. 7d. cost of lighting, £79 for insurance, and £33 miscellaneous expenses, and books, printing, &c., £47 11s. 10d.?—Yes.

840. I see in one case, and in only one, you pay head-rent?—Yes, in the case of Castle market.

841. You pay there £310 a year?—Yes; and we have only seventeen or eighteen years of the lease to run.

842. The Castle market is, I think, for the sale of vegetables and fruit?—Yes.

843. And is that the only market which is not on your own freehold?—Yes; that is the only one.

December 13, 1876.

Dr. Samuel Browne examined.

844. Mr. Exham, Q.C.—You are the consulting sanitary officer of the Corporation?—I am.

845. How long have you occupied that position?—Since December, 1874.

846. I believe you were a long time a member of the Corporation?—Twelve years.

847. Had you anything to say to the sanitary arrangements of the city, before the Act of 1874 came into operation?—I was appointed medical officer of health in 1845 and 1849, and again in 1853 and 1854.

848. Then practically you have had to a great extent the superintendence of the sanitary arrangements of Belfast, over a series of years?—Yes; I may say that in conjunction with the late Dr. Morgan, I instituted the first sanitary inquiry into the state of Belfast in 1848.

849. And have you been looking after it ever since?—Well I have taken a great interest in it.

850. Chairman.—After the Act of 1874 was passed was not the staff all remodelled?—Yes.

851. And after that of what did the staff consist?—The staff consisted, before the Act, of an inspector and five sub-sanitary officers.

852. Since the Act was passed of what does the staff consist; of how many and what officers?—There is a consulting sanitary officer—that is myself; Mr. Scott the executive sanitary officer, then there are six sub-sanitary officers, and there are the nine medical officers connected with dispensaries, who are called sanitary officers. Six of these are within the borough, one in Ballymacarrett and two whose districts are partly rural and partly urban—Numbers 9 and 10 districts.

853. Does Mr. Scott devote his entire time to his duties?—Yes; he gives his entire time as executive sanitary officer.

854. There are seven sanitary officers within the town and two partially outside?—Yes; seven, counting Ballymacarrett. Numbers 9 and 10 districts are partly outside and partly inside, as you will see by my report.

855. Mr. Exham.—Do the six sub-sanitary men under Mr. Scott give their time exclusively to sanitary work?—Yes.

856. And the medical portion of the staff—that is, the dispensary doctors—are they paid by the poor law authorities?—They were sanctioned by the Council—they are *ex-officio*; they are paid by the Poor Law Guardians. They are *ex-officio* sanitary officers as dispensary medical officers under the Act of Parliament.

857. And, I presume, the salaries paid are sanctioned by the Local Government Board?—Yes; all of them.

858. What duties do the sub-sanitary officers perform—the six men?—Well, the town is divided into districts, and each one has charge of a district. They alternate their duties occasionally according to Mr. Scott's arrangements. They have to go out and observe any nuisances that may be reported, and to make a report upon them; to serve the various notices that Mr. Scott issues; to see that they are carried into effect; to report the date on which they are executed; and also, if they have not been executed to make a report.

859. Chairman.—Do they report in the first instance to you or to the dispensary doctor—*i.e.*, the sanitary officer?—They do nothing with the sanitary officers at all except take reports from them and bring them to the town hall.

860. In other towns the consulting sanitary officer has had nothing to do with them—but your system seems to be quite different?—Every morning one of the men calls at the dispensary of a district and obtains from the medical officer of that district whatever report he may have had occasion to write regarding nuisances and other matters. There are several of these reports and one of them is the report of what zymotic disease (if any) occurs during the preceding twenty-four hours.

861. Mr. Exham.—Are these reports brought down to you or to Mr. Scott?—The nuisance reports go directly to Mr. Scott, and the reports regarding disease come directly to me.

862. Do these six men look after lodging-houses?—Yes; they inspect the lodging-houses regularly.

863. And report their condition to Mr. Scott or to you?—To Mr. Scott; and if any questions arise Mr. Scott refers to me. There are 102 licensed common lodging-houses.

864. Do these men to your knowledge see to the carrying out of the by-laws—I suppose there are by-laws for the regulation of common lodging-houses?—Yes; you should have a copy of them. [They were handed in.]

865. Do these six men see that these by-laws are carried out?—Yes; they see them strictly carried out;

Belfast. Jan. 22, 1878. — Dr. Samuel Browne.

and if there should be any infringement they report to Mr. Scott and he refers to me.

866. Do they see that these houses have the necessary accommodation?—They have been carefully examined by Mr. Scott, and where there was any doubt on the subject he made a measurement of the rooms and submitted it to me, and where he had any doubt on the subject he took my advice. I may observe that the by-laws relating to common lodging-houses are approved of by the Local Government Board.

867. And what is the lowest number of cubic feet allowed according to the by-laws in the lodging-houses?—300 cubic feet for each inmate—that is the minimum, but I generally have much more.

868. You mean you generally have more, but you are never below the minimum?—We observe that strictly.

869. Then is there proper ventilation in them all?—There must be proper means of ventilation.

870. Are they limewashed regularly, according to the by-laws?—Yes.

871. Then are all the by-laws strictly carried out?—Yes, strictly carried out. (Copy of by-laws handed in, and also the ticket that is put up in each of the rooms of the lodging-houses.)

872. With regard to the bakehouses, are they regularly inspected by these men?—There are fifty-seven bakehouses inspected regularly by these men. Indeed I may say that Mr. Scott always undertakes that inspection himself. It is done by night. He inspects these bakehouses along with one of the men—the man belonging to the district.

873. As far as the lodging-houses are concerned, have they got water-closets, privies, or what?—Water-closets, or rare accommodation, in that class of houses.

874. What is done where they have not got water-closets?—They must not be without privy accommodation and ashpits.

875. What arrangement is there for the removal of the refuse?—The arrangement is that which exists throughout the whole town. They are occasionally cleansed according as they may be noticed.

876. Are they cleaned out by the Corporation?—The parties have them cleaned out, and the Corporation carts remove the refuse.

877. How are the lodging-houses supplied with water? Is water laid on to them generally, or are there taps out in the street?—They are generally supplied with tanks—not by a tap or a rain. In fact that is generally so in that class of houses.

878. Then they have always water on the premises?—Yes.

879. Pipe water?—Pipe water is laid on to all the houses.

880. Mr. Scott, you say, sees that the regulations with regard to the bake-houses are carried out?—Yes; and he visits to see once a week if there is any infringement.

881. With regard to the bake-houses, what is the amount of cubic space insisted upon?—300 cubic feet, that is the minimum.

882. And you adhere to that minimum?—Yes; and generally I go much beyond it. For instance, where we have three workpeople in a room, and the amount of cubic feet goes near to that minimum, we have one of the parties taken out of that room. If there is 1,000 cubic feet of space, we will only allow two parties in that. I may say that probably there is scarcely a lodging-house or bake-house in Belfast that has only the minimum.

883. Chairman.—Did the council, acting under your advice, fix a space for each room of a lodging-house?—Yes.

884. Is there any difficulty in procuring lodging-house accommodation here?—I am not aware that there is.

885. Have you had many infringements of the bake-houses Act?—There are fifty-seven bake-houses, and we have very seldom had an infringement of the Act. There have been only two cases in which we had to remonstrate with persons for employing work-people under age.

886. Mr. Ekman.—With regard to the slaughter-houses, are they regularly inspected?—There are thirty-two licensed slaughter-houses inspected regularly.

887. I suppose they are inspected regularly by the subsanitary officer?—Yes.

888. Is any manure allowed to remain in the slaughter-houses for any length of time?—The owners are obliged under the licensing regulations to have it removed within a very short period—I think it is twenty-four hours.

889. Are the slaughter-houses properly supplied with water?—Yes.

890. With pipe-water?—Yes; there might be, perhaps, in Cromac-street one or two where a pump is used. Whether it is so now I cannot say.

891. They are, at any rate, properly flushed and cleansed with water?—You are aware that slaughter-houses must have a good supply of water, and I believe they have that here. They are obliged to have a cistern containing a certain amount of water.

892. I suppose there are proper connecting sewers to the main sewer from those slaughter-houses?—Yes; there is immediate connexion—there are connecting drains. I am now speaking of licensed slaughter-houses, but we have private slaughter-houses as well. There are also public abattoirs. I remember at the time the regulations were passed we had a dispute as to the size of the tank. At that time I was a member of the Corporation. Before I leave the subject of the lodging-houses, I may mention that there were only two cases of contagious disease occurring in lodging-houses during the past twelve months. That is a matter of great importance. The owners are obliged to report the occurrence of any case of infectious disease.

893. The public slaughter-house is the Corporation slaughter-house, I presume? Is it furnished with all proper appliances with regard to sewerage, and so on?—They are very satisfactorily worked. We had a difficulty in the early part of the summer with regard to some nuisance collected, but that has been overcome since. There was a complaint made regarding the slaughter-house, and I consequently went down and inspected it. I found that there was some cause for the complaint, and the nuisance was immediately removed. I have heard of no complaints since.

894. Who has the actual charge of the public slaughter-house—the looking after it?—There is one man who looks after it specially. I think there are three slaughter-men for the slaughter-houses, and then of course they have subordinates, and there is almost daily inspection by one of these officers.

895. There is then any almost daily inspection by some of your subofficers?—Yes; a man of the district nuisance division looks into that place very frequently.

896. Are there many dwelling-houses in the neighbourhood of that public slaughter-house?—It is a considerable distance from any inhabited house. It was built specially with a view to avoid proximity to any of the inhabited houses.

897. You have school-houses here—are they inspected?—Yes, all the public school-houses under the Board of Education are inspected repeatedly by the staff—by the men belonging to the districts.

898. Are they well supplied with all the necessary accommodation?—We have had complaints regarding the accumulation of night-soil, but that matter has been attended to as a rule after the notice was served.

899. There are some graveyards still within the limits—intra-mural?—There are four within the borough still, but three of them are nearly entirely closed up. The Shankhill graveyard—one portion of it is entirely closed up under order in council, and a large part of Friar's Bush is also closed up under order in council. The new burying ground behind the poor-house was also partially closed, and as far as I know there has been no infringement of the Burials Act brought under our notice, except in two instances in both of which we instituted prosecutions.

900. That is part of the duty you say that is looked

after specially?—Yes; a report is made once a week to the committee, which sits weekly, and at whose meetings I am always present.

901. You have already mentioned that the sanitary doctors used to report almost daily?—Whenever a case of disease occurs they always make a return—at least I understand they do.

902. When they send in their reports do they go to Mr. Scott?—Yes, all on nuisances, immediately.

903. And does he act upon those almost immediately?—He acts promptly, except in cases where there is a doubt regarding them, and they should consequently be brought before the committee.

904. Does he serve a notice for the abatement of the nuisance?—Yes, and follows that up immediately, if it be not attended to.

905. And then we have it that there are two legal crown solicitors appointed by the Corporation to prosecute in these cases?—Yes; in all cases connected with the Town Council, and attending both courts—the custody court and the summons court—as they are required.

906. I suppose a report-book is kept as part of the records of the Corporation in which those reports of the sanitary officers are entered?—There are a large number of books kept for this purpose.

907. Then with regard to the order of the council upon that, I suppose there is a record kept of that?—That is entered on the minutes of the committee.

908. Does anyone then report as to whether what is ordered to be done is done?—Mr. Scott, the executive sanitary officer is held responsible for that.

909. Does Mr. Scott actually furnish to the sanitary committee a report as to whether what they have directed or you have directed is done?—He follows that out and reports.

910. In a case where the sanitary medical officer reports that there is disease of a contagious character, what course is adopted then?—We endeavour to have the party removed to hospital as soon as the party can be removed from the place where he or she is lying; and the infected place itself is after the removal fumigated, and if it be a serious case of disease, the bedding is destroyed. We disinfect and deodorise all houses where there is infectious disease.

911. Do you find as a general rule, that the people are ready to go to hospital?—No; but there are exceptions. We have some parties that will refuse to go to hospital under any circumstances.

912. Are you ever obliged to resort to the 26th section of the Public Health Act of 1866, by which you are enabled, if in the opinion of the medical officer, the party has not sufficient and proper accommodation, to force his removal to hospital, by obtaining an order from a magistrate for the purpose?—We have not done that; but in a case at a lodging-house, we did it at once without waiting for an order from a magistrate.

913. Is there any hospital provided specially by the Corporation?—None.

914. What hospital accommodation is there?—That provided by the Poor Law Guardians—an extensive, ample, and well-managed hospital.

915. Are there any cars provided for the purpose of removing the sick?—The Poor Law Guardians have cars for the purpose. There is, I may mention, a bye-law of the Council which prevents any car from off one of the public stands from taking a person suffering from infectious disease at all, under a very heavy penalty.

916. I suppose there is no difficulty in getting the means of conveyance through the relieving officer for cases of sickness?—Not the slightest.

917. CHAIRMAN.—There is no conveyance, you say, kept specially by the Corporation for the purpose?—No; the Poor Law Guardians have taken the entire charge of that portion of the sanitary duty.

918. Is there not sometimes a difficulty then arising from the extent of the borough?—Well, I may tell you that such has been found occasionally to arise. For instance, in periods of severe epidemics such as in 1847, 1848, and 1849, I had to hire special cars for which the Poor Law Guardians, or Board as it was then, paid.

919. By the Act of 1874 you will remember that you are empowered, as the urban sanitary authority, to maintain an ambulance for this purpose?—Yes; but we have had no necessity.

920. Has the Corporation provided a place for the purpose of having a disinfecting apparatus erected?—That was under consideration and engaged a good deal of attention, and it was found that it would be too expensive a proceeding. At the Board of Guardians they have a place for the purpose of disinfecting clothes, and they do so after they are sent to them at once.

921. I suppose there is a conveyance there for the purpose of carrying infected clothing?—I cannot say that they are taken in that way. The parties themselves take their clothing with them when they go to hospital.

922. But what about the bedding that is left behind?—We invariably pay for it, and destroy it if recommended by the officer that it ought to be destroyed.

923. What is the distance of the workhouse infirmary, where the disinfecting apparatus is kept, from the centre of the town?—About a mile and a quarter—barely a mile and a quarter.

924. Then it is within the borough boundary?—Yes. A mile and a half within the borough boundary.

925. Have you felt the want of one in a more convenient situation?—No; we have not felt the want of it nor do we think it necessary; and I am sure the Council would erect one if a necessity arose for it.

926. Is there a mortuary provided by the Corporation?—There is.

927. In the town?—In Arthur-square—near the Town Hall—a place to which dead bodies are removed. We have no mortuary devoted to the purpose of having bodies removed to who have died from infectious disease at their homes.

928. But what do you do in cases where persons die at their own homes of infectious diseases?—We endeavour to get them interred as soon as possible; and the house is then fumigated and cleansed.

929. You have power to erect a mortuary under the Public Health Act of 1866?—We have; but it would be a very difficult matter to carry it out. The prejudices of people would be very much hurt.

930. What you call a mortuary is in fact a morgue?—It is a place to which bodies found in the river and other places are removed. The Coroner's Court is adjacent to it.

931. I don't know whether you have "wakes" here or not?—I think that is nearly abolished in Belfast; but in such cases I have issued very strong cautions to the people not to intermix with people living in places where infectious disease has been prevalent.

932. Suppose a case of fever breaks out in one of those small habitations in which children live, and so on, if the party does not go to hospital, are any precautions taken to prevent the spread of the disease—are the children removed, or any steps taken to separate the healthy persons from the infected person or persons?—We have not interfered by force yet. We endeavour to do everything by persuasion, and I may give as a reason for that, that we don't wish to make our department unpopular by using what is called force. We take every precaution by advising the people as far as possible to avoid contact with contagion, and we have the rooms in which such sickness occurs disinfected. I have gone to the houses and cautioned people myself personally very frequently.

933. What is the sanitary condition of the houses of the lower orders in Belfast—what accommodation have they?—There is a very large number of houses inspected, of the working classes, which are very good, but there are others in a lamentable condition.

934. Are many without privies?—There were at one time upwards of 4,000 houses in Belfast without

Belfast.
Oct. 15, [illegible]
Dr. Samuel Browne.

Belfast.
[illegible]
Dr. Samuel Browne.

rary accommodation. There are at the present time somewhere about 1,500 still in that condition.

935. And in their case what has been done?—A large number have been swept away of late, and others have been made to get common accommodation—that is, a privy for the accommodation of four or five houses. We have endeavoured to do the best we could under the circumstances. I may tell you that we used very often to notice parties to close houses that did not possess proper sanitary accommodation, and we followed that up by getting an order from the magistrates, and that worked very well for a period, until a case was referred to the Recorder, who gave his decision against us; and since then I myself did not like to interfere, and Mr. Black advised me not to interfere with these houses until we have some ample means to deal with them. I look upon it as much to be regretted that that decision went against us.

936. Mr. Exham.—The Recorder, I believe, was of opinion that the Act of Parliament did not apply to any house built at the time of the passing of the Act?—Yes; and where disease had not actually occurred on the premises.

937. Was that Mr. Otway's decision?—Yes.

938. The practical effect of that would be that you could not force people to put up privy accommodation in houses so long as the inhabitants of those houses had not had fever?—I am not sure that it went so far as that.

939. In the case of the houses, 1,500 or 1,600, that you say are without privy accommodation, what do the people do there?—They have to deposit night-soil on the streets, and then by doing so they are infringing a local Act, and if they are discovered they are brought up and fined; and they have been repeatedly discovered and fined of late.

940. I see by your report that you have been calling the attention of the Corporation to this matter with the view of trying some plans to get rid of this nuisance?—Well the plan that has been adopted has been to get the people to leave the manure out in the street in the morning and the Corporation carts will come and take it away; but unfortunately parties still very often leave it out after the carts have passed round.

941. Chairman.—Are you aware of the nature of the pail system in use in Rochdale?—Yes; I know of it, but we have tried no regular system here. We are, however, anxious to try any system that would do away with the evil.

942. Mr. Exham.—Are the streets scavenged on Sundays?—No, they are not.

943. Then if this stuff is put out on a Saturday after the carts pass round it must remain out during the whole of Sunday?—Yes; either it must remain in the people's houses or out in the street; that is one of the evils of the want of rear accommodation.

944. Are the owners of the houses required to make connecting drains between their houses and the main sewers?—I should mention, before passing on, that all the streets are swept very late on Saturday nights.

945. Are there connecting sewers with the main drains?—Yes; all houses that have water-closets must have drains.

946. Unless they have cesspools?—We have no cesspools in connexion with water-closets.

947. You do not permit that?—No; as far as possible not within the town. We would not permit cesspools to be made within the town.

948. If the house is situate within 100 feet of the main sewer you make the owner put down a connecting drain?—That has been done invariably; that is a point that has been looked after very specially.

949. What is the water supply of the houses without this accommodation?—The greater number have a tap inside the door. There is a stopcock—a cock that must go on running unless it is immediately turned off.

950. Have they to pay for that or is it supplied to them free?—The landlord under certain circumstances pays for the water. The Commissioners of course charge all parties for the water. I may say as a rule that those houses are very well supplied with water.

951. Are there supplies of water to the public fountains in the streets?—A large number.

952. Are they paid for by the Corporation?—No.

953. How are they paid for?—They are given gratuitously by the Water Commissioners. There are a large number of drinking fountains for the use of the people and also for cattle.

954. Any private wells?—Yes; a large number in the Cromac district.

955. Are they largely used by the public?—Largely sold and used by the public.

956. Was the water in these wells been analysed?—Repeatedly; and found to be very good. I think, however, there were two wells found not to be pure and we ordered them to be closed and they were closed. The Cromac water is looked upon as the best in the country.

957. In what condition are the main sewers?—They are in a good condition where there is a good fall. Of course if you take some low-lying sewers you must have a large deposit from the want of a fall, and I do not think then that the flushing of such sewers would be of much advantage. All the low-lying sewers must be cleansed out, and it costs a great deal of money annually for the cleansing of those sewers and it is one of the evils we cannot avoid.

958. Are they opened by the Corporation periodically and the accumulation taken away?—Wherever there is any suspicion, the sewer is immediately opened and cleansed by the surveyor's department.

959. Are there any traps in these sewers for the purpose of letting off all the sewage gas?—They have open ventilating grates; but they are trapped at the sides where the water goes in.

960. That helps to take away the sewage gas and it also takes away the pressure from the houses?—Yes; and we have "manholes" in the principal sewers in order to enable the men to get down and cleanse them.

961. But you are only able to do that within a short distance of the "man-holes"?—I have known the men to go through the whole sewer.

962. Do any of the sewers go into the river?—Nearly the whole of the sewers go into the river.

963. What is the condition of the famous Blackstaff?—It is sometimes very bad, and sometimes not very bad, according to the amount of water running down it. You would not find it very bad at this season of the year, but if you were here in June you would find it unpleasant.

964. Has anything been done with regard to the condition of the Blackstaff?—Nothing, except cleansing it out, levelling the edges, removing obstructions, but not anything to keep the sewage out of it. You are aware that there is a plan before the council regarding it which has been practically adopted.

965. Chairman.—Is the Blackstaff the outlet for a great portion of the sewage of the town?—For a large portion, but not a great portion.

966. Mr. Exham.—It is in a bad state in the summer?—Unquestionably.

967. Well, as sanitary officer, is its condition in summer, in your opinion, dangerous to public health?—I must say that in the neighbourhood of the Blackstaff I never found that we had more disease than anywhere else, even in times when there were epidemics, strange to say.

968. Some years ago you made a strong report against its condition to the corporation?—It has been reported on repeatedly.

969. Mr. Lawless.—Have those reports ever been acted upon?—Main sewerage to divert the sewage out of it has never been made yet; but upon that point you will get full information from the surveyor.

970. Is the Blackstaff in the same state now as

when you reported upon it?—Precisely; in the summer it is in the same condition, or even worse than it was when I reported on it, because the amount of sewage going into it increases annually, and a large portion of that sewage comes from the mills, which mills get a great deal of cooling water from that stream.

971. CHAIRMAN.—Are there no intercepting sewers?—None.

972. Mr. EXHAM.—There has been nothing, I believe, done upon a large scale with regard to the condition of the Blackstaff for several years?—Nothing practically done for several years.

973. What is the outlet for that portion of the sewage of Belfast that does not go into the Blackstaff?—The Lagan is the receptacle for all the sewage, because the Blackstaff runs into the Lagan.

974. Do you consider its condition is rather dangerous to public health?—I consider its condition very dangerous to public health.

975. If an epidemic broke out, might it not be a source of contagion?—Yes, although, as I have said, during epidemics, we did not find the neighbourhood of the Blackstaff any more dangerous than other localities.

976. Since the last Public Health Act came into force, have you reported against the condition of the Blackstaff?—The matter was last referred to me when the scheme for the removal of the nuisance from the Blackstaff was submitted to me.

977. Did you approve of that scheme?—I did approve of that scheme decidedly, although perhaps I do not approve of the water-closet system as a rule.

978. You approved of most of the features of that scheme?—Yes.

979. But that scheme has not been adopted?—Not yet; there has been a difficulty about an outlet between us and the Harbour Commissioners. The system comprises two levels—one high and one low. The low level will require to be pumped, and the high level will discharge itself by gravitation. It is the high level I refer to now.

980. Do you think the Corporation will carry out that scheme, provided they get the consent of the Harbour Commissioners?—I am sure the Corporation will do anything that is practical in the matter. I must, at the same time, tell you that there have always been great difficulties in these cases in connexion with the outfalling of the town sewerage, which has always been one of our greatest difficulties.

981. You have had, I find from this report which has been handed to me, 5,141 streets and lanes inspected with respect to the sanitary regulations from the 1st of January of the present year?—Yes.

982. That is eleven months, and there were in that time twenty houses provided with back yards, and the necessary accommodation?—Yes.

983. And it goes on to say that there were 2,666 feet of pipe drains laid, connecting house drains with street sewers; 100 house drains constructed, eighty-five privies and ashpits erected, and 204 re-built; twelve water-closets erected, and twenty-seven repaired, and 1,373 house drains cleansed?—That is correct; and I may as well tell you that with regard to the water-closets, that was where they had not formerly existed, that of course does not refer to new houses being built.

984. Have all these matters reported and referred to have been done at the instance of the owners or complaints under your directions?—Yes.

985. Then there were I see 118 stench-trap grates put on house drains; 810 yards rolled and skew-sewers repaired; thirty walls cemented to prevent offensive matter soaking into the adjoining premises, eighty back passages cleaned; forty-five houses provided with water spouts; six pools of stagnant water abated, and three accumulations of offensive matter removed; thirty-two roofs repaired, eight houses closed up which were unfit for habitation?—That was done by consent of the parties after being noticed.

986. Do the Inspectors examine the roofs?—In going round they observe dilapidations of any kind, and it is reported to the surveyor's department, and attended to.

987. There were also I perceive three chimneys raised to abate the smoke nuisance?—There were chimneys found to be too low.

988. There are also said to have been 1,899 houses whitewashed, and 1,690 privies and ashpits cleansed; and 257 houses fumigated and whitewashed where contagious diseases occurred?—Yes; we have had very little contagious disease as you are aware during the last twelve months.

989. Did you not report a number of houses unfit for human habitation, specially mentioning Smithfield?—Yes, that is the place I reported as unfit for human habitation, but now a scheme is being considered for the improvement of dwellings of that class.

990. Mr. Black mentioned that the artisans' dwellings scheme was under the consideration of the Corporation, and are we to understand from you that the Corporation are about taking proceedings under the provisions of the Artisans' Dwellings Act for the improvement of artisans' dwellings?—Yes; and here is the joint report of the sanitary and town improvement committees of the 20th of September last, with my reports to them on the subject recommending the Town Council to declare the districts therein referred to an unhealthy area, and that a scheme be prepared for its improvement. (*Vide* Appendix No. 4, page 210.)

991. Is there any company established in Belfast for providing such dwellings?—None whatever.

992. Mr. LAWLESS.—Are the lanes and alleys where the poorer portion of the population live well attended to in the way of scavenging?—Yes, there the scavenging is very fairly done. As I said before there is a difficulty occasionally experienced from the fact of the parties themselves not being of very cleanly habits, and from the circumstance that they pitch things into the streets, and so on.

993. Have the Corporation provided any public conveniences?—Yes, in connexion with our markets they have provided places of public convenience.

994. CHAIRMAN.—In your report you say that the narrow streets, courts, alleys, and backyards of places inhabited by persons of dirty habits are not so carefully kept, from a sanitary point of view, as they should be?—Yes.

995. But as far as the scavengers can attend to it is the work well done?—Yes; as far as I can see it is well done. Every morning the men go round, and we have an inspector and two sub-inspectors attending to this duty.

996. Mr. EXHAM.—Is there as much attention paid, in the way of cleansing, to those parts of the town where poor people live, as there is to the portions of the town inhabited by rich people?—That does not come under my view, so I cannot say.

997. CHAIRMAN.—There is, you say, daily supervision exercised, but in consequence of the untidy habits of the inhabitants, it is impossible to keep those poorer quarters of the town as clean as you would wish. Is that what you wish to convey to us?—Yes; if you examine the Chairman of the Police Committee he will be able to tell you with regard to many of those points; they do not come under my observation.

998. From a sanitary point of view would a better supply of water be advisable?—We never could have too much water in the town, but I do not complain of the water supply to the inhabitants.

999. I mean that the Corporation should have at their command a better supply of water for the flushing of those small lanes and alleys, so as to have them washed and cleansed?—In my opinion there should be an almost unbounded supply for cleansing purposes.

1000. Mr. LAWLESS.—Do you think the Corporation have at present a sufficient control over the water supply for sanitary purposes?—They have no control over the supply.

1001. CHAIRMAN.—I suppose it is a question of price?—It is as you say; they have no power of using the water themselves.

BELFAST.
Dec. 13, 1877.
Dr. Samuel Browne.

BELFAST.
Oct. 12, 1877.
Dr. Samuel Browne.

1002. Mr. Exham.—Is there an ample supply of water for all purposes?—I think generally speaking that they have no ample supply for the inhabitants.

1003. Suppose the Corporation themselves were owners of the waterworks, is there a sufficient water supply for the houses?—I think there will be, but I think myself that there has not been hitherto, and, as you are probably aware, on two or three occasions we have been nearly on the point of a water famine. That is not, however, the fault of the Water Commissioners. The growth of Belfast has been so rapid that it has been almost impossible to overtake it with regard to the water supply.

1004. They have a new reservoir for the water supply made?—Yes, it is thirty years ago since the first was made.

1005. They have got a couple of extra ones since?—A number of new dams have been made since, they are down in the neighbourhood of Carrickfergus.

1006. Then taking all that into account you still don't think the water enough for the increased growth of Belfast in population?—Not at all, and I imagine the Water Commissioners anticipate getting a larger supply.

1007. Chairman.—Do the Corporation get any supply of water for the purpose of washing the streets and sewers from the river?—We used to pump up water from the river for the streets in summer; but as that was not a very wholesome proceeding, I always advised them to get clean water for the purpose, and to buy it from the Commissioners.

1008. That would be of course far better than using the water of the Blackstaff?—But the Commissioners have to be very chary of giving too much water; because they might run the public dry in the summer, as that is the time when there is a greater demand for water, and the Commissioners have been very careful on that point. During the past few months the Commissioners have instituted a house to house examination with a view of preventing the waste of water.

1009. I see you, as consulting sanitary officer, go a great deal further than anyone in your position that we have yet met elsewhere in Ireland; you send in regular reports and you don't wait to be invited to attend meetings of the Corporation?—I consider the late definitive, and I consider it my duty to do all I can without waiting to be asked for advice; I look on that as part of my duty, and I do not merely wait to be asked for my advice. I come to the town hall every day, and consult with the executive sanitary officer, and once a week with the committee, regarding what is best to be done. I make a report once a month, and a general report every three months.

1010. You are provided with a proper office and clerks I suppose?—We have very good apartments in the town hall; there is a private apartment for the executive sanitary officer, and one for myself.

1011. And are reports kept regularly and filed there?—Yes.

1012. You apparently act as general advising medical officer?—Yes; such as there is in Liverpool, Manchester, and so on.

1013. Practically, you are the medical officer of health?—Yes; practically I am.

1014. Mr. Exham.—In every way in their power, exclusive of the Blackstaff, the Corporation seem to have done everything in their power to improve the sanitary condition of the town?—The Corporation are most anxious and willing to do anything in their power for the improvement of the sanitary condition of the town.

1015. In your report for 1876 you call attention at page 16 to the main drainage, sewering, and paving of the streets. You state in that report:—

"I am aware that within the last few years the main drainage, sewerage, and paving of the streets have been greatly extended. These most important works should not be curtailed or delayed, but every effort should be made to have the main sewerage and drainage effectively carried out; while the streets that have not yet been properly formed, paved, and drained, should, without delay, be put into the condition that would allow surface-cleansing to be effectively performed. On this subject of surface cleansing, I may say that while the great thoroughfares are kept properly swept, the narrow streets, courts, and lanes (especially those without back-yards), and where are usually inhabited by persons of careless, if not dirty habits, require a closer supervision with regard to their cleanliness. This very much depends upon the inhabitants themselves, and I regret to say they are not nearly so careful as they should be."

As far as possible have these suggestions been carried out and that work done?—There has been a very large amount done during the past twelve months.

1016. You said that public accommodation had been provided by the Corporation in the markets. Have they also provided such accommodation in those poorer places to which you refer in your report?—They have accommodation in various places. They have not done it themselves, but they have compelled such places to be erected.

1017. So as to lessen the nuisance?—These 1,500 houses, I may mention, have not often a public place in connection with them; and on the other hand, in many streets one of the houses has been taken down for the accommodation of the others, and a properly built place put there.

1018. Have a large number of public urinals been erected?—Yes; a large number.

1019. Chairman.—With regard to the public slaughter-house, I asked was it in a thickly populated part of the town, and I was told it was not, and that the only person who complained of it was the gas engineer. You have inspected that place, I presume. Is it kept in a proper and wholesome condition?—The man in charge of it appears to be most anxious to keep it in good order. I know myself that the manure is removed from it very frequently; I think every second day.

1020. In your judgment is it to any extent a nuisance and dangerous to public health?—Not to the smallest extent. It was built with the view of obviating any public offence.

1021. The depot at which the manure and the refuse of the streets is kept is also within the town, I understand, and near to houses?—Not very near any houses; the nearest are some houses in Stewart-street.

1022. Is its locality an objectionable one, or one that is calculated to make it a nuisance and dangerous to public health?—It would be better if it were removed outside the borough decidedly; and I know that that is a question that has come before the committee. I imagine that as far as they can see their way they will have that attended to.

1023. Have you found injury to public health arising from its present position?—None whatever.

1024. But still you think it should be removed for better security for the public health?—As a matter of prevention, I think all these places should be removed outside the city.

1025. Mr. Exham.—Have the Corporation ever tried to take steps to prevent the owners of house property, and so on, from draining into the Blackstaff?—No; at least I am not aware that they have.

1026. Because the refuse of the mills, where there is a large population daily employed, must necessarily pollute and foul the river; and also, can you say, if any steps have been taken to make such owners form large cesspools?—I am not aware; that does not come under my observation.

1027. Under the Sanitary Acts it might come to be your duty to see that these owners should not be allowed to drain their refuse into the river?—You are aware that under the present Act we are a very short time in operation, and we have not had much opportunity of taking all the necessary steps. I think it would be a very proper thing if all the sewage were diverted out of the Blackstaff. Unquestionably these mills should be prevented from using the water of that river also.

1028. Are there a separate set of carts provided for sanitary purposes as distinct from the scavenging?—No.

1029. They are always able to get rid of the nuisance?—Yes.

1030. There is no difficulty in getting what carts

Belfast. Dec. 12, 1876. Dr. Samuel Browne.

and horses are necessary for the purpose of removing the night-soil?—Not the smallest.

1031. Does it ever happen here that horses are kept in the houses of the people, or anything of that kind?—If we find anything of that kind, the people are instantly noticed to remove them.

1032. Are pigs ever found under such circumstances?—There is a difficulty about pigs in the town; but we take as much precaution as we can to prevent pigs being kept in the houses; and if they are complained of as nuisances the people are immediately ordered by Mr. Scott to have them removed; or if the medical officer reports them, they are immediately ordered to be removed. I may observe that we have had from the inhabitants during the year 1,800 complaints all of which have been attended to; 2,298 notices have been served, and these were all attended to; and we had to summon ninety-three parties—in some cases we got convictions, in others not.

1033. You have a public analyst here?—Yes; Dr. Hodges, and you are aware that the food and drug department have been put under my charge, and whenever I have reason to suspect anything wrong with food or drugs, I get a man to take a sample to Dr. Hodges, who makes the analysis and reports to me, and the committee or myself may order a prosecution, or any paid solicitor.

1034. Do you think there is a sufficient staff for the working of that Act?—I would suggest that there should be a man specially set apart for that work. He might have combined with it the inspection of some portion of the markets. In consequence of the sickness of the clerk of the markets, we have not yet got an arrangement with regard to the services of a man, but it will I am sure, work very satisfactorily. I think before the end of the year we will have it all arranged and combine the two duties.

1035. There has been apparently very little disease?—Yes; the zymotics have been very low. The death-rate during the first quarter was 21·97 of the estimated population; that is for the year 1876.

1036. In 1875 it was 29?—You will find that the death-rate was high in all towns in that year. We were decimal point one above Dublin last year.

1037. Chairman.—According to these returns you were ·1 below Dublin last year?—For this year the first quarter is 1·74, and the second 2·3. We have had very little zymotic disease this year, but the early part of 1875 was high in that respect.

1038. Had you a good deal of scarlatina and fever?—Yes, and a great deal of measles. This year we have had a great deal of whooping-cough and diarrhœa among the better classes, and a singular immunity among the poor. You can ascertain that by comparing the numbers returned by the dispensary medical officers, and the amount of deaths by the registrar-general's returns. I do not think our natural death-rate would be more than about twenty-three.

1039. Have you found much adulteration of food here?—Well, principally in milk. We have taken up some butter and flour, but as a rule there has not been much food adulteration. We have had about 100 specimens examined.

1040. Mr. Lawson.—Are complaints from the inhabitants brought before your notice?—If the occasion requires, but not otherwise.

1041. Supposing the executive sanitary officer does not do what the complainant requires, what does the complainant do then; can he bring it before you?—Yes; and before the committee, and the committee will attend to any complaint that has not been attended to by the officers. Mr. Scott, in any case of doubt, always comes to me about it and consults me. We work very harmoniously in our department.

1042. As a rule are the complaints of the public attended to?—When well founded they are invariably attended to, and as far as possible the cause of them removed.

1043. Chairman.—Are they at least always investigated?—Yes; some of them are very trifling—a wrangle between two women, and that sort of thing.

1044. Mr. Lawson.—In your opinion are the meetings of the sanitary committee held sufficiently frequently at sufficiently short intervals?—I think so, decidedly; because in the meantime we do all that is necessary. The meetings are regularly held every Thursday.

1045. Mr. Exham.—Do a sufficient number of the committee attend to form a quorum?—We have always a quorum. We never have had any adjournments. Three form a quorum in all committees. I may remark that the sanitary committee makes a full report to the council.

1046. I suppose the water supplied by the Water Commissioners is good water?—Excellent water, and it has been frequently analysed. The water supplied through Belfast is principally the drainage of pasture and upland, and that next to spring water is about the best.

Dr. James Aitchison Alexander examined.

Dr. James Aitchison Alexander.

1047. Chairman.—You are, I believe, an alderman and have been a member of the Corporation for several years?—Yes, fourteen or fifteen years.

1048. You are the chairman of the police committee, I believe?—Yes; since Mr. Black became solicitor to the Corporation; he preceded me.

1049. And that committee has charge of the cleansing and lighting of the streets, I believe?—They have.

1050. Do the town surveyor and the officer who has charge of the cleansing and sweeping of the streets, the street inspector, act under the directions of that committee?—They do.

1051. Are the streets well swept and cleansed in your judgment?—They are.

1052. Are the back lanes and back alleys attended to as well as the main thoroughfares?—The back lanes, narrow lanes, and places of that kind are swept regularly daily, early in the morning.

1053. Did you hear by Dr. Browne's evidence on that point, that in consequence of the uncleanly habits of the occupants of the lanes and alleys it was impossible to keep them as clean as was desirable?—It is, very often; and I think our police force do not do what they should in that respect, by enabling us to bring up people who deposit things on the streets immediately after they are swept. We have appointed men to look after that, in addition to the police, to prosecute parties who deposit nuisances on the streets.

1054. Have any communications passed between you and Captain Bailey the chief inspector of the police force on that subject?—Yes.

1055. And has he expressed himself as willing and desirous that the police should act in that capacity?—I cannot say just from memory now so exactly as to that or not, but there have been frequent communications between us, and Mr. Bailey has been always willing to aid us and has given orders that these things should be carried out.

1056. Mr. Black has told us that the police do not do some of these duties very satisfactorily?—I might say it was the unanimous voice of the town that the police do not act as they are expected to do in carrying out the requirements of the local Acts and the by-laws. There is one thing that is much complained of—the regulation of the traffic.

1057. And though your committee is styled the police committee, it has nothing whatever to do with the police beyond drawing cheques for the yearly accounts. Really and truly the duties of your committee are to take charge of the cleansing of the streets and the lighting of the borough. Are not those the main duties?—Yes; those are the main duties. We find it very irksome to have nothing to do at all with the police but pay the accounts when presented. We have nothing to say with regard to the accounts, and we contend fairly enough, I think, and it is generally admitted, that where there is taxation there should be representation, but we have no

BELFAST.
Oct. 15, 1878.
Dr. James Andrews, Alderman.

voice in the matter at all. I think the principal reason for that is the large payments for extra police brought in on special occasions here. The police payments last year amounted to £14,000, while a few years back they only amounted to £8,000 or £9,000, and we cannot estimate for these payments at the beginning of the year. We have no control over them whatever, and when the extra police even have been brought here they have been retained much longer than we thought was necessary; and I may just state that it is the almost universal opinion of the inhabitants of the town that the regular force we have here would be quite sufficient to preserve the peace of the town, aided by the military, whom we have always here. The general opinion is that the military would be much more successful in keeping the peace of the town than an extra force of police would, and the former would cost us nothing. If it could be done we would be willing to pay something to the military if they were called out, because we would then save the travelling expenses of the police to and from long distances.

1058. We understand that a redistribution of the force cannot take place until July next?—There ought to be a revision. The people expected at least that they would obtain some assistance by this inquiry, in order to get some alterations made with regard to the police.

1059. All we can do is to take a note of your objections from a financial point of view. I think we cannot travel beyond that.

1060. Witness.—You will permit me to mention that the police committee have the charge of the fire brigade. Soldiers have been permitted to come out and assist at fires, and we have found them very efficient, and paid them the usual charge for helpers. We therefore think that they might be allowed to come out on some occasions to quell riots, and we would be quite willing to pay in the same way for the duty that would be involved in their so doing. I heard an observation made with regard to the manure yard. It is the intention of the committee to provide a better site for it if they can obtain one. They have been doing all they could to get other places in which to deposit the manure taken out. We have had no objections raised occasionally, but very seldom, about the present locality; but at the beginning of this year we raised a wall around the yard considerably, and we have heard no objection to it since then.

1061. Dr. Browne stated that you, as a medical man, would give us your opinion as to whether it is injurious to public health where it now stands?—I frequently visited it, and never could say that it was injurious to public health.

1062. Do you agree with him that it would be better in a less thickly populated neighbourhood?—The neighbourhood is not thickly populated. It would be better outside the town than in it; I quite agree with him in that.

1063. And it is at present under consideration if you can get a convenient place for it?—Yes; it has been under consideration for the past two years. We endeavoured to get a tramway laid, so that it could be sent out from the Central Railway, which runs adjacent to the manure yard; and we intended to have rails laid there, so that trucks could run alongside and the deposit be taken outside the town altogether.

1064. Has the scheme of main drainage and the purification of the Blackstaff come specially under your observation as chairman of the committee?—Not specially.

1065. It has come under your observation, I suppose, as a member of the Corporation?—Yes, as a member of the Corporation.

1066. Would you tell us what are the difficulties and the obstacles as to carrying out that scheme?—I frequently asked information on that point myself, and I have always been told that private interests have prevented the Corporation from carrying out what they wished to do. They have no authority to do what is necessary.

1067. You say "private interests"—do you mean that there is opposition to it on behalf of private individuals?—Not at all. Those having property adjacent to the Blackstaff have water rights and interests in the river. It is the mill owners and others, and I may as well state that in my opinion if there was not a single sewer discharging into the Blackstaff it would be polluted, because the water is used several times for cooling purposes in connexion with the mills, and it gets mixed up with the oil and other matters, and heated, so that in that way it becomes a nuisance of itself even without any sewage matter passing into it.

1068. What is your idea of the best outlet for the sewage of the town—the best means of preventing the water from being infected?—My own opinion is that it should be carried as far down the river as possible; but we are prevented from doing that, I believe.

1069. How—by the Harbour Commissioners?—Well, expense is one cause, and getting the drainage through private property is another, and carrying it two or three miles down the river would be very expensive.

1070. That is part of the scheme that is now under the consideration of the Town Council to carry out the sewage to a certain point, and that is what the Harbour Commissioners object to your doing?—They wish us to carry it much further down the river than the point where we intended to discharge it. My own opinion is decidedly that the further it is carried down the river the better, because if it is deposited at certain places it is liable to be brought up again. One objection to the system of drainage is that so much slob land will be bared, and if the river was narrowed at certain places, and did not leave any ground uncovered with water I think it would improve that very much.

1071. Mr. Lawson.—In other words if that slob land were reclaimed?—Raised, and the river narrowed.

1072. Chairman.—Do you think the Corporation are really desirous to carry out an effective system of sewerage for the town if they can see their way to doing so without involving themselves in litigation?—Every member of the Corporation is as anxious as any other person could possibly be.

1073. Mr. Lawson.—I suppose the use of the water of the Blackstaff is considered necessary by the mill owners for cooling purposes?—Yes.

1074. And then their proprietary interests would interfere to prevent them consenting to any change in the present state of things?—Just so. But I know some of them would be very glad if improvements were carried out, provided the dams were made higher up so as to give them a supply of water for their mill purposes.

1075. If it happened that some of those gentlemen were members of the Corporation, would they be as willing as others to carry out these plans?—I have spoken to some who are members of the Corporation, and some who are not, and one, at least, has expressed his willingness that improvements should be carried out, and said he would contribute towards the expense of making impounding dams; others said they had already expended a good deal of money themselves, and that, therefore, they could not be expected to contribute anything towards the cost of the dams.

1076. Chairman.—There was one point in Dr. Browne's evidence to which I wish to refer you, and I wish to ask you if it has been considered by you or other members of the Corporation. He mentioned the difficulty experienced in accurately determining the health statistics in districts Nos. 9 and 10, because they are partly outside the urban sanitary authority, the municipal boundary; and he states, I observe, that if the portions of 9 and 10 districts could be joined to the other urban districts to which they are adjoining, it would tend to greater convenience for the purpose to which he alludes. Has the question as to whether that suggestion could be carried into effect ever been considered by the Corporation—by reducing the number of the districts and adding 9 and 10 to the adjacent districts?—It has been talked of, but whether by the Corporation or not I do not know. It was talked of by the Poor Law Guardians and by the dispensary committee that regulates the district; but I do not know whether the question has ever been considered by the Corporation.

1077. Of course that could not be done without the consent of the Local Government Board. Any re-distribution of these districts would have to be submitted to the Local Government Board, would it not? —I cannot speak as to that of my own knowledge.

1078. If you are desirous of getting accurate returns of the vital statistics of the borough, the carrying out of Dr. Browne's suggestion would be a convenient thing, would it not?—I think the present returns are incomplete, and anything that would contribute to their being made more reliable, would be desirable. With regard to the scavenging of the town, I wish to observe that we have a contract for a certain number of horses, and we supply the carts. We have a contract for the horses by the year. If the number is less than the contract at any time, the inspectors have instructions to employ others, wherever they can get them, and at whatever price they can get them at; and the instruction of the police committee has been—"Employ any number that may be necessary at any cost." They are not restricted; and we wish to carry out the regulations as well as we possibly can.

BELFAST. Dec. 23, 1876. — Dr. James Alexander Browne.

1079. They are not obliged to wait for another meeting of the committee for extra horses, if they require them?—Not at all.

1080. The manure is sold fortnightly, I believe, so that it is not allowed to accumulate?—Yes, it is sold fortnightly by auction.

Mr. Conway Scott examined.

Mr. Conway Scott.

1081. Mr. Exham.—You are the executive sanitary officer here?—Yes.

1082. And by profession you are a civil engineer? —Yes.

1083. You were appointed immediately after the passing of the Act of 1871?—I was appointed just two years ago at the beginning of next year—the first of the month.

1084. Do you give your entire time to the Corporation—to looking after the sanitary operations?—Yes; I give my entire time to looking after the sanitary operations.

1085. Are they all carried out under your direction? —Yes, I am responsible for them to the sanitary committee.

1086. You have six subofficers. Five at 25s. a week, and one at 30s.?—Yes, and he got an increase lately or will get one.

1087. Have you authority yourself to act in the ordinary cases without waiting for the action of the sanitary committee?—Yes, I act at once in all ordinary cases. Such a notice as this is served (hands in form of notice).

1088. You serve the necessary notice, and certify the time at which it is to be done or proceedings will be taken against them?—Yes; and proceed against them.

1089. In other cases than the ordinary ones what do you do?—If I could not go myself, or if I had some doubt about it I would send to the dispensary officer, and he would go and report.

1090. Do you yourself personally see that in all cases of complaint the cause of complaint is removed? —As far as practicable I do. I would select a certain number out of the weekly reports, and go round and see them made right.

1091. Do you send a subofficer to see the other places?—I would keep check by their not knowing to what place I intended going to see. The weekly report would be in this form—(hands in form of the weekly report).

1092. Do you give this in every week?—Every week. I send them every Thursday morning.

1093. As I understand this you report the entire work done under your direction?—Yes.

1094. At the end I see reports of a number of nuisances, and these cases were withdrawn the nuisance being abated?—Every week the sanitary committee have a record of what is done the week before, and they have a full report of the work that is carried out.

1095. Chairman.—What is the nature of your inspection of schools?—We find it is very desirable to inspect the National schools where there are a great many children, and we endeavour as far as possible to see that there is no overcrowding. Sickness very often begins in the schools.

1096. Is twenty-nine the number of slaughter-houses?—I think it is about thirty-four.

1097. You never seem to inspect less than twenty-nine in the week?—Some of them would not require as much inspection as others.

1098. And you inspect from seventy to eighty lodging-houses in the week?—Yes.

1099. Mr. Lawless.—6th December, 1876, 119 streets and lanes are inspected for sanitary purposes. I suppose the men under you give returns of what they do?—Yes, and then there is a summary made out.

1100. Chairman.—There appears to be not a single week in which less than 100 to 110 privies or ashpits have been cleaned out?—Yes; it takes the greatest care to see that it is done.

1101. Mr. Exham.—In the portion of the town where there are no privies or water-closets what do you do?—I could not say that there are any houses in Belfast with none. They may have confined accommodation, five or six of the houses having the use of the one pit; and in such case I would call on the landlord to clean that pit. We have not got many water-closets amongst the poor classes in Belfast.

1102. About how often are these pits cleaned where you say there is one common pit to five or six houses?—We would try to get them cleaned once a week.

1103. Are they covered-in places?—The privy would be covered in, but the pit would be the usual open pit.

1104. I understand from Dr. Browne that there was a considerable portion of the town in which the people could do nothing except throw the filth in the streets? —That would require explanation. They throw it in the streets to prevent us from noticing them to cleanse the pit. Even if they have accommodation they will throw it in the streets. Of course there might be some houses where they might have no accommodation, but they are very few.

1105. Are the houses which have water-closets connected by drains with the main sewers, where there are main sewers within 100 feet of the houses?—I think as a general rule the water-closets are connected with the sewers.

1106. Have you made an examination from house to house to find that out?—I have not. That is a thing I could hardly tell. I examined the Antrim-road, and I found the houses were connected where they possibly could be connected. Some of them were more than 100 feet from the main sewer.

1107. Did you see that those beyond 100 feet from the sewer had cesspools?—They made all the arrangements they could.

1108. With regard to the scavenging of the smaller lanes and alleys of the town, do you see that it is properly attended to?—I have nothing to do with it. It is done by the scavenging department.

1109. Do you find any difficulty from not having a sufficient supply of water for public purposes in carrying out the sanitary operations—flushing the sewers or washing the streets?—I could hardly give an opinion as to that. It would not come under my notice.

1110. What about the Blackstaff?—I think there is a good deal depends on the cleaning of the bed of the Blackstaff. When we notice any accumulation in the river we send word to the surveyor's department, and they send the men to clean it.

1111. Have you taken any steps to prevent any persons—millowners or anyone—from sending matter into the river—I do not mean the refuse from the mills, but the sewage matter?—I would hardly like to say to our newy anything for doing what is done all over the river. Up to the present I have taken no steps in the matter. I would not exactly know how to go about it. The thing has gone on for a long time.

1112. You say the bed of it is cleaned out occasionally?—Very frequently, when the tide is low, they send men to clean out that black sediment that accumulates in it.

1113. Is it sent down the river or put on the shore?—It would be put on the slabs and carted away as far as I know.

1114. Are complaints made to you about the condition of the river by people near it?—I do not think there was ever a formal complaint lodged in the office about the condition of the Blackstaff.

1115. Then the action of the sanitary authority in getting it cleaned comes from themselves, and not because complaints are made by the inhabitants?—I do not say there is not a good deal of public feeling about it, but I do not think there was ever any complaint lodged in the office complaining of that particular thing.

1116. While things remain as they are it must continue as it is?—It will always be the same as it is until some arrangements are made to prevent the sewage matter from going into it.

1117. I suppose you see that the lodging-houses comply with the by-laws?—I measure them every year to see that they fix the number of lodgers. I measure each room—the number of feet in it.

1118. In case of infectious disease, do you see that the houses in which it takes place are afterwards disinfected?—Yes; we notice the landlords to have the houses whitewashed and fumigated. In a great many cases they take chloride of lime and try to get the people to go to the hospital.

1119. With regard to the clothes, do you see that they are destroyed?—We burned clothes a short time ago—the bedding and mattress—in a case of small-pox. We do that when the doctors say that it is required.

1120. Have you known many cases of infectious disease where the parties would not go to the hospital?—I think the prejudice against the hospital is rapidly being removed. There used to be a great prejudice against it. The people used to be very unwilling to go to the hospital. I do not find that to the same extent now.

1121. Are you always able to get a car from the hospital to have them removed?—They keep a horse and car, and send it down to the place and have the people taken away if they are willing to go at all.

1122. CHAIRMAN.—Have they got more than one ambulance?—I am not certain about that.

1123. As a matter of fact you have not found any difficulty in getting that ambulance when required?—We have not.

1124. Mr. RUBEN.—In the case of a person dying of any infectious disease, what do you do with regard to the body—do you do anything?—We never had any occasion to take any steps. I think there are legal powers which would enable us to remove the body, but we never had occasion to do so.

1125. CHAIRMAN.—You have no authority to which you can remove the body of any person dying of infectious disease?—No; there is only the Morgue.

1126. Mr. KAVAN.—Has anyone reported that there are six open and offensive drains near where they lived?—They would be drains that people were getting cleansed. Where there is a drain running along a field for a long distance it would be too much to expect them to pipe it.

1127. CHAIRMAN.—Dr. Browne said they were outside the borough boundary.

1128. Mr. KAVAN.—Are these six drains in the populous parts of the town?—No; they are not inside the town.

1129. I see you had a good many houses this year in which there was contagious disease, for you fumigated 257?—Yes, by the owners; and sometimes we get them done ourselves.

1130. Did that number of cases of contagious disease exist this year?—I have no doubt of it. That, no doubt, included measles, and so on. We generally returned anything that the doctor returned to us as contagious disease.

1131. CHAIRMAN.—Would that, then, embrace the houses in which there were cases of measles and whooping-cough?—Yes. We generally like to get the houses cleansed, and I would take that opportunity to have it done.

1132. Mr. BAXTER.—From your personal knowledge of Belfast, are you able to say that the sanitary condition of the town is improving?—I am certain of it. I think it is.

1133. Mr. LAWLESS.—I see here in the sanitary work ending the 6th September, 1874, you have had five places provided with yards and accommodation. Do you mean to say that the Corporation gave additional premises for making these?—I would notice the man to give additional accommodation. There might be property in the rear which he got into his hands, and after he did so he would be made to provide sanitary accommodation. A good many were done in that way. If a space in the rear of the house is purchased by the owner he is made to get yards and privies constructed.

Mr. JOHN JAMES MONTGOMERY examined.

1134. CHAIRMAN.—You are the borough surveyor?—Yes.

1135. And have been surveyor for fifteen years?—Yes.

1136. You are, I believe, a member of the Institute of civil engineers?—I am.

1137. Have you charge of all the engineering works and the repairs of all public works within the borough?—Yes.

1138. A great many streets we heard already, within the last five years, have been opened and sewerage made—those that apply to the town on both sides of the river—the part in the county Down and the more important part in the county Antrim?—Very much in the county Antrim and very much in the county Down.

1139. The 79th clause in the Belfast Act of 1865 provides that Ballymacarrett and Ballynafeigh are to get £5,000. Was that sum set apart for them?—Very much more than that has been set apart for them.

1140. Last year it would seem that upwards of £7,000 was expended upon Ballymacarrett?—Yes; about £15,000 have been spent in drainage works in Ballymacarrett, but a large portion of that comes from the owners of property. More than £5,000, however, has been set apart out of the funds of the Corporation irrespective of what was recovered from the owners of property. It was at my own suggestion that that £5,000 was put in the Act, so that I know all about it.

1141. The 77th section provides that the cost of the sewers shall be apportioned 1s. 3d. on the general purposes rate, and the residue on the district sewerage rate, and on the owners of property, as provided by the 80th section of the Belfast Act of 1865; does it come under your department to see that that is done in all cases?—Yes.

1142. There is another clause in this Act immediately following the one referring to Ballymacarrett, which gives power to clear a passage in the rear of the Belfast Bank, between Donegall-street and North-street, has that been done?—I must explain that. At the time of the passing of that Act we were not quite aware of the exact position of the place of ground that we were to get, and the banking company would not positively give an undertaking to set the bank back within any given time; but in point of fact, they have entered into an agreement with the Corporation in pursuance of the powers of that Act, and strictly within the powers of that section by which we have agreed with the owners of the bank. They have given the Corporation ground to widen North-street, and entered into an agreement with the Corporation, either to set the bank back, or to give the Corporation a sum of money (£1,500) towards the continuation of the widening of North-street, which has already taken place, adjoining the bank. In the immediate neighbourhood of the bank you will see that considerable improvement has been carried out, and at any moment the Town Council wish to call upon them to contribute this £1,500 towards the widening of the street in the neighbourhood of the bank, they will pay it, and we are now in treaty with owners of property to do so, as far as £1,500 will go. They have already paid £650 for improvements out of the £1,500.

1143. The real object of course was to widen the street?—Yes. We were most anxious that the bank should be set back, but unfortunately the bank some time ago lost £150,000, and that has prevented them from rebuilding, but I have no doubt the bank will be rebuilt soon, and set back as intended.

1144. Mr. EWART.—Will they be obliged to set it back after giving you the £1,500?—Yes; there is a clause in the agreement providing for that. In that case we are bound to disgorge the £1,500.—(hands in agreement between the Corporation and the Banking Company.)

1145. CHAIRMAN.—Was it not you who prepared this scheme for the drainage of the borough?—It was. [For summary of this scheme see Appendix No. 9, page 210.]

1146. Did you consult Mr. Bazalgette on the subject?—Yes; he came to Belfast and examined that scheme, and reported in its favour, and afterwards assisted us in promoting a Bill in Parliament to carry it out. He substantially adhered to my scheme.

1147. Did you prepare any estimate of the cost of that scheme?—That scheme was prepared in 1866, and it would therefore cost a very much greater sum now. I have apprehensions as to the applicability of that scheme at present. It only proposed a system within the borough, and it was to have cost then £160,000; but in my report other works were included which were intended to remove annoyances from water under which the people of Belfast suffer—the water from the Cave-hill Mountain that causes floods was not dealt with in this £160,000. It was laid down in the scheme, but not included in the estimate of those works. The impounding reservoirs that were proposed in that scheme to save the town from so much flooding would have cost at least £100,000; and it was hoped that we would have been able to turn into a blessing, from being as they now are a public calamity, those waters from the mountains, and be able to give the mill-owners an abundant supply of water. I think I heard it mentioned here that we were in treaty with the mill-owners as to a joint scheme for impounding the water. We had two or three meetings at which Sir Charles Lanyon and myself were present, and we did all we could with them; but we could not go on. There was a third part of the scheme to prevent those floodings. A great question was how to dispose of the sewage; and that was not included in the estimate because we proposed to waste it in the tideway—a most injudicious course of proceeding. Supposing that this scheme was carried out it would have cost £500,000. That would not save us from the flooding, but would create the greatest nuisance in the harbour. However, I do not pin my faith to any works of the kind because I honestly believe that one-third of the scheme would be very little use, and it was rather fortunate we did not get that scheme without the reclamation and the irrigation.

1148. Your chief object was, of course, to make the water your servant and not your master?—Yes. You have heard a great deal of the Blackstaff, but really the Pound Burn is the worst portion. From time immemorial it has been used as a common sewer for a large portion of Belfast. You know this river was the conduit to carry all the refuse water of that district, and it is so still. When I was appointed to the office of surveyor, the town was subject to flooding three or four times every year. I and my assistant had to give orders for boats and carts to rescue the people out of their dwellings. Durham-street was flooded often. The people were in danger of their lives. Subscriptions were got up to relieve the sufferers. I was very much amused to hear any-one say that this state of things is not decidedly better now, because the works that the Council have carried out reduced the flooding very nearly as much as they will be able to reduce it at any time. It is true that when the whole county was flooded part of Belfast was flooded, but nothing in comparison with what it was in previous years. I say that since those works were completed the flooding is abated, except in isolated cases—for instance, cellars built thirty years ago below the level of the drains and below the level of the tide. I have got some of them built up. Before we got the Act of 1865 we had very little power over persons laying out streets and buildings; and two or three streets some years ago were laid out below the level of the tide, and those streets were completely flooded the other day, and will be always flooded. We do not allow anything of that sort to be done now. We insist upon all the floors being laid above the level of the tide.

1149. You got those powers under the Act of 1865 and 1868?—Yes. I saw by the newspapers the other day that the passage under the Record Court was flooded the other day. The architect of those buildings, without consulting me, as he should have done, made a subterranean passage below the level of the tide. That passage should never have been allowed to be constructed, and the sooner it is filled up the better.

1150. Does this passage lead to the cells?—It is the way by which they bring the prisoners to the cells. I should have mentioned to you that dealing with this plague part of ours, the Blackstaff, the council have constructed four great lateral overflows from it—short cuts towards the tideway of the Lagan—and that is what has abated the floodings. There are four of them; a man can walk in them from one end to the other; they are three or four feet high, and when great floods come those channels take away the water down the tide-way, and without exaggeration, I may say that nine-tenths of the floodings have been abated by providing those four additional outlets. This river is cleaned out—I can't say every month, because the tide won't allow us, but it is cleaned out frequently—when the men can get at, and the lowering of the bed has contributed greatly to the carrying off of the water, and therefore immensely prevented the floodings. I prepared a very careful report on this matter many years ago, in which I advised that the bed should be brought to a uniform level, that a uniform fall should be given from end to end, and after that that it should be made into a wholesome open river. I contended that a wholesome open sewer with the river flowing through it is much better than any sewers that are being suggested.

1151. Is the Blackstaff a rapid stream?—At times exceedingly rapid. It has its source in a mountain 1,640 feet high; this sends torrents of water down it. Some persons wished to cover it over, and I advised them not—that it was better to regulate it, and keep it open. A scheme was prepared, and we got Mr. Harrison, our counsel, to come down to Belfast, and he with our solicitor and myself spent two days over this notable scheme, but we found the rights of the millowners so strong in this river, and our rights so weak, that we could not touch it without an Act of Parliament. The bed of the river has been raised artificially for impounding water for the mill-owners' purposes at all the great mills. We proceeded rather injudiciously to

BELFAST.
Dec. 15, 1868.
Mr. John James Montgomery.

remove one of these mill dams that had been diverted, and we were served with a notice from Chancery; and we had to go back to the jury and ask pardon, and put back the rubbish. Mr. Harrison's advice was that we would have to pay compensation to every mill owner upon the stream; and therefore the scheme for regulating the river fell through. They then told us to go to Parliament for this scheme; but some of the inhabitants got alarmed at the cost, and they did not proceed with the bill. It was promoted in 1870 and 1871, and the preamble had passed standing orders. It was first withdrawn in consequence of a divided opinion as to what was to be done, and that divided opinion still exists. Glasgow, Birmingham and Manchester are in the same state and don't know what to do with their sewage.

1152. By your scheme, at what point below high water would you discharge the sewage?—At the farthest point away from the borough we could go—to discharge into the most deepest channel, and only to discharge it at the top of the tide, so that when the tide was ebbing, it would carry it out to sea, and that would involve pumping by steam engines.

1153. Have not the drainage works you have carried out in the borough cost some £30,000 within the last few years?—Yes; and they are a subsidiary portion of our main drainage scheme, so that we have not been idle.

1154. Can you say to what extent the number of houses in the town and the population have increased since your appointment as town surveyor?—The population is almost doubled; the increase in the population between 1861 and 1871 was over one-third; the number of houses in 1861 was 18,505, and the population 121,602; and in 1871, the number of houses was 27,691; and the population as against that of 1861 was 174,394.

1155. You have had a great number of houses built since 1871?—About a thousand every year on an average for several years; and if you take 6·2 as the proportion of persons to each house, you will have an increase in the population of about 6,000 a year; and I am sure I am within the mark. If you take the new houses and add them to what we had in 1871, you will find that you have now a population of about 210,000—if you go by the new houses.

1156. That would be 210,000 in 1876, as against 121,000 in 1861?—Yes.

1157. Has proper drainage been provided for all the new houses that have been built?—can you undertake to say that?—Yes, with this qualification; that there are new houses in the suburbs where we have not been able as yet to push arterial drainage. We have drained the roads, but there are still roads where cesspools have to be used; but they are very limited. We are just finishing a large portion of the sewerage of a district, which will relieve us from cesspools.

1158. When houses are built more than 100 feet from the main sewer, do you always insist upon the construction of cesspools?—Yes; and to have them cleaned out as often as we think necessary. We also insist upon the house being connected with the main sewer when practicable, and, before anyone can proceed to build, the drawings and particulars are deposited with the town surveyor.

1159. The building clauses of the Act of 1865 are enforced, I suppose?—Rigidly enforced.

1160. Mr. Lawless.—Do you enforce what is set forth in the 95th section?—Yes; particularly about the drainage. That section in particular I have to be satisfied about.

1161. Before you allow the foundation of any house to be made?—Yes.

1162. Do you see that the provisions of that clause are enforced in every case?—In every case the first thing we look after is the drainage of the houses.

1163. This portion of the clause requires that the drain is to be constructed before laying the foundations of the house?—We do not insist upon that if it be carried on simultaneously with the building of the house. The plans give the levels and lines and all the particulars of the sewer, but I do not insist upon its being constructed before commencing to build.

1164. Chairman.—But before the house is occupied do you see that there is a proper sewer constructed?—Every house built is inspected, and there may have been cases—a case will occur now and then—where work has been scamped over, but I think on the whole the building regulations are honestly and fairly carried out, and that the builders show a disposition to help us.

1165. Suppose you have a building where this portion of the clause is not complied with simultaneously with the building of the house, what do you do then?—We first notice the parties and then issue a summons to have the thing remedied. If it is a wilful violation, in which a penalty can be enforced, I do not notice them; but if it is a thing to be remedied, and I find the people willing to do it, I do not summon them. There are some cases in which the penalty is enforced at once. If a man leaves the public street in a dangerous state at night we enforce the penalty. There is hardly a week that we have not cases in the police court, but still we get a great many of these things remedied without having to go to court.

1166. Then you say the objects of the Act are carried out?—They are substantially carried out very fairly indeed. I do not say that all the regulations we ought to have are included in them, but such as they are they are honestly carried out.

1167. Is there not some provision with regard to persons occupying houses before the streets are paved or properly drained?—We occasionally allow houses to be occupied when the works are in progress or being carried on; there is a great demand for houses in Belfast, and they are often occupied quite too soon. For many years the sewage works, street works, and all works were at a stand still owing to the Chancery suit. When we got our powers enlarged and amended in 1865 an enormous quantity of work had to be done; and the pressure of that work was so great that you will see we have not been able even yet to overtake the whole of it. I should think at this moment there are one hundred streets built on, and not yet completed. There is great difficulty often in getting material and workmen; but I do not think in any town in the three kingdoms—I know a great many of them, and I do not know any in which more work has been done to private streets than we have done here.

1168. You sewered and paved no less than seventy-nine last year. We see last year that a very large sum of money was expended on that particular outlay?—Yes, at the cost of the owners; that is where the houses are inhabited before the streets are paved. The town has been growing rapidly, and it was so long—seven years—neglected.

1169. Mr. Lawless.—In those cases in which houses are occupied before the works are finished, are the Corporation still engaged in sewering them; or do they allow these works to remain at a stand still, and do nothing?—The Corporation issue compulsory orders in all such cases. When a few houses are built in a street this order gives the owner a certain time to do the work, but in a great majority of cases the owner carries out the works under my supervision and that of my staff.

1170. You expended £30,000 on sewerage, paving, and other street works?—That does not include the works we are talking of; the works we are talking of are done at the cost of the owners. The Corporation pay a very small portion of it.

1171. Chairman.—You mean there is a great deal done that would not come into this account?—I should say there has been £100,000 laid out on streets within the last few years which does not appear in the Corporation accounts at all. I merely certify the cost to the owners when we do it, and they pay it.

1172. Irrespective of this £30,000, was that large

sum which never appeared in the accounts expended by owners alone?—Yes; especially during the last two years; sometimes we had fifty such streets going on together, solely at the cost of the owners or almost.

1173. And yet at the same time entirely under your control?—Every item of the work must be done under my control and that of my staff. I have a large staff.

1174. You have charge of all the municipal buildings generally, including the markets, cemetery, the slaughter-houses, and gasworks?—All the works of the Council except the gasworks. If there was a quay to be constructed or anything of that kind I would superintend it.

1175. The markets have been considerably enlarged since you have been the surveyor?—Indeed they have been reconstructed; every year a considerable sum of money has been expended in attending to the markets.

1176. You say there have been seventy-nine streets sewered and paved in the last year?—I say that there have been 750 streets sewered and paved at the cost of the owners during the last ten years; that would give an average of seventy-five streets each year.

1177. What is the length of highway which you repair within the municipal borough?—Ninety-one miles.

1178. And have you what you consider an efficient staff for that purpose?—I have.

1179. If you require more have you any difficulty in getting more from the Council?—Not the slightest. There is a resolution of the Council authorising me to employ another assistant, but I have never employed him; I have every facility afforded me by the Council.

1180. If you want additional labourers for these special works—of pressing works that require immediate attention—can you employ extra hands?—The Corporation have given me full control to do what I like in that respect—or what I may deem necessary. I have always employed my own staff; I buy my own materials. The Corporation have everything by contract, but we are very peculiarly situated in Belfast, there are many things which we can't do cheaply by contract. The Corporation have never found fault with what I have done, and I have never had to complain of want of money in carrying out the public works and improvements of the town.

1181. Is the stone-yard under your control?—Yes.

1182. Tell me the system there. I see £17,000 of material for repairing streets, and you expended, that is, you gave out materials valued at £16,000. You have always apparently a large stock of materials on hand?—Yes, a large stock.

1183. To which you keep adding?—We generally advertise, and enter into contracts for the supply of materials. We advertise largely in England and Scotland, as well as in Ireland, for the supply of setts. We made a contract with the Penmaenmawr Quarries. I thought them the hardest and cheapest setts we had got. They are taken from the vessel into the yard. There is a storekeeper in the yard; he keeps the day-book. That day-book is brought every day to my office, where I have a bookkeeper, and he divides the materials under their proper headings from the day-book, and charges them to their proper work. This is checked by the general accountant of the Corporation, Mr. Woods. It is a very elaborate and careful system that we have in the store-yard. We take stock once a year, sometimes oftener. Nothing can be given out of the yard except upon an order signed by me or my chief assistant; so that a very careful system is kept up there.

1184. Are all these large purchases made by contract?—There are some things which we find it cheaper to purchase without any contract; take pebble paving-stones, for instance, we can get quite too many here; they are the wreck of the sea, and at certain times they are tossed up in large quantities on the coast of Ireland; the poor fishermen run us with a lot of them into Belfast, and we should have money in hand to buy them on those occasions when we require them.

1185. That is a comparatively small item—only £350?—Take again the broken stuff for roads. An attempt was made by the lord of the soil, Lord Donegall, to get a monopoly of these works. He said they were his manorial rights, and he took legal proceedings against everyone who meddled with them. This matter was going on for years. The Corporation always considered this an open market for stones, and they were accused of violating his lordship's rights, but we made it an open market, and we bought from everyone that came in. In that way, by making a great competition between the railway who bring in wagons and the farmers all around Belfast, we are able to buy stones at about half the price they are bought at in England. We have stones carted and laid down on our streets for, at an average, 3s. 6d. the ton. The consumption of broken stuff is something enormous here. Some years it used to be 50,000 tons per annum; but then this system of open market allows the poor farmer who is coming into town to make some purchases, to bring in a load of stones, and to take out a load of manure.

1186. With what committee are you most frequently in communication?—My principal committee is what is called the improvement committee; it takes charge of almost the whole of the surveyor's department; under other committees I am occasionally called in; we have a great many committees here—a committee sometimes every day. Mr. Scott seemed to be in some doubt about the water-closets; all the water-closets are connected with sewers; we should not tolerate one connected with tanks; I do not know an exception; there might be a very old house in the suburbs, or a villa, where there is a tank, but practically all water-closets are connected with the main-sewer, and it would not be tolerated without that being done. [Witness hands in statement of work done in his department last year.—See Appendix No. 10, page 211.]

Mr. Arthur Wellesley Calcott examined.

1187. Mr. Lawlor.—Are you the registrar of the borough cemetery?—I am.

1188. When was the cemetery formed?—It was formed previous to August, 1869.

1189. How many acres does it contain?—Forty-five altogether.

1190. Is it divided for the interment of persons of different religious denominations?—It is divided into two portions, one for Protestants and one for Roman Catholics.

1191. Chairman.—Has there not been some portion set apart lately for the Jews?—There has.

1192. Mr. Lawlor.—What are your duties as registrar; do you receive applications for interments?—I do. I receive all cash in connexion with the purchase of graves and interments.

1193. I suppose you have some people employed under your superintendence?—There are.

1194. For the purpose of keeping the cemetery in proper order?—Yes; the staff consists of a superintending foreman, sexton, and twelve labourers.

1195. Your salary I think is about £80 a year?—£80 as registrar of cemeteries.

1196. What were the receipts last year?—The total amount was £1,681 11s. 2d. That includes the fees, the purchase moneys, and the foundations of vaults.

1197. And receipts of all kinds?—Yes.

1198. Whose duty is it to see that the place is kept in decent order—of course the cemetery is enclosed?—It is with a stone wall about six or seven feet high.

1199. It is, in fact, kept in decent and becoming order?—In beautiful order; it is kept like a garden at present.

Belfast, Jan. 13, 18[illegible].

Mr. [illegible] Lanyon [illegible].

Mr. Arthur Wellesley Calcott.

BELFAST. Dec. 13, 1876. Mr. Arthur Wellesley [illegible].

1300. CHAIRMAN.—How many acres have they set apart for Falls Park?—There are forty-five acres in the Falls Park, and there are forty-five in the cemetery; and then there are about eleven acres of surplus ground in connexion with it.

1301. Then the cemetery ground was about 100 acres?—About 100 acres.

1302. All the money passes through your hands?—Yes, and it is checked every week by the audit committee, and lodged with the Commissioners every week.

Dec. 14, 1876. Mr. John James Montgomery.

DECEMBER 14, 1876.

Mr. JOHN J. MONTGOMERY re-examined.

1303. Mr. SEXTON.—Were any steps taken to prevent the drains from being discharged into the Blackstaff. The question was asked yesterday in your absence?—The Town Council have constructed several very large sewers which have intercepted and diverted from the Blackstaff and the streams a very large quantity of the sewage. I may also say that in every case where plans have come in for streets and buildings we have objected to any fresh sewage being discharged into these streams, and have generally succeeded in preventing it; but in exceptional cases we require compounds to be constructed in such a way as to minimise the evil.

1304. It was mentioned by some one that a good many large mills discharge their sewage matter either into the Pound Burn or into the Blackstaff River—is that so?—It is so.

1305. Is that not beyond all doubt a nuisance?—Beyond all doubt it is.

1306. Then the inspector of nuisances would have absolute power to compel them to make a compound in some way or other and not allow it to go into the stream, if it amounts to a nuisance. It may be said that it would be very hard to do so, they having their mills constructed as they are now, but that is their own look out. They should manage their sewage in some way so as not to discharge into the Blackstaff and Pound Burn in the way they do?—I am aware that was the object of the Pollution of Rivers Inquiry, and some large towns in England are situated just as Belfast. Hitherto none of those large manufacturing towns have [illegible] this work. They are all puzzled now.

1307. Is there not ample power to prevent them from discharging the sewage of their mills into the river in the way they do under the Public Health Acts and Nuisances Removal Act?—I don't know as to that. All the large towns are in hopes that the Parliament will assist them in abating these nuisances. We have gone as far as we thought we could safely go in the matter.

1308. CHAIRMAN.—Have you enforced the regulations with regard to all new houses?—Certainly. I may mention with regard to the water, that I would be very glad to have water for washing the dirty lanes. I never refused to take it, but in the winter time we did not need it.

Dr. Samuel Browne.

Dr. BROWNE recalled.

1309. CHAIRMAN.—You wish to say something?—Yes; I wish to contradict a statement made regarding the evidence I gave before you yesterday, as to the Blackstaff and the Lagan. I did not say that they were not productive of disease. I believe they are injurious to health, and I have stated that for the last twenty years over and over again.

1310. Is it then your opinion that they are injurious to health?—Most decidedly. I should say any such streams must be injurious to health. I want to convey that opinion most distinctly.

1311. Would you say that the districts through which these rivers flow have suffered more from disease than other parts of the town?—I have not found so from statistics, but I must say that any such streams must be injurious to health. I have said so over and over again, and I say so still.

Mr. James Stelfox.

Mr. JAMES STELFOX examined.

1312. Mr. LAWLOR.—I believe you are the manager of the Belfast Corporation gas works?—Yes; since the 1st May, 1873.

1313. They became the property of the Corporation on the 30th June, 1874?—Yes.

1314. Were you engaged in any gasworks before?—I was engaged for about ten years as assistant to my father, who was manager of the works for the Belfast Gaslight Company.

1315. Are all the people employed there under your supervision and management?—They are.

1316. By whom are the materials for manufacturing the gas purchased?—Tenders are invited by public advertisement, and are sent under cover to the town clerk, who submits them to the gas committee, and selections are made by them under my advice in matters affecting the manufacture of the gas.

1317. Have you anything to do with the payment of those purchases?—I have not.

1318. Mr. SEXTON.—Are samples of the articles required sent with the tenders?—Generally.

1319. Mr. LAWLOR.—Do you superintend the distribution of the gas through the town?—I have the general oversight of it, but there is an inspector of meters who reports to me. In case of anything particular arising I visit the place myself.

1320. Are the workmen at the gas works under your control and superintendence?—They are.

1321. Have you an assistant engineer?—I have one.

1322. Do you superintend the sale of coke and other residuals?—I do.

1323. Are they sold at the gas works?—They are.

1324. How are they sold?—The coke is all sold from day to day. The tar and ammoniacal liquor are sold under a two years' contract which is now about to expire.

1325. Is it proposed to sell the tar and liquor under a new contract?—Yes; the advertisements have been already published inviting tenders.

1326. How is the coke disposed of?—A portion of it is disposed of for cash at the office in the works, and the cash received for it is accounted for nightly. The amount of each day's sales is brought into my outside office where it is checked by a clerk, and a weekly return is made by him to the cashier of the gas works.

1327. I see by your reports that there is a considerable sum derived from the residuals produced in the manufacturing of the gas?—There is.

1328. For the year ending 30th June, 1874, you used coke at the works to the amount of £4,144 0s. 9d.?—Yes.

1329. How is the price of that fixed?—It is charged to the account of the making of the gas at the same price as we sell it for. I should explain that many companies do not put that item in their accounts at all.

1330. In the accounts here you describe £21,667 18s. 8d. as the amount of residual products of which £4,144 0s. 9d. has been used in the manufacturing of the gas?—Yes; the price which is charged for the coke used in the works is the same that is given for it by public buyers.

1331. How much is your salary?—£600 a year.

1332. And your assistant's salary is £193 14s. 3d.?—That was only for a portion of the year. He is to be paid £200 per annum. He is only recently appointed; up to that time my salary was £500, and the remainder is portion of his salary.

1233. Your salary has been raised?—Yes, since the 1st July £100.

1234. For the year ending June, 1876, I find the wages of the men employed in the manufacture of the gas amounts to the sum of £3,783 2s. 3d.?—Yes. There are other wages besides. That is only one class of wages.

1235. What are the salaries of those engaged in its distribution?—For gasfitters and inspector, inspectors and clerks in departments, £628 15s.

1236. What are the salaries of those employed in the collection of the gas rents, &c.?—The salaries of the cashier, accountant and clerks, office-keepers and messengers are £1,379 15s. 10d. The collectors are paid by salaries and not by fees, and these are £516 for the year.

1237. That makes the total expenditure for salaries and wages of all kinds connected with gas manufacture and works £6,814 1s. 3d.?—Yes.

1238. What office did you hold with the old gas company?—I was cashier and book-keeper about the year 1838.

1239. What was the gas rental then?—I could not tell now, but the auditor can from the books.

1240. Do you keep accounts of the amounts received for gas?—We do.

1241. What were the gas receipts for the year ending June, 1876, exclusive of the cost of lighting the public lamps?—£73,813 11s. 8d. less £4,781 1s. 5d. allowed for discount, and £281 0s. 0d. estimated for bad debts, but some of those debts were since recovered.

1242. So that the net receipts for the year under the head "sale of gas" were £70,733 7s. 3d.?—Yes, and in addition we received £2,926 5s. 2d. for public lighting, and lights under agreements.

1243. I find by the 56th section of the 37 and 38 Vic., chap. 125, the corporation are authorised to allow discount to certain consumers of gas?—Yes.

1244. Chairman.—What is that discount?—There is a regular scale according to the quantity consumed, which is as follows: On a consumption of 10,000 cubic feet, and not exceeding 50,000 cubic feet, 2½ per cent.; above 50,000 cubic feet, and not exceeding 100,000 cubic feet, 5 per cent.; above 100,000 cubic feet, and not exceeding 200,000 cubic feet, 10 per cent.; above 200,000 cubic feet, and not exceeding 400,000 cubic feet, 15 per cent.; above 400,000 cubic feet, 20 per cent.; provided the account be paid at the office, 25, Queen-street, on or before the 20th day of January, April, July, and October, in each year. It is the same rate of discount that we had formerly.

1245. Your receipts for the rent of meters were £4,118 11s. 6d., and allowing for discount and bad debts, your net receipts under that head were £4,093 0s. 11d.?—Yes.

1246. The amount of the residual products was mentioned already. Then there is the sum derived from the sale of tar and so on, and a small amount allowing for value of coke sold and used, and that of the other residuals, making your receipts for the year ending the 30th June, 1876, on the gas account were £107,800 14s.?—Yes.

1247. The items of expenditure, including cost of materials, salaries, and law charges, &c., amount to £78,734 12s. 9d., leaving a balance to be carried from the gross revenue account to the net revenue account of £29,166 2s. 3d.?—Yes.

1248. Do you know what the law charges, which amount to £461 11s. 11d. were?—A portion of them were taxed costs.

1249. What for?—During the transfer of the works to the corporation law costs were incurred—Mr. Black's costs.

1250. Do you expect an increase for the future in your residuals?—Yes. At the present time there is a net receipt from them of about £16,000 a year. The present price at which they are sold is much below the present market value. They are now sold under a contract made eighteen years ago by the old corporation, which we were obliged to take up.

1251. To whom is the item of £12 for the audit paid?—To the Local Government Board, for Mr. Hamre auditing the accounts. Belfast. June 13, 1876. Mr. [illegible]

1252. By whom is the account [illegible]?—I believe they send an account for £24 altogether, one-half of which is charged to the gas, and the other half to the other accounts of the corporation. The trouble is very considerable in going through the accounts, though they appear in a very simple form here.

1253. Your profit and loss account shows a balance of £13,913 13s.?—That balance is brought forward from the preceding year.

1254. And to that is to be added the profit on the present year, ending June, 1876?—Yes, that is £29,166 2s. 3d., which makes a total of £43,081 2s. 6d., less £581 6s. interest allowed by the bank, and that is applied as far as is necessary to the payment of the purchase-money and loans for the year ending 30th June, 1876.

1255. How much was applied for that purpose?—£21,216 13s. 1d.

1256. What is the item £581 6s. for bank interest?—Interest allowed by the bank on money deposited there, which was raised before it was paid off, and the bank allowed us that premium for interest upon it.

1257. The net profit on the last year's working was £7,949 9s. 2d.?—That is quite correct.

1258. There is a balance on the revenue account of £21,864 10s. 7d. since you bought the gasworks?—Yes.

1259. Has the quantity of gas increased?—Yes; the consumption for the last two years has averaged about ten per cent. per annum increase. For the year ending June, 1876, the increase was a little over twelve per cent., and as far as we have gone this year there appears to be an increase of about four per cent. on that.

1260. Mr. Evans.—What is the illuminating power of the gas which you supply?—The standard quality is sixteen-candle gas. Of course in order to have that at all times we are obliged to make two or three candles over it.

1261. Do you supply gas to the public at the full standard of sixteen candles?—It is always in excess of that.

1262. Mr. Lawless.—Are there any complaints made of the quality of the gas?—Of course we cannot say that we have no complaints; we have about 14,000 consumers and perhaps we have fewer complaints than are to be met with in most places. We have often found that when complaints were made the parties themselves were to blame for having defective pipes and burners.

1263. Has there been a decrease in the number of the consumers, and if so has that been, so far as you know in consequence of complaints as to the bad quality of the gas?—I believe a number of parties (very small consumers) gave up using gas last year, owing to the very low price of mineral oils, but in the present season, the number of our small consumers is on the increase, as I believe from the increase in the price of oil. I believe it was owing to the cheap price of oil and not to the quality of the gas that the number of small consumers decreased.

1264. How many cubic feet of gas do you get from a ton of coal?—We got last year about 10,000, and we were paid for about 9,300.

1265. Mr. Evans.—Can you get seventeen-candle gas from that?—We can by using six per cent. of Lesmahagow coal. We can get from that coal almost 13,000 cubic feet per ton; but we use only a small portion of that coal, as the price of it is 40s. per ton free-on-board in Glasgow.

1266. What was the total amount of arrears of gas-rent for the year ending June, 1876?—£709 1s. 7d. Of course you will understand that we make up our rental to the 30th June, and those sums only just falling due go to the following year.

1267. The number of consumers last year was 13,815?—Yes. The number was larger the year before from the cause that I have referred to, but the general consumption was considerably more.

Belfast. [illegible] — Mr. [illegible].

1268. What is the present price of gas per 1,000 feet?—The maximum price is 4s. 11d. with meter rent, and the discount on which in some cases is twenty per cent.

1269. Do you expect to be able to reduce the price of gas?—We hope so. The committee were very anxious last year to make a further reduction, as trade was in a very bad state in town. They thought it well to feel their way rather than reduce their price to a sum at which they could not continue it.

1270. By whom are the wages in connexion with the gasworks paid?—By the cashier.

1271. Are they paid in cash?—Yes.

1272. What is the weekly amount?—The maximum is about £400, and the minimum about £290. The list of wages is presented every week to the committee, certified by me as corresponding with the wages-book kept at the works, and a cheque for the amount is issued in the usual way by the committee, and received and disbursed by the cashier.

Mr. Alexander [illegible] examined.

1273. Mr. Lawless.—You are the cashier of the Belfast Corporation Gasworks?—Yes.

1274. What are your duties as cashier?—I receive all moneys on account of gas and meter rent and the amount of the coke sales at the works. I pay all accounts, the interest on mortgages, the salaries, and the weekly wages, and I also superintend the business of the town office, and attend to the local correspondence.

1275. What is your salary?—£300 per annum.

1276. The gasworks were purchased in June, 1874, by the Corporation?—They were transferred to the Corporation on the 1st July, 1874.

1277. The amount expended on the purchase of the gasworks was £131,387 14s. 6d.?—No; it was £386,550.

1278. The Corporation were authorized to raise £500,000 on the security of the gasworks, the gas rents, and the police rate?—That is their granted borrowing power.

1279. How much of that was actually raised, and how?—They raised on mortgage £468,784, and on annuities £2,340 14s. 11d.

1280. Was that £471,139 14s. 11d. the amount of loans altogether on both loans and annuities?—Yes; that is correct, but it includes £140, the purchase-money of the [illegible] property, which we sold and carried to the capital account.

1281. Why was that £140 brought into the gas account?—Because it was required by the Act of Parliament. It was settled in that way under Mr. Black's direction.

1282. By the Act of 1874?—Yes. Of the £471,139 14s. 11d., £386,550 was applied in purchasing the gasworks. There was a balance left of £84,847 13s. 6d.

1283. Are you able to state how that balance was applied?—You have the particulars of expenditure on the other side.

1284. Can you tell me how that £84,847 14s. 6d. was applied. I suppose a considerable portion of it was applied in defraying the costs of the Act of Parliament?—You have the particulars in the gas account for the year ending June, 1875. (Hands in the account referred to.)

1285. I find in this account for the year ending June, 1875, this item—"By gasworks, meters, &c., valued at net cost, £432,003 4s. 2d.;" now, beside the purchase-money of £386,553 was there any additional separate sum to be paid for the plant and machinery and meters?—I cannot give evidence on that point. You will require to refer to the manager.

1286. With respect to the purchase?—Yes. I can speak with respect to the amount of the purchase-money.

1287. You will find on the credit side of this account, "gasworks, meters, &c., £432,003 4s. 2d." Were the "meters, &c.," paid for separately from the gasworks? Was it the gasworks only and not the plant that was purchased for the £386,553?—I think that purchase-money covered everything.

1288. Mr. [illegible].—The purchase-money authorized to be paid for the gasworks by the Act of 1874 was £386,553.

1289. What did that represent?—That was made up by twenty-two and a half years' purchase on the [illegible] dividends of the old company. That makes up exactly £386,550.

1290. If you look to the account for the year ending June, 1874, you will find in the capital account—the first item on the credit side—"By gasworks, meters, &c., valued at net cost, £432,003 4s. 2d.;" explain how that is made up?—That is £386,553 and £50,000 which the late company raised on mortgage. There was some deduction which I must refer to the books to say about exactly.

1291. To Mr. [illegible].—Do you pay the interest on the mortgages?—Yes.

1292. And all the current expenses of carrying on the works?—I do.

1293. Have you a form of the payment for the weekly expenditure on the works?—Yes. (Hands one in.)

1294. Do you give any security?—Yes.

1295. With sureties?—Yes.

1296. For what amount?—£500 by the Guarantee Society.

1297. Do you pay the weekly expenditure in cash?—All accounts under £5 are paid in cash by me weekly.

1298. Do you pay them out of your receipts in cash?—Out of the receipts during the week, and then it is refunded to me by a cheque passed by the gas committee at the end of the week.

1299. I do not exactly understand that. If they are paid out of the receipts, how is it there is anything to be refunded to you?—I am required to lodge all receipts for coke and gas weekly; whatever I pay they refund to me, and I lodge the cheque I receive as part of my cash.

1300. How are the accounts over £5 paid?—By cheques signed by three members of the town council and the town clerk. (Hands in a copy of monthly list.)

1301. Are the accounts over £5 paid monthly?—Yes, as a rule. Sometimes there is an necessity for passing a cheque at the weekly meeting of the gas committee.

1302. Are the accounts for gas and meter rents made up by you?—They are all made up by me every quarter.

1303. Is the town divided into different districts?—Yes; into thirty-eight districts, and for each district there is a ledger and cash-book.

1304. How are the consumers' accounts collected?—They are payable in the office within the month after each quarter, and after that the collectors go out and collect all accounts unpaid.

1305. How often do the collectors make returns to you?—Daily, of the cash received.

1306. How often do you make lodgments in the bank?—Daily, to the credit of the Belfast corporation gas account. (Hands in bank-book.)

1307. How often do you balance your rental, so as to ascertain the amount outstanding?—The rental is balanced quarterly, when we ascertain the amount of arrears outstanding at the end of the preceding quarter.

1308. What was the amount of the gas rental for the year ending June, 1876?—£70,759 7s. 6d.

1309. And of the meter rental?—£4,092 0s. 11d.

1310. During that time what was the price of gas per thousand feet?—4s. 2d. per thousand for that year, and 4s. 6d. the year before.

1311. For that year, 1876, the amount received for public lamps was £3,939 8s. 5d.?—Yes; the total revenue including coke charged to works was £107,[illegible] 16s.

Belfast. Oct. [illegible]

Mr. Alexander Turnbull.

1312. What was the total amount of arrears for the year ending 30th June, 1876?—£790 1s. 7d.

1313. Has any portion of that since been collected?—Yes, a large portion of it, perhaps nearly the half of it. There was a large amount of it collected before Mr. Simson made his report.

1314. What is the net balance available at the end of the year's work—the year ending June, 1876?—£7,049 5s. 3d.

1315. What is the present amount of capital debt on the gasworks and the police fund?—£471,129 14s. 11d.

1316. That is the entire amount that was raised on mortgages and annuities?—Yes.

1317. Is the entire amount of that still due?—It is all due with the exception of one payment which has been made to the bank of England of £11,000.

1318. What was that made on account of?—On account of a loan of £220,000.

1319. Does that go to part reduction of principal as well as interest?—Entirely for principal. I have remitted interest on account of it.

1320. Will that payment be a deduction from the £471,129 14s. 11d.?—Yes.

1321. Did Mr. Simson audit the account for the year ending June, 1876?—He did.

1322. Did he audit the account for 1875?—He audited both years. You will find his certificate in the accounts which I handed in to you.

1323. Mr. Rankin.—Are you to pay £11,000 every year?—Yes. We have already borrowed from the bank of England £220,000, repayable in twenty years by instalments of £11,000 per annum. We have not yet made any provision for a sinking fund. We are in the first year which we are required to provide for it. At the end of this third year we will make provision for it.

1324. You will have to borrow the money every year?—We will have to borrow the money if we go on paying off the bank of England, but we expect to borrow on better terms and to pay off the bank of England.

1325. You paid £11,000 out of the two years. You did not borrow that?—We paid that out of our surplus cash. No money has as yet been set aside as a sinking fund.

Mr. Thomas M'Clelland.

Mr. Thomas M'Clelland examined.

1326. Mr. Lawless.—You are a solicitor, I believe?—Yes. In the year 1873 I contested the borough for the situation of assessor. I considered that I would be paid for my services, and I went to some expense for that purpose and was elected. I sat for ten days successively, revising the burgess roll of the borough with the then mayor and another assessor. It was then discovered for the first time that there was no power for the Corporation to appropriate any portion of the borough fund for the payment of assessors, and I think that very hard, because as I understand in the other corporate towns in Ireland, the assessors are all paid. I sat for ten days, and afterwards I was re-elected to the office and sat for six days. I thought it right to bring the matter forward here in the interest of my profession, as something ought most certainly to be done. It requires a certain amount of knowledge and skill, and the duties of assessor are not picked up without some considerable trouble, and the Corporation have great difficulty in getting any gentlemen to take the position upon them. There was a time when professional barristers were appointed and paid high salaries, but Mr. Black who was anxious to do what was right in the matter took Counsels' opinion, and they were of opinion that there was no power to pay assessors out of the borough fund.

1327. Mr. Black.—Mr. M'Clelland says the Corporation have great difficulty in getting gentlemen to take the office of assessor. They have nothing whatever to do with the appointment of assessors.

[Mr. Woods handed in returns showing the purposes to which the loans on the police fund were applied; also a statement showing the sources from which the payments in discharge of the primary and secondary mortgages had been made; and also a statement showing the amount of irrecoverable rates from vacancies and other causes, and the rates upon which discounts were allowed—on valuations not exceeding £8, and payable within one month].

1328. Chairman (To Mr. Woods).—These returns are I presume issued from your office?—Yes; and I can certify as to their correctness. (Appendix No. 13, p. 313.)

Mr. James Coleman.

Mr. James Coleman, 91, Falls-road, examined.

1329. Chairman.—Are you a ratepayer?—I am a ratepayer and owner of property in that part of the town, where the inhabitants have taken a great interest in the establishment of the Falls-road Park, and in other questions of sewerage and sanitary reform with regard to that district.

1330. Are we to understand that you on your own behalf and that of other ratepayers and owners of property in the neighbourhood of the Falls Park desire to be examined for the purpose of showing that the Town Council have not carried out the provisions of the Local Government Order Confirmation Act of 1873, so far as relates to the Falls-road Park, and the road leading thereto and the surrounding district, and that they have, to a certain extent, neglected their duty so far as sewerage and other sanitary reforms are concerned?—Just so.

1331. What provisions of the Act do you say they have neglected?—I state that the third clause of that Act has not been carried out.

1332. That is the clause that recites that the governing body were authorised to purchase ground for a cemetery under the provisions of the Burial Grounds Act; and whereas under the provisions of the Act money had been laid out in the purchase of burial ground, part of which was not required for the purpose, that the part which was not required was valued at £5,000, and was suitable for the formation of a public park—it is ordered that the governing body shall apply the same under the provisions of the Public Parks Act. That is the substance of the clause?—What I say with regard to that is, that the surplus grounds of the cemetery outside the cemetery walls should be dedicated to the purposes of a park according to the Local Government Order Confirmation Act, and according to the resolution passed by the Town Council, and that instead of dedicating all these grounds outside the cemetery walls the Corporation have caused to be staked off some thirteen or fourteen acres—the most valuable portion of the ground, and have not complied with the Act or with their own resolution, but have retained that portion of the ground there for purposes which I cannot define. They may have reasons for it, but we, as ratepayers in that part of the town, say that this portion of the Act has not been carried out, and further, that there is no intention on the part of the Corporation to carry it out.

1333. I think we have evidence to show that 103 or 105 acres were purchased originally for the burial ground, forty-five of which were retained as cemetery, forty-five were devoted to the Falls Park, and thirteen acres or what would make up the remainder of the quantity, were retained as surplus lands?—These figures are substantially correct.

1334. What you object to is the retention of these thirteen acres as surplus land instead of their being thrown into the park?—Quite so. I would direct your attention to a resolution passed by the Town Council on the 1st of November, 1869, complying with the terms of the Parks Act, and confirmed according to the Public Parks Act on the 1st of January, 1870. (Witness handed in resolution).

1335. I now have those resolutions before me. The first is to the effect that the Council shall establish and maintain two public parks—one in the Ormeau demesne and the other on the Falls-road, adjoining the new borough cemetery; that they will prepare the Ormeau Park for opening to the public, and that it be ready by the 1st of April, 1871, and on that day a resolution was passed at a meeting of the Council authorizing the sale of the park lands on the Falls-road, which sale was advertised to take place on the 29th of April, when the inhabitants memorialized against it?—Yes; and the memorial they presented was signed by 3,000 ratepayers of the locality, and was presented by the largest deputation that ever appeared before this Town Council.

1336. Then in consequence of that memorial and the deputation the council abandoned their intention of selling the ground of Falls Park, and arranged for the opening of it as a public park as soon as possible?—Just so; and I would draw your attention to the reason why they were going to sell these grounds, which was that there was not sufficient land to make a park, while now they say there is too much, and they want to retain thirteen acres.

1337. Mr. Exham.—Are these grounds excluded actually at present from the cemetery?—I think for the satisfaction of the Commissioners you should have a map of the cemetery and the grounds before you. If you had you would see that there is a stone wall seven feet high around the forty-five acres that constitute the cemetery. Outside of that is the park ground which we allege according to the intention of the Act of Parliament, and according to the opinion of Mr. May, Q.C., cannot be used for any other than park purposes.

1338. Chairman.—Then instead of the park being limited to forty-five acres, it should be fifty-eight; in other words the whole of the ground that is not in the cemetery should be thrown into the park?—Precisely.

1339. With regard to the park itself have you any objection to the mode in which it is now kept?—We say that apathy is exhibited with regard to it by the Corporation, and there is not sufficient money spent upon it, that it is left unproductive, and in fact all that the council have done up to this shows that there is apathy with respect to it, and that they would rather in fact take it from us altogether than comply with the terms of the Act of Parliament. If I might draw your attention (in confirmation of what I say that sufficient money is not being expended on the Falls-road park) to the expenditure on the parks at page 54 of the accounts, you will find that for the year 1873 £2,974 3s. 6d. has been expended on the Ormeau park, including rents, while on the Falls park only £333 has been spent.

1340. Yes, but of the £2,900 expended on the Ormeau park, £2,158 is for rent?—Just so; but that leaves a balance of nearly £1,300 expended on the Ormeau park against £333 laid out on the Falls park.

1341. Part of the expense of the Ormeau park applies equally to the Falls park, for instance, the salary of Thomas Dickson who superintends both parks, so that you see that item of expenditure applies to both parks. I am not sure whether there is any other item applicable to both parks?—I think that is all.

1342. What is the extent of the Ormeau park?—One hundred acres, and they allow us only forty-five acres, while the whole of the ground due to us is fifty-eight, which we claim, as authorized by the Local Government Board Order Confirmation Act, and according to the opinion of Messrs. May and M'Donough who both advised that this land could not be appropriated to any purpose other than the park.

1343. Mr. Exham.—Have they planted the Falls park at all?—I may state that a great deal of those grounds were planted by the former proprietor, I think Mr. Sinclair, and I suppose I might say that one-third had been already laid out in his time, and a good road made up to the other portion of the ground. Since then they have removed from the cemetery some plants and young trees, which they have planted in the park.

1344. Chairman.—The Amending Act of 1872 gives the governing body of a town, who had acquired land for the purpose of establishing public parks, in addition to anything contained in the Act of 1869, power to dispose within five years by auction of any portion of the land not required for such public park. We are not here to discuss the law, but we are here to take any objection that may be raised by any ratepayer as to the mode in which it is carried out, and as to the mode in which the funds or property of the town is administered?—We admit that that is so according to the Amended Parks Act, but the Local Government Board Act of 1873 was obtained under peculiar circumstances; the first Parks Act, passed in 1869, was obtained at the suggestion of the town council, by Messrs. M'Clure and Johnson, the representatives of this borough, and there was an objection raised subsequently by the present solicitor to the corporation, Mr. Black, that that Act would not give power to make parks outside the borough—this, the Falls park, is outside the borough. Thereupon the town council asked Messrs. M'Clure and Johnson to bring in the amending Bill which the Government took in hand in 1872, and power was given by the amended Act of 1872 to make parks outside the borough. Another objection was then raised by Mr. Black, that, under the 10th section of the Local Burials Act of 1856, this surplus ground had better be sold to the highest bidder, that transferring it from one committee of the corporation to another was not a sale within the meaning of the Act, and that it had better be sold. In order to get over that difficulty a meeting of the corporation was held, and they petitioned the Local Government Board to send down an inspector for the purpose of holding an inquiry into the matter, and accordingly, Mr. O'Brien, the Local Government Inspector, came down here and held an inquiry in February, 1873, at which the town surveyor, the town solicitor and several members of the town council, as well as several ratepayers, myself amongst the rest, were examined, and all gave evidence in favour of this park. There was not a dissentient voice at that commission of inquiry, and the upshot of it was that a provisional order was issued; and at that inquiry (I have not got the notes of evidence before me), I think the town surveyor gave evidence to the effect, that the corporation had cemetery ground sufficient for the next sixty years; and Mr. Carlisle, who was then a member of the town council, gave testimony to the effect that in his opinion they had sufficient cemetery ground for 100 years. After this inquiry the Local Government Board order was made, which shows the necessity of this ground for a park. When this Local Government Board Act was passed, an opinion was obtained, that the amended Parks Act of 1872 was rendered inoperative, as the Local Government Board Order Act directed that all this ground outside the borough wall should be converted and allocated to the purposes of a public park.

1345. The Act of Parliament says—It is ordered that the governing body shall apply said land so remaining and not required for the purposes of said cemetery, to the purposes of a public park, under the provisions of the Public Parks Act of 1869, and the Public Park Amendment Act of 1872, and shall have power to apply the sum of £5,000, and so on. It says that the land shall be devoted to the purposes of a public park under the provisions of the two Acts that I have quoted. We are not here to discuss the law, or to give us an authoritative opinion of the law upon the subject, but to take a note of your objection, that they have not carried out the law, which can be considered by the House of Commons. By whom was the case submitted to Mr. May, Q.C.?—By the Town Council. I presume the case was drawn up by Mr. Black. The opinion of Mr. Macdonogh, Q.C., was also obtained by the Corporation, and their opinions agreed with that of Serjeant Armstrong, which the ratepayers had taken. There is another point to which I would like to refer you. I wish to show you how much the ratepayers prompted the Council into making this park. At first they were very plausible and agreeable to us when we were regarding the formation of the Falls Park, but latterly when the Ormeau Park was opened in 1871 they went out with the mayor and Corporation in all their splendour and the different trades of Belfast, and the park was opened by the gentleman who was mayor at the time, who presided on the platform that was erected, and the proceedings were carried out with great ceremony. What I complain of is, that after the Local Government Board Order Act was obtained, and after three opinions were obtained, we had even then to go into the Court of Queen's Bench and take the first step for the purpose of getting a mandamus to compel the Corporation to make this Falls-road Park.

1346. Was it not until the preliminary notice was given that the Corporation yielded?—Only then.

1347. And they have since made a park?—Yes; and they put us to the expense of the bill of costs, which we had to pay; of course we didn't want to go to extremities with the Town Council. On the 1st of February, 1878, they commenced to lay out the park; but instead of laying it out in the manner they should have done, they have staked off that thirteen acres; and now, according to the resolution of the Town Council passed on the first of this month, they intend to look for powers to take this thirteen acres back into the cemetery, even to the extent of going to the expense of looking for an Act of Parliament, which Mr. Black instructs the Town Council is necessary; and they are doing all this after having got three Acts of Parliament to enable them to make the park; and now they are going to the expense of yet another to take that land again from us.

1348. Is the view you wish to represent to us that they are not fairly carrying out the formation of the park as a public body?—Yes. They have commenced making the park in a sort of way, and are making a road through it, which I think will be a disgrace to any common man to make, for it is a road that runs round the grounds, and no two vehicles of any description could pass abreast; and how they intend to make that a road for a park I do not know. I know it will be stated on behalf of the Town Council that they want the ground for cemetery purposes, but I deliberately say, and I believe I speak the feelings of a vast number of the ratepayers of Belfast, that they have ground amply sufficient for burial purposes in the forty-five acres within the walls, if they are re-allotted. There is no doubt that some of the allotments, such as Nos. 6 and 5, and 1 and 2, have been used for graves, and are exhausted; but there is one-third of the ground which has never been touched by a spade, and never opened for graves, and there is a great deal taken up with shrubberies and such like. They have only to go to the brow of the hill where there are only eight or ten vaults. Interments, too, have taken place behind the vaults in the back portion of the grounds; but we say, with regard to the cemetery grounds, that if they are re-adjusted or re-allotments made, there is sufficient, according to the testimony of the town surveyor given early in 1873, for more than sixty years, and of the town councillor, on the same occasion, for perhaps one hundred years. We also say that there are fifteen acres of this ground which remain lying without being used at all; that is, fifteen acres out of the forty-five. Some waifs and strays of the Catholic religion in Belfast, without the pale of the church, have been buried there, but the fifteen acres to which I allude were allocated for the burial of Catholics, and that portion of ground remains unused.

1349. We understand that the cemetery was divided into two portions, one for the Catholics, one for the Protestant community, and a small portion for the Jewish community, for which there was a payment received by the Corporation?—Thirty acres are allocated to Protestant burials, and fifteen acres were set apart for the burial of Catholics, and out of the thirty acres, I think there is a small space walled off, given to the Jews, of which I think there are only a few families in the town.

1350. Do you complain of that allocation of the fifteen acres for Roman Catholic burials, and can you say why they are so sparsely occupied by them?—That ground is not occupied by them at all; there is no Catholic buried in it except those outside the pale of the church, because the church prohibits burials there. There are not more than six or seven interments of persons who are outside the pale of the church.

1351. Do you know why it is not used by the Catholic portion of the community when it was set apart for them?—I know the reason perfectly well. The reason is that the Town Council would not give the necessary powers to the Catholic Bishop over the grounds. The question with the Catholic Bishop was this, whether the ground was for Catholics alone, and if so, had the Catholic Bishop and his clergy powers of ascertaining that the persons buried in that portion belonged to the Catholic religion. That ground is retained, and cannot be used but for Catholics, and it remains unproductive; and if an arrangement could be made with the Catholic bishop, probably this fifteen acres could be made available for Protestant purposes, inasmuch as the Catholics have since got a cemetery of their own.

1352. The resolution of the Town Council of December, 1878 [?], is to the effect that additional ground is required for the purpose of making graves, and it recommends in consequence that the ground in Falls Park be taken for the purpose?—Yes.

1353. You say that an equal quantity of ground could be got to supply the deficiency alleged by the Corporation by using the ground set apart for, but not occupied by the Catholic?—Yes; and by re-apportioning the Protestant portion of the ground.

1354. In addition to the thirty acres set apart for Protestant burials, there are you say fifteen acres at present unoccupied?—I say there are thirty acres appropriated for the burial of Protestants, and if those thirty acres were properly reallotted according to the various gradations, sufficient ground would be obtained, even without resorting to the fifteen acres set apart for the Catholics. I say in the first instance that there is too little ground for a certain class of graves, and too much for other classes. There is ground there that must lie unproductive for generations if it is not re-allotted. The fifteen acres to which I have already referred has been lying practically unused since the cemetery was opened in 1869. I remember in that year the contention between the bishop and the Town Council, and I was one of those who went with the bishop before the Privy Council with regard to the Catholic portion of the cemetery, when Judge Keogh asked what was the reason why the bishop and the Catholics of Belfast could not be given by a resolution of the Corporation the powers which the bishop wanted. The Town Council however remained steadfast, and refused to comply with the bishop's requirements, and yet they afterwards allowed that small portion that I have previously mentioned, to be walled off and given to the Jews on the very same terms as those the bishop wanted with regard to the ground originally intended for the Catholics. That is my belief. I say now that the Catholics have cemetery grounds of their own independent of this altogether, and if this fifteen acres could by a compromise being effected between the Catholics and the Town Council, be used for Protestant purposes, it would save the necessity for looking for ground elsewhere.

1355. What powers did the Catholic bishop require?—I believe there was a document handed in to the Town Council at the time fully stating what the bishop required.

1356. You say that the Roman Catholics have a cemetery of their own?—They have.

1357. Was that in existence before 1879 [?], or was it got since?—It was got since. When the bishop could not get the portion of ground allotted by the Corporation for Catholic burials upon the conditions which he desired to impose, he bought ground of his own. The Privy Council said it would have been hard to get

Belfast, Jan. 15, 1880.
—
Mr. [illegible] Callaghan.

BELFAST. [illegible] Mr. James Colligan.

liberty to open another cemetery, but under the circumstances these powers would be granted to the bishop.

1358. When was the application made to the Privy Council?—In 1869, in the year that the cemeteries were opened; another objection was put forward by Mr. Finlay MacCance, a gentleman who came with us on one of these deputations, of which there were many, with regard to the cemetery, and he said "We object to any more cemetery grounds being put on the Falls-road; we say if you want more cemetery grounds go to another part of the town which will be more convenient, and do not be bringing all the dead of Belfast up the Falls-road, and injuring our property there. We say if in addition to these forty-five acres there is more cemetery ground wanted, the Town Council could go to the Antrim-road, the Shore-road, or any other road, and procure ground there, which they have power to do under the Burial Grounds Act of 1866."

1359. In what part of the town is the Catholic cemetery?—It is exactly opposite the Falls-road Park grounds, a little further up.

1360. Mr. Exham.—What quantity of ground did the Catholics take there?—Eleven acres. Mr. [illegible], the chairman of the parks committee, has always acted in the best manner, and endeavoured to keep the Town Council right in this matter.

1361. The motion of the Town Council that has been referred to, to appropriate part of this surplus ground, was carried by thirteen votes to six?—Yes.

1362. Did Mr. [illegible], the chairman of the parks committee, vote against it?—Yes.

1363. Have the Roman Catholics erected a mortuary chapel?—Unfortunately they have not; they have no rates to depend on. Although the Catholics are one-third of the population and pay rates for the Corporation burial-ground, it has been refused to them, and in addition to having to buy ground of their own, they have expended between £450 and £500 on the drainage of it, and other work.

1364. You live on the Falls-road. Are there many houses there?—Yes; and the owners of property complain that our houses are greatly injured by the conveying of the dead to the cemetery day after day.

1365. Do you object to the funerals passing by your property?—I do not object to that.

1366. Do you object to the number being increased?—Yes.

1367. Chairman.—Do you also object to the mode in which the sewerage of that part of the town is carried on?—Yes.

1368. Is your property situated inside or outside the borough?—Half a mile inside—it is half a mile on this side of the cemetery.

1369. I see there is an item of £[illegible] in the accounts, on account of a contract for building a temporary reception of the dead. Is that only for the reception of the dead in the borough cemetery?—Yes.

1370. Is that building used for religious services, prayer, &c.?—Yes.

1371. Is it fitted up with seats, and so on?—Yes.

1372. Then it is a mortuary chapel?—Yes.

1373. Is there one built for the Roman Catholics in their part of the cemetery?—There is not.

1374. Did they ever apply to have one built?—No; because they never could use this ground on the terms they wanted—with a view of having Roman Catholic supervision over it.

1375. Is the Roman Catholic ground divided by a railing or wall?—It is divided by a sunk ditch, which cost £300, and a stone-faced wall.

1376. Then it comes to this, that the Roman Catholics pay for the interment of the Protestant dead, but the Protestants do not pay for the interment of the Roman Catholic dead?—Yes.

1377. And the Roman Catholics derive no benefit whatever from this public cemetery?—None that I know of.

1378. With regard to the sewerage, I believe that you wish to offer some evidence on that point?—I think our portion of the town is badly sewered. Although the Falls-road is some half a mile long, and a very important thoroughfare with a number of streets abutting it on each side, I think I am right in stating that there is no main sewer in that street at all.

1379. Mr. Exham.—If that be so, how are your houses drained?—The end of my houses abuts on a street called Springfield-road. In that road there is a two feet six-inch sewer, which was, I believe, put into it by Mr. [illegible], the owner of the ground; he is my head landlord. It is a brick barrelled sewer. There are a number of streets as well as my property that drain into that sewer. There is Malcolmson-street, Spring View-street, and Colligan-street. There are thirty or forty houses. We have water-closets running into this two feet six-inch sewer, and the sewer goes into the middle of the Falls-road. At one time this drain used to go across the Falls-road into an open field called Dunville's field where it emptied itself, and the sewage went away wherever it liked until the place became so much a nuisance that representations were made to the Council about it, and they then got put down from this two feet six-inch drain on the Falls-road a six or eight-inch pipe—I do not think they could be larger, which they ran down the Falls-road, instead of going down the Grosvenor-road, until they came to Dunville-street, which was paved and sewered by the owners. It was then taken down Dunville-street, about sixty perches, after which they turned it round another street and brought it back into the Grosvenor-road—bringing it a circuitous route of from fifty to sixty yards from where it started.

1380. Chairman.—The gist of your complaint is that they bring this sewer a circuitous route into the main sewer, and that instead of the drainage being carried through large pipes it is brought through small ones?—Yes.

1381. How long have these houses on the Falls-road been built?—Some of them longer than I can remember; my houses were built in 1867.

1382. Because it is an important element in comparing with Mr. Montgomery's evidence, for he stated that wherever new streets had been made he had taken care that new sewers were also made there?—Yes.

1383. With regard to sanitary matters, do you wish to be examined on that subject?—I do. I have to complain that sanitary matters are not attended to in any district as they should be. For instance, near the Lunatic Asylum there is a large convent on the other side of the Falls-road. Connected to this convent is the Catholic National School, as well as schools for private pupils, and attended by a large number of scholars. Well immediately opposite the convent there is a large pond which was formerly used for brickmaking purposes, and which could, in my opinion, be easily drained. Indeed I believe that a man could do it in three or four hours. Last summer the prioress of this convent sent a note to me in which she pointed out that a dreadful effluvia was emitted from this pond which was then about three feet deep. I went and viewed the pond, and saw in it dead dogs, cats, pigs, and other animals all exposed there. The stench was very great, and when there was wind in that direction it would not only affect the people in the asylum and convent but affect the people living in the houses in the Springfield-road. Well, I went to the sanitary medical officer of the district and I told him about that. I went to the dispensary doctor, who lives in one of my own houses, and he very kindly went and saw the pond of which I complained, and he told me that evening or the next morning that its condition was intolerable, and that he had sent a note down to the sanitary inspector's office about it.

1384. Who would that note be sent to?—I do not know, but the result of that was, that a man came with a drag and dragged out a portion of the dead animals, and took them away and buried them; but I visited the place on the next day, and I saw that there was still a number of these animals left there, that were

Belfast. Jan. 13, 187–. Mr. James Colligan.

imbedded in the ground under water, and what I wanted the medical sanitary officers to do was, to get the pond drained off and filled up, for it was there for no useful purpose, as no brick-making or any other work has been carried on there for the last two years. As I have stated, this pond was once used for keeping water for brick-making purposes, but it is now unused, and there it stands from that day to this, and it never has been drained. We have to complain of it very much, and what is more, there are several other ponds of the same description adjoining populous places in the same neighbourhood.

1355. Do you mean to say, with regard to that pond, that nothing further was done than partially dredging it?—Nothing further.

1356. Is it in the same state still?—Yes; it is less offensive now, and will, doubtless, remain so until the warm weather comes, when it will be as obnoxious as ever it was. I anticipate there would have been no difficulty in making drainage, and carrying away the offensive water and other matter.

1357. Where could they run it to?—To the river which runs close by.

1358. Have you ever made any written application at all to Mr. Montgomery, or to the committee who have charge of the sewerage—the sanitary committee, with respect to the defective drainage which you have already described to us so fully?—I cannot say that I have.

1359. You never brought any formal complaint either before the executive officer or before the committee?—No. There is another matter to which I wish to direct your attention, and of which I have to complain, and that is with regard to the expenditure of the rates in our portion of the town. Some three years ago we were promised that there would be a flagging put down on the Falls-road, one of the most important thoroughfares in Belfast, indeed I might say it is the leading thoroughfare. There is a footpath two feet wide, and we have been promised from time to time that there would be a flagging put down along that line where the traffic is very great, with people walking to and from funerals, and from Ballymacarrett. We were promised three years ago by the corporation that they would flag the thoroughfare to the extent of two feet wide for the accommodation of foot passengers. That has not been done, and I know that long since that promise was made to us similar flagways have been put down in other portions of the town. The flagway on the Shankhill-road was put down within a very short period of time compared with the time when we were promised it. A portion of ground was got opposite the convent for £25 by the corporation, and they promised to make a footpath there, and also that all the footpath would be flagged in this way, and that was reported to the town council at its next meeting—that £25 was to be given for the ground, and the footpath laid down, and it was remarked by a member of the corporation, that the flagging would be put down the whole length of the Falls-road, inasmuch as it was the thoroughfare to the cemeteries. There is another matter which happened recently, and which shows that there is an inclination to spend as small a portion of the rates as possible in our neighbourhood. It is plain to everyone that large sums of the rates for years back have been spent on some parts of the town, while other parts have been sadly neglected. An instance of this was furnished in the case of Milford-street, which has densely inhabited streets on each side of it, and is an important thoroughfare leading from Divis-street to Albert-road (being the continuation of the first-named thoroughfare), there was a plot of ground not built on, and at this time a party had taken it for building on. The town council had for a long time wanted to prevent people from building on this ground, but at last they granted permission, and the complaint we make is that the Town Council should have in the first instance prevented owners from building on that ground, and afterwards permitted them to do so, when the ground ought to have been preserved in order to perfect the communication between these two thoroughfares—Milford-street and Albert-road. For some reason or other the parties who owned the ground at last succeeded in getting their plans passed. It came to the knowledge of the people residing in the locality that this ground was not to be kept open. They sent down to the Committee a deputation, which included clergymen of the Protestant, Catholic, and Presbyterian Churches, and they stated that it would be a public convenience if this piece of ground was left open. What we wanted the improvement committee to do was to pay the party for this piece of ground about £150, and to form it into a street joining Milford-street to Durham-street for the accommodation of the people of the locality and those using the churches in the vicinity—Catholic and Presbyterian. Dr. Browne, who was the chairman of the improvement committee, fell in with our view, and said that that course should be attempted as far as they possibly could, and that they would endeavour to keep this piece of ground open. Mr. Black resisted that proposition, and said the Corporation had no money for such purposes. I said I could not understand that, that there was surely money for making public improvements. I knew that in different parts of the town large sums had been expended, and I could not see why such a policy upon us this could not be advanced. The chairman of the committee favourably entertained our case, and a sub-committee was, in fact, appointed to go with the deputation to the ground and examine it. Before they came back with the deputation they consented to give £50 if we would buy the ground ourselves—that is, that the Town Council would give £50 towards the cost of it. Well, the subcommittee went with the deputation and examined the ground, and so convinced were they of the reasonableness of our request that they went back and reported to the full committee, and urged the committee to increase their grant towards the expense from £50 to £75, which was accordingly agreed to. We set about making arrangements to buy the ground, but the party, seeing that there was some anxiety manifested to get the piece of ground, he was hard to deal with, and, as a matter of fact, we could not deal with him at all. The result is that half the street is built over. I should tell you that the Town Council then reduced their offer from £75 to £25, and I believe the result was that a collection was made to do this, which, I say, should have been done by the Corporation, and the expenditure on which would have been money well spent.

1360. Have you got the thoroughfare open now?—The result is that only half the thoroughfare is kept open now, and it is a disgrace and an eyesore to the town, and would be to any place like Belfast.

or is it actually completed, because it makes a great deal of difference?—The Fallsroad Park was formerly a bleach ground, the property of Mr. John Sinclair, and the water was conveyed down from the mountain in a pipe for bleaching purposes. In the portion of the park that has been staked off—this thirteen acres—there is fresh spring water fit for bleaching purposes. There is also part of a road that was made by Mr. Sinclair, with trees growing on each side of it; that is continuation of that up to rising ground there is a kind of a chaussée road about the breadth of one carriage, but that road is not formed in a respectable manner, nor is it sufficiently wide to allow one carriage to pass another.

1394. What I want to know is this. The Ormeau Park, you say, is a better park than the Falls Park?—Yes.

1395. But is the Falls Park now finally completed by the Corporation, or are they going to do more, and to put it in the same position as the other park. Have they in fact left off decorating the Falls Park, and finishing it? I think they are improving it still a little, but they are doing so with the greatest reluctance possible. That would be shown if the estimates for the Falls Park for next year were produced. They would show what are the intentions of the Corporation with regard to that park.

1396. Is there any other matter on which you wish to give evidence?—There is nothing else with the exception that I do not wish to go too fully into this park question from feelings of delicacy. I understand well the reasons why this park has not been properly made, but I don't like to speak so elaborately as I would wish.

1397. Keep as much as possible from attributing motives and give us the facts?—Well I know as a matter of fact that some of the members of the Town Council live at Ravenhill convenient to the Ormeau Park. There is no member of the Town Council who lives near the Falls-road, and consequently the Corporation have no interest there, and they don't seem to care much for making improvements where they have no interest.

1398. Are there not several good houses on the Falls-road?—There is a good class of houses, but the principal factories and foundries are situated there, and there are a number of mill girls working there. The heat in these mills is very great and the smell of all is most oppressive. I tell you candidly I could not believe until I ascertained it that there were such close choking smells in these mills. These places are adjacent to the park, and what we wish is that these working classes—who cannot come before you and have their interests represented—should have what they badly want—a place where they can go and enjoy themselves in the open air. I speak now on behalf of this class of people especially that this park is a great public necessity.

1399. That this park is especially a necessity for these poor people?—Yes. They want some relief from the heat and noxious smells they have to endure all day.

1400. You know that these mills are inspected, not by the officers of the Corporation, but by the factory inspectors?—I am aware of that.

1401. So that the state in which they are kept rests with the factory inspectors?—Yes; but this park is the only convenient place for the recreation of these workers.

1402. Do many of the workpeople live close to the Falls Park?—Yes; very many; they could not go to the Ormeau Park for the want of sufficient good means, and besides that the distance is too far. Owing to the proximity of Lough Neagh and the Black Mountain the air in the neighbourhood of the Falls Park has been found to be more pure than any other air about Belfast—that is one of the great advantages we claim for it.

1403. Then the air is peculiarly suitable for a public park?—Yes.

1404. Is there any point with regard to the sewerage or drainage of the district upon which you wish to give evidence?—I wish to allude to a pond which is situate on the Falls-road immediately at the flour mills. I got a memorial signed by a large number of the inhabitants, and Dr. Heaney said that this pond was a public nuisance and dangerous to health in summer. The water in it is used for the purpose of condensing steam, and the water comes by a circuitous route. It is also used very often for the purpose of raising steam at one of the mills, and goes to Mr. Alexander's flour mills. In summer the smell of that water is very offensive, and the water is poisonous. As I have said I brought a memorial to the Council about that.

1405. How long ago?—The summer before last. I may tell you that the nuisance of this pond is such that those living or working in immediate proximity to it in the summer cannot have an open window as the air outside is worse than the air inside. Two members of the Council, after the memorial was presented, came and examined this pond. Nothing, however, has been done since that time beyond the raising of the wall around it—the pond remains the same, and in the summer proper the those living on the Falls-road and paying taxes have to endure the dangerous effluvia from it. The nuisance is not abated although the memorial I presented was signed by the clergymen of the different religious denominations, and several inhabitants of the district, and two members of the Council examined the place. The only thing done as I have said was the raising of the wall which, however, is not higher than a man's head. You cannot see the pond now owing to the height of the wall, but the offensive smell is the same.

Mr. Black re-examined.

1406. Mr. *Black*.—I wish to state that the Harbour Commissioners do not prevent us from carrying the sewage into the Lagan; the only difficulty with the Harbour Commissioners in connexion with the sewage scheme is as to the point of discharge.

Adjourned.

DECEMBER 15, 1876.

MR. SAMUEL KEAFLEY examined.

the matter, but you have not visited the pond yourself?—Yes; I have not visited it myself lately.

1413. Surely, under the circumstances, it is the first thing you should have done?—Two years ago the Council called this a nuisance, and nothing has been done since, so far as I am aware, to abate it; the nuisance remains there still.

1414. Is it your property that drains into that sewer?—I have no house property in that street. It belongs to other parties, but the drainage of my houses further up on the Antrim-road goes into that sewer and into the pond.

1415. In fact the sewage of your houses goes there?—Quite so; and my attention was not drawn to this matter until between two and three years ago. The Council then called it a nuisance. When this street was first made I paid £40 or £45 towards the work, believing that it was correctly done. I find that this new sewer was made northward instead of southward. The main sewer is at the south end.

1416. Does the sewage go into the pond instead of into the main sewer?—Yes.

1417. Since the Council pronounced it a nuisance have you done anything to draw the attention of the sanitary inspector of the district to the fact that it remains still in the same state?—I wrote to Mr. Scott, the executive sanitary officer upon the subject, immediately after the Council adjudged the grievance, two or three years ago. I have heard nothing about it since.

1418. And you have done nothing since?—It was stated by Mr. Hastings, the engineer who examined the state of the sewage of that district that it was a piece of bungling. I am a civil engineer myself.

1419. Mr. Lawless.—When and to whom did you pay your contribution for the making of that sewer?—I gave it shortly after it was finished to Mr. Kent, who owns a large property on the Antrim-road to pay with his own, for making the new sewer in this new street.

1420. That was two years ago?—It was six or seven years ago.

1421. By whom was the sewer made? Was it by the Corporation?—Their men had the management of it.

1422. Mr. Kent is not an officer of the Corporation?—Not that I am aware of.

1423. You paid the contribution to him as a private owner of property?—Yes.

Belfast. Oct. 14, 18[illegible]

Mr. Edmund Keatley.

Mr. Montgomery recalled.

Mr. John Lanyon Montgomery

1424. Chairman.—Have you heard the statement of Mr. Keatley as to the sewer in Richmond crescent?—I have.

1425. Can you give us any explanation about it?—I can. The owners of property there made that sewer. I hold in my hand the plan of certain streets near Richmond-crescent, the property of Messrs. Phillip Johnston and Company. This plan was submitted to me in July, 1866, and after being frequently disapproved of by me in my written reports it was ultimately approved on the 6th February, 1867. My objection to this scheme was that there was no proper outlet for the drainage—that we ought not to allow any houses to be built there, nor any streets to be laid out, until a sufficient mode of drainage was provided. This was immediately after the Act was passed to enable us to divide the upper area of the borough into districts (the Act of 1866), and to impose two-thirds of the cost of each district on the inhabitants. It was urged by the owners of property there that the district was young, and so for a year or two the drainage was staved off, but it was ultimately accomplished.

1426. What drainage?—The Antrim-road drainage district. The owners selected my predecessor, Mr. Hastings, a man of great experience, who assures me that the drainage has been a very great success, and it is the first time in my life that I have ever heard any charge of bungling brought against it. Mr. Hastings had a conference with me, and by putting our heads together we thought that a method of drainage by tanks might be made. The tanks were drawn out on this plan by Mr. Hastings, who was then acting in a private capacity for Mr. Johnston, the owner of the property. He says, "These tanks will be removed a sufficient distance from the houses." These tanks have been constructed, but not until the Council threatened hostile measures against the owners of property. They are not quite finished yet. The Council made complaints to the owners that the system had not been fully carried out as undertaken in the plan. We did not press the matter for some years, and I will tell you why, because the great bulk of the nuisance that used to flow past Mr. Keatley's property was intercepted and taken into the district sewer some time ago.

1427. Is there a main sewer?—There is a great main sewer passing along the high road in front of Mr. Keatley's houses at such a level as would drain most of the nuisance complained of, but not all Mr. Keatley's houses.

1428. Are there connecting drains from the houses to the sewers that you speak of?—I will explain that. When additional houses were being built the evil became conspicuous. We called on the owners for amelioration, and Mr. Hastings agreed some months ago to remedy the defect in the sewerage, and those works are still in progress. That, I think, disposes of the private question. It was adopted as a temporary expedient until such times as we could impose a sewage rate on the district, and thereby make an effective system of drainage.

1429. What question do you say that disposes of?—The private question. It is a matter done entirely by the owners of property; but I may say on behalf of the Corporation that we are ready at any time to make a new sewerage district which will include these houses.

1430. Your point is that these are drainage works not constructed by you, but with your consent (your reluctant consent), until the drainage rate could be imposed?—Yes.

1431. Mr. Exham.—You say yourself that the main sewer down the Antrim-road is constructed at such a level that the backyards of the houses there cannot be drained into it. Is that so?—That is what I am now coming to.

1432. Chairman.—Mr. Keatley told us that he contributed what he was told was his portion of the cost of the drainage. Did any of that come into the hands of the Corporation?—Not one farthing. The head landlord has sub-let this property in building leases.

1433. The head landlord is Mr. Johnston?—Yes.

1434. Mr. Keatley paid to the person whom he held under?—Yes.

1435. To Mr. Kent?—Yes; Mr. Kent holds from Mr. Johnston.

1436. Was any portion of that £45 paid by Mr. Keatley paid by Mr. Kent to the Corporation?—No.

1437. Mr. Lawless.—There is one thing I want to know before you go any further. Do you admit it to be the case that the sewer in Richmond-street has no connexion with the main sewer?—It has none nor can the sewerage be sent into it without the aid of a steam engine.

1438. Is it true that the outfall from that sewer is into the open pond?—Yes.

1439. How long has that state of things existed?—Since 1867.

1440. Has there been a sewer rate laid for that district since that time?—There has, and there has not. That requires explanation. Do you observe this line on the plan? (Producing plan.) That represents the taxing area for this drainage district (the Antrim-road district). The property in question all lies outside of that boundary and has not been rated except Mr. Keatley's own row of houses (he has three, and there are four others—seven altogether) which are within the drainage district. The ground floor of these houses and all the floors above the ground floor could be drained into the main sewer, but the ground falls so rapidly that it would have been abominable bungling to have made this arterial sewer at such a level as would have drained the cellars, and the town surveyor who would have done it should have been dismissed. The whole estate, now is being rapidly divided into drainage districts, of which the Antrim road is one. Four of those districts have been completed and half a dozen of the leading roads have been designed like the Antrim-road at proper levels. It happens, with respect to those half a dozen houses, that owing to the great fall in the ground the kitchens are in the front of the houses which front to the Antrim-road sewer, and a very great difficulty arose about the rating—whether or not such houses, in which only portion of the back and yard were drained were to be entirely rated or only the parts which would get the benefit of the drainage, and whether that part should be charged not only with the sewer rate but with the frontage charge.

1441. What is the frontage charge?—The centre of Belfast had all been drained; there are drains in every street in the centre of the town, and in 1865 the Council cast about for an equitable way of draining the immense suburbs that were being made after the American war, and we found an Act of Parliament, the "Towns Improvement Clauses Act, 1847," which contained provisions suitable for our purpose. We then put clauses into our Act of 1865, as to the charge for district drains which Parliament passed, and we divided that charge into three portions, one-third was made a general charge over the borough payable out of the general purposes rate—one-third was charged on the occupiers of houses in the district, and the remaining third was charged on persons having building ground and houses fronting the main sewer who by this means escaped the necessary duty of constructing a sewer for their own property.

1442. Has it been doubted whether you could charge the same party the drainage rate and the frontage charge?—The one is a money payment, and the other is a rate. After proper legal advice, and full consideration the Council came to the conclusion that they were bound in such cases to make the double charge; and a very leading gentleman in town in this very district contested it with us. He took advice on the subject, and after a good deal of hesitation and delay he paid it.

1443. Who was that?—Mr. William Thompson, secretary of the Harbour Board. Therefore we go on charging it and we find it to be equitable for this reason—The health of every district is important, and you not only make your property better and more valuable, but you improve the health of the inhabitants of that district, and health is so much gain.

1444. Mr. Baman.—But in this case the houses are built nearly ten years and the tanks are not made yet, so there has not been any gain to the health of the inhabitants?—You that is so.

1445. Why have you allowed ten years to elapse without requiring this to be done, Mr. Johnston. As I read the Act of Parliament you ought to have made proper sewers at once?—I think seven or eight houses would do very little additional harm to a river which drains seven or eight miles. The river discharges a large volume of water and carries off the nuisance from these houses. It is not a drain as represented but a watercourse.

1446. Was there ever any direction given by the Corporation to have that particular portion of the river cleaned out so as to abate the nuisance caused by it?—It is really the first movement that I heard of a general complaint in reference to this river.

1447. But you stated just now that it was a nuisance?—Yes; but I had not heard any general complaint of it.

1448. Was there ever any direction given to have it cleaned?—No; nor did I hear it was necessary.

Mr. Alexander Tyrrell recalled.

1449. Mr. Lawless.—What rate do you charge private consumers for gas?—3s. 11d. per thousand feet.

1450. Do you supply gas outside the municipal boundaries?—Yes, to a considerable extent.

1451. Do you charge them the same price?—We do.

1452. Although they are not subject to the municipal taxation?—Yes.

1453. Chairman.—Did the Corporation supply it to outsiders at the same rate as the former gas company?—Yes; and we gave them the same reduction as we gave to those inside the borough.

1454. It was quite natural that when you took over the works with the price at 4s. 6d. that you should supply the consumers outside the borough at the same rate, but when you reduced the charge to consumers inside the borough it does not follow that you should reduce it to those outside. There is a great difference between the charge you made then and now?—The opinion was that there should be a uniform price. The matter was frequently under discussion and one reason given for reducing it was that the great bulk of the consumers living outside the borough are also merchants and traders connected with the borough.

1455. Mr. Lawless.—You found that system existing when the gasworks were taken over by the Corporation?—Yes.

1456. Have you laid down any new mains since the Corporation became owners?—Yes, we have expanded the mains outside the borough boundary.

1457. Did you require any contribution towards that work from the residents there?—Yes; it is a matter of arrangement in the Sydenham district—consumers there contribute one-half of the expense of the work.

on any account like the Town Council should have any power of revaluation.

1463. The Town Council have no power over it?—Nor would we like them to have.

1464. Do you say that there should not be a revaluation?—Yes; and if we should have a revaluation, that the Town Council should have no power over it. From the year 1860 the extent of property has doubled, and yet our rates keep on increasing. One would think that the great increase in the population of Belfast would reduce the rates, but it has not done so.

1465. Mr. Lawless.—Would it not be very much to your advantage that the rates should be reduced, and this might be effected by a fair revaluation?—Yes, but we are afraid to allow the Town Council to have any control over it.

1466. Supposing that property in 1860 was valued at £80 and £90, and that at present it is let at £120, do you not think it should be valued higher?—Certainly; and so it is. I think there may be fifty or 100 cases of that kind.

Mr. Black recalled.

[Mr. Heenan read report of the 17th September, 1873, of the sub-committee of the law and sanitary committees, of which Mr. John Brown was chairman, with regard to the Blackstaff. In that report the committee point out that the nuisance is actually caused and originated by the Town Council themselves in some respects by emptying the town sewage into the stream, by the mills and other manufactories discharging the polluted matter into the stream. The millowners pumped the water into their engines, which, after being used by them, was discharged into the river.]

1467. Mr. Heenan.—I call attention to the report principally because of the statement made by Mr. Scott, the executive sanitary officer, that he never heard any complaints made about the state of the Blackstaff.

Mr. *Black*.—You will bear in mind that Mr. Scott is only the executive sanitary officer of the Corporation since the passing of the Public Health Act, 1874.

1468. Mr. Heenan.—I am aware of that, but a memorial was sent up to the Local Government Board by a number of medical men regarding the state of the river, and yet Mr. Scott stated that he had not heard that there were any complaints made about the Blackstaff. The report goes on to say that the Blackstaff and Pound Burn are converted into open sewers, and that they receive the whole of the sewage of the districts through which they pass, as well as a large quantity of most offensive matter from some of the buildings near the streams; that the water is taken by the numerous mills and manufactories along the course of the Pound Burn, and after being used for condensing purposes is sent back to be taken and used over again further down, and when thus returned to the river at a higher temperature was then more offensive. The committee say that during the time they were making their inspection "it was almost impossible to remain more than a few minutes on the banks of the river the effluvia was so intolerable." The sub-committee were of opinion that at many points where the sewers were discharged into the river they might easily have been turned in another direction. I want to know has anything been done since 1873 regarding the matters stated in this report?

Mr. *Black*.—If you turn to the Act of 1845 you will find by section 90 that the Corporation had power to use the Blackstaff as a common sewer.

1469. Chairman.—Why was not the report of the sub-committee entered on the minutes?—It was not adopted by the committee at all.

1470. But why is there not some record on the minutes as to its having been brought forward?—I will be able exactly to give you the facts connected with it.

1471. Mr. Heenan.—Then there follow the suggestions made by the sub-committee regarding the mode of remedying the nuisance, and also a resolution passed by the committee to the effect that the suggestions of the sub-committee should be referred to the borough surveyor to consider if they were practicable.

Mr. *Black*.—The suggestions of the sub-committee were absolute impossibilities, for you cannot make sewers run up a hill.

1472. Chairman.—But the sub-committee report the Blackstaff and Pound Burn to be a nuisance.

Mr. *Black*.—And I am not here on the part of the Corporation to deny that the Blackstaff is a nuisance; but the difficulties hitherto in the way of our remedying that nuisance have been so great that so far we have been unable to overcome them. An effectual remedy does not lie in those petty suggestions made by that sub-committee, but by the construction, as Mr. Montgomery has suggested by his scheme, of a system of main drainage for the town, and this system the Corporation have been prevented from carrying out owing to the difference existing between the Corporation and the Harbour Board as regards the outlet for the sewage, and also the serious expense that would be incurred in constructing the works. When the town is prepared to meet those difficulties, the work, no doubt, will be carried out. No suggestion has ever been made about dealing with the Blackstaff nuisance or any other nuisance that was not carefully considered. I may say further than that, that the opinion of the present Attorney-General (Mr. May) was taken on the subject, and he personally with myself inspected the entire Blackstaff and the Pound Burn for the purpose of seeing if there were any way of remedying the nuisance, or if we had any rights in the river beyond what we already exercised.

1473. Mr. Heenan.—Did the Attorney-General (Mr. May) tell you that you had no power of preventing the millowners from sending all the filthy sewage of their factories into the Pound Burn and the Blackstaff?—I am prepared to say that he did. If you refer to section 90 of the Act of 1845, and section 61 of the Act of 1850, you will find that the Corporation were empowered to make sewers and to run these sewers into any river or stream. The Corporation of the day exercised that power, and unfortunately, for after generations used the Blackstaff as a common sewer; and we were advised that until we took the drain out of our own eye we could not insist on the millowners taking the mote out of theirs. When we have got suitable main sewers, no doubt the millowners will run their sewage into them.

1474. Have you got the opinion of the Attorney-General upon that point?—Yes. (Hands in the opinion of the Attorney-General.)

1475. When you say that the Corporation carefully considered every suggestion that was made about the Blackstaff, will you tell me was anything done to carry out the resolution of the 29th October, 1873, as to the committee's carrying on its investigation, and as to employing an engineer to consider the matter with them?—There was not anything further done as to that. The Corporation were waiting to have one comprehensive scheme of drainage.

1476. Do you think that under the 51st section of the Act of 1850, to which you have called our attention, the Corporation have the power and right to turn the public sewers into the Pound Burn and Blackstaff rivers?—I do.

1477. Do you notice that the section says "but so that the same shall in no case become a public nuisance or annoyance to the neighbourhood." How can you justify this when everyone admits that those rivers are a frightful nuisance and caused in a great measure by the sewers which the Corporation have constructed discharging filthy matter into them?—I think still they have the power of doing so.

Mr. WILLIAM AGNEW examined.

1478. Mr. LAWLESS.—You reside in Belfast?—Yes; in No. 4, Henry-street.

1479. To what do you wish to call our attention?—To the state of sewage of Henry-street, abutting on Corporation-street. The nuisance we have to complain of arises from the discharge of the water used by the York-street spinning mill into the Blackstaff, and which passes by the houses in my street. The effluvia arising from this is very offensive.

1480. Who is the proprietor of that mill?—It is a limited company. The water when used in that mill passes down the main sewer in my street. There is a smell rises from a grating in the street near my own house, which I have felt in my own dining room.

1481. How long have you perceived this nuisance?—For years. I set to work myself and got the sewer cleansed.

1482. Does that smell arise from the heated water from York-street mill getting into the main sewer?—Yes. They use the sewer for carrying off their water and sewage.

Mr. MONTGOMERY recalled.

1483. CHAIRMAN.—Have you noticed this grating that has just been referred to by Mr. Agnew? Has your attention ever been drawn to the matter?—Not to that case, but such matters are frequently the subject of complaint. When the owners of houses put in proper traps and proper pipe sewers, no smell can arise. There is a general question about the condensed water going into the sewer. It is used for condensing purposes in the mills, and sent out again in a warm state, and I apprehend that we cannot prevent it. I have put in several hundred ventilators in the sewers and it is very much better to allow the smell to escape by them to the surface than to allow it to go into the houses. You must have sewers to dispose of bad smells. I can construct an entirely new system of drainage for the borough at a cost of half a million of money which will cure that.

1484. Were many of the connecting drains made before you became surveyor?—Yes.

1485. Is it not the duty of the parties making them to put themselves in communication with you or your staff to see that they are properly made, and that they enter the sewer at the proper place?—Yes, and to see that the traps are properly made.

1486. In the case of old houses have you no means of knowing the state of the drainage until it is brought under your notice by the owner?—The sanitary staff take the trouble of examining the houses to find out if there is a bad smell. In the house where I reside they took active steps to make the landlord attend to the drainage, but generally speaking notice is given to the sanitary staff about bad smells and then steps are taken to have the nuisance abated.

Mr. FOSTER CONNOR, J.P., examined.

1487. CHAIRMAN.—You wish to give evidence?—Yes; I wish to say something about the Blackstaff and Pound Burn. I am the only factory owner on the Pound Burn, using the water for mill purposes, and I have heard it stated here that all nuisances and offensive matters are discharged by the mill owners into it. Now I wish to say that I do not discharge any into it because I was advised by the Town Council many years ago not to do so, and I do not. They take away the offensive matter every morning from my place.

1488. When were you noticed by the Town Council not to send the water into it?—Long ago. I am the only person on the Pound Burn who uses the water for mill purposes. The Corporation cart away the offensive sewage matter every morning from my place ever since they gave me notice.

1489. Do they send their carts to remove it?—Yes.

1490. Do they empty your cesspool?—Yes. With regard to the condensing water, of course I take it from the river and discharge it again after I have used it. After it is used by me it becomes more offensive by being heated. I admit that. I think the remedy to prevent all that would be by making two sewers—one for the sewage proper, and one for conveying the water itself down the stream. The water is supplied directly from the Falls-road district. The Falls river comes down past the distillery, and I would suggest that the water should be conveyed from the mill-dam down to the Pound Burn, and discharged into the Blackstaff in a pure or comparatively pure state, which could be done. The offensive matter could be taken down by a separate sewer and discharged into the street sewers. Mr. Montgomery, who is very conversant with this question, said that it is impossible to run water up a hill, but if you raised the sewers it would meet that objection.

1491. Is the water from your mill offensive?—No doubt it is.

1492. Is that because the Pound Burn receives the sewage of houses above you?—Yes.

1493. Are there many?—Two or three streets, and besides there are a great many houses on the Falls-road that drain into it.

1494. What you wish to convey to us is, that you do not add to the impurity of the river by your own sewage, and that the water, in being used in your mill, is only rendered more impure, as it is impure before you get it at all?—Precisely so. The Blackstaff in itself is really not a nuisance—in fact it is impossible that it could be a nuisance. It is the Pound Burn emptying itself into it which makes it a nuisance.

1495. Mr. LAWLESS.—After the junction of the two streams does the Blackstaff become a nuisance?—Yes; in the summer time it becomes a great nuisance, but at the present time it is not so. I am the only one in the Pound Burn, and but for my interest in it it might be closed to-morrow.

1496. Have you raised the height of the water by a weir?—Yes, that has been done about twenty-five years ago.

1497. Does that give your mill the use of the water?—Yes.

1498. There is no question in the world but that the Pound Burn would be relieved by the system of two sewers which I have referred to—one to carry off the water and one to carry off the sewage matter.

the cause of the floods, for on the 6th of this month (last Thursday week) we had very heavy rain, and the lower story of my house began to be flooded five hours before high water, and there were several inches of water in the basement long before high water. I am satisfied that the upper sewer with which my sewer is connected is not sufficient to carry off the water. In the row in which I live there are underground areas which are flooded, but it has been stated that the reason was that they were at a lower level than any of the other houses with underground areas. Mr. Young, the civil engineer, made a survey of the place and he found that they were in some cases four feet higher, and in others from five to seven inches higher than the underground areas of houses in Howard-street and Donegall square, South, and those places are not subject to be flooded as we are.

1503. Are the other places you mentioned also in the vicinity of the Blackstaff?—Yes.

1504. Should not they be flooded as you were if it arose from the rains?—I should say so, but I do not know exactly the construction of their sewers. I believe they are connected with another main sewer.

1505. Can you suggest how this flooding might be avoided?—If the sewers from our houses were connected with the main sewer very close to us in Howard-street, which goes in another direction it would very considerably relieve the flooding.

1506. Have you ever represented this matter to the sewage committee?—Yes; my friend Dr. Ferguson and I attended before one of the committees at the suggestion of the borough surveyor. He recommends that in the case of our row of houses in Donegall-place a valve should be put at the junction of the sewer from the houses with the main sewer. This was done. The sewers from the houses were all remade at the expense of the tenants by the Town Council during last summer, but we have been twice flooded since it was done.

1507. You find it had no effect?—It has had no effect. I might add that the lady who lived in the house which I now occupy for fourteen years had no flooding during the time that she was there. I am living in it about eleven years. I think the same thing exists as regards the house in which Dr. Ferguson lives.

1508. Of course we have had an extremely wet season. Is it from that cause only or do you think there has been some action by the Corporation or their surveyor in the meantime which caused the flooding to exist more than during the occupancy of the previous tenant?

1509. Dr. *Ferguson*.—There has been a new sewer constructed, and since it was constructed the flooding has been worse.

1510. Dr. *Smyth*.—A number of new houses were erected and the work thrown upon the sewer has been more than it is able to bear. It was extremely hard for medical men to get houses near the centre of the town because they are nearly all made into shops.

1511. Dr. *Ferguson*.—I wish to corroborate all that Dr. Smyth has said.

1512. Did you attend before the committee and laid the matter before them?—I did and on the suggestion of the surveyor a valve was placed at the junction of the sewer with the main sewer at our expense; even their trying that was the result of three or four applications in the one year, and it gave us no relief.

1513. Mr. LAWLESS (to Dr. *Smyth*).—Is it your opinion that if the main sewer was enlarged sufficiently to do the duty now cast on it from the increase of houses the flooding might be stopped?—Yes.

1514. CHAIRMAN.—If Mr. Montgomery's scheme for the main sewerage was carried out, would it have the effect of removing your cause of complaint?—Yes; if there was any prospect of its being carried out, but until it is so we think that something should be done to put us in the same position we were in some eight or ten years ago when the then existing sewers were sufficient to protect any houses from being flooded.

1515. Have any representations been made to the Town Council on the subject which have not been attended to?—I came here some six or seven years ago as a deputation and have been frequently here since, and I am sure they were not in ignorance of any cause. That was only as regards three houses in Donegall-place, and did not refer to me at all.

Jan. 16, 1875.

Dr. Bryce Smyth.

Mr. MONTGOMERY recalled.

Mr. John James Montgomery.

1516. CHAIRMAN.—You wish to say something with regard to this matter?—Yes. In the first place I wrote a letter to these gentlemen, informing them that the high level sewer which he alludes to would not prevent them from being flooded. I think I advised that if each house would make a proper system of piped drains to the main sewer, and put valves on them at the expense of about £4 or £5 per house, no flooding would, I believe, arise from the sewer, or at all events that it would be greatly abated. The work was done, and I assert fearlessly that it will greatly abate the flooding. The occasion of the last flood was in consequence of the extremely high tide, which was a couple of feet higher than I have recorded since the time I became surveyor. The tide was so high and the flood so great on that occasion that many contrivances which had lasted for years failed, and amongst the rest Dr. Smyth's place; and in point of fact it was the surface water from the streets and the overflow water from the tide that got into these areas, which should never have been made at all. The surface of the ground there is scarcely above the tide level. Under no circumstances shall we be able to prevent such cellars from being flooded. When the river overflows, in consequence of high tides, the water will find its own level and go into low passages and kitchens. No system of drainage will prevent it.

1517. Could there be relief given in the way suggested by Dr. Smyth—by connecting that sewer with the other sewer he mentioned?—The levels were taken, and there is not fall sufficient. I for one would not be a party to making a sewer without some fall. Owing to the improved drainage, it is a fact that a much larger quantity of water comes down in a given time than used to come down, and this is caused by the ordinary rainfalls and the improved drains, which send down the water more rapidly than before, and any new sewer that we could construct could not carry off the whole of that water at all times.

1518. Dr. *Smyth*.—If the open basements in Donegall-square, South, are four feet lower than the area basements of our houses, how is it that after all the work was done it did not stop the flooding of our houses?—The one set of cellars are, I should say, a quarter of a mile from the other. The two sewers are entirely distinct.

Mr. WILLIAM COATES, J.P., examined.

Mr. William Coates, J.P.

1519. CHAIRMAN.—You wish to give some evidence about the Blackstaff?—Yes. I was a member of the Town Council several times. I believe that the reason the Blackstaff is such a nuisance is owing entirely to the Pound Burn being allowed to go into it at all. If there is any scheme could be devised to divert the Pound Burn into the main sewer that runs down High-street there would be no nuisance at all in the Blackstaff. It passes through property that I have in a pure state, and would continue to be pure but for its being contaminated by the millowners, who use it for engine purposes, and also by the quantity of sewage discharged into it.

1520. Mr. BEGGAN.—Would there be any difficulty in sending it down the main sewer in High-street?—I do not know the levels, but my impression is there would not, because the ground is higher.

1521. CHAIRMAN.—It seems to me that it would be a tremendous thing to turn the Pound Burn into a common sewer?—A good portion of the Pound Burn at present goes into the main sewers. I should like to put it all in.

1522. Mr. Exham.—Do you wish to say anything with regard to the collection of the rates?—Yes. It would be a good thing if all the rates were struck and collected at one time as they are in Dublin. Owing to the way it is managed here there are a great many collectors of different rates, and so many rates to be collected that you are never free from a tax collector coming to you for something.

1523. Mr. Lawless.—Are not all the municipal rates collected at the one time?—Yes; but the water rate and all the other rates should be struck and collected at the same time—as they are in Dublin.

Mr. James Hart examined.

1524. Chairman.—You are a member of the Town Council?—Yes. I have been on the Town Council since 1864. I have attended particularly the meetings of the sanitary committee of which I have been a member ever since I joined the Council.

1525. And you are on it now?—Yes; I am on it now, and I have heard all that the engineers have suggested during that time for the improvement of the Lagan and Blackstaff. I am probably one of the most regular attendants at the Council meetings. [The witness handed in a report of a scheme of his own for the cleansing of the Lagan.]

1526. What you suggest is that the river Lagan requires to be cleansed from the first lock on the canal to the quays. How would you do that?—By dredging in the centre and throwing the sand and gravel out on each side. This would cause a good scour, and then noxious matter would not lodge in the bed of the river and create a smell. The tide coming up always brings something bad with it, and noxious smells are created if all the sediment is not carried away by the receding tide.

1527. Was this report prepared by you at the request of the sanitary committee in February, 1878?—Yes.

1528. Was it entered on the minutes of the corporation?—It was not.

1529. You contributed this report as an individual member of the committee?—Yes.

1530. Do you know why it was not entered upon the minutes?—I do not.

1531. Was the plan considered by the committee?—It was. It was in part approved, and in part it was not.

1532. Has any action been taken upon it?—Nothing of any consequence has been done. There has been some cleansing, but what I contend is that it should be sustained on the bottom with something like flagging, or smooth material of some kind.

1533. No doubt, if you could asphalte the bottom, it would be a very nice thing?—Flagging might be cheaper than asphalting. I am opposed to the great long sewer that is proposed to take the sewage five or six miles down the river, and if they keep it by the road they will not have sufficient fall to answer the purpose.

Mr Samuel Black re-examined.

1534. Chairman.—What do you say in reference to the first point dealt with by the evidence of Mr. Colligan, concerning the intended allocation of a portion of the Falls Park as additional ground for cemetery purposes, instead of for park purposes?—I may state in reference to that, that on the 1st of November, 1869, a resolution was passed by the Council to establish and maintain two public parks for the use and enjoyment of the inhabitants of Belfast, one the Ormeau Park and the other on the Falls-road adjoining the borough cemetery. That resolution was subsequently confirmed on the 1st of January, 1870, by a majority. Subsequently, however, the Corporation seemed to be of opinion that it was not desirable to establish the Falls Park, inasmuch as the distance out of the town was so great, and steps were taken to put the ground adjoining the cemetery into the market for public sale. On the 22nd of April a deputation from the ratepayers and inhabitants of the Falls-road district attended upon the Council, and represented their views, and thereupon the Council directed the proposed sale not to be proceeded with. However, there were two legal difficulties in the way of establishing a park there: first, the Public Parks Act of 1869 only gave power to establish parks within boroughs; second, our own Burial Grounds Act of 1866 required that the land not to be used for cemetery purposes, should be sold, and I advised the Corporation that a mere transfer or a nominal transfer from one committee of the Corporation to another, would not be a sale within the meaning of the Act. Mr. M'Clure and Mr. Johnston, the members for the borough, took a very active part in obtaining a public Act in connexion with the Parks Act. A bill was passed in 1872 (the Public Parks Amendment Act of 1872) by which Corporations got power to sell surplus lands that might not be required for the purposes of a cemetery. That Act, therefore, removed the first objection. Then came the removal of the second. The Corporation were anxious to get several additional powers by amendment of their local Acts, and application was made to the Local Government Board for a provisional order, and eventually the provisional order was obtained, and an Act confirming it. That provisional order removed the second difficulty as to the sale of the surplus lands for the purposes of park.

1535. That Act specified the sum to be given for the surplus ground to be £3,600?—It did. It never was intended that the entire of the surplus lands on the Falls-road should be devoted to the purposes of a park. The intention of the Corporation always was that under the provisions of that Public Parks Amendment Act of 1872, the portion of ground adjoining the park should be sold for building purposes.

1536. The same way as at the Ormeau Park?—Precisely. Previous to the Council going for the provisional order, the committee considered the question fully, and on the 24th of October, 1872, a plan—which I now hold in my hand—was prepared, showing how that surplus land might be disposed of to advantage, and laid out for building purposes.

1537. Was that plan submitted to the Local Government Board when the provisional order was applied for so that they had before them at the time the proposed allocation of this ground?—That plan was before the Inspector who was sent down to make the inquiry upon our application for a provisional order.

1538. Can you tell whether it was before the House of Commons when the Act was passed?—I don't know. I don't think it was. There was no opposition to the provisional order and it passed merely as a public Act. In framing the provisional order, the words which you referred to, or one of the Commissioners referred to, embodying the Public Parks Amendment Act of 1872, were considered by the counsel for the Corporation to be sufficient to enable the ground to be sold in the ordinary way.

1539. They were introduced expressly for that object?—Yes.

1540. You have since had an opinion from Mr. May, Q.C., that they do not effect that object?—Just in the same way that doctors differ we have had different opinions on the subject. Mr. May said they did not, and Mr. MacDonogh gave an opinion to the effect that they did. Some new members came into the Corporation from time to time from 1873, and certainly some members were of opinion that it was not then desirable to establish the park there at all, and in addition to that the ground in the cemetery was being taken up and occupied much more rapidly than we had at all anticipated, and we found that if the ...

rate of interments continued as at present, and for some time back, in six years' time we would not have a single grave to dispose of unless we went into the reserved portion of the cemetery—the ornamental part and what was reserved for walks.

1541. In point of fact how much of the forty-five acres is reserved as ornamental ground?—I could not really tell you the quantity.

1542. Mr. Colligan said in his evidence that if a proper allocation of the cemetery ground was made sufficient space could be found for a considerable number of years for the interment of poor persons—in fact the class of persons for whom this ground is wanting. Have the Corporation considered that?—Some of the graves are now first-class graves; there are second-class graves and so on, and the price varies from £9 per grave down to £3. I understood Mr. Colligan's statement to be that if we reduced the higher priced portion of the ground we would have enough of the poorer class of graves for a considerable time.

1543. We will ask Mr. Colligan. (Addressing Mr. Colligan.) My impression is that you said in your evidence that if the present allocation of the ground was altered there could be a sufficient portion set apart for the interment of poor persons at a low charge to last for a considerable number of years?—Mr. Colligan.—You are quite right.

1544. Then I understand that you also proposed to allocate for the like purpose the whole or part of the ground set apart for Catholics and not used?—You are quite right.

Mr. Black's examination resumed.

1545. Has that view ever been presented to the Corporation and considered by them?—I have no recollection of that view ever having been considered by the Corporation.

1546. Have they been applied to to consider that view?—Certainly not; they have never been applied to. It would totally destroy the ornamental character of the cemetery if you did so.

1547. I want to know if Mr. Colligan's objection and the objection of Mr. O'Neill and those they represent with reference to this reserved thirteen and a half acres, has been represented to the Corporation, and whether the Corporation could not by a fresh allocation of the cemetery grounds obtain all they require for the burial of poorer persons at a cheaper rate without infringing on the ground which was originally intended for a public park?—I think not.

1548. This matter has not been considered by the Town Council?—No, it has not.

1549. Mr. *Colligan*.—We think it is the duty of the governing body to reallocate the present burial ground before they go and seek for other ground.

1550. Chairman.—We want to know whether any representations had been made to the Council on this subject. Mr. Colligan has stated that it is a very short time since Mr. Montgomery and Mr. Carlisle gave evidence with regard to these grounds.

1551. Mr. *Black*.—Under our present arrangement we have space for only about 3,370 graves available, and taking the ordinary average of the sales of ground six years would dispose of every one of these graves.

1552. At the rate you have been going on lately?—Yes. We have still about 4,800 additional graves in places which have been reserved in order to give convenient passages to those graves which have been let. If these have to be used, the result will be to a certain extent to shut up the ones that are occupied and taken, and will do away with the facilities which exist at present for getting to them.

1553. Of course many of these are vaults, not single graves?—Yes; enclosed with railings.

1554. Which will be required to be open for other members of families?—Yes.

1555. In order to use that ground available for the 4,800 graves, do you say you would have to use the ground now occupied to a great extent by walks and approaches to the existing graves?—Yes.

1556. In point of fact the ground in the Protestant portion of the cemetery has been used to a greater extent than the Corporation anticipated when they set apart forty-five acres for this purpose?—Yes, that is the case, although the cemetery was only opened in 1869, we have had about 10,000 interments. The exact number is 9,878.

1557. And the only space left, according to the calculation you have made, without encroaching upon the roadways and ornamental grounds, is 3,370 graves, or about six years' requirements?—In the public ground—where a poor person is buried on payment of 2s. 6d. we have plenty of room.

1558. What do you say to the evidence given before the Local Government Board inspectors at the inquiry by Mr. Montgomery and Mr. Carlisle, which was mentioned by Mr. Colligan?—I do not know what evidence they gave.

1559. When you propounded the scheme of devoting this thirteen and a half acres to cemetery purposes, did you mean that ground to be used for the free burial of poor persons—as public ground?—Certainly not. There are numbers in town of the poorer class who don't like to have their friends buried at the public expense. I think as far as the public ground is concerned there is space enough for a considerable time. After the lapse of fourteen years we can reopen the graves in the non-proprietary portion of the cemetery—that is the time specified by the Act.

1560. At the time the provisional order was obtained, you did not anticipate having to add to your cemetery?—Certainly not.

1561. What you intended was to sell off as building ground the surplus portion of the land?—Yes.

1562. But you now desire to devote it to cemetery purposes?—Yes; exactly so; and Mr. Macdonogh advised us that we had power to do so, and Mr. May considered that we had not any such power.

1563. I see there is marked on the plan of the cemetery, the site of the Protestant and Roman Catholic mortuary chapels. Why was the chapel not erected on the Roman Catholic portion of the ground the same as on the Protestant?—The Protestant one has only been erected within the past year, and the other would have been erected at the same time had the Roman Catholics availed themselves of the portion of the cemetery allotted to them, but they declined to do so.

1564. Why did they not avail themselves of the portion of the cemetery allotted to them?—An application was made on behalf of the Roman Catholic bishop, that certain rules should be made by the Corporation, which rules I have in writing. They required firstly, that the sexton and gravedigger for the Roman Catholic portion of the cemetery should be Roman Catholics, subject to the approval of the Roman Catholic bishop for the time being, and also be dismissed by him without his being obliged to assign any cause for so doing; secondly, that persons who committed suicide should not be buried in that portion of the cemetery, nor should any person be allowed to be buried there who should be deemed by the said bishop, or person authorised by him for such purpose, to be unfit to be buried there; and that in the sales or lettings, a clause to that effect should be inserted in the conveyance.

1565. That is the sale of any portion of the Roman Catholic ground for interments?—Yes. Thirdly, that an annual stipend should be paid by the Corporation to such Roman Catholic clergyman as should be nominated by the bishop to act as chaplain of the cemetery at the burials of Roman Catholics. These were the rules that were proposed on behalf of the bishop to the Corporation, and also some other rules subsequently, very much to the same effect.

1566. What was the answer of the Corporation to that?—That as the Corporation were trustees for the public they could not delegate their powers to any authority outside the Corporation.

1567. Did the correspondence then cease?—By no means. The bishop went to the Privy Council and tried to get the rules I have detailed to you established, but the Privy Council refused his application.

1568. Is that the last feature in the case?—As far

Dec. 18, 1876.

Mr. Samuel Black.

BELFAST.
[illegible]
Mr. Samuel Black.

as I know that is the last feature. Before the application to the Privy Council there was an application from the bishop or his solicitors to purchase from the Corporation those fifteen acres so as to get absolute control over that ground. That was made in 1869, prior to the application to the Privy Council, before the rules were passed for the regulation of the cemetery.

1569. Was the application to purchase outright before the application to you to grant the bishop those powers which you declined?—It was.

1570. The first application from the Bishop was to purchase the ground. That was not in consequence of the refusal of the Corporation to grant his proposals?—No, but it was declined.

1571. And then came the application for those powers?—Yes.

1572. And when those powers were refused him he applied to the Privy Council?—He did. The case was argued on behalf of Bishop Dorrian and the Council, and the rules as proposed by the Corporation were approved of. The Privy Council, on the application of the Corporation, at that time virtually closed up the other burial grounds within the borough, except in certain cases, where interments were allowed in proprietary graves.

1573. And the intra-mural burial-grounds were closed?—Yes.

1574. Were we correctly informed when we were told that since that time no Roman Catholics have availed themselves of the privilege of burial within that cemetery, except some persons who were considered outside the pale of the Church?—As a matter of fact very few interments have taken place in the Roman Catholic portion of the cemetery—not more than six or seven. They have established a cemetery of their own very close to ours. Had the Roman Catholics availed themselves of the cemetery the burial rate would have ceased at a much earlier period than it actually did. Next year will be the first year that we can do without a burial rate; that would have arrived several years ago had the Roman Catholics availed themselves of our burial-ground.

1575. We were told yesterday that a small portion of this ground had been set apart for the burial of Jews. Is that so?—Yes, but it was a later transaction altogether, and done with the sanction of the Lord Lieutenant. It is a total fallacy on the part of Mr. Culligan to say that that has been done on the same terms as proposed by the Roman Catholic bishop. The Corporation retain the absolute control of that portion of the cemetery. The Lord Lieutenant in Council approved of the allocation. The thing was done in the most regular manner possible.

1576. Was there any favour shown to the Jewish community that was refused to the Roman Catholic community?—Certainly not.

1577. How many burial rates have you levied?—Since we purchased the cemetery every year, down to and including the present year?

1578. What has been the highest rate?—I think 3d. Last year it was 1d.

1579. Is it 1d. this year?—1d. this year, and 1½d. last year. There will not be any rate next year.

1580. Mr. Kernan.—Are the rules I hold in my hand the rules afterwards sanctioned by the Privy Council?—No; these are the second set of rules proposed by the bishop.

1581. Did you ever make any rules yourself with regard to the Roman Catholic portion of the cemetery?—We made rules applicable to all the portions without distinction.

1582. Were the rules you made the same for Roman Catholic and Protestant burials?—Quite so.

1583. Was it simply because the Roman Catholics did not make use of their portion of the burial-ground that you have not erected a mortuary chapel?—Upon that ground alone.

1584. Are the Corporation ready to erect a mortuary chapel as soon as the Roman Catholics avail themselves of their portion of the Corporation cemetery?—That has not been decided upon, but I am sure that if the Roman Catholics would only avail themselves of the ground allocated to them, a mortuary chapel would be erected for them forthwith.

1585. Would the Corporation give them the same amount of money to build a mortuary on their own ground?—I cannot say that.

1586. Were any rules submitted by the bishop before your rules were made?—These rules were submitted by the Roman Catholic bishop, and were brought before the Privy Council in opposition to the application of the Town Council for confirmation of the rules made by them for the allotment and management of the ground. The Privy Council disallowed the cases drawn, and confirmed the views of the Corporation. The Roman Catholic bishop's rules were made a *sine qua non*, and we could not possibly adopt them.

1587. Did you make any objection to the first rule of the bishop's? Can you give us the answer of the Corporation to the bishop?—I suppose it was in writing?—I believe the terms of the answer are on the minutes. I know they were taken into consideration by the Council, and they could not by any possibility adopt any of them. The Privy Council confirmed that view.

1588. The proposed additional rules came after your answer to the first?—They did.

1589. Chairman.—The first thing was that those rules that you read were submitted?—Yes.

1590. Then you sent an answer declining to accept any of them, and then was followed by a further set of rules very much to the same effect as the first?—Yes, very much in the same sense as the first—in fact the essential difference between the Corporation and the bishop was that the bishop insisted upon having the absolute control of the Catholic portion of the burying-ground in his own hands, and the Corporation, as trustees under the Act of Parliament for the public, were advised that they could not possibly yield that control.

1591. Were those plans of the graveyards submitted to the Privy Council, with the sites of both mortuary chapels marked on them?—Yes; and there was a *bona fide* intention to carry out that plan, which intention will be performed, and a second mortuary chapel built, I have no doubt, whenever it may be required.

1592. We will now proceed with the next complaint. You appear to think that Mr. Macdonogh's opinion is at variance with Mr. May's. Do you think you are right in that, because the case on which Mr. Macdonogh gave his opinion assumes that the Corporation thought a public park was unnecessary there? Did the Town Council ever pass a resolution that it was unnecessary to have a park there, or that those thirteen and a half acres were unnecessary for a park?—Oh, no. They passed a resolution declaring that there should be the forty-five acres for a park, and that the thirteen and a half should be reserved for building purposes. I think Mr. Macdonogh's opinion fully justifies their doing so.

1593. Mr. Culligan says that he and many others in his district are of opinion that less is done by the Corporation for the Falls Park than for the Ormeau Park, and for the Falls-road neighbourhood generally than for other parts of the town?—Well, I think that opinion is incorrect.

1594. Chairman (addressing Mr. Culligan).—You said yesterday that you considered less was done by the Corporation for the Falls Park and for the inhabitants of that neighbourhood rather because, as I understand you, the poorer members of the Roman Catholic community live out in that direction. Is that the impression you intended to convey?—Well, I didn't use the words, but really that is the impression on the minds of the majority of the inhabitants of that district; and if I wished to push the matter further, I could get evidence to prove that certain members of the Town Council have made use of expressions which bear me out in the impression I have formed.

Mr. Black's examination resumed.

1595. Chairman.—What do you wish to say with reference to that allegation?

1596. Mr. *Black*.—I think if you will take the accounts for the past year, you will find that that impression is totally erroneous. The Ormeau Park is 160 acres in extent, while the Falls Park is only forty-four or forty-five. If you take the rentcharge and taxes out of the sum spent on the Ormeau Park, you will find the outlay is only £1,113 17s. 9d. in the last year. We have a rent of £106 0s. 9d. to pay on the Falls Park.

1597. The rent that you have to pay for that park is a charge on the cemetery ground generally, is it not? —No; it is exclusively a charge on the park grounds.

1598. How is that?—Because we could not have the cemetery ground subject to a rent, and under the Burials Act of 1866 Lord Donegal was enabled to release the cemetery from the rent, so that it is a total fallacy to say that the rent is not payable out of the Falls Park. The expenditure of £1,113 17s. 9d. on Ormeau Park from the receipts of £396 11s. 4d., leaves a net balance of £717 6s. 5d., and that on Falls Park during the same period very nearly £480.

1599. Then you have been expending more money within the last twelve months than is shown in the audited accounts before us?—Oh, yes.

1600. In fact nearly double?—There is in the printed account only half a year's expenditure.

1601. When did you commence work on the Falls Park?—Not until after February, 1875, the accounts for both parks terminated at the same part of the year, but the expenditure on the Falls Park didn't commence till the middle of the year. The total expenditure on the Falls Park for that year, including rent and taxes, was £665 0s., less miscellaneous receipts amounting to £103 13s. 6d.

1602. Was that from the sale of grass and so forth? —Yes; leaving the expenditure £555 13s. 6d.

1603. That is from August, 1875, to August, 1876? —Precisely; and if you deduct then £106 0s. 9d., for rentcharge, it leaves the net expenditure, on the Falls Park, £479 12s. 9d. Having regard to the quantities of land in the two parks, I think that is a very reasonable sum for the Falls Park.

1604. That is £479 12s. 9d. for the forty-five acres? —Precisely.

1605. Now give me the same expenditure from August, 1875, to August, 1876, on the Ormeau Park? —The net expenditure on the Ormeau Park, exclusive of rents and taxes, was only £718 1s. 3d., for the same period.

1606. Were those sums of £718 1s. 3d. and £479 12s. 9d. respectively the net expenditure from the rates for the parks?—Yes.

1607. What was the total expenditure from the rates on the Ormeau Park for the year 1876?—£968 11s. 3d. One of the inducements held out to the Corporation by Mr. O'Neill when they were establishing the Falls Park was that it required no expenditure. That was before the park was established, now they take a different view. In addition to the expenditure on the Falls Park, we had a large quantity of shrubs and young trees in the cemetery which were originally planted thicker than they would afterwards be required to remain, so we transplanted them to the Falls Park and have not charged for them.

1608. What are the estimates for the next year's expenditure upon the two parks?—For Ormeau Park £1,030, and for Falls Park £460.

1609. I perceive you estimate the receipts at £250 on the Ormeau Park and £100 on the Falls Park?—Yes.

1610. Irrespective of the evidence you have given as to the expenditure on the two parks, was the Corporation ever influenced by any such motive as that which has been suggested in their relative expenditure on one park as against the other—any sectarian motive? —I think there is no sectarian motive or any other motive influencing the Town Council in any way in their expenditure on the respective parks but a considerable number of the members of the Council thought it was altogether a mistake to make a park so far out of town as the Falls Park, and would much prefer that one more generally available for the inhabitants of the borough should be provided in lieu of it.

1611. Is it a fact that the Corporation at one time decided to offer all that ground for sale, and to provide 100 acres elsewhere, but gave up that plan, from representations made on behalf of the inhabitants of the neighbourhood?—That is a fact.

1612. As far as you know are the Corporation prepared honestly to carry out the formation of that park? —They are *bonâ fide* carrying it out, notwithstanding the fact that some members of the Council feel it is a mistake to have a park there at all.

1613. Mr. Culligan has stated that there has been no disposition manifested by the Corporation to spend the rates on the Falls-road neighbourhood; that some time ago the people were promised that a certain portion of the Falls road should be flagged, and that was not done, although the Shankhill-road was flagged. Is that so?—That is incorrect; as a matter of fact the Corporation have been most anxious to lay the entire flags in a continuous line on all the important thoroughfares leading to the borough, but unfortunately want of funds has hitherto prevented them carrying that out to the extent intended. The flagging upon the Shankhill-road has been done, simply because the owners of property there have given ground to the Corporation to widen a portion of the footpath. In such cases, we either make the footpath for them, and gravel it if it is a considerable distance from the centre of the town, or we flag portion of it if it is near the centre, according to the value of the ground, and any gentleman who gave ground for the purpose of widening the road would get the same flags. The convent proposed to give us some ground, which was accepted; and I paid money for it in place of flags on behalf of the Corporation. They gave the ground, but in place of taking the value of it in flagging they preferred a gravel path, and curb bricks.

1614. That will not prevent you from flagging it eventually?—Certainly not.

1615. Millfield street was referred to yesterday?—That was purely private work to prevent the street from being built up, and in order to render the property in that street more valuable to the private owners. Of course to a certain extent it would be very advantageous to the public, but we have been most unwilling to establish the principle of opening up private property at the expense of the public rates, but when the owners of property come forward, and consent to pay a portion of the expense, the Corporation join them in keeping the ground open. It was complained here that we did not give the entire amount originally intended. The amount proposed to be given in the first instance was for leaving open the ground the full width of the street, but we were unable to get that, as the owner of the property had sublet a portion of it to another, and we could not deal with him, as his terms were ridiculously extravagant. Before the thing was at all spoken of, the landlord had let to the subtenant. We had no power to act in this case except as a matter of arrangement between the parties. We had no power to take these lands compulsorily.

1616. The impression conveyed to us was that by an earlier communication with the landlord and subtenant you could have got this ground?—We could have got it by paying an extravagant price for it.

1617. Mr. *Sexton*.—What do you call an extravagant price when the ground was for opening up the street to such a public place?—£140.

1618. Chairman.—Has not £100 been given within the last four or five months to the Water Commissioners for the purpose of allowing the Town Council to level a small bridge which rises over their main in Donegall Pass, and makes the street unsightly, and not so valuable to the owners of property?—Yes; that is quite true, and by means of that expenditure we have taken away one of the greatest eyesores from a leading thoroughfare in the town. The Water Commissioners had an aqueduct across one of the streets known as Donegall Pass, leading to the gas-works. It was actually dangerous, and they met the Corporation readily in the matter, and accepted £100 to provide a pipe to carry the water across. That outlay has removed a dangerous structure and a public eyesore.

Belfast,
Dec. 14, 1876.
Mr. Samuel Black.

1619. Have you not expended at University-road, in making a culvert, a very large amount of the public money? Where is University-road?—It is near the Queen's College; there was a watercourse belonging to the Commissioners crossing the street, and at a very small expense we were enabled to throw a culvert over that watercourse, and allow a continuous traffic across the street, instead of having it thoroughly blocked. It was a great public improvement, and one called for by the wants of the town, and the expense of it has been comparatively trifling.

1620. Mr. Galligan complains that even some small part of the money produced by the rates is not laid out in his part of the town. For instance, have the Corporation done anything with regard to the flagging of the Falls-road?—With regard to the flagging of the Falls-road, terms were made with the convent people, which amount to this—they gave thirty or forty feet of their ground, and the Corporation gave them £25, and they, the Corporation, were to complete the footpath, which they did with gravel. The improvement committee, in reporting their work for the month to the Town Council, reported that they had done certain things, and that they were going to run two feet of flagging there.

1621. But I want to know if they put down any flagging where Mr. Galligan says it was promised?—Not yet.

Mr. Montgomery, Borough Surveyor, re-examined.

1622. Chairman.—A comparison has been instituted between the Shankill-road and the Falls-road. How much of the Shankill-road has been flagged, if any?—None of the Shankill-road has been flagged, except where the owners of property have contributed portion of the cost of the laying to do it; and the same thing has been carried out on the Falls-road in six or eight different places.

1623. Do you flag only opposite the houses of individuals who give you ground?—Sometimes we pave and sometimes flag. Not one of the leading streets was paved a few years ago, and one of the earliest we took up was this very Falls-road. It has several names, and it is one of the great leading lines of road leading from Castle-place. Since the time that I was appointed the Corporation commenced paving all the great leading roads, and the Falls-road was one of the first. It is seven or eight years ago since we paved it with Welsh sets; from Castle-place to Park-street. Now, speaking offhand, that would be £5,000 worth of work. There is a great arterial sewer made in it from Castle-place to Durham-street, and we are engaged at the footways still. From the time of the complaints of the inhabitants of the Falls-road, a great many places have been repaired and curbed, and crossings been put in. We have had a great many applications from the Falls-road, and at every time something has been done. I assure you I never heard a promise given that the Falls-road was to be flagged, except when it was in the power of the Corporation to do so. I have had no complaints of want of drainage in the remainder of that road. It occupies a ridge, and there is a valley on each side of it, and a great number of new streets have been laid out, either on or abutting on that road. I, myself, have paved and drained a great number of them, and it happens curiously enough that there is no flooding on that road, as there are so many cross streets with sewers running in both directions, that the pressure is carried off and flooding is avoided.

1624. That applies to the surface-water only?—All the houses built are drained, and until yesterday, I have had no application for a main sewer on the Falls-road.

1625. How are these houses drained?—There are a great number of streets on both sides; they all are sewered, and the sewers fall towards these valleys.

1626. It is a sort of spine, as it were?—Yes; it falls both ways. There are two valleys, and the streets are drained efficiently, although there is not a main sewer. The water is taken off by gully drains. One reason why the Falls-road district has not been more sewered is that there has been no pressure put on the Council. Immediately pressure is put on the Council, additional sewers will be made in that sewerage district, like the other four districts. The plans have been partly prepared, and were suspended, because we have had no complaints.

1627. As the houses are built along that road, you are surely bound to see, if you have not got a main sewer, that there are proper conduits for the accommodation of such houses?—These houses are drained into the existing sewers; they drain backwards; there are no complaints.

1628. Do you dispute the assertion that in the Falls-road there ought to be a main sewer which would be discharged into this main arterial sewer?—The time will arrive, and may already have arrived, when a sewer should be made in the Falls-road itself, because several of the streets on the right side of the road have only temporary contrivances, in the shape of six-inch and twelve-inch pipes. There is a twelve-inch pipe laid as a temporary contrivance for conveying the sewage of several streets, on one side to the outlet on the other side of the road. There are a number of streets near Mr. Galligan's house from which the sewage falls into the Falls-road, and passes across it by means of a twelve-inch pipe, which ultimately discharges itself into the main sewerage system of the borough. This pipe was laid, because it answered as a temporary contrivance until the proper time arrives for laying the new sewerage. It has never been inadequate to its work, and until now I never heard any complaint of it. If the owners of property in the neighbourhood like to have an expensive sewer, the Council will not prevent them. At three or four places along the road these temporary connexions have been made from the streets on one side to the streets on the other, in order to take off the drainage for the present. This is the first time I have heard a complaint; and now that a complaint has been made, I am sure the Corporation will be delighted to make the Falls-road into a drainage district. I am certain they will not prevent it. Their reluctance to do so only arose from the fact that they did not want to put the owners of property in a sparsely populated district to so great expense.

December 19, 1876.

(Before Mr. Cherry, Mr. Lawless, Q.C., and Mr. Exham, Q.C.)

Dr. Dorrian, Roman Catholic Bishop of Down and Connor, examined.

1629. Chairman.—I believe you wish to give us evidence as to the grounds on which the Roman Catholic people of Belfast do not avail themselves of the portion of the cemetery set apart for their use by the Corporation?—Yes, I have attended for that purpose, and I may direct your attention to the Act of Parliament by which the Corporation were empowered to possess themselves of land for the purposes of a cemetery. That Act of Parliament not only makes provision for the allocation of parts of that cemetery to the different religious denominations, but it also makes a very striking provision—namely, that the head of each religious denomination shall be at liberty to bless or consecrate for the use of his people the portion of the cemetery allocated to them. It confirms me, therefore, that the Legislature could not have intended to make the Act [illegible] for me by offering me power to consecrate the ground if in reality I had substantial reasons in my own conscience not to do so. I had an objection to consecrate the ground so allotted to the Roman Catholics, because our ecclesiastical law books [illegible] both the cemetery and the Church

BELFAST. Oct. 25, 1864. — Dr. Dorrian.

are the same, and subject to the same rules; and I could, therefore, no more consecrate a cemetery or graveyard without a title or lease, or some assurance that I could protect it from desecration, than I could consecrate a church. No bishop could think of doing such a thing, and no religious denomination would have a church without a tenure that would justify them afterwards in retaining it for the purpose for which it was intended. I was, therefore, anxious to know from the Town Council what was the rule by which it would be governed. The town clerk very politely informed me that as soon as the rules would be made regulating the cemetery he would supply me with a copy of them. My object was to see if the rules contained anything which would give to the bishop for the time being the right to prevent the ground which was intended for Catholic interments from being desecrated. I came over to the office of the town clerk to look at the map or tracing, in order to ascertain what was the portion allocated for the Roman Catholics, and on looking at the map, I thought it was very objectionable that the Catholic portion of the ground was, as traced, in a kind of horse-shoe form, the centre portion of which was to be retained for the interments of Protestants and Presbyterians. This portion was decidedly far away the best portion of the whole ground; and I found then that the Roman Catholics were thrown on one side as a counterpart for the poor Presbyterians who were thrown on the other side, and one day on the grounds, in the presence of the mayor and the chairman of the cemetery committee, and I think the town solicitor, I objected to that, but I was told that the Protestants and Presbyterians had arranged to bury promiscuously. "Oh," I said, "if that be so, I am therefore precluded from making any objection, though otherwise I might have a fair right to have a share for the centre as well as the sides." I was present in the town clerk's office at an investigation held by Dr. Knox, Poor Law Inspector, and heard a member of the Town Council state that the Protestant bishop was going to consecrate a portion of the cemetery for himself, whereupon the town solicitor, addressing that member of the Town Council, said—"Sir, you have no business to make use of a private observation." I did not know at the time that the Protestant bishop was going to consecrate a portion of the ground for his people, and I considered that if that statement was a truthful one faith was not being kept with me, for I was distinctly told that Protestants and Presbyterians had arranged to use the ground promiscuously, whereas in reality it turned out afterwards that the Protestant bishop has since then consecrated a portion of the cemetery for the use of his people. However, I waived that, and simply asked the cemetery committee to treat us fairly by at all events drawing a line straight up from the road to the extremity of the cemetery, and to give us a fair chance of whatever of the centre would fall inside it. They said that was fair, and could not be objected to, and it was done; but there was another misstatement made that was injurious to me, which was that I had required a wall twelve feet deep to be built between the portion allocated to the Roman Catholics and that allocated to the other denominations.

1630. The statement made to us was that there was to be a small fence, but not that you required a stone wall?—I merely required that there should be a simple line of demarcation—a chain for instance, which I thought would be sufficient for all practical purposes. I then stated to the committee, that my greatest objection was—what would be the assurance that I or the bishop coming after me would have hereafter, that that ground if consecrated by me could not be alienated for any other purpose, or used for the purpose of other interments. I knew by the law of my church that I was precluded from consecrating the ground, unless I had some assurance of that kind. I then made four different offers to the Corporation.

1631. We have had before us two sets of rules?—At all events I may state to you that there were four offers on my part. The first one was the written set of conditions in which I showed what I as Catholic bishop must require. That is, that the ground should be under the care of a sexton appointed by the bishop. The other offer was that I would take the portion allotted for Catholic interments at the price it cost the Corporation, and pay them the money for it. That was refused. Then I was told to put my propositions in writing, and that I would get an answer. Another proposal I made was that the Corporation should retain sanitary control over it as far as the walks, and so forth were concerned, to pay them a yearly rent, and to take a lease in perpetuity, but insisting on the appointment of a gravedigger to be under the control of the bishop for the time being. Evidently the sexton would not have much to do with it; the gravedigger was the person who should open the graves, so that unless he was responsible to the bishop for the time being, the ground might be used against our laws and Church government; and the last offer I made was that as they had surplus ground outside the boundary wall I was prepared to take fifteen acres of it, and to give up all claims on the ground allocated to us inside the boundary wall, and pay them what it cost. That was refused—in fact, every one of the proposals I made was rejected and there never was a proposal of any kind made to me, nor any kind of assurance given to me, that I or the bishop that might come after me, would have any control over that ground, beyond what the Corporation might be pleased to concede.

1632. Were the rules you proposed submitted to the Council by you, or by your authority?—Yes, by myself.

(The Chairman then read the rules submitted by the bishop.)

1633. Those are the first set of rules?—Those rules embody everything that I have been saying. The point about the chaplain receiving annual remuneration, I argued on the strength of the fact that, at Liverpool the Roman Catholic bishop had received the same—given under the sign manual of the Home Secretary, and I look upon that as good as any lease or bond. If I had got anything of the same sort or any assurance from the Corporation as to the ground, I would have gladly accepted it, as marked out and intended.

1634. After submitting the first set of rules, did you receive any answer in writing from the Town Council?—The answer of the Town Council was invariably to the effect that my proposals could not be entertained.

(The Chairman read two letters from the Bishop to the Town Council, and also the resolutions on those letters.) See Appendix No. 11, page 212.

1635. Your letters do not seem to refer to any rules of the Town Council?—I think the rules of the Town Council were rather an answer to my rules.

(The Chairman read the report of the cemetery committee, dated the 10th July, 1863.)

1636. Was the application to the Privy Council to sanction the Corporation rules?—Yes.

1637. Did you then try to get the Privy Council to sanction yours?—Yes, and they adjourned the argument from Wednesday until Saturday to see if some arrangements could be come to. On the first day Mr. Justice Keogh suggested to the committee of the Town Council that there was nothing to prevent their going home and passing a resolution on the books, giving the Bishop what he wanted. That was stated by Mr. Collins, and it was quite true. Mr. Justice Keogh by making that statement satisfied me that the Town Council had power to do what we wanted if they chose to exercise it. Mr. Bates, in his statement before the Privy Council, suggested that they should give the longest possible time before closing Friars Bush burying ground, in order that we might either come to terms with the Town Council, or go to the Court of Queen's Bench for a mandamus requiring that the Corporation as trustees for the public should make the ground really useable by the Catholics, which it was not in that condition. On that application they adjourned the case until the 25th of November.

1638. Did Mr. Barr settle your rules?—Yes. The Privy Council also suggested that we would have the opportunity in the meantime of looking out for a cemetery of our own in case the Town Council did not come to terms with us. I did not ask anything but what had been conceded elsewhere in Limerick and at Liverpool.

1639. Did the Town Council after that make any further proposal to you?—No; and when I saw they were not disposed to come to terms with me, or give me any assurance of protection over the ground that I might consecrate, I felt a conscientious objection to consecrate the ground, and the law of my Church obliged me to follow that course. I was still anxious to come to terms upon which I could use the ground if possible, but finding that hopeless, I then adopted what I considered the peaceable mode of settling the matter—that was, when the Town Council would not come to anything like reasonable terms with me, to withdraw from their ground, and seek out a cemetery for ourselves. A little inaccuracy took place on the last day this matter was before you. It was stated that we had expended £500 on the sewerage of our cemetery. Our cemetery cost us £4,100, and for sewerage fourteen feet deep, and not four feet, as was stated, it cost us £3,000 in addition, in all £7,100, including the cost of making the main entrance to the road. At the same time that we have paid that money for our new cemetery, we have to pay our share of the taxes for the other cemetery, which we cannot use.

1640. Mr. Exham.—Does the £7,100 include the cost of the purchase of the land?—Yes, it does; £4,100 was for the purchase of the land, and the rest for the sewerage and the fencing around, and the road-making. We were, therefore, enabled to open our cemetery in proper time, when I found it was practically useless to have any further correspondence on the subject, as the Town Council were not disposed to do what we were advised they could do, that is, make the ground useable for the persons for whom they were trustees, and in order to make it useable it should be consecrated by me. I do not think the Legislature meant to insult me by saying to me, "You may consecrate that ground, but it must be at the peril of your own conscience, for it may be desecrated." I don't think any fair man would do so.

1641. When were the rules which were prepared by Mr. Barr given to the Corporation?—I think they were handed in during the adjournment of the Privy Council in Dublin. I may observe that Mr. Macdonogh stated to the Privy Council, as counsel for the Corporation, that his clients would be most willing to make any arrangement they could, with the view of bringing about a satisfactory settlement of the matter. That statement gave us hopes that there would be an arrangement arrived at, but unfortunately those hopes were not realised, though I did my best to make a conciliatory arrangement in the matter.

1642. There is one thing you should be aware of. We found that there was no Roman Catholic mortuary chapel on the grounds, and we asked the reason of that. Mr. Black told us that the site for that chapel was fixed upon at the time the Roman Catholic ground was marked out, and that the only reason the chapel had not been built at the same time as the Protestant mortuary chapel was in consequence of your having opened another cemetery of your own, as the Roman Catholic population would not avail themselves of the cemetery of which the Town Council are trustees, and he undertook that if the Roman Catholic portion of the cemetery was used the Corporation would provide the same kind of mortuary chapel in the Roman Catholic as in the Protestant portion?—The Corporation surely could not expect that I would hand over to their custody a church or cemetery that I would consecrate. A mortuary chapel is not of so much importance to us as the burial ground, for this reason, that at all our funerals the office or requiem takes place in the church near which the person dies, and then the funeral goes away.

1643. Did they ever tell you that they were willing to put a resolution on their books, that for all future time the ground should be dedicated to the use of the Roman Catholics?—Never, and the great difficulty is this—who is to be the judge of who was a Roman Catholic. Surely the Town Council were not to be constituted judges as to whether certain persons were Roman Catholics or not.

1644. Did you ever receive any proposal from them after the conclusion of the case before the Privy Council?—Never. It was my anxiety on my part to try and get any arrangement made by the Town Council to settle the matter.

Mr. William John Scott examined.

1645. Chairman.—You are the chairman of the committee of the Belfast Water Commissioners?—Yes, for this year.

1646. The Belfast Water Commissioners are incorporated under the Act of 1840, with amending Acts?—Yes.

1647. Have you been a member of the Water Commissioners' Board for some time?—Yes, for three years.

1648. In the course of the evidence before us, it was stated, that in consequence of the price charged by the Water Commissioners to the corporation, the latter were unable to obtain a sufficient supply for flushing the sewers and watering the streets without an expenditure that they did not feel justified in incurring. We wish to know on what terms did you offer to supply water to the corporation for that purpose?—We have never been applied to by the town council officially or otherwise, as far as I know, or as the records of the books of the water corporation show, for water for that purpose exclusively.

1649. Or the watering of the streets?—That is another question.

1650. It was stated that there was a higher rate charged to the corporation than to the general public?—The terms upon which they have received water for watering the streets, by special contract, is 4d. per load. Their carts hold something like 250 gallons. That is a higher average charge than we are in the habit of charging for water for other special purposes. We made this contract with the corporation, and they know the grounds of it well. It was based upon the 67th section of the Belfast Water Act of 1865; the town council knew perfectly well the price they were to pay for this water when they made the bargain for it.

1651. Have you got the contract with you?—I am not sure whether there was any written contract; but both parties were aware of the arrangement. In connexion with the matter I may add, that we do not think the charge of 4d. a load, which they now complain of, for this water is too high, and we offered them other good water at 1d. per load of 250 gallons, which is 70 per cent. cheaper than the ordinary scale for selling water for special purposes.

1652. Do you not supply water at 6d. for every 1,000 gallons to private consumers?—Our charge varies from 1s. 6d. to 6d. Here is our scale of charges. (Hands in document.)

1653. Is there an actual contract?—There is simply a written resolution to supply the corporation at 4d. per load of 250 gallons for watering the streets.

1654. Am I to understand that at the same time as you offered them the water at 4d. per load, you also offered them water from another of your sources at 1d. a load?—We did. We have works that are now useless for the supply of the town, owing to their being at so low a level. We offered to give them water there at 1d. per load of 250 gallons. It is not because it is bad, but it is because we are not able to utilise this water that we are able to offer it to them

Belfast. Dec. 16, 1876.

Mr. William John Scott.

so much cheaper. It is better spring water than some of the water we are now using.

1655. Could you have given them an ample supply of water from that source for watering the streets?—Yes. I may add, that there is a great waste of water in filling the carts from the hydrants, so that the quantity taken from us is considerably more than the quantity paid for. Of course we do not complain about that.

1656. Is this your last proposal in writing dated 21st April, 1876, and addressed to Mr. Graham?—It is, and states that the application of the Town Council for watering the streets is granted on the same terms as last year, 4d. per load from the fire plugs and 1d. a load from Basin-lane. That is the north works.

1657. Is it equally easy for the Town Council to get their supply from Basin-lane as from the fire plugs?—It is equally accessible; it is in a leading thoroughfare, and they could fill their carts in a few moments.

1658. Would it incur additional and what expense?—I have heard it stated that the reason why the Town Council preferred taking water from the pipes, at what Mr. Black called an exorbitant charge, was the saving of expense, as the drawing of water from Basin-lane works would cost on the average from 10d. to 1s. a load of 250 gallons, and therefore that our high pressure supply was cheaper.

1659. What causes the difference?—If they draw water from the north works they may have to draw it two miles or more; it is a long distance to parts of the Antrim-road and the Falls-road.

1660. The best proof is which water do they take?—The pipe water, and they take it in summer when it has been a question with the Commissioners whether they could give it at any price, inasmuch as our supply for some years past has been insufficient, and it has become increased in consequence of new works. It was a great question whether we could give it or not to the Corporation, but rather than stand in the way of what would be for the general benefit of the town, we risked our position as Water Commissioners with the ratepayers in giving this water for that special purpose when we were unable to supply it for domestic purposes, according to the Act of Parliament for the twenty-four hours of the day.

1661. What was the price charged to the Council for watering the streets in 1868 or 1870?—I cannot tell you that.

1662. Mr. Lawless.—By your printed statement of charges I find that for the supply of two millions of gallons the charge is £58 10s. 4½d. a quarter. How many gallons would the Corporation take in a year?—Upwards of five millions.

1663. And it is stated in that scale that any quantity in excess of two millions of gallons taken in any one quarter shall be 5½d. per thousand?—That refers to people taking it all the year round.

1664. If they consume more than two millions, why do you charge them in excess of the prices put forward in your statement of prices?—These charges are fixed as yearly charges, but payable quarterly by persons taking large quantities of water for the use of mills and factories, whereas the Corporation want it only for a short time, perhaps for two weeks or one quarter, as the case may be. We have other private charges much higher, for instance, the charge for water for shipping purposes—8s. 4d. for the first thousand gallons, and 5s. for the subsequent ones.

1665. The 97th section of the Act of 1874 declares that you shall provide, and keep constantly laid on (except as therein) a sufficient supply of water for the cleansing of sewers, drains, for cleansing and watering the streets, and for supplying any public pumps, baths, or washhouses that might be established for the use of the inhabitants, and that same shall be paid for as therein provided. Are you not bound to supply water for the flushing of the sewers and the watering of the streets?—Yes, but we are to be paid for it; and besides before we give water for any special purpose we must be in a position to supply the ratepayers' dwellings inside the borough with water for each of the twenty-four hours in the day.

1666. Was it ever suggested that the Corporation should have the price of the supply of water for the purposes of the borough regulated by two justices of the peace?—Not to my knowledge.

1667. Was it always a matter of contract between you?—Yes. I always understood so.

1668. Did they know your scale of prices?—Yes; they had copies of all our public documents.

1669. There is a resolution of the 18th August, 1874, requesting the Corporation to take all the water for the streets from Basin-lane. Was not that practically making them pay 10d. to 1s. a load including cartage for the water you were giving them for a penny?—As we were bound to provide a sufficient supply for the ratepayers, we asked the Corporation to stop taking water from the pipes. The supply was getting deficient through, and it was on that ground alone they were asked to do so. They were charged as long as we could spare it to them, 4d. per load for the high pressure water, and afterwards a penny per load from Basin-lane. In our original agreement we reserved the right to stop the supply from the pipes at three days' notice, and we did so. We take away the fire plug water from the Corporation when we are likely to be short for the ratepayers, but not otherwise.

1670. Mr. Exham.—Did you take it away from the mill owners at the same time?—I think that would be the next step very likely, but we did not do so then, because it would be a very injurious matter to the town of Belfast; it would be injurious to the portions of the town where the people might be turned out of the mills for want of water for condensing purposes.

1671. Chairman.—These are the facts, in April you made a proposal which was accepted, that you would supply the corporation with water at 4d. per load from the fire-plugs. In August, you gave them notice to terminate the supply from the fireplugs, and unless there was a fresh agreement they were entirely dependent upon Basin-lane for their supply?—Yes.

1672. And that was owing to necessity?—Yes, otherwise we would not have taken that course.

1673. I understand you to say that you had entered into no agreement with the corporation with regard to flushing of the sewers?—I wish to state that it is a fallacy on the part of the town council, or any of their representatives, to put a matter like that before you, as they did in regard of want of water for flushing the sewers. It is well known to the borough surveyor, and though Mr. Black does not, he should know that it is impossible, owing to the construction of the sewers of Belfast, to introduce our high-pressure water to flush them in the proper sense of the term. The sewers are not constructed for that purpose, and in the second place, the great majority of the sewers on the low level districts of the town are lying at a lower level than the main sewers that form their outlets, and the result is, that these sewers have from eight to ten inches of solid matter and stagnant water lying in them all the year round, and in order to flush those sewers before you fill the outlet portions, as a matter of course you will have the low-level sewers flooding the people's houses, and driving all the injurious gases into their apartments, and all the stagnant matter into their back yards through the gratings. I have further to add, that I know sewers in Belfast, even in a high-level district of the town, where actually the water staying in the sewer is within eighteen inches of the fire that the people cook their meat upon. I speak now of the north-west districts of the town where the sewers will not deliver their contents.

1674. Could you mention a district in which that is the case?—In Little York-street the stagnant matter is lying all the year round in the sewer eight and nine inches deep, and the way in which it is got rid of is, that it is opened periodically in long lines, and the stuff thrown out in the streets and carted away. All

M 2

BELFAST.
Oct. 18, 1876.
Mr. William John Kemp.

the using the Water Commissioners present would not flush a sewer like that. Of course you would destroy the people's property in every way if we were to give a supply of water for flushing sewers which are not constructed in a way that it is possible to flush them.

1675. Has any application been made to your board for water for the flushing of the sewers, and have the difficulties you have referred to ever been described to the corporation?—I am not aware personally.

1676. Is the water always available for the purpose of extinguishing fires?—Yes.

1677. Have there been disputes between the Water Commissioners and the Corporation with reference to the fire-plugs?—That is a very serious matter, perhaps in some respects more important than the other. We have from time to time as a Corporation separate from the Town Council, been endeavouring to do our utmost to prevent any such altercations between the Water Commissioners and them, and also to provide water for fire purposes in as large quantities as our works could furnish it. We have given special attention to that, which I think you will say is right and proper. We have in the entire borough of Belfast 1,061 fire-plugs. It has been stated by Mr. Reilly, the superintendent of the fire brigade here, that these fire-plugs are not in sufficient quantity. We have the quantity I have named in the limits of the borough. We have an additional quantity of fire-plugs provided in private warehouses and mills, which any manufacturing establishment can have on application to us by paying 10s. a year, which we charge for the maintenance of such fire-plug and its appurtenances. These 1,061 fire-plugs cost us £8,300. The Town Council should have paid for them according to our interpretation of the terms of the Act of Parliament, but they have not.

1678. Have you applied for payment?—Yes, by letter of the 9th March, 1876, for any plugs.

1679. Mr. LAWLESS.—When were the fire-plugs put down?—Some were fixed when the high pressure water was laid on, and additional numbers since. The 30th and 31st sections of the Act of 1840 clearly show that the Town Council are liable for the cost of those plugs; and I may also refer you to the 39th and 40th sections of the Waterworks Clauses Act of 1847. As they have not paid for the plugs I suppose they owe us the £8,300. I will read you a copy of a resolution passed at the Water Commissioners' Board, and sent to the Town Council on the 9th of March, 1876, which should have prevented any misunderstanding with regard to these hydrants for taking water for fire engines—at least we thought so:—

"Belfast, 9th March, 1876.

"DEAR SIR,—I am instructed by the Waterworks Commissioners to write to the Police Committee of the Town Council, that in accordance with the request made by the deputation which waited upon them on the 18th of January last, they directed their engineer to report to them as to the fire-plugs of the borough, which report has been made, and before proceeding further they request to refer the Police Committee to the 39th and 40th sections of the Waterworks Clauses Act of 1847, and to know if the Corporation is prepared to pay the cost of additional fire-plugs.

"I am, dear sir, yours faithfully,

"J. S. M'KENNA, Secretary.

"James Guthrie, Esq.,
"Town Clerk."

1680. Did you get an answer to that letter?—We have never got an answer to that polite note. We have never heard anything about it, although they complain of insufficient facilities for getting water for fires.

1681. You got no answer?—No; although we are prepared to provide all that is necessary. I may further call your attention to the meeting of the Belfast Water Commissioners published in the *News Letter* of November 10th, 1876, at which Mr. Gaffikin, a member of the Town Council and of the Board of Water Commissioners, gave us a very high character in connexion with the supply of water for fire purposes. The statement of Mr. Gaffikin was as follows:—

"Mr. Gaffikin said he had the pleasure of being present on Saturday last, when the men belonging to the fire brigade went through a course of drill for the purpose of exhibiting their efficiency. He saw the hose attached to a [illegible] main for the purpose of ascertaining the pressure of water. The supply was most copious and convinced them what could possibly come through the hose by an engine. The water was able to be thrown a distance of seventy feet. The fire brigade would not want a steam fire engine if they had a [illegible] main through the principal streets in the town, and he hoped the Board would be able to see their way some time or other to have large mains all through the town for the purpose."

1682. How did the question arise that caused that statement to be made as to the fire brigade with reference to the water supply. Was there any question before the Water Commissioners with regard to the supply of water for extinguishing fires?—No; at that moment there was a particular reason for the remarks I have read to you. The fire brigade superintendent takes out his engines periodically at times to try them and to see if they are in good working order, and in the course of the drill a line of hose was attached to one of our ordinary water-pipes, and that was the result produced. I may say that very likely what led to that remark of Mr. Gaffikin's, was this—we have had several complaints from sufferers at the time of fires of the want of water, and when we inquired as to the real cause of these defects we found it was on account of the superintendent not having given proper notice to the man specially appointed by the Water Commissioners, and approved of by the Town Council, to look after the fire-plugs, and turn on the proper valves for each fire. We generally found that this man was not sent for, but could not find out the reason. I know that very recently a deputation of our body waited on the Committee of the Town Council to discuss this question with them, owing to a serious matter that occurred at a fire in Kingan-street, as was alleged by Mr. Reilly, from the water not being turned on at the proper time. We found in that case that the wrong valves were turned on, and that sent the water through a very circuitous route to the required spot, in place of having the valve turned on that would have sent the water direct to the place, and it was not caused or was represented generally by the want of water, but the fault of mismanagement. The man's name who turns on the valves for fire purposes is M'Clenton. He gets his ordinary wages from us, and £7 10s. extra for the plugs, and he is entirely under Mr. Reilly's control for fire purposes.

1683. Is it his duty to turn on the fire-plugs, or the duty of the men going with the engine?—It is the duty of this man, on being informed of the exact place of the fire. He knows the proper valve to turn on. It is the duty of M'Clenton.

1684. The 42nd section of the Act of 1847 (the Waterworks Clauses Act) requires the company supplying the water to keep the mains always full for fire purposes. Do you do this, or is it necessary under your system to have the required supply of water turned on to the plug from which it is necessary to work?—The large mains are constantly charged, except in case of accident, &c.; but in streets where there are lesser ones the water is turned off constantly for repairs and other purposes, and then by the man getting notice of a fire the water is at the spot as quick as the fire brigade.

1685. Except for repairs are the mains and service pipes to which the fire-plugs are attached always kept full?—Nearly all are; but some of the service mains are not always kept full. They can, however, be filled at a moment's notice.

1686. But that is one of your obligations?—Well, we have occasion to turn it off for reasons of our own, and which we cannot avoid.

1687. Is that the cause of the deficient supply?—In some cases it may occur in that way, and for repairs. If a pipe in a house breaks, the landlord or owner will send for a plumber to get it repaired, and in that case the water is turned off.

1688. Is the water in some parts of the town turned off for parts of the day?—Yes, sometimes in the winter time, and in summer, when the supply is limited and intermittent, that is also the case; but it is not so in certain streets. Our present high-service reservoir, from which we get our principal supply for the centre of the town, is 250 feet above the ordnance datum, and gives 40 lbs. of pressure on the pipes. That will explain Mr. Gallagher's description of the height the water was thrown at the time he saw the fire brigade being exercised. The supply is equal to 5,650,000 gallons a day coming into the town—that is, twenty-five gallons per head per day. I make this statement to show you that we have really a comparatively sufficient supply of water, and that our pipes are not deficient, as represented in some cases. We are now at the present time spending £4,000 in running an eight-inch main pipe from a new reservoir that is just completed to the Ardoyne district, where they never before had water from the Water Commissioners. We have also in the course of completion two additional reservoirs, which will add considerably to the supply of the town. They will increase the present supply to 6,000,000 of gallons a day, and will be completed in a short time. We improve the main pipes where they are too small by laying larger ones, and so on. This will be equal to seven months' supply for the town of Belfast—that is to say, we will have provided sufficient storage, when these two works are completed, to supply the town of Belfast at the rate of 5,000,000 gallons per day for seven months.

Belfast.
Jan. 22, 1878.

Mr. William John Scott.

1689. Mr. Exham.—Without any rainfall?—Yes; that will be the result of our storage.

1690. Are there fireplugs in all the streets of Belfast?—Yes. I don't know about the lanes, but there are some in all the public streets.

1691. At what distances are they fixed in the streets?—We have a great number fixed on the average at about eighty yards distance from each other throughout the main streets of the town. As a rule, the mills are provided with them if they think proper to apply for them. (A map showing the mains laid throughout the town was produced by the witness and shown to the Commissioners.)

Mr. Robert Carlisle examined.

Mr. Robert Carlisle.

1692. Mr. Lawless.—You wish, I understand, to give some evidence with regard to the water supply of this town?—Yes, and also with regard to some sanitary matters.

1693. Are you a Water Commissioner?—Yes, from 1867 to 1871, and I was a member of the Town Council from 1870 to 1873, and I was also general inspector for the Water Commissioners for one year. I am now Public Works contractor. As a member of the Town Council and also of the Water Board I took a very active part in connexion with the general working of both trusts. The Mayor of Belfast is an ex-officio member of the Water Works Board, but I am sorry to say that very few mayors ever attend. Before 1865 the greater portion of Belfast was supplied by what is known as the Smith Side Works. It was a low-level supply pumped up at two points. The springs yielded very small quantities, and the greater portion was pumped out of the Lagan, a polluted stream into which the refuse of Lisburn and Lurgan and some other towns flows. In 1865 the Commissioners were empowered to borrow £145,000, having previously borrowed some money under the Act of 1840, thus making a total debt of £314,000. The works that were designed under these plans were for supplying 4,000,000 gallons per day, but unfortunately the borrowing powers were not sufficient, and rather more than half the works were not carried out for want of borrowing powers, and the suggested supply was not obtained.

1694. Were the borrowing powers exercised?—Yes, and £14,000 was paid out of the rate over and above. The Water Commissioners finding that the 4,000,000 gallons of water secured in 1865 was not sufficient went again to Parliament in 1870, but the Bill was lost; they went in 1874 for further powers which they obtained, and these works are at the present time being carried out.

1695. Under the Act of 1874?—Yes, and when the works are completed they will be able to put the full powers of their Act into force and give a sufficient supply.

1696. Does the Act of 1874 enable them to raise further capital on loan?—Yes; it enables them to raise £130,000 in addition to that borrowed previously.

1697. Did they under the powers obtained by the Act of 1874 enlarge or make a new water supply?—Yes; the works are now in progress. As well as expending the amount of money which they are entitled to borrow they have expended on laying mains and pipes through the town, from 1865 to the present time for fire and general supply purposes, in round numbers rather over £36,000 out of the rates, and they are still going on as the former witness (Mr. Scott) stated laying these pipes. New mains are being laid at the present time, and I presume they intend to go on until the whole thing is completed. While they were doing all these works they reduced their water rate from 1s. 3d. to 1s. in the pound.

1698. Is that the rate for the domestic supply?—Yes, and they reduced the fire rate from five pence to two pence in the pound. With regard to the special rates I may say that when I was elected I found the special supplies in a very bad state, and a committee was appointed to inquire into and fix them.

1699. Will you explain what you mean by special supplies?—Water used by parties other than domestic consumers.

1700. Does that include the mills?—Yes; unfortunately they do not use much clean water. I took some trouble to procure a uniform rate to be charged all parties. I had letters written to the principal towns in England, Ireland, and Scotland, and got their tariffs of charges, and afterwards this book was compiled which covers all cases, and has given I believe general satisfaction. We afterwards found that a great number of people in the town were taking the water without paying anything for it. In some cases I myself found it out, and in one large mill I found they had a branch pipe directly fixed to the Water Commissioners' pipe, and they were using the water for condensing purposes. I thought that the Commissioners' men could not be doing their duty, and I took some trouble myself to find matters out. I child up late in the evening, and got up early in the morning, and I found the men were doing their duty. I then knew there must be something wrong, as the water was still being used, and was unaccounted for. I had a suspicion that some of the water of the Commissioners was being taken without their knowledge, and I took men with me to this mill, and we broke up their floors, and discovered their pipe. The parties were brought before the magistrates and fined, and a great many others were fined in the same way. That was partly what led to the compiling of this book, which has answered the end we had in view. In some cases the Commissioners had considerably to reduce the special rates, and in others they had to raise them so as to bring them all as nearly as possible to the same price.

1701. Mr. Exham.—You say your fire rate is now reduced to two pence. Do you keep any separate account of that, and apply it to the keeping up of the mains?—No, it would not pay for the keeping up of mains. There is no separate account kept. It is not required by the Act of Parliament. With reference to the flushing of the sewers, there is always in winter a large amount of water running waste to the sea, and the Commissioners believed this would be useful for

Belfast.
Jan. 19, 1878.
—
Mr. Robert [illegible].

washing out the sewers. I myself brought the matter before the police committee of the Corporation, so that with the consent of my brother Commissioners that we would gladly give the water that was then running to waste for flushing the sewers.

1702. In what year did you bring it before the committee?—I believe that was in the year 1871. Mr. Montgomery was sent for at the time, and he stated that there was plenty of water for flushing the sewers from the ordinary rain-fall, and that in reality the sewers were not constructed to be flushed out as I proposed or in some English towns.

1703. Did you propose any resolution at the meeting of the police committee?—No.

1704. Is there any record of what then took place upon the books of the council?—No; nothing was done. I know now of my own knowledge that the sewers are so constructed that the principal streets of the town could not be flushed out. The reason I know them so well is, that while I was inspector of the water commissioners, there was a great deal of wasting of water, and I had to open the sewers in a great many places over the town, and I found all the principal streets round by Victoria-street, Anne-street, and Corporation-street, up almost all occasions choked full of water; when the tide is in they are entirely full. The sewers from Dock Ward and Corporation-street I found in a very filthy state, with the water resting in the most part of them, so much so that we were not able to trace the run in any way, and could not ascertain where a burst in the main-pipes took place. Since that the corporation never asked the commissioners for any water for flushing the sewers, and had they done so up to the time I left the Board, they would have given it to them in the winter time free of charge. In the summer time they had not enough for domestic purposes on account of the works not being finished. I may say, the commissioners have always given the corporation a full and free supply of water for what is generally called sanitary purposes—viz., flushing the street urinals, and a supply for drinking fountains or water troughs put up by the town council and the humane society.

1705. CHAIRMAN.—Are you not bound to give a certain amount of that by the Act of 1871?—No.

1706. Is there not some provision of that kind in the Act?—Not that I am aware of. Up to the year 1868, before I was a member of the town council, so far as I can remember, they were in the habit of pumping water for watering the streets from the river Lagan, from the waste in connexion with the starch side works; this water was very filthy, and when used on the streets, particularly in the very hot weather, it caused a very bad smell, and was injurious to the health of the town. There was then an arrangement come to for one year between the water commissioners and the corporation, that they were to take the water at 3d. per load from Basin-lane. Finding that they could save a large sum on cartage, the corporation arranged to pay 4d. a load for water from the fire-plugs. In some cases they had to cart the water from Ballymacarrett or the Lagan, a long distance, and could only draw twelve or fifteen loads a day, while from the fire-plugs they could cart perhaps forty or fifty. It was in 1870, or perhaps 1871, the arrangement was brought about by which they were to pay 4d. a load.

1707. Was that the first arrangement?—Yes.

1708. Was there no arrangement before that to take it at 1d.?—Yes, but they used that water only in the streets in the immediate vicinity of the Basin-lane works. Mr. Hiltrick and another inspector went into the matter, and found that by taking water from the fire-plugs at 4d. per load it would save the Corporation £400 or £500 a year. You will find the report in writing in the records of the Corporation. One reason why the Water Commissioners charged so much was on account of the great waste in taking the water from the plugs, but they are not very particular about the quantity taken; they allow them to count the loads themselves. There was also a proposition made that if the Town Council would put ordinary valves on the plugs to save waste the Water Commissioners would take the reduction of the rate into consideration, and an arrangement was come to that they would go to that expense, but unfortunately I was not a member of the Boards then, and the arrangement was not carried out. I am sure that the Water Commissioners have tried, and are still trying, to assist the Corporation in every way in their power, and if those valves were put on, I have no doubt they would reduce the rate, for I believe from what I saw myself that there was more water wasted than was carried away in the carts. Before the special rate of charges was compiled the Water Commissioners had special rates for summer and winter, but they found the people were not satisfied with that, and they made it uniform, and those who only take the water in the summer are charged an additional rate.

1709. Is water which is taken only for the summer made a matter of agreement?—Yes; the only other water supply which comes into comparison with that for watering the streets is that for shipping. It is taken out of the plugs in the same way. They charge a good deal more for it than they do for the water for the streets.

1710. Are you not obliged to keep people specially for working that supply?—Yes, and that is on account of the waste also. We are obliged to keep one man, but even without his wages being added, the shipping supply is still very much dearer.

1711. Is the shipping supplied at one place only or all along the quay?—All along the quay. I may further tell you that the supply of water here can scarcely be considered a sanitary matter, for the Corporation never get any except the principal streets of the town watered. In the streets where the shops and warehouses are, their owners only pay the 3d. rate, and they are watered twice a day, while the streets in other portions of the town are never watered at all, and yet the residents there have to pay the 6d. rate, and therefore it is hardly fair that the people who pay the highest rate should water the streets for those who only pay the lower rate. The former get their streets well watered and the latter never get theirs watered at all.

1712. Do you mean the private streets where there are nothing but private houses?—Yes.

1713. Do you mean to say that these streets are never watered by the Corporation?—Yes; I mean to say that they are not watered at all.

1714. Mr. KEMAN.—Do they water High-street and the principal streets?—Yes.

1715. Do they not pay any other rate there?—No; nothing but the 3d. The people who have those places live outside the borough, and pay no water rates at all. In a great many cases I know the residents never see the water-cart at all, and in a great many cases the streets are well watered elsewhere. It is hardly fair to call what is done by the Corporation in this respect a sanitary matter. The water for legitimate sanitary purposes is given free by the Water Commissioners.

1716. Do you know whether the Corporation use the water from the Pound Burn for watering the streets?—Yes; up to 1869 they watered the streets out of the dubeary, where the Lagan and the Pound Burn, both empty. At one time it was taken out of the mill-dam, which is the worst part of the Pound Burn for watering the streets. It may have been done last year also, but I believe it was not.

1717. Is there high pressure enough in the pipes at night, in case of fire?—Yes, in all the principal streets.

1718. Is it confined to the principal mains?—It is in the mains in all the principal streets. The whole system is this. It is equally divided on three districts—the low, high, and middle. When the whole of the works are completed, which they are carrying out as quickly as possible, these districts will have separate and distinct reservoirs, so as to equalize the pressure. They will also have direct connexion with all their works and mains, so as to be able to turn on a greater pressure in the case of fire, to any place required.

1719. Mr. Lawlor.—Would it not be necessary to have a man on the spot to do that?—They have a man called M'Cadden, who has been a long time in their service. He is paid £7 10s. a year by the Corporation. When the Corporation came to the new building M'Cadden could not hear the alarm-bell ringing, and an arrangement was made by the Corporation that one of the firemen in the yard should go at once and knock M'Cadden up. All the time I was a member of the Water Commissioners there never was a complaint of the want of water in case of fire except once—when a complaint was made (since I ceased to be a Town Councillor or Water Commissioner) which was examined into, and it was found that M'Cadden had not been knocked up by the Corporation men for some years.

1720. Mr. Exham.—Did the Corporation, to your knowledge, ever complain that the branch pipes were shut off from the mains at night?—Mr. Kelly, the superintendent of the fire brigade, would much rather have them constantly on; but that cannot be done, for if it was you could not get water in the summer to supply the town.

1721. Is it on account of the insufficiency of the supply?—It is only since 1865 that the Commissioners have got any supply at all. The town is growing very rapidly, and there is leakage also, which lessens the supply.

1722. Do they leave the branch mains turned on during the winter months when they have plenty of water?—As much of them as they can safely. There should be no difficulty in turning them on at any moment, and I never heard any complaint when M'Cadden was there.

1723. But if he was not there?—I never heard of a case in which M'Cadden was not there if he was sent for.

1724. Is he not your officer?—He is the officer of the Water Commissioners for town-cock purposes, and the officer of the Town Council for fire purposes. If any complaint was made they would inquire into it, but there were only two complaints I ever heard of. I wish to add, that the people here are unanimous in wishing that the Water Board should be kept separate from the Corporation.

1725. I find on the 18th March, 1870, there was a report which is signed by James Sinclair, one of the street inspectors, that "there would be a saving of from fifteen to twenty per cent. by taking the water for watering the streets from the fire-plugs as compared with the cost of taking it from the pumps?"—Yes; and you will find another one after that showing the annual saving on the year by taking it at 4d. from the fire-plugs. When I was a member of the sanitary committee there were complaints made frequently with reference to the Blackstaff and Pound Burn. A special committee was appointed by the Town Council, of which I was one, to inquire into the matter. This special committee then appointed Alderman Hughes, Mr. Dixon, and myself as a sub-committee to inspect the Blackstaff and both branches of the Pound Burn, and to make a report to them. This was about the summer of 1873, and we made a unanimous report to the committee, which ought to be on the books of the Corporation.

1726. Mr. Dixon gave us the draft report, but it appears that the report was not put on the minutes in extenso?—No; Mr. Black advised it should not be put in, as it would do them harm.

1727. Were you a member of the Town Council then?—Yes; and a member of the sanitary committee, and appointed on the special committee.

1728. Then why did you not get the report put on the books?—The meeting of the committee was adjourned by a side motion (we understand these things pretty well in Belfast), and there was a large attendance at the next meeting of members who were not in the habit of attending. They were there to prevent it from going on the books.

1729. Mr. Lawlor.—Do you complain that your recommendations were not considered at all?—My complaint is that the nuisance is still existing. There were some places where we could not stand on the banks owing to the smell, and people were living quite close to it. I had no idea it was so bad as it was until I went and examined it. They would not put it on the books at all. They positively refused to allow our report to be put on the books.

1730. This is the minute of the meeting of the special committee on the Blackstaff improvement on the 17th September, 1873, Mr. Dixon in the chair:—"The special committee having inspected the entire line of the Blackstaff and Pound Burn, suggested that one sewer should be connected with another, and then resolved that the suggestions agreed upon should be referred to the borough surveyor to consider if they were practicable, and would take the sewage out of the Blackstaff and Pound Burn, or if he would recommend any steps of a like nature."

1731. Mr. Exham (to Mr. Black).—I think there must be some mistake about this. Was there a report made by the special committee?

Mr. Black.—I cannot say.

1732. Mr. Exham.—Does the minute I read last refer to a meeting of the special committee only?—Yes.

1733. Mr. Lawlor.—The next record in relation to this, after the meeting on the 17th September is a meeting of the Blackstaff committee on the 31st October:—

"Resolved.—That the committee stand adjourned till this day week, in order to enable the special committee to confer with the surveyor on the subject of the report made by the special committee on the inspection of sewers on the 17th September last."

Then the next meeting is on the 28th October, 1873. Meeting of the special Blackstaff committee. Minutes of the Blackstaff committee of 21st were read, when the surveyor submitted the following report upon the suggestions in the committee report of the 17th September to the committee. The surveyor's report is then read. It is a very long report, but the sum and substance of it is that the report of the committee is impracticable. Then there is a further meeting of the sanitary and sewerage committees on the 29th October, 1873. Minutes of the meetings of 17th September and 21st October read, and also a report from the special committee:—

"Resolved.—That the following be reported to the Council:—That your committee have considered carefully the entire question of the Blackstaff nuisance, and a scheme of sewerage [illegible] to the practicability of the suggestions made by the special committee they request permission to continue their inquiries, and if necessary to employ a qualified engineer at a cost not exceeding £100.'"

Did this Committee—that is the sewerage and sanitary committee—read your report made to the special committee?—Mr. Carlisle.—Yes.

1734. Was anything since done by the Town Council or the sewerage and sanitary committee in pursuance of this resolution?—Nothing. I left the Corporation shortly afterwards, and nothing was done after I left.

1735. Did they not appear to you in October to be disposed to follow out the report of your sub-committee or at all events to have the matter considered?—No doubt they appeared so at first, but unfortunately I and the other members who were active in the matter were put out in November, and things got back into the old groove again. All that time we were most anxious to get our report on the minutes, but we could not manage to have it done.

1736. On the minutes of what meeting did you try to have that report entered, and which you say was refused?—The joint meeting of the law, sanitary, and sewerage committees.

1737. Mr. Exham.—Were you present at that meeting?—I was.

1738. Mr. Lawlor.—Do you mean to say that you

BELFAST. [illegible] Mr. Robert [illegible].

and others applied to have that report put on the minutes, and that the others refused to do so?—I do positively, and they did so on the advice of Mr. Black, the solicitor. We considered it was a most important report to have put on the minutes, so that our opinion of what we had seen might be recorded, and something done with it. We found on examining it, that it was so much filthy sewerage going in it that caused the bad smell. It was caused from the sewerage and other matter being emptied into this reservoir, and taken into the mills and heated, and then sent out in a hot state. The smell arising from it was something very bad. After it was sent out from one mill, it was taken by those further down and heated over again, and sent on to the north, so that it was gradually getting worse and worse.

1739. Mr. Exham.—Must not the using of this water, mixed with sewerage, in the state you describe, for the purposes of generating steam in a mill, have been very injurious to the health of the people working there?—Very injurious. I observe from the reports in the newspapers that Mr. Conner gave some evidence here with reference to his factory in contradiction of our report. I may say that we did not find anything wrong in his factory—it is mills up the Falls-road that are the worst. We found they all used polluted water, and further polluted it themselves. The factory we found the worst is the one in Agnes-street. Unfortunately they are mostly all aldermen and town councillors who are connected with it.

1740. Mr. Lawless.—How do you mean connected with it?—Connected with it as directors.

1741. Is it a joint-stock company?—Yes.

1742. What is the name of it?—It belongs to the Brookfield Linen Company. In its own neighbourhood it is known as the Agnes-street Weaving Factory.

1743. Mr. Exham.—Is that the place where you broke up the floors and found the four-inch pipe?—Yes; they made a reservoir called a cinder inside the gate. It is enclosed all round by rows of workmen's houses.

1744. What is the extent of it?—It is about as large as this hall. All the sewerage matter from some streets there is now piped into it, and that is used for condensing and boiler purposes. There is also a spring that arises in a field a little further up called the Fairy well stream, piped into it so as to thin it a little, for without it the sewerage stuff would be too thick for boiling.

1745. Mr. Lawless.—Is it used for condensing purposes?—Yes; the sewerage of Haliday-street, Shaftesbury-place, and in fact, of the whole district around it is drained into it, and used for that purpose.

1746. Mr. Exham.—Are the houses round it drained into it?—Not that I know of.

1747. Mr. Lawless.—Do you say that the water from that reservoir is used for condensing purposes?—Yes; and after being used there the overflow is brought down to Hudson-street. Formerly a small river from that spring ran down there, but now it goes down with the sewerage to Hudson-street, and the factory there uses it also in a like manner, and the people there have complained frequently of the bad smell of the steam.

1748. What is the depth of the cinder in Agnes-street?—I do not know; I could not see the depth of it.

1749. Mr. Exham.—Did you see the water run into it?—I turned on the water in the people's yards and saw it running in; I made myself sure about it.

1750. Mr. Lawless.—You said that some of the drainage of these streets were conveyed by pipes into that reservoir?—Yes.

1751. By whom were those pipes laid?—I presume by the company, Shaftesbury-place belongs to them.

1752. But not by the Corporation?—No; by the Brookfield Linen Company. The Corporation permit of the sewerage pipes going across to that reservoir instead of making them discharge into the sewer.

1753. Does any stream run through that reservoir?—Yes; that small stream that runs from the Fairy Well mixes with the sewage and runs with it—that is the stream I described as arising in the field.

1754. Mr. Exham.—Do you know what the Hudson-street people do when this stuff is sent down to them?—They cannot help themselves now; they have to use it as they get it.

1755. Did they never do anything to prevent the people above from polluting it?—It seems not. After leaving Hudson-street factory it goes down the Shankill-road and it would find its way into the public sewers there, but the Corporation to oblige them put in a glazed pipe a little bit further up the Shankill road so as to send the water down the original stream bed. It is then used in Townsend-street foundry (now Mr. Owen's foundry), at least I think it is that foundry uses it. It then becomes lost in the sewerage of the Shankill-road, and the sewerage pure and simple is then taken from the Shankill road and sent down to another mill. It then goes down to Mr. Hardman's mill (that is, Smithfield mill). That is one branch of the Pound Burn, and it finally empties into the main sewer at Millfield. There is another branch of it in Mill-street. It is a branch off the Pound Burn (it is not called the Pound Burn) in Mill-street, where the Smithfield mill has placed a cinder. We went there to examine it.

1756. When?—At the time we were making the report. I examined it myself. It is just as bad a place as you could see. If you wish to see the cinder at the Brookfield Linen Factory it is there fully exposed. The stuff in it rises to within one foot of the houses, and perhaps it may be half a year in this state. In fact it is just as bad as bad can be. They draw their water for condensing purposes out of that and send it back again when they have used it into the same place in a heated state. The whole of that river is very bad. The dam at Millfield is as bad as possible, and very often it is allowed to overflow its banks into the street and past the people's doors. The matter was brought by myself before the Corporation but we were still met with the statement that they had no power to abate it. I did not believe that, however; my opinion was that under the Sanitary Act they had ample power to act.

1757. Was it ever brought before the Corporation since you left the body?—I do not think it was.

1758. Did you bring it before their notice since?—No; I did not since I left the Corporation. I think that is all I have to say with reference to the sewerage. It would repay the Commissioners to see some of these places. I would be very happy to go with them at any time.

1759. Mr. Lawless.—Is there any other matter you wish to refer to?—There is one small matter with reference to the closeness with which the town is allowed to be built up. I do not know of any town being built up so close, which is composed so much of the working classes as Belfast is. I think the Corporation should be compelled to purchase some patches of ground for parks or gardens, so as to ventilate the town. If they allow this to go on, and the town grows as it has been doing, it will be very unhealthy by-and-by.

1760. Are the houses built in such a way that the rows are placed too near one another?—Yes, it was tried to allow a passage of say four or five feet at the back of the houses, but it was found by the Corporation to be a nuisance, because carts could not enter them, and the people generally threw out their nuisance into these places. Instead of their public parks outside to which the people of the town cannot go, if there were small parks of one or two acres I believe it would be of very great advantage to the health of the people, such as in London and other towns.

1761. Do the Corporation require that proper privy accommodation should be built in every house?—Yes; I think they do. If they gave more privy accommodation I believe it would be more of a nuisance than anything else. I think they require them to be provided with sufficient privy accommodation. The people do not keep their yards as clean in Belfast as they do in other towns.

1762. Mr. Dunbar.—Do the Corporation clean out the yards?—The country people nearly always come and take away the manure when a sufficient load is collected. After a great fight I got a scale fixed of from 1s. to 1s. 6d. a load for cleaning out these yards. My impression is that the Corporation ought to clean them out free of charge.

1763. Do the Corporation see after it and make the people clean them out?—Their inspectors make them clean them out. I believe the officers of the Corporation do their work very fairly.

Mr. Isaac John Murphy examined.

1764. Mr. Exham.—I believe you wish to give us some evidence about the Blackstaff?—Yes.

1765. You are owner or part owner of a very large mill on it?—I have been. That is now the property of a joint stock company, in which I am not interested.

1766. What do you wish to say?—It is with regard to two branches of the nuisance. The one is a nuisance such as was described by Mr. Carlisle, from which a very bad effluvia arises, produced by sewerage matter from the houses going into it; and the other is the liability of the river to floods. It is utterly impossible that it could be dealt with as a flooding nuisance by covering over the river, as it would be absolutely necessary to make a separate vent for the flooded water in a different direction from that in which it runs at present.

1767. What about the sanitary condition of the river?—Supposing that there was such a flood-vent constructed as I speak of, and the present channel of the river left to conduct the ordinary flow of water along it—what may be called the summer flow of water—it will still remain an open sewer; but if it is relieved from the flood water there is nothing to prevent it from being covered in, and that would completely do away with the nuisance.

1768. Would not all the sewage matter then be carried into the Lagan?—Yes; but then I think it must go into the Lagan in any case. I do not know where it can go if not into the sea.

1769. Mr. Lawson.—As long as the present system of sewerage existed?—Yes. The line by which the channel of relief (as I may term it) should be brought must be through high-lying ground, from about the position of the distillery beside the Ulster Railway to the Lisburn-road or Donegall-pass.

1770. And do you think that scheme could be carried out at a reasonable expense?—It would require an Act of Parliament.

1771. Supposing it was got, do you think it would be of advantage proportionate to the cost?—I have no doubt it would cost a great deal, but I do think it would. There is no other town in the world of 200,000 inhabitants in which it would not be done.

1772. As far as you know the general wish of the ratepayers and people in the town, do you think they are anxious that it should be done?—No; I think it is not a question that has been before the people at all. It is an idea of my own.

1773. Have the people had before them and considered a good many schemes about this?—When I was a member of the Corporation, a good many years ago, it was thought that they were not in a position to take up works of this kind. I was a member of two committees appointed to inquire into this subject, and I advocated something like the scheme which I have laid before you. There is no doubt but that it could be carried out.

1774. Mr. Exham.—We have been told about the shocking condition of the water that is used by the mills and factories for condensing and other purposes. Could not the mills get water from the Water Commissioners for boiler and other purposes by paying for it?—I have no doubt of it—that is, if the Water Commissioners have the water to spare.

1775. Would much water be required for the use of one of the mills if proper appliances were adopted?—A steam engine with a cooler would require a large amount of water, but you can use the same water over and over again—that is, by using a cooler. The position that I take with regard to the rights of the mills along the river is that they have the right to use the water, and you cannot take that right from them without compensating them for it, and doing so would not get rid of the nuisance. There is no doubt the nuisance is made worse by being used and heated over and over again; but you have dirty water to begin with, and if there was not a single mill along it the Blackstaff is nothing more than an open sewer.

1776. From your own knowledge as a millowner, can you say that the nuisance is worse and worse as it comes out of each mill?—It is. It is bad from beginning to end.

December 20, 1874.

Mr. James Kennedy, J.P., examined.

1777. Chairman.—Are you a justice of the peace, and do you reside at Belfast?—Yes. I am a borough and a county magistrate, and live close to Belfast.

1778. What is your opinion with regard to the taxation of Belfast?—In my opinion it is very excessive, as compared with towns in England and Scotland.

1779. We know what the municipal rates are in the town. On what particular matters do you consider that the taxation is expended?—That would be going too much into the conduct of the Town Council. I only take results, and if I went into the details of the question I might be blaming a member of the Town Council, or some of the officers, unjustly. I only know this, that in Manchester their 8d. rate is opposite our 3s. 7d. one, and their 1s. rate is opposite to our 1s. 7d. rate, and the same thing exists in Scotch townships as well as in Manchester. I know that in Edinburgh the rates are 10½d. and 1s. 2d., and in Glasgow only a penny or twopence more than that. I have a son who lives in London whose house is valued at £100, and his taxes only amount to £17. He lives at Whitmore House, Upper Norwood. His taxation is only half what it is in Belfast, on the same valuation. I think we labour under a heavy debt, and have to pay a heavy sinking fund. My object in giving evidence is only to stimulate the Town Council to try and reduce the same.

1780. How do you consider your rates in Belfast as compared with Dublin and Limerick?—I think they are about the same as Dublin. I don't know about Limerick. In Cork I believe the water rate is only 4d., and the whole rates 4s. Now, our rates upon a good house valued at upwards of £20 amount to 4s. 6d. or 4s. 7d., and our water rate was 1s. 6d., and is now 9d.

1781. One gentleman said the rates were 4s. 7d., but he lived in a district where there was a special drainage rate. May I take it that 4s. 4d. is the municipal rate, except in special drainage districts?—Yes. There is another thing to which I wish to call attention, the way in which the death rate is kept in Belfast. I do this for reasons connected with the sanitary condition of the borough, as the sanitary authorities are always saying the death rate is so low. It is not kept for the borough, but for the whole union. The outside district is out of the borough entirely, and, therefore, the death-rate for the borough appears to be a great deal less than it really is. There ought to be one kept for the old borough, and one for the out districts, for nearly all our merchants, large shopkeepers, and town councillors, reside in the country, and the

BELFAST. Feb. 28, 1878. Mr. James Kennedy.

farmers of the neighbourhood are in comfortable circumstances. The true drawbacks to Belfast borough could then be seen.

1782. The next point to which I believe you desire to call our attention is the failure of the Corporation to fulfil the Act of 1853 as regards Ballynafeigh?—Yes.

1783. That is the Act which put the county Down on the same footing as the county Antrim?—Yes; we opposed that Act, and got it thrown out in 1847, and it was re-introduced in 1853. The reason we opposed it was this—in 1845 they raised for the town of Belfast £150,000; in 1846 they raised £30,000 for gas purposes, and in addition to that, Mr. [illegible] forgot to tell you, inadvertently, no doubt, that there was £44,000 borrowed without any authority whatsoever, and the whole of the £224,000 was spent on the town of Belfast. They levied the borough rate and other small rates off the county Down, and they never spent one shilling upon it. Therefore we objected. We were willing to pay our own rates, and for our own lighting and watching, but we objected to pay the rates and for lighting and watching of the town of Belfast. We objected to pay interest on the sinking fund of this debt, at least our proportion of it, and we opposed the Bill in Parliament; but the Committee of the House of Commons would not let us off, though we wanted to make our district into a separate township, the same as one of those about Dublin. We thought we could manage our own affairs for half the town taxes of Belfast, but the Committee of the House of Commons passed the Bill.

1784. The 28th clause provides that the corporation shall forthwith proceed to put in force the powers of the Belfast Act of 1845, and of this Act, for the purpose of completing, sewering, and repairing the several public streets within that portion of the borough situate in the county Down?—Yes.

1785. And the 29th clause is to the effect that £8,000 shall be set apart and applied as a contribution towards the sewers as in the townlands of Ballymacarrett and Ballynafeigh?—We thought that because the term "forthwith" was used in the 28th clause, that that meant at once and without any appeal. We appealed, however, to the House of Lords, and they inserted the 29th clause.

1786. By which they were to set apart £8,000. Did they not do so?—They did not. They got a main sewer made in Ballymacarrett that cost £17,000 or £18,000, and by the Act of 1853, and the universal practice all over the borough, the council paid one-third of the cost of the main sewer, and the owners of property in the neighbourhood paid two-thirds.

1787. The owners of property paid two-thirds in a certain way—one-third directly, and another third in the form of a special drainage rate?—We have received no favours in Ballynafeigh, nor have the streets been put in order in our district. We say that Ballymacarrett has had no advantage of that £8,000, and nothing has been spent at Ballynafeigh. There is no sewer in all Ballynafeigh.

1788. The answer given is, that more than £8,000 has been spent on sewerage and paving on that side of the river, either in Ballymacarrett or Ballynafeigh?—That must be a mistake, for there was nothing done but that main sewer, which was not done under the Act of 1853, and if there was any paving I believe the owners of property paid for it.

1789. Do you complain that whatever has been spent in Ballymacarrett, nothing has been spent in Ballynafeigh?—Yes.

1790. Is Ballynafeigh a distinct townland?—Yes.

1791. Why has the money been spent on Ballymacarrett and not on Ballynafeigh?—There has been only £4,000 spent on the former place, but that has been spent according to all former practice, and according to the Act of 1845; that is, that the corporation spent £6,000 on the sewer there, and the people paid the remaining 12,000. Ballymacarrett has not received one farthing of the money. I say that in fairness the £6,000 should be spent upon the two townlands, say £3,000 upon each.

1792. Do you say that the sum should be divided into fair proportions between the two townlands?—Yes; something like that. I do not object to getting something more for Ballymacarrett. That £4,000 under that Act of 1853 was never really expended as intended on special works in Ballymacarrett and Ballynafeigh. They did nothing but spend the £6,000 towards the sewerage of Ballymacarrett, which was no more than would have been done for that district according to their ordinary practice, as an ordinary drainage district; and it is therefore, I say, most unfair for them now to say that the £6,000 they spent on the sewer of Ballymacarrett was a *bona fide* compliance with the 29th section of the Act of 1853.

1793. Do I understand you to say that they have spent £6,000 in Ballymacarrett, but that it has not been in special works?—Yes; they have spent £4,000, but it has not been in special works, as provided by the Act.

1794. Do you consider, as regards Ballymacarrett, the town council have complied with the duty imposed upon them under the Act of 1853?—Certainly not. I would like very much to refer you to the 6th clause of the Act of 1853.

1795. Has that clause been contravened in practice in any way?—Well the owner of a valuable house with forty acres of land is not rated in respect of his demesne or mansion house, while a man who has no land at all pays 4s. 7d. local rates, water rates, from which the other is exempt.

1796. That is not the fault of the Town Council; that is the act of the Legislature?—Yes; but they promoted the bill which works this injustice.

1797. What you say is this—that the 6th clause of the Act of 1853 creates a hardship, inasmuch as a person who owns forty acres of land in a part of the borough where no streets have been formed, and on which no other dwelling-house is built in the immediate neighbourhood is liable to escape with a smaller amount of local taxation than the occupier or owner of very much smaller premises in a part of the town that has been built over?—Yes.

1798. Mr. Lawlor.—Do you complain of the unequal local taxation caused by this 6th clause?—Yes. It so happens that three committees claim exemption in a small district. There is a very curious fact with regard to the Blackstaff that has not been brought out. As you were told by Mr. Green the Falls-road sewer goes ultimately down Hightown, and then passes over a weir into the Pound Burn. When there is plenty of water, in wet weather—that water passes over that weir, but when there is no water at all, the Pound Burn is filled chiefly with sewage matter, which goes through a considerable district of Belfast.

1799. As compared with the taxation of the towns in England are you aware whether or not the valuation upon which the taxes are assessed is the same. Is it not the case that the principles of assessment differ?—Ours is the Government valuation; theirs is, I believe, a local valuation.

1800. Is it not upon the letting value?—I think not.

1801. Is it upon a local valuation?—Yes, at least several of my friends have told me so. I believe they do not take twenty-five or thirty per cent. off the letting value as they do here, which is a very good rule.

1802. With respect to the amount of the taxation of this town, and with respect to the expenditure of it—do you consider that the expenditure of the rates of this town upon the staff employed by the Corporation is excessive. I include the entire staff of every kind?—I do not think it is. With regard to that, what strikes me is, that some of the officers do not do their duty—particularly the sanitary officers. I think that is very clear from the evidence of Mr. Scott the other day.

1803. Chairman.—Do you think the salaries are excessive for a town like Belfast?—I think not.

1804. Mr. Lawlor.—Have you had considerable experience as a millowner?—Yes, it is fifty years since I went to the business.

1805. Do the mills and factories here to your know-lodge our water from polluted sources, and into which sewage matter has been discharged, for the use of the mills?—The mills and factories using the water which ultimately discharges into the Blackstaff must and do take polluted water, for they have nothing else. I have given up business for the past ten years, but I know that before that, if we could have got an abundance of water at a cheap rate we would have used it. It would be far cheaper for the mill-owners to pay for good water, if they could get it at a moderate price, than to be using the water of the Blackstaff, because it is so prejudicial to health, and it destroys one's boilers and machinery.

1806. Do you think it is prejudicial to the health of the workpeople?—Very much so. I knew a great many people who left the neighbourhood on account of the smell. The Rev. Dr. M'Ilwaine told me he [illegible] in his house in Howard street, and had to go, in consequence of the offensive smell, to live in the country. I built two mills on the Blackstaff in Brunswick street and Bedford street, and had to sell them afterwards, and my successors have built a very large warehouse, and I understand they are leaving those premises, because the young men are continually getting ill there.

1807. Are the majority of the mills within the area in which the Water Commissioners deliver pipe water?—At first they were not. Now they are.

1808. Would you have been willing to pay a fair price for pipe water instead of using the polluted water of the Blackstaff?—Yes; the last mill I had was a small one, and the price of water was, we thought, outrageously high. I, however, forget at this moment what it was at that time. I knew Mr. Foster Connor, who was examined here, and I inquired from him as to the price charged for the water, and I came to the conclusion that it was outrageously high. Besides that we knew that the Water Commissioners could not give us a supply adequate to the requirements of the millowners and guarantee to continue it.

1809. Was the price then asked practically prohibitory?—Yes.

1810. Would you have preferred getting it from the pipes instead of drawing it from the Blackstaff and the Forth River if you got it at a reasonable price?—Yes.

1811. Could you tell me the price at which the Water Commissioners would have supplied you with water?—I could not. They are not able to keep their mains always full. They have not the water.

1812. Do you say that they asked a price that was excessive?—Yes. I forget the price now because it is twenty years ago.

1813. It was before 1865?—Yes.

1814. They had not then the powers they have now?—They had not. I would be very sorry to cast any blame upon the Water Commissioners, because they have done their duty very well.

1815. CHAIRMAN.—Is it by choice the millowners take this polluted water or not?—They began to use it when carts were drawing water into every street in Belfast. Every one who could buy Cromac water used to do so. I used to purchase a barrel of that water every day for the use of my workpeople whom I would not allow at that time to drink the town water which was nothing else but the Lagan pumped up. At the same time, however, the Town Council or their officers were not to blame for that.

Mr. John Dwyer continued.

1816. CHAIRMAN.—I believe you wish to give evidence as to the neglect of the Corporation to carry out sanitary matters of importance?—Yes; it occurs to me that you have not all the facts relating to the Blackstaff before you. I saw the memorial from the medical gentlemen published in the Belfast *Northern Whig*, and as I happened to be the chairman of the subcommittee of the Corporation that took up the matter formerly I thought it right that you should have the report which came from them in order that you might understand the views they held on the subject of the Blackstaff at that time. (Hands in draft report.) There is one thing that you ought to have before you, and that is the reply given to the medical gentlemen, and the report made by the borough surveyor regarding the Blackstaff. If you recollect there was a memorial signed by a number of medical men sent to the Local Government Board. That memorial is dated the 15th of February, 1873, and with it were sent extracts from Mr. Montgomery's report of the year 1868, and that of the law and sewerage committees of the Town Council approved of on the 1st November, 1870. (Documents handed in.)

(The witness handed in the report of these matters contained in the *Belfast Weekly News*, of February 22, 1873.)

1817. *Witness.*—As chairman of the subcommittee of that time, I endorse every word of that report. I find that the 10th section of the Sewage Utilisation Act, of 1865, expressly prohibits under pain of indictment any person polluting a watercourse which is within the jurisdiction of the sewer authority, and the 11th section expressly prohibits the sewer authority from using the river as a watercourse. Now, from the report that was made at that time by the subcommittee we found that this law was violated, and we then came to the conclusion that we could not urge the injunction of the Corporation when they themselves were liable to be prosecuted.

1818. If I understand rightly it was upon that ground, Mr. May based his opinion, that they could not proceed against those parties, because at the time they were violating the law themselves?—I am not aware. I was told that there was an opinion of Mr. May stating that nothing at all could be done about the Blackstaff, but I never had an opportunity of seeing Mr. May's opinion. I now say that in my opinion the Town Council have not discharged their duty as public corporators—that there has been an apathy, an indifference, and a culpability in the discharge of their duty. I think the Town Council as a sanitary authority should be no longer trusted, and that the Local Government Board should be empowered to have those works that have been so long unattended to, promptly and efficiently done, and that the authority and control should be at once removed out of the hands of the present Corporation.

1819. That could not be done without an Act of Parliament?—If a Corporation are guilty of neglect, I think the Local Government Board have some authority, but if not the matter ought to be rectified for the sake of the people here at all events. In 1868 after we had the report of our borough surveyor relative to the drainage of the entire town, the object of the subcommittee was to abate this nuisance [illegible], and to allow the drainage of the entire town to be done by degrees, and not to saddle the town with so heavy an expense, all at once.

1820. There are certainly very considerable engineering difficulties?—Yes, there may be.

1821. Mr. LAWLESS.—At what time did you cease to be a member of the Corporation?—In November, 1874, I resigned.

1822. The last notice taken of that report made by the subcommittee of which you were chairman, was in October, 1873?—It was. I don't know whether I should go into further particulars about what took place, but the whole thing was pooh-pooh'd.

1823. Was it not brought before the Council again?—Not the report we made. The subcommittee's report was shelved at once. But I may tell you that the suggestions we made from an engineering point of view were done in accordance with the plans before us, and with the full concurrence of the [illegible] of the Corporation. I may further state that we had a very good [illegible] engineer, a member of the Corporation.

1824. Mr. Montgomery, however, entertained your plan subsequently?—Yes.

1825. Mr. [illegible].—Did they refuse to place this report upon the minutes of the Town Council?—Yes.

BELFAST. Jan. 22, 1878. Mr. John Gibson.

1826. CHAIRMAN.—Was there any motion made with reference to the adoption of that report?—No; it was postponed at once.

1827. MR. LAWLESS.—I have before me a minute of the Corporation of a resolution passed by them on the 1st of November, 1870, after reading the report of the 28th of October, 1870. The resolution is to the effect, that the following members of the Council be appointed a committee to inquire into the best means of abating the Blackstaff nuisance, and the removal of the cause of the flooding in the town, to report to a special meeting of the Council to be held on that day fortnight; and then follow the names of the committee of twelve appointed. Do you know whether anything was done in pursuance of that?—Nothing; the matter is getting worse and worse every day. I say the Blackstaff should be remedied, but they want to make it an excuse for a grand drainage scheme for the whole of the town. I say abate this murder nuisance, and then go over the rest of the town if it is required.

1828. That committee reported on the 15th November?—Reports and complaints have been made from time to time, since 1847, but nothing has been done.

1829. CHAIRMAN.—Have you any other matter you wish to mention?—Yes; I will not characterise the course that has been pursued by the Corporation with reference to the Parks Act; but I say that had it not been that I happen to be a member of the legal profession, I do not think the Falls Park would have been made. After the provisional order was obtained in 1873, and after the promises made by the Town Council, and the resolutions from the year 1869, up to the year 1873, I think it was a very hard thing that some members of the Town Council should attempt to (I am sure they would not do it in their individual capacity) repudiate their acts and break good faith with the public. Even after the provisional order was obtained there was the strongest possible attempt made to prevent the formation of the Falls Park.

1830. Did they not, however, yield to the memorial of the inhabitants?—They did not yield to the memorial at all, but I suggested that proceedings should be taken against them, and it was not until they were threatened with a mandamus that they complied.

1831. Did they not yield before the mandamus was applied for?—Yes; but not until they knew it was going to be applied for. There is another matter with regard to the park to which I think it right your attention should be directed. The chairman of the sanitary committee took a very active part in opposing the Falls Park. He is an old corporator, and he made use of the argument that the park was too near the cemetery, and that the result would be that people coming with funerals, and so forth, would not like to hear indecorous or unseemly behaviour when passing the park. Although that argument was made use of, strange to say, since they found it was mandatory to have a park made there, they have passed a resolution allocating the portion of the ground which the Act of Parliament requires to go for building purposes, for the purpose of a cemetery. I think that, knowing as I do what took place at the discussion on the parks question, is the most extraordinary proceeding of which I have yet heard, and if you refer to the Burial Act that was passed, you will see that it was never intended that the borough of Belfast should be confined to one burial ground, which is away at the very outskirts of the town. The present cemetery is in a most inconvenient position for the people living on the county Down side of the river, and I think they have a right to demand a burial-ground of their own, and not be compelled to travel three or four miles to have their people buried in the present cemetery.

1832. Have any of the county Down people applied for an additional cemetery on that side of the river?—I believe there was such an application, but nothing has been done.

1833. Did you apply to the Town Council for redress and failed to get it?—No; I wish to show that the Parks Act should not be violated by the granting of the additional ground they now claim for burial purposes, and that there is the absence of a burial-ground on the county Down side.

1834. MR. LAWLESS.—I wish to draw your attention to the 8th clause of the Act of 1866, which specially provides that the Act is not to prevent the establishing of a second burial-ground?—Yes.

1835. "And the council may proceed to provide the same by the purchase of land, &c."?—I live in the county Down, and I know the feeling of a large number of the inhabitants there, and I have no hesitation in saying that it is their feeling that there should be a second cemetery on the county Down side. There are fifty acres of surplus ground at Ormeau Park now unproductive, it appears—a beautiful park by nature—but owing to the Blackstaff nuisance it is not resorted to as much as it should be, and fifty acres of the ground are lying idle.

1836. Is the Ormeau Park on the county Down side of the river?—It is. Under the Parks Act they have a right to deduct one-fourth of the ground allocated for the park. There are 175 acres altogether, so that under the Parks Act they could sell for building purposes one-fourth of that. I only mention that matter for the purpose of showing that there is plenty of ground for a cemetery on the county Down side of the river, and that ground is lying unproductive, owing very much to the apathy of the Corporation and want of good government by them of that side of the town.

1837. Has anything substantial been done towards making the Falls Park into the condition of a real park, because I find the expenditure is very small under that head?—What has been done is quite insignificant; it is only a colourable proceeding. As a matter of fact, whether it is owing to the reluctance or not of the Town Council, but very little has been done at all, and nothing for a long time past. They were going to do away with the Blackstaff in 1847. I don't know whether they are going to make this a park or not.

1838. Do you think they failed to carry out the Acts of 1845 and 1865?—Yes; there is one subject on which I ask your special attention in a sanitary point of view, and I think it is a disgrace to the Town Council to allow this to go on, where fever is produced by their inattention and neglect to carry out, and their acting in violation of, the Act of Parliament. The Town Council is to a certain extent governed by committees, and there is what is called an Improvement Committee. The Improvement Committee have to inspect and pass all plans for public buildings, and they have to be approved of by the borough surveyor before any house can be erected. I wish to draw your attention to section 75 in the Act of 1845, and to the penalty imposed by the 25th section of the Act of 1848, and for the violation of the Act—"In case any house or other building erected after the passing of this Act shall be inhabited contrary to the 75th section of the Belfast Act of 1845, the owner for the time being shall be liable to pay, and shall pay to the Corporation a sum of 10s. per week for every week during which such such house shall continue to be inhabited." I ask any person acquainted with the town of Belfast to look around them and say whether the provisions of both Acts of Parliament are violated or not. Look at the number of streets unpaved and unsewered, and yet the houses are inhabited, to the knowledge of the Council and their officers. I ask you to require from the town clerk or the surveyor the number of houses inhabited in streets that are unpaved or unsewered, and whether there was a single proceeding of the owners. It is no wonder that we have disease prevailing in our town, and the death rate so heavy.

1839. CHAIRMAN.—It was admitted by Mr. Montgomery that the law was not carried out, but he gave his reasons for it?—Yes; but those reasons have not gone forth to the public. I never heard any reason assigned.

BELFAST. Jan. 28, 1879. Mr. John Dinnen.

1840. The violation of the Act was admitted, and it was put upon the extent of pressure for better accommodation in Belfast, but in the meantime it had reference to the convenience of the inhabitants that the Act had not been carried out. We need not therefore ask you to explain the points as to the fact of the Corporation having violated the Act ?—I do not wish to cast the slightest imputation upon any individual corporator, nor do I wish to speak disparagingly of the improvement committee, but it is a curious coincidence that upon that committee there are five timber and slate merchants and two builders. There is one other matter which I wish to refer to, under the Act of 1865, sec. 32.

1841. That is with regard to the passage at the rere of the Belfast Bank; do you wish to give some evidence regarding that ?—You have had an explanation regarding that, which I have read very carefully, and I was rather surprised that that explanation was given in the way it was. I happened to be present before the Committee of the House of Commons when this clause was discussed, and most unwilling were they to allow any public passage to be blocked up or stopped, and the plans were required to be submitted of the improvements projected, and I recollect well that it was expressly stated that Bridge-street was one of the leading thoroughfares, that the Belfast Bank projected very much and interfered with the traffic of the day, and that if it were put back it would be a great public advantage. The plans were shown to the committee and the evidence was given, and that is all on record, and now what do you find, that notwithstanding that obtainable statement, the Belfast Bank, who happen to be the treasurers of the borough, have made arrangements and bought up the obtainable statements for money.

1842. What are the arrangements you refer to ?—Before the Committee of the House of Commons it was decided that this public building, the Belfast Bank, should be set back and the ground dedicated to the public. Instead of that the Corporation by resolution, which I opposed vigorously, have passed a resolution allowing them for money consideration to close up the passage, and gave them some ground instead.

1843. The Corporation have not availed themselves of the powers given in the second part of the clause ? —They have to a certain extent. They sold the obtainable right of claiming from the Belfast Bank the right of putting the building farther back in front.

1844. What the Corporation have done is that they have closed up this passage ?—I complain of a breach of faith on the part of the Corporation in allowing the passage to be closed up without getting the consideration agreed upon, namely, the setting of the bank back. The evidence given on that occasion is on record, and I would beg of you to look at it, and see whether it is consistent with the resolution passed by the Corporation in allowing their powers to pass out of their hands for a money consideration.

1845. Mr. *Black*.—If you wish the evidence, we have it. Mr. Dinnen totally mistakes it.

1846. CHAIRMAN.—There is an agreement bearing date the 31st of March, 1878, between the Bank and the Corporation, by which they were allowed to retain the present site of the bank, closing one passage and opening another ?—Yes. (See Appendix No. 18, page 314).

1847. Mr. *Black*.—Mr. Dinnen contends that there was a violation of the Act.

1848. Mr. *Dinnen*.—I do, most certainly.

1849. *Witness*.—Before passing from this Act of 1865, I can only endorse what Mr. Kennedy has said with regard to the expenditure of money in Ballymacarrett, that the Act has not been complied with.

1850. CHAIRMAN.—With reference to Ballymacarrett and Ballynafeigh ?—*Witness*.—They are both on the same side of the river, and about a mile from each other. They have done nothing for Ballynafeigh, and they have levied the rates there ever since.

1851. Don't those townlands touch ?—No; the park lies between them. The boundary is the Logan village on the Ballymacarrett side, and Ballynafeigh does not commence until about half or a quarter of a mile from the other townland.

1852. Mr. *Montgomery*.—As a matter of fact, I say those townlands adjoin each other the whole way.

1853. *Witness*.—I do not know whether you have had an explanation relative to the rate which the Council have the power to strike for compensation for malicious injuries. Under the Act of 1853, at the separation of the borough there was power given to the Corporation to strike a rate. I merely want to direct your attention to the fact that the Corporation in case the amount claimed is £1,000, have power to strike a special rate. I don't know whether you heard that in 1866 the rate was first struck, and if you refer to the estimates for each year you will find that £1,000 has been put down for the payment of these malicious injuries, and that has been going on from 1853 to 1876. I think there was no occasion to strike a special rate.

1854. Do you mean to say that £1,000 has been put apart in each year for that purpose, and it has accumulated ?—It ought to have accumulated. They have accounted no doubt for the money. Some years we know the claims did not amount to £20, and other years £10; and no doubt if the amount they have in hand was calculated, it would be found that they have had in their hands a sum more than sufficient to pay the amount of the compensation, and therefore they had no occasion to strike a special rate at all for that purpose.

1855. Mr. LAWLER.—The Corporation are bound up to £1,000 for malicious injuries, and for any amount beyond £1,000 they have power to strike a special rate. The malicious injuries were ascertained to amount at a certain assizes to something like £2,377. There was then a rate struck, and I understand that rate was struck to meet the balance of £1,377 over and above the £1,000—that is £2,377. A certain portion of that was applied in discharge of claims for malicious injuries, and the balance remaining was carried over in the hands of the bank, standing to a separate account, bearing separate interest, and there is now about £900 of that fund ?—But what I want to call your attention to is that you have not had an explanation about where this £1,000 that has been annually included in the estimates, has gone. The 43rd section of the Act of 1865 provides that if any year the sum paid by the Corporation for malicious injuries exceeds £1,000, the Corporation shall, in the then next ensuing year, levy a sum to pay the excess beyond £1,000; and the 60th section provides that the Corporation shall include in their yearly estimates the sum of £1,000 to pay the amount of compensation for malicious injuries; and the 43rd section, as I have already said, provides that that £1,000 should be actually in the hands of the Corporation to meet any contingency that might arise in consequence of riots, or anything of that kind. Therefore, they had no right to strike a special rate to meet that £1,700, or whatever the amount was, for the accumulations of the £1,000 each year during previous years, would have more than paid the deficiency of the one year. The Corporation also have power to appoint a Recorder for the borough, and to establish a Recorder's court, and there are certain salaries payable by the Corporation in connection with that court.

1856. What is the point you want to raise ?—The point I want to raise is that this court was established for the purpose of meeting the public requirements, and from that time to the present the Corporation have been paying the salary, and the public have not been getting any benefit. Furthermore, the court does not meet the requirements of the public, inasmuch as the sittings are held at inconvenient times. Instead of the court sitting on regular days, for two or three days at a time, it comes on just before the quarter sessions, and people are kept waiting on hand from ten days to a fortnight. It thus monopolises the

BELFAST. [illegible]. Mr. John Dinnen.

quarter sessions business. That I now say on behalf the inhabitants of the town, who complain of this matter, because the court is paid from out of their rates. At the time the Recorder's court was established, it was done for the purpose of facilitating the recovery of small debts promptly, and not one single farthing have the Corporation derived from that court in fees. They pay the salaries, but they get no fees.

1657. Mr. Black.—It is a matter over which we have no control.

1658. Witness.—I will show you that you have control. You pay the salaries under the Act of Parliament. The salaries are fixed at £[illegible] for the Recorder, and £[illegible] for the clerk of the peace. But you will find under the Municipal Corporations Act that where a Recorder is established for a borough, that the Corporation is required to fix the fees; instead of the fees going into the hands of the Corporation, they go into the hands of the clerk of the peace, and the result is that instead of getting £[illegible] a year, the clerk of the peace is getting £[illegible] or £600. I think the town should have the advantage of the difference between the salary allowed under the Act of Parliament and the fees.

1659. Can you tell us what fees are paid in the Recorder's court. Are they the same as at quarter sessions?—There is a table of fees under the Act of Parliament, but there are fixed charges that are not under the Act of Parliament, such as fees on spirit licences, and on affidavits filed in court, and things of that kind.

1660. Is it your proposition that all fees payable, assessable or otherwise, should go into the coffers of the Corporation, in aid of the Recorder's salary paid out of the city rates?—Yes; not only that, and I think that a portion of the stamp duties in the court should be applied in liquidation of the salary of the Recorder. I say that the Corporation have not done their duty under the Municipal Corporations Act in not setting apart the fees which should go into the corporate funds under the Municipal Corporations Act.

1661. Does the clerk of the peace draw his salary as well as the fees?—Yes.

1662. Mr. Lawless.—Do all the fees go to the clerk of the peace in the Recorder's court?—Yes.

1663. Mr. Kernan.—Does Mr. Owens, the Recorder, hold a monthly court?—No; it is held every six weeks. It is not half often enough; but not only that, but it is so arranged as to catch the quarter sessions business, and the result is, that it prolongs the court and renders the Recorder's court (small) inoperative.

1664. Mr. Lawless.—Have the Corporation power to regulate the sittings of the Recorder when they appoint him?—I can only refer you to the Municipal Corporations Act. I cannot answer that question, because I have not given it sufficient consideration; but I know this much, that the Recorder would be only too glad, if it were properly represented to him, to try and arrange the court to sit oftener.

1665. Has any application been made to the Corporation to represent the matter to the Recorder?—I know it has been greatly commented on.

1666. But has any application been made to the Corporation?—I am not aware; I think not.

1667. Chairman.—Have you any further evidence to offer?—There is just one other matter, and it is a reform which I consider is much required in the Corporation with the view of lowering the taxation of the town. I believe the Corporation to be a huge political engine, worked by the officials of the Corporation, who are paid out of the rates of the town.

1668. If you can produce facts in evidence to substantiate that assertion, we shall be happy to take such evidence; but do not make statements unless you are going to support them by evidence?—The officers I look upon to be the ruling spirits in the Corporation. They nominate, canvass, pay runners and agents for the purpose of having men of their choice returned as representatives to that body.

1669. Who do you say do that?—The officials of the Corporation.

1670. Can you name the person or persons who do this?—I will name one person; but I do not like to individualize.

1671. But how can these statements be answered unless you do individualize?—Then, I will individualize for my present purpose. There is the cashier who has been before the public. This cashier commenced on a salary of £[illegible] a year, and you will find on referring to the printed accounts that his present salary is greater than that of any other person, I will venture to say, in the town of Belfast, holding a similar position, if not double what such a person would receive.

1672. What is his salary?—£[illegible] was the salary originally, now, I believe, it is £[illegible], and I consider that the Corporation acted in an improper manner with respect to him.

1673. Is it in raising his salary?—Yes; and especially when he has taken an active partisan part—one that was not in keeping with the position of a public officer, paid out of the rates of people of all denominations; and knowing how the Corporation officials were going on, I moved a resolution in the Corporation to prohibit any officer of the Corporation from taking an active part at any election.

1674. Mr. Lawless.—Can you give the date on which you moved that resolution?—It was shortly after I was returned in 1871, or it might have been in 1872. Yes, it was at a meeting of the Council held on the 1st of February, 1872. I hold in my hand a summons to attend that meeting. I may observe before going further, that I thought it was my duty to try to have politics avoided in the Corporation. I thought it was a perversion of the municipal trust to allow it in any way to be mixed up with or influenced by politics. The moment I introduced my motion into the Council, immediately the cry was raised, "Oh, this is introducing politics," although the very opposite was the reason that induced me to bring it forward, which really was for the purpose of trying to have the same system adopted in the Corporation as exists under the Local Government Board, where no officer is allowed to interfere in election matters, save by recording his vote. I thought that an official of the Corporation had no right to take up a partisan position, and to interfere in the election of members for the Corporation, more particularly when he is paid by the public money. Well, that was the notice of motion I gave; and I may take the opportunity of mentioning in passing, that there was some little good done in the way of reform during the time I happened to be a member of the Council, as I find that this same summons contains another notice of motion to obtain the transfer of the gasworks to the Corporation, a scheme that met with considerable opposition, but which ultimately was carried into effect. This is the notice of motion I gave: "Councillor Dinnen to move—'That it be an instruction to the employés of the Corporation not to take any active part prior to or at any municipal or parliamentary election beyond recording their votes.'"

1675. Was that resolution moved and considered?—It was moved, seconded, and discussed, and on being put to the vote was rejected by 17 to 4.

1676. Mr. Kernan.—At the time you moved that resolution did you state any instances within your own knowledge to the members of the Corporation of officers who had so interfered at municipal or parliamentary elections?—Yes; and not only that, but one councillor, who happened to be recently returned, although he did belong to the same party, identified this particular gentleman as having taken part against him, he being a new member.

1677. Chairman.—Did you state these facts in support of your desire to have the resolution, of which you had given notice, adopted by the Council?—Yes; I am stating my recollection of what occurred at the time. I know at that time there was a very strong feeling in the town that the officials were interfering improperly in returning members of the Corporation. In consequence of this resolution being rejected, I believe the spirit has still become stronger, and that instead of the officials being told not to interfere, that they now, to a very large extent, actually have the control of the return of the members of the Corporation in their own hands.

1678. In what way have they the control?—They control both the nomination and the election of representatives for the municipal borough.

1679. Do you mean to say that they receive instructions from the Corporation to take an active part in the nominations and elections?—I say that they receive instructions indirectly, that there is an inner circle of the Corporation who manage the entire borough, and the others are but mere tools in their hands.

1680. Do you mean to say that the town council give instructions to their officers to take an active part in the elections?—Yes; and so much so that it is looked upon as a kind of political refuge for old hacks who have been doing tory work, when a situation happens to be vacant.

1681. Who are these gentlemen who give these instructions, because it is a very grave charge you make against them, and it is but fair and right that you should mention their names, in order to give them an opportunity of defending themselves if they can?—I am making a charge against the officials.

1682. But you say that the officials are acting upon the instructions of members of the Corporation. You should give us the names of the officials who so act, and also the names of the members of the Corporation from whom they derive their instructions?—There is a difficulty in that, especially when you have not given us an opportunity of cross-examining any of the witnesses that have been called on behalf of the Corporation. I have no hesitation in stating that I believe I would have no difficulty in being able to elicit those facts if I had an opportunity of cross-examining some of the witnesses that were brought up before you; and without having afforded others as well as myself that opportunity, I consider it would be hard to name any particular person as the person who gave directions, but I can state as a fact that the Corporation officials not only go so far as to nominate aldermen, but that the gentleman to whom I refer had the audacity, when asking for an increase of salary, to go to the late Mayor, Sir John Savage, and say that he should support the application he was making because he was the man who got Sir John Savage into the Corporation, and was the means of having him made Mayor.

1683. Who is the person who you say said this?—The cashier. In order to have the exact words which he made use of, I would refer you to the newspapers of the 2nd of February last, which contain an account of the proceedings, fully published, at which the statement I allude to was made.

1684. Mr. Rynam.—Did Sir John Savage state at that meeting that the individual you allude to made those observations?—Yes. As a matter of fact Sir John Savage was castigating him in a speech that he was making, in the course of which he said, that the official in question went so far as actually to have the audacity to state that he was the person who got him returned to the council. I say that some of the officials have a certain power in their hands which I contend ought at once to be removed.

1685. Chairman.—Who are the other persons included in what you have designated as the "inner circle"?—Well, there are what are called the rate collectors of the borough. These men have in their power the manipulation of the burgess lists.

1686. Do you include all the rate collectors?—Yes; all the rate collectors. There are rate collectors for each ward. They have in their hands the returning to the town clerk of the names of the different people who are entitled to be on the burgess roll, and they also know the different parties who should be put on as claimants. This state of things gave the greatest possible offence. I mean the belief that the rate collectors were abusing (though I do not mean to say that they are doing it to the same extent now as formerly) their powers. I find it on the minutes of evidence in the Blue Book (which I can give in evidence if you desire it) at the time the Act was passed in 1864, that that state of things existed, and the Council from that time up to the present, notwithstanding the opposition given by the independent ratepayers of the borough, have violated the promise they gave to the Committee of the House of Commons, on the faith of which the preamble to the Indemnity Act was passed, namely, to introduce a public Bill to do away with these rate collectors and have a collector-general appointed, and for other purposes. The evidence will show that the preamble of the Bill was passed on the faith of a public Bill being introduced by the Corporation. I may quote an extract from that book where the Chairman of the Committee stated—"That the great object of the Committee was that, if possible, some measure should be introduced to prevent a continuance of the grievances and heartburnings which appeared from the evidence on both sides to prevail in the borough of Belfast."

1687. Who was the Chairman of that Committee?—Mr. James Milnes Gaskill. Well, the result of the discussion before the Committee was an understanding that a public Bill should be introduced, and that these town collectors who have the manipulation of the burgess roll, should be abolished.

1688. Mr. Lawson.—Was any public Bill introduced?—None. I mention these minutes of evidence, taken before the Committee of the House of Commons, for the purpose of showing what was the feeling of the Committee when that Indemnity Bill was approved of on the faith of a public Bill being introduced. I say that the terms of that public Bill were to be the abolition of the rate collectors of the different wards, the appointment of a collector-general, and further arrangements for the improvement of the town to be arranged by general arbitrators. I say that that has not been done, and that there has been a breach of faith on the part of the Corporation in not carrying those contemplated changes out.

1689. Chairman.—These minutes of evidence are on the records of the House of Commons, and we can refer the Select Committee of the House of Commons to those minutes of evidence by date, and it will be for the Committee to draw their own inference?—I may tell you that one of those rate collectors was notoriously a district ward agent and a well-known political agent before his appointment, and he still continues in that office up to the present time. He also occupies the position of deputy grand master of an Orange lodge at the present time.

1690. What is that collector's name?—Charles Noah Davis.

1691. What ward does he collect for?—The St. George's ward.

1692. Is there any other collector to whom you object?—I hope you will understand me as not making any objection to Mr. Charles Noah Davis or to any particular individual rate collector. I am only attacking the system, and I do so for the purpose of showing that those gentlemen who hold offices of that kind have a certain amount of control in their hands which, I think, ought to be removed. And having stated so much I think that until some change takes place in the government of the town by the removal of the present Corporation, you will never have the public comforts and the public good of the town considered. I think you have had sufficient evidence of their neglect in sanitary matters. I think I have shown you conclusively that there is improper conduct going on in the inner circle, as denounced by Sir John Savage; and until the Local Government Board or the Government step in and take the control of the town for some time out of the hands of the Corporation, I say it is my deliberate opinion we will never have any peace or good for the inhabitants of the town of Belfast.

[illegible] Dec. [illegible], 18[illegible].

Mr. John [illegible].

BELFAST.
Jan. 25, 1878.
Mr. John Pyper.

1893. Is there any other individual whom you desire to name except the cashier?—The cashier was denounced by Sir John Savage.

1894. I want you to name those who you say are guilty of corrupt practices in the Corporation—for your charge amounts to that. You at first, if I remember, clearly said there were three officials. Do you limit the charge to three?—I do not limit it at all.

1895. Will you name the others? Who are the three?—The cashier.

1896. That is only one?—I have mentioned the position of Mr. Noah Davis.

1897. That makes two. Who is the other?—I cannot at present name a third. I say the entire body are more or less tainted.

1898. But that will not do. You should not make so grave a charge as that which you have preferred without being fully able to substantiate it. You have charged certain members of the Corporation and certain corporate officials with corruption. It is not fair play if you do not individualize. You know you could not make a graver charge?—I reiterate that charge, that the Corporation permits its officials to take an improper part in the municipal elections. I cannot give you details or the names of each party, particularly as no opportunity has been afforded of cross-examination.

1899. I think you should name whom this "inner circle" consists of that you say exercises this control over the Corporation. That is practically a charge of corruption, and you should now support that charge by naming the persons to whom you allude. If you decline to do so, then of course your statement falls to the ground?—I think the statement on the authority that I have named, that there is a political influence or advantage in the hands of the officials of the Corporation is enough.

1900. I want to know who these persons are. If you make this public charge the people against whom you make it should in fairness have an opportunity of coming forward to give evidence in their own defence, otherwise as I have said before judgment will go by default?—I have referred you to the statement made by Sir John Savage. I think a statement coming from a gentleman occupying the position of an ex-mayor that the corporate officials were exercising that improper authority should be sufficient to satisfy you that there was something wrong.

1901. I want to know who those other parties were?—Well, it is difficult to go into that.

1902. You have brought a charge against a particular officer of the Corporation, who has had his salary increased from £70 to £400 because you allege that he has "worked" the Corporation, or the "inner circle" of the Corporation, by exercising undue influence or corruption at the elections of the Corporation. Well, it comes to this, that he is the only person you will name?—He is the only person of whom I have personal knowledge.

1903. Then your charge falls to the ground with regard to all the other persons except the cashier?—If any evidence I have given affects any other person I withdraw it.

1904. Is your object to prevent the officials of the Corporation from being allowed to take any part in political contests?—Clearly; that is my entire object, and to prevent them from using their office improperly and their influence too with regard to elections.

1905. Mr. Exham.—With regard to the minutes of evidence taken before the Select Committee of the House of Commons, has there or has there not been any change in the carrying on of the practices that were at that time made the subject of complaint before the Committee?—The same state of things exists; but I am in justice bound to say that the rate collectors have been more particular in the collection of the rates, and that the same system is not carried on as heretofore as to disfranchising voters.

1906. Has your complaint against the rate collectors, as far as it goes, reference to the past and not to the present?—Yes; but it has reference also to the power that they still have in their hands.

1907. Do I understand you to say that at the present time the system prevails of rate collectors disfranchising certain persons, and putting on others?—They have it in their power, but I do not say that they do it at present to the same extent; in fact, it is not done at present to the same extent. The public bill was to provide for that and other matters, and it has never been carried out. The bill was passed on the faith of the undertaking given before the Committee, but they have never carried it out. With reference to the wards, I think the town is not properly divided. If you look at the map of the wards you will see that they are arranged in a most extraordinary way—one running into the other, &c., and so they have remained since the Act was passed, notwithstanding the undertaking on the faith of which they got the bill.

1908. Mr. Lawless.—When was there a re-distribution of the wards?—In 1853. A commissioner was sent down; there was no representation on one side, and the wards were divided in a way that gave and give great dissatisfaction.

1909. Chairman.—We have had it already that the wards are unequal in point of rateable value, and in point of the number of burgesses?—You will see at once that it is almost impossible for any person who attempts to assert an independent position to fight at a small expense a ward containing as many burgesses as some of the county towns in Ireland.

1910. Do you think that the wards are too large?—Far too large. The number of wards should be increased, and by the bill that was to have been introduced, the town was to be arranged in a manner somewhat similar to that in which the wards are arranged in Dublin, where, I believe, they have fifteen wards. I would say that if a change is to take place the number of wards in Belfast should be from ten to twelve.

1911. Mr. Lawless.—What was the population of Belfast when the re-distribution of the wards took place?—From 110,000 to 120,000. Now, as you are aware, the population is 200,000.

Belfast. [illegible] Mr. John [illegible].

1919. Is there any flagging?—No. The only way the people have of passing from door to door is by a footway formed of cinders which the foreman threw out.

1920. How long have these houses been inhabited?—About a couple of years. They have all been built since 1866.

1921. Have these streets been opened as a public thoroughfare?—Yes.

1922. Mr. Ewart.—Who are the owners of that property?—The Grosvenor-street property is owned by Mr. Thomas Lawson Brown, who is a member of this council.

1923. Is he the owner of those three streets?—Yes. He is also a member of the town improvement committee. I wish to refer you to a property in Ballymacarrett. I visited four streets there last night, and found the lower part of Mountstreet in a very bad condition. There are also Dunmore-street, and Langan-view-street, and Fenton-street, and they are in the same condition, they are perfectly impassable. You could not go through them without going into thirteen or fourteen inches of mud.

1924. Are there any footpaths there?—Yes, but they are not completed—they are in the same state. It is almost impossible to pass over them. The curb-stones are laid down, but there is no paving yet, nor any sewerage that I am aware of. It may exist, and if so the surveyor can tell, but I do not know of it.

1925. Who is the owner of the streets?—I cannot say whether it belongs to one individual or not. The party building there at present and who owns some of the street is Mr. Peter Quinn. He holds that property from Mr. John Brown, who is the chairman of the town improvement committee. Mr. Quinn is not a member of the Council. Fenton-street runs off Mount-street.

1926. Chairman.—How long have these streets been open to the public?—I cannot say.

1927. Twelve or six months?—I cannot say; there are people living in them now.

1928. Are there any other streets there in that condition?—These are the only ones.

1929. Has any representation been made to the Town Council or the improvement committee, as to the condition of those streets?—I am not aware that any complaint has been made about it.

1930. Mr. Lawson.—Do you consider it is the duty of the Town Council to prevent those streets from being opened until they are finished?—I do, and it is a duty imposed on them by the law.

1931. Mr. Ewart.—Does the sanitary officer go there to see after the condition of the place?—I do not know, but it is the duty of the sanitary officer to make a search and see after such things. If he did go there he has not done anything to the place.

1932. Are you satisfied with the arrangements of the town generally, as to the sanitary matters and the condition of the streets?—Mr. Montgomery gave an explanation as to the town increasing so rapidly—that they were not able to keep pace with the demand for houses, but if you refer to the [illegible] section of the Act of 1865, you will find that it is the duty of the owners of property to make all these improvements.

1933. Upon an order from the Council?—Yes; and therefore it is the fault of the Council. My own impression is that the remissness on the part of the Town Council is, because there are a certain number of gentlemen on the improvement committee who are timber merchants and builders.

1934. Mr. Lawson.—Are there many timber merchants and builders on the improvement committee?—Yes; there were seven last year, and I believe the same number this year.

1935. What is the number of the improvement committee?—Fourteen Councillors and five Aldermen, and I think seven of those belong to the timber and building trade.

1936. Chairman.—Is there any other point to which you wish to draw our attention with regard to the sanitary arrangements—any special complaint?—Of course, I would like to mention something about the Blackstaff. I reside in that neighbourhood, and I have to pass over it twice a day on the Cromac-street side, and sometimes more frequently for the last fifteen years, so that I have had a sufficient opportunity of seeing that river. I have heard numbers of people say they would visit the park but for the nasty smell that arises from the river—Ormeau Park I mean. I think it keeps people from visiting the park, and it is also injurious to the interest of property-holders in that neighbourhood, and the health of the people.

1937. Does that state of the Blackstaff in your opinion prevent people from using Ormeau Park?—Yes. There is another matter that I noticed in the evidence of Mr. Heath. In reply to a question from Mr. Ewart, if the river was cleansed out occasionally, he said "Yes; frequently," but I say that is not a fact. There is certainly what I may describe as a cess-pool immediately between what was the weir of an old mill and the paper-mill bridge, and perhaps once in the summer they put a number of men there and carry away a few loads of the stuff, but it is impossible to take anything out of the course of the river from that to the Dublin-road bridge on account of the great number of stones lying in the bottom of it, and there is nothing done with that portion of it. It would be a great deal better for them not to stir up the mud in the river; they only make it worse while they are doing it. All the cleansing the river gets is a mere bagatelle. I wish also to express my opinion to the same effect as the last witness as to the size of the wards. They are not equal, and a redistribution is most requisite and necessary. As Mr. Dixon stated, I might as well contest a borough, or in fact some of the counties in Ireland as some of the wards here, on account of the great number of burgesses in them. There is also another matter—Mr. Kennedy said that the salaries were not excessive, but in my opinion the salaries are much in excess of what they should be. I should say that one-half the present salaries would be sufficient, having regard to the way competent persons of the same class are paid here.

1938. Do you mean the salaries generally or any one in particular?—The salaries generally. They are on too high a scale.

1939. Mr. Lawson.—Are you a member of the Town Council?—I am happy to say I am not, at least at present neither, but I am a ratepayer.

Mr. Robert Stewart examined.

Mr. Robert Stewart.

1940. Chairman.—You reside at 75, York-street, Belfast?—Yes.

1941. Are you a ratepayer and burgess?—Yes.

1942. What is your profession?—A Scotsman vintner.

1943. Do you wish to say anything as to the mode in which the collectors perform their duties, or their mode of collection?—Both; but first I wish to say something with regard to the police force of Belfast.

1944. Are you satisfied with the manner in which the police discharge their duties?—Yes, perfectly satisfied. I would not have them changed on any account, or put under the control of the corporation. I know, as a matter of experience, that when we had the police under their control, a great many of them were open to accept bribes and used to wink at acts of misconduct, and I know that the present Royal Irish Constabulary are a very superior body of men, and discharge their duty very efficiently, and are impartially considered of all sects. I think that if the local police were again brought into Belfast they would be a partisan force, as they were before, instead of a police force. I think there is no evidence on record that Mr. Bailey ever refused to give assistance to the Corporation. My object in stating this is, in consequence of what was stated by Dr. Alexander, because I believe that what he said was a matter of opinion.

1945. What objection have you to the mode in which the collectors perform their duties?—The,

BELFAST. Jan. 28, 1876. Mr. Robert [illegible].

collectors are paid a percentage on the collection of the rates; that per-centage is excessive, for it enables them to employ deputies. In the ward for which I pay rates there is a person appointed collector who is an ex-member of the police force, and superannuated. He is appointed collector, and I think the only credentials he had was, that he was a member of the old local police. He is a man advanced in years, and I take it for granted he is unable to discharge the duties personally.

1946. Why?—Because he employs a deputy. I have paid taxes to the Town Council for four or five years, and during the whole of that time Mr. Rankin, the collector appointed by the Town Council to collect them, never was in my house. I complained frequently to several members of the Corporation, and drew their attention to this fact, but no redress followed. I think it is a great grievance that men should be paid large salaries for doing nothing but sitting in their chamber, not as tax collectors, but as tax surveyors.

1947. Does he employ more than one person?—I only know of one who collects my rates. I am not speaking with any degree of personal knowledge, I am speaking of the ward in which I live. I believe that a similar system is adopted in at least two of the other wards.

1948. I want to know whether it is one or more deputy he employs?—It is one deputy.

1949. Has that man, to the best of your knowledge, always accounted for his receipts, or have you had any cause to complain?—I think he is a most efficient collector.

1950. It is not from any objection you have to the deputy that you complain?—It is not.

1951. Mr. LAWLESS.—How much does he receive?—In the Dock Ward the commission on the collection amounts to about £270. They get seven and a half per cent.

1952. CHAIRMAN.—What is the name of the collector?—George Rankin. I have just been informed that he was a member of the Royal Irish Constabulary. He pays out of the commission which he receives £60 a year to this deputy.

1953. Do you know that?—Yes.

1954. From the man himself?—Yes.

1955. Does that deputy give security?—No, he does not. Rankin is responsible to the Corporation, and I believe entered into a bond for the due return of the money, but I hold that a collector should not be appointed unless he is able to discharge the duties in person, and see that every person is properly registered on the burgess roll. I do not object to him. I object to the principle which enables him to employ a person as deputy by paying a larger salary than he is entitled to. I think it is calculated to lead to abuse. I was about to say that there is a system of disfranchising the people in Belfast carried on (I do not say deliberately carried on), but it results in disfranchising the people. The tax collectors allow persons to be too late in paying their rates, and those persons are generally persons opposed to those collectors in politics, and I need hardly say here that those collectors are always appointed through political influence exclusively.

1956. Is that your opinion?—Yes; and the opinion of many others.

1957. Do you mean that they delay collecting the rates for a particular object?—Yes; from some persons, and those persons are always opposed to voting in the direction of their masters.

1958. Cannot those persons always pay or tender their rates?—Yes; but as a rule the people are not sufficiently versed in municipal matters to know that they will be disfranchised by not paying them in time. In Smithfield Ward last year there were a number of persons who were willing enough to pay their rates, and who were never asked for them until it was too late to enroll them on the burgess roll. I know as a matter of fact that upwards of 100 voters were disfranchised. I was a candidate at the last Smithfield Ward for a town councillor, and the people who imagined they were on the roll complained very bitterly of this important fact, and I could, if necessary, bring up at least fifty people who could state that they were never asked for their rates.

1959. Were those people of the poorer class?—Persons in moderate position.

1960. Were they people of whom the collector could have no doubt?—They were people who were perfectly solvent.

1961. I want to know if they were persons in the poorer classes and solvent?—There are many of the persons to whom I have referred that are very solvent.

1962. Men whom the collectors would have no reason to be indulgent to, because they might not be able to pay?—Not the slightest. The municipal taxes, so far as I understand, must be paid on the 31st of August of each year.

1963. Have you ever known an instance in which the collectors refused to receive the rates?—No, never. The next point to which I wish to refer is with regard to the mode and manner in which the costs of the town solicitor, and the several other solicitors employed by the Town Council, are paid, and the manner in which the amount of their costs is ascertained. I wish to say that I was reading very carefully the report of the evidence given by Mr. Black. He said that he was paid no salary, and that his bill of costs were always taxed by the taxing master in Dublin, and that a solicitor who was only paid his taxed costs was certainly not overpaid. Mr. Exham said he was well aware of that, but I will try to convince Mr. Exham that he is well paid. In the year 1873 Mr. Black's taxed costs alone amounted to £2,605 13s. 9d.; in the year 1874 to £1,705 12s. 8d., and in 1875 (last year) to £1,381 8s. 5d. Now, the ordinary ratepayer imagines that that is a very fair salary for a solicitor. In addition to that, Mr. Black has an extensive private practice; he is permitted by the Corporation to have it, and he is also supplied with a suite of rooms, which are at least valued for £80 a year, being in the centre of the town, well ventilated, and capacious.

1964. Are they in this building?—Yes. He is also supplied with stationery free of charge, and everything considered it would be best that Mr. Black should be paid a fixed salary. I think that the better course would be that the Town Clerk should be a solicitor, and that he should conduct all the legal proceedings, and money would thus be saved for the ratepayers. I may also say for the information of the Commissioners that there are three solicitors employed by the Corporation, the others being John Coulter, and James M'Lean, one is the sessional Crown solicitor; they each receive £164 annually.

1965. Is that a salary from the Corporation?—Yes. I believe the town solicitor as town solicitor should discharge all those duties. I believe there should not be three solicitors. In the year 1875 (I think it was 1875) Mr. M'Erlean preferred an indictment against the Corporation, and it must have appeared to Mr. Black and those two other gentlemen to be a very serious indictment, for they brought in a fourth solicitor. This fourth solicitor defended the suit, and the three other gentlemen remained silent.

1966. Mr. EXHAM.—When was that prosecution?—In December, 1875, before Mr. O'Donnell. The prosecution was for opening a graveyard full of dead bodies before Mr. M'Erlean's door. The bill of costs simply says, "bill of costs," so much.

1967. Do you know Mr. Black's costs?—I mean the amount of the costs.

1968. Do you think the particulars of the several items should be given?—I think the particulars should be given in every instance, of every class of items, in dealing with a company or a corporation. We have no evidence to show that Mr. O'Rorke, who was called in by the three salaried solicitors, did not get paid out of the taxes of the town. If they stated that they paid him out of their own pockets the ratepayers would have been satisfied; but if not, why should the Council pay him for helping the other three.

1969. Do you think it is a thing that requires explanation on the face of the accounts?—Yes; some particulars of the items of law costs should be set forth, so that there should be no mystery about them.

1970. Did Mr. O'Rorke get them off?—It fell through.

1971. CHAIRMAN.—Do you wish to say anything with regard to the way in which the municipal elections are held in Belfast?—I do. They are all presided over by Tory aldermen; there is very little else in the Corporation now, except Mr. Bernard Hughes, and he is going very rapidly in that direction. I refer to the class of men who preside over elections in Belfast. The booths are so constructed that a portion of them is let off to Tory candidates—as for instance, in the case of the Smithfield Ward election. I was a candidate for one of the vacancies on the 25th November last, and there were two agents employed by my two opponents. I may state that I am a Presbyterian and Independent. There were four candidates in the field for two vacancies, Messrs. Haslett and Ewart my opponents, and also Mr. Rea; and I say that the booth was so constructed as to give an advantage to my opponents. When I entered it I found a large construction of wood in the form of a counter, and behind this counter were two agents of the Tory party. As each voter came in he was asked for his name by these men, and when he gave the desired information, he was given a ticket (the tickets were supplied by the Conservative candidates), on which was the number representing his name on the burgess roll. When they got this number, they were handed a paper on which was printed "Vote for Haslett and Ewart."

1972. You say they were handed a voting paper on which it was suggested how they should vote?—Yes; it was a "thimbly rigmarole." Each voter as he came into the polling booth was handed this bill, and at the same time he was instructed to go inside and mark the voting paper. I remonstrated with the aldermen, with regard to those men being permitted to remain there, and he was so extremely Tory (Mr. Bernard Hughes was the alderman) that he would not interfere. He refused to remove the agents from the polling booth, as he said he received his instructions from the town clerk.

1973. Did he offer you any similar accommodation?—He did not. He was not so generous.

1974. Mr. LAWLESS.—Did he tell you he received his instructions from the town clerk?—Yes, and that he would not interfere. I should have stated that across the street from where the polling booth was situated tally rooms were taken by those candidates, and a regular system of communication was kept up between the agents who were behind the counter which I have already described and the persons across the street.

1975. How?—By means of messengers going across and giving the names of the persons who had voted.

1976. CHAIRMAN.—Was word sent to the other side how the polling was going?—Yes; as each person voted his name was struck off, and the information was sent to the tally rooms so that they knew who had not voted, and messengers were sent to hunt up the other voters. I immediately proceeded to protest against the irregularity.

1977. Did they offer any of these papers to any gentlemen whom you expected to vote for you?—Yes. I should say that Mr. Rea's electoral friends and my electoral friends, though they never went to the tally rooms of our opponents at all were still handed the papers. I protested against this conduct, and pointed out to Mr. Hughes one or two sections of the Ballot Act, and he said I should put my objections on paper, and I did so, and retired from the election, and proceedings are now being taken to have the election declared null and void in the Queen's Bench. I believe all the trouble that I have been put to is in consequence of the officials of the Corporation (one or two of them) being active in conducting the election.

1978. Will you name the officials to whom you refer?—I include some individually, and I exclude some, because they are all one and the same.

1979. Do you decline to mention names?—I do.

1980. You said one or two of the officials?—Yes.

1981. Are you unable to individualise?—I could individualise remotely.

1982. What do you mean by individualise remotely?—I decline to mention names. I believe it is not advisable at present. I could give names but I have reasons for not doing so, owing to a suit which I have pending in the Court of Queen's Bench, with regard to this election, and mentioning the names now, which I could do now, might prejudice my proceedings in that court, and for that reason I do not wish at present to mention the names. There is one thing which I omitted to mention, and it is this—Mr. Black stated that his costs were taxed by the taxing master in Dublin. I am convinced from information which I received, and which I believe to be very reliable that that statement is not correct. I believe that costs were taxed by an official of this Corporation, and I think you should receive evidence on that point.

1983. Can you specify the bills of costs? There should be no difficulty in seeing whether you are right or wrong. If you can give us the bills to which you refer the thing can be cleared up in a moment.—I will do that. I intended to say there should be an increase in the number of wards, also how I think they should be divided.

1984. That is a question entirely for the House of Commons and not for us.

1985. Witness.—I see in the account—"Johns, Hewitts, and Johns, for taxing costs, £33 1s."; "Samuel Black's taxed costs, £357 11s., and Johns, Hewitts, and Johns, for attending at the taxation of costs, £33 1s."

Belfast. Jan. 20, 1879.

Mr. Robert Stewart.

Mr. BLACK recalled.

Mr. Black.

1986. Mr. LAWLESS.—Were these costs taxed as between attorney and client?—Yes.

1987. Were Johns, Hewitts, and Johns directed to attend on the part of the Corporation on the taxation of these costs?—Yes, and they reduced every item that they could. My costs were all duly taxed.

DECEMBER 21, 1878.

Jan. 21, 1879.

Mr. ROBERT STEWART recalled.

Mr. Robert Stewart.

1988. CHAIRMAN.—What is the next point upon which you wish to give evidence?—There is just one alteration which I would like to make in my evidence of yesterday, and that is with regard to the rooms occupied by Mr. Black. I said that the Corporation allowed him free rooms, free gas, and free coal, and that the estimated value of these would be about £50 a year; but I am now in a position to state, and also in a position to put it in writing, that the offices I have referred to would let at £200 per annum. I have also been informed that Mr. Black is the attorney for a building society, and that while being so he assisted in passing all plans for the erection of houses. I have been informed of that fact.

1989. Mr. LAWLESS.—Can you mention any instance of his assisting to pass plans?—No.

1990. CHAIRMAN.—We have heard a good deal already about the paving of the streets. If you wish to mention anything with regard to that, you may as well do so now?—John-street, Berry-street, Little Donegall-street, Mustard-street, Union-street, Waterloo-street, Smithfield-square, and many of the streets leading off the Shankill-road, which I need not mention, are paved with very large paving stones, and are very uneven and unlevel, which causes large pools of water to collect in them, so that the people cannot possibly pass through those streets without being wet. In some places you would go knee-deep in them.

1991. Are there any crossings in those streets?—No.

1992. Are the footpaths paved?—They are paved with Kelsey paving stones. In North-street and York-street there is a third kerbstone on the footpaths. The street leading from the town hall here to Ann-street, yesterday morning and this morning, has been a perfect sea of mud and dirty water, and I think that arises from the very imperfect surface drainage.

1993. Are the street channels alongside the footpaths kept in good order?—There is an utter want of flagging, or paving either. In those streets that I first mentioned the traffic is impeded materially when brick carts pass through them.

1994. Have those streets been long built?—They are the oldest streets in Belfast. The houses are very old. Frequent complaints have been made as to the state of those streets, and of the labour on horses in dragging laden carts over the boulder-like paving stones. The police office and the courts adjacent are in a bad condition owing to the state of the sewerage, and since they have been built a great deal of money has been spent in remodelling the buildings, which were only recently erected, with regard to the Recorder's court.——

1995. That is a building we have already heard of, the basement of which was flooded?—Yes; I just wish in confirmation of what I say to draw your attention to a paragraph published in the *Northern Whig* of the present month (handing in copy of the *Northern Whig* newspaper).

1996. Mr. Lawless.—Is this about the prisoner who was nearly drowned in a pool of water when coming from his cell to stand his trial before the Recorder?—Yes; and I may say that the Recorder concurred with the remarks made on the occurrence by Mr. Rea.

1997. Chairman.—You next wish to give evidence with regard to the conduct of the cashier and wish to say with regard to the cashier that he is a great political power in this Corporation.

1998. How does he use that power?—He assists directly and indirectly in the return of all the councillors to the Corporation, and by reason of his political services, and in consequence of the action which he takes in election matters there is no difficulty whatever in his managing to have his salary increased from time to time on such terms as he may think proper to put forward, and of which he thinks he requires to give only momentary notice. In confirmation of the truth of what I say I would call your attention to the following report published in the *Northern Whig* on the 2nd February of the present year:—

"The Salaries Question.

"The town clerk read the minutes of the Council at which the salaries question was considered. The only alteration from the report presented on the 1st January was that the salary of Mr. Woods, the accountant, should be increased from £250 to £300 instead of £400, as originally proposed; and the salary of Mr. Cobain, the cashier, from £400 to £500 instead of £550, as originally proposed.

"Mr. Thomas R. Browne moved the adoption of the minutes of Council in committee, which were unanimously [illegible].

"Sir John Savage said there was no vote taken but they were not unanimous.

"Mr. Rodgers seconded the motion.

"Mr. R. H. Thompson said he had a great objection to propose an amendment to anything done by the Council in committee, but he had been unavoidably absent from the meeting, and if present would have taken objection to part of what was done. He would move an amendment [illegible] that part of the report which it was proposed to reduce the increase of Mr. Wood's salary from £100 to £50. This increase was well considered by the Finance Committee, and the Committee thought that, considering Mr. Woods was giving a six years' engagement £100 was only a fair increase. There was objection to other advances, but there was none to that of Mr. Woods, and a compromise should not have been entered into prejudicial to the interests of a valued officer. No officer in the Corporation better deserved the increase than Mr. Woods. The Corporation [illegible] had often [illegible] to the [illegible] officers to which the books were kept, and indeed they all knew this for themselves.

"Mr. R. Thompson seconded the amendment.

"Dr. Alexander said that if the matter was to be opened up for discussion he would propose that no increase should be given for the present year. It was an invidious thing to propose that the salary of one officer should be equal to the amount originally proposed and another not.

"Mr. Galligan was opposed to any increase of salary at present. It the gentleman who advanced money, considerable efforts for a few dozen in [illegible] were aware of the difficult [illegible] people had to contend with in paying the taxes they would not be thinking of big salaries. One of the officers in particular (Mr. Cobain) had caused all the row and all those meetings with regard to salaries, and he spoke [illegible] as a political or [illegible] point of view, did not justify his claim upon the Council.

"Mr. [illegible] said this was not the fourth day they had had the question before them. Mr. Galligan had mentioned about Mr. Cobain, but in what other Corporation was the accountant paid higher than the cashier.

"Mr. Haslett said that if they postponed the matter for a year they would be in a better position to consider it.

"Sir John Savage availed of the opportunity of saying a word or two on the subject. He regretted that Mr. R. H. Thompson had not seen his way to fall in with the views of the Council in committee, but, notwithstanding, nothing had been said to alter the opinion that he had taken upon the matter. He agreed with Mr. Haslett that salaries should be raised gradually instead of in a lump sum with percentage, giving £50 or £100 increase at once. Any gentleman who thought himself under-paid had nothing to do but send in his resignation (hear, hear); but he did not know that a single one of those gentlemen were underpaid. On the contrary, they were paid up to the full capacity of their ability; but he was willing, for the sake of peace, to agree to a compromise. Mr. Cobain, he had heard, had stated that he (Sir John) had shown great ingratitude, as he (Mr. Cobain) had put him into the Council the first time he stood for election. He gave that an unqualified contradiction. He would be ashamed to be a nominee of Mr. Cobain or of any man (hear, hear). He stood there as an independent man, and no man was fitter to tell Sir John Savage. He had been independent all his life, and never was a nominee. That man that he put into the Council having the right to vote against him—he knew other Town Councillors and Aldermen—he stood up and oppose him when he came for an increase of salary. How could a man who was of good birth stand as a nominee or say he was treated badly? He did not want to be severe (laughter), but he had an [illegible] the [illegible] of [illegible], and would put any to marry men on the Treasury to act independently.

"Mr. Thompson's amendment was then put, and lost by a majority of twenty to seven."

The rates are principally misappropriated by reason of these large salaries. I say the salaries of the officials are tremendously in excess of what they ought to be paid. I say there are two exceptions, and these two are the town clerk and the clerk of markets. I think the salaries of those officials are not excessive, because their duties are onerous and intricate. These are the only two that meet with general approval outside this hall. The accountant has £300 a year, and there is no accountant in Belfast, or in any of the Commissioners' offices, who has more than £150 a year that I am aware of. I say his salary ought to be £150 a year. I say it is one-half too much. There are also five apprentices of the Town Council, all of whom get £60 a year, and I consider that too much.

1999. Do they not begin at £20, rising up to £60?—I say they should begin at £10 a year, and be raised £5 each year. With regard to the salary of Mr. Conway Scott——

2000. He is the executive sanitary officer?—He is. I say his salary is excessive, and that he is not competent for the office.

2001. Is not his salary approved of by the Local Government Board?—Yes; but I say the Local Government Board approve of many things they should not. Any recommendation of the Town Council is sure to meet their approval. This Mr. Scott used to measure gravel on the roads and was not a proper person to be appointed as executive sanitary officer of a place like Belfast. With regard to the appointment of Dr. Browne; he is a magistrate and was once a member of this Corporation, and mayor of Belfast. His appointment was made when he was at the same time resigning his position as honorary physician for the Belfast Royal Hospital in consequence, as he said (and as persons that present heard him state), of advanced years and declining health. I say therefore his appointment was very unsuitable and improper, and I am in a position to state that an efficient consulting sanitary officer can be obtained here for £100, instead of £300 a year.

2002. Was not Dr. Browne's salary also approved

of by the Local Government Board?—That makes no matter. The taxpayer ultimately pays it. In the year 1870, I find the sum of £124 3s. 3d., expended in cleansing, painting, and gas supplied to the Albert Memorial. My objection is that the amounts are excessive. Mr. Fitzpatrick's charge is £35 for cleaning the statue, and Mr. J. Lynn, for reporting on repairs, the sum of £13 13s. I say that no Corporation should have sanctioned the passing of that £13 13s. for work that any ordinary individual would have done for £1.

2003. Do you know Mr. Lynn?—No I never heard of him before. The charge is nearly as much as that of the man who did the work. Then there is £20 for keeping the clock in order, and I say that is a waste of money. The clock may be of use in the daytime, but at night it is of no earthly use, unless you are standing in the street beside it. There is £71 12s. 5d. worth of gas yearly consumed in illuminating it, which was money thrown away, considering you cannot see it at any distance. In the year 1874 there is charged for the removal of the Earl of Belfast's statue, 1s. 6d. for candles and some other items. You will observe that they had to remove the statue after dark for fear of the gentlemen of the Pound who might very likely attack it. For the removal of the statue itself £3 15s. 6d. is charged.

2004. Did not Lord Donegal pay all the expense of that?—If he paid it, why should we be charged, as we are in the accounts.

2005. But you will see from the other side of the account, that Lord Donegal paid more than was expended?—Then I think it was unfair for them to receive more than they paid. The expenditure with regard to the Albert Memorial, and the statue of the Earl of Belfast, I contend the Belfast Corporation should never have incurred, and I say that the rates were misappropriated, because these statues were put up to perpetuate the memories of men whose opinions the majority of the ratepayers did not agree with; that they should not be supported with public contributions, and that they should not be cleansed, repaired, &c., at the expense of the ratepayers. I say that the charge upon these statues was a useless expenditure of money. I complain of large sums of money being charged under the head of sundries. I think it is calculated to mislead. If sums to the extent of £2,000 or £3,000 are paid away, I say that the persons receiving the payments should be specified distinctly in writing and in printing, and also what the payments were for, and that these payments should not be set forth in globo.

2006. Do you mean to say that the accounts as published do not give sufficient information to the ratepayers?—I do, and I also say that items appear here and there through the entire reports setting forth high sums for wages and cartage, and that it is a system of book-keeping which is at the least open to suspicion.

2007. Do you not know that these accounts are audited by the Government Auditor. These items appear before him, and any ratepayer can attend the audit and make any complaint he may have?—That is quite true; but sometimes it is not convenient to attend. We have an instance of the Government Auditor passing sums he should never have passed if he had known his business.

2008. Mr. Lawless.—I understand you to mean that the accounts submitted every year to the auditor should be full accounts and not abstracts of the accounts?—Yes.

2009. Chairman.—Are there not full accounts submitted to the auditor?—There may be; but my argument is that they should be published, and furthermore, I wish to state that the receipt which every ratepayer receives on the payment of his annual taxes should distinctly set forth all the items which he pays for. It should be set forth more distinctly. Coming under the head of general purposes rates, people do not know what they are paying for at all.

2010. I would next refer you to an item of £86 1s. 6d. which appears in the expenditure side of the police fund, for the year 1873. "Mr. James Henry, umpire for courts and repairs to robing rooms."

2011. Do you object that he was then a member of the Town Council at the time?—Yes; and is still. Then there is £137 10s. 9d. for cleansing the Blackstaff, and I think you have sufficient evidence before you to show that it has not been yet cleansed, and that that money has been uselessly expended. In the same year (the year ending 31st August, 1873), £18 8s. 3d. has been spent for the cleansing of the Blackstaff. In the year 1874, I also find that Mr. James Henry has been paid the sum of £27 6s. 6d. for building and materials. I observe by the list of expenditure published in the year 1878, that this item appears in the miscellaneous account: "Cost of erection of platform in the Botanic Gardens, on the occasion of the knighting of the mayor and chairman of the Harbour Commissioners, £8 16s. 6d." It is not said to whom it is paid.

2012. Do you object to it as being an improper charge on the rates?—Yes; and if it is a proper charge, that the name is not given of the person to whom the amount was paid.

2013. Did you or anyone else appear before the auditor to object to these items?—I did not appear, nor anyone else on my behalf, but surely the auditor should have disallowed them himself. I have only seen them a very short time ago, when I commenced to look into these matters, with a view to this inquiry, but when I saw it I thought there was something wrong. I would state, with regard to the publishing of the book of expenditure and receipts, that I suppose there are not fifty ratepayers in Belfast, outside the town hall, who know that such a book is published yearly. I think a public notice should be placed in different parts of the town, saying that that book is published yearly, and can be obtained on the payment of 1s. I went into the office last year, and asked the town clerk to show me the minute-book, and after he had showed it to me he came forward and said I should have to pay 1s. for looking at the book. He said this just as I was getting the information I wanted. I thought the proceeding was very queer.

2014. Mr. Lawless.—That contract with Mr Henry bears date 4th January, 1873. Do you object to the amount that was paid to him?—The contract was paid when he was a member of the town council, —the payment was made for that contract within two months after that date. I believe that Mr. Harvey, who was a town councillor, made an award with regard to the payment of the amount, and that award and this payment were both made when Mr Henry was a town councillor.

2015. What sum was paid under that award?—I think it is £27 6s. 6d.

2016. Chairman.—I find "J. Henry for building, &c., £27 6s. 6d.—charged to the police fund account"?—In the year 1874 a sale of the surplus grounds at the pork-market took place. Messrs. Archer and Sons prepared plans for it, and I find charged in this account—Messrs. Archer and Sons, £9 10s. 6d., "for plans of the surplus grounds at the pork-market." (This is in the police fund account.) There were two sums of £21 each paid to William Hastings and George M'Anlis for a valuation of the ground. Mr. Black's law costs in connexion with the sale of the ground were £78 8s., and £33 1s. 2d. is charged for advertising it for sale.

2017. What is the total amount?—£163 18s. 8d.

2018. Do you know if any of these items were objected to before the auditor?—I am not sure.

2019. Not to your knowledge?—Not to my knowledge, but I now say that the amount paid to Messrs. Archer and Sons for preparing the plans was uselessly expended, there being a surveyor and an assistant surveyor for the borough of Belfast paid an annual

[illegible]

Belfast. Jan. 22, 1878.

Mr. Robert Stewart.

salary for doing such work as this, and I say they ought to have prepared the plans of this ground.

2020. In the year 1871, under the General Purposes Fund, I find Mr. Louis M'Cammy, civil engineer, "for plans of reclamation of slob lands and general drainage plans" paid £140, and Mr. Meshinney, for plans, £27 4s. Now, I say that our two surveyors should have prepared the plans, and saved the town that sum of £167 4s. I think you will find, from Mr. Fagans' report on the audit, that no objection could be possibly taken before him to the conduct of the corporation. The report is of the most satisfactory character, and is so complimentary to everyone, I wish it could be put on the notes of this Inquiry, and placed before the select committee of the House. In the years 1872, 1873, 1874, and 1875, we have sums of money paid to Alderman Henderson for printing and advertising.

2021. Was he an alderman in those years?—Yes.

2022. Was that paid for advertising in the *News Letter*?—Yes; while he was alderman, and you will understand me as objecting to the amount charged by him as being in excess of that which is charged by the other three newspapers. Workmen's wages also appear here and there and everywhere in the books, and whether or not such wages are paid is a matter for the auditor; but I say there is no regularity in the way of keeping the books, and that they are open to suspicion. With regard to the law costs for the year 1873, under the head of "General Purposes Fund," I find that Mr. William Kisbey, with respect to the claims for malicious injuries, for professional services rendered, is paid £120 19s., and to Mr. M'Clean, solicitor, £10 12s., and to Messrs. Johns, Hewitt and Johns, £23 1s.; and then there is an item for "sundry persons for damage done to their property, £3,777 11s. 8d." I say that such an extravagant sum of money should not be set forth under the head of "sundry persons," but the names of the persons and the sums of money paid to them should be given.

2023. And the amount claimed by each individual?—Certainly; and I hold that the personal services of Mr. Kisbey were not required, for we have a town solicitor, who, according to evidence as yet uncontradicted, is worth £3,000 or £4,000 a year.

2024. Did not the claims amount to £14,000 or £16,000, and were they not reduced to £3,777?—Yes. I say that those particular claims should be heard before a judge and not before the Corporation. These were claims arising out of party riots, and should not have been adjudicated upon by the Corporation, and paid for by them. Latterly the Corporation have allowed a number of individuals to erect expensive stalls in the public streets, which are decked with flashy sign boards.

2025. What are they?—They are called "Irish Temperance League coffee stands."

2026. Are they an obstruction to the footway?—They are erected by the consent of the Corporation, several of whom are members of that association. There is one of them erected in Pottinger's entry, and I say that they are erected with the view to monopolise the commercial enterprise of ratepayers who keep hotels and lodging houses, and pay very large taxes. People go in there and get a cup of coffee, but it is not so much harm to the inn-keepers as to the common lodging-house keepers.

2027. Do people sleep in those stalls?—I do not know; they seem to be of mysterious construction. They provide food at a much cheaper rate than the lodging-house keepers, and the association can dangle a purse of £3,000 in the eyes of the ratepayers and say that they do not care.

2028. Are they an obstruction?—They are, most unquestionably, and they have no right to be there at all. Several prosecutions were instituted within the last three or four months by the police regarding the sale of oranges and apples on the public highways, and it was proved in evidence that those were injurious to the interests of the shopkeepers, and the magistrates convicted the street sellers.

2029. Mr. *Black*.—They have only one stall in the town, and it is a temporary erection, that can be removed at any time.

2030. Mr. *Stewart*.—With regard to the Recorder's Court, I agree with every sentiment expressed yesterday by Mr. *Dawson*. We have a clerk of the peace who pockets about £100 a year on an average for licensing applications.

2031. Mr. Bruce.—I find on looking at the book that the items of compensation for malicious injury in the accounts appear to have been gone into most minutely by Mr. Fagan, the auditor.

Mr. John Brown.

Mr. John Brown examined.

2032. Chairman.—Are you chairman of the town improvement committee?—Yes. There were some statements affecting me made in evidence on the previous day to which, in justice to myself, I wish to refer. It was stated by Mr. Morton that four streets in Ballymacarrett—namely, the lower part of Mountpottinger, Dunvegan-street, Lagan-view-street, and Paterson-street, were in a very bad state, some of them being quite impassable from mud; and that Mr. Peter Quinn, who was building there, held the property from Mr. John Brown, the chairman of the improvement committee. Now, I wish to say that Mr. Peter Quinn does not hold the property under me. It does not belong to me. Mr. Quinn took a number of acres from Mr. Corry, one of the members for the town, and under his arrangement Mr. Quinn was himself to make those streets. It is a filled-up street—filled up slob ground, and it takes time to consolidate such ground; so that if the improvement committee made Mr. Quinn finish it at once it would sink, and they would have to put stuff on it afterwards. Therefore they have to wait for a little time until it is properly formed. Those streets referred to are no thoroughfares. If you went a little way onwards you would go into the tide. They are only part of the way built upon. I do not think there is one of the houses quite finished or occupied yet.

2033. Mr. *Morton*.—Certainly there are. In Lower Mount-street, Dunvegan street, &c., there are houses occupied.

Mr. Joseph G. Biggar, M.P.

supply and at the same time sell the water at a more liberal price. Since the Act of 1874 was passed their powers are extended, and they will be able to give a larger supply and to lower the price. In addition to that there is another point to which I wish to refer. The Corporation wanted the water for the purpose of watering the streets always at the time it was scarce. Now, at that time of the year, the water is running to the sea. They would gladly give the water at much less than 6d., but in the summer time they should get a higher price. There is always a risk that the manufacturers would need a supply. I think that upsets the argument made use of with regard to the question of the conflict of interests between the Town Council and the Water Board—and on which we have had a good deal of controversy in the newspapers and during the time I was on both boards——

2035. Were you on both at once?—Yes; there was also more or less trouble in supplying water in the case of fires; but there were two parties concerned, and when you have one set of men watching another set of men you are very likely to find where the fault was. Each one set out where he thought the blame was, and the result was that the public got at where really the blame and fault was.

2036. Where did you come to the conclusion the fault was?—I think more or less on both sides. Of course this took place some years ago. Mr. Reilly's complaint was that the Water Commissioners' men did not go to open the plugs. He ought to know where they were as well as the Water Commissioners' men.

2037. We have heard that they are working well enough at present?—Mr. Black said, in his evidence, that this controversy took place some three years ago and that the two boards should be amalgamated.

2038. The real grievance complained of was that two boards should have a right to open up the streets, that two jurisdictions should be over the streets. He said they were working harmoniously together now?—It is strange I did not take notice of that in Mr. Black's evidence; but after all, the matter you refer to would not, I think, be of sufficient importance to bring about such an issue. As well as I remember the Water Commissioners opened a street when they required to do so, and they closed it up in a temporary way, and then gave notice of the matter to the Town Council who, I suppose, were paid the amount of their claim, so that I do not think that reason sufficient for what was proposed. There was another question raised by Mr. Black not in connexion with the water board, and really I would be disposed to take a very different view of it. He said there was no reason why the Harbour Commissioners and the Town Council should not be joined. I do not know if this question about the Harbour Board exactly comes within your province, but I wish to state one matter about it. There is a very material conflict between the Harbour Board and the Town Council on one point, and it is a most serious matter for Belfast. It is with regard to the outlet for the sewage, and it was referred to by Dr. Alexander. We have had a great number of complaints here, and before the inquiry ends you will have more about the defective state of the sewerage of Belfast. There is a great difficulty in getting a proper outlet for the sewage, and this is a vital question—much more serious than that of the paste of water, &c., and with the view to having a proper outlet I would hazard the opinion that it would be desirable the two Boards should be joined. The question is—how is it to be done? That is—how are you to get rid of the sewage?

2039. I have already said that the question of the Blackstaff being a nuisance is proved beyond all doubt, and we have had several schemes laid before us to remedy the evil, but we are not here to determine between rival schemes—it is not a question for us. We will take a note of your opinion, that with the view to having a proper outlet for the Blackstaff, the Town Council and the Harbour Board should be amalgamated.

2040. *Witness*.—I do not wish to raise any rival schemes. I am in favour of a thorough scheme of reform for the sewage and not for one of these temporary remedies. They paid too much for the gas-works. It was a dear bargain. I think if the gas-works were not in the hands of the Corporation now we would have gas at a lower price than we are paying for it. With regard to the houses being occupied when the streets were not paved and sewered, I may say that there are many such places. I know that the excuse of Mr. Montgomery is that the increase in the number of streets is so large that it could not be kept pace with, and I think it is not a very unreasonable excuse after all. On the very important question raised here by Dr. Dorrian, about the graveyard, I may say that the opinions and wishes of a large portion of the population of Belfast were not considered or consulted at all, but were set aside altogether. The Roman Catholics were all of the bishop's opinion, but the members of the Town Council being all Protestants, except one or two, they set the opinion of Dr. Dorrian and the Roman Catholics of Belfast at defiance. The laws of the Roman Catholic Church could not by any possible means be carried out, because of the decision come to by the Town Council.

Dr. MICHAEL R. O'MALLEY examined.

Dr. Michael R. O'Malley.

2041. CHAIRMAN.—Do you reside in the Ballymacarrett district?—I reside in the town.

2042. You wish to give us some evidence with regard to the sewerage of the Ballymacarrett district?—Yes.

2043. We heard yesterday that the sewerage there is very imperfect?—Yes. I am physician to the Nazareth convent there.

2044. Will you state shortly the evidence you wish to give as physician to that convent?—As a matter which concerns the public health, and at the request of the superioress of the convent, I want to say something about the defective state of the sewerage. The convent, until about twelve months ago, was a private residence. Now there are between sixty and one hundred inmates in it, and the tank into which the sewerage flows is merely a cesspool.

2045. Was the house made originally for a private family?—Yes.

2046. Is the tank large enough now when there are so many inmates in the convent?—No; and the consequence is, that there is a frequent overflow from it, as there is no main sewerage in the neighbourhood, and it endangers the health of the people very much.

2047. Is there not any main sewerage there?—There is no main sewerage into which they can drain.

2048. Have you inspected it yourself?—Yes, I saw the cesspool.

2049. Can you state that it is very prejudicial to the health of the inmates of the convent?—Certainly.

2050. And also to the immediate neighbourhood?—Yes. This convent is established for the reception of old infirm people, and young children who are orphans, foundlings, and incurables of all creeds.

2051. Have you ascertained for yourself that there is no means of connexion with any public sewer in the neighbourhood?—I have done that. I have made inquiries about it, and there is no main sewer with which a connexion could be made.

2052. Has any representation been made by the superioress of the convent, or by anyone on her behalf, to the borough surveyor on the subject?—Yes; I have it from the superioress that a communication was made, and that Dr. Browne was out there; I am not certain, but I think the surveyor was there also.

BELFAST.
Oct. 21, 1876.

Dr. Richard E. O'Malley.

2053. Did Dr. Browne inspect the place?—Yes.

2054. Mr. KELLY.—Has anything been done since that?—No.

2055. When did Dr. Browne go there?—I do not know the exact day.

2056. Was it within the last few months?—Yes. There is also the Magdalene Asylum on the other side of the road, and a number of private houses that are similarly inconvenienced.

2057. CHAIRMAN.—Do they also complain of the want of sewerage?—Yes.

2058. Have they cesspools?—No, I think not.

2059. How do they dispose of their sewerage?—I think there are no cesspools. I think it is removed from time to time.

2060. You only speak of what you believe to be a fact?—No; I know of one house I am positively certain about.

Mr. James Dempsey.

Mr. JAMES DEMPSEY examined.

2061. CHAIRMAN.—What material points are there to which you wish to direct our attention?—Upon the question of expenditure. I don't think the improvements in the town are at all commensurate with the money they have cost, and I consider that the salaries paid to our officers are altogether too high. For instance, our borough surveyor is now paid £450 a year, while in 1865 he had £300; and the assistant surveyor who had originally £100 is now paid £275.

2062. Do you think that the increase in the salaries is more than commensurate with the increased work?—Yes. The borough surveyor has now a large staff and two assistant surveyors, and the Act only contemplated his having one. There is the surveyor of highways, and a clerk in the surveyor's office, and a large staff, all paid very high salaries.

2063. What staff has he except his assistants and the labourers who receive weekly wages?—They are put down as weekly wages, but I think they are very fair salaries. For instance, you have the weekly salaries of the inspectors—Bradley, £3 10s.; James Donnelly, £3; George Zachary, £2, Samuel M'Kenny, £1 15s.

2064. Are not these men all employed for scavenging purposes?—They are not.

2065. At what work are they employed from time to time?—I do not know.

2066. At what are they employed, Mr. Black?—Mr. Black.—The workmen vary, but these men are inspectors and do not vary; they are permanent; they are foremen.

2067. Witness.—But my observations do not apply to these men, but to the salaries of the superior officers.

2068. Would you specify whose salary is excessive?—I think the salary of the borough surveyor is very excessive. The surveyor of buildings of Customs Board, in London, receives only £500 a year, and of the Inland Revenue Department, London, £400 per annum. Taking the capabilities of these officers into account, I think our borough surveyor is greatly overpaid. Indeed I think that the whole of the superior corporate officers are overpaid.

2069. Are their duties similar to those gentlemen you have named?—I should say that the duties of the London officers are more onerous.

2070. Have you any special knowledge as to what the duties of the borough surveyor are?—I think it should be much less critical supervising the plans of small houses than performing the duties which those officers in London whom I have named have to discharge. In 1865 the salaries in the borough surveyor's office have amounted to £605, while in 1875 they were £1,637. There might be some exception taken to that, because in the borough surveyor's list of salaries that I have before me, Mr. DeCobain's is included. I have also included the officers employed in the sanitary department, in the £1,637. Mr. DeCobain in 1865 received £75 per annum; in 1875 he was receiving £300. I think that is excessive.

2071. Is he in the same department now that he was in at that time?—No; but he is classed with the salaries. The fire brigade in 1865 cost £398, and in 1875, £1,161. I think the increase of salaries has been the principal increase of the cost of that department also.

2072. Can you give me the number of new houses built in Belfast during the last ten years?—I cannot; but there is not so much difficulty in passing plans for new houses; they are generally passed in batches. I don't think many of them are ornamental, and many of them have been built on and without any proper foundation for them.

2073. Has the work of the fire brigade been heavy?—Fires have not increased very much, I am happy to be able to say. The accountant's salary appears to have increased very much. His salary at present is £350. I think that is very much in excess of what it ought to be. I think that looking at the state of things that is now prevailing it would seem that the officers first appear to have got their salaries increased, and then they appear to have assistance. I question very much whether there is much more done in some departments than signing letters, they have so many assistants.

2074. Then you complain not only of the increase of the salaries but of the increase of the staff?—I do; I think the whole thing could be done much more economically than it is. I think the work of the staff is very light. The total list of salaries is about £10,887.

2075. Does that not include wages?—No; it does not.

2076. Does it include the salaries of the gasworks officers?—Yes.

2077. But that is altogether distinct?—I think that there is no more work in both departments than there is in the Customs Department of Belfast, which employs gaugers, landing officers, and others, and I think they ought to be better paid than the corporate officers.

2078. Have you compared these salaries with those paid in any other incorporated borough. Do you find the same proportion of salaries paid elsewhere?—I have not been able to do that, but I have compared them with the public service, and I find they are in excess of that. There is, for instance, the salary of an officer who has been recently appointed, Dr. Hodges, the borough analyst. He receives £150 per annum, and yet he charges £30 for materials.

2079. Has he been appointed under the recent Act of Parliament?—Yes.

2080. Do you complain of that amount as excessive?—I think so; I especially complain of the £30 for materials in addition to his large salary.

2081. Is not that also submitted to the Local Government Board?—I suppose so. His first report showed that he had analysed twenty-eight samples. I have estimated that they should not cost more than 10s., and I think that £30 is decidedly excessive.

2082. Mr. Black.—That amount is charged for retorts and things of that kind. The money was for utensils, and, I think, the town should pay for them.

2083. Did you ever object to these things before the auditor?—We never heard that there was such a thing as printed accounts.

2084. But you knew there was a public audit?—We knew nothing of that. We have no information on that subject.

2085. Are not the public newspapers open to everyone?—It is not published in the newspapers I say. I think if we had some representation on the Council we would know more of these matters. It appears that the paper it is published in—though a valuable paper in the evening—is not published until after the people have gone home.

2086. Does not the auditor publish it in more than one paper?—I do not think he does, and I do not think that it is for the purpose of bringing that any publication is made. I think the salary of the present town clerk is an excessive one. From £350 in 1865 it was increased to £450, and now it is £[illegible]. I understand he does not approve of the principle of employing apprentices.

2087. There is no obligation on the auditor to publish a notice of the holding of his audit, but do not the Corporation publish the notice of his audit in the newspapers?—I do not think the ratepayers know anything about it. I object to the number of apprentices, and the rate at which they are paid. I think the superintendent of the fire brigade receives too much salary. It is at present £150, and I think his qualifications have been derived from his having been a fireman. I object to these officers being paid so high out of the rates of the town when officers of the public departments are not paid anything like the same salaries. There has been a great deal of congratulation about the gas question, but I don't think it was stated that the cost of lighting has considerably increased. With coals about the same price we had gaslight in 1863 at about 3s. 9d. per thousand, whereas we now pay 3s. 11d. Up to very recently we got it from the gaslight company for 4s. 6d. I object to the commission charged for the collection of the gas rates as being too high, and I also object to a reduction being made in the price of gas to large consumers. I think there should be a discount given to those who pay in proper time, but not an excessive discount. I would allow a discount for prompt payment, but not twenty per cent. to large consumers. I object to allowing anything over two and a half per cent., and that only for payments within a month's time. I think the salaries paid in the department of the gas works will prevent a reduction in the price of gas to the proper standard. The manager gets £600 a year, and the assistant manager, £250—it costs £[illegible] for the management of the gasworks.

2088. Mr. Rea[illegible].—What did he get from the company before?—I am sure the salaries have been increased, but I don't know how much. The manager's office costs £1,[illegible] per annum, and the salary of the cashier is almost equal to that of any collector of customs in any port—£[illegible] a year. The salaries of the clerks are as high as staff officers of the army. I also object to the erection of a temperance [illegible] coffee stand in the public street.

2089. What is your business?—I am a vintner and wholesale spirit dealer. I consider that these temperance league people are organizing a crusade against the traders to which I belong, and it is not fair for the Corporation to assist a body against a section of the trading community, either by advertising or otherwise.

2090. Do you consider that the coffee house where it now stands is an obstruction to the public thoroughfare?—Most certainly; there was a passage way for carts where it now stands, and there is not one now. What I object to is that this is probably only the beginning of many of them. My principal object in giving this evidence with regard to the salaries is, that at the very last meeting of the Corporation there was notice given for a further increase of salaries, but I suppose that in consequence of the visit of this Commission the matter has been allowed to lie over for the present.

Mr. J[illegible] M[illegible] examined.

2091. Mr. Lawson.—Where do you reside?—At 37, Millfield-street, Belfast.

2092. And you are a ratepayer of the borough?—Yes.

2093. Do you wish to give evidence with regard to the question of the neglect of the corporation in managing the public streets?—I do.

2094. What is the point on which you wish to give evidence?—Millford-street is a long street, leading to the Falls-road and into Albert-street; when the ground at the end of it was about to be built on, Mr. Browne, the chairman of the improvement committee, came and looked at the spot where this building was being put, and told me to go before the improvement committee and complain about it. I did so, but they, nevertheless, let the man build on that piece of ground and passed his plans.

2095. Was the building on it when Mr. Browne saw it?—It was partly up. What I understand was, that the improvement committee objected to this in the first instance, and then passed the man's plans afterwards. Alderman Hughes, a member of the improvement committee, told me that the plans were approved of, by which this obstruction was created in Millford-street and the Quadrant-road. He told me they were passed by favour to the contractor.

2096. Mr. E[illegible].—Who was the person who erected the plans for the works?—His name was Craft.

2097. When were these plans passed?—Two years ago.

Mr. Montgomery re-examined.

2098. Chairman.—What do you say as to this complaint about Millford-street?—For some years I endeavoured to prevent that block of buildings being erected. Mr. Browne never stated that he put any of the blame on me. We had been endeavouring to prevent it for years, but the owners of the property erected that building in defiance of the town council. After three or four years of persistent effort on my part and on the part of Mr. John Browne, the owners took their own course, on legal advice, and built the house on the place which is a continuation of Millford-street. The corporation was not allowed to continue the street straight through, for the owners built up a row of houses which made the street narrower at one end than the other. We have applied to a number of the owners of property to co-operate with us in making these streets all through in continuation, but not one of these owners would give us any assistance, and I do not think the rates are applicable to the purpose. There are many instances such as that to which I have now referred.

the value of property in this town at least 25 per cent., owing to the want of confidence that there would be in the administration of the force.

3104. Mr. LAWLESS.—Do you think the same state of things that prevailed in 1864 would be likely to be restored?—Yes, I do. I believe that if the police force were under the control of the Corporation, and there was a contested municipal election, and I took part in it in virtue of my rights, and used my influence in favour of one of the candidates, the police force would use their powers against me as police, and my business would be injured. We cannot do anything here. We have no representation on the Town Council for Catholics.

Mr. THOMAS H. BROWNE examined.

3105. Do you wish to make a statement about the unfinished streets alluded to by Mr. Moreton, in the first of which there are twenty-nine houses occupied?—Yes. He said they belonged to Messrs. L. and T. Browne.

3106. Do they belong to you?—I am the joint owner of them with another party. He said they were neither sewered nor paved, &c. They are perfectly sewered, and the drains in the backyard go into the main drains, and the footways are formed and flagged ready for paving.

3107. He said they were not sewered so far as he believed. He said he did not think they were from the state of the street?—The roadway is also made ready for paving. I may mention that the houses are not ours now. They were built by us about two years ago, and we sold them to another party, and are now only ground landlords.

3108. The exact complaint was this—that you being a member of the improvement committee of the Town Council had sufficient influence to allow this street to be opened before it was in a proper state to be opened?—I deny that entirely. If members of the improvement committee of the Town Council happen to have the misfortune of being owners of property, they are more particular not to show any favour to themselves than any other property.

3109. Did you, as a matter of fact, exercise any influence with regard to the opening of this street?—Certainly not. The other streets are sewered and channel, and the footways made all to paving. Of course they will be done with the approval of the town surveyor.

3110. When were the houses built and when were they sold?—The houses were built two years ago, and they were sold—part of them three months ago and part a year ago. The streets were so far made before the houses were sold.

3111. Was there any question with the parties to whom you sold them as to whether or not the street should be opened immediately?—As soon as the other side of the street was built.

3112. Did you, or would you, derive any benefit, directly or indirectly, from the street being opened before the time specified by the Act?—Not the least.

3113. Was it a condition with the parties to whom you sold these houses that they should go into occupation immediately?—Yes, it was.

3114. Mr. EVERARD.—Don't you know perfectly well that the section states that the surveyor is not to allow the houses to be occupied until the street is completed, and that the party is liable to a penalty of 20s. a day for every day it is occupied?—Yes.

3115. Mr. KEITH.—That section has never been enforced in Belfast.

3116. Is it your excuse, Mr. Keith, that the Corporation knowingly violated the law since the time they themselves obtained their own Act?—I admit it was not carried out.

3117. Mr. EVERARD (to the Witness).—Do I understand you to say that before these houses were used the street had been thoroughly drained and sewered, although it had not been paved?—Yes. These houses are now in perfect sanitary condition. They are new houses, and they are perfectly sewered.

3118. Did you not know at the time you sold them that the 75th section of the Act of 1865 had not been complied with?—I knew that it was not to the full extent.

3119. Why then did you make it a condition, as you say you did, with the parties to whom you sold the houses, that they should be occupied immediately?—Because the streets were sufficiently finished, and the sewers were complete.

3120. Did you do anything or interfere with the opening of houses further than you have stated?—I had nothing further to do with the matter. I deny that as a member of the Improvement Committee or as a member of the Town Council, I used any influence whatever in having these houses opened.

Mr. O'NEILL re-examined.

3121. CHAIRMAN.—Do you wish to say anything about Mr. Browne's houses?—I live in sight of those streets in question. I paved Peel-street at a cost of £73; Rose-street, at £37, and I am now paving Mayor-street at a cost of £26 6s. All these streets are in sight of the streets that Mr. Browne has been examined with reference to, and I say deliberately that not one of the streets to which Mr. Browne referred is half-made or made but above paved. There are kerbstones running along, but no paving between them and the houses. Outside that stone there is mud and slush, and no bottom. It was a swamp some time ago, and is so still and from passing. I know that these houses are inhabited for a long time. I state now of my own personal knowledge that the statement made by Mr. Moreton is substantially correct.

3122. Did you complete the paving of your streets before the houses were let?—They were let before I bought them. There was a kind of paving on them a long time before, but I was forced to pave my streets when I bought them.

3123. Who compelled you to pave your own streets?—I was made do so by an order of the Corporation.

3124. Do you positively say that these other three streets in view of yours have not yet been done?—Yes; I was made do mine at once because I was not a Town Councillor.

3125. Were you allowed a shorter period before you were made do your streets than Mr. Browne has been allowed for his streets?—I got a much shorter time. The place is at a low level and very like a swamp. It was drained, and the Messrs. Browne built these houses on ground which is still a kind of swamp, and some of the houses became pied. I think they are built about two years.

3126. Did they come down upon you as it were and make you dig and pave your street without giving you the same time or about the same time they are supposed to have given to Mr. Browne?—My time was very much shorter. I was made do it at once. My streets had been accommodated for years past before the paving took place, but when I got the notice for the paving—the notice was put up at the corner of the street—I had to get it done at once. There was a kind of paving on my street, and it was in better order than Mr. Browne's were. I had to pay £73 in one case; in another £37, and in a third £26 for paving the streets. I objected that I should be made a "scape-goat" of, and when an arte complaint I was served with a summons and placed on the part of the Corporation in reference to this paving. I went to the office of Mr. Bruce about it, and when he told me I would have to pay £3 10s. costs, I replied I would never pay a farthing, and I have never been asked to pay a shilling of it since. Mr. Browne's houses are built on a swamp.

3127. Do I understand you to mean that the place is a swamp now?—Yes; the streets are not paved.

3128. The CHAIRMAN read a memorial he had received from a number of the ratepayers residing in the neighbourhood of Millfield, complaining of a nuisance existing in a milldam there, which he handed to the officers of the Corporation for an explanation.

Adjourned.

[illegible]

Mr. Samuel Black.

3129. CHAIRMAN.—You made a note of the points on which you wish to reply?—I did.

3130. There is a very important portion of the evidence given to which I wish to draw your attention. Mr. Dixon says in the course of his evidence (reads):—"I consider the Corporation a large political engine, worked by the officials who are paid out of the rates of the town." What is your answer to that?—My answer is that it is untrue.

3131. Can you produce any facts in evidence contradicting it? He also said (again reads from the evidence of Mr. Dixon):—"The officers of the Corporation I look upon as the ruling spirits, who nominate, canvass, and pay runners and agents for the purpose of having the men of their choice returned as representatives of that body." Speaking for yourself, Mr. Black, can you say whether or not you ever did any such thing?—I can state most distinctly that since the day I became solicitor to the Corporation I never interfered, either directly or indirectly, with political affairs within the borough.

3132. Can you say of your own knowledge whether any officer of the Corporation at any time nominated, canvassed, or paid agents for the purpose of having men of their own choice returned?—I can say that as far as I know it is perfectly untrue.

3133. I pressed Mr. Dixon on the subject, and I could only get him to name one person, the cashier?—The cashier will answer for himself.

3134. To the best of your belief has the cashier interfered as to the elections in any way whatever?—I don't interfere with them myself, and I do not know anything of his interference.

3135. Did he ever interfere in elections by your instructions?—Certainly not; neither he nor any other officer of the Corporation.

3136. Can you say whether or not any members of the Corporation have given any instructions to any official to take an active part in elections?—Never to my knowledge.

3137. Do you know of other persons who have so interfered?—I do not.

3138. Do you know of any "inner circle of the Corporation" which governs the rest of the body, as stated by Mr. Dixon?—I do not know of any "inner circle of the Corporation."

3139. Can you tell us the circumstances under which the salary of the cashier was raised from £70 a year to £300 a year?—I think it was a mistake to say it ever was £70 a year; when he came here he was simply a clerk in the cashier's office; he was appointed at a salary of £70 a year as clerk.

3140. Was he appointed first simply as clerk?—Yes, and not as cashier; he was subsequently appointed as cashier, and his duties increased greatly.

3141. MR. LAWLESS.—About what time?—It was about 1866; after the passing of the Act of 1865 the revenue of the Corporation became greatly increased, and we found it necessary to considerably increase the staff at that time.

3142. CHAIRMAN.—When was he appointed cashier, and at what salary at first?—Mr. Fisher Oulton was the accountant and cashier at that time.

3143. The two offices were combined then?—They were.

3144. What salary was Mr. Oulton paid?—My impression is that he had £250 a year.

3145. Do you remember when Mr. Colvin was appointed cashier?—About the year 1866, I think.

3146. Can you tell at what salary?—£100 a year.

3147. Has it since been raised to £300 a year?—It has.

3148. Was it raised at one time or at different times?—At different times: when the gasworks were taken over by the Corporation, the cashier of the company was paid £400 a year: of course we had to take him over on the same terms; Mr. Colvin, the cashier of the Corporation, said he filled a corresponding office of one and the same importance and labour, and that the salary he had then of £150 a year was not at all equal to the duties he discharged; therefore, he applied for an increase of salary. The salary he then had was £150 a year.

3149. Was there a proposal afterwards to raise it to £250?—There was.

3150. Was it raised to £300?—Yes.

3151. MR. LAWLESS.—Do I understand you to say, that because the cashier of the gasworks received £400 a year for his salary, Mr. Colvin became dissatisfied with his salary, and applied for more?—He put that forward as a reason for getting more.

3152. CHAIRMAN.—Mr. Dixon said that Mr. Colvin's salary was raised for services rendered in connexion with the municipal elections. Is that true?—That is perfectly untrue.

3153. MR. EXHAM.—Were you present at the meeting of the Corporation when there was a resolution moved by Mr. Dixon to prevent any officer in the Corporation from taking any part in elections, save recording his vote?—This is the resolution. (Reads resolution referred to.)

3154. Were you present when that resolution was moved?—I was.

3155. Was it moved, seconded, and discussed; and upon being put to the vote, was it rejected by seventeen to six?—Yes, that is quite correct.

3156. Can you say why that resolution was rejected, and what were the grounds urged against its adoption?—There was a good deal of discussion about the matter. I think it was a resolution that might have been fairly passed, and I think it would have been passed, but for the injudicious course adopted by some of its supporters. They brought charges against the officials which were shown to be totally groundless, and without foundation.

3157. Were the grounds urged for its adoption similar to those made the other day by Mr. Dixon?—Yes; the Council simply refused to adopt any such resolution on such grounds, and said they did not wish to interfere with the private rights as citizens of any of their officers, but at the same time they never gave them encouragement to take an active part in political matters in the borough.

3158. CHAIRMAN.—Mr. Dixon said, in reply to Mr. Balson, that he had when moving his resolution cited instances of this. Was that so?—The members of the Corporation knew of their own knowledge that his statement was untrue.

3159. Did the Corporation make any inquiry into Mr. Dixon's charges?—No, they knew them to be groundless.

3160. Mr. Dixon also said that he believed the action of the officials had grown stronger since his resolution was rejected, and that they now had complete control over the election of the Corporation. Do you deny that statement is correct?—Yes.

3161. Are you present at all meetings of the Corporation?—Yes, I am at almost every meeting of the Corporation.

3162. He also says that this is done by the inner circle of the Corporation. Have you any knowledge of this?—I have not.

3163. I asked him to name any official beside the the cashier, and the only other persons he named were the collectors?—Two of them were referred to—Mr. Charles Noah Davis by him, and Mr. Rankin by Mr. Stewart. It was stated that voters of one party were disqualified by the collectors by their neglect in applying for payment of the municipal taxes. Now I find the number disqualified for the last year for non-payment of municipal taxes in the dock ward in which Mr. Rankin is the collector, were eighteen. In Ecclesfield ward, where Mr. Davis is collector, only fourteen were disqualified for non-payment of

Belfast. Dec 22, 1876. — Mr. Samuel Black.

municipal taxes, but ninety-seven were disqualified for non-payment of poor-rates.

3164. Were any voters disqualified by reason of the collector not having returned their names?—I can't tell. I dare say there were, but that would not interfere with the collectors; they get the names from the clerk of the Poor Law Union, and they are not responsible for that in any way.

3165. Did the Corporation pass rules in the year 1866 with regard to the collection of rates?—Yes. (Hands in rules.)

3166. Are they carried out?—They are.

3167. Do you say of your own knowledge that the rules are carried out?—Yes, strictly; and I think it would now be well for me to state the practice as to the collection of municipal taxes. The rates are all struck on the 1st of January in each year, and the rate-books are at once put into the hands of each rate-collector for collection. The first month in each year is occupied principally in receiving taxes from the landlords of property, who are entitled to a discount of twenty-five per cent. for prompt payment, and therefore the collectors are obliged to remain in their offices during that month. Immediately after they serve notices on the ratepayers with as little delay as possible, stating the particulars of all the municipal taxes leviable and requiring payment. If the taxes are not paid by the 1st of May, notice is published in all the newspapers requiring payment, and informing the parties in arrear that proceedings will be taken against them to recover the amount due. After that each of the collectors is obliged at every meeting of the finance committee, which takes place once a fortnight (if not more frequently), to bring in a list of the first fifty names on the rate books of the persons in arrear, and he is obliged to account for the collection of the rates, and the collector himself then serves a further notice on the parties in arrear and demands payment personally, and if the rates are not paid he then issues summonses against them. A fresh list is brought in from time to time of the next fifty names, and so on until the whole books and all the parties in arrear are gone through. There is no favouritism in the matter. The names are taken in regular order from the rate books as they occur.

3168. If these instructions are carried out it is impossible that any person could be disqualified by reason of their not being called upon to pay their rates? —Quite so; they must, in fact, receive two notices.

3169. Mr. Lawson.—Are the names of the persons taken alphabetically?—No; they are taken just as they occur in the book; such are the instructions given to the collectors, and such I believe to be carried out. I think that, on the whole, in no town in the three kingdoms (and I have a good deal of knowledge of them) are the rates so well collected as in this.

3170. Mr. Exham.—Is not this one of the rules— "No deputy or assistant shall be employed by any collector for any other purpose than assisting in filling up notices and receipts, preparing returns to the accountant's office, and other office work, it being the intention of the Council that each collector shall be the personal collector of the rates of his ward?"—I am aware it is.

3171. Do you know that the collector for one of the wards (I think the Dock ward) does not collect the rates personally, but employs and pays a deputy to go out and collect them for him? Is that within your knowledge?—It is not. It is the first time that ever I heard of such a thing.

3172. To your knowledge have instructions been given by the Town Council themselves in accordance with these rules to each collector that he is to collect the rates in person, and that his deputy or assistant is only to assist him at the office work?—I know that those are the instructions given by the Council, and we always thought they were carried out. I may state that Rankin, the man referred to, is I believe one of the best collectors we have. He collects his ward extremely well.

3173. We heard nothing against him or the manner in which the rates were collected. The complaint was that he collected the rates by deputy, which is in direct violation of the rules. Is it without your knowledge or within the knowledge of the Town Council, as far as you know, that he employs a deputy?—As a matter of fact we know that he employed a deputy for particular purposes, but we never knew he employed that deputy for the purpose of collecting the rates.

3174. The statement made by Mr Stewart was that for five years Rankin never came to demand or receive a rate from him, and that he (Mr. Stewart) always paid his deputy. He also said that the deputy told him (Mr. Stewart) that Rankin paid him £60 a year for collecting the rates for him. What do you say to that?—Rankin is in regular attendance in his office, and out about his district, but whether he called for Mr. Stewart's rates I do not know.

3175. But surely if this has been going on for five years one would suppose the Town Council or their officers would know it. I want to know whether he acts as alleged, and if so whether he does so with the knowledge of the Council?—Certainly not. Perhaps you will allow me to explain that so anxious were we that no person should be disqualified for non-payment of rates, or from not being properly rated, that we actually advertised in all the town papers within the last year, requesting all firms and others to see that the names of individuals were returned properly, and to send them in to us at the town hall. In many instances the rate-books were corrected in this way.

3176. Otherwise you take the names from the Poor Law Union books?—That we are obliged to do.

3177. Does each collector report to the town clerk every Saturday whenever there has been a change of occupancy or residence, as he is bound to do under the rules?—I know that they frequently made reports, but whether they did so once a week or not I really cannot say.

3178. Chairman.—Were they instructed to make such reports?—They were.

3179. Mr. Exham.—Is the 3rd rule carried out; "these books" (that is the collector's rate collecting-book) "shall at the close of the collection for the day be lodged in the accountant's office"?—I believe that rule is strictly carried out. In St. George's ward only twelve voters were disqualified for non-payment of the town rates.

3180. Chairman.—Is there any quarter of the town which is more inhabited by Roman Catholics than the others?—There is a place called the "Pound" which is principally occupied by Roman Catholics.

3181. Which ward is that in?—I must confess my ignorance of that. My impression is that it is either in St. George's ward or Smithfield ward. In fact I believe it to be in both of those wards.

3182. There is another general rule here which says that "no application, report, recommendation, or proceeding relating to the salary or pecuniary allowance of any officer shall be taken into consideration at any other than the monthly or quarterly council meeting next after the quarterly or monthly meeting at which such report, application, or recommendation shall have been made or submitted to the Council"—so there must always be a month or quarter elapse between the notice and the voting on it. Has that rule been always adhered to?—Yes; any such application must be brought forward at one meeting, and taken up at the next.

3183. Mr. Exham.—Were you present at the meeting when a member of the Council (I do not say who) complained that Mr. Cohain said that he ought to vote for his increase of salary, because he (Mr. Cohain) helped to return him as a member of the Town Council? —I was present at the meeting when Sir John Savage made a statement to the effect that it had been stated to him by some one else that Mr. Cohain had observed that he (Sir John) should support his application for an increase of salary, because he had assisted him, or voted for him at his election.

2184. Was Mr. Colvin then asked whether he made use of such a statement or not?—Mr. Colvin was asked by me, and he said he never made such a statement.

2185. Did Sir John Savage make the statement to that effect in Mr. Colvin's presence?—He did.

2186. Did he in this council-room make a charge that Mr. Colvin had said that?—He did.

2187. Was Mr. Colvin called before the Council to answer or explain this statement made by Sir John Savage in open Council before the vote was passed to increase his salary?—He was not. I remember that a number of the salaries were proposed to be increased at that time, and the matter was referred to the Town Council in committee for consideration. It was suggested at the meeting of committee, that the increase should be simply one-half instead of the whole amount. That was accepted, and after it came up again at the subsequent meeting (anything done by the Council in committee must be confirmed in open Council), it was proposed, notwithstanding that compromise, that the salary of Mr. Woods, the accountant, should be made £— a year as was originally proposed—because the Town Council as a body thought that he was performing very important duties. Sir John Savage I think was annoyed at the matter being reopened, and made that statement which has been alluded to with regard to Mr. Colvin.

2188. When that charge was openly made before the whole Council by a gentleman of Sir John Savage's position against an officer of the Corporation, was any inquiry made by them as to whether or not he (Mr. Colvin) had made such a statement?—My impression is that the Council took it as a joke.

2189. Is it the statement of Sir John Savage?—Yes.

2190. You say that he distinctly denied to you that he made use of it. Did you ask him about it?—Yes, and he distinctly denied that he made such a statement.

2191. Mr. Lawless.—Was Mr. Colvin's salary increased beyond the amount that had been agreed to by the committee of the Council?—Certainly not.

2192. Was Mr. Woods'?—No, but a motion was made to that effect. There was a question asked me about the collectors reporting changes of occupancy or residence. I have now before me the book in which those changes are reported from time to time to the town clerk. He makes a note of them. They are entered in that book alphabetically by the town clerk himself. (Hands in book.)

2193. These seem to be reports made every day?—Every day.

2194. This is only for the last quarter?—Yes.

2195. Have you any regulations as to the duties of the town surveyor, because we had it in evidence yesterday that other surveyors were called in occasionally?—The town surveyor is to make all plans; but occasionally a leading engineer has been called in to advise and assist him in important matters, such as the main drainage scheme. On one occasion (about the year 1870) the Council proposed to carry it out, and also to clear lands for irrigation purposes. The town surveyor was totally unable either by himself or by his assistant to prepare all the plans for that. We had applied to the then Government to advance the money to carry out the irrigation scheme, and certain plans were required for the purpose, which the surveyor could not possibly prepare in time, and therefore assistance was called in.

2196. For what were the two persons paid £21 each for making valuations?—That is a total fallacy. It was with reference to the sale of the Park market ground which adjoins this place.

2197. Chairman.—Were not two sums of £21 paid, and if so, for what purpose?—Those sums were not paid for plans, but for valuations. I advised the council that it would not be well for them to put grounds of such value into the market without having the opinion of at least two competent valuators as to their annual value, and two leading valuators in town (Messrs. Hastings and M'Ardle) were brought in to put a price on the grounds. They were paid £21 each, and I consider that was a very moderate charge.

2198. Was that done on your advice?—Yes; there was also a charge of £9 10s. for plans. There was a plan prepared by the surveyor, but we required to attach to it all the particulars and the conditions of the sale. We required about 200 copies of it, so that it would be utterly impossible for the surveyor, unless he was a lithographer, to get these ready. A lithographer was, therefore, employed and paid. It might have cost five or six times the amount paid for the work if it had been done by the surveyor, and may be could not have been done by him in the end. (Plan produced.)

2199. Does Mr. Montgomery prepare all the plans for the Corporation? Is he always required to do that?—Yes; and his entire time is devoted to the work of the town. He is not permitted to take any private business whatever.

2200. What were the occasions on which other solicitors were called in?—I am merely paid according to the amount of work done, and not by salary, and would be very glad if I had a salary instead of payment for work actually done by me.

2201. What was the occasion of calling in other solicitors?—I merely conduct what I may call the office business of the Corporation. It would be totally impossible for me to attend to their petty sessions and other local court business, and accordingly Messrs. M'Lean and Coulter attend to the local court business, and get £150 a year each for it. The reason there are two employed is, because there are two courts sitting at the same time, and each has his own business to attend to. Sometimes cases will be going on in each of the courts at the same time, and the magistrates were of opinion that one solicitor could not possibly attend to them both. As to the calling in of others, there was a case brought by Mr. M'Gillan against the Corporation for an indictment, and Mr. O'Rorke was called in to assist the local gentlemen in the court.

2202. Not to assist you?—No; I had nothing to do with it. Mr. O'Rorke attended during that case. It is the only case that I know of where he was called in. Mr. M'Lean, etc., was also referred to as having been brought in to assist in the malicious injury claims, but he was only brought in on one day, I think, when counsel was away. The list of 157 claims amounted to something about £14,000, some very small sums, and some large ones. One gentleman thought he was entitled to £1,375. The counsel employed for the Corporation was obliged to go away, and Mr. M'Lean was called in to assist me for one day, and only for one day, in the business.

2203. Was there any discussion in the council on the resignation of Mr. Beals, who had been the solicitor conducting the prosecutions for the Corporation, as to whether the business might not be conducted by one solicitor?—There was, and it was the unanimous opinion of the Town Council that it would be better to have two, and the reason was to have the courts worked efficiently.

2204. Mr. Lawless.—What business had the magistrates to express any opinion on the subject?—The magistrates were asked about it (the magistrates sitting in the courts), and they gave it as their opinion privately that it would be very desirable to have two solicitors instead of one.

2205. Mr. Keenan.—I could understand it if there were cases going on every day in the two courts. I would like to know who asked the magistrates privately for their opinion on such a subject, and who were the magistrates that gave it?—Several of the Corporation asked members of the bench.

2206. Chairman.—Do you know the members of the bench who put any expressed that private opinion?—I was not present; I, myself, privately asked one of the resident magistrates, and he told me that in his opinion it would be desirable to have two solicitors.

2207. Who was that magistrate?—Mr. Orme.

Serjeant. Dec. 22, 1875.

Mr. Samuel Boyd.

2208. You say you asked Mr. Orme, and that members of the Corporation asked other magistrates?—Yes.

2209. Can you name who the other magistrates, and who the members of the Town Council, were?—I cannot name them.

2210. Mr. Lawless.—Did you communicate what Mr. Orme said to the Town Council?—I did.

2211. Mr. Bulkan.—Is there any resolution on the books to the effect that the magistrates having considered it would be desirable to have two solicitors to attend to the courts they should be appointed?—There is a resolution, but I cannot say what it is. There was originally only one court instead of two, and one solicitor who was paid a salary of £200 a year. He resigned.

2212. Mr. Lawless.—When?—I think about three years ago. He resigned, and the two gentlemen were appointed at £100 a year each. They subsequently complained that their salaries were not a sufficient remuneration for the duties they had to perform, and it was raised to £150 each.

2213. Chairman.—I asked you about Mr. Montgomery's duties. It was referred to here yesterday by Mr. Browne, who came forward to give an explanation about some streets which were opened contrary to the Act of Parliament, and afterwards Mr. O'Neill came forward. I want to know whether these notices are given by the improvement committee, or whether the borough surveyor acts on his own responsibility in calling on parties to do any species of work?—The surveyor brings before the committee any case in which he considers an order should be made. It is entirely within his discretion, and as a matter of course in every case that he brings forward there is a report sent to the council that an order should be made, and the order is made. I know nothing of the streets referred to.

2214. Does the order originate in practice with the committee?—In 99 out of every 100 cases it originates with the surveyor.

2215. Have you ever known any case in which the borough surveyor brought forward applications for the owners of property in a street to be compelled to do certain work, and in which the order was refused to be granted by the committee?—I cannot recollect a single instance. I may also add that since the present sanitary committee came into existence under the Public Health Act they have taken up this question, and where they see from time to time that streets would be improved by being completed they send forward reports to the improvement committee, which were attended to.

2216. Mr. Bulkan.—Did the improvement committee direct the surveyor not to carry out the Act of Parliament?—The 12th section was found impossible to be carried out in practice.

2217. You got the Act of 1863 yourselves, and made its clauses more stringent by the clauses of the Act of 1868. Why was that section not asked to be repealed if you found it could not be carried out, instead of being made more stringent by the Act of 1868?—It is merely a question of cost to the owner as to whether he will carry out the Act of Parliament or not. By the Act the owner is not to allow any persons to inhabit the houses until the terms of the Act are carried out. I want to know why the improvement committee and the surveyor do not carry them out?—The council tried to carry out that section, and they had such representations made to them as to the inconvenience of doing so, that they have not enforced it.

2218. Why did they enforce it in the case of Mr. O'Neill and his streets, and not in the case of Mr. Browne, who was a member of the improvement committee, and his streets?—I know nothing about Mr. O'Neill's streets.

2219. Mr. Lawless.—By whom were these representations made to the council?—By owners of property in town.

2220. Was not that really by the builders?—Yes. I believe there is no town in the three kingdoms in which the owners of property are obliged to make the streets first.

2221. Mr. Bulkan.—Probably that is because they have no such Act of Parliament.

2222. Mr. Lawless.—Did you ever enforce the Act and prevent the owners from allowing their houses to be occupied until everything was done?—I do not recollect.

2223. Mr. Bulkan.—The borough surveyor can stop up those streets. He has only to put a bar across and say to the owners, "You cannot occupy the houses until everything required by the Act is done"?—That is quite true, but it could not be carried out.

2224. Chairman.—Mr. Bulkan asked you a very pertinent question: "Why, when you found the Act of 1863 could not be enforced, you did not get a clause amending it?"—I was not solicitor for the Corporation then.

2225. Was not the town spreading rapidly between 1863 and 1868?—Yes, very rapidly.

2226. But not to the same extent it has done since?—It was spreading more rapidly between 1863 and 1868.

2227. Mr. Lawless.—Was there ever any instance to your knowledge in which a builder of houses, who was a member of the Corporation, when his houses were built, had notice served on him to complete the paving of the street before his houses were occupied?—I have known many instances in which we required them to be completed. As a matter of course, an order was made.

2228. Can you give us the names of builders who were members of the Town Council and who were ordered to comply with the Act?—Certainly, but not at the moment.

2229. Did you ever know a case in which application was made by the borough surveyor for such orders in which they were refused?—Certainly not.

2230. Do such matters come within your knowledge?—I think I would have known that had it been the case.

2231. Why then was not Mr. Browne made to complete the streets in which his houses are before they were occupied?—That I cannot tell.

2232. You wish to give evidence on some questions relating to your law costs?—Yes. I wish to draw attention to some matters personally affecting myself. I was appointed solicitor to the Corporation in March, 1871. I find the payments to me for the years 1873, 1874, and 1875 have been referred to. You will see the purpose for which that was done when you take into account what I received for the preceding years. In the year 1871 I got nothing at all. I do not mean to say that I did not earn it, but I was not paid anything that year, and my costs were not taxed until a year subsequent.

2233. In what year were you appointed?—In 1871. In 1872 I only got £373 14s. 1d. In 1873, 1874, and 1875 it is quite true I got the amounts referred to—£2,394 18s. 7d. in 1873, £1,423 17s. 6d. in 1874, and £1,580 13s. 1d. in 1875.

2234. Can you tell me how much you were out of pocket of these costs?—It would be totally impossible for me to do that at the moment. The amount for 1873 included the costs connected with the investigation of the claims for malicious injury amounting to a very large sum. It also included the Parliamentary costs in opposition to the Central Railway Bill and certain other matters in which the town was concerned. The amount for 1874 contained further Parliamentary costs, and the costs of negotiations about the sale of the gasworks and opposition to the Gas Bill, and other things, which amounted to a very large sum. The amount for 1875 included the costs of the Gas Act, and also the provisional order and the Act confirming it. It was also stated here that my costs were taxed by the officials of the Corporation. How that error crept into the mind of the person who made it I cannot say.

[illegible] Mr. [illegible]

2235. That is not the case?—No. It was also stated that I got stationery from the Corporation, but I never got the value of a sheet of paper. It was also said that I was solicitor for a building society, and that I assisted in passing their plans. It is true I am solicitor for a building society, but the business of that society is to lend money upon buildings erected, and if they ever passed plans for building it is certainly unknown to me.

2236. Are you empowered by the terms of your appointment to take no other employment?—No. I am happy to say that my private practice is as good as my public practice.

2237. Of course I need not ask you whether or not much of these costs are costs out of pocket—but you cannot say how much?—A very considerable amount were costs out of pocket. Unfortunately we are sometimes brought into court, but up to the present we have been always successful.

2238. Mr. Rylands.—I think it is only fair to say that the Corporation seem to have adopted the best course—that is to employ a well-known firm of solicitors to attend the taxation of Mr. Black's costs.

2239. Chairman.—Was every bill of costs taxed by the proper officer?—Yes. The rate for the militia-barracks was referred to, and Mr. Hanna said that £1,000 was included in the estimate for each year. Now, of course, at the beginning of the year the Council estimated what the probable expenditure will be during the year, and very frequently they included £1,000 in the estimate, and at the end of the year, if it is not expended, it goes into the balance of the general purposes fund and reduces the estimate for the next year. If you take the year 1871 for instance, you will find that we estimated our contribution to the county Antrim Grand Jury at £7,000. Unfortunately we had to pay £8,883 0s. 7d. In 1872 we estimated £9,000, and paid £9,226 1s.; in 1873 we estimated £10,000, and paid £12,165 0s. 3d.; in 1874 we estimated £11,000, and paid £14,623 0s. 6d.; and in 1875 we estimated £11,000, and paid £16,817 16s. The clerk of the peace was also accused, but if you refer to the 194th section of the Act of the 3 and 4 Vic., cap. 108, you will find that by that section the fees are payable to the clerk of the peace himself, and not to the Corporation. So far as his salary is concerned we have nothing to do with it. The Lord Lieutenant fixes his salary, and we are obliged to pay it.

2240. How long did Mr. Seeds do business in the two courts. Did he get any assistance?—Yes, he occasionally got assistance from his legal friends.

2241. Do Messrs. M'Lean and Coulter attend at the courts every day, or do they ever go to the country on their private business, and get their cases postponed?—It is of very frequent occurrence for persons practising in these courts to get cases postponed for some other day, and they may occasionally get it done.

2242. It is said they get cases put off altogether for the purpose of enabling them to go and earn money elsewhere. Do you know if that is so?—I cannot say.

2243. Mr. Lawless.—How often do these magistrates sit?—Every day.

2244. At what hour in the morning?—At eleven o'clock.

2245. How long do they sit?—They sometimes sit very late. I have heard them complain of the gaslight.

2246. How many hours in the day, on a rough average, do they sit?—Some days they would have from thirty to forty cases to attend to on the part of the Corporation, and on some days not one. There was also a complaint made about the salary of Mr. Stelfox, the manager of the gasworks and his assistant. When we took over the gasworks his father had £750 a year, but we made an arrangement by which a reduction was made, and his son was appointed at a salary of £500 a year. This was increased to £600 last year.

2247. Were the united salaries of Mr. Stelfox and his father £1,100 a year?—Yes, and now the salaries of the manager and his assistant are only £850. The sub-manager gets £250 a year, and Mr. Stelfox, £600.

2248. Was there any pension given to Mr. Stelfox's father?—None whatever.

2249. Do you owe him any money?—Not a farthing. The old man thought he had worked long enough. He resigned, and his son, who was a most efficient officer, was appointed in his place. The book-keeper, Mr. Charles Stelfox, had a salary of £170 a year.

2250. Is he a brother of the other man?—Yes; and he is a most efficient officer.

2251. Was there any stipulation by Mr. Stelfox on his retirement that his son was to be appointed in his place?—There was, and we had no objection to him. With regard to the expenditure on the clock and the Albert memorial being an illegal charge, if you will look to section 160 of the Act of 1845 you will find we have full power to make the expenditure. With regard to the observation that we had sustainable powers to prevent the end of Mill-street from being built up, I have to say that we have no such powers, and could not prevent it. We had no power to prevent the street from being closed, and when we found that we could not absolutely prevent it we made an arrangement by which the open space was not built on, and the Corporation thought it was only fair that where private property was materially to benefit by this that the owners of it should contribute a certain amount of the expenses. (One gentleman contributed £100 towards the widening of Hill-street, because it was of advantage to his property); and a gentleman, the chairman of the committee I think, gave £5 towards the £35 required to keep the end of Mill-street open. In addition to the Corporation giving the public money, some of its members gave a subscription from their private purse.

2252. Up to the time when the Corporation appointed Mr. M'Lean and Mr. Coulter as their solicitors in these courts they had Mr. Seeds acting in the two courts at a salary of £400 a year?—Yes.

2253. From whom did the proposal for the change come?—So far as I know it was from the committee themselves.

2254. Did they seek to remove Mr. Seeds or did he offer to resign?—He offered to resign. It was entirely at his own desire, and his resignation was accepted with reluctance.

2255. Was he a competent man?—Yes.

2256. Why then were two gentlemen required to discharge the duty which one had theretofore done properly?—It was considered better to have two instead of one.

2257. Did the Corporation advertise for a successor to Mr. Seeds when he resigned, or how did it happen that these two gentlemen were appointed?—They were gentlemen practising in the town. I never would think of advertising for a solicitor.

2258. Were there any other competitors for the place?—Never that I heard of.

2259. Did these gentlemen offer to do the work for £100 a year?—I do not know. The committee offered a salary. Here is the report of the police committee presented to the Town Council on the 1st December, 1873. (Hands in report.)

2260. What was the general way of giving intimation of a vacancy for any office?—As far as I know there may have been an advertisement.

2261. Was there any intimation given of the intention to appoint a successor to Mr. Seeds?—The committee's report appeared in all the public papers on the 2nd December, 1873.

2262. When did it come before the Council?—On the 1st December, 1873. The report is dated 27th November, 1873, to be presented to the Council on the 1st December, 1873, and it says:—

"Mr. Seeds having resigned the office held by him for many years as petty sessions solicitor, the committee recommend the Council to approve of the following as the terms, conditions, and duties, subject to which a new solicitor shall be appointed in his place.

"Conditions.—That the annual salary shall not exceed £300, to commence from the date of appointment, to be payable quarterly.

and three months' notice to be given in writing by the Council of petition, previous to terminating the employment. That the duties shall be performed personally and not by deputy; that the solicitor shall take his instructions from the officers of the Council, and prepare all agreements, [illegible] bills, and documents connected with the same, and if [illegible] by the Council or committee of Council, to personally attend and advise the Board as to any matter [illegible] or appointment or application, and to appear on behalf of the Council or any of their officers, or any party [illegible] their employment, or police, at any petty sessions court held in the borough, or coroner's court, or [illegible] inquiry and recorder's or quarter sessions court in relation to Corporation business. Also to [illegible] from any [illegible] or [illegible] of any such court. That all costs ordered to be paid by any court in any case in which the Corporation have costs, shall be paid over to the credit of the Corporation. And they further recommend that intimation be given in the usual way of the vacancy in said office, and appointing a day for the Council to fill up the vacancy."

I will now read you the resolution of the 1st January, 1874—

"Moved by Councillor Dunn, and seconded by Councillor Aitchison, that the report of the police committee adopted by the Council on the 1st December last, which provides for the appointment of a petty sessions attorney, at a salary not exceeding £[illegible] a year, be rescinded, and that two attorneys be appointed—one for each court, at a salary not exceeding £[illegible] a year each, or such other arrangement as the Council may approve of on the subject; passed. [illegible]"

At the same meeting of Council, 1st January, 1874—

"Moved by Councillor Dunn, and seconded by Councillor Aitchison, that the appointment of petty sessions solicitor be postponed until next meeting, and then be the committee to advertise, be [illegible] in accordance with the resolution just passed for the appointment of two solicitors."

2763. There is a further report of police committee presented on the 1st January, 1874, as follows:—

"Notice was published in the newspapers of the intention of the Council to appoint an attorney to attend the petty sessions business of the Corporation, in the room of William Seeds, esq., resigned. The following gentlemen have intimated their willingness to undertake the duties if appointed, John Coates, E. O'Rorke Hickey, John Coulter, James M'Lean, junr., and Charles Stewart, and the committee request the Council to make a selection."

2764. That occurred between the 1st of January and 2nd February?—Yes; the next I find is a motion moved by Councillor Aitchison, and seconded by Dr. Alexander. There were eight aldermen and twenty-three Councillors present on the occasion.

2765. Did you attend that meeting?—I did. I see I was present.

2766. A notice of motion was given by one gentleman to appoint two solicitors?—There was a resolution to appoint two instead of one.

2767. Was that carried?—It was.

2768. Is there any reference made in it to the statement of the magistrates?—There is not.

2769. Was there any communication made to the public in any way of the change in the arrangement of the intention to appoint two solicitors instead of one as formerly?—I am not aware of any.

2770. Mr. Exham.—Were they to be appointed on the terms of the original report; because the original report of the police committee you can see practically required the man to be at the courts every day?—I hold that they are bound to be there every day.

2771. Mr. Lawless.—Were they appointed under the terms of the report of 24th December, 1873?—Certainly. They accepted their engagement in accordance with the terms of that report.

2772. How soon after the appointment was the change made on the salaries from £100 a year to £150?—I think the £150 was only made during the present year.

2773. Was there an advertisement put in the newspapers?—Yes; then comes the appointment of Messrs. M'Lean and Coulter. You see the appointment was not made without notice, though I was not aware of the fact.

2774. Mr. Exham.—It appears that the report of the police committee was adopted on the 1st December, 1873. What notice is required that a decision of the Council is sought to be set aside?—Notice must be given on the summons paper to every member of the Council of the intention to rescind any resolution.

2775. Mr. Lawless.—Was there any notice given of Mr. Dunn's motion?—Yes; it must have appeared on the summons paper. Before you pass from that subject I would just like to call your attention to the summons sheet, and to read you another resolution—

"Meeting of Council, 2nd February, 1874. Moved by Councillor Aitchison, seconded by Alderman Alexander—'That Mr. James M'Lean, junr., and Mr. John Coulter, be appointed to conduct the business of the petty sessions, quarter sessions, and Recorder's court, and that it be referred to the law and police committee to make the necessary arrangements with these gentlemen. Passed unanimously.'"

2776. Did the Corporation ever advance a sum of £5,000 or £3,000, or any other sum to Dr. Browne himself, or to him and other members of the Corporation, and if so, to whom, and for what purpose?—I cannot fancy anything to which the question you have been required to put to me refers, except it be with reference to the mayor's salary, which was paid to six of the mayors who filled that office. The mayor's salary was £1,000.

2777. Was the mayor not paid here for some time?—No, he was not.

2778. In what year was it that a mayor received a salary?—In the year 1865.

2779. Was any mayor paid up to that year?—No.

2780. Give us the names of the mayors who received the salary of £1,000 each?—Yes; John Lytle, 1865; William Mullan, 1866; David Taylor, 1867; S. M'Causland, 1868; F. H. Lewis, 1869; and Dr. S. Browne, 1870. Mr. Lytle gave his salary towards the erection of the Albert memorial.

2781. Has any mayor been paid any salary since 1870?—No.

2782. Mr. Exham.—Did each of those gentlemen, including Dr. Browne, receive the £1,000 during their year of office?—They did.

2783. Were those payments made by resolution of the Council?—Yes.

2784. Was there any report from any committee suggesting to the Town Council that the mayor should be paid a salary the same as in other places?—It was discussed fully in the Corporation at the time, and a resolution was passed.

2785. Was it a resolution for a year only?—Simply for the year. It was discussed fully in the committee for each year.

2786. Was it renewed for the other years you mentioned?—Every year there was a fresh vote taken.

2787. Has it ceased since the year 1870?—It has.

2788. Did they cease to pay the salary by a resolution of the Council?—There was a division in the Council on it, and they decided that they would not pay the salary.

2789. Who was the mayor of Belfast then?—Mr. Philip Johnston.

2790. Was the matter brought forward since 1870?—The question was not brought in again.

2791. Did each of the gentlemen you named receive in his year of office the £1,000, and no more?—Just so.

2792. Was any extra money paid to any of those gentlemen on any pretence whatever?—Not a farthing that I know of, except what has been paid to Dr. Browne as consulting sanitary officer. Mr. Stewart mentioned an item yesterday which appeared in the borough fund account for the year 1873 as the cost of erection of a platform in the Botanic Gardens on the occasion of the knighting of the mayor and chairman of the Harbour Board; but he forgot to draw your attention to the opposite side of the account, where you will find that the amount was repaid—the workmen of the Corporation were employed to do the work, but the cost was repaid.

2793. Were you in the Corporation in the year 1864?—I was.

2794. Do you wish to give any explanation with regard to the statement that has been made that the Corporation never carried out the pledge that they certainly appear to have given to the Select Committee of the House of Commons with regard to bringing in a public bill?—I am not aware of anything requiring the Cor-

[illegible]

Mr. Samuel Black.

poration to bring in a public bill for any purpose. The Corporation might bring in a private bill.

2295. After the bill of 1864 was passed, was the question of promoting a public or private bill relating to the regulation of the affairs of the borough ever considered by the Corporation?—I am under the impression that it was considered by the council; but I believe they never settled the heads of any bill.

2296. Were any steps taken by the council with reference to getting the heads of any bill settled by the arbitrators named to the Select Committee in 1864?—I have no recollection of any steps having been taken for that purpose.

2297. Had Mr. Lytle to whom the Corporation first voted a salary as mayor, been engaged in any litigation with Mr. Rea before that vote was passed?—Yes; he prosecuted Mr. Rea at the assizes here and got a verdict of guilty against him.

2298. Did he get costs?—Yes.

2299. How much?—I could not tell you.

2300. Was Mr. Mullan one of the special respondents in Mr. Rea's information against the Corporation?—I think not.

2301. Was Mr. David Taylor?—I think not.

2302. Was Mr. Samuel M'Causland?—Yes; I am under the impression that he was one of the special respondents.

2303. Was Mr. Lewis? He was a special respondent in that case.

2304. Was Dr. Browne a special respondent?—He was. I may add that Mr. Philip Johnston who was mayor in 1871 was also special respondent, and he got no salary.

Mr. W. C. CUNNINGHAM examined.

Mr. W. C. Cunningham.

2305. Mr. LAWLESS.—Are you the clerk of the peace here?—I am.

2306. When were you appointed clerk of the peace?—In the year 1847. Belfast was then created a separate jurisdiction under the Municipal Corporations Act.

2307. Do you mean the Act of 1840?—Yes.

2308. By that Act the power was taken from the old Corporation and the appointment put into the hands of the Lord Lieutenant?—Yes; it was vested in the Lord Lieutenant. There are two appointments—the clerk of the peace and the registrar to the recorder. The Lord Lieutenant appoints the clerk of the peace and the recorder appoints the registrar.

2309. How is your salary fixed? At the time of the passing of that Act (3 and 4 Vic., chap. 108) all clerks of the peace were paid for their duties (both criminal and civil) by fees, and by the 194th section of that Act the Town Council are to settle the amount of fees as thereby provided. In that Act they simply provided for the court then in existence, and not for any court that might afterwards be constituted. I took the opinion of counsel on the subject, and he advised that the machinery there provided for fixing the salaries of clerks of the peace could not be carried into effect, because the fees should be fixed by the council six months after the election of the Corporation under the Municipal Corporation Act.

2310. Were there any table of fees in existence when you were appointed here?—No. In point of fact I did duty as clerk of the peace for a year and a half in the criminal court, and only got as fees the amount of the crown summonses.

2311. Was any table of fees fixed?—No; and if there had been they would have gone into my pocket.

2312. Were the fees paid by the tables of fees in the county Antrim?—No; by the 6th and 7th William IV., the fees for criminal business were charged by the Irish Grand Jury Act, and provision was thereby made for the payment of salaries to clerks of the peace in Ireland for discharging the business, and those salaries are still paid; but after the 31st and 32nd Vic., my salary was fixed by the Lord Lieutenant in pursuance of its provisions at £200 a year. I get this salary for certain specific duties for which I was not before paid. I prepared a statement of what those duties are, and beg to hand it in to you.

2313. Does this statement contain any of the fees you received?—It refers principally to duties for which I was paid nothing—for the summoning of jurors, the discharge of criminal business, the preparation of indictments at the borough sessions court, the arraigning of prisoners, and for performing all the duties of clerk of the peace in connection with the criminal business of the borough quarter sessions court.

2314. What amount of fees or fees do you receive in the Recorder's Court?—I get fees for the duties discharged under the Parliamentary Voters and Jurors Acts; also certain sums for Crown summonses and other matters at the Crown side, and these fees were never intended to be paid to the Corporation. With regard to the sittings of the Recorder's Court there was a very extraordinary statement made, but I can show that he is only bound to hold six courts in the year. He holds four courts as county chairman.

2315. Under what legal obligation is he only bound to hold six courts in the year?—By the memorial to the Lord Lieutenant's warrant. To show you that Mr. Dixon is mistaken, and that the courts are held as nearly as possible at equal intervals, I will just call your attention to the courts held by Mr. Otway last year. He held a county court as chairman on the 13th January, a borough court on the 11th February, and one on the 13th March; a county court on the 13th April, a borough court on the 16th May, and one on the 17th June; a county court on the 10th July, and, after vacation, a borough court on the 25th September, and county court on the 29th October, and a borough court on the 5th December.

2316. Mr. ELMES.—Is it a fact that before the borough of Belfast was taken away from the county Antrim Mr. Chichester got from the Grand Jury a salary of £370 a year besides fees?—Yes.

2317. Does he get the same salary still?—Yes.

2318. Does he also get the fees?—Yes.

2319. Were not the duties and work of the clerk of the peace for the county greatly reduced by the taking away of Belfast from the county Antrim?—Yes.

2320. Then he gets the salary of £370 a year, and the fees, and £200 a year is paid by the borough to you as the clerk of the peace for the borough besides?—That is so.

2321. Do you discharge your duties in person as clerk of the peace for the borough?—I do. I was only absent from the borough court at one sessions.

2322. Have you power to appoint a deputy?—I have for the civil side of the court, but not for the criminal side, except in case of illness. The clerk of the peace is one person and the registrar is another. In Cork he is the same person. I am bound to attend in person as clerk of the peace, but not bound to attend in person as registrar. In point of fact I have no deputy. I have an assistant, but I sign every decree.

2323. What power have you as registrar to appoint a deputy?—I have the same power as other clerks of the peace in Ireland. It has been done by every registrar.

2324. Have you ever allowed your business to be performed by deputy except in case of illness?—Yes. I have frequently in the case of civil business, but in the case of Crown business I feel myself bound to attend. I was not appointed by the Town Council. Twenty-one out of the twenty-three members of the Grand Jury signed the recommendation in my favour, and that was the way I got my appointment. The Government would appoint no person except a solicitor.

2325. Is not the result that there is an increase to the salaries of £200 divided between Mr. Chichester and you for the very same work which he did before, and the people of Belfast pay this, and Mr. Chichester in addition gets all the fees?—Yes.

2326. Mr. LAWLESS.—How much did you receive for the last two years from spirit license applications?—I received £163 14s. 6d. from that source last year.

The Reverend Isaac Nelson examined.

2327. Mr. Lawless.—You are, I believe, a Presbyterian clergyman?—Yes, and a large ratepayer residing here.

2328. Do you complain of the severing and the paving of the streets?—Yes; I happen to be part owner of property in several streets—Commerce-street, Capar-street, and Mountjoy-street. I did everything, as I understand, that the Corporation required in Commerce-street, and was the first person in that street who had completed the work in connexion with his property over which the Corporation had any control. At the end of some time, however, they took proceedings against me in the Court of Queen's Bench for £21 for work they alleged they had done for me. I did as much myself for £4 or £5, I should say.

2329. Were not those proceedings taken against you in 1872?—I believed I had finished that street in 1870, and these law proceedings were taken in 1872. Here is a letter I wrote to Mr. Black on the 30th of July, 1873:—

"Sir,—In November last you issued a summons and [illegible] against me, repeating me to finish Commerce-street, of which you knew nothing [illegible]. As guarantee for the safety of £5 or £6 you require the sum of £21 [illegible] to be placed in the [illegible] of the Council, and you [illegible] for your own [illegible]. I [illegible] three members of the Improvement Committee would come and decide on the mode of doing the work. This you refused, but in [illegible] you granted a delay of three weeks to finish the street. I completed the work within the given time, and under the [illegible] of [illegible], the only surveyor who [illegible] to take any interest in the work. You now [illegible] me with a bill of costs, and [illegible] to [illegible] judgment in the action. I [illegible], and will [illegible] nothing for the advice at your good [illegible], and at the [illegible] of the Town Council, [illegible] to proceed further [illegible] until I am informed distinctly and legally whether or not Commerce-street has been accepted as completed and done by the Town Council. When you lay this communication before the Improvement Committee and hand their answer, you will hear more from

"Isaac Nelson.

"Mr. Samuel Black, Town Solicitor."

Up to this hour I have never received an answer as to whether or not they consider the street finished. There is a communication of a hurried sort from Mr. Black, saying that he would accept the street as finished; but I believe that if they chose to proceed to put me to law again, I have no means of proving that the street is finished. With respect to Commerce-street, I complain that I have been subjected to unnecessary expense by the Corporation. They went so far as to direct me to bring the water from the Shankill-road to Commerce-street.

2330. Mr. Exham.—Did they require you to make a sewer?—They did, and I made it. The sewer they ordered me to make I objected to make. With regard to Capar-street, that street is not finished to this hour, owing to the confused and absolutely preposterous manner in which first one and then another gives directions as to what they require. Some of the houses in Capar-street are not tenanted.

2331. Is Capar-street completed?—It is not; and yet the expense for doing so was paid to the town collector.

2332. What have you paid?—About £10 or so.

2333. What work was to be done for that?—I cannot say. But my complaint is that they put me to law expenses without any necessity for it.

2334. Has the work for which the £10 was required been done?—In a great measure, but not all. They wanted me to build a parapet wall which would be about four feet up in front of my houses, but I refused.

2335. What has been done with regard to Mountjoy-street?—In that street the work is unfinished. It has cost me in law expenses about £17 or £18. The people opposite me have not done their work, but I have.

2336. Cannot you call upon the Improvement Committee to make these other people do their portion of the work?—I declined ever to appear before the Improvement Committee until they determined the truth or untruth of my original statement.

2337. Are you dissatisfied with the way in which the Corporation officials carry on their work in regard to the streets?—I am dissatisfied with the outlay; we are plundered by the way they go on.

Mr. William O'Hara examined.

2338. Are you a ratepayer in Belfast?—Yes; for the last twelve years.

2339. And are you engaged in any trade or business?—I am a merchant tailor and general draper in Old Lodge-road.

2340. Is it in relation to that street that you desire to give evidence?—Yes. It is a street about an eighth of a mile long, and there is only one crossing—at Townsend-street—the entire length of the thoroughfare, which is crossed by, I should say, from ten to twelve streets. Immediately opposite my door a stream passes—the stream in relation to which Mr. Cartwright gave evidence—that goes from Agnes-street to Fairy's Well. At the point opposite my door there is an open barrel sewer into which it flows. In Portingall-street there is no sewer, except an open gutter, and the water flows down from it into this place, and the water also coming down the Old Lodge-road, runs into it, and three or four pipes empty into it also. Well, the result is, that if there is an hour's continuous rain the doors of the houses all along the street for a considerable distance are flooded two feet up. In some of the private houses I have seen the doors covered with dirt and clay three feet up during heavy rainfall in the middle of summer. Indeed at night the people are sometimes roused up out of their beds in consequence of the flooding of their houses.

2341. Mr. Exham.—Is this an open sewer? Is there sewage matter there?—Yes; there are three sewerage pipes running into it opposite my door.

2342. Where do these pipes come from?—One carries away the sewage matter from the property adjoining the place near where I am living.

2343. What is the name of that property?—It is part of the Old Lodge-road; the houses commence at 176 and run up to 180 or 200; and the sewage matter from that property is conveyed by the pipe I have alluded to.

2344. Who owns that property?—Part of it is owned by a gentleman named Hale.

2345. Is there any main sewer in that road?—I cannot speak definitely with regard to that; my own impression is that there is not.

2346. Is there a bad smell arising from this open sewer?—Yes, very bad.

2347. Have the sanitary officials ever looked after it?—Yes; from the King-street factory down to this point it was formerly open the whole way. Recently it has been piped down and now there is just a sort of rough opening left where it gets into the old barrel.

2348. Have you got the benefit of the open sewer opposite you?—Yes.

2349. Is there any pipe sewer from your house?—I have a pipe sewer into the Bedeque-street sewer; but whether that is connected with the main sewer or not I cannot tell.

2350. Mr. Lawless.—Is the Old Lodge-road long built?—I suppose it is one of the oldest thoroughfares in the town. The upper portion is not, however, so long built. I may observe that there is part of the footpath just behind the county court-house, on the opposite side of the street from the county court-house which is nothing more or less than a mud embankment. There is not even a kerbstone along the edge of that portion of the footpath.

2351. How long has that remained so?—It has been in that condition ever since the road was made. There has never been anything done to it since the property was built.

2352. Mr. Lawless.—Who is the owner of it?—I do not know.

2353. Mr. Exham.—Did you ever complain to the Corporation about it?—No, I did not. With reference to some of the streets referred to in evidence yesterday evening—Lady-street, Tea-street, and Slade-street, I may remark that I am perfectly familiar with the condition of them, and all that has been stated about them is true.

2354. What do you know about these streets?—

Well, they were described as a swamp. I do not think that term describes them at all; they are a perfect nuisance. Lady-street in particular, is one perfect mass of nuisances of every description. I suppose there are upwards of thirty cart-loads of rubbish deposited there off the streets of the town.

2355. How long have the houses there been inhabited? —About three years ago they were first tenanted.

2356. Has the road been left in the condition you describe all that time?—Yes; I have passed through it week after week, and when I heard Mr. Browne give his evidence I felt as if a blind had passed over my eyes, and after the Court rose I went again and looked at these streets, and saw the state they were in; and I now state positively that they are in a fearful state. The only attempt at the formation of a road is the laying down of a kerbstone on the edge of each footway, but the roadway itself is as I have said a perfect mass of nuisances of every description. Owing to the quantities of road dirt deposited there, the roadways are on a level with the kerbing, but if you want to walk on it you would sink down at least ankle deep in the filth.

2357. How long do you say the houses in these streets have been inhabited?—About three years as far as my recollection goes, that is about the time Lady-street was inhabited. The houses were inhabited as soon as a fire could be lit in them.

2358. Do the people pay rent?—Oh, yes.

2359. To whom?—I do not know.

2360. To whom do these houses belong?—Some of them to Mr. Browne who is a member of the Improvement Committee. I may observe that in my opinion the whole surface water from the fields appears to be conveyed into those streets, and if it was taken away by proper sewers, then Lady-street, Rose-street, and Ruthven-street would be better fit for habitation.

2361. Is the owner of these houses a man of means sufficient to enable him to do his portion of the work? —There can be no doubt about his ability, if he has the inclination to do what he is bound to do.

2362. Is there a sufficient fall from these streets to enable them to be drained?—There is; they could easily get a proper level for the sewer.

Mr. Thomas Gaffikin examined.

2363. Mr. Lawless.—Are you a member of the Town Council?—Yes.

2364. What are the points upon which you wish to be examined?—I wish to state that I have known the Logan for the last sixty years, and have been walking in its neighbourhood during that time. I remember the time when fish were alive in it. As the population in its vicinity increased and mills were built, the stream became polluted. The principal sewage that pollutes it is taken at the south-west side, where there is great drainage from the warehouses, colleges, &c., and that is taken into the Logan. If the Pound Burn was diverted before it joined the Blackstaff, the Blackstaff would never be polluted.

2365. Mr. Exham.—Do you know any reason why the Pound Burn has not been diverted?—Well, since 1870 the Blackstaff has been the subject of a variety of schemes. In that year Mr. Montgomery produced a plan—I believe it was approved of by Mr. Bazalgette —for a new system of sewerage for the entire town. That would cause an increase of the rates to a very large sum. By that scheme, to a portion of which I was opposed, it was intended to relieve the Blackstaff, by taking the nuisance of the Pound Burn out of it, at a high level by sewer, and it would, to a very great extent, have that effect; but no plan has as yet been adopted.

2366. Do you think that this plan would, to a certain extent, carry out that end?—Yes, a portion of that plan, if carried out, would have relieved the Blackstaff and Pound Burn; but in connexion with that, I may say that the Blackstaff was made a lever for a whole number of Acts of Parliament, and the Blackstaff has got more blame than it deserved. It was made use of when it was proposed to go in for an Act of Parliament in 1870, for the sewerage of the entire town, and the reclaiming of the sloblands of the river at Holywood on the one side, and Macedon on the other. That scheme would have been a source of great expense, and the Town Council, in my opinion, had nothing to do with it.

2367. Mr. Lawless.—How is the Blackstaff polluted by the Pound Burn?—The Pound Burn goes no more from being a clear stream, which used to run through the fields where cattle were depastured. As mills and factories were built, and the population increased, the sewage was diverted into it, and it has been made an open sewer for the last thirty years. It flows into the Blackstaff, which is also polluted in a similar way, and that increases the nuisance, and the Blackstaff then, with the addition from the Pound Burn, flows into the Logan.

2368. How many mills are now along the Pound Burn?—Several. I may say that the drainage from them and the several streets which discharge into the Burn has made it a nuisance, and in some places, an open sewer instead of a clear stream.

2369. Is the sewerage stuff in the Pound Burn used for mill purposes?—Yes; the works of the mill owners being close beside it, it is used for mill purposes. At the present time of year, however, the Blackstaff is not objectionable. There is no more nuisance in it at present than there is in the water down the Belfast Lough.

2370. Have you been a long time a member of the Corporation?—Yes; nearly twenty years.

2371. Was there any influence or power existing in the Corporation that prevented them from setting to work and organising the cleansing of the Pound Burn, and preventing it going into the Blackstaff?—I do not know of any.

2372. Do you believe there was anything of the kind? Do you believe there was any influence in the Corporation that prevented the Pound Burn from being properly drained, and prevented it from running into the Blackstaff?—I am not aware of any.

2373. Mr. Exham.—Are you on the improvement committee?—I am. I was its chairman for some time.

2374. Is there any influence there which prevents the provisions of the Act of 1865 from being carried out with respect to not allowing houses to be occupied until the streets, &c., are made as required by 76th section of the Act of Parliament?—I do not know of any.

2375. Why then do not the committee carry out the provisions of the Act?—That I cannot tell.

2376. Mr. O'Neill told us yesterday that he was called upon by notice by the improvement committee to do some paving work or something of that kind in Rose-street, Parker-street, and Mayo-street. There were some other streets in the neighbourhood which were the property of Mr. Browne or one of the firm of which he is a member. Mr. O'Neill was made to complete his streets long ago, while Mr. Browne's are not completed yet. I want to know was the question of ordering Mr. Browne or his firm to complete their streets ever brought before the improvement committee?—I don't recollect distinctly, but when I was chairman of the committee I certainly did my best to get those streets completed.

2377. Were you overruled when you wanted to have them completed—were you out-voted?—I do not recollect how it happened.

2378. Is it a fact that there are five timber and slate merchants and two builders on the improvement committee, and that they are concerned largely in building operations in the town, and derive a large profit from such buildings, and that by the influence of those persons the surveyor does not put the Act of Parliament into force with regard to the streets where they have built?—I do not know that those persons could have much influence on the city surveyor, but at the same time I must confess that I would on many occasions have preferred that there

BELFAST. Dec. [illegible]

Mr. William O'Rane.

Mr. Thomas Gaffikin.

[illegible]

were not so many men in that line of business on the improvement committee.

2379. Mr. O'Neill informed us yesterday that he bought some property in that district, and that before he got it at all the houses were inhabited and the street paved to a certain extent, but that he was called upon notwithstanding that to do it better, and he stated that an action was brought against him for £60 for the cost of his share of the work, while an action was not brought against Mr. Browne although he owed £30; and he complained that while the improvement committee took these proceedings against him they had allowed Mr. Browne to set his houses without having made the streets or provided the sewers required by the 13th section of the Act, and that his houses are inhabited for the last three years, while he has never been made to comply with the Act. Do you know anything of that?—No; those three or four streets were laid out, and had become built and inhabited while I was absent from the Council. I was only re-elected again last year.

2380. Were you present on the 2nd of February last at a meeting of the Town Council when a discussion took place with reference to an increase of the salaries of some of the officers of the Corporation?—I think I remember that.

2381. Did you ever see a report of your own speech on that occasion. Do you remember the question of the salary of Mr. De Cobain being increased?—Yes. I was opposed to that.

2382. Was it suggested at that time that there was any increase of duty or labour cast upon Mr. De Cobain which justified an increase of salary to him?—It was not, and I was not aware of any.

2383. It has been stated to us that you spoke as follows at that meeting:—

"I am opposed to any increase of the salaries of the officials at present. While the gentlemen who occupied their comfortable offices for a few hours in the day were aware of the [illegible] business people had to contend with in paying the rates they would not be clamouring for big salaries. One of the officers in particular, Mr. De Cobain, had [illegible] all this year, and all these messages with respect to salaries [illegible] and his qualifications, except in a political or electioneering point of view, did not justify his claim upon the Council."

Is that a correct report of your observations on that occasion?—I think that is correct.

2384. Did you consider Mr. De Cobain justified in applying for an increase of salary?—I did not.

2385. Was there any allegation made at that time, or statement put forward upon his part as stated here today by Mr. Black, that the salary of the cashier of the gasworks was £360 a year, and that Mr. De Cobain considered that he ought to be placed upon something like an equality with that officer?—I do remember something about that.

2386. Why did you state that Mr. De Cobain's qualifications were of a political or electioneering character?—Because I knew them to be so.

2387. In what way?—By his canvassing in every way in his power, by his attending Conservative meetings, and making himself as influential as possible with reference to every change that took place in the Town Council.

2388. Do you know that of your own knowledge?—I do.

2389. Were you a member of the Town Council when Mr. Dempsey moved his resolution to the effect that none of the officials should interfere in political matters save by recording their votes?—I was, and I voted for that motion.

2390. Is it a fact that when Mr. Dempsey brought forward his resolution at that meeting, and stated it as his belief that the officials of the Corporation did interfere in election contests, that that statement was emphatically contradicted on the part of the officers, and that the reason why the resolution was not carried was alleged to be that it was unfair to be unjust to assert that the officers interfered in political matters?—Yes, but I voted for the motion because I knew the statement to be true that the officers did interfere at elections.

2391. Were you put out of the Town Council?—Yes.

2392. When were you put out?—I was out all of the year 1876. I was put out in November, 1875.

2393. When did you get in again?—In the next November.

2394. You said you were aware that Mr. De Cobain interfered in election affairs; of your own knowledge did Mr. De Cobain interfere adversely to you in the election at which you were put out?—He did.

2395. Did any other officers of the Corporation?—There was a feeling among the officers that I should not be in the Town Council.

2396. Do you include Mr. Montgomery or Mr. Black in that statement, as you named the officers of the Corporation in general?—No, I do not; I do not call those gentlemen officers of the Corporation. They are independent professional gentlemen.

2397. Was your reason for saying that on many occasions you would have preferred fewer gentlemen in the timber and slate trade and builders being on the improvement committee, that their own personal interests used to interfere with the discharge of their duties as members of the Corporation?—Well yes; but not greatly; but to some extent there is no doubt that it did.

2398. When you say there was a feeling among the officers of the Corporation that you should not be re-elected, had you done anything directly or indirectly beyond what you believed it to be your duty to do against those persons?—No; quite the contrary.

[illegible]

Mr. MICHAEL SHIELS examined.

2399. Are you a ratepayer here?—I am; and I have expended about £3,000 in building in the outside districts of Belfast.

2400. Do you wish to give evidence as to the condition of any particular part of the town?—Yes. Mr. W. Biddell and Mr. Ewdale, two very large ratepayers and I, went before the gas committee last year and requested them to have the gas light extended as far as the borough cemetery on the Falls-road. It is the width of a road immediately outside of the municipal boundary.

2401. We were told that if we could give a guarantee that the tenants that would occupy the houses that I then had built would take the gas, that they would take the matter into their consideration, and that at that time, as it was the light season of the year, perhaps they would see their way to extend the main fifty yards, which is the distance from the last lamp, to accommodate my tenants.

2402. Was anything done after that?—There has been nothing done yet.

2403. Did they ask you to join in the expense of the mains?—I had no right to do so. I will certainly dispute the payment of the police rate unless I am lighted as well as watched.

2404. Are your houses to which you wish the benefit of the gas extended within the municipal limits?—Yes, considerably, a quarter of a mile.

2405. Why do you want it brought outside?—I do not want it brought outside.

2406. Did you not want it brought to the borough cemetery?—Yes; but only as far as the municipal boundary extends, which almost adjoins the cemetery. In other portions of Belfast, where aristocratic people live, they have the gas much further extended than we have.

2407. Is there not any supply of gas now from the Corporation works to the locality where your property is situate?—No.

2408. Mr. Eccles.—What length of road is there without a lamp?—After you pass my door there are no lamps for a quarter of a mile from the boundary.

2409. And are there lamps for that distance?—There are.

2410. Is the lamp at your door the one farthest out along that road?—Yes, the farthest. I have, I any taxation, other property, even fifty yards further out, and I cannot get light for it. I also say I think there should be £1,000, or at least £500 a year struck off the salaries of the overpaid officials of the Town Council, and that the men who are doing the real work—the hard-working men—should get advances to their present salaries. I also am of opinion that the position of an officer of the Corporation should be properly valued, and that on his appointment he ought to know the salary he would receive, and he said that he should not be asking for advances.

3411. Do you say that salaries should not be increased when once the men are appointed, no matter how long they may have served?—I do. After having been in Europe, Asia, Africa, and America, the large amount of taxation which I am liable for here makes me afraid to look at the pile of houses I have built, and makes me often wish I could have my money back and leave the town.

Mr. JAMES WALLACE examined.

3412. Are you a ratepayer in the town?—Yes.

3413. And you wish to give evidence with regard to the police?—Yes; I would be very sorry to see the Royal Irish Constabulary force here superseded or removed, and I do not at all coincide with anything that has been said about their maladministration. We could not do with less than 400; and the £16,000 which they cost by no means represents what would have to be paid for a local force. A local force of 400 men would cost more than the present force. The sum that would have to be paid for a force, even equal in number to the present, would be much larger than the present expenditure.

3414. Do you think it is better that the control of the police force in this town should be in the hands of the Government, and not in the hands of the Corporation?—Unquestionably.

3415. Can you say of your own knowledge that that feeling is largely shared in by the ratepayers?—I think it is pretty largely shared in. There are some parties who would wish them superseded and a new force appointed under the control of the Corporation, but I think that wish is from a partisan point of view. With reference to the complaints on the subject of the Corporation not having sufficient water to flush the sewers, I complain that there is a large quantity of water that could be collected and used for that purpose if proper means were adopted.

3416. Do you then complain of the present management of the Corporation in this respect?—I do.

Mr. WILLIAM M'CORMICK examined.

3417. Are you a ratepayer?—I am.

3418. What do you wish to give evidence in relation to?—In the first instance with regard to Victoria Park.

3419. Where is that park?—It is at the extreme end of Ballymacarrett, on the county Down side of the borough. I am here to complain that it has not been made a public park.

3420. Is it the property of the Corporation?—It is not, but I believe it ought to be, and there is a difficulty between the Harbour Board, as to who ought to be the possessors or holders of the park. The Harbour Board in 1851, obtained an Act of Parliament for the purpose of enabling them to reclaim ground in that neighbourhood, on the express condition, that portion of it was to be made into a public park for the people, and I know that at the time they were getting signatures to their memorial to go before Parliament, they had accompanying that memorial very pretty plans of a park made out, and in that way they obtained signatures to the memorial with which they went before Parliament. The ground has been reclaimed, but the park is not yet made. The matter has been several times brought before the Corporation, but the park has never been handed over to the Council.

3421. Was it to have been handed over to the Corporation?—Yes.

Mr. SAMUEL BLACK re-examined.

3422. Can you explain the reason this park has never been handed over to the Corporation?—I can explain that. There was an omission in the Act obtained by the Harbour Commissioners. There was no provision made in the Harbour Act of 1854—the 17th and 18th Victoria, chap. [illegible], sec. 20,—by which the Commissioners could hand over the park to any one, but we have lately applied under the provisions of the Public Parks Act for this park to be handed over to the Corporation, and the Harbour Commissioners have referred the matter to a committee of their body, so that the matter is in fact in process of arrangement at the present time.

Mr. WILLIAM M'CORMICK re-examined.

3423. I am glad to learn that that is so, as this park would be the most healthy part of Belfast, as it is some miles down the lough. With regard to the manure depôt, I think it is most deplorable that that nuisance should be allowed to exist. It is at the central railway, along the bank of the Lagan, quite convenient to the [illegible]. It is one of the principal thoroughfares by which people go into Belfast, on the county Down side of the river. It is also lying close to the public markets, and I think that the Town Council should take immediate steps for the purpose of having it removed. It is almost impossible to go across that central railway bridge in summer time, the effluvium is so great that arises from it. In summer the effluvium is never away from it, and it is intolerable when one passes along that central railway bridge which is twenty or thirty feet above it.

3424. Are there any houses in its proximity?—There are—a great many by the side of, and all around it. I wish also to state that between one-fourth and one-fifth of the ratepayers of the town are entirely unrepresented on the Council. The majority of the working classes, ratepayers of this town, think it very strange that they are denied privileges in connexion with the franchise that are enjoyed by their fellow workmen in England and Scotland.

3425. I believe you desire to make a statement concerning the assessors?—Yes. The working classes of this town some years ago put in a gentleman in whom they had confidence, and, strange to say, what was hitherto unknown in the Corporation of Belfast, the fee that had been paid by the Corporation up to that time was refused to him.

3426. Can you give the date when that occurred?—I cannot say exactly; four or five years ago.

3427. Who did the working classes elect?—Mr. Charles H. Ward as one of the borough assessors.

3428. Do you say that the Corporation refused to pay him his salary?—Yes; and he occupied the position for two years. The working classes of the town were most indignant that he was not paid.

3429. Did the Corporation refuse to pay him for the entire time?—They did.

3430. Upon what ground?—I cannot say. The salary had been paid for years before to men who were considered by some to be in a better position than Mr. Ward was.

Dr. E. D. GARDNER examined.

3431. Mr. LAWLESS.—I believe you are a physician and surgeon?—I am.

3432. Do you wish to be examined in relation to the sanitary state of the town?—Yes. I wish to state that for the last quarter of a century, and above that period, I have been practising as a physician and surgeon

BELFAST. [illegible]

Dr. E. D. [illegible]

ence in that town, and I know in the course of my practice that fever has occasionally cropped up, and sporadic cholera has also appeared, in the district adjoining the Blackstaff. My attention has been directed to watching these diseases for some years past, and I have seen ten, fifteen, and twenty cases of these diseases in that neighbourhood. There has been nothing done by the Corporation in the way of mitigating the evils attendant upon the condition of the Blackstaff.

3453. Do you attribute the prevalence of these diseases to the condition of the Blackstaff?—Well, I have remarked when the cases first cropped up they occurred in the vicinity of the Blackstaff. I recollect the disease attacking the people living on one side of [illegible]-street, and also some families in the neighbourhood. I would suggest that at a small expense the evil might be greatly mitigated. I am aware that many members of the Town Council are as anxious as I am to mitigate the evil. I attach no blame to the sanitary committee, nor do I attach any blame to the sanitary officers that are now connected with it. I have had on different occasions to apply to them in order to have grievances remedied when they came under my notice, and I always found them most anxious and painstaking officers. I would suggest that at a small expense the evil might be mitigated or abated. Supposing they commenced at the Corporation property—the gasworks—and flagged the bottom of the Blackstaff, and filled up the deep cesspools that are to be found along its course, and made an uniform level, so that when a high tide would rise it would sweep down all the offensive matter that had collected. This could be accomplished by deepening the channel below the Corporation property at the gasworks. I also wish to refer to the smoke nuisance. I know a respectable family living in an adjoining street, and adjoining their premises is an establishment in which are four smoking compartments. In these places the saw-dust used are sawdust and wheaten straw. From the imperfect combustion which takes place when you expose these two articles to heat a noxious fetid vapour is given off that is almost unbearable. That smoking process is carried on there for the smoking of American hams and bacon. The nuisance is generally carried on at night, and the fetid vapour is intolerable.

3454. Is it dangerous to health?—I really believe it is. I know one establishment where four smoking rooms are in operation. I attach no blame to the Corporation staff. I did expect that there would be some remedy for it, but the person who committed the nuisance got into the Town Council, and I believed it was useless to appeal to a Board where one of the judges was the culprit.

3455. Do you mean to say that the gentleman who was carrying on this establishment and causing this nuisance was a member of the sanitary committee of this Corporation?—Yes, I know that of my own knowledge.

3456. Was his attention ever called to it?—Often; and that party is at present the owner of the establishment which adjoins the parties' private dwelling house to which I have alluded, and I have not the least doubt that it is injurious to health.

3457. Are there more of these establishments in the town?—I have only referred to this one, which has come under my observation. I believe if the gentleman had not been a member of the sanitary committee, the evil would have been removed long since.

3458. Did you call the attention of the sanitary officers to this matter?—I did, both to-day and yesterday. He is not to be blamed; if he could have remedied it he would have done so long ago.

Mr. John Ross

Mr. John Ross examined.

3459. Mr. Lawrence.—I understand you wish to give evidence as to the differential rate between large and small house property?—My opinion is that it militates very much against the better description of property in Belfast.

3460. Can you shortly state in what respect you think so?—There are a class of property owners who find that the large taxes injure their property to a considerable extent. Of course an increased tax will considerably militate against the letting of the property they are building below a certain class, and consequently it increases the rate upon the better classes of property.

3461. Do you think it is a kind of premium upon the better class of property?—Yes, a kind of premium.

3462. Do you say that from their construction and build the houses are not valued at so fair a valuation as if they were better built?—Of course when they come under a certain value it decreases the valuation considerably.

3463. According to your knowledge of Belfast, is a re-valuing of the entire borough desirable?—I have no doubt of it.

3464. Do you think, having regard to the present day, that the rateable value of the town has increased very much?—Yes, on some properties—properties which have been valued a long time since.

3465. Do you think that the old property is not paying its fair share of rates according to its present letting value?—It certainly is not. I think the differential rate bears very heavily on the owners of property. Independent of that the Water Commissioners seem to have arranged charges in such a way that the large properties will ultimately pay the entire of the water taxes; in fact I had it from their clerk yesterday that that was their aim. I can give you evidence that would convince you of it. (The witness here gave some details as to the different rates for water charged by the Water Commissioners, but we do not insert it as we considered it beyond the scope of our inquiry.) There is one thing in connexion with the sanitary matters to which I desire to call attention. The fire of which I am a member has a place where many of our young men lodge, and unfortunately a person who manufactures tobacco is next to us. He has turned an ordinary chimney of his premises into a flue which he uses in the manufacture of tobacco. I hold that where young men have to sleep the air ought to be kept as pure as possible, and when the chimney of a dwelling-house close beside them is used for the purpose I have named, the Council ought to interfere. I brought the subject under their notice, but they have done nothing in the matter. As I have said the ordinary flue of the house has been turned into a chimney for a furnace employed in the manufacture of tobacco. I think that is dangerous both to property and health, for there is a high flame and sparks coming out at the top of the chimney. I am astonished that the Council have not interfered in this instance, and put a stop to this dangerous nuisance. There are a number of things in connexion with our town matters that I think should be changed. I think it puts a great deal of labour unnecessarily upon our town surveyor to have the purchasing of materials of a great many things without advertising for them. Hundreds of pounds worth of materials of different classes are evidently bought in this way, for there is not an advertisement of any kind for them, and I think that is a system which is liable to lead to a great many abuses. I think it is open for people to contract for these materials. Take stone, for instance. I assert that our surveyor takes stone without regard to quality, and that is quite injurious to our streets. I think the Council should advertise for that material. They take these stones irregularly as they get them, and they have men to spread them, who sometimes are standing idle for hours, not having any to spread. I think that is a department in which there should be advertising, and that a great deal of money would be saved for the town in the way of labour alone.

3466. Do you think the streets would be kept in better repair by contract?—Yes; or otherwise that they should advertise for all the materials.

Mr. SAMUEL BLACK re-examined.

Belfast. Dec. 22, 1876. Mr. S. Black.

2447. What do you wish to state in answer to Mr. Robb's evidence on this point?—I wish to state that everything is taken by consent where it is possible. We have got some by consent, frequently. The fact is, we took some stones from Mr. Robb himself, but they were too coarse for us.

Mr. ROBB'S examination resumed.

Mr. John Robb.

2448. The quality of the stone is very indifferent, one load being good and another bad, and these are supplied one beside the other. From what I have heard from others they have only one contractor, who seems to be a favourite with the Town Council, for making stones, and I have heard several contractors complain and say that he was evidently a favourite, and that there was no use in their attempting to obtain any work from the Council.

2449. What is his name?—Campbell. I think from the great number of materials ordered by the town surveyor I think they should be advertised for, and more narrowly looked after for the benefit of the town.

2450. Did you never see an advertisement for these materials?—Never.

2451. Would it be possible to get good stones delivered in the town?—I do not see any difficulty in the way of arranging to get them from four or five individuals, so that they might calculate upon the men being employed. There is another matter I have to complain of. At one time we put in plans for a projecting window in a house in Castle-place, before the Town Council, and they were approved of. After we had gone to the expense of putting it up we were noticed to take it down. Afterwards the matter was fought out, and it was arranged ultimately that it should be allowed to remain; but to the present day I see a number of places equally as bad, nor do we hear of them being taken any notice of at all, and they remain undisturbed. I could mention as one instance of that, a house in Queen's-square which is worse than ours, and it never was deemed an obstruction.

2452. Upon what grounds were you noticed?—The Town Council, in their absolute power, judged it an obstruction.

2453. What was the obstruction?—We got notice about our premises on account of a small circular projection into the street. After we went to the expense of constructing it, they wanted us to take it down, and we refused because they had passed the plans, and we showed them the note we had from them to that effect. We, of course, refused, having gone to about £1,000 worth of expense in the matter, and had ordered our circular plate-glass. Well, they judged it an obstruction, and because they did so they thought they could make us do away with it. They proceeded to law, and it could not be taken from us. But there are, as I have said, many other obstructions with which they have not interfered.

Mr. S. BLACK re-examined.

Mr. S. Black.

2454. Mr. Robb forgets to state to you that when his plan was submitted with this projection it was disapproved; but it is quite true that a circular was sent to him from the town clerk's office, stating that the plan was approved, instead of stating that it was disapproved. It came before the Council immediately afterwards, and the plan was disapproved, and the fact was published in the public prints, and Mr. Robb's attention called to it, but after that he went on with the building. He relied on the technicality that was afforded him by the error contained in the circular that was sent him. As far as the presumption is concerned there was no truth in that.

Examination of Mr. ROBB resumed.

Mr. John Robb.

2455. I want to show that there appears to be an espionage as regards the Town Council, because there are other obstructions equally as great as ours, of which they do not take any notice.

2456. Do you think that course arose from a feeling of animosity?—I have long come to that conclusion, and so have other people as well. They proceeded against us about six lamps outside another building of ours, which they also deemed an obstruction. If every person was treated alike I should not object, but they are not.

Mr. BLACK re-examined.

Mr. S. Black.

2457. If they had consented to keep these lamps alight as long as the ordinary street lamps we would not have objected, but they wanted to put them out when the premises were closed for business, and then the lamps became an obstruction.

DECEMBER 23, 1876.

Dec. 23, 1876.

(Before MESSRS. LAWLESS, Q.C., and EXHAM, Q.C.)

Mr. JOSEPH BIGGAR, M.P., re-examined.

Mr. Joseph Biggar, M.P.

2458. Mr. LAWLESS.—Do you wish to give us further evidence?—I do, about what is called the "Timber Ring" of the Town Improvement Committee, that I wish to speak.

2459. Have you heard that expression before?—I was a member of the Improvement Committee for three years, during the chairmanship of Mr. Guffikin, who was examined here last night, and Messrs. John Brown, Thomas Brown, Dixon, and Lowther were also members of the committee. I think Lowther and Dixon were only part of the time members of the Council, but the Browns were all the time. These four gentlemen are timber merchants and building speculators. It is the general opinion (I don't say the universal opinion) but it is a very general opinion that these gentlemen use their position as members of the Improvement Committee to benefit themselves. It is a very difficult matter to prove in any individual case whether or not they are fighting really for themselves, although not apparently doing so, because owing to their position as timber merchants they come very closely in contact with the builders and owners of houses which are being built, and they may be fighting for the business of friends, and in that way indirectly benefiting themselves, while the other members of the Improvement Committee would not know they were really doing so. In one or two cases that I can remember I have seen them act in a way which, I believe, was directly to benefit themselves.

2460. Will you mention those cases?—I will, before I am done. I may say that, so far as I can form an opinion, Mr. Montgomery was always disposed to do what was right. So far as I can form an opinion he reported fairly and correctly to the Improvement Committee, but I have repeatedly seen his recommendations overruled, and in such cases he would say, "Well, of course, gentlemen, I must do as I am instructed, but you will please to take a note of the fact that I have recommended differently." I have often seen Mr. Montgomery do this. There is one case in which Mr. Dixon bought a strip of ground from the Harbour Commissioners which lay in front of a row of houses which have been occupied for some years, the houses being the property of Mr. James Glenn. This ground could only be used to build houses of an inferior description on. There is a rule that no streets shall be formed of less than thirty feet wide for occupation by dwelling-houses.

3461. If they were limited to that rule, was there only room for houses of an inferior description?—Yes, that was the width from front to front. An application was made by Mr. Dempsey to build a public house of an extensive character at the end of this street, on the ground which Mr. Dixon had bought. His plan was so extensive that it would leave less than thirty feet of the street in front of these dwelling-houses. The application was objected to in the first instance when it came before the committee—Dempsey's plan I mean.

3462. Was it brought before them in the usual way?—Yes. It was brought by Mr. Montgomery before the committee. It was objected to in the first instance, but by perseverance the majority was got to report in favour of it.

3463. Did Mr. Montgomery when he brought that plan before the committee approve or disapprove of it?—I believe he disapproved of it, for the thing was objected to in the first instance. If he said "This report is all right" there would have been no discussion, but I remember there was a great deal of discussion over this business of Dempsey's. By perseverance the majority of the improvement committee was got to report in favour of the plan being carried, the result is, that the width of the street in front of the dwelling-houses is fixed at about twenty feet. The large building is built at one end of the street, which is there only twenty feet in width, and that fixes the line for the remainder of Mr. Dixon's houses upon that strip of ground.

3464. What street is it?—New Andrew-street.

3465. Can you give the date of that?—I really cannot tell you. I left the Town Council about three years ago; it is about three years ago.

3466. In the record of this in the minute book?—Yes.

3467. Then, in that case there has been a direct violation of a settled rule?—Exactly. I may say there are a number of rules. One is that the street should be thirty feet wide, and another that there should be no cellars deeper than the sewers of the premises. It is a very common thing at the committee for special applications to be made for leave to infringe some of these rules; but I believe the invariable practice of Mr Montgomery has been to report against any infraction of the rules, and then the party who sent in the plan would come before the committee and make a fight, and get leave to do what Mr. Montgomery objected to.

3468. Can you give us an instance?—In Messrs Ward and Greenway's place beside the Blackstaff the cellar was made deeper than the Blackstaff which adjoins it, and there is no doubt that Mr. John Ward and Mr. Brett came before the improvement committee at least six times, and at last they got leave to make it. I am told that it requires to be pumped out by a steam engine to keep it from being flooded with water.

3469. Can you give us any further instances?—I remember a particular case of Mr. Thomas H. Brown about a sewer that was recommended to be made by Mr. Montgomery somewhere in the neighbourhood of the Ballymacarrett-road.

3470. Was this plan passed by Mr. Montgomery?—No; he recommended that certain improvements should be made by the owners of the property, and the result of it was that Mr. Thomas H. Brown came before the improvement committee, of which he was then a member, and made a most determined objection to incurring the expense which he was asked to incur, and the result was that Mr. Montgomery's recommendation was not carried; so far as I remember the result was that no order was made, and the matter dropped.

3471. Was Mr. Brown then owner of the property?—Yes. I remember a case in which it was considered desirable to widen and straighten the footpaths in Donegall-pass.

3472. What was done about that?—Mr. John Brown, chairman of the improvement committee, had a piece of ground in front of some of his houses, which stood out on the footpath, and he wanted to make very much of a Jew's bargain with the committee—that is, he stood out against it. His was the only house that was beyond the line for houses, and he held out for better terms than the owners of the neighbouring ground were content to take.

3473. Was there any compulsory power to purchase the ground for improving the street?—No, they expired about the year 1830, but very often there is some compensation given for pieces of ground to improve the streets, and very properly. I remember a case; it did not come under my notice in my capacity of Town Councillor; but there is a piece of property owned by two members of the improvement committee, Mr. John Brown and Mr. Lowther, one of the tenants complained very much to me that these landlords would not be got to finish the streets although they had let the houses, and had bound themselves to the tenants to make the streets.

3474. What street is that?—It lies near Lisburn-road, between it and the New Lodge-road.

3475. Are Messrs. Brown and Lowther in partnership?—They are in partnership, and joint confederates in these ground speculations.

3476. Were there tenants occupying houses in the street that was not completed?—Yes; it was not completed, it was simply marked off; that is what gave rise to the great deal of discussion that took place here, namely, the landlords' contracting to make the streets and not doing so. In this case they had plenty of money and should have done so. The poor man cannot go to law with the rich landlord, and I think the remedy for these complaints which are really very general, about the conduct of the Improvement Committee, would be that when the Town Council are fixing their committees there should not be more than two members of the timber trade put on the Improvement Committee. I think there should be two; for these gentlemen know a great deal about the value, &c., of property, and their opinion on many matters with which the Improvement Committee have to deal is worth much. It is desirable that on any committee like this where these members form a quorum, that there should not be more than two, for the interests of these gentlemen very often clash with the general interests of the public.

3477. Do you think that the experience of two members of the timber trade would be of public advantage on that committee?—I think there could be no objection to it.

3478. Mr. Exham.—The 16th section of the Act of 1865 provides for the width the streets should be?—Yes; and there are by-laws and rules which ought to be as binding as the Act of Parliament, to give you an example, the Town Council once resolved that the footways of the streets should be flagged instead of laid down with round paving-stones, and that is a law which of course (until it is rescinded) should be binding in morals and fair play on the Improvement Committee, but they do not carry it out, for they are canvassed by people who wish to get these things done in their own way. I will give you another instance as to the way in which the committee is influenced. When the Tramway Company got authority to lay down their tramway, they bound themselves to make the roadway of a certain quality, and Mr. Montgomery frequently reported against the way in which the work was done, and he was as constantly thwarted by members of the committee, whom I do not at present remember, but it was the case. He reported over and over again that the work was improperly done, but it was not stopped. I do not wish to say that all the members of the Corporation are not desirable men, but I think the great fault is the want of a sound public opinion here. We have no representation of minorities. There is another small matter which was referred to by the Chairman, that is, as to the Local Government Board approving of the salaries of the sanitary officers. Those gentlemen made a remark about the salary of Dr. Browne, and Mr. Corbett said that it was confirmed by the Local Government Board, and he seemed to think that because that was so it must be all right. I think it would be judicious, and very likely it might be proposed that the powers of the Local Government Board should be extended, and I think that the Local Government Board is very good for some things.

2479. Mr. Lawlor.—I think this is going beyond the scope of our inquiry.

2480. Witness.—I would not have referred to it but Mr. Corbett said, or seemed to think, that because the Local Government Board sanctioned Dr. Browne's salary it must be all right. I say the Local Government Board are not competent to decide whether Dr. Browne has a fair salary or not. I am not competent myself to decide upon his duties or salary. I think it is an insufficient tribunal for business of that sort. I think it would be very good for matters which have turned up in the course of this inquiry; where the owner of property in a street pays to have the street past his own house made, and the owners made, while the remaining part of the street is not sewered or paved. It would be a very good thing for the Local Government Board to see that the street was made.

2481. Mr. Lawlor.—Is not that a matter which should be attended to by the Town Council?—Yes; but when they neglect it the Local Government Board would be a competent authority to see that it was done.

Belfast, Dec. 22, 1876. — Mr. Joseph Rogers, J.P.

January 8, 1877.

Jan. 8, 1877. — Mr. Robert Stewart.

Mr. Robert Stewart re-examined.

2482. Mr. Lawlor.—You went very fully into the several matters to which you referred when you were examined here last, and we must therefore request you will not go into any matter you mentioned before. What do you now wish to state?—Mr. Black gave evidence on the 22nd December regarding some evidence which I gave affecting a rate collector named Rankin, and inasmuch as Mr. Black's evidence is misleading and untrue, I think it right in the interests of public justice to refer to it. He said that in my evidence I charged Mr. Rankin with disqualifying a certain number of voters. I did not make any such statement in my evidence. Mr. Black said that Mr. Rankin is constantly in attendance on his duties, and I say, and am prepared to prove, that this is not true, and that members of the Town Council know about it. Mr. Rankin never called upon me in my house or elsewhere for rates. Mr. James Crozier was the person who always called upon me and the other persons in Dock Ward for the rates, and I have ascertained that in the entire of Dock Ward Mr. Rankin does not collect the rate from a single person, excepting three establishments—namely, the Belfast Harbour Commissioners, the Northern Counties Railway Company, and the York-street Spinning Mill.

2483. Do you mean to say that his collecting the rates by deputy is known to certain members of the Corporation?—Certainly. George H. Crane, a town councillor, living in Dock Ward, pays his rates to James Crozier; Daniel Dixon, Samuel Lowther, David Corbett, and William Harvey, all town councillors in the same ward, also pay their rates to him, and so does Dr. Alexander, the alderman of that ward. This fact is, I think, sufficient proof of my statement.

2484. Do you mean to say that these gentlemen were aware of the fact of Rankin acting by deputy?—Certainly, and they actually pay their rates to Crozier as his deputy, and have done so for many years past. I do not know for how many years, but I can say for some years.

2485. Have you the receipts for the rates which you paid?—Yes.

2486. In whose handwriting are they?—In Rankin's.

2487. In his own handwriting?—Yes; my allegation is that he himself never calls for the rates. It is always the deputy. I merely wish to make this statement in correction of the evidence given by Mr. Black. I have made inquiries with regard to two other collectors employed by the Corporation, and I find that they both employ deputies.

2488. Name them?—Charles Noah Davis employs a deputy.

2489. Do you know this of your own knowledge?—I do. I do not know the name of the deputy whom he employs, but he is his brother-in-law, and there is George Miller, the collector for Cromac Ward, who had in his employment a deputy up to the first of the present year.

2490. Do you know that of your own knowledge?—I do.

2491. Do you know whether he has ceased to keep the deputy collector?—I do not know that he has ceased to do so yet.

2492. Do you know his name?—I do not know his name.

2493. How do you know that the rates are collected in those other wards by deputies?—I saw them collected by them.

2494. Mr. Exham.—Have you been in the houses and seen the people pay the rates to the deputy?—Yes; I saw the deputies giving receipts in the ratepayers' houses in those wards.

Mr. James Lamrock examined.

Mr. James Lamrock.

2495. What complaint have you to make against the officials of the Corporation?—I wish to corroborate the statement already made by Mr. Dickson and Mr. Gaffikin. Having seen in the local newspapers that Mr. Cobain, on the 23rd December last, said that the evidence regarding him and his interference in political matters was unfounded, in self-defence I think it my duty to come forward and corroborate the evidence given by Mr. Dickson.

2496. Mr. Exham.—We want distinct evidence—evidence that you know of your knowledge—not what you know by hearsay?—The greater part of the evidence which I intend to give now was formerly given by me on oath before the Recorder in a case which I had against Mr. Cobain for wages due to me.

2497. Mr. Lawlor.—Did you bring an action before the Recorder against Mr. Cobain?—I did.

2498. When was that, and what was it for?—It was in 1870. You will see it all in the newspaper. [Newspaper produced.]

2499. Were you ever employed by what is called the Conservative Registration Association in Belfast?—Yes, I was, from 1869 to 1871.

2500. In what capacity?—As political agent, parliamentary and municipal agent for St. Anne's ward.

2501. By whom were you employed?—By the Conservative Registration Association.

2502. Can you name any of the individuals acting in it?—I cannot in every case, for this reason—that there was a new association formed every year; consequently I cannot name them.

2503. Was Mr. Cobain a member of that association?—He was.

2504. Was he a member during the time that you were employed as agent?—Yes, from 1869 until the present time.

2505. Did that association act in relation to the municipal elections?—Yes, and the revision of the burgess and parliamentary voters lists.

2506. Were you ever present at any meetings

BELFAST. Jan. 5, 1877. Mr. James Lennon.

for the purpose of naming candidates for the Town Council?—I was repeatedly.

2507. Have you ever seen Mr. Cobain present at any of those meetings?—Yes, I have.

2508. Have you ever known him to nominate any person as a candidate?—I did.

2509. Can you remember the name of the candidate nominated by Mr. Cobain on the occasion to which you allude?—Yes, Mr. John Harrill, J.P.

2510. Were you ever employed by Mr. Cobain as a member of that association to do work connected with it?—Yes, I was employed by him to do special work in Cromac ward.

2511. What were you employed to do?—I was employed to make what is called an after-inspection, and to post up the books and prepare the list and conduct the burgess revision for Cromac ward, which I did.

2512. Were you specially employed by Mr. Cobain to do that work?—I was.

2513. When?—I do not remember the date, but it was in 1871.

2514. Were you to be paid for that?—Mr. Cobain said he would see me paid.

2515. At what rate were you to be paid?—There was no sum mentioned as to what I was to be paid, but it was to be afterwards ascertained what I should be paid.

2516. Out of what funds?—I do not know; out of the general subscription.

2517. Did you do that work yourself, or did you employ some person to assist you in it?—I did it, but I also employed a man to help me, and promised him 30s. for one week.

2518. What is the name of the man you employed?—James Clarke.

2519. Is he living still?—Yes. He is living at 75, Hopewell-street.

2520. Did you pay him that 30s. which you promised him?—I did not. I said when I was employing him I would pay him when I was paid.

2521. Were you paid?—I was not.

2522. Did you apply for payment?—I did.

2523. To whom did you apply?—I applied to Mr. Cobain, and I asked others to apply as well as myself.

2524. Did you apply in 1871, or any time after 1871?—Yes, I did.

2525. How many applications did you make to him?—A good many; but when I found it was useless I got a solicitor to apply for me.

2526. Did you bring an action against him?—Yes.

2527. For how much?—For £15; in the summer of 1874 at the quarter sessions.

2528. Before the Recorder?—Yes.

2529. What was the result of that action?—It was dismissed without prejudice on some technical point.

2530. Did Mr. Cobain defend that action?—Yes, he did.

2531. Did he deny your claim?—Yes.

2532. Were you examined in the case?—I was.

2533. Was Mr. Cobain examined?—He was.

2534. Did he deny your claim?—He admitted that I did the work, but he did not admit that he employed me to do so.

2535. Did he admit that you did it upon his employment—his retainer, as it were—or did he merely dispute the amount?—He disputed that he ever personally promised to pay me.

2536. Had he promised to pay you?—If Mr. M'Erlean, who was my solicitor in the case, was here, he could tell you all about it.

2537. Your own recollection is as good as Mr. M'Erlean's?—He disputed paying it because he did not look on it as an employment in his own name.

2538. Were you the only agent employed upon that occasion?—I do not remember.

2539. Did you ever know of any other agents being employed by Mr. Cobain?—I did; Mr. Whiteman was one. He gave evidence in my case also.

2540. Do you know of anyone else being employed by Mr. Cobain?—Yes; Mr. Clarke and Mr. Connor.

2541. Was that Mr. Connor the deputy of Mr. Rankin, the rate collector?—Yes.

2542. Were these men employed by Mr. Cobain to render similar services to those which you were appointed to do?—I know that Mr. Clarke and Mr. Whiteman were, but Mr. Connor was not employed by Mr. Cobain, but he promised him a bonus in the same year of £20.

2543. Who promised the bonus?—Mr. Cobain.

2544. Who did he promise it to?—To Mr. Connor.

2545. A bonus for what?—The salary was too small, and he promised him that bonus for doing some work in Dock ward.

2546. Do you mean in addition to what he received as deputy for collecting Rankin's rates?—Yes, for acting as ward agent, the same as I was.

2547. Was it for being ward agent that Mr. Cobain promised him the bonus?—Yes; that was what the man swore to.

2548. Did he ever pay that to Connor, or ever procure it for him?—No, he utterly denied it.

2549. Were any witnesses examined in that action brought against Mr. Cobain by you?—There was Mr. Clarke, Connor, and Whiteman.

2550. Did their evidence sustain your case, or Mr. Cobain's case?—My case; that I did the work.

2551. What was the technical point on which your case was dismissed?—Simply that Mr. Cobain did not guarantee any payment. That it was simply in the name of the society he made the appointment, and that they and not Mr. Cobain personally were legally liable to pay me.

2552. Were you ever present at any of those ward meetings—what did you call them?—Some were meetings of the general committee, and others were ward meetings.

2553. Were candidates nominated at them?—Yes.

2554. Have you known Mr. Cobain to take as active part such as any other elector would take in proposing or nominating or objecting to any candidate?—Yes; repeatedly. In all those cases he took a most prominent part.

2555. Have you known him to take an active part in the municipal elections here?—I have.

2556. In what way?—He canvassed; and got lists for that purpose, and afterwards came in and made reports to the committee as to the result, the same as any paid agent would do.

2557. Have there ever been any collections made for any of those purposes?—There was a collection made every year.

2558. Have you ever known Mr. Cobain to make a collection?—I have known him to go out for that purpose when any financial difficulty arose, and he always got money.

2559. Have you got a letter dated the 8th October, 1873, from Mr. Cobain?—I have (hands in letter).

2560. This is the letter:—

"Rugby-road, Belfast.

"8th October, 1873.

"SIR,—In reply to the communication with which you have favoured me supporting a claim for £15, which you allege is due you for the help rendered in the revision of Cromac ward in the year 1873, I have to inform you that I know nothing of the claim in question; you were never employed by me, nor was any other person for the purpose you mention. I [illegible] myself to your [illegible] [illegible], and did all I could to have you appointed for the [illegible], and while you were an employee of the Conservative Society I did all in my power to have your services recognised in the most generous manner. I did what in a very large [illegible] in the [illegible] I [illegible] by your [illegible]. I [illegible] the [illegible] [illegible] for the [illegible] [illegible] [illegible]. If this money is really due you should at the time have preferred your claim to the proper quarter. You are perfectly aware I never had any connexion with the duty of employing and paying the [illegible] [illegible], and I therefore decline entirely to take any responsibility in the matter.

"I am, sir, yours truly,

"E. W. DE COBAIN."

After that you brought the action?—Yes; it was in the year 1874.

2561. Are you able to state from your own knowledge that Mr. Cobain has taken an active part on more occasions than one in the election of members of the

Council?—Yes; in every year that I was ever employed as an agent.

2362. Was he during all that time outside of the Corporation?—Yes; and he is still, and he was publicly regarded as a prominent man in politics.

2363. Mr. KERNAN.—Did you yourself ever see Mr. Cobain fill in objections to ratepayers?—I did in 1871, and I also assisted him. We had to do it in a hurry, because the form of some of them was spoiled by the old man in charge of Cromac Ward, and we had to fill them on the very last day that they could be posted.

2364. Have you ever known any person whom Mr. Cobain actually canvassed for his vote in any municipal election?—I do not recollect.

2365. Were you ever present when he did such a thing?—No, I never was.

2366. Can you state the name of any councillor for whom he ever canvassed?—I did not take notes on that point. I cannot swear to an individual, but I know he did it. I did not take notes of it.

2367. How long did the meetings generally last?—Sometimes they would last two or three hours; it was according to the importance of the business.

2368. How many people were generally present at them?—At the meeting of 1870 there was only four burgess electors of St. Ann's Ward present.

2369. Was that when Mr. Hamill was the candidate?—Yes.

2370. Mr. LAWLESS.—Can you give the names of those present?—Yes. Mr. Henry voted. There were two for and two against Mr. Hamill, and the chairman, Mr. Thomas M'Clinton, gave a casting vote in favour of Mr. Hamill.

2371. Who proposed and voted for the second man?—I know Mr. William Gray was present.

2372. Was Mr. Hamill put forward as a candidate?—He was.

2373. Was he elected?—He was on that day.

2374. Was there any book kept of the records of that society, whatever it was?—[No answer.]

2375. Did you ever see any entries made in a book? Did you see a book?—I did repeatedly. In a couple of years (1869 and 1871), the society became totally bankrupt, and the landlord of the offices which they occupied confiscated all the books, papers, and office furniture for payment of his rent.

2376. Have you seen Mr. Cobain present at more than one of those meetings?—Yes; at more than fifty meetings.

2377. Were they about municipal elections or parliamentary elections?—Municipal in particular.

2378. Did you hear discussions, or what was done at those meetings?—It was simply the workings of the association.

2379. What were the workings of the association? Were there lists of the voters and ratepayers there?—Yes, regularly.

2380. What was done?—Simply looking over the workings of the association.

2381. Were returns given in as to who promised to vote and who did not?—Yes; there were lists made out—canvass lists as it were—and these lists were given to canvassers, and reports were made by them almost every night at the ward meetings as to the chances of success of the candidates.

2382. Do you mean to say that you yourself saw Mr. Cobain present at those meetings when the reports were given in?—I do.

2383. Give us the names of some of the persons who you say were present as well as Mr. Cobain?—That I cannot give, for the reason that the canvassers for the wards were, with the exception of myself, generally volunteers.

2384. Did you hear Mr. Cobain give instructions to those persons?—Yes.

2385. What was the nature of the instructions?—To take their lists and canvass the wards according to the lists to see who would vote, and who would not vote for the selected candidate.

2386. Who opposed Mr. Hamill then?—I do not remember at present.

2387. In 1870 did you make out any canvassing lists for Saint Ann's Ward?—I did, street lists.

2388. Was it by Mr. Cobain's directions, or by the directions of anyone else?—By the whole committee of the ward.

2389. Who else was on the committee besides Mr. Cobain? Was Mr. Davis?—Mr. Davis was one, and my own brother was another.

2390. Who is Mr. Noah Davis?—One of the rate collectors.

2391. Charles Noah Davis?—Yes.

2392. Did you refuse to act for the candidate Mr. Hamill?—I did.

2393. Why?—I refused on principle, in accordance with the rules of the association. That was my principal point.

2394. What was the principle upon which you refused to act for Mr. Hamill?—Because of the fifth rule (I have the rules at home). The fifth rule said that there was to be no one returned for Parliament or the Town Council except he was a supporter of our Orange and Protestant principles.

2395. And that being the rule you refused to support Mr. John Hamill?—I did.

2396. Did Mr. Davis give you any canvassing lists upon that occasion?—No; but Mr. Davis made use of the lists I had then made out.

2397. In other words did you give your lists to Mr. Davis?—No; but he took them as a member of the society.

2398. And did he make use of them in the interests of Mr. Hamill?—Yes.

2399. Mr. KERNAN.—I am, if the report of this trial is correct, that his Worship the Recorder would not allow Mr. Cobain to be asked the question whether or not he himself had selected candidates for the Town Council. It was objected to by Mr. M'Lean that the question was irrelevant. The question was—"Do you swear, Mr. Cobain, that you yourself have not selected candidates as members of the Town Council for political purposes," but on the trial the Recorder would not allow that question to be put to him.

2400. Mr. LAWLESS.—Have you known Mr. Davis to take an active part on behalf of the Conservative Society in the year 1873?—I did.

2401. What part did you know him to take?—I have known him to give a list of the names belonging to George's ward; that is, the names and addresses—some seventy, I should say, to the then solicitor of the society, Mr. Bates, to be claimed for.

2402. To be put on the burgess roll, is that what you mean by "to be claimed for"?—Yes.

2403. Have you known Mr. Davis of your own knowledge to interfere with the revision of the burgess lists?—Yes, repeatedly.

2404. Have you seen him do so?—I have repeatedly as a member of the Conservative Society.

2405. Have you known Mr. Cobain to attend to the revision of the burgess lists?—Yes; in any particular year to see that it was correctly done. I have seen him go over them in my own house.

2406. Is it not the duty of the officers of the Corporation to attend the revision of the burgess roll?—It is the duty of the collectors to attend the revision.

2407. And the town clerk?—Yes; and also the clerk of the union.

2408. Do you know what the duty of the collectors of the municipal rates at that revision is? Is not the duty of the collectors simply to state to the court of revision what persons' rates are paid, and what are not paid?—Yes; and also to answer whatever questions it may be thought proper to ask.

2409. Have you known any of these rate collectors, or any officer of the Corporation, take a part in the revision of the burgess roll beyond his regular duty?—I have, almost every year. I never remember it otherwise. Mr. Davis could let nothing pass without interfering in every disputed point in the burgess revision. At the very last burgess revision, when I myself was arguing a point, he interfered, and had to be reminded of his position by the town clerk.

BELFAST. Jan. 8, 1877. Mr. Angus Lennon.

2610. Was that to stop his interference?—It was.

2611. Mr. Exham.—Was he going beyond telling whether taxes were paid or not, or answering questions?—He was, and was merely interfering. It had nothing to say to the payment of taxes.

2612. I see by the report in this paper that you had an interview in this hall with Mr. Cobain—was that so?—No, it was not in this hall. It was in the surveyor's office in the old town hall in Police-square.

2613. Was it there that you say he directed this after inspection to be made?—It was.

2614. And you state that he told you to do it, and that he would see you paid?—Yes.

2615. And his evidence was, that if you did the work, you should be compensated for it?—Yes.

2616. Did Mr. Noah Davis ever give assistance at these meetings to your own knowledge?—Yes.

2617. When was the last time you knew Mr. Davis to take such a part?—The last time was in 1871.

2618. Mr. Exham.—Do you know anything of Sir John Savage's election?—I did, for I was his principal working agent.

2619. Did Mr. Cobain assist in his election?—He did, just the same as any of the rest of the Committee.

2620. Was he one of the Committee?—He was, undoubtedly; from 1869 up to the present he was a member of the Committee.

2621. Was Mr. Noah Davis on the Committee?—He was and is.

2622. Mr. Lawless.—Do you remember the occasion when Mr. Carlisle was a candidate?—I do.

2623. Mr. Exham.—When he was put out?—I remember all about it.

2624. Mr. Lawless.—Did Mr. Cobain take any part in that election?—I do not remember; I will not travel beyond what I know to be facts.

2625. Mr. Exham.—Do you know anything about Mr. Griffith's election?—I do not remember very much about it.

2626. Mr. Lawless.—Used Mr. Cobain to give in reports in writing?—He gave in verbal reports.

2627. Had he anything written down on paper?—Yes; he read the reports from his memorandum and my directions.

2628. What became of them afterwards?—Oh, they were generally burned; they were of no use to them afterwards. As Mr. Cobain read out the names of the list of voters they were checked off on the roll.

2629. Mr. Exham.—Do you mean to say that Mr. Cobain came in having a list with the voters' names on it and that he read out the names of the voters from it?—I do; he used to read out the names of those who promised and those who refused.

2630. Were the names then taken down in books kept for that purpose?—They were checked off on the list—on the rolls of voters.

2631. Who checked them off while he was reading?—The chairman, or secretary, or some member who was present, as the case might be.

2632. Can you say who it was checked them off?—I cannot say. I cannot mention the individual; different persons did it on different occasions.

2633. Mr. Lawless.—Was there a chairman elected every day?—No, every year, and in his absence some other person would act.

2634. Mr. Exham.—Was there a secretary?—There was.

2635. Can you now recollect his name?—I think it was Mr. Clinton for the year 1870.

2636. Do you remember Mr. M'Clinton?—Yes; he was chairman for St. Anne's ward.

2637. For that year?—Yes.

2638. How often used the Committees of each ward to meet?—Generally once a month, and oftener before an election.

2639. Where were the meetings for St. Anne's ward held which Mr. Cobain used to attend?—I believe it was in the Victoria Hall, in Victoria-street.

2640. As you say you were there constantly, surely you must know?—I was, but they changed their offices so often that I cannot now remember distinctly.

2641. Did any other officer interfere beside Mr. Noah Davis?—Never, directly to my knowledge or indirectly. I omitted to say that in 1871 Mr. Cobain and Mr. Davis compelled the agent for Cromac ward to send objections to Charles H. Ward, solicitor, and Thomas Ward, flax buyer.

2642. Who is the agent for Cromac ward?—A Mr. Henry. The list that I referred to as given by Mr. Davis is held in duplicate by Mr. Dinnen, and if he was here I could get the duplicate. Mr. Dinnen can corroborate that.

2643. You can get it from Mr. Dinnen?—Yes; I am prepared to verify the foregoing list on oath.

Mr. Black re-examined.

2644. Mr. Lawless.—A communication has been made to us that on 26th December last there was a resolution passed by the Law Committee of the Corporation with reference to the attendance of the officers of the Corporation, and their giving evidence before this Commission—was there such a meeting?—There was.

2645. Have you got the minutes of it?—I have.

2646. Will you let me see them?—(Minutes produced.)

2647. This is the resolution passed by the Law Committee on the 26th December last, and I find that part of it was communicated to us, but only part of it:—

"Minutes of Law Committee, 26th December, 1876.

"Present—Councillor R. Thompson (in the chair), Councillors Lawther, Mullan, Bellew, and J. R. Thompson. Moved by Mr. Mullan, seconded by Mr. Greenhill, and resolved—That the sitting of the Commissioners having been adjourned until a future day, without the evidence on behalf of the Corporation having been brought forward, and the parties against them being heard by the Commissioners, this Corporation considers it most desirable that rebutting evidence should be heard by the Commissioners, and urge upon Messrs. Cobain, Lawless, and Exham to give them the opportunity desired, and that a copy of this resolution be forwarded to them."

Well, that is a very proper resolution, but there follows (and I cannot speak of it in the same terms, as it does not seem to me a proper resolution to be passed by the Committee) another resolution:—

"Resolved—That the several officers of the Corporation, except the Town Clerk and the Borough Surveyor, be informed that the carriage of the evidence to be given at the inquiry is in the hands of the solicitor, and that they be requested not to interfere directly at the Commission except under his advice."

In that resolution the word "carriage," which is written over an erasure, shows that it was substituted for some other word, and I may say that that suggestion is strengthened by the fact that the resolution, a copy of which was privately sent to us, has instead of "carriage" the word "course"?—The resolution was prepared by me, and the reason there was an erasure was because the one word was mistaken for the other, and copied wrongly into the book. Then, of course, it had to be erased and corrected. That resolution was drawn up by me.

2648. Have you got the draft of it?—No; I have not. I found that the word was written "course," and I had to correct it when I came to see the mistake.

2649. Mr. Exham.—Some one, at all events, must have taken a copy of that before the erasure was made?—Certainly. When it was read before the Committee I found that the word was miscopied.

2650. Mr. Lawless.—A copy of this was sent to us this morning in which the word is "course," and not "carriage"?—That was the original word.

2651. Mr. Exham.—Some one must have taken it from the original and sent it to us?—It was marked off and sent to the different members of the Corporation.

2652. Mr. Lawless.—I must say I consider it would have been better if that portion of the resolution had not been passed. It appears to me to show on the part of the Corporation a desire to keep back their evidence from us, or only to bring forward such portions of it as may suit themselves. It is impossible not to come to that conclusion?—On the first day that you sat here I said that my instructions were to lay before you every document and every evidence in our possession, and also to produce before you all the officers of the Corporation that you wished to examine. Such has been my practice throughout, and such shall be my practice as long as you continue to sit. On the last day you were here certain officers of the Corporation sent in communications wishing to deny certain charges which they thought implicated them, and by which I thought they were in no way implicated, and I thought that they (Mr. Cobain for instance), would come forward and force their evidence at a time when the Commissioners were not prepared to hear them. It was with the object of preventing that and with that object alone that the resolution was passed. It was drafted by myself and advised by myself to the committee.

2653. Taking your statement that it was done with the intention of facilitating matters here, I give you credit for it, but I think it would have been better that it should not have been done?—On the last day after half an hour was occupied in discussing the matter I had to get up and express my concurrence with the opinion expressed with reference to Mr. Cobain's coming forward then and giving evidence, and under the circumstances I thought it absolutely necessary that the committee should give instructions upon it.

2654. Mr. *Greenhill*.—I objected to that resolution being passed unless it was understood that full liberty should be given to all the officers who were charged to vindicate themselves from such charges.

2655. Mr. Exham.—The terms of the resolution are that they are not to come forward unless Mr. Black agrees with their doing so, but we have power to ask them to come forward and give evidence whether the Corporation like it or not.

2656. Mr. *Black*.—They all wish to come before you.

2657. Mr. *Greenhill*.—Mr. Black stated that he would give full liberty to them.

2658. Mr. Lawless.—I cannot understand why any of them should want liberty from Mr. Black or anyone else.

2659. Mr. *Greenhill*.—I was perfectly satisfied with what Mr. Black said after I objected.

2660. Mr. Exham.—Every one knew that we wished to give the fullest opportunity to the officers of the Corporation to come forward and vindicate themselves, and we will take care they shall do so if they please.

Mr. William Cosgrove examined.

2661. Mr. Lawless.—Are you a ratepayer in Belfast?—Yes; I am a ratepayer.

2662. Where do you live?—In Greenmount.

2663. What do you complain of?—Of the making of streets. I have laid out about fifty acres of ground myself for building, and have made some fourteen or fifteen streets. The first I had to do with were in the Shankill district.

2664. What year was that in?—It is at least fourteen or fifteen years ago. I then had the ground abutting on one street, about 800 feet in length. It was made and macadamized, and devoted to the public use, as streets were then laid out and accepted as corners (Crimea-street for instance). The Council occasionally cleaned, but never permanently took charge of them.

2665. Do you speak of this particular street?—I have only one complaint to make with regard to this street. Four years afterwards they ordered it to be paved, and sewered, and kerbed. My complaint is this—that when I took and built on it, and the houses were occupied, and having sufficient drainage, that the Council put me to the expense of about——. I cannot exactly say the expense, but the length of the street will testify to the amount it cost me.

2666. In what way were you overcharged?—The street was macadamized, and laid out, and appropriated to the use of the public, as streets were then. There were many streets at that time which were macadamized and laid out in the same way, and they put me to the expense of re-making my street, while they did not make others do the same to their streets.

2667. How long were the houses occupied at the time this was done?—Three or four years.

2668. Had any sewer been made through that street?—I already said that I had sewage.

2669. You say they then compelled you to remake the street?—Yes.

2670. Were the footpaths made at the time?—No; the upper end of the street, for about forty feet, abutted on a portion of ground that the Council wanted to go through. I several times submitted plans to build—they never refused to allow me to build—but they would not approve of the plans, and I took that as a refusal. Latterly I went before them, and the surveyor and one of the committee went with me to the ground, and eventually we agreed that the Council should pave and sewer the portion of the street running across my ground there. Mountreath-street was 800 feet long, and subsequently the Council cut off about 340 feet to close up the street at the end. Previously it was laid off as a street 800 feet long, but subsequently a portion was let to a foundry, and the Council closed it up, and only left me 450 feet.

2671. Mr. Exham.—Do you mean after that street was paved and completed?—After it had been approved and laid out, they altered it. It was a loss to me though I do not complain of it.

2672. You said you had some complaint to make about the conduct of the officials of the Corporation?—I have nothing but what I put before you.

2673. Is Mr. Black your solicitor?—He is.

2674. Has he been your solicitor long?—Yes, for five or ten years.

Mr. Constantine O'Neill re-examined.

2682. Chairman.—Mr. O'Neill, what statement do you wish to make?—I wish to make a statement in relation to the weaving factory, which adjoins the Belfast District Lunatic Asylum, near the Falls-road.

2683. Who is the owner of the factory?—Mr. Lindsay. I inspected the place on the 1st of January, and I saw that at the side of the factory, between it and the asylum, the sediment of the workers comes out into the stream. The heated water from the same factory comes out a few yards below that; the sediment and the hot water mix together, and then run down an open drain which is in a parallel line with the asylum wall, and separated from it by a distance of only four feet.

2684. Do the sewage and the water used there for condensing flow together into the open stream?—Yes; They don't leave the factory in the same drain but unite shortly afterwards and flow down past the asylum.

2685. Where does it run to?—It discharges itself into the Blackstaff. On the 1st of January there was such a smell from it that when it came in contact with my palate and stomach it had such an effect that I was not quite well till after I had got a sleep.

2686. Mr. Ekman.—How far does it run in that direction?—About 300 yards before it falls into the Blackstaff.

2687. How many people are working in that mill?—About 200.

2688. Do you complain that Mr. Lindsay is allowed to have this drain containing sewage matter open when it should be in a covered channel?—My complaint is that it should be culverted so as not to be a public nuisance.

2689. Are there many people passing up that way?—No, except the workers. I have a house of mine close by and I was summoned for not having spouting on it, and there is a small yard which I got notice to have cleaned. I got the notice which was very proper from the sanitary officer, and what I complain of is this, that I am so visited by the law, and that the drain which is such a public nuisance is not taken any notice of by the Council. I complain that the law is put in force against me, and not against Mr. Lindsay.

2690. Mr. Lawless.—You don't complain that the law has been put in force against you?—I say that if it was put equally against all I would not complain.

2691. Mr. Ekman.—Is Mr. Lindsay a member of the Town Council?—Yes; and he has been mayor.

2692. Was this place built since 1845?—Yes; and I say that I feel very much aggrieved that I should be so treated, and that a man who is a member of the Council and a great moral reformer should be allowed to have such a nuisance in sight of my house. I wish to let you know that your coming here is a God-send to many persons who are oppressed, and whose redress would be very small indeed if you were not here to listen to them. There is one other thing that I want to refer to. There was great talk in the Council about a change of the police in Belfast.

2693. Mr. Ekman.—You need not say anything about that. I did not understand Mr. Black to make any complaint about the police. It is extraordinary how this matter is misunderstood. What he said was that the town should have a larger police force free. He showed that Belfast was not getting, under the Act of Parliament, its proper number free, and that if it did there would be a saving of £3,000 a year to the ratepayers. He said that the matter was brought under the notice of the Chief Secretary, and that it would be considered in July next when the number of the free police force to be stationed over Ireland will be allocated.

2694. Witness.—Dr. Alexander said that the Council should have control over the constabulary.

2695. Mr. Lawless.—His idea was that fewer of the constabulary with the assistance of the military would be sufficient.

2696. Mr. Ekman.—Have you reported the complaint about the factory to the sanitary authorities?—I never did, and for this reason: some time since I made a report which was signed by two doctors and by clergymen of different religious persuasions about a nuisance in the same district, and we got no redress.

Mr. Robert Forbes Dill, M.D. (Borough Coroner), examined.

2697. Chairman.—On what point do you wish to give evidence?—Owing to the enormous amount of walking which the coroner has to do I think that there should be power given to appoint a deputy coroner.

2698. Mr. Lawless.—Are you appointed by the Corporation?—It is owing to that fact that I present myself.

2699. Are you paid by fees?—Yes; and I would like also that the Corporation should have power to pay a fixed salary. I think it would be more satisfactory for all parties. A very considerable amount of talk has been indulged in by certain persons as to the holding of certain inquests, and if there was a fixed salary that talk would be done away with. Eighty-five might be about the average number of inquests held in the year, and then there are returns of about fifty that the coroner does not consider to hold inquests on. I think that there should be some remuneration for the work done in connexion with those cases on which I don't find it necessary to hold inquests. I would allow the deputy to be paid by the coroner in proportion to the amount of work that he did during the year.

2700. What is your fee?—I am paid £1 for each case.

2701. Supposing the inquest is adjourned from day to day?—I only get the one fee per case.

2702. Chairman.—I am afraid this matter hardly comes within our jurisdiction.

2703. Mr. Ekman.—Have you formed an opinion as to how the Sanitary Act is carried out here?—I think that the officers themselves are only groping their way. The town is so extensive, and of such growth, that I believe there will be very great difficulty in overtaking that work, and while every one of the sanitary officers is disposed to do his duty, at present he is only getting into the knowledge of what he should do. The work under existing circumstances could not be done all at once. I believe you have not had evidence regarding the flooding which takes place in certain parts of the town, and which I believe could be prevented by stopping the flow of water in one direction, and enabling it to run down in its natural channel.

2704. Do you know anything yourself of the mills using sewage matter for the boilers?—It is generally admitted to be a fact.

2705. In your opinion, as a medical man, is the using of that water detrimental to the health of the people working in those mills?—I think it is more injurious to the people outside the mills than those inside. I do not believe the injury overtakes the persons inside as it does those outside. The vapour and steam from those mills escape back again into the sewage, and then gets into the atmosphere.

2706. In your opinion, as a medical man, is the vapour arising from the steam generated in these chimneys contaminated to a dangerous extent?—Yes, most dangerous.

2707. Do you think the sanitary authorities are carrying out the law at all if they allow that to go on? Have you known them to attack it in any way?—From a general knowledge of the meaning of the word nuisance, I should say not.

2708. Are you aware of any steps having been taken to prevent this dangerous nuisance?—I do not believe there have been any steps taken, and I believe the only steps that could be taken to remedy that would be to prevent the mills using the stuff they do, and to have a constant supply of water furnished by the Water Commissioners to the mills.

2709. Do you know do they heat the rooms in those mills with hot vapour or hot water pipes?—I am not so well acquainted with that matter as I am of the point I have spoken of. If the vapour comes from that sewage water, it must be equally detrimental inside and outside.

BELFAST. Jan. 8, 1878.

Mr. Robert F. Dill, M.D.

Mr. WILLIAM O'HARA recalled.

Mr. William O'Hara.

2710. Mr. EXHAM.—Do you know whether the rooms in which the people work in the mills are heated by hot vapour?—I cannot tell from what source the water is taken, but the spinning of yarns cannot be carried on unless the rooms are constantly filled with vapours. In point of fact when the workers come out of those rooms their clothes are literally wringing.

2711. Are the rooms heated by hot water pipes?—No; a damp atmosphere is required for the purpose of spinning.

2712. Does that remark apply to the mills on the Falls-road and along the Pound Burn?—It applies to all spinning mills.

Mr. LUKE MACASSEY examined.

Mr. Luke Macassey.

2713. CHAIRMAN.—You are principal engineer to the Belfast Water Commissioners?—Yes.

2714. How long have you been in that capacity?—Since the year 1874.

2715. Did you attend the meeting of the ratepayers yesterday?—Yes; I was present at that meeting.

2716. Did they pass a resolution to this effect—"That we, the water-ratepayers of Belfast, in annual public meeting assembled, do hereby return our best thanks to the Belfast Water Commissioners for reducing the dwelling-house rate from 1s. 6d. to 1s., and the fire rate from 6d. to 2d., and we earnestly request the Water Commissioners to take all such proceedings before the Municipal Royal Commissioners and the Select Committee of the House of Commons as may be necessary to prevent the Town Council obtaining any of the powers now vested in the Water Commissioners." Was that passed in your presence?—Yes; I was present when that resolution was moved, seconded, and passed.

2717. Mr. LAWLESS.—What quantity of water can the Water Commissioners send into Belfast daily?—Well, at present we are sending in five million gallons per day. In the summer season we go down to four and a half millions, and last summer we went down as low as a two hours' supply. That was not altogether due to the shortness of water in the reservoirs but to the fact that we were carrying on extensive works, and we required the water to be kept in the largest store reservoir at a low level for the convenience of the contractors.

2718. On an average summer are you reduced to a four and a half hours' supply a day?—Yes.

2719. Do you supply private consumers at a certain rate fixed at a certain assessment?—Yes.

2720. Do you also supply the owners of large establishments who take the water at a certain rate?—Yes.

2721. Are those rates contained in a book setting forth the tariff?—Yes.

2722. Has there been a question between your body and the Corporation as to the supply of water for watering the streets?—Yes. They require a summer supply only, and we agreed to give it at the rate of 1½d. per 1,000 gallons from the fire-plugs, and 4d. per 1,000 from the south side works.

2723. Is the latter an inconvenient source of supply?—Yes; for a certain portion of the town.

2724. And expensive?—Yes; in cartage.

2725. Was there ever any arrangement between the Water Commissioners and the Corporation for supplying water for the streets all the year round?—I am not aware of any.

2726. How many reservoirs have you?—We have six, and we will have more. The storage of our present reservoirs is equivalent to 539,000,000 gallons, and our new storage will enable us to store over 1,274,000,000 gallons.

2727. When will you have that new supply?—We have some of it already, but after next summer we will have a constant supply of up to thirty gallons per head per day.

2728. Mr. EXHAM.—Independent of that, what can you give the mills?—That is the greatest supply we will have for all purposes. The present supply is from twenty-three to twenty-four gallons per head per day. This scale of measurement has been arrived at in Glasgow by the Water Committee there after careful experiment. They allow fifteen gallons per head per day for domestic use only; that is considered ample. The next item is general allowance for the public, three gallons per head per day. The next item is for trades and special, seven gallons per head per day. That would make altogether a total of twenty-five gallons per head per day. Then the allowance for waste is five gallons per head per day, which makes a total of thirty gallons per head per day which we will be able to give when our works are completed.

2729. Mr. LAWLESS.—In case of fire, how is the water supplied?—As stated already by the chairman of the works committee there are some 2,000 fire-plugs in Belfast.

2730. By whom are they put in?—By the Water Commissioners at their sole expense. I think the exact number is 1,960. Those plugs form part of the system, and are kept in repair by the Water Commissioners.

2731. Are they always kept supplied with water?—They are when we have water; but previously to this last summer there were occasions when the water was not on in certain districts.

2732. Are they supplied from mains or service pipes?—From mains. There are not fire plugs on the service pipes. The service pipes supply the water to the houses. There are two kinds of mains. There are some service mains which are not always kept full. As a general rule, they are in all the principal streets.

2733. What officer has control of them?—The Town Council can open them if they like, by the fire brigade officials.

2734. Have they a key for opening them?—Yes.

2735. Can they make them always available?—Yes; provided the water is let on.

2736. Supposing the water is not let on, and it becomes necessary to let it on in any of the service mains, whose duty is it to do that work? Can the men of the Town Council do it?—If any of their officials know where the valves are, they can do it.

2737. Is there any one whose duty it is to do that?—Yes; there is a man called M'Cuddon in the employment of the Water Commissioners, and paid by the Town Council for doing this special work. He is always at their call, and he is a very efficient officer, and knows all the valves; and as soon as he is apprised of a fire by any of the officers, he turns on any necessary valves to supply water.

2738. Is he the man who is paid for doing it and who has the necessary keys?—Yes.

2739. Have any other officers of the Corporation the means of turning on the supply into the empty service main?—The fire brigade officers have the means of turning on the water. I don't know whether any other officers of the Corporation have besides the fire brigade officers.

2740. Have the fire brigade the means of turning on the water if the service main is empty, without applying to M'Cuddon at all?—I believe they have; but I believe also that if they don't apply to him they won't understand how to turn on the water, and instead of turning it on they might turn it off, which was exactly what did take place on one occasion, and they did more harm than good.

BELFAST. Dec. [illegible]. — Mr. [illegible].

3741. Are there not any men in the employment of the Water Commissioners for that special duty?—No one that I am aware of except M'Crudden. There is a great deal in the turning on of water and opening the proper valves, some of which are for the purpose of concentrating the pressure in a certain spot in case of fire. Of course all the waterworks are at the service of the fire brigade when they are wanted.

3742. Mr. Exham.—Have the Water Commissioners ever objected to allow the Town Council to train as many men as they like to become acquainted with the turning of the cocks?—By no means. The cocks are there for them to use as they please.

3743. If they train men and let them have keys, have you any objection?—Not at all. We would be glad to see it. If the fire brigade department were under the control of the Water Commissioners there would be always an ample water supply.

3744. Mr Lawson.—Are you aware of complaints having been made of the supply in the case of fire not having been sufficient?—I am not aware. I have made inquiries since I went into the employment of the Water Commissioners, in connexion with every fire that has taken place, as to whether there was a sufficient supply or not, and I found that there was. I heard of one fire which occurred in the Messrs. Lind-say's, Donegall-place, where there was a little shortness of water; but some of the fire brigade people had cut off the water instead of putting it on. The public thought there was a shortness of supply, but the water was there, and was turned off.

3745. Mr. Exham.—Have all the service mains fire-plugs?—Yes; the plugs are either on the mains or on the service mains, with the exception of a few short service mains where a plug would not be necessary. We have a population of 200,000, and we have 2,080 fire-plugs, which you will find is an average equal to that of any other town, and in a few cases there are private fire-plugs in the premises of manufacturers. There are some thirty of them, and I think they should be more general. I believe all the large warehouses ought to be provided with fire-plugs. The Commissioners will supply water for them, at a charge of 10s. a year. The fire-plugs would then be in easy reach, and the water would be much more effective before the fire is allowed to spread, and would do more good in the first five minutes than Mr Boyd and his forces could do in a whole night afterwards. Warehousemen should go in for these and have fire-plugs on their premises.

3746. What quality is the water? Have you had it analysed?—Yes; by Dr. Hodges, and his analysis is very favourable. Sometimes in winter our water is muddy. Our conduits get deranged under the river; but when the new works are completed we will draw our water from a new upper point, so that the objection which is now made to it in winter will be removed.

3747. Are the Commissioners about to raise more money under their borrowing powers?—Under the Act of 1874, we have borrowing powers to the sum of £120,000. Our present works will take £70,000. We have power to increase our drainage area to the extent of 1,500 acres, and construct two new reservoirs. This would give us a supply of eight million gallons per day, and these powers are still in force.

3748. Will that new supply be introduced at one level or at different levels?—Well, the water from Woodburn will all come in at one level. That is our great source of supply. There is a portion of water we get at Ardoyne, and then there is a part of the supply we take from the Cavehill. All along that district there will be a pressure main which will be always charged, and which will be a great accommodation to the ratepayers, and will be a great security against fire in the factories in that district and on the Crumlin-road.

3749. Will you be able to give the mill-owners a water supply for their boilers when your new works are completed?—We will, and I look forward to the mill-owners giving up the using of the dirty water they now use, and using our water.

3750. Do they use in these mills this horrible sewage stuff?—I would not go the length of stating that they use sewage. If you have a mill on the stream and that you use the water of course when it leaves your mill it is more impure than when you get it. Certain kinds of oil and lubricating stuff gets into the water, and when it comes to my mill I use it, and send it on down. By the time it passes through a dozen of mills, it is neither good-looking nor good-smelling.

3751. If it happens in its course to receive contributions from the public sewers and other sources, is it improved?—By no means.

3752. Do any of these mill-owners take water from your body for condensing purposes?—I don't know that they condense with our water, but they get it to dilute other water.

3753. Is that because it was too thick to use without being diluted?—Yes.

3754. If each mill in succession returns back its refuse into the source that supplies the mill lower down, what a nice position the last must be in?—It does not follow that it all goes back. A great deal of it will go into the public sewers. I can hardly believe that any mill-owner in Belfast would take water for condensing direct from the public sewers.

3755. We have it in evidence that some of the public sewers are discharged into the Forfar Burn, and that it supplies some mills. Must not that be most injurious and dangerous?—I think it would be better for the private mill-owners to give up using this supply, and get our clean water. It must be bad for their boilers to use this supply.

3756. Mr. Kennedy says that it wears out the iron. Is that so?—Yes; it will corrode it.

3757. Mr. Lawson.—I think you mentioned that there is no contract between you and the Corporation for flushing the sewers?—Yes; I said so.

3758. It was said here by a member of your company, that the sewers were not made to be flushed?—Yes; the chairman of the works committee made a statement to that effect, as to the low level sewers.

3759. Do you wish to make any statement about that?—As to the flushing of the sewers, we send into the town two acres of water ten feet deep, in the day. That would be ninety per cent. going into the public sewers after being used by the consumers. With such a quantity of water going into the public sewers, if properly utilized the sewers ought to be sufficiently flushed. Any further supply which the Commissioners could give or will be able to give, if run through the sewers in the way the present supply is or the way they are constructed would not properly flush them. Our main conduit bringing our water into town from Woodburn, is a three feet six-inch chamber, capable of running eight million gallons per day. If that was distributed through all the sewers in Belfast, it would not have much effect in flushing them, unless properly applied for flushing purposes. As far as I know the Town Council have not constructed any apparatus or made any provision whatever for specially flushing the sewers. Some of them have very good fall, and of course, a small quantity of water coming down will keep them clear. The other sewers are so flat in the fall that they cannot be thoroughly flushed without providing a special apparatus as has been done in London. The mode in which that is done generally is this:—A temporary sluice is put in the sewer, and the water is allowed to gather there for a time, then they let it rush away with great velocity, and it clears out the sewerage. I therefore state advisedly and professionally, that all the water they could get will never flush the sewers as at present constructed except some provision be made for that purpose. A number of the sewers have flat gratings, so that when the tide rises in the river, it sends back water over the whole district. They cannot help that. I don't blame the Town Council; but I object to the Water Commissioners being blamed for not flushing the sewers.

3760. According to your evidence there does not

want the means of efficiently flushing the sewers?—It does not exist, for the simple reason that it has not been provided.

3761. Is there anything more?—I wish to say that the Water Commissioners in improving the supply have had great difficulties to contend with. The town has been growing enormously both in population and in streets and houses. The Commissioners have taken trouble individually and as a board, in trying to keep pace with the improvement of the town, and to keep up the water of the town; but although they have had a great many difficulties to contend with, there is no board at present so popular—from the fact that they are painstaking, and I think efficiently, to keep pace with the increase of the town.

3762. Mr. Nuzam.—Is the supply that you offer at all at a level to enable you to accommodate the mills?—Some of them might get supplied from it.

3763. Are not those the mills which get the worst of the water?—Yes, that which is got by the mills on the banks of the Blackstaff.

3764. Would not that be a better quality of water than they are getting?—Decidedly.

3765. Would there not be less nuisance to the mill-workers from using that water?—Decidedly.

3766. Would they have to pump it up?—Not all, for the mills on the low level we could do it by gravitation.

3767. What quantity could you give them?—I suppose from two to three hundred thousand gallons per day.

3768. Would it cost each mill £1,000 a year to get a supply of water for their mill purposes?—I could not say that on the moment, but I could easily give you evidence upon the point.

3769. However, you could give it to them?—Yes, we could give it to them. I may state that it was given in evidence before you that this water was valueless. We pay for that south side water £300 a year, and we sell some of it in the form of specials to builders and contractors who are putting up houses. In some few cases we put it for domestic supply, so that it is not entirely valueless, as has been said.

3770. Do you know where they got the water to water the streets last summer when you wrote to stop their supply?—I do not. I don't think the water was stopped.

3771. Mr. Lawless.—It was stated that the water was stopped because of an apprehension of scarcity?—Not so much on account of scarcity. We were constructing a large reservoir, and we were compelled to keep the water at a low level. We wanted to get an embankment made whereby to keep the water for the town, and there was a notice put into the newspaper asking the people to be as economical as possible. The following is the notice:—

"Wednesday, August 23rd, 1876.

"Notice.—In consequence of the present dry weather the Water Commissioners request the inhabitants of Belfast to economise the water for a few weeks, while they hope to have a supply of water from the new works available.

"S. Maitland, Assistant Secretary."

3772. Had that notice any effect?—I imagine it had. With the present works we can give them a plentiful supply.

3773. Mills and all?—Yes, mills and all.

Bennett. Jan. 3, 1877. Mr. Luke Hanaway.

January 4, 1877.

Mr. Colligan re-examined.

Jan. 4, 1877. Mr. Colligan.

3774. Mr. Lawless.—You have intimated to us that you wish to make some statement as to the non-performance of their duties by the Town Council, with reference to their allowing houses to be occupied without being properly finished. Is that so?—Yes.

3775. What is your complaint?—I allege that they have neglected, either through negligence or favouritism, to carry out the 37th section of the Act of 1850—the 13th and 14th Victoria, cap. 102.

Mr. Lawless reads section of the Act referred to.

3776. Witness.—I will give you the numbers of eight houses situate in Spring-view-street—Nos. 43, 44, 45, 47, 49, 51, and 53; and my allegation with regard to those houses is—that the rooms on the ground floors are made with common earth, and have never been made of wood, flags, tiles, or asphalte, as required by the provisions of that Act.

3777. How long have they been built?—They were built in the beginning of 1869, and inhabited ever since.

3778. Have you seen the rooms that you refer to?—Several times; last time I saw them was on Friday last; I examined two of them. I went into them; three of them are now unoccupied, for no one could live in them at all. In one that I examined, an old woman showed me a place in the room beside her bed where she had a bit of carpet about two feet square, and she complained that the moisture came up through the earthen floor, and the damp that came up through it was very dangerous.

3779. Was that room used as a bedroom?—Yes.

3780. Did you see these rooms yourself?—Yes, I saw two of them in that condition on Friday last, and I am convinced the whole eight are just the same.

3781. Where are these houses situated?—Close beside the Falls-road, in a very thickly populated district, in Spring-view-street; there are about sixty houses there altogether.

3782. What is the rating of these houses?—About £4 or £4 5s.

3783. Mr. Exham.—Are they two-story houses?—Yes; there is a kitchen and a little room down-stairs, and two rooms up-stairs, and yards to those houses. I believe it is the law that the yards should be paved or tiled—but if not, I know it is the rule with the Town Council. These yards are not paved or tiled, they were just filled in with earth heavily when the houses were built; I was brought in to see them, and there are ponds of water in them.

3784. What size are the yards of these houses?—The yards are large enough, they are the size required by the Act of Parliament—ten feet, I think; what I complain of is that they are not properly paved or tiled.

3785. Have they privies in the place?—Yes, they have; but they are in a very bad condition, in one that I examined, the manure place of the opposite privy was completely falling down.

3786. Do you know the owners of these houses?—The owner of these houses is a building society.

3787. Mr. Lawless.—What is the name of that society?—I had rather not give the name, as I have good reason for not doing so. I objected in my capacity as Town Councillor sometime ago with regard to not taking their complaint, and I know the result of that; so that I would rather not mention names. I am perfectly sure however that they belong to a building society of which Mr. Browne is the agent.

3788. Who is Mr. Browne?—He is a land agent.

3789. Is he either of the "Messrs. Browne" whose names were mentioned here before?—No; he is not. The reason I am bringing this before you is because I consider that the way in which these houses have been got up by speculators, one of whom was before you yesterday, assisted by building societies, is a grievance which should be put a stop to, and dealt with as the law directs. But unfortunately there are a large number of cases which are not so dealt with. A speculator in building ground goes and gets a number of acres for that purpose, and he then builds a few houses.

3790. We know all that.

3791. Witness.—What I say is that it is a very unfortunate circumstance; they merely open out the streets, perhaps, either at the bottom or the beginning to form the sewer; and then they let them out in small lots, perhaps making £20 or £30 out of the transaction. These houses were built by a man who, I know, did this

BELFAST.
Jan. 4, 1877.
Mr. Gilligan.

2792. Mr. LAWLESS.—It is exactly to meet such a state of things that the "Belfast Building Acts" were passed. They are sufficient to meet this if they are enforced, and if they are not the Council are responsible for it. I can fully appreciate your reasons for bringing these cases forward. Can you show us any further instances of what you complain?—What I complain of myself is that the Town Council don't compel parties who take the ground to form the streets before they let it out in these small lots. They let it in these cases to parties who have to go to building societies for accommodation—to parties who are going by these means to build small houses on speculation. They go to timber merchants who generally belong to the building societies (I have reason to believe that most timber merchants in town belong to these societies). They then get accommodation from them, and the timber merchants get their trade from these people. The result is that a man with a small capital has no chance against these people; their houses are ruined by this class of houses being put up in the streets, and the matter is generally winked at by the Town Council.

2793. It is your complaint that in many of these cases the Town Council don't carry out the provisions of the Act?—Yes.

2794. Can you give us any further instances of what you complain?—I built some houses there myself, and after some time the other houses became occupied by a worse class of people than it was intended they should be occupied by. The result is very bad for my houses and others of a similar class.

2795. Were your houses in every case built in accordance with the requirements of the Act?—Yes.

2796. Were the others not?—They were not.

2797. Mr. EXHAM.—Did you ever complain of these eight houses?—Yes, I did; I complained to Mr. Frazer who was the assistant in the surveyor's office.

2798. When—about how many years ago?—About four or five years ago I complained of it; I drew his attention to these houses and he said he would have the matter attended to, but he never did that. Perhaps it may be said that it was not part of his duty to do it; but I may tell you that he thought it his duty to come to me when I was building my houses, and make me go down to the town surveyor to show I had actually complied with the law in every respect before the plans for my houses were passed.

2799. Did you complain to him that he was not making the builders of the other houses comply with the law while he was making you do it?—Yes.

2800. It appears to be the opinion here from remarks I have heard made that complaints should be made to the Town Council or their officers that the law is not being enforced before they ought to take action. Is there anything in the Act of Parliament that you know of to show that they are not to stir or compel the law to be carried out until or unless some one makes a complaint to them?—There is nothing of that kind in any Act of Parliament, and that is my complaint against them. They act differently towards some from what they do towards others.

2801. Is not the object of these building clauses for the preservation of the health of the people by having proper houses for them?—Yes; most certainly.

2802. Mr. LAWLESS.—What is the second head of your complaint?—*Witness.*—The second head of my complaint is that the Town Council have been for some years back, and still are, creating a great and dangerous nuisance in a field lying between the Falls-road and Grosvenor-road. This field contains about three acres, and slopes down from Falls-road to the foot of it; and I suppose it is probably fifteen feet below the level of the streets at the low end, and it comes gradually up until it comes to Falls-road (as you heard from the town surveyor, the Falls-road lies on a ridge). The Town Council have been carting into that field the sweepings of the streets, with privy and yard manure, and emptying all together for some time back, and on Monday last I saw them doing so.

2803. How long have they being doing this?—I think it is five or six weeks since they commenced to do it, and they have probably seven or eight hundred loads of this stuff in it by this time.

2804. Is the slope of the lower part of the field towards the Grosvenor-road side?—Yes, and runs by the new street called "Roumania-street."

2805. Is that street inhabited?—No; it is not.

2806. Are there many houses near it which are occupied?—Yes; and some good houses.

2807. Who is the owner of that field?—Mr. Dunville.

2808. Is it being filled up to make it fit for building ground?—Yes.

2809. Is not that laying the foundation of cholera for the houses?—It is. You will observe from Dr. Browne's evidence that there are 1,800 houses without privies, and of course the night-soil of these houses is thrown in the streets, and the matter is all brought to this place. During the time I have mentioned there have been 800 loads of this stuff put into it; and, worse than that, at the bottom of this street there is a sewer which takes away the surface-sewerage from the field, and the effect of emptying it there is to completely stop up the sewer, so that there is a large pool of water there now, which you could not leave again, and which is likely to remain there and become stagnant. I called upon the sub-sanitary officer on Monday morning, and mentioned this matter to him.

2810. Who is he?—I do not just know his name; but he is the sub-sanitary officer of the district. He told me he had reported it to Mr. Scott, and that he had also reported it as a nuisance, and that the Improvement Committee had it in their hands. I also spoke to Dr. M'Connell, the medical officer for the district, about it, and he said he had reported it as a dangerous nuisance. Notwithstanding it still continues to exist, and they are increasing it every day.

2811. Do you positively say that the sub-sanitary officer and Dr. M'Connell both told you they had reported it as a nuisance?—Yes; and the sub-sanitary officer said he had reported it some time since—probably some short time after they had commenced to use the place for emptying the stuff in. What I complain of with regard to this nuisance is, that though it was reported, nothing was done to stop it, and the place has been for some time nearly covered. With regard to the nuisance mentioned yesterday by Mr. O'Neill, an expense of £50 would cover that nuisance from the Blackstaff to Mr. Lynch's factory, and steps should be taken to abate it. I have also to mention that plans were put in for certain houses in March, 1873.

2812. By whom?—By a man named James Cooke; and with regard to this, I would ask the surveyor to bring up his notebook with the objections that were raised to the plans.

2813. Were the plans objected to?—They were.

2814. Mr. EXHAM.—Before you go further, I have here a report from Dr. M'Connell, dated 5th December, 1876, in which he says:—"My attention having been drawn by the sub-sanitary officer to what I consider to be a dangerous nuisance in Dunville's fields, I beg to report the same, and I recommend that the field be fenced in to protect parties from passing through the nuisance to the risk of their lives." What has the Improvement committee to say to that?—The Improvement committee has not taken the reports of the doctors.

2815. Is it not the business of the sanitary authority? Are not Dr. Browne and the sanitary staff responsible if it is a nuisance?—The police authorities have communicated the Town Council with regard to the danger caused by this place.

2816. You say that the plans you mentioned a few minutes ago were rejected?—Yes; I saw in the improvement committee's report of May 2nd, 1873, that by the consent of the committee, and by the advice of the surveyor, the plans are approved or disapproved. Under the head of those plans I saw these houses were disapproved of.

2817. Mr. LAWLESS.—Does it give the reasons for disapproving of them?—Yes.

Belfast.
Jan. 5, 1877.
Mr. Colligan.

2818. Were they disapproved of by the committee's adopting the surveyor's report?—Yes.

2819. Were these plans for building six houses afterwards adopted?—Yes.

2820. When?—Nineteen months afterwards. I see in the report of the improvement committee, that they were brought up in the same manner at the Town Council meeting on December 2nd, 1871, and that report commences by saying, "that by the advice of their surveyor they approved of these plans."

2821. How do you know that they were the same plans?—I called yesterday at the surveyor's office, and asked upon what grounds these plans, which in 1873 were disapproved of, were then passed; and I was told if the houses were built it would close up the thoroughfare.

2822. I find by the report that the plans were rejected.—"The plans of James Cosby, of Killen-street, for building six houses in Albert-street, were disapproved of because they would close the end of Milford-street."

Mr. Montgomery.—The plans were not passed by me, but they were passed by the improvement committee. They were passed by the committee without my sanction. The widening of the thoroughfare was not accomplished. I asked the agent the price for which they would sell the ground, and he said 3s. 6d. per foot per annum, and the committee declined to pay that price. We had absolutely no power under the Act to continue that street, and many such streets have been blocked up in spite of us.

2823. How was the space now left vacant acquired for the public?

2824. Mr. Colligan.—By the Town Council paying £35.

2825. Mr. Montgomery.—The chairman of the committee, one of the members, and some other gentlemen raised a subscription for that purpose.

2826. To whom did you apply concerning the price of that ground?—A Mr. M'Auliffe; he asked 3s. 6d. per foot per annum, but the committee would not give it. We found we had not means of purchasing the ground, and the matter remained in abeyance for some time until we persuaded the people by coaxing them, as in the case you heard of yesterday. The plans were sent in again, and we found we could not legally resist them.

2827. At the time these plans were brought in was the space private property?—Yes.

2828. Were the plans afterwards passed by the committee.—Yes. Attention was called to the fact that this space was about to be closed up, and a deputation waited on the improvement committee, and a very strong case was made that it should be left open. They endeavoured to have it opened, and the committee again renewed their offer that they would contribute if any arrangement could be made to keep the whole of the street open. The committee had no funds for buying ground of that sort, and in the exercise of their discretion they refused to give the money, but some of the members in my presence offered to subscribe, and the ratepayers contributed some.

2829. How much was given for that ground?—There was £70 offered for the whole of it.

2830. Was it given for the half of it, or was it for the entire?—It was afterwards given for the half.

2831. Were the plans passed before that £70 was agreed to be given?—They were, and I will tell you why——

2832. Was it after the plans were passed that the portion of the street was thrown down?—It was long after. If we don't make any decision on the plans they can carry them out in spite of us; if there's any departure from the plans, and we bring them before the magistrates we have nothing to rely on.

Mr. Colligan.—There is the Catholic house of worship in Milford-street, and it is the best building for a house of worship in Belfast.

2833. Mr. Exham.—Is this your complaint—that the Corporation being offered this piece of ground so as to continue Milford-street for £140, they would not give that sum, and that if they had given £140 they would be able to continue Milford-street through this place?—Yes; they got half of it for £70, and they could have got the other half for £70 more if they pleased.

2834. Mr. Black.—You may assume that we could have got it for £140.

2835. Mr. Colligan.—Under the 92nd and following sections of the Act of 1858, they would have power to refuse to pass these plans. (Reads section referred to.) The 85th section as amended by the 23rd section of the Act of 1868, gives power to impose penalties. In the first instance I say they should have given £140, and I also say that they had power to refuse to pass these plans.

2836. Mr. Exham.—What is the width of the place referred to?—The street is about twenty feet wide, and it spoils the appearance of the street. I say that under the 83rd section they had power to refuse to pass these plans. I wish to say also, that the Corporation have powers under these Acts to lay out in improvements of this description £1,500 a year. They can raise £1,500 a year for this purpose; and for £140 out of that £1,500, laying aside altogether the question of whether they had power to approve or disapprove of these plans, they could have bought this bit of ground. I say that they should have paid this £140, and have this ground kept opened. It is an important place in the town, and the money would have been well laid out. I will draw your attention to the fact that they are laying out hundreds of pounds in the present year for improvements not so great, and for the reason that they are in the aristocratic portion of the town occupied by a different class of people. In University-road they are laying out at the public expense a sum of £100 at the present time, in culverting over the water-course and building a wall along the Water Commissioners' ground there. That has been done at the expense of the Corporation. They are also laying out a sum of £100 in Donegall-pass, by lowering a hill along which the Water Commissioners' water passed. They are now lowering that—certainly for the public accommodation, but it will also make property of considerably more value to the owners there.

2837. Mr. Lawson.—Are these improvements in University-road and Donegall-pass, really substantial improvements to the parts of the town for which they are made?—They are. I do not wish to object to these being made, because I wish to go in for all improvements; but I think they should be equally distributed over the town. In Rosemary-street they have spent money in purchasing property in order to set back the street and widen it. I say they have this £1,500 a year, and that they should equally distribute it over the whole town; for we pay our portion of the rates and ought to have our portion of benefits from the public funds. It is said by all the people in the neighbourhood, that it is because this place which I first referred to, is inhabited by a certain class of people, and because it would be a particular accommodation to the members of people who attend the services at the church there, having to go through that street, that they refused to spend the £140 upon it.

2838. What are the class of people to whom you allude?—I allude to the Catholics.

2839. Is the church to which you allude a Catholic church?—Yes; and it is the best religious building of any sort in town. I may just say with regard to the money, that the Corporation gave only a sum of £35; Mr. John Browne, the chairman of the improvement committee, has given £5; Mr. Bernard Hughes £5; Mr. M'Caisy £5; and there was a poor man present who gave his bill for £20 to make up the difference, and that bill has been renewed from time to time.

2840. Do you wish to give evidence about the cemetery?—I wish to call your attention to rules 4 and 7 of the Lord Lieutenant and Privy Council's Order. (See Appendix No. 11, p. 712, for rules.)

2841. Mr. Exham.—Do you say that the Corporation have violated these rules?—Yes, I do. I say that they have violated numbers 4 and 7 of these rules by burying five corpses in one grave, which they continued for five years.

2842. Do you mean five corpses not members of the same family?—Yes.

2843. By the rules the grave is not to be opened within fourteen years?—Yes; but I say they continued to open them from 1869 to 1874.

2844. Mr. Lawlor.—When was the cemetery opened?—In the year 1869. It is a wider and larger question than you seem to imagine. It was proposed to take in ten or eleven acres of additional ground which would cost some £10,000 or £12,000 to the ratepayers; and I heard if the grounds already possessed by them were properly allocated, there would be cemetery ground for fifty years to come. Another great hardship is, that if the money is to be spent there is a class of ratepayers that would have to contribute their portion although they would get no benefit from it.

Mr. Thomas H. Dixon examined.

2845. Are you a ratepayer in Belfast?—Yes. I am a timber merchant and general merchant. Mr. Biggar complained that in consequence of my brother being a member of the Council and a member of the Improvement Committee, we were enabled to have plans passed which would not otherwise have been passed; that statement I give a direct contradiction to.

2846. Have you been a member of the Town Council?—No, I have not been.

2847. Mr. Lawlor.—Do you know the plans to which he referred?—Yes; the property in Whitla-street for which I prepared the plans.

2848. When?—I could not give you the exact date. It was brought before the improvement committee in the absence of my brother.

2849. Was your brother then a member of the improvement committee?—He was.

2850. I thought these plans were not put before the improvement committee, but referred to the surveyor?—I brought them before the improvement committee directly.

2851. Were these plans disapproved of?—Yes.

2852. By the surveyor?—Yes; and also by the improvement committee.

2853. Did you bring them personally before the committee?—Yes.

2854. Was your brother sitting on the committee at the time? No, he was not.

2855. Will you state the grounds upon which these plans were disapproved of by the surveyor and the committee?—I asked them for an explanation of the reason why they refused to sanction the plans, and they said that they did not object to the plans, but that before passing them they would have to dedicate ten feet of ground for the purpose of widening New Andrew-street. I told the committee that they had no approach to New Andrew-street, and that we did not desire any entrance to it, and that we did not see that we should give our plot of ground and get no profit from it. The answer was that the owner of the houses in New Andrew-street had only left twenty feet for the street, and had built his houses contrary to the recommendation of the town surveyor and the town improvement committee, and that in order to make amends for his misdeeds we were asked to give this piece of ground, and to get no remuneration. (Witness produces plans referred to.) The plans for these buildings were not passed until they made large of that ground for ever.

Dr. James Moore examined.

2856. Mr. Exham.—We have already heard about the Royal Hospital building, and it is not necessary to put anything more in the notes?—Very well. I am about thirty years surgeon to the Hospital, and have been deputed to come here and speak to you about the smoke nuisance.

2857. In what street is the hospital?—In Frederick-street.

2858. Will you describe what the nuisance is to which you refer?—The hospital building is like a three-quarter square, and at the end of York-street there is a funnel which pours out smoke in dense volumes. It belongs to a stone manufacturer. The smoke comes up from his place into the area in front of the hospital, and floats about in such a way that we can't keep the windows open on account of it; there is also a bread-manufacturers' bakery nearly opposite which pours out smoke, and it curls into the space in front of the hospital. The place I refer to is on the opposite side. It pours into the front when the windows are open, and the health of the patients is very much impaired thereby. We would like very much to be able to give them fresh air, but unfortunately we can't do that on account of the smoke nuisance.

2859. How long is the first one in existence?—Well, I should say some few years.

2860. How long is the second?—There were a number of old houses made into a bakery; we do not feel it so much in the daytime, but there is more smoke coming from it at night.

2861. Are the funnels that you speak of old chimneys?—Yes; they pour out such an amount of smoke, that standing in the hospital in the Charter wing and looking over towards the other wing, you could not see the windows in it owing to the density of the smoke.

2862. Has this only occurred since the bakery was established?—Yes.

2863. Mr. Lawlor.—Is the other nuisance to which you referred as bad?—Nearly so. It is a stone-cutter's work-place; it is worked by machinery. There is an industrial school beside us, and the children there have suffered very much on account of the smoke. When persons are brought to the hospital suffering from consumption we are not inclined to take them in because of the smoke, and thus you will see it is a very great hardship indeed.

2864. Why do not the hospital authorities indict these people?—I have spoken from time to time at public meetings about this. The remedy is to make the proprietors of these places throw their smoke higher, so as to carry it away clear of the hospital. We think the Town Council should have the nuisance put a stop to. They are the sanitary authority.

and have been in the improvement committee ever since.

2868. Are you aware that plans for building are brought before the improvement committee?—They first receive the sanction or disapproval of the town surveyor, and then they are brought before the improvement committee.

2869. Is it the usual course for the improvement committee to act upon the recommendation of the surveyor?—No, it is not; but I was very seldom present on the passing of plans. Other gentlemen generally did not come to the meeting for an hour after ten, and for perhaps an hour there would be only three or four present. We used to get through the minutes, and I generally retired between one and two o'clock, and the plans for buildings were generally passed afterwards.

2870. Did the persons who proposed the plans attend before the committee?—He and his architect generally did.

2871. Did they apply to have the plans passed, and bring forward objections to the decision of the surveyor if it was against the plans?—Yes; I think that was the course usually adopted. I did not know anything about Millfield-street until two or three places were built up. I went to make inquiries about it, and saw Mr. Cook, the architect, with whom I was acquainted, and I said, "This is a very bad job," and he said that since he had got his plans passed he would make us pay for the ground.

2872. Used parties, whose plans were rejected, give notice of their intention to attend before the improvement committee?—It was always understood they would attend.

2873. Are the plans usually brought up after some of the members of the improvement committee have left?—Yes, after the majority have left. I was very seldom there at the passing of plans.

2874. Mr. Exham.—Who were the members of the improvement committee who used to sit?—Generally at one o'clock ten or twelve members came in, when the real business commenced. Some came in later. Previous to this the minutes were read, and the accounts considered and passed.

2875. The gentleman to whom you spoke said that now he had got his plans passed he would make you pay for the ground?—Yes.

2876. Were you aware at that time that those plans had been disapproved of before?—No. When I heard what he said I came back to Mr. Montgomery and spoke to him about it, and he said, "Mr. Hughes, I tried to prevent them from passing it two or three times." He did prevent them from passing them for some time, but they were afterwards passed.

2877. Were they passed in spite of him?—Well, I do not know if they passed in spite of him.

2878. Mr. Lawless.—Was Mr. Montgomery always obliged to attend when plans that had been rejected were brought up again?—He generally attends, but when he does not he has another young man who attends for him.

2879. Mr. Exham.—On that occasion did he give you to understand that he did not wish those plans to be passed, and that notwithstanding his wish the plans were passed?—Yes; but he did not say who passed them, and therefore I do not know who did. They would be initialed by the chairman if they were passed.

2880. Mr. Lawless.—Have you, as a matter of fact, known plans to be passed in opposition to the wish of Mr. Montgomery?—Not of my own knowledge, except in the case of the tramways. He objected to them and would not pass them, and still they were passed. With regard to that street, I may say that Mr. Harvey was the man who got those passed. I brought five or six of the gentlemen on once to the place and showed it to them, and they said it was very bad, and that they would try to get it remedied, and the consequence was, we found the man had bought the ground, and that he had a right to build when the plans were passed. Mr. Harvey said on the following day, when I was bringing the matter forward again, that they had no interest in it, and that it was the people up there who had an interest in it that got them passed. That is the reason why I say he got the plans passed. Those gentlemen whom I brought to look at the place—Mr. John Browne and others and myself—subscribed to prevent the other half of the street from being closed up.

2881. Mr. Exham.—Was there only part of the work done then?—Yes.

2882. If they thought it was such a very bad thing why did they not induce the Town Council to give £140 and prevent the place being closed up?—It could have been originally prevented by paying £140 or £150; in fact I think it could have been got for £120. I told Mr. Cook that I would guarantee to give my cheque for the money if he would take down the bricks and not give such annoyance. I also said "you will find some horse and cart will run away and knock it down," but he said he had begun it now and would go on. I afterwards sent my son and went myself to say that I would guarantee the expense.

2883. As a member of the improvement committee I ask you do you think, having regard to the fact that it was to be used as a public entrance to Millfield-street, it was worth while for the town to pay £140 for the people of that district?—I do. There has been £400 or £500 laid out in other parts of the town on improvements not so useful as this would have been in my opinion. There was £300 or £400 laid out in Rosemary-street.

2884. Was it ever suggested that this particular portion of ground should be bought?—Yes, and the Council afterwards gave £35 towards buying part of it and we raised £10.

2885. Admitting there was £35 given for part was there any proposal to sell the whole of it for £140?—The owner of it told me that he went to the Council and offered it to them for £110 before he let it to Cook.

2886. Mr. Lawless.—Was the £35 given in pursuance of a resolution of the Council?—I do not know.

2887. Mr Exham.—Would the people have subscribed £70 if the Corporation gave £70?—Yes, and the Rev. James Young would have given something. Mr. Peter Quinn was made take down two houses that he had built. He was ordered to do so by the chairman. He brought forward plans.

2888. Where were these houses?—In Short-strand, Ballymacarrett.

2889. Were the plans approved of?—Yes; on the conditions that he built them according to the plans. He built two houses and they summoned him for not building them in accordance with the plans.

2890. Mr. Montgomery.—These houses were built without any plans being passed and the magistrates convicted him, and they were ordered to be pulled down. I wish to say in the presence of Mr. Browne, that he was there and had the plans, and they withdrew the complaint on condition that he would go to take down the two houses, and build them in accordance with the plans passed.

2891. To Mr. Hughes.—With regard to the laying down of the tramways, was Mr. Montgomery's opinion overruled by the improvement committee?—Always.

2892. In what way?—He said the work was not done well.

2893. Did he, therefore, refuse to pass them?—That was it. The Government engineer came down here, and Mr. Montgomery would not pass the work, and then afterwards the Council or the town improvement committee let it pass over.

2894. Mr. Lawless.—This report of the town improvement committee carries out at all events what you say, Mr. Hughes, about this opening. If keeping the half of it open would effect a desirable improvement to the thoroughfare it would be much more so by having the whole of it open?—Five times the money would not buy it up in a dozen of years.

2895. During the time you have been on the improvement committee were there many members of it interested in the building trade directly or indirectly? —Yes, six or seven of them, but I do not believe any of them would be influenced by that in an improper way, and I believe they were of more use on the committee owing to their professional knowledge—provided there was no underhand work. They were generally in the timber trade, and Mr. Harvey was a builder, and that led me to think he was interested in getting these plans passed for this man Craft.

Mr. Robert Carlisle re-examined.

7896. Witness.—I wish to add a little to the evidence which I gave when I was before examined.

7897. Chairman.—On what point?—On two or three points. The Blackstaff is one.

7898. I think we have had quite enough evidence with regard to the Blackstaff?—Well, this is not exactly on the point of the Blackstaff being a nuisance; that is, I think, admitted; but it is with regard to the reason that has prevented the Town Council from abating the nuisance.

7899. Well, if there is anything to show that the Corporation have not done their duty, that we will hear?—That is the point I want to give evidence on. When I was a Town Councillor the question was always discussed at the Council, of making catchment basins or dams for the purpose of abating the floods. The Blackstaff is a nuisance in two ways, by the flooding and by the millowners using the sewerage water. The Blackstaff is quite pure until the point where the Pound Burn falls into it. A section of the Corporation was always for making catchment dams at the expense of the ratepayers, to procure pure water for the millowners instead of the sewerage water they are now using. I was always against that; and my proposition was that by the powers they had of making a district sewerage, they should take the sewage out of the Pound Burn, and then to compel the millowners if they polluted the water to send it back by filtration in a pure state. And I believe if it had not been for the way in which the millowners had been favoured, that it would have been remedied in that way long since.

7900. Is it then your opinion that the influence of the millowners prevented the Council from taking that course which you say would have been the proper one?—Yes; and I think it would be very unfair to make the town pay for good water for the millowners instead of that they are now using.

7901. How many of the millowners were members of the Corporation?—A great many. If I had the list of the names I could point them out at once; but I believe that the millowners outside the Corporation wield greater influence in these matters than those who were inside the Council.

7902. When were you a member of the Corporation?—From 1870 to 1873.

7903. Can you tell me the names of any millowners who at that time influenced the Corporation?—Well, I consider there was a general influence.

7904. Can you name any?—Yes; I consider that Mr. Duffin influenced them considerably, also Mr. Ewart, and Mr. Mullan.

7905. Mr. Lawless.—Do you mean that you know it?—Well, I know it in this way, that the improvement committee, which I know to be the parent committee in the Corporation, contrary to the evidence given here, did their best to break up the sewerage committee, and we brought up resolution after resolution for that purpose, but there was always a beat up of members to defeat us. That committee was the cause of the delay in making the improvements in the Blackstaff and Pound Burn, and we did our best to break it up, so that the improvement committee could deal with the nuisance.

7906. Chairman.—Who were the members of the sewerage committee then?—Well, I think Dr. Browne and the borough surveyor were the principal heads, although it required three to make a quorum. I was put on the sewerage committee, but I objected to remain on when I found I could not do any good.

7907. Did not the town surveyor attend in his capacity as surveyor, and not as a member of committee?—Yes.

7908. Was Dr. Browne then a member of the Council?—Yes. Had it not been for that sewerage committee and the obstruction given by it to the improvement committee, I have no doubt but the proper remedy would have been applied long since.

7909. Mr. Lawless.—Was there any application ever made to put your powers under the 1865 Act in force?—There was not. The powers would be insufficient, and the best way was simply to take the Corporation sewers out of the Blackstaff, and then compel others to do the same.

7910. According to Mr. Griffith the Blackstaff has been relieved by some drains?—I think that was not by Mr. Montgomery's plans; I think that was done by Mr. Harvey, myself, and some other members.

7911. Chairman.—Well, the material fact will be, if you can prove to us that some scheme was moved in committee, and that it was resisted by the millowners who were members of the Corporation. I have turned over the minutes here now, to see if any such proposal was brought forward by any one, and I cannot see that there was?—It was brought forward in an indirect way. A report was made on the subject, but we found that we could do nothing, and the members who were most anxious to have the Pound Burn purified found that they could do nothing except by breaking up the sewerage committee.

7912. Mr. Lawless.—Was that before 1873?—It was.

7913. Was the constitution of the sewerage committee altered then?—It was; and a different set of men were put on it.

7914. Chairman.—What I want to know is, if there was any proposition made in committee or elsewhere to prevent the millowners polluting the river and which the millowners defeated?—There was nothing direct ever brought forward of that kind; but we tried to break up the sewerage committee, because we believed it was obstructing the improvement committee. The result of that was, that a compromise was made.

7915. Mr. Lawless.—What was the compromise you refer to?—It was by putting a great number of the members of the improvement committee on the sewerage committee.

7916. The Chairman read the names of the members of the sewerage committee, and the witness stated that two of them, Messrs. Mullan and Duffin, were millowners.

7917. But the object of your coming forward to give evidence is to show that the schemes which you referred to were prevented by the millowners from being carried into execution?—Yes.

7918. But you should be able to give us some dates?—The minutes will show a resolution by which we made an effort to break up that sewerage committee.

7919. Mr. Lawless.—Was the motion to break up or to dissolve the committee?—It was to abolish it, and transfer its functions to the improvement committee.

7920. Do you say that the influence of the millowners was brought to bear to defeat that motion?—No doubt of it.

7921. Chairman.—But you ground it on this, that the sewerage committee had influence brought to bear on them by the millowners to defeat any proposition to abate this nuisance?—We were most anxious to get sewers made in certain places, and it was more to get outlets for the sewers that the improvement committee wanted this for the purpose of passing streets, and it was very awkward for the improvement committee to be passing plans and not knowing where the sewers would run. For instance, in the case of the Antrim-road district sewer, the improvement committee was passing plans, and there was no way laid out by the sewerage committee for the falls in these plans. A large scheme was prepared by the borough surveyor, and that scheme was brought before the Corporation, and I, myself, upset that scheme effectually, and in such a way that on the day on which it was brought forward they could get no seconder for it, and it broke up the whole scheme. We were met by the objection from the surveyor and others that there was no other outlet but to bring it through Donegall-street and Waring-street.

2922. Well, we don't want the details of the scheme.

2923. The minute book showing members of sewerage committee in 1870 was produced, and Mr. Carlisle said the only mill-owners on it were Alderman Lindsay and Sir John Savage, and Councillor E. H. Thompson, interested in that branch of business. In 1871 Alderman Carlisle, mill-owner, and E. H. Thompson, were on the sewerage committee.

2924. Now, do you mean that Alderman Carlisle and Sir John Savage, for the interests of their business, obstructed motions which would have the effect of purifying the Blackstaff?—Yes; and Mr. Ewart also.

2925. Mr. Ewart was not a member of the committee?—Well, in council he was obstructing.

2926. But you said the sewerage committee obstructed?—Yes, by doing nothing.

2927. Is Sir John Savage's mill on the Blackstaff?—Yes, it is.

2928. Tell me any other mills on the Blackstaff in which members of that committee had an interest?—Sir John Savage's, the Brookfield Spinning Company, and the dye works of Alderman Carlisle, of which Mr. Mullan is a director.

2929. Who moved this resolution to abolish the sewerage committee?—I believe it was Mr. Osborne, and it was seconded by myself.

2930. On what grounds?—Simply that they were not doing their duty, and were obstructing the improvement committee in not giving proper outlets for the sewerage.

2931. Mr. Kaylan.—Do Sir John Savage's and Mr. Carlisle's mills discharge their sewerage into the Blackstaff?—Yes, they do by the Pound Burn. The fact of it is that above where the Pound Burn falls into the Blackstaff the river is pure, and it is the Pound Burn creates the whole nuisance.

2932. Chairman.—Can you point out any movement with the exception of this of merging the sewerage committee with the improvement committee which you say would have prevented or was brought forward to prevent the flooding or pollution of the Blackstaff or Pound Burn, and which was rejected by the influence of the mill-owners?—No; because we could scarcely bring forward a resolution of that sort. I believe there were two resolutions brought forward on two occasions in Council.

2933. Was there none in committee?—After the overflow was taken from the Blackstaff there was very little flooding there.

2934. Was there any resolution proposed which was rejected by the sewerage committee, and which would prevent the flooding or improve the Blackstaff?—No.

2935. Then what do you come forward to prove?—That the sewerage committee for 1870 and 1871, and a great part of 1872, did nothing with reference to the district sewers of the town, and that on the other hand the improvement committee were making exertions to do so. After the additional members were put on the sewerage committee they took an active part in making other sewerage districts—it takes a long time to make a sewerage district—and before we got the length of the Falls district I left the Council and I don't know what has been done since.

2936. But what you say is, that owing to the influence of the mill-owners these efforts were obstructed, and I want you to point that out?—Well, the sewerage committee did nothing for these two years.

2937. I want you to prove that anything was rejected?—It would be very difficult to prove it, as I was not a member of the sewerage committee.

2938. Mr. Lawson.—In order to show that you should be able to prove that some scheme was proposed and rejected?—The only thing was a recommendation that was conveyed to the sewerage committee, and it would not be allowed to be put on the minutes.

2939. Chairman.—But you cannot show that any sewerage scheme was rejected?—No.

2940. Then you are only wasting our time?—I know that all the time I was in the Council the improvement committee did their utmost, and they were upset entirely by the sewerage committee.

2941. But you have not given us one instance of it. We have referred to the minutes and we have not found anything to bear that out. What did you come to prove?—What I came to prove is this: that the Town Council could, if that committee had done their duty, have abated the nuisance in connexion with the Pound Burn and the Blackstaff, and my impression is that, that that was owing to the influence of the mill-owners.

2942. But impression is a very different thing?—Well, as a general rule mill-owners have influence. Well now evidence was given by Mr. Murphy here. He stated that the price of water was such that mill-owners were compelled to use sewage water. Now the only mill that uses the Water Commissioners' water for condensing and boiler purposes is one in King-street, a flax mill belonging to Mr. Neill. He gets water from the Water Commissioners, supplied by meter, and the whole account last year was something under £30, both for cooling and for boiler purposes. Mr. Hind, a mill-owner, also has taken water for boiler purposes, not for condensing, and it cost a small amount indeed. Mr. Neill's is a very large concern, so that the price of the water cannot be the reason that the mill-owners use in their boilers the sewage rather than they do. Another point I want to draw your attention to is the way in which the Gas Act is being carried out. My impression is that it is being carried out in the same way as the Harbour Commissioners carried out their works for a certain time—that is, they have a large number of works that are short-lived. Their pipes will only last twenty-five years. That is about the average length of time that they will last in the gasworks.

2943. Were you a member of the gas committee?—No; the Corporation hadn't the gasworks then. You will find by the report of last year the small amount for pipes. The amount that the pipes would cost would be £160,000, and the outside time that they will last will be thirty years. The Corporation should set aside a sinking fund as a renewal fund that would renew them in thirty years. The Harbour Commissioners did the same, and at the end of thirty years they had to double their rates for the purpose of renewing their works, and the same thing will occur with the gas if they don't take precautions, and have a fund for renewal. They are now putting down mains, and they are not charging enough to revenue, but far too much to capital. The result will be that they must strike a large rate in some time, or raise the price of gas to meet the expenditure. I wish also to refer to the political influence which some officers of the Corporation exercise. I know this of my own knowledge. It is seven years ago since Alderman Mullan was re-elected alderman. At that time I attended a meeting in the Victoria-hall for the purpose of taking part in the election. It was a conservative meeting, and was called by advertisement. I was there as a member of the party. I saw a considerable number of the officers of the Corporation there, and Mr. Coburn in particular. The object of the meeting was to select an alderman to the Town Council for St. Anne's Ward. Mr. Mullan was the alderman going out. Before that he had sworn himself to be a whig, and I thought it was very strange, and I said so much on the subject that Mr. James Alexander Henderson was nominated, but, strange to say, although it was a very considerable meeting of ratepayers, some parties took it upon themselves to change the nomination from Mr. Henderson to Mr. Mullan. At that meeting Mr. Coloain was present, taking an active part, and what I want to draw your attention to is, that the gas was turned off to give me a beating. It was done by some of those in the place, and Mr. Coloain was taking an active part in the meeting.

2914. Mr. Lawlor.—Do you mean to say that Mr. Coloain was taking an active part in canvassing or nominating candidates there?—I saw him speaking to a great many of the people who were taking an active part in the meeting.

2915. Chairman.—Did he speak?—Not publicly; but he took an active part. He was at the meeting, and spoke to parties who spoke publicly. Well, in reference to the opposition of Sir John Savage to me in 1872. At that time I knew very well that I would be returned had it not been for the influence that Mr. Coloain used for Sir John Savage amongst some of my own friends on the Shankhill-road. There is no doubt but I was defeated that year by that influence.

2916. What proof have you of that?—Well, some of the parties who asked me to stand against Sir John Savage, because he did not do his duty in reference to the roads, actually voted against me afterwards.

2917. Did any of those parties say that it was the influence of Mr. Coloain changed them?—No, they did not say that directly, but they said as much.

2918. Well, what proof have you that Mr. Coloain used that influence?—Well, I don't wish to bring the parties forward. I would rather let it go for what it is worth.

2919. Then the charge falls to the ground?—Well, in a meeting in Dock Ward, when Dr. Alexander was changed from being a councillor to an alderman, Mr. Coloain was there, and taking an active part. I saw him canvassing for Dr. Alexander, and I heard him distinctly saying that Dr. Alexander should be the alderman for Dock Ward.

2920. Did you hear him influence persons to vote on behalf of him?—I heard him influence them before the election by stating that he was the proper man to make alderman.

2921. To whom did he say that?—Oh, I could not say.

2922. Mr. Lawlor.—Were they voters?—Yes, I presume so.

2923. Chairman.—Could you not name one person to whom he said that?—I could not. I want to mention also in reference to this, that in 1872 all the officers' salaries were revised. They were revised, and a few of us considered that the proposed increases were too high. It was then considered better to have an amicable arrangement, and that we should reduce the whole of the increases by one-half. We all agreed to that. However, to our surprise, when the salaries came up, and it was moved that the report should be adopted with the compromise, Dr. Alexander proposed, and I do not know who seconded, that Mr. Coloain should get the full amount of increase given at first. I voted against that, and I said I could not see how we should pick out one and not give the full amount to another. That was in 1872. I went immediately after that to the News-Letter office, as I had business with Mr. Lilburn, the editor, and he told me that in consequence of my opposition to Mr. Coloain he would write against me until he would put me out.

2924. Well, what have we to say to this?—Well, Mr. Henderson, the proprietor of the News-Letter, and Mr. Coloain are brother orangemen. The editor told me that he would write against me until he would put me out of every board in the town. I told him that I only did what was my duty, and I believed Mr. Coloain was fairly paid at the time. That is the only instance I will mention.

2925. We know nothing about the Belfast News-Letter, and Mr. Lilburn has no connexion with the Corporation, so what can we have to do with that?—Well, it shows this, that influence was brought to bear on the News-Letter. I can go no further than the facts.

2926. Mr. Lawlor.—Were you written against in the News-Letter?—Yes, I was, and they refused to publish a reply from me although they published a correspondence on the other side, and in some of the reports of my speeches afterwards they made me speak nonsense, and made it ridiculous, carrying out the object in view.

2927. Chairman.—Oh, well no matter about that; we cannot take any notice of it.

2928. Witness.—Well, before I go I want to say this, that I believe the gentlemen in connexion with the improvement committee have done their duty to the best of their ability, and I believe that this talk of a "timber ring" is incorrect. So far as I could see, for the three years I was on that committee, there was no timber influence brought to bear. I had no connexion with any of the timber merchants, and I believe that they did their duty to the best of their ability, and that they have done so without favour.

2929. Mr. Lawlor.—Is all that Mr. Biggar said incorrect then?—I do not know, but so far as I saw I could find no fault with the members of the timber trade on the committee, although sometimes they were in opposition to my views.

2930. Chairman.—Did you see any favour shown to any builders on that committee?—Quite the reverse. Now, with reference to Mr. Brown's buildings on the Donegall-pass, I know that, so far as I could see, Mr. Brown was perfectly right, for he was giving a strip of ground to the Corporation, and he only asked what other people were getting—that the footways should be kerbed and that flagging should be put along the footpath; and the sub-committee recommended that he should get the same as other people, and then it was done at once. The only other case I can mention is one in Donegall-place. The borough surveyor had served a notice in connexion with a board where there was an overhang, and the gentleman had a signboard on it. The house belonged to Mr. William Ewart, a member of the Corporation, and the borough surveyor ordered the board to be taken down. It came before the improvement committee, and they examined into the whole matter, and they gave directions contrary to the borough surveyor. No doubt there was influence brought to bear on the borough surveyor to have the board removed, but the improvement committee ordered that nothing should be done to it, as it had been there for twenty years or more, and instead of being a nuisance, as alleged, it was the means of preventing a nuisance at that place.

2931. The borough surveyor had influence brought to bear on him, you say, to remove it?—Well, the tenant of the house wanted a window put up where the board was, and that tenant was a tenant of Mr. Ewart's. I believe that improper influence was brought to bear on the borough surveyor to get the board removed.

2932. Mr. Montgomery (borough surveyor).—That is perfectly untrue; I deny that.

2933. Mr. Carlisle.—Mr. Montgomery denies that. Well, first I say that Mr. Montgomery served a notice, and that summonses were issued, or about to be issued, when the gentleman whose signboard it was came before the improvement committee, and when they heard how it was they stopped the prosecution, and would not allow Mr. Ewart any favouritism more than any other; so that I always found the improvement committee showing favour to no party.

2934. Chairman.—I want to know what questions arose in which any of those builders, being members of the improvement committee, were themselves concerned, or with reference to apportioning expenses to be charged to themselves, whether they took part in the proceedings in the committee?—They never interfered, and, as a general rule, whatever Mr. Montgomery recommended or disapproved of, was accordingly adopted or rejected, and, as a rule, builders never interfered with reference to their own plans.

2965. When such questions were brought forward before the committee, did those members who were interested in the matter retire or act?—As a general rule builders' questions were decided in the same way as others.

2966. Do you ever recollect an instance in which it was sought to throw expense on a builder who was a member of the committee, in which he remained to vote, and influenced the others to vote against it?—No, never.

2967. CHAIRMAN (for Mr. *Colligan*).—Can you say why it was that Mr. Cosgrove, who complained that he had only one house in a street was compelled to pave it, while Mr. T. H. Browne, a member of the improvement committee, has streets open for three years and has not paved them yet?—Well, materials in many cases could not be got, or men could not be got to pave the streets all at once; and what was generally done was to take up those streets that were worst. One thing stopped the improvement committee, and that was that a street could not be made until there was an outlet for the sewerage. In many cases the improvement committee were sorry that they could not make streets on account of there not being an outlet for the sewerage.

2968. Mr. KERAN.—Are you more or less connected with the building trade?—No; my business is in connection with earthworks, and for the last year only.

2969. Do you know that certain streets belonging to certain parties were paved by the Corporation years since, and the owners had writs issued against them for the cost, while adjoining streets belonging to other parties had nothing done to them up to the present?—Well, it was impossible to pave all the streets at once.

2970. Surely it was not impossible to put an obstruction at the end of them until the Act of Parliament was complied with?—Well, there was not enough houses for all the people. I think there were recommendations put on the books to pick up the worst streets first.

Chap. xxiv. Jan. 5, 1877. Mr. Robert Carlisle.

Mr. JOHN REA examined.

Mr. John Rea.

2971. CHAIRMAN.—Are you a solicitor and ratepayer of this town?—I am a solicitor residing here and practising in this town, and throughout Ulster. I have been a member of the Corporation twice for a period altogether of three years. I was also a member of the Water Commissioners Board for six or seven years, and a Poor Law Guardian for one or two years.

2972. Well what are the particular points with reference to which you wish to give evidence?—I wish to say first, with regard to the burying ground question that I entirely agree with the Town Council in reference to their proceedings relative to Dr. Dorrian's demand to have an influence over the public cemetery which would not be allowed by any Corporation, and had not been asked by any Presbyterian or Protestant priest. I believe a large body of the Roman Catholics approve of the action of the Town Council in preventing Dr. Dorrian from having that which a compliance with his demands would give him, viz. a virtual ownership of the graves. With regard to the Blackstaff nuisance, I want to say in fair play to the Corporation, that I believe the Corporation are substantially right with regard to the Blackstaff nuisance. (Mr. Rea then entered into a lengthened narrative of the history of Belfast municipal affairs for the past twenty years, which the Commissioners held to be irrelevant to the present inquiry. In 1863 the Corporation, he added, voted a salary of £1,000 to the then mayor, Mr. John Lytle, for the purpose of paying the costs of litigation with Mr. Rea. No salary had up to that been paid by the Corporation to the mayor. That was a misapplication of the ratepayers' money. For six years each mayor was paid £1,000.)

JANUARY 6, 1877.

Mr. MONTGOMERY re-examined.

Jan. 6, 1877. Mr. Montgomery.

2973. CHAIRMAN.—As questions affecting your department have been raised I think it will save time if I allow you to answer them in the order in which you have, I believe, taken notes of them?—By your directions, as I was not allowed to reply at the time I have taken notes of them. First, with regard to Mr. Smyth's, the water commissioner, evidence about the flushing of the sewers. Mr. Scott and Mr. Carlisle both said that these sewers in Belfast could not be flushed, and quoted the borough surveyor as their authority. It would be convenient now to say that their engineer, Mr. Macassey, stated that they can be flushed, but that the Council had not constructed any apparatus suitable for flushing them. Now I say that a great many of them can be flushed, or I would rather use the word "scoured." I never said that the sewers of Belfast did not require water, on the contrary I put in my printed report on the drainage, dated November 22nd, 1866, in which, on pages 18 and 19, you will find I said, "In addition, a standing supply of water should be afforded for the cleansing of the sewers, and this is indispensable for their proper working;" and on the next page—"It would be impracticable to attempt large floods in any case; moreover, in dry seasons when water would be most wanted it could not be obtained under the present wasteful system;" and at the bottom of that paragraph—"watering the sewers could be effected by this plan." Therefore Mr. Scott made a mistake. He alleged Mr. Carlisle informed him that I said water was not wanted for the cleansing of the sewers. It is simply untrue. I say that Mr. Scott informed this tribunal that his authority was Mr. Carlisle, and that he had told him this idle story. It is utterly untrue. Many of the drains can be scoured, but some of them must have their deposit removed by workmen. That is the statement I originally made—that in some sewers in Belfast which admit the tide what is called flushing would increase the evil instead of removing it. In England we found that fully proved some fifteen or sixteen years ago.

2974. Is it a fact that the majority of the sewers in Belfast lie below the level of the river?—That is not true. Water flowing through all the sewers in the town would be useless although it might in some of them remove the deposit.

2975. Mr. LAWLESS.—Is it true as stated that there is no apparatus for flushing?—The new sewers are so constructed as to be self-cleansing. It would be an admission that they were wrongly constructed to say that they wanted flushing. It was said that the sewers in the low levels and some of those in the higher districts generally have ten inches of stagnant water lying in them, and that statement I wish to correct, and also that many of them were lower than their outlet, and that for example the sewer in Little York-street was in a high district, and that the water lies within eighteen inches of the level of the fire-places in the houses. Each and all of these statements I contradict. In the first place all the sewers have a fall towards the sideway (these sewers alluded to), and where the tide falls below the bottom of the sewer these sewers were designed to be empty. This does not occur on every day, for on many days the tide does not leave the sewer at all.

2976. In spring tides?—On a great many days. For some days sometimes it will not leave the sewer.

2977. Are these sewers at low water free from sea water?—Yes; they are then clear from sea water.

2978. *Is that only at low water of spring tides?*—

BELFAST. Jan. 5, 1877. Mr. Montgomery.

That is a matter of levels. These sewers have valves which provide for keeping the tide out, and while those valves are closed the back water accumulates, and, therefore, there is back water in them. These sewers, unless they are cleansed by manual labour or mechanical contrivances, will have a deposit. All that is fully stated in my report. Unless the valve is opened to give egress to a dirty sewer there must be stagnant water in it.

2979. How recently have these sewers been constructed?—They were constructed before I came to Belfast in 1861.

2980. Are they the oldest sewers here?—Yes, in dry weather, when there is a bad smell from some of these sewers, washing them with clean water would abate it. I do not lay much stress upon flushing these sewers, for I do not think it would be a very successful operation.

2981. Mr. EXHAM.—If you say they are full during a great number of months in the year they are so during the neaps also. The spring tides run out more than the neaps?—Yes; but they are never blocked up, they are empty to within about two feet. One-half of them are empty. You will find the facts carefully stated in the report. All cities built on estuaries are the same. The sewer in Little York-street has no valve on it at all, and is open the whole way to the tideway. Unless it is cleansed water might gather in it. There is no valve, and in dry weather nothing to prevent an accumulation of deposit in it. If it is scoured with water it would be to a large extent relieved from the deposit that Mr. Scott complains of.

2982. I understand his complaint to be that there is a sewer under his premises, and that the water comes up to within eighteen inches of the fire-place?—Mr. Scott's house sewers are made with so little fall that they contain the deposit, and I believe that is the reason why it goes so near his fire. I could make that all right for a few pounds, but it is the duty of the ratepayers to do it.

2983. He says the water is within eighteen inches of his kitchen fire, and, therefore, the sewer must be within eighteen inches of the kitchen fire. Is that so? —At the time of high water the sea comes up this sewer, which is in fact an open channel, in which there is no valve, and it comes not only to within eighteen inches of the ground, but it sometimes arises to the level of the street. I want to show you the recklessness of the statements made. It was said that this was one of the highest districts of the town, and to that I give a direct contradiction, and under no system that I know of can you prevent the tide from rising. If you carry out a large scheme of drainage, and employ plenty of pumping power, we can abate that, but they must not cry out about those works unless they give us the money.

2984. Is the curing of this defect in the sewers part of the large scheme?—Yes; and it cannot be remedied by any small work in any particular locality. What I would ask water for is for cleansing the streets. There are multitudes of old, dirty, filthy courts and lanes in Belfast, and if they were washed with a hose and jet as you know is done in some large towns, it would be a very great matter. It would be extremely valuable indeed. I would make them a present of the flushing if those streets were washed from the fire-plugs with a hose and jet, for it would not only cleanse the surface in dry weather, but it would also cleanse the gullies and sewers that I have recommended to be scoured. We do not want it in wet weather for we have plenty of water for those purposes then.

2985. Mr. LAWLOR.—Do you think the town wants that?—I am only giving you my own opinion—there are a great many things in Belfast that we have not got, but want.

2986. CHAIRMAN.—Will the Water Commissioners, by their new reservoir be able to increase the supply to the town very largely?—Of course they will.

2987. Do you not expect this deficiency of water to be supplied when the new reservoirs are completed?—I have no doubt they will. I am not complaining even of the deficiency, but I think the price that is charged of 1s. 6d. per thousand gallons in the dry season when we want it is practically a prohibition.

2988. Will they be able to supply you from the fire-plugs when they get the increased supply?—Yes; I am sure they will. With regard to Mr. Carlisle's evidence—it is, so far as I am concerned in my department, a repetition of the statements that were made by Mr. Scott.

2989. Is it a fact that the Corporation use the water of the Pound Burn for watering the streets?—The superintendent of the scavenging department will be here afterwards to give you full particulars as to that. With regard to the report of the sub-committee before referred to by Mr. Dawson, the facts are, Mr. Carlisle very improperly, during my absence in England, came into my office and got hold of some plans I was working above.

2990. Was he then a member of the Town Council?—Yes; and on the sub-committee, but he was utterly incompetent to judge of such plans. He got these plans from my assistant. They had the lines of existing sewers marked on them, and certain other works of indication. He noticed that the Pound Burn came between the ends of sewers, and it was very obvious to any person not educated in this particular business that if you drew a line from sewer to sewer it would be a very handy way of connecting them. He produced such plans that it really took all my official gravity to enable me to discuss. However I sat down to answer all his recommendations as gravely as I could, for I never forgot that he was a member of the council. When I came home I had to answer this extraordinary report, and I did so, but I am afraid that Mr. Carlisle showed some animus against me for doing my duty. He seemed to have a notion that he could make water run up a hill. He had some influence with certain persons, and he took a great deal of trouble from time to time making this foolish proposition. When he would not take my advice I said "perhaps you will take Mr. Rawlinson's (the inspector and engineer of the Local Government Board in England), which confirms mine." The Central Railway Company wanted to interfere with the sewage of the town, and they proposed the same sort of sewer-pipes under their railway tunnels. I was to be the judge under the Act of Parliament, and I condemned their plans, and got the matter referred to Mr. Rawlinson as the highest authority on the subject. We were taken to London, and Mr. Rawlinson decided that I was right, but even that would not be taken as enough by Mr. Carlisle, and the report was sent before the committee, and my report had to go to contradict it. That is the whole of this subject.

2991. Mr. EXHAM.—One portion of the complaint was that when he and two others were appointed to consider the matter the report which they made was refused to be entered on the minutes?—I have nothing to do with that. I forget all the little details of the matter. With regard to the Fairy Well stream—this miniature Pound Burn—it is an old water-course, and the people who have property on its banks have a right to the use of its water, and we cannot take it from them without paying them compensation, and that answer applies to all of these cases. I need not repeat that Mr. Harrison (now Judge Harrison) was brought here specially to go over these rivers. We went into this matter and we were advised that we could not prevent the mill-owners from abusing these streams.

2992. Do you say, as a matter of fact, that you were advised you had no right to prevent the mill-owners from polluting the streams. I can understand that they have a right to use the water and send it back again as they get it, but not that they have any right to pollute it. Mr. May's opinion was, that the Town Council were the first offenders themselves, and that, therefore, they could not prosecute others; that opinion I can well understand?—Well, I admit that, but Mr. Harrison himself came over the river, and his attention was chiefly directed to the submerged weirs or contrivances for raising the rivers, and creating a nuisance in them. The [illegible] of taking and returning the water to the stream after use was not the main question at that time. The other was the important question.

2993. CHAIRMAN.—Was a written opinion given by Mr. Harrison?—I have no doubt that some written opinion was given.

2994. Are you speaking from or referring to a conversation that you had with Mr. Harrison when you were inspecting this river together, or from your having read his written opinion?—I should say from both.

2995. If there is a written opinion we must have it produced?—I am sure there was.

2996. Mr. EXHAM.—Do you say that the present Judge Harrison advised that the Corporation had no power or right to stop the pollution of the rivers by the millowners?—I do not mean that.

2997. But Mr. Carlisle's complaint is, that they were knowingly allowed to pollute the water, and that in addition, the Corporation themselves polluted it?—I admit that. You will find it in my printed report. Fortunately I have everything down. As to the Fairy Well, it is quite true that they do run it, and it is a miniature Pound Burn. The sewers also are discharged into it, and have been before I became surveyor, but it is now altogether covered over.

2998. One complaint was that when the Council were constructing sewers (main sewers), they allowed the polluted watercourse to run on in its existing channel to supply some of the manufactures? Of course we did. If we had stopped any of that water we would have been threatened with an action.

2999. CHAIRMAN.—Did you threaten to stop it?—Yes, I did, and had a warning notice from the York-street Spinning Mill, and Mr. Reid, the managing director of the company set a watch on me day to day to prevent our interfering with it, and yet this water is not so clean as we would like it. After the Fairy Well stream was last used we diverted it into the public sewers, and a great blessing it is to the public sewers which it passes through, because it scours them. Another complaint was, that after it was diverted into the public sewers the rest passed on to Mr. Crawford's works, and that we put on a [illegible] pipe and certain contrivances for giving him the best of it. This water-course, which has been diverted into the main sewer, was used by manufactories. I was very anxious—the district was rapidly increasing, and the sewer was becoming more and more polluted and unfit for manufacturing purposes, and many new streets were being drained into it on the Shankill-road, so I advised the Council to prevent it from coming down Townsend-street and going into the Pound Burn, which was subject to floods at that time. It is not subject to them now. I advised them to divert it from the Pound Burn, and to take it down North-street, to the tide. That is one cause that I say has greatly abated the nuisance in the Pound Burn, and one of the causes which has greatly diminished the flooding. Of course it was necessary to give a supply to those people who have a legal right to it, and they got it. I plead guilty to that charge, but I would do it again.

3000. Do I understand you to say that a part of the water is sent down a glazed pipe to the foundry in Townsend-street and down to Smithfield mill, and that another portion of it is diverted from the Pound Burn? The complaint is that the Council send down sewage matter into that river, and down to those factories, where it is used, and returned again in a much more polluted state, from being heated, and that they actually supply other places by this glazed pipe with sewage water. Is that the fact?—What I said was, that while we conducted this water down North-street, and so into the tide, we were obliged to leave the manufactories who were using this water what they needed. This pipe was so contrived as to give them the best of the water from the Fairy Well stream, which had become polluted.

3001. Mr. EXHAM.—Was there a new sewer made on the bed of the Fairy Well stream?—No. The complaint is, that whereas they had a right to have it come down its original channel, and no one had a right to divert it, that it was turned by the Corporation themselves into the sewer higher up, and that these persons then said, "You are taking it away from the usual bed here, and you have a right to give us water."

3002. CHAIRMAN.—Do you give them as pure water now as they formerly had from the Fairy Well?—I think purer. I would rather say less polluted.

3003. Mr. LAWLESS.—When was that done?—About four years ago. I say the water is the same.

3004. CHAIRMAN.—They say that the Corporation, through their officials, give water more polluted to the millowners than they previously had?—I do not think it is more offensive.

3005. Mr. LAWLESS.—Could it be worse?—It could be worse. It will be getting worse every day. With regard to Alderman Carlisle's cooler. He charged Alderman Carlisle that in one of his manufactories he had a cooler, and that the sewage of the houses which are built around it was discharged into it, and that the plans for those houses were passed by the borough surveyor. To that I give the flattest contradiction. It is totally devoid of any particle of truth. The plans were passed, but when they came into me I called attention to that cooler.

3006. CHAIRMAN.—Then do you say that in point of fact, the cooler existed when the houses were built?—Yes. The houses drained into the adjoining street sewers. I had the place inspected the other day, and the manager of the factory will be here to prove that the houses do not send the drainage into that cooler. I spoke to Alderman Carlisle on the subject, and he denies it. As a matter of fact they have a pump and they use that pump-water, and do not use that filthy stream. He says that at present they are using the pump. The manager is here and you can examine him. These houses are all drained into the street sewers. Our men saw them. If any person had surreptitiously put a four-inch pipe into the reservoir, and Mr. Carlisle had informed me I should have sent a man to examine it.

3007. We understood Mr. Carlisle to say that the house drains communicated with the reservoir which led into the cooler. Is that so?—I say not—at least not to my knowledge.

3008. Have you ever sanctioned any plans which drained those houses into the reservoir?—Certainly not. It would be a monstrous thing to do so.

3009. Mr. EXHAM.—It is alleged that there is foul matter in it plain to be seen by anyone. Mr. Carlisle has even asked us to go and judge of it for ourselves. Surely if you go up yourself you can see it, and tell us whether or not his charge is true?—I do not deny that if the whole of these coolers are not frequently cleansed, they will give off an offensive smell.

3010. CHAIRMAN.—Did you sanction the construction of those drains that are complained of in Haldane-street and Shaftesbury-place?—I not only did not sanction them, but if I found such a state of things existing as was complained of I would order the parties to be prosecuted.

3011. Do you believe that the sewage matter finds its way from Haldane-street and Shaftesbury-place and the surrounding streets into this reservoir on Alderman Carlisle's premises, after passing through the cesspool into which they drain in the first instance?—I have no knowledge of it, and I do not believe it.

3012. Mr. LAWLESS.—Do you know anything to the contrary?—I do not. I sent a man up to examine into this matter, and he reported to me that there are no houses drained into the cooler.

3013. CHAIRMAN.—It is alleged that those houses are drained into the cesspool in their rere, from which cesspool there is communication into the cooler?—If that is so it is very improper, but I have no knowledge of it being the case.

3014. Mr. Carlisle.—I assert that the drains from,

BELFAST. Jan. 4, 1877.

Mr. Montgomery.

these houses run into this cesspool which discharges itself into the sewer.

3015. Mr. *Montgomery*.—I know nothing of that. I know of nothing but the Fairy Well stream, and I do not believe what Mr. Carlisle states to be a fact.

Mr. Donnelly, the inspector of sewers and foreman of works, on the day after the statement was made, went to the place and examined it and inspected it, and if you wish you can examine him upon the question.

Mr. James Donnelly.

Mr. JAMES DONNELLY examined.

3016. CHAIRMAN.—Are you the foreman of works under the borough surveyor?—Yes.

3017. Did you inspect this place referred to?—I did.

3018. Did you find any drains from houses running into this reservoir which has been referred to, and which contains sewage matter?—No; I examined it carefully and found none.

3019. Can you undertake to say that there is none?—I can.

3020. Mr. BARLAS.—Is there a tank or reservoir in Alderman Carlisle's yard?—Not that I am aware of.

3021. Did you hear Mr. Carlisle say that there was a tank into which the liquid filth from Haldane-street and Hirtesbury-place discharged itself?—I am not aware; there may be a tank in the yard.

3022. Is there any communication between the sewer and the tank in the yard?—None. I examined it carefully, and it was very low at the time.

3023. How can you be sure of that if you do not know whether or not there is a tank in the yard?—Well I don't believe there is.

3024. Was the sewer empty?—No.

3025. Were you the overseer who saw the sewers made?—I was.

3026. Did you hear any complaints made in reference to Landscape-terrace?—I did.

3027. Mr. *Montgomery*.—But that is a mile away from this place.

3028. CHAIRMAN (to Mr. *Carlisle*).—Did you give any notice of this matter to Mr. Montgomery at the time?

3029. Mr. *Carlisle*.—I brought the complaints of the neighbourhood before the Corporation about this particular spot, because the complaints were terrible about it.

3030. Was that after you had made these examinations?—After I examined it I made complaints about it two or three times, and it was well known to the members of the Corporation as well as to Mr. Montgomery that the drains ran into that place.

3031. Mr. *Montgomery*.—I never heard of this complaint before from any person until I heard Mr. Carlisle make the statement here, and I do not believe the statement was ever made at any meeting of the committee.

3032. Mr. *Carlisle*.—I remember distinctly bringing up before the sanitary committee the complaint with reference to Haldane-street and Hirtesbury-place.

3033. CHAIRMAN (to Mr. *Donnelly*).—Could you, as a practical man, have suffered a pipe to cross the sewer from those houses and discharge itself into this reservoir?—I certainly would not do that at all.

3034. It must be within your recollection whether or not such a thing did occur?

3035. Mr. *Montgomery*.—I do not believe this complaint was ever made at any committee meeting.

3036. CHAIRMAN (to Mr. *Carlisle*).—How long is it since you ascertained the fact about this reservoir?

3037. Mr. *Carlisle*.—At the time this sewer was made.

3038. How long is that ago?—Six or seven years ago.

3039. Did you make any report of that to the Town Council?—I did not report it in writing. I simply brought before the committee the complaints of people that I heard.

3040. Were you a member of the Town Council at the time you made these complaints?—I was.

3041. How long ago is it since you ascertained that the pipe which drains Landscape-terrace was continued into this reservoir?—Six or seven years ago.

3042. Did you make any report of that fact to anybody?—I repeatedly brought the matter before the Corporation.

3043. Did you bring the matter as to this pipe being continued from Landscape-terrace houses into the reservoir instead of being carried into the main sewer before the Corporation—did you report that?—I reported generally that the sewage was being piped into that reservoir, and was poisoning the neighbourhood all round.

3044. Was it while you were a member of the Town Council you did this?—Yes, while I was a member of the Council.

3045. Then in point of fact this sewer has been made a long time?—It has.

3046. Mr. *Montgomery*.—The street in which this sewer is will be completed one of these days, and then any sewer in the street will be connected with the main sewer.

3047. Mr. LAWLESS (to Mr. *Carlisle*).—Was it to the improvement committee you made the complaint of this state of things?—I have no doubt it was to the sanitary and improvement committees. I remember distinctly bringing it before the sanitary committee on one occasion.

3048. CHAIRMAN.—Was Alderman Carlisle a member of the committee at that time?—He was a member of the Council. I understand that the chairman was manager of this [illegible], and that he is here to contradict this statement.

Mr. Montgomery.

Mr. MONTGOMERY'S examination continued.

3049. Mr. *Montgomery*.—Hardman's dam is lower down on the same stream. I can vouch for it myself as a very impure stream. It creates a bad smell in the neighbourhood.

3050. Mr. LAWLESS.—Is it remediable by any means in your power—by anything you or the Corporation can do to prevent it?—Yes; but then comes the leading question—it should be closed up at once. I got some pipes put in to prevent the flooding in Smithfield, and it ceased to be continuous. The flooding has ceased more or less but the nuisance remains.

3051. Suppose you adopt some engineering means to prevent the flooding, would the use of those prejudice Mr. Hardman's water rights?—Decidedly.

3052. CHAIRMAN.—Is there any other point upon your mind upon which you wish to give evidence?—Yes. You have taken evidence with regard to the streets being too narrow, and there have been different opinions expressed upon the subject. Those streets have been laid out under my supervision, and I do not consider that thirty feet is too narrow. I differ in opinion from those who say it is; for workmen's houses two stories high, I consider thirty feet is quite sufficient, and I have had some experience of such matters.

3053. Mr. *Carlisle*.—I never said that they were too narrow, but I said the town was built too closely together, and that there should be more open spaces.

3054. Mr. *Montgomery*.—It was stated here that the houses were built back to back, but that is utterly untrue; there are no back-to-back houses in Belfast. I agree with Mr. Carlisle that there should be more space between the houses. My object was that there should be a passage which would allow the people to wheel away the house excrement. When I was appointed the law did not require any plans of buildings to be submitted to the surveyor, but after a good deal of agitation I got the Council to apply for powers compelling the parties to produce plans and they got them. I strongly advocated that back passages should be provided, and that we should have power to insist upon it, because then the contents of privies and ashpits were being carried through the rooms in the houses where families lived and ate their food. I thought that a most indecent condition of things. Very great opposition was given to me about that amongst other things, and I was not able to carry it out. In point of fact that is the great blot upon the present system of workmen's houses. Mr. Carlisle is of opinion that the back passages are a nuisance.

3055. He said that at one time it was tried to get passages between the houses and it was found to be a great nuisance?—I assure you that in Bradford, Liverpool, and Manchester, these passages are not found to be a nuisance; they are kept very clean.

3056. However that is a matter of opinion, you need not trouble yourself to answer that any further?—I wish to add that if you can assist in getting the making of such passages compulsory you will render a great service to the town. In Hopewell-street there is a block of houses that form a hollow square, without yards, and I am informed that Mr. Carlisle is the owner of them. The houses surround the square and there are some common privies for the use of all the houses. I think that that arrangement for the working classes is a very bad one.

3057. Were those houses to which you refer built in your time?—I believe they were, but I may tell you that some time after the passing of the Act of 1866, things were done that we do not do now. Previously I was single handed in grappling with these matters, but we have got proper machinery since then, and things are properly carried out now. If the charge is made that things were done improperly at that time I plead guilty to it. Everything had to be created, and we are now working in something like the way we ought to do.

3058. Was the block of houses in Hopewell-street, built shortly after the passing of the Act of 1866?—We have tried to trace them but cannot. I think Mr. Carlisle began to build them without any plans, and I objected to them at the time.

3059. Would you allow houses to be built now in that way?—No; nor would I then, but the houses were commenced and I did not prosecute him for them; however the fault is not mine. That disposes of the matters relating to the defects in buildings. Here is a document (handing in same) which will explain the complaints about Hopewell-street; we are required by the Act of Parliament to see that there is a yard to every house, but before we got the new powers we had no power to insist upon plans. With the staff I had I could not watch the building operations properly.

3060. Is there any passage through which the refuse of these houses can be taken away except through the houses themselves?

3061. Mr. Carlisle.—Yes; there is a gate-way.

3062. Mr. Sexton.—Had you not power under the 12th section of the Act of 1845 to deal with the matter?

3063. Mr. Montgomery.—At the end of six months after the commission of the offence against the law there is no power to take proceedings. With regard to Dr. O'Malley's complaint about the cottages at Ballynafeigh, I may say that it is another instance of building houses without lodging plans. Some seven or eight years ago it was quite a common thing but it is never done now.

3064. Chairman.—If it is necessary for the owners of houses to make a larger tank so as to prevent the overflowing of the sewage into the road, it is incumbent on the Corporation to compel them to do so?—I have advised such steps to be taken in this case.

3065. How long ago?—About three weeks ago.

3066. Mr. Sexton.—How long has the nuisance existed?—The first complaint to me was from my deputy. There are some seventy or eighty people there who are engaged in washing clothes, and the liquid from it is allowed to run on the highway. Of course they could be prosecuted for this. I thought the nuisance should be taken across the public highway, by a six-inch pipe, but since that time other complaints have come in about the drainage.

3067. Mr. Lawlor.—In that district?—In that which has been covered by cess-pools, and I believe some of the inhabitants are anxious to have it made into a drainage district, and are willing to undergo the heavy charge thereafter. I have got orders to prepare a scheme for the district of Ballynafeigh, and to report whether or not I think it advisable just now to make it into a drainage district.

3068. When did you get those instructions?—Since you heard the complaint.

3069. Previously was it your advice to take it by means of a pipe to the other side of the road?—Yes.

3070. Chairman.—Would you advise the Corporation to go to the expense of making it a drainage district?—Yes; if we had the majority of the people willing to go to the expense. With regard to Mr. Stewart's complaints as to the pavement. A great many of the old streets are paved. It is rough paving but that is all that is wrong with it—it is wholesome, good paving but rough. I wish we had money to put down flagging instead. There was a complaint about Victoria-street and Ann-street being flooded, but the whole of that place has been thoroughly drained and paved, except the footways, and I have over and over again called attention to the fact that those footways ought to be flagged at the cost of the owners of property, and for this reason; the Town Council sold the adjacent lands by public sale to certain persons who were about to build, and the consideration was partly in work, and partly in money. They paid so much money, and they were to flag the footways. They have partially done so, and I advised the Corporation, before you came here, to take proceedings, and compel them to carry out their contract. The improvement committee on two occasions passed peremptory resolutions, calling upon the owners to do this work. I think after this, that Mr. Black will not be to blame if he issues writs against them. The real complaint is that the improvement committee are too lenient.

3071. Mr. Lawlor.—Who are the owners?—There is a whole lot of them—six or seven.

3072. Chairman.—Are any of these members of the Town Council?—I think not. The members of the Council have done theirs. Sir John Savage is the only one who is a member of the Council along that line, and he did his part many years ago.

3073. Mr. Sexton.—If he did it many years ago why were the others not made do theirs?—Here is one reason that was given. One gentleman (a Mr. Charles) came to the committee and said, "I have an architect engaged and I am preparing to build a pile of warehouses on my ground. I will lodge with you a sum of money to do the imperative part of the work—the kerbing and channel, and I'll do the rest as soon as the warehouses are completed." The committee thought that was a reasonable proposal and agreed to it, but he undertook to go on with his building much sooner than he has done, for he has not begun yet. He paid to the cashier the money for the portion of the work that had to be done then. With reference to the great complaints about this building and its drainage, I have to say that the drainage of the courts was not executed under my direction, nor was it for some time found to be defective. The architect who was paid for this work must not have attended to the drainage as well as he ought to have done. I have had to look after that as well as I could.

3074. Have you done anything to remedy the cause of complaint?—Yes, everything I could do.

3075. Have you tried to prevent the flooding of the basement?—I have puddled a large portion under the floors, and since that has been done I have not heard of any flooding. With regard to the Albert Memorial, £18 10s., the charge of Mr. Lynn, the sculptor, was complained of. This Albert Memorial and statue were erected by the Corporation. The sculptor, Mr. Lynn, furnished the statue of the Prince that stands in front, and owing to some bit of carelessness the hole of a Lewis bolt used for raising the statue got filled with water. This water probably froze and expanded and burst the head of the statue, and it became dangerous to passers-by. Up to that stage I had nothing to do with the matter. My attention was called to it—the passers-by thought if it fell it would kill some one, and at a meeting of the committee I advised them to take steps either to take down the statue or to make it safe, for the next frost would probably split it altogether. There was a long discussion about what was to be done, and I advised that as the statue had cost a sum of £600 and was public property the best plan would be to consult Mr. Lynn about the right way to cure the evil. He accepted it, and advised a certain course of procedure. When the work was finished he sent in an account for £16 16s. The committee thought it was rather high, but he declined to make any reduction as he considered that for an artist of his standing it was a very moderate charge. It is alleged that the money of the ratepayers is wasted for the cleansing of Blackstaff, but, if my opinion is worth anything, the cleansing has been of immense advantage to the town. I said already that the town was repeatedly flooded in the neighbourhood of Durham-street, and Mr. Connor and others allowed me to carry out some work by which the flooding has been greatly abated. No money has been wasted on that cleansing. I was offered another assistant over and above what I had. When Mr. John Lytle was mayor he proposed that as the work was so very greatly increased and so large I ought have a third assistant——

3076. What was your reply to that?—It was left over for consideration—to take my advice, and I said I could do if I only got temporary assistance. That has saved a couple of hundred pounds a year. The extra expense in my department has been very slight.

3077. What would have been the least you could have got a competent man for in your judgment?—Three guineas a week; and I have done without him.

3078. Was that the reason why you required temporary professional assistance which cost £300 or £200 within the last ten years?—I do not think it cost £100. With regard to Mr. Dempsey's complaint. The cost of the staff in my office is greatly less than in any town in the three kingdoms, where similar works are carried on. In Newcastle the salary of the surveyor is £1,000 a year, in Birmingham it is £1,000 a year, and the staffs are in proportion very much larger. In Liverpool the assistant has £600 a year. I never in my life, directly nor indirectly, solicited an increase of salary. It is alleged that the rates are wasted paying my salary and that of my staff, but in no town in England are the officers paid so low. I never complained of my salary or asked for an increase. For fear you might not understand what I mean by saying that the Town Council is too lenient, I may tell you that this Mr. Dempsey violated the building regulations, and the improvement committee, contrary to my advice, agreed, if he would give a written guarantee that he would make the alterations within the year, they would not take immediate proceedings, on condition that he complied with the surveyor's wishes. That year has not yet quite expired, but it will in a month or so. I mention that to show you that they are not expedited in being lenient.

3079. Do you attend every committee meeting?—Every meeting, unless I am absent in England.

3080. Have you ever seen any instance of favouritism shown to any of the members of that committee with regard to the streets in which works were being carried on?—I have not, and I have been thinking over it carefully. I do not recollect any case where a member of the Council got concessions or favours shown to him that were not on other occasions given to the very bitterest of their opponents. I think that several times a sort of fear of being supposed to go against opponents has made them unwilling to put their powers in force to the extent they might otherwise have done. I do not think that party or religion has anything to do with their actions in the Town Council.

3081. Has the fact of their being on the Town Council?—I think it is the very reverse, and with regard to the carrying out of the Acts of Parliament, I think they are carried out more stringently in Belfast than in Bradford or Blackburn, or any of the other rising towns, and in point of fact, the number of streets paved in Belfast within the last ten years, is greater than what has been done in any other town. There has been a greater proportion of new streets paved at the cost of owners of property than in any other town that I know of.

3082. What do you think is a reasonable time to give persons to carry out the Act of Parliament with regard to paving or laying out new streets, suppose the words of the Act of Parliament were that the man should do the work "within a reasonable time"?—I think it would vary in nearly every case that arose. I think that in every case when a well-founded complaint reaches us a compulsory order is issued. I hardly know of a case where a complaint was made to the committee in which an order was not issued.

3083. Does the Act of Parliament say that a complaint must be made? It says a certain thing must be done, and until that is done the houses must not be inhabited. It is in evidence before us that at all events, several houses have been inhabited for years in streets in which the requirements of the Act of Parliament have not been complied with?—That is so; that is admitted.

3084. I want to know how long do you say this is to go on? It has gone on for over three years in several instances—is it to go on for thirty years? The legislature thought it was right that people should not be allowed to inhabit houses until there was a proper way provided for their getting into them. I want to know what in your view is to be the limit within which you think you ought to enforce the law?—I have given you my view. I think in some cases one year would be ample, but I think that in some cases it might require much more.

3085. Under the Act of Parliament you are directed to shut up the street and not allow it to be opened, nor a single house in it to be inhabited until it is flagged to your satisfaction, or the footways made, and the road macadamised. Is it of your own free will that you do not enforce the law, or do you refrain from doing so by the orders of the improvement committee?—I never got any such instructions from the committee. That section of the Act was put in by Mr. Bruce contrary to my advice. I do not know of any other town where such an Act is carried out.

3086. Do you act on your own responsibility?—Yes. I got one or two sections of that Act repealed, and may be I will get this one also.

3087. Do you know that Mr. O'Neill said he was noticed years ago to lay out and repair footways of his own, and that the Corporation did it when he refused and brought an action against him by Mr. Brown, their then solicitor, and he had to pay £33, while other persons similarly circumstanced had not any action taken against them. He further told us that there were streets in some places three or four years inhabited without roads or footways, and that you did not compel the owners of them to comply with the law, and he named Mr. Brown as the person who was responsible for not carrying out the law in some of them?—I heard him say so.

3088. CHAIRMAN.—We want to know was any favour shown to Mr. Brown about that?

3089. Mr. EXHAM.—Mr. Brown said he was not now interested in the houses?—When I came to Belfast Peel-street and Mary-street (the streets complained of) were then old streets. I have always advised that old streets should be properly completed and adopted as highways. We are not compelled to adopt them, but I have always advised that the older streets should be taken the first, unless there is some good reason for pursuing a different course with regard to them. The streets that the Messrs. Brown are interested in are quite new—it was a green field quite recently. I think however the time has arrived when an order should be made for these streets, although they are very partially built on yet. We like to allow the people time to get rents. The Messrs. Brown had completed one of these streets, M'Donald-street, which is the leading street to the old streets. Peel-street and Mary-street were in an unwholesome state, stagnant water was lying in them, and they had never been completed and adopted. The usual course in all these cases is to serve an order, and if the party is aggrieved he has the right to appeal. If he can show that they were properly completed that ousts the jurisdiction of the Corporation completely. The officer who first served the notice about Mary-street is standing here, and he says that when he served it on Mr. O'Neill he said he was very glad that Mary-street was about to be paved.

3090. CHAIRMAN.—His complaint is, that he was called upon to do what others were not called upon to do at all?—I am not here to defend the Messrs. Brown, but surely the question of time is something. Some few months ago I presented to the improvement committee a list of ninety-two streets which had been ordered to be paved and sewered, and the surveys and estimates prepared by me and my staff. I advised that before any new orders were issued these streets should be taken up and done, and, regardless of the complaints of the owners or people interested in them, that writs should be issued and the money expended should be got in. Our solicitor spent every week close in my office with myself and my deputy arranging about taking legal proceedings against these men, and a great many of them have been put in motion, but the owners of property came every day to the committee asking time, and saying that it would ruin them if these orders were enforced, and pressure was brought to bear on the committee to grant a delay. Mr Hilton was given three or four months since the complaint was made to you. He is a Catholic gentleman.

3091. Mr. LAWLESS.—What sort of pressure is brought to bear on the committee?—Entreaty. The usual course is this: the sites of houses in this town are not the property of capitalists. A class of middlemen come in and rent a piece of ground, and undergo a heavy rent. They are not able to get their houses up as quickly as they would like. They are still under rent, and suppose a writ is issued against these unfortunate men their property would be confiscated.

3092. Suppose the creditor of one of these middlemen was a member of the Town Council, would he go to that man to use his influence?—I should say he would.

3093. Suppose a member of the council was a middleman?—I should say from what I have seen that that member of the council would be more narrowly watched than any of the others.

3094. CHAIRMAN.—Do the members who are described as the "fender ring" generally take part in the deliberations of the committee, or vote when these questions are brought before the committee?—I think there is generally a feeling that a man should not sit upon his own case. I have known the Messrs. Dixon to retire so as not to influence the other members of the committee, or vote when their brothers' interests were involved. I opposed a large scheme of Councillor Dixon's for building on reclaimed lands on the county Down side, as I thought the houses should be raised higher above the tide.

3095. In Ballymacarrett?—Yes. We had several interviews and arguments about it, and I succeeded in getting him to raise his houses higher than any of those that had been previously built in the neighbourhood, and at a very heavy cost. From that day to this I never found out that Mr. Dixon's countenance was set against me. That is not a single case. It is alleged by Mr. Biggar and others that the surveyor is coerced.

3096. He said it was generally known that these gentlemen used their position as members of the improvement committee to benefit themselves; that so far as he knew Mr. Montgomery was always supposed to do what was right. Is it the case that your recommendations were often overruled by the improvement committee when you reported that such and such steps should be taken, and that the members mentioned by Mr. Biggar were on that committee, Messrs. Brown, and Lowther, and Dixon, and that owing, directly or indirectly, to their influence your recommendations were rejected?—Well, there, I give it a flat contradiction. I heard Mr. Biggar's remarks about the "fender ring," and I contradict them.

3097. Mr. LAWLESS.—Have your recommendations ever been over-ruled?—Certainly; but the recommendations of every town surveyor in the Three Kingdoms have been over-ruled.

3098. Have they on those occasions been over-ruled by those gentlemen named by Mr. Biggar?—I have not the recollection of a single case. I do not believe that such a thing ever occurred. There is no town surveyor infallible, and my recommendations did not always meet with the approval of the Town Council. They did not think my recommendations must be always right and all others wrong. I think I have been better supported in Belfast than any other town I have been in. I know nothing of these charges of corruption, and I do not believe one of them.

3099. There was one case mentioned in which Mr. Dixon was concerned. He bought ground for building a row of houses, and an application was made by Mr. Dempsey to make a public-house at one end. It was brought before the committee and rejected in the first instance, but by perseverance it was afterwards got passed. Do you remember that case?—I do.

3100. Will you tell us exactly what the circumstances were?—If you understand my last answer I wish by it to convey that the committee were acting in the conscientious discharge of their duty.

3101. Yes; I quite understand that is your belief?—It is.

3102. To the best of your belief has any improper influence been exercised on the committee?—Yes. Many years ago (ten or twelve years), when our powers were exceedingly limited, a Mr. Alexander built a row of houses on his own ground without first laying out the street.

3103. Was that before the passing of the Act of 1865?—Long. He submitted a plan at my request. On that plan were two streets that I agreed to and approved of, and disapproved of the row of houses unless the street was laid out. This was a place fronting the ground of the Harbour Commissioners; the ground lay between Alexander's houses and Whitehouse-street. Notwithstanding my disapproval and the committee's disapproval, this row of houses was built during the time of the Chancery suit. I reported the matter at the time, and we were advised that it could be cured when the opposite row of houses was built. The Harbour Commissioners in due time sold their strip of building ground, which was bought by the Messrs. Dixon. They brought in a plan to me of a large pile of warehouses, which I disapproved of, and the committee backed me in that, and there was some disagreement between us which I may remark the Messrs. Dixon never remembered against me. They contended, as I think you heard from Mr. Dixon that this ground touched on Whitehouse-street and to one of the rows of houses, and Mr. Glenn thought he should not be compelled to give ten feet of his ground towards a street that was of no use to him. The dispute was solved in this way. After he sold the ground to Mr. Dempsey, plans of houses were passed in Mr. Dempsey's favour (plans produced). A sort of compromise was come to—that he should build within thirty feet of Mr. Glenn's houses. He was to surrender ten feet in addition to the twenty. He said, "I'll enclose that ground. You may have the right to restrict me in the building, but the ground is mine, and I'll hold it till you pay me." We can buy that ten feet at any time to widen the street.

BELFAST.
Jan. 8, 1872.

Mr. James Alexander Henderson, J.P.

Mr. James Alexander Henderson, J.P., examined.

3104. Chairman.—You are a Town Councillor?—Yes.

3105. And have been for some years?—Yes; I was two years Mayor.

3106. And I believe you are proprietor of the *News-Letter*?—Yes.

3107. Mr. Carlisle, who was giving evidence here yesterday, mentioned that shortly after the vote about Cobain's salary was come to he had business in the *News-Letter* office, and that Mr. Lilburn told him that, in consequence of his having voted against the increase of Cobain's salary, he would write against him. I asked what had Mr. Lilburn to do with the Corporation, and it was suggested that you were proprietor of the *News-Letter*. I want to know is that the case?—I need hardly say there is not a word of truth in it. I would be exceedingly sorry to direct the editor of the *News-Letter* to do so. It is perfectly untrue. I have this morning had a conversation with the editor of the *News-Letter*, and he told me he never had a conversation with Mr. Carlisle that could possibly bear the slightest tinge of truth in reference to that statement, and I know he is a gentleman who is far above anything of the kind.

3108. In any way, directly or indirectly, have you caused Mr. Carlisle to be written down?—Certainly not.

3109. Or were any steps taken by you, or anyone in your employment, to prevent Mr. Carlisle being returned?—That is a different thing. An argument we canvassed strongly against him, as he attempted to put out Sir John Savage at the time, and I think it was most improper to attempt to put a person out who had been mayor from serving on the Corporation. I personally canvassed against him in favour of Sir John Savage.

3110. There has been something said of an inner circle of the Corporation, and although the gentleman who has mentioned it declined to give names, Mr. Rea, who was addressing us last night, said he would give the names, and he mentioned your name as one of the four. I want to know if in any way you have ever instructed Mr. Cobain, or given him any authority on behalf of the Corporation, to exercise any influence at the time of the elections?—Certainly not, in any way whatever.

3111. Have you been cognizant of the fact that he has been so acting?—Certainly not. I believe there has been great exaggeration about that.

3112. Do you remember a proposal being made—I think by Mr. Dixon—that no officer should be allowed to take part in the elections except by voting?—Yes, I remember the resolution. It was proposed to gag the officials of the Corporation, and we allowed them to use their free rights as citizens; but I believe the officials of this Corporation are as free from anything political as any Corporation can be. In fact we rather congratulate ourselves that neither politics nor anything of the kind is introduced into the Corporation.

3113. Have you or any members of the Corporation, to your own knowledge, ever desired Mr. Cobain or any other officers of the Corporation to use their position as officers in influencing the elections?—Certainly not. If it has been done, it has been done contrary to my knowledge and to my wishes.

3114. Mr. Exham.—Were you present at the Council on the 1st February last year, when Mr. Gaffikin opposed the increase to Mr. Cobain's salary on the ground that he had to his own knowledge actively interfered to put him out of the Council?—I really do not remember, but Mr. Gaffikin had a feeling——

3115. Mr. Gaffikin has stated to us that he knew the facts he stated of his own knowledge?—I recollect well Sir John Savage's statement.

3116. His statement was that Mr. Cobain had said to some friends of his that Sir John Savage was most ungrateful in opposing the increase of his salary, as he had been instrumental in securing his return?—Sir John Savage seemed to be annoyed at any member of the Corporation saying his influence had got him into the Corporation.

3117. Was anything done by the members of the Council to have an investigation of the charge then made by Mr. Gaffikin and Sir John Savage as to the conduct, not of a member, but of a servant of the Corporation?—I don't remember. We did not think it necessary to go into that matter. Mr. Gaffikin's charge was not made at that time.

3118. You are in error—it was on the same day?—Sir John Savage was very warm, but we did not think——

3119. Chairman.—Were you present when he was warm about it?—Yes; I think it was at the meeting of the Council.

3120. Were any steps taken by members of the Council then present to investigate the truth of the allegation which Sir John Savage made?—No steps were taken, as we did not consider it necessary.

3121. Mr. Exham.—I suppose, Mr. Henderson, you would do Sir John Savage the justice that he would not make that charge unless he believed it to be true?—I am positive he would not. He was a little annoyed that anyone would take it upon him to say such a thing.

3122. When a member of the Council who had been mayor made that statement, did not it occur to you that it would be well to ask Mr. Cobain to give an answer to it, or to have an investigation about it?—I don't know.

3123. Chairman.—In your opinion was Mr. Cobain's salary increased on political grounds?—Certainly not.

3124. Did you vote for it on those grounds?—I voted for it because I felt that his salary, when he commenced, was low, and that he was a very excellent officer. It was solely on the ground of his services in the particular position he occupied, but certainly not at all in connexion with any political duty or what he may have done in a political point of view.

3125. Mr. Lawless.—Was there any increase of duty imposed on Mr. Cobain?—There was. The amount of money coming into his hands was considerably increased; and when his salary was compared with those of other officers it was found to be very much lower.

3126. Do you mean with the officers of other Corporations or your officers?—Particularly with the gasworks.

3127. Chairman.—Do you consider he is overpaid for the duties he is fulfilling, compared with the other officers?—Certainly not. I consider him a very efficient and respectable officer. We never had the slightest reason to complain of Mr. Cobain.

3128. I understand you to say that it was solely on the ground of his services and the proper fulfilment of his duties as cashier you voted for his increase of salary?—Solely; and I believe it was solely on that account the majority of the Corporation increased his salary.

3129. Mr. Lawless.—You voted against the resolution that the officers of the Corporation should not be permitted to interfere in political affairs, but not to take away their rights as voters?—There were different views in the Corporation on that subject. It was thought that if we put the resolution on that ground it would be a sort of admitting there had been such conduct on the part of our officials, whereas we denied there was anything of the kind.

3130. Was it not openly asserted at the time that there was something of the kind?—It might by those who brought forward the resolution. I believe it was greatly got up by exaggerated statements outside the Council, and by some of the newspapers.

3131. Chairman.—Was it not stated by Mr. Dixon at that meeting as the ground of his motion that the officers did interfere?—Mr. Dixon has very particular views; he may have said such things, but I can't tax my memory.

3132. Mr. Lawless.—I don't suppose the resolution was brought forward without the statement being made,

Mr. James Alexander Henderson, J.P.

and I suppose the gentlemen who voted for it believed it to be true?—I suppose so.

3133. Mr. Kernan.—Supposing it is a fact that Mr. Cobain did, at a certain ward-meeting, propose a certain gentleman as Town Councillor against another person who was a Town Councillor, do you think that would be a right interference on his part as an officer of the Corporation?—I think it would be very unwise if he did so. It would have been much better if he had not, and much better if the officers kept out of those things.

3134. Mr. Lawless.—Did you ever hear, except on that occasion, of Mr. Cobain interfering in municipal elections?—It was repeatedly stated over and over again.

3135. Chairman.—Did you ever take the trouble to investigate the truth of it?—I have been very observant of his conduct, and specially during the two years I was in the position of mayor, and I could see nothing of it whatever. I always found him most attentive to his duties.

3136. Did you ever see anything to justify the imputation that he was interfering at the time of the elections?—Certainly not.

3137. Mr. Kernan. Supposing it was proved or stated to you that Mr. Cobain prepared ward lists and canvassed and returned lists, what would you say to that?—If such a thing had been stated to me I would have found it my duty to have spoken to Mr. Cobain.

3138. Chairman.—Do you not think the resolution proposed by Mr. Dixon was a proper one?—I think it was a very improper resolution, as we did not believe there was any truth in it.

3139. Do you think it a proper thing that officials in the Corporation should or should not take part in elections?—Certainly; I think it is very improper, except to record their votes.

3140. Mr. Rea.—Mr. Henderson has contradicted my evidence about the inner circle, and several ratepayers have been allowed to suggest questions for cross-examination, and I desire to make a suggestion to the Commissioners. I wish leave now to suggest, with regard to the contradiction given to my most positive testimony, that Mr. Henderson be asked when I stood for Dock Ward in 1875, against Alderman Carlisle, whether he did not, about two o'clock, go down to the ward with Mr. Noah Davis to take steps to keep me out.

Mr. *Henderson*.—I don't remember anything about it, and I don't believe it was the case.

3141. Chairman.—Do you remember going down?—I was not at the tally booth.

3142. Mr. *Rea*.—I did not see him in the tally booth, for I was there and saw him speaking to Noah Davis across the street.

3143. Mr. *Henderson*.—I would not speak to him about the matter, for if I saw Mr. *Davis* there at that time I would tell him to go about his business.

3144. Mr. Lawless.—Did you take any part at that time against Mr. Rea?—I had a conversation with several gentlemen of the ward. I could name some of them, and I did take part against him.

3145. Mr. *Rea*.—I want Mr. Henderson asked whether or not he ever furnished accounts to the Corporation in the name of Mr. Spiller for work done for the Corporation, he being a member of the Corporation at the time, and getting the money for the accounts, Mr. Spiller being the manager and head clerk in the *News-Letter* office.

3146. Chairman.—Have you ever done so?—Certainly not. I never have done any printing for the Corporation since I have been a member of it.

3147. Mr. *Rea*.—Does he believe Mr. Spiller did it, and if so doesn't the money Mr. Spiller gets go into his pocket?—I don't believe Mr. Spiller did anything of the kind, and I hope the money he gets comes into my pocket.

3148. Chairman.—Did you vote for any of these £1,000 payments to the Mayor?—I think I was in the Corporation at the time.

3149. Were they unanimous votes?—I think they were until some persons objected to them, and then they gave way. I think it is most unaccountable the Mayor does not get a salary, because there are so many expenses connected with his being Mayor.

3150. Do you know on what ground the first was voted? Was it to recoup Mr. Lytle for the costs he had incurred in proceeding against Mr. Rea?—It could not be, because he handed it over to the Albert memorial.

3151. Mr. *Rea*.—Can Mr. Henderson recollect being at any political meetings where Mr. De Cobain was present?—I may have been, but I don't remember.

3152. Chairman.—Well I think we require nothing further with you, Mr. Henderson.

3153. Mr. *Henderson*.—Well as you have allowed a great many matters to be introduced here will you allow me to introduce what I consider to be a great abuse, and that is this—that at our municipal contests one person can come forward to contest five different wards although he can only sit for one if elected, and that all the expenses of these elections comes out of the rates.

3154. Chairman.—Well these are matters we cannot go into.

3155. Mr Lawless.—There is only one question I want to ask you. As a matter of fact did any articles appear in the *News Letter* against Mr. Carlisle?—Well I think that articles did appear against him when he endeavoured to put out Sir John Savage at the time he was Mayor, but I am perfectly certain that Mr. Lilburn never did any such thing as Mr. Carlisle stated. Mr. Lilburn has positively told me so this morning.

3156. Mr. *Robert Carlisle*.—I am positively certain that Mr. *Lilburn* did.

3157. Mr. *Henderson*.—Well I gave him no authority to do so.

Mr. Montgomery, Borough Surveyor, was then re-examined.

Mr. Montgomery.

3158. *Witness*.—I want to explain about Mr. Kennedy's evidence as to the money that should have been expended in Ballymacarrett. His statement is that under the Act of 1868 the Council were bound to spend £6,000 in certain works at Ballymacarrett. Mr. Kennedy must have been misinformed. There have actually been expended on the works contemplated in the section, £6,700. Then it was said that a fair share of that was not spent in the townland of Ballynafeigh. As a matter of fact there were only some £300 or £200 spent in that townland, and I never heard that complaint made till I heard it before you. Ballynafeigh is a rural district. In laying out the £6,700 we took the leading roads nearest to Belfast, and a good deal more would have been laid out, but as you heard owners of property on the Newtownards-road would not facilitate us. I had authority to spend £700 more on that road, and could not get the ground.

3159. Mr. Kernan.—What was done to Ballynafeigh?—There were new footways, flagging, and channels made. About the outfall of the sewage the reason that is on your books is not correct. Mr. Kennedy said the Harbour Commissioners objected to the drainage of that district of Belfast generally, because it would be a nuisance. That is not the reason. The reason given was that the Chairman and some members of the board wished the sewage discharged upon the slob lands. My scheme proposes to discharge it into the tideway. That was the issue.

3160. Chairman.—Has it been in consequence of the absence of main sewerage, and pending a scheme being carried out that the delay has been caused in making the private sewers in the streets mentioned by Mr. Moran?—That was one of the chief reasons. At the moment the complaint was made about Mount-street, Loganview-street, and the other

BELFAST. Jan. 4, 1877. — Mr. Montgomery.

stream mentioned by Mr. Morton the committee had on their minutes the directions to the surveyor to have orders prepared for their completion, and those orders had been prepared before you heard the complaint. With regard to the nuisance complained of at Parkinghouse[illegible] the solicitor had got instructions to compel the owners of property in that street to carry out the compulsory order of the Council that was issued some years ago, and I think they will put more pressure on now.

3161. Mr. *William O'Hare*.—What I complained of was that, with the connivance of the Town Council the pipes were laid down there recently at Fairy Well, and were discharging the sewage into the stream. There is a bad smell arising out of the sewage there in consequence of the pond.

3162. Mr. *Montgomery*.—And this order will remedy that. The Fairy Well stream has been polluted for twenty years.

3163. Mr. Exham.—But Mr. O'Hare says that there is a large new drainage pipe put down there, and that all the sewage is allowed to collect there, and that is done by the Corporation.

3164. Mr. *O'Hare*.—I say that the Council are privy to it.

3165. Mr. *Montgomery*.—There is no other way to drain it now, but when we will be able to cover over the Fairy Well stream this will be removed.

3166. Mr. Exham.—Have you sanctioned the drainage into the stream?—Yes.

3167. Then that is putting new sewage into the stream, and what right have the Corporation to do that?—I am endeavouring to have the scheme carried out that will remove this. There is at present no drainage near the line would drain the district.

3168. If there are 100 houses in the street, is the sewage from these to be added to the stream, and the mills to be obliged to use it?—I think that is generally understood as the custom in Belfast.

3169. Chairman.—What we want to know is, if you are taking any steps to prevent it?—No steps, except a proper drainage for the whole town.

3170. Mr. Exham.—Are you not encouraging the pollution of the streams by others by polluting them yourselves?—That was always the system here, and I might leave Belfast if I did not continue things as I got them. The same thing prevails in Bradford and other places.

3171. All I can say is, that I have been asked by several persons if it is the fact that the millowners are allowed to use polluted streams in their mills in Belfast, and that in addition the Corporation themselves pollute them?—It is the general complaint in all the manufacturing towns that it is done. I think it an improper thing for the sake of the public health, and that the people who are complaining should agree to carry out proper drainage works; but what I say is, that it is exceedingly unfair to be bringing charges of this sort against the Corporation of Belfast, as it is a matter of notoriety that it is done in every town in the three kingdoms.

3172. Chairman.—Could it not be remedied by constructing a main sewer?—Not a main sewer, but a system of main drainage for the whole town. With reference to the complaints about University-street, the moment the Council got leave to go through private property I and my men were up and commenced at those works which we are accused of neglecting. We had no power to order the sewers to be made through private property, but the very moment we got possession of the ground we commenced the work, and we are going on. The next charge is that of Mr. Robb, who complained that a favourite was employed as a contractor for the paving of the streets, and that no other man had a chance. Well that contractor got it on the lowest tender by public competition, and he was a Roman Catholic. Mr. Biggar says that Mr. Ward's cellar was below the river. Well I objected to the plans and the committee objected, and Ward Brothers gave an undertaking that the cellar should be used only for stores or something like that; and they gave a guarantee to indemnify the committee for anything that would happen.

3173. Mr. Exham.—But Mr. Biggar's complaint was, that the plans were passed in spite of you, and there is nothing in the Act that objectionable works are to be allowed on a guarantee being given to the committee?—Well, I do not think there is anything wrong in it. I must say that I approved of what took place in this case.

3174. But you had objected to it at first?—Yes, *pro forma*, and I say that fearing an improper use might be made of this basement story, the Messrs. Ward, a very eminent firm in this town, came and said that they would undertake to drain this place, and I think the committee did wisely in acceding to their request.

3175. If a poor man, who cannot give a guarantee, applied for the same privilege, would the committee refuse him?—No. Mr. Dempsey got leave to make a similar place for cooks in a house he built near the borough boundary, on the Shore-road, in the premises in which I had to prosecute him for having a dangerous flue. As to another complaint. There was a projected street, Moscow-street, intended to go forward into some grass land. Messrs. Grant Brothers wished to put up a manufactory on the site that was intended to be devoted to one of these private streets. The subject was discussed, and as there were so many streets parallel, permission was given to the Messrs. Grant to build on this land, and Mr. Cosgrove said he did not object to it, but he wanted that rule to be applied indiscriminately to all the streets, and in the event he wanted it, it would have been a great public inconvenience, and, moreover, owners of property having land fronting that street objected. Mr. George Clarke waited on the committee and warned them that he did not permit the street to be closed, as they refused Mr. Cosgrove permission to put a house on the site of the street. He complained that Crimea-street had been unsewered[illegible]. It was improperly made, and the works were ordered in the usual way. Mr. O'Neill gave evidence yesterday that there was a nuisance at the Messrs. Lindsay's factory, near the asylum. All I can say is, that there was a nuisance there several years ago. This factory was built without any approval or consent of mine. There were several very injurious clauses in the Act of 1866, and one of them was that anyone building a house fifty yards from a street need not submit the plans to me. I got that clause removed. The Messrs. Lindsay discharged their refuse water into an open drain that flows towards the river Blackstaff, and that has been a very great thing; but if anyone has any complaint of a nuisance, it should be sent to the sanitary inspector. This is rather a private place, but it would be his duty to examine it and report upon it.

3176. Mr. Exham.—I read a letter in the papers today from the Messrs. Lindsay, and it does not meet Mr. O'Neill's charge at all.

3177. Mr. *Constantine O'Neill*.—There is a great nuisance there where the drain and the stream meet a little below the mill, and I repeat what I said before that, when I visited it there were two dead cats lying there. It was most offensive.

3178. Chairman.—How did you become aware of it?—It was brought to my attention and I went there to examine it on the 1st of January. It is close to the walls of the asylum where there are 180 patients.

3179. Mr. Exham.—Did you not say that from 300 to 400 persons are continually working in the factory?—Yes, there are. What I complain of is that I am visited by the law very sharply and that Mr. Lindsay gets off scot-free.

3180. Mr. *Montgomery*.—Before the Act of 1866 a great many irregularities occurred, but now that does not occur. There is a proper inspection now and such a thing cannot occur in future, and I never was aware of this nuisance until I heard it in this room.

3181. Chairman (by Mr. *Gilligan*).—Had you a proper staff in your office to see after works in connexion with your department when these buildings were erected?—There was immense additional work thrown upon us then, and I plead guilty to carelessness in this respect, and I am sorry for it; but I think when the whole town is raked up for complaints the result is very slight.

3182. Mr. *Calligan.*—I venture to say I can hunt up 200 cases.

3183. Mr. *Montgomery.*—Mr. Alderman Hughes made a mistake about the houses he referred to. He said that Mr. Peter Quinn erected two houses on a site which had been passed by the Town Council for a street. These houses were built without any plans being approved of and legal proceedings were taken against him, and the magistrates after hearing the case deferred their decision until he came before the committee. He did do so, and he is taking the houses down now. The last matter I have to mention is a charge that Mr. Robert Carlisle made against me. He said he believed improper influence had been brought to bear on me to get a board removed in Donegall-place. I asked him to give me the date of that, but he did not, and I cannot recollect anything about it. But Alderman Ewart is a man that is incapable of trying to influence me, and Mr. Carlisle's statement is an atrocious slander on him and me. I don't know anything about the board.

3184. Mr. *Carlisle.*—I stated facts, and I would like to know what did influence Mr. Montgomery to serve the notice. The orders are on the improvement committee's minute-book not to proceed further with the case. Mr. Craig, who was Mr. Ewart's tenant, wanted to put a window where the board was, and after it had been pulled down several times by Craig and put up again by Mr. Carswell, who owned it, Mr. Montgomery served the notice. The gentlemen then came before the committee, and they went into the whole matter, and decided that they would not interfere between Mr. Ewart's tenants and Mr. [illegible].

3185. Mr. *Montgomery.*—There never has been any undue influence brought to bear on me, and I'll stake my character against Mr. Carlisle's.

3186. CHAIRMAN.—You need not mind that, but you say that you were never unduly influenced by Mr. Ewart?—Never.

3187. Will you endeavour to find from your records what the circumstances were?—I will.

3188. Mr. Carlisle said that some schemes for the purifying of the Blackstaff were opposed by the influence of the mill-owners, and I want to know whether that is so or not?—I know nothing of this alleged secret work; I don't believe it, but I have heard it stated repeatedly. Mr. Charles Duffin was always in opposition to the Council. If any schemes were rejected I believe it was by my advice, and through my influence. I believe they have confidence in my judgment at all times.

3189. Mr. EXHAM.—We have got a letter within the last two hours from Jaffe, Brothers. This is what they write:—

"GENTLEMEN,—Observing from the reports in the newspapers that you are receiving evidence on the sanitary condition of the town, we beg to state as large ratepayers that there is no sewer in Linenhall-street, in which we hold several tenements, and that we have been frequently troubled with offensive smells in consequence."

What do you say to that?—There are sewers in Linenhall-street, but they are not efficient sewers. A compulsory order was prepared for this very piece of street, Linenhall-street, and there was a dispute as to whether the street could be sewered in any degree at the expense of the owners of property. Our solicitor held that it could, but Mr. Carroll and some others objected, and contrivances were adopted for rendering the sewers. A large sewer was not made in the street.

3190. CHAIRMAN.—Why?—In consequence of this dispute. I admit the facts as alleged in that letter, and I think there should be a sewer there, and in every street in Belfast too, but it would take some time to do it.

3191. Why don't you proceed to make it when you admit it is wanting. Has there been any complaint before about this?—Well, I have not had a complaint about Linenhall-street, and I am intimate with the Messrs. Jaffe.

3192. Into what do all these sewers drain?—Into the main sewers of the town; sewers that were made thirty years ago. There is no flooding there that I ever heard of. The temporary works that were made there were a great improvement.

3193. Mr. EXHAM.—We were told yesterday that in a field belonging to Mr. Dunville, in which there is a declivity of some fifteen feet, the Corporation are carting stuff off the streets, and that that contains not only sweepings off the streets but most offensive nuisance matter. That appears to have been reported to the medical sanitary officer, who reported it to the sanitary board, and they referred it to improvement committee. Do you know why this is done by the Corporation?—The only complaint that reached me, and the only one the improvement committee would take cognizance of, was as regards the fencing of the place as it is dangerous. I was asked to consider if we could compel the owner of Dunville's field to fence it all round, and we have not had an opportunity of seeing to it since. It is not in my department, except as regards the fencing.

Mr. JAMES M'KEOWN examined.

3194. Mr. EXHAM.—You are the street inspector of this borough?—I am.

3195. Dr. M'Connell made the following report—"My attention having been called by the sub-sanitary officer, William Duff, to what I consider a dangerous nuisance existing in a plot of ground, known as Dunville's field, on the Falls-road, I beg to report that I have examined same, and I recommend the field to be fenced to prevent parties from going there to the danger of life." Mr. Calligan says that he saw the Corporation carts drawing stuff off the streets and most offensive nuisance stuff besides and putting it into this place. Is that so?—Yes; the stuff of the streets is going into it since the beginning of winter, but there is no offensive matter put into it.

3196. CHAIRMAN.—Why is not this matter brought to the proper depot?—Well we have no place to bring it, and we put it into every hollow that we can get. But this is only the scrapings off the streets.

3197. Mr. EXHAM.—But surely there must be droppings of a large number of animals in it?—Yes; but I don't think that is a nuisance.

3198. Mr. *Calligan.*—Dr. M'Connell distinctly told me that he saw yard stuff emptied in this place, and I saw myself rotten stuff, which was taken from dunghills, emptied in it.

3199. CHAIRMAN.—Is that so?—Yes, but it is not put there by us, and it was a place used for nuisances long before we put anything in it.

3200. Mr. *Calligan.*—There never was any nuisance there before. Formerly it was used by cricketers.

3201. CHAIRMAN.—What do you say to that?—Well, I have to say, that before we put anything there we took dead animals out of it many times. I was requested by the sub-engineer of the borough to put the stuff there, and as a matter of economy it is of been a value of £3 a day to us to put it there.

3202. From whom did you get permission to put it there?—From Mr. Wakeford, and he got it from the trustees who have the ownership of the field.

3203. Mr. EXHAM.—Are you aware that all open places of that kind should be paled in?—I am not.

3204. Mr. *Robert Carlisle.*—When I was a member of the Council there was a general rule on the books of the improvement committee that all open places of this kind should be paled in, and I believe it was carried through the Council.

Mr. E. St. W. De Courcy examined.

3305. *Witness.*—The first statement I wish to reply to is a statement made by Mr. Dunne as to the salary I received from the Corporation. He said that my commencing salary as cashier was £70 per annum, and that statement was not correct. I was appointed at that salary as assistant to Mr. Pinto Collins, who was both cashier, sub-treasurer, and accountant, and upon his resignation the offices of cashier and accountant were divided, and I was appointed cashier, my salary being increased.

3306. Mr. Lawless.—What was your first salary?—I think it was £100 a year. Subsequently the Act of 1863 came into force, and under the provisions of that Act the collections of county cess within the borough were abolished, and a general purposes rate was imposed, which very largely increased the revenues of the Corporation, and correspondingly increased my duties and responsibilities, and in recognition of this my salary was increased further, as also were the salaries of the other officials. That was somewhere about the termination of the year 1866 or the beginning of 1867. My salary was at this time increased to £130 and afterwards to £150. The Corporation subsequently acquired the cemetery and public parks, while the town itself kept rapidly extending; and from time to time, the Corporation, in acknowledgment of these facts, increased the remuneration of their various officers, mine among the rest; but not at a greater ratio than that of the other officers of the Corporation.

3307. Chairman.—What were the several increases you got?—I was raised first to £100, and then successively to £120, £130, £175, £250, and ultimately to £300.

3308. Was the third rise in consequence of the cemetery and public parks being acquired?—Yes, and the rapid extension of the town. These increases were given in consequence of the labour in my department being more than that in any other, and my remuneration, as compared with the rest of the official staff, was beyond all comparison, the lowest paid to any officer in the service of the Town Council.

3309. Did you apply for the increase, or was it volunteered?—In one or two instances it was given without application, and upon one occasion, on the revision of the salaries, it was given without application. Mr. Dunne stated my salary was equal to, if not double of that of any official holding a similar position in Belfast or Ulster. The published accounts of this Corporation for 1855 will show that the gentleman who was then known as sub-treasurer in the borough, and whose duties were analogous to mine, was paid a salary of £350 a year, though the corporate revenues at that period were not one-third what they are now, and all the other officials' salaries were paid at a very much lower scale than they are at present. The sub-treasurer then was the present town clerk, and he received £300 a year. Besides, the cashier of the gas works receives £500 per annum, while I, as chief cashier of the borough, receive only £300 a year. The Harbour Commissioners, another of our local boards, pay their chief cashier £450 per annum, though the revenues and disbursements of that body are not much more than one half of those of the Council. In Cork the officer who discharges the duties of the office I fill receives £520 per annum.

3310. Mr. Kenan.—Who is he?—The treasurer.

3311. His duties are not analogous to yours at all. He keeps the whole of the accounts and books of the borough and receives the rates there?—Well, the treasurer of the Dublin Corporation receives £1,000 a year.

3312. Chairman.—I don't think your duties and his are at all analogous. The comparison may be a fairer one with the chief cashier of the Harbour Commissioners or with the cashier of the gas trust?—Well, in the English Corporations the cashier is called the sub-treasurer, and in all towns of the same magnitude as Belfast, the salary is, at least as far as I know, double what I receive. I regret very much to have to enter into this question, but I think it necessary in order to disprove the assertions that the Corporation paid me in acknowledgment of political services, and I want to show that in the responsibility and labour of my office there is sufficient warrant for the increased salary. In my capacity as public officer I have never interfered directly or indirectly with political affairs—that I undertake to affirm if necessary on oath.

3313. Is it true that you ever said to any person that you had been instrumental in returning Sir John Savage to the Council?—If you permit me to follow that in order I will come to that.

3314. Mr. Kenan.—What do you mean by that last sentence that as a public officer you never interfered?—I mean as an officer of the borough in Council there. I have never directly or indirectly, or in any shape or form, interfered with political affairs, but as a citizen and ratepayer I have exercised the rights and privileges conferred upon me by the law of the country.

3315. Chairman.—You say you have not considered it inconsistent with your position as cashier for the borough to take part in elections of members of the Corporation in your private capacity. You draw a distinction between your public capacity and your private capacity. I want to know if you do not consider your rights as a citizen are qualified by your position as cashier of the borough in regard to elections for members of the Corporation?—Certainly not.

3316. Have you, in your private capacity, taken an active part in municipal elections?—No.

3317. Have you in Parliamentary elections?—Well, I have exercised my influence for several Parliamentary candidates, and occasionally for municipal candidates.

3318. Have you taken an active part in ward meetings?—Well, not an active part. I have been on the committees.

3319. Mr. Brien.—Have you proposed candidates?—Never. I have never received any instructions from the Council, or any member or members of the Council, in reference to political matters, nor do they, as far as I know, interfere with or touch political affairs. If you wish me to explain, if there is any difficulty with regard to that, I don't mean to ignore the fact that at ward meetings I may have come into contact with gentlemen in this Corporation who happened to be in the room, but I mean to say that no section of the Corporation have endeavoured to influence me in public affairs as a public officer. I know nothing of, nor did I ever hear of, an inner circle which managed the affairs of the Corporation, and I consider that statement a deliberate and malicious slander. The statement that I or any official ever nominated any alderman or councillor is also devoid of truth.

3320. Do you recollect the occasion on which Mr. John Hamill was proposed?—I will come to that directly. It is also utterly false that I ever stated that I returned Sir John Savage as Alderman, or to any office whatever. That statement is simply a fabrication from beginning to end. I never had a conversation with Sir John Savage, or any other person, in relation to the subject to which Mr. Dunne referred. I never stated to Sir John Savage that I either returned him or caused him to be returned, nor did I ever use language which was capable of such interpretation. I have no doubt that Sir John Savage, when he made the statement, believed it to be true, but if he had conferred with me before he made the statement, I would have given him a most emphatic denial, but not being afforded the opportunity I could not do so.

3321. Chairman.—Did you afterwards correct it?—Well, I wished to have an opportunity for repudiating it; but, acting on the advice of others, and having regard to the fact that I was an officer of the public, I refrained from doing so, though my own inclination was for doing so. Mr. Gaffikin's evidence that I have contributed to put him out of the Council is incorrect.

3222. Did you take no part against Mr. Gaffikin, at the election?—I did not.

3223. Mr. Kenan have read the evidence of Mr. Gaffikin, as to Mr. Coburn's having actively interfered against him of his own knowledge, and having attended ward meetings relative to municipal elections. What reply do you give to that?—I can inform the meeting that the secretary of the Conservative society is here, and has the minutes of these ward meetings, and that will afford evidence that I was not at, and took no part in them.

3224. Chairman.—Mr. Gaffikin was asked how he knew that, and he stated that he saw you present at those meetings?—Well I have attended meetings of the Conservative party, and I have already told you that I have exercised my voting power. I have exercised my political privileges as a citizen.

3225. In respect to the election of members of the Town Council?—In relation to all public officers for all public offices. I would decline to remove any appointment that would deny me that. Mr. Gaffikin, was not put out of the Council. He was not nominated, and he refused to allow himself to be nominated. I was not present at any meeting to nominate candidates, and did not use any influence against him. I may say now that for the last three years, I have not been present at any ward meeting for the nomination of candidates. I don't at all mean to imply by that that I don't consider myself perfectly entitled to do so.

3226. Have you indirectly used your influence to promote the election of one candidate as against another?—Oh, I never considered when candidates solicited the suffrages of a public constituency that as a citizen I was bound to keep silent and express no opinion as to the merits of the candidates. I would consider that a state of political bondage which in a free country could not exist.

3227. Do you mean to say that you record your vote but have not taken any further part in municipal elections?—No, I have not; not by canvassing, otherwise than by expressing to friends my opinions of the parties who were nominated.

3228. Then you have tried to influence other persons as to their votes?—No; if you mean by influence a systematic attempt to influence votes, I say no; but as to a general expression of the merits of the candidates I have done so. I have never considered myself politically dead.

3229. Previously to the last three years had you taken a more active part?—Yes.

3230. Had you canvassed?—Oh yes; I have canvassed in relation to candidates for all public offices. I was going on to say that Mr. Gaffikin stated that I canvassed against him, and my reply to that is this, that if a gentleman retires and does not seek re-election, there can be no canvassing against him. It is reported, and I believe correctly, that one of the principal reasons that he did not wish to be nominated was that he refused to pay the printing and postage of his circulars for his former election.

3231. Mr. Lawless.—I confess I don't consider that material.

3232. Mr. Kenan.—Do you think it right or proper to make that statement against Mr. Gaffikin?—I am stating a fact that is ostensibly the ground on which he was not nominated for the office.

3233. Chairman.—I think you had better not go into that?—Well if a town councillor is so envious or malevolent——

3234. Go on with your statement and do not make such remarks?—If you permit me I will. Another reason that contributed to Mr. Gaffikin's not seeking re-election was because he contested St. George's ward for a vacant aldermanship against a gentleman in town who was the senior councillor for the ward.

3235. What occasion have you for going into this?—Excuse me, I am now endeavouring to defend myself against a very gross, improper, and impudent attack against my character, and if I am not permitted to pursue the course of evidence that I consider necessary, I'll decline to go further.

3236. I simply give you my opinion that it is a most unwise course for you to take?—Well I consider that I am on my defence now. I would also say that besides this Mr. Gaffikin's opposition to the granting of a site for Dr Cooke's statue had so embittered public feeling against him, that in retiring from the Council he made a virtue of necessity. Mr. Gaffikin's statement that he voted for Mr. Dixon's motion to restrict corporate officers from interfering with elections is also incorrect, and instead of voting for Mr. Dixon's motion he voted against it. Mr. Gaffikin also frequently omitted to say that he considered I was quite unpaid, considering the importance and responsibilities of the duties I had to discharge. Subsequently to that he retired from the Council.

3237. Mr. Lawless.—What was the amount of your salary at the time he said that?—Well, I could not say. Mr. Gaffikin made that statement more than once.

3238. Chairman.—When your salary was at £220 there was a question whether it should be £250 or £300. Had you any conversation with him at that time with respect to your salary?—Well, I have stated that I cannot identify the time at which this took place, but I have a clear recollection that more than once Mr. Gaffikin made that statement. With regard to James Larmour's evidence, I will state in how far it is true, and in what respects that witness must have knowingly perverted the facts. I was, as Mr. Larmour stated, a member of the Conservative party, which party employed him. I never personally employed him for work of any kind politically or otherwise in any capacity, and the Chairman of Quarter Sessions held so, and he dismissed his case against me. This man made it a rule to disturb gentlemen in their offices, and he came to me notwithstanding that I told him not to do so in office hours. Mr. M'Master, who accompanied him at the time he alleges he held that interview with me in the car inspector's office, though summoned as Larmour's witness, proved I did not employ him, and he can state that I reproved him for coming to my office on such business. Larmour stated I nominated the late Mr. John Hamill. I never did so, and not being a member of St. Anne's ward committee, could not do so. The nominations for each ward are made by burgesses within the ward.

3239. Mr. Kenan.—Mr. Larmour did not say that you nominated him?—Oh, yes, he said so. He said I nominated the late Mr. Hamill.

3240. No; but he said that at a meeting of the ward committee you proposed that he should be adopted as the candidate?—I did not nominate him, or propose that he should be nominated—I never did so. That also disposes of the statement he makes, that I acted on Sir John Savage's committee. I never was present at a meeting of that gentleman's committee in my life. I was not canvassing for his return, nor did I actively interfere in that contest. He stated that I employed other persons for political work. That statement is grossly untrue. All these persons were employed by Mr. Condon, the secretary of the Conservative society. That I signed notices of parliamentary objections to voters is an unqualified falsehood. If I had done so I would be obliged to go into the Revision Court to prove that, and anyone who is conversant with revision law would know that. He stated that I made returns of street canvassers to the chairman of the meeting. That statement is deliberately false. I challenge him to bring up any such chairman of meeting. In relation to the question put before the Recorder, as to whether I had ever selected or nominated any candidate for the Town Council I declined to answer, and the court ruled I should not answer that question, not that I was afraid to answer it, but I considered it impertinent. But I now most emphatically state I never did so. This man brought his action against me knowing I was a public officer, and hoping to intimidate me on that account into the payment of the money. At the time he sued me Mr. William John Johnston, the hon. treasurer to the conservative society held a receipt in full for all moneys due Lavener by the conservative society. I was simply a member of committee of that society. I never collected money for the conservative party. He said I signed objections against Messrs. E. H. Ward and Thomas Ward. That statement was false. I heard it stated such notices were served, and when I heard it, I expressed, as a member of the conservative party my condemnation of it to the secretary of the society.

3341. CHAIRMAN.—Did you take any part in that?—I never heard of it until they were signed. Mr. Robert Carlisle stated I was present at a meeting where Alderman Mullan was nominated for St. Anne's Ward, where he suggested the name of James Alexander Henderson as candidate. I never was present at such meeting, nor did I ever hear of the turning out of the gas, or the threatened beating of Mr. Carlisle until I read it in this morning's paper.

3342. Mr. *Carlisle.*—I know you were.

Mr. *Colvin*—I claim your protection against the gross impertinence of anyone to contradict my evidence, and I am prepared now to give this evidence on oath.

3343. Mr. *Carlisle.*—Mr. John Stephenson was in the chair at the meeting.

3344. Mr. *Colvin.*—Mr. Carlisle also said that he would be returned for St. Anne's Ward but for the influence I used in favour of Sir John Savage. I have previously stated that I did not interfere in this election, and I never spoke to an individual on the Shankhill-road for or against either of the candidates. I was present at a meeting where Alderman Dr. Alexander was nominated, but I am prepared to prove in the most solemn manner that Mr. Carlisle was not at that meeting, and that he never saw me speak to any one in relation to Dr. Alexander's nomination—in fact no speaking was necessary, there was perfect unanimity on the subject. I may further say that it has been a matter of bewilderment to myself the supposed omnipotence and political influence that has been attributed to me. I never understood myself to exercise such marvellous power in reference to political influence as it appears I possess until I have read the evidence given here; and my own impression is this, that these statements arise from the wildest illusions on the part of the persons who make them.

3345. CHAIRMAN.—Have you finished your statement?—Well, I have no further information to put before you.

JANUARY 6, 1877.

Dr. BROWNE recalled.

3346. CHAIRMAN.—You want to explain something with regard to the way in which the death-rate is taken?—Yes. Mr Kennedy was in error when he said the death-rate was taken on the union at large. It is only taken on the nine districts. The difference of population between the borough proper and the country portions of two of the districts is about 5,000—that is the only difference. The ninth and tenth districts are not all within the borough. In England they allow for the increase of the population from the time the census was taken to the time the public report is made. For last year I took the difference between 142,000 by census of 1871, and the corrected population (203,000) giving a death-rate of 25·1, and in this year we find by the registrar-general's returns that the death-rate is 24·17, which on the corrected population would be 21·33. This you will admit is rather low. It will likely be less than that when we allow for the increase of the population during the last twelve months, which I have not yet done.

3347. What do you say as to the complaint made of the water discharged from a factory belonging to the Messrs. Lindsay, which it was said causes a nuisance outside the lunatic asylum walls?—My attention was never drawn to that, nor was my advice asked about it, and you are aware that it is my duty when a case is reported to examine it, and give my advice about it. It is not my duty to go and inspect all nuisances.

3348. Can you say whether it is a nuisance or not?—I suspect, as the whole of that part was flooded. There was an allegation made which was not correct, namely, that it was no use applying to our office. So far as I am aware no application is ever overlooked. Mr. Smith immediately acknowledges receipt of complaint, and gives notice to the parties against whom the complaint is made, and such matters are always attended to at once.

3349. Have you ever visited that factory of Messrs. Lindsay?—No.

3350. What do you say as to the removal of a quantity of street refuse to Dunville's field?—That was reported to the sanitary committee. Dr. M'Connell was requested to report, and he said it was a nuisance dangerous to the parties crossing the field, and that it ought to be cleansed.

3351. Was his report brought before you?—Yes. I asked the superintendent what was the nature of the stuff they were putting into it, and he said it was simply the scrapings of macadamized roads. Belfast has not a good foundation. In the low-lying districts of Belfast the alluvial deposit is very much like what the road scrapings are.

3352. Ought it not to be covered with concrete?—I do not know much about the use of concrete.

3353. Is it not a very bad sort of foundation?—There is no doubt about that. Nearly all Belfast has bad foundations.

3354. Mr. KAVANAGH.—Supposing it is dangerous to the life of people passing, should not the improvement committee fence it in?—I thought it was fenced in.

3355. Mr. LAWLESS.—Are you aware of a nuisance being caused at the Belfast Royal Hospital by smoke?—Yes. We immediately served notice on the parties, and had it abated, and they promised not to reproduce the nuisance. I am not aware that it has been reproduced since then.

3356. The doctor complained of the nuisance caused by a bakery opposite the hospital, which still exists, and is injurious to the health of the people in the hospital?—They have been noticed to raise their chimneys, which are too low. We have had no complaint, I think, since the month of June. The smoke from it can only affect the hospital when the wind is due west.

3357. Mr. KAVANAGH.—The doctor said they had actually been obliged to refuse to take a certain class of patients into the hospital on this account, and that they cannot open the windows because of the smoke?—I am not aware of that, but the matter has a very simple remedy. The parties must be noticed and made raise their chimneys. There is another point to which I wish to refer—the charge made that I was incompetent—from physical causes, I think it was said, and that I resigned my office in the Belfast hospital from ill-health. I did not resign from ill-health, and I am not aware that I am advanced so far in years as to render me physically incompetent.

3358. CHAIRMAN.—There is also another matter. It was stated by Mr. Carlisle the other day that when you were a member of the improvement committee he took some notice with regard to the sewage, and it was mentioned that you and the borough surveyor frequently transacted business by yourselves?—If you find that on the minutes I'll say it is right.

3359. I want to know if you ever did transact business unless there was a quorum present, and did you ever know the committee fail to meet?—We may have had no meeting in consequence of members not attending, but I think we had generally four members. I never transacted any business without a quorum.

3360. You generally found there were four or five present?—Yes.

3361. Mr. Exham.—Suppose it is a fact that a pipe—a six or nine inch pipe—has been taken from the public sewer and put into the old course of this Fairywell stream to supply a mill below, do you think it would be an arrangement prejudicial to the health of the people?—It depends upon how the water is used.

3362. Mr. Kennedy stated it is boiled up, and that it is used for mills and boilers?—I think any mill-owner would be very foolish to use bad water when he could get clean water. It depends upon whether or not it was sent through the mills, but they must have pure water for spinning purposes.

3363. The complaint is that when four or five mills have used the water it has been taken by a pipe to the public sewer and sent down to another mill, where it is used again?—I should say it is very wrong to do such a thing, and if it is brought under our notice, and the law permits us, we will prevent it.

Dr. M'Cartell continued.

3364. Mr. Exham.—Are you a sanitary officer here?—Yes; for the district in which Donville's field is.

3365. Was your attention called to it by the sub-sanitary officer?—Yes.

3366. Did you examine it?—Yes.

3367. Was it a nuisance at the time you examined it?—It was.

3368. Do you mean merely a nuisance dangerous to people who might walk across the place or a nuisance from the smell?—I mean dangerous to the people who were attempting to go across it. That was my idea at the time I made my report, which I forwarded, calling the attention of the sanitary authority to what was going on. In the summer time I would undoubtedly have reported it as a nuisance dangerous to health.

3369. Chairman.—At every time of the year was it dangerous in the other way?—Yes; and it was a place that people frequently crossed.

3370. Mr. Exham.—Did you see any yard manure put into that place?—I saw something that I thought was yard manure but could not be sure. Unless I went knee-deep into it—I could not examine it minutely. The sweepings of the streets were certainly put there, and it ought to be remembered that there are a good many small houses in the neighbourhood which have not got proper accommodation.

3371. Did you state that in the report?—I did.

3372. Mr. Colligan told us the reports mentioned about the street sweepings?—That was what I intended to convey. That was my idea.

3373. Mr. Colligan also said you told him that you saw yard manure thrown into it?—Yes; my original intention was to call attention to the spot.

3374. Mr. Colligan.—I say that if any three gentlemen in the room visit the place, and afterwards state that there is no yard manure there I will undertake to pay £50 to the Royal Hospital before six o'clock this evening.

Mr. Montgomery re-examined.

3375. Chairman.—You wish to make a further statement?—Yes; with regard to the statement made by Mr. Carlisle that there was some improper influence brought to bear upon me by Mr. Ewart with regard to a shop in Donegall-place about getting a board removed. That statement is altogether false. I hold in my hand a plan which was submitted by Mr. Adam Craig in August, 1870, of alterations to a shop front in Donegall-place. The plan is indorsed and signed "David Taylor, chairman, 17th August, 1870; approved." It was approved by the improvement committee when I was absent on leave, and Mr. Bowland, my assistant, attended the committee, and the plan was approved of by Mr. Bowland, my deputy, during my absence.

3376. Was Mr. Craig the owner of the property where the board referred to was?—Yes; he submitted that plan as the owner of the property. The plan says, "The part coloured red to be devoted to the public." Now, I have ascertained on refreshing my memory by looking over the books, that the improvement committee having had their attention called to a board that ran from one point to another, shutting out from public use what was given to the public by this plan, passed this resolution—"Resolved, that Mr. Robert Carswell be required, within seven days, to remove a certain obstruction recently erected by him, from the public footway in Donegall-place." The obstruction cut off, from public use, a portion of the footway which is the part coloured red in the plan submitted by Mr. Craig and passed by the committee.

3377. Is Mr. Carswell Mr. Craig's tenant?—He is in possession of the shop adjoining that one. It was represented to the committee that the board which formed the obstruction was being removed or repainted—so far as I recollect I heard that it was being removed or repainted, and the committee thought proper to remind Mr. Carswell that this place was their property, and that two years having elapsed the compact ought to be carried out. Mr. Ewart is here himself to deny that we had any correspondence about it.

3378. Had you any communication with Alderman Ewart on the subject?—Never. I think it is plain now there is not a shadow of foundation for the charge. This is really a personal matter. Mr. Carlisle has given me a great deal of annoyance, and I now charge him with malice in the matter.

3379. Was that plan lodged by Mr. Craig in your charge as owner of the property?—Yes.

3380. I asked you to ascertain if it was true that the sewage instead of being carried into the main sewer is carried across to supply water to Alderman Carlisle's reservoir?—I have examined into that since last night. It is from that drain—a very old drain, two feet square, which arose from the spring—a tributary of the Fairywell stream as I thought it was previously crossed by the line of our sewer. That drain was opened and examined and it was seen that it was water, and that it went into the then Fairywell stream which was used by mill-owners, so it was restored and treated as a branch of the Fairywell stream which has also become polluted more or less by the house-drainage from Landscape-terrace. There is an order made for making new drains in Landscape-terrace, for taking the sewage out of that and discharging it into the main sewer, and bringing it into the main sewer.

3381. Mr. Exham.—Why was it not done long ago, and why has this been allowed to go into Alderman Carlisle's mill?

Mr. Ireland.—These works were done seven or eight years since. At the time that water was going down the square culvert it was nearly pure. It is really a branch of the Fairywell stream, although it has become polluted by houses being recently built.

3382. Chairman.—At the time you restored it to connexion with the reservoir was the water in a pure state?—Yes.

3383. Did the sewage from Landscape-terrace go into it?—No.

3384. Mr. Exham.—Did Mr. Montgomery approve of the plan of the sewage going into that stream, which you say you know went into the culvert?—He did.

3385. Chairman.—Do you know how the sewage got into that ancient watercourse?—No.

3386. You knew of the watercourse crossing your main sewer?—Yes.

3387. Were those Landscape-terrace houses built at that time?—They were; some of them were.

3388. Or were in course of building?—Yes.

3389. Was the sewage of any of those houses dis-

Belfast.
Jan. 8, 1877.
Mr.
Montgomery.

charged into that watercourse at that time?—Not to my knowledge.

3290. But you must know or ought to know where it went. You were acting as Mr. Montgomery's deputy?—The water was running pure, and I was not aware of any sewage getting into it.

3291. How did it get into it. It could not get into it without your knowledge?—(No answer.)

3292. Mr. Ewean.—You should have had plans of it. Did you get them?—I don't remember.

3293. Were there houses in Landscape-terrace at the time?—Yes.

3294. Did you ascertain where they drained into before you made this two-foot sewer, and allowed the water to run into the tank?—I was not aware of any drain in Landscape-terrace.

3295. Did you examine and see where the drainage of Landscape-terrace went at the time you were making this new sewer?—There have been a lot of new houses built since, and there is a complaint that the sewage is allowed to be taken into that tank.

3296. Mr. Montgomery.—I admit that the house sewage goes into the stream, and is used by the mill owners.

3297. Mr. Ewean.—The complaint is that the sewage is not kept separate from the Fairywell stream, and that what was at first pure is by that means polluted?—I admit that. I am not aware yet that it goes into the cooler. I have inquired from Mr. Carlisle, and this gentleman has inquired at the factory, and their statement is that they do not use this water. I prepared an order for the making of a new sewer in Landscape-terrace for these houses. That order was printed and published, but legal proceedings arose in that very terrace—there was a suit in the courts in Dublin about it, and owing to one difficulty or another that order has never been carried out. As a matter of fact the order is on the books of the Council, and I am not to blame because it is not carried out.

3298. Chairman.—It has not yet been explained to us how this watercourse has become polluted with sewage matter, and we want you to do so.

3299. Mr. Ewean.—And the reason why it continues to be polluted with sewage matter is because the Corporation who ought to be the prosecutors cannot do so as no jury could convict any person who was prosecuted for polluting the stream, for they would say you polluted it first yourselves?—I am not here to defend the people of Belfast. In every case in which a complaint was sent in you will find in this book a warning that this will ultimately go into one of these systems. Until we get a main system of drainage for Belfast there is no other way of draining the town. We could have done nothing else unless there was a system of drainage for the town.

3300. Supposing that one mill owner — the first on the stream—got the water in a perfectly pure state coming down from the Fairywell. Suppose he indicted the Corporation for putting a sewer from this new street into it, what answer would you have?—All I know is that I am not to blame.

3301. Have you issued your warning rules against this nuisance, and did the Corporation refuse to attend to it?—The fact has been there since I was appointed.

3302. Mr. Black.—The Act of Parliament expressly authorises the Corporation to run the sewage into the streams.

3303. Mr. Ewean.—I think you are in error in supposing that, and Mr. May's opinion is in direct opposition to any such notion.

3304. Chairman.—I ask you supposing the water was pure at first how was it allowed to be polluted with sewage matter?

3305. Mr. Montgomery.—I prepared an order for preventing the sewage of Landscape-terrace from going into it. Difficulties arose about carrying out that order, and I washed my hands clean of those difficulties.

3306. Mr. Welsford (assistant surveyor).—I wish to contradict most positively the statement made by Mr. Dinnen, that I ever approved of the special committee's report on the Blackstaff. That report was prepared quite independently of me, and my opinion was never asked or given. I deny most positively that I approved of it.

3307. Chairman (for Mr. Rea) to Mr. Montgomery.—During the fifteen years of your surveyorship did you ever apply to or know of an application being made to the Water Commissioners for water to flush the sewers of Belfast, or any of them?—No, never.

3308. During these fifteen years did you ever apply or direct an application to be made to the Water Commissioners for water to cleanse any of the filthy courts, lanes, and alleys that you admit have remained in a frightful sanitary condition for the last fifteen years?—I object to the statement in the question. I never made any application for water to cleanse the courts, lanes, and alleys, nor did I ever say that they were in a frightful sanitary condition.

3309. Have you ever been refused water?—No. I never applied for it; it is not in my department; it is in the scavenging department. I cautiously abstained from passing the slightest reflection on the Water Commissioners.

3310. Have you, as the surveyor having charge of the sewers, ever reported to any committee or subcommittee of the Corporation, or to the Corporation itself during the past fifteen years that application ought to be made to the Water Commissioners for water to flush the sewers, and to cleanse the courts, lanes, and alleys of Belfast?—I think I have often suggested that the courts and alleys might be cleansed with water.

3311. Was the suggestion made in writing or verbally, and if verbally, to whom?—It was by verbal communications, and also in the printed report on the general drainage of the town.

3312. Can you say whether or not during these fifteen years, the necessity of flushing the sewers being so apparent, and the necessity of cleansing these places being so apparent (in the summer time at least), you ever wrote a short report to any committee, or subcommittee, saying, "Gentlemen, from what I have seen of these places you ought to make some application for water"?—I have never made a written report in connexion with any department of the Council for which I was not responsible.

3313. Have you suggested that it would be desirable to do so?—I have, frequently. I have not the slightest control over the scavenging department.

3314. Chairman (for Mr. M'Erlean to Witness).—Who is the contractor for the timber supplied to the Town Council?—Mr. Fair.

3315. Who is the contractor for the timber supplied to the gas-works?—I do not know.

3316. Will you undertake to say that the timber purchased by Mr. Fair does not come from a member of the improvement committee of this Council?—I do not know where he gets the timber.

3317. Is not Mr. Fair a small builder convenient to May's-fields?—Mr. Fair carries on business near May's-fields.

3318. What is his business?—He is a builder.

3319. Has he a large business as a builder or a small business?—I am not sufficiently acquainted with his business to say. He is not a famous builder.

3320. Can you say whether or not it comes from a member of the improvement committee?—I do not believe for a moment that it does. I would not take timber coming from a member of the improvement committee.

3321. Do you say it does not come from a member of the improvement committee?—Most decidedly.

3322. Will you undertake to say that the timber does not come from Mr. Brown's yard?—I never followed the timber to see where it came from. It was advertised for publicly in the newspapers, and the committee got tenders sent in. Mr. Fair's was accepted, as I believe he was the lowest.

3323. Mr. Kehoe.—Do you know, as a matter of fact, that his was the lowest?—I am just reminded by Mr. Bradford that it was decided by schedules of estimates. There was some difference of opinion at the committee meeting, and it was decided that Mr. Fair's schedule of prices would come lowest.

3324. Mr. Lawless.—How long is the contract for?—For one year.

3325. Chairman (for Mr. M'Erlean).—Did you ever oppose plans that were afterwards passed in spite of your protest?—Yes, I am quite sure there must have been, because I am sometimes wrong in my advice.

3326. Chairman (to Mr. M'Erlean).—Mr. Montgomery previously stated that the committee were almost invariably guided by his opinion.

3327. Chairman (for Mr. M'Erlean).—When a case of that sort occurred did you take any notes of it?—I think the records show those notes. This book (produced) is the only official one I have. I have no private notes. There is nothing but what is in the official book. I always entered the matter in the official book before it came before the committee.

3328. When you were overruled by the committee did you take any note of it?—I simply drew my pen through my recommendations, and substituted the decision of the committee.

3329. Before you put anything in the official book did you ever make an entry in a private book?—I assure you I have no records but the official book.

3330. Mr. Kehoe.—I see that in one case a plan was approved of and disapproved of in the same day?—People came before the committee with fuller information. Sometimes they made amendments on the plan before the committee, and then it would be passed.

3331. Chairman (for Mr. M'Erlean).—Did you approve of the widening of the Antrim-road in 1874—convenient to Carlisle-circus?—Yes.

3332. At the time you approved of it did you approve of the removal of a portion of a graveyard from where it was, contrary to the Privy Council rules, so as to widen the street?—I know now the case you refer to. I felt it my duty at a meeting of the Charitable Society and the Town Council to call attention to the fact that there might be some difficulty in widening the road at that point, as I was informed that interments were made there many years ago. I mentioned that two or three times, and it was represented to me that the interments had taken place long ago, and were at the same time so few that there would be no nuisance, and no public exception adversely directed to it, and I was led to believe that any human remains which had been there would have vanished entirely, and therefore I ceased to urge my objections any further. There was a very strong feeling in the Charitable Society that the ground ought to be given for the purpose of widening the road, and negotiations had been going on for a long time.

3333. What was the Charitable Society?—A public body, a corporation who have the care of certain lands given for charitable purposes by the Donegall family. It is a sort of alms for poor people of the better class.

3334. Was this graveyard on their premises?—There is a public graveyard on their property, and outside the public graveyard there was a bit of ground that once, I am told, belonged to the county road, and in making improvements many years ago, this bit of ground was walled in, and became a sort of "nobody's land." It seems that at one time (during the outbreak of cholera, I think) some bodies were interred in that vacant ground outside the wall of the graveyard, and I believe the bodies of suicides had also been interred there.

3335. And in consequence of what you heard concerning it, you said it would be impossible to throw it into a public road. Is that what you say?—Yes. At a meeting of the Charitable Society and a deputation from the Town Council, the Charitable Society said they would undertake all the responsibility on that account, and in point of fact this portion of ground was then added to the footway, and while the work was going on some coffin lids or boards, and some human bones were discovered, and they were re-interred in the graveyard.

3336. Chairman.—Not where they were interred before, but inside in the graveyard?—Yes; inside the graveyard. Mr. M'Erlean and some others were opposed to it, and the Corporation were brought before the police court. There was a long trial, and the case was dismissed by the magistrates.

3337. Mr. M'Erlean.—Informations were refused to be granted on the matter.

3338. Chairman (for Mr. M'Erlean to Witness).—Did you approve of the plan for the widening of this portion of the Antrim-road?—I made the plan myself.

3339. Where were the remains removed to?—The churchyard.

3340. Do you know that to be true?—I saw several bones interred in the public graveyard.

3341. And what became of the soil and the coffin lid?—The soil that was taken from it was removed to a hollow place some fifteen or sixteen feet deep. It was tipped there because the hollow place was given to the Corporation for that purpose.

3342. Mr. Lawless.—That was not in the graveyard?—No.

3343. Chairman (for Mr. M'Erlean).—Are you aware that at the time they were removed from that place the boards were damp with human remains?—I cannot say.

3344. At what distance were they and the soil removed to from the residences in [illegible]-park, Lincoln-avenue, [illegible]-street, and all about there?—Two or three hundred feet perhaps. I am not exactly certain, but I'll measure it for you if you wish.

3345. Was it more than two and a half perches from the nearest house?—I think it was about two hundred feet from the nearest house.

3346. Can you say if at the present moment the ground containing the human remains and the coffins is advertised to be let?—I do not know. My impression was that no human remains were there, but only some bones. That is my recollection.

3347. Mr. Kehoe.—When it was removed was the smell offensive?—No.

3348. Chairman (for Mr. M'Erlean).—At the time that offensive matter (as it was considered by many people to be) was removed, who was the sanitary authority in the town?—The Town Council.

3349. And the Town Council did the work?—Certainly.

3350. And in the proceedings in the police court, was not the Town Council the defendant?—Yes, of course.

3351. Mr. M'Erlean.—I'll hand this memorial to Mr. Montgomery to read for you. (Hands same to witness.)

3352. Mr. Montgomery.—(Reads)—"16th December, 1874. We, the undersigned inhabitants on the Antrim-road, believe that the removal of the graveyard soil from where it was, and placing the same in [illegible]-park is a common nuisance."

3353. Chairman (to Witness).—Did you ever see that before?—I dare say I did. It would go to the sanitary committee.

3354. You say there were some bones interred inside the graveyard?—Yes.

3355. Is this a copy of the document sent in?

3356. Mr. M'Erlean.—It is the original document itself.

3357. Mr. Lawless.—I presume the original document would be sent in?

3358. Mr. M'Erlean.—That is it. It bears the original signatures.

3359. Chairman (for Mr. M'Erlean to Witness).—Will you undertake to say that the action of that church did not prove before the magistrates that in making a hollow to remove those bones to, they happened to remove portions of graves outside the graveyard?

3360. Mr. *M'Erlean*.—My contention is that they took portions of the remains out to make room for other remains. Do you not know, Mr. Montgomery, that in so doing the Corporation violated the third subrule of rule three.

3361. CHAIRMAN.—As I understand this was not done by the Corporation.

3362. Mr. *M'Erlean*.—All was done by the Corporation.

3363. Mr. *Montgomery*.—The bones that I spoke of were being interred in the graveyard when I saw them.

3364. CHAIRMAN (to *Witness*).—Did you see any others displaced to make room for them?—When I went there there was a pit dug and the bones were lying in the bottom of it.

3365. Mr. LAWSON.—Was that in the graveyard?—Yes; I saw a good many bones in the bottom of a little square pit, and I do not know a single thing more about it than that. I understand they are all removed from the "Potter's field" into the graveyard—into the consecrated ground.

3366. Did you see more than one place of reception for these bones?—No, only one.

3367. CHAIRMAN (for Mr. *M'Erlean*).—Were you aware that the place made for their reception was formerly a graveyard?—No.

3368. Were you aware that in removing it at all the Council violated rules that they would punish others for violating.

3369. Mr. LAWSON.—That is a question of law; it is hardly fair to put it to him.

3370. Mr. *M'Erlean*.—I myself was the plaintiff in the case, the soil having been left at my very door.

3371. CHAIRMAN (to Mr. *M'Erlean*).—You reside near it?—Yes.

3372. Were you one of the persons who signed this memorial?—Yes.

3373. CHAIRMAN (for Mr. *M'Erlean* to *Witness*).—Would you permit houses, providing the ground was taken for building houses, to be built on the place to which the soil was removed?—I shall certainly object to the building of houses upon any field or ground in which, to my knowledge there is anything unwholesome, or any street sweepings.

3374. Is there any order of Privy Council closing it as an old graveyard?—Yes. It is under the third rule.

3375. Mr. KERNAN.—Is that the one already mentioned?—I cannot say.

3376. Was this graveyard ordered to be closed?—It is an old pestilence burial ground.

SIR JOHN SAVAGE examined.

3377. CHAIRMAN.—I am glad you have come forward to be examined. Your name has been mentioned several times—by Mr. Carlisle, I think—as one of the gentlemen who influenced the Corporation as a millowner, to prevent any improvement being made in the state of the Blackstaff and its tributaries?—There is not a word of the truth in that statement.

3378. Did you ever do so?—No, never.

3379. Are you a millowner on the Blackstaff?—No; not on the Blackstaff.

3380. On the Fairy Well stream then?—I am a millowner on the water going down the Old Lodge-road. It goes down from Mr. Lyons' place.

3381. He said that Sir John Savage's mill, and Mr. Carlisle's bleach works did all the harm?—There are no dye-works in connexion with Mr. Carlisle's place. I believe they bleach yarn, but that would not pollute the water in any appreciable degree.

3382. Do your works discharge water into the Pound Dam?—Not at all.

3383. Have you used any influence in the Corporation to prevent any purification of the Blackstaff?—Neither directly nor indirectly have I ever used the slightest influence for that purpose.

3384. We have had your name mentioned rather more prominently in connexion with Mr. Cobain's salary. In reference to a conversation about his salary?—I do not know that it was a conversation. It happened one day that the mayor was absent from the meeting of the Corporation, and I took the chair in his place—as a matter of arrangement they voted me into the chair.

3385. Perhaps you will tell us what the facts were?—I was aware that a considerable amount of excitement prevailed about Mr. Cobain's salary. I thought Mr Cobain was carrying the matter to an undue extent, in endeavouring to influence the members of the Council to increase what I considered to be a fair salary for the work done. Before I went into the chair, a most respectable member of the Corporation informed me that Mr. Cobain had gone so far as to assert that it was most ungrateful on my part to oppose the proposed increase of his salary, because as he said, he had largely influenced my return as Alderman for St. Anne's ward. I denied the truth of that statement then as I do now, and I said I believed it had no existence in fact.

3386. You do not believe that he had any influence on your return to the Council?—I cannot tell what influence he exercised in a proper way. I believe it would have been in my favour, but I was not aware, nor am I now, that he so influenced the election as to cause my return. I would be ashamed to be the nominee of any man.

3387. Have you read in the newspapers his denial of the statement imputed to him?—Yes, but he draws a very proper distinction about his official and unofficial position.

3388. Mr. KERNAN.—He said it was utterly false that he ever made such a statement to any human being?—I believe the member of the Council to whom I refer.

3389. CHAIRMAN.—He said that if he had had an opportunity to speak to you first, he would have been able to satisfy you that he never said so?—That is quite possible. I believe him to be quite trustworthy in his word.

3390. He said it was utterly false that he ever stated that he returned you or exercised any influence whatever to cause your return to any office, nor did he use language which was capable of such interpretation. He also said he had no doubt that when you made the statement you believed it to be true. Have you made any other inquiries since which enable you to say that you were under a misapprehension?—Not in the slightest degree. I thought it was a proper thing to rebuke him for if it were so, and it was quite open for him to come forward and contradict it, even in the open Council if he chose. I did not make any inquiry about it.

3391. Has Mr. Cobain, with your knowledge and consent, at any time, or to the best of your belief with the knowledge or consent of any member of the Corporation, taken an active part in municipal elections?—I hope not with that of the regular members of the Council.

3392. With any member of the Council?—Well, I can speak for myself, and certainly not to my knowledge, nor with my consent. Such had been alleged against Mr. Cobain before, and immediately after the election I had a conversation with and told him my mind with regard to any official of the Town Council taking the slightest part, are or not, with regard to the return of a member of Council, or doing anything that might bear a partisan or political character.

3393. Was it your opinion that such conduct was to be highly disapproved of?—Yes; I told him so, and said that if he ever attempted such a thing he would certainly lose my confidence and support as an official.

3394. Did he admit that there was any truth in the charge on that occasion?—I could not say as to that. The conversation took place years ago, and I could not say.

3395. Mr. KERNAN.—The other day you were reported as having said that you would be no member

Belfast. Jan. 4, 1877.

Mr. John Savage.

... sentimentality prevent you from doing what you thought was right, and that you met Mr. Cobain in the street, and, like the Priest and the Levite, he turned away from you?—That was said in a playful manner.

3396. Did he pass you by in the street in that way?—I could not say that he did it intentionally.

3397. Mr. Lawless.—You said that Mr. Cobain was carrying the matter a little too far in endeavouring to influence the members of the Council to vote for his increase of salary—was that your opinion?—Well, it was. I am opposed in every case to canvassing the members of the Council, which I thought Mr. Cobain was doing. How far that went I could not say. I regard him as a highly respectable member of the Town Council otherwise, and my advice to him was to abstain from doing anything of that sort.

3398. Chairman.—Was it a question of raising his salary to £350 or £300 a year?—I thought it was going a little too far to raise it so much at once; but as to any parallel between Mr. Turnbull and him, it does not exist, for Mr. Turnbull has fully three or four times the amount of duty to perform, and is a very efficient officer.

3399. And a very old officer?—Yes.

3400. You voted for raising the salary to £300 a year?—I did. I do not wish to force my opinion on other people.

3401. Do you think he is overpaid at £300 a year, considering the moneys that pass through his hands?—I do not know.

3402. If Mr. Cobain had really the power and influence that some people attribute to him of procuring the return of members of the Town Council, do you not think that would give him considerable influence in getting those persons to vote for increasing his salary?—I should not say so with any gentleman of high moral principle.

3403. Mr. Lawless.—Do you remember Mr. Dinnen's resolution, prohibiting any of the officials of the Town Council from interfering in politics?—Yes.

3404. What side did you take in voting on that resolution?—I believe I voted against Mr. Dinnen's resolution upon the grounds that I did not believe they did what was attributed to them. Immediately after that the conversation took place in which I advised Mr. Cobain strongly that if he ever had done so not to attempt it again, or he certainly would not retain my friendship.

3405. Chairman (by Mr. M'Erlean).—At the time the question of salaries was before the Town Council were you of opinion that the increase was unnecessary, they being already fully paid?—I never made such an assertion as that. I was quite willing to pay every man a full salary for the work done.

3406. Did you say that in your opinion they were paid up to their full capacity?—Yes; bearing in mind the duties to be performed.

3407. Did you believe that at the time?—I really cannot recollect all that I said at the time. My impression at the time was, that the increase was uncalled for, but notwithstanding that I submitted to the opinions of others in giving a moderate increase.

3408. Did you agree to a compromise?—I did; undoubtedly I may have taken a view of the fairness of their salaries that was too tight, so to speak, and with the view to not having so large an increase given at once. I may have thought it was uncalled for, but at the same time I was quite willing that every man should be paid up to the full measure of his abilities.

3409. Did you make use of the expression attributed to you in the newspaper report about the servants having the money of the Corporation?—I believe I did.

3410. Mr. Kernan.—Were you of opinion that the Corporation was the servant of the officials?—I had no such idea.

3411. Chairman.—Did you ever see Mr. Cobain at your election, or at any other election, bring in voters, or was he in the habit of bringing in voters?—Never, to my knowledge; I never saw any such thing.

3412. Mr. Kernan.—Mr. Cobain has made wisdom to say that whatever member of the Council told you that he had said it was very ungrateful of you not to vote in favour of increasing his salary, because he had influenced your return as a member of the Town Council, had stated a downright falsehood. I think it is only fair we should have the name of the member of the Town Council who said it.

3413. Mr. Lawless.—Who was the gentleman who told you that Mr. Cobain had made that observation about you? (No answer.)

3414. Mr. Kernan.—You have said it was a member of the Town Council; Mr. Cobain said that whatever member of the Town Council said so made a downright misstatement?—Well, in that case I may as well tell you who he was. It was Mr. Thomas Gaffikin.

3415. Are you aware that for many years mill-owners have taken in the sewage water, and used it in their mills for condensing purposes?—That would be excessively imprudent on the part of the mill-owners if they could get clean water.

3416. Chairman.—Are you inclined to doing it?—Not at all. The upper mill-owner would have it as pure as I have it.

3417. Chairman (for Mr. Roe).—Did you, or did you not, believe at the time you made the speech about the salaries in the Council that three or four persons were in constant communication with Mr. Cobain as to who were the persons in town who should be suggested for nomination to the Conservative committee?—Not at all.

3418. Mr. Lawless.—Do you believe, or do you not, that at any time any person was kept back from being nominated, or that any person brought forward as candidates was put into the Council by Mr. Cobain's influence?—To my knowledge I believe not.

Mr. William Evans.

Mr. William Evans examined.

3419. Chairman.—Your name was mentioned by Mr. Carlisle as one of the persons who influenced the Corporation as a mill-owner to prevent improvements from being made in the state of the Blackstaff. Mr. Carlisle spoke of "gentlemen," and I asked him to give names, and he then mentioned you amongst others?—I read this statement of Mr. Carlisle's yesterday morning, so I came here to ask for an opportunity of giving it an emphatic and distinct denial in every respect. So far from doing anything against the improvement of the Blackstaff, I have at all times done my best to have it improved. I have used my influence in that direction. I believe the Blackstaff is a very great nuisance, and ought to be improved.

3420. Are you a millowner on any of those streams?—Yes; I am a mill-owner on the Glen stream.

3421. Is the water impregnated with sewage matter before it is used by you?—Very little. It comes down from Mr. Girvan's dyeworks, and it is used by Messrs. Johnston, who have a weaving factory there. I do not think there is any sewage matter in it.

3422. Has your influence been directed to the purifying, and not to the pollution, of the Blackstaff?—Yes.

3423. Did you ever try to influence Mr. Montgomery in any way with regard to the removal of a board in front of premises in Donegall-place, of which, I believe you are the landlord?—I never influenced Mr. Montgomery in the slightest degree. I never saw the plan until I saw it here to-day. The statement to which you refer is totally incorrect.

3424. Mr. Kernan.—Are there many houses now above your mill, between your mill and Mr. Girvan's?—There are.

3425. Do you know whether the Corporation allow any of the sewage of those houses to go into your stream before it comes down to you?—I do not know.

3426. Chairman.—Is the stream in a very polluted state in the summer season after it leaves your mill?—No.

3427. Is it in an unfit state for condensing purposes?—No; it is used by some forty concerns after it leaves us. In the most of them the water is boiled—the fine is bubbled, so that it becomes somewhat worse every time it is used. The only cure is to bring in an additional supply of water to save the town from the floods in the winter time, and store it up in the summer.

3428. Does the overflow from the tank, which is the receptacle for the sewage, go into the stream?—Yes.

3429. Mr. *Carlisle*.—What I meant to convey was that by doing the mill-owners influenced the Corporation to prevent the purification of the Blackstaff.

3430. Mr. Lawless.—That was what you meant?—Yes.

3431. Chairman.—Have you made use of Mr. Cobain or been cognisant of any influence used by Mr. Cobain in municipal elections?—Never; I never influenced or was influenced by him.

3432. Mr. Lawless.—Did you ever see his influence or power?—No.

3433. Nor availed yourself of it?—Never.

3434. Mr. *M'Erlean*.—I wish you to put this question. Assuming this gentleman (the witness) to be a member of the Conservative Association, and that Mr. Cobain is also an active member of it, and that none but their nominees are returned as members of the Town Council—did he ever speak to Mr. Cobain upon the subject of elections.

3435. Chairman (to witness).—Have you ever discussed the subject of elections with Mr. Cobain?—I have had political talks with Mr. Cobain, but never any special conversation as to who should be brought forward as a candidate.

3436. Has Mr. Cobain ever been a tool or agent of yours or of any of the members of the Corporation in municipal elections?—Oh, never; I do not believe that Mr. Cobain is capable of anything of the sort.

3437. Mr. Exham.—What Mr. M'Erlean wants to know is—did Mr. Cobain, to your knowledge, actively interfere in municipal elections by canvassing or otherwise?—I do not think he did. A long time ago I had a talk with Mr. Cobain about Parliamentary affairs and the like of that.

3438. Chairman.—We want to know whether or not, to your knowledge and belief, Mr. Cobain, with the cognisance of members of the Town Council, ever took an active part in municipal elections?—Not that I know of.

3439. Chairman (for Mr. *M'Erlean*).—Are you able to say that you never spoke to Mr. Cobain with reference to municipal elections—to the management of municipal elections?—Never.

3440. Has Mr. Cobain ever collected any money from you towards the Conservative Association for political purposes connected with the Town Council?—I do not believe he has ever collected money from me with reference to that object. I do not remember ever giving him any money.

3441. Chairman (for Mr. *Rea*) to witness.—Were you not a member of the Town Council for twenty-five years?—I believe so.

3442. Were you not one of the special respondents in the second information?—Yes.

3443. Chairman.—Are your and Alderman Carlisle's mills within the borough?—Yes.

3444. Have they been at any time exempt from the police rate?—Yes; they are not exempt now. The outside part of the borough was not brought in to be lighted and watched for a long time and we were not taxed, but as soon as the Town Council thought it would pay to bring it in they did so.

3445. When were they brought in?—I do not know; it is a long time ago, more than twenty years ago I think. At the time referred to our mill was in the country; now it is in the town.

3446. Was there a motion made to bring them in?—There was a motion made to extend what is called the lighted and watched area.

3447. But it did not extend to your place beyond lighting?—No.

3448. Mr. Lawless.—When did you commence to pay the police rate?—I do not recollect; a very long time ago.

3449. Was it more than ten years ago?—Yes.

3450. Chairman (for Mr. *M'Erlean*).—Did not the lighted and watched district of the town extend at the time you were not paying the police rates up to your mill?—I believe it did not.

3451. Was it close to it?—I do not know really where it was.

3452. At the time your mill was so exempt, were you not a member of the Town Council?—I was.

3453. Was there any influence brought to bear by you upon your brother members of the Corporation to keep your mill outside the lighted and watched district?—No. The mill at the time may be said to have been in the country; it was a long time ago.

3454. Will you undertake to say that no parties further outside had to pay for lighting and watching?—I just recollect now, that the end of the lighted and watched district did not come near our mill at the time, because the millowners had erected lamps and they did not want it.

3455. Before they took the matter into their own hands, had they to get the consent of the Town Council?—I presume we had. The district was not lighted, because it would not pay to light us. It is twenty years ago and more.

3456. Mr. *M'Erlean*.—That means that the men in the Town Council got permission of themselves to do it.

3457. Mr. *Ewart* (*witness*).—That application with regard to putting up those lamps was made to the gasworks, who had all the power in their own hands, I believe, to open up the streets when it was wanted to put up lamps.

Mr. William Mullan examined.

3458. Chairman.—Are you a member of the Corporation?—Yes. I am senior alderman.

3459. How long have you been a member?—Since 1858.

3460. You are mentioned by Mr. Carlisle as a mill-owner who influenced the Corporation to prevent the purification of the Blackstaff?—I never used any influence directly or indirectly to prevent the purification of the Blackstaff or its tributaries, but on the contrary when I had any opportunity of promoting its purification I did my utmost to have it done.

3461. Have you ever directly or indirectly taken any part through any officer of the Corporation (I mean Mr. Cobain in particular) in influencing the municipal elections?—Never.

3462. Chairman (by Mr. *Carlisle*).—I want to know are you a director of the Brookfield Linen Company, Limited?—I am not now, but I was one of the directors.

3463. Mr. *Carlisle*.—Is he aware that the Brookfield mill is the original polluter of the Pound Burn?

3464. Chairman.—In what way?

3465. Mr. *Carlisle*.—By their mills on both sides. Agnes-street factory is the worst, and also the bleach-works. I wish you would ask the names of the other directors.

3466. Chairman (to witness).—Are you aware that the Brookfield Linen Company, Limited, by their mills are the principal polluters of this stream?—I am not aware of it.

3467. Do you believe that they pollute the Pound Burn otherwise than by taking the water and boiling it and sending it out again?—That I believe is the only way.

3468. Did the Brookfield Linen Company, when you were a member of it, send the sewage into the Pound Burn?—I do not believe they did, except in the case of an overflow of the tank.

3469. Mr. Exham.—Are you aware that there is a tank in the yard into which the sewage from the street higher up is conveyed?—What yard do you refer to?

BELFAST, Jan. 8, 1877.

Mr. William Mullan.

3470. The yard of Hyrne-street factory?—I am not aware of it, nor do I believe it. Of course there is a tank, but I do not believe the sewage goes into it.

3471. We have had it proved here this morning that the houses in Landsdowne-terrace were drained by a piped sewer which leads into a sewer of two feet square, and this discharges into the tank in the yard of the factory?—I am not aware of that. It may be so; it is three years since I was connected with the establishment.

3472. While you were a member of the Brookfield Linen Company were you aware of the source from which the water came into the cooler?—I was not aware.

3473. Was there any influence brought to bear by the company to preserve that old watercourse?—Not that I am aware of.

3474. CHAIRMAN.—Were you aware from what source besides the *Fairy Well* stream the water to supply the mills of the Brookfield company was obtained?—There are concerns owned by the Brookfield Linen Company. The mill proper—Brookfield mill, Agnes-street weaving factory, and another factory. I am aware of the fact that a very large pump or well was sunk on the premises of the company for the purpose of supplying water to the factory.

3475. Was that well to which you refer sunk at the expense of the owners of the place?—Yes, at a great expense.

3476. Did you derive a supply of pure water from that?—Yes, I believe so.

3477. Can you say if that water was used for condensing purposes?—Yes, and after the water has been so used it may be passed back again to the pump and reused for steam purposes.

3478. Would you, as a matter of choice, use sewage water or pure water?—The water to be used for the purpose of getting up steam must be quite pure. I would much prefer cold water.

3479. Mr. LAWSON.—Is it only as a matter of necessity you would use sewage water?—Yes; fully three-fourths of the manufacturing places in the town of Belfast would be compelled to cease working if that kind of water to which you refer was not used.

3480. CHAIRMAN.—Under existing circumstances is it a matter of necessity?—Yes.

3481. How long has the Brookfield Linen Company been formed?—It was formed as a limited liability company about the year 1868.

3482. Mr. *Carlisle* (to Chairman).—Will you ask Mr. Mullan for the names of the directors of the Brookfield Linen Company?

3483. CHAIRMAN (to Witness).—Can you give us their names?—Yes; their names were, Mr. Lindsay, Mr. Harter, Mr. Elliott, Mr. Jaffé, Mr. Smith, Mr. Riddel, Mr. Simms, Mr. Carlisle, and myself. Messrs. Carlisle, Smith, Simms, and I were directors. There was a statement made before you here about the existence of an "inner circle," or managers of the Corporation. Will you permit me now to say that I am not a member of any "inner circle" or managing party connected with the Corporation. I know of no such "inner circle" existing in the Belfast Corporation, nor was I ever aware of it.

3484. WITNESS.—Will you permit me to correct the names of the directors of the Brookfield Linen Company. They were myself, Mr. Harter, Mr. Simms, Mr. Elliott, Mr. Jaffé, Mr. Smith, and Alderman Carlisle was managing director. I was really puzzled as to what evidence had been given about the tank in Agnes-street. I have inquired and find that no sewer passes into the tank, and Alderman Carlisle will prove it. The supply from the tank has been long discontinued, and the water used for steam purposes is the water procured from the well on the premises.

3485. CHAIRMAN (for Mr. *Rea*).—Did you vote for a salary for the first time to Mr. Lytle as mayor of £1,000, in his second year's mayoralty?—I did.

3486. Was that after Mr. Lytle had been for two years in litigation with Mr. Rea?—I do not remember.

3487. Were you the person who moved it?—No, sir, I was not, nor do I remember taking an active part in that.

3488. Do you remember the ground on which it was voted?—I do; it was in the ordinary course of business.

3489. Do you recollect that before the salary was voted Mr. Lytle complained that he was being ruined by the litigation that Mr. Rea was carrying on?—I do not, and I believe he never did.

3490. Do you recollect that some time after the salary was voted to Mr. Lytle he died in very poor circumstances?—Mr. Lytle died, and I know something of the circumstances, and I believe the whole statement is erroneous.

3491. Do you know that before Mr. Lytle died, and before the salary was voted, he complained bitterly through the town that the Lindsays had betrayed him, for that they had induced him to file an information to attack their opponent, and that a salary would never have been voted if a subscription had been raised?—I can say, sir, most distinctly, it is the first time I ever heard of a subscription being got up for such a purpose, and I know of no man who would more emphatically have repudiated any contribution of the kind than Alderman Lytle. I have been his friend, and we were boys and came to Belfast together fifty years ago. I never heard from him that he expected any contribution to pay his expenses, and I know that his first year's salary, the salary spoken of, was given freely and voluntarily by him without solicitation towards the erection of the Albert Memorial which adorns this street here.

3492. Was that salary voted to indemnify him for the expenses he had been put to?—Not in the slightest degree.

3493. Do you know whether or not there was a subscription got up or tendered to Mr. Lytle?—I never heard of it.

3494. Why didn't Mr. Lytle get the £1,000 the first year when he was appointed mayor, and why did you vote for the £1,000 the second year after Mr. Lytle was put to those expenses by litigation?—I never heard it was on account of those expenses.

3495. Was the question raised the first year?—Not that I recollect.

3496. What was the ground on which you voted for the salary when it was so many years in abeyance?—The question was discussed for a long time, and the members of the Corporation found that mayors were paid elsewhere, and it was considered by the majority of the Corporation that the mayor should not out of his own private purse pay expenses and outgoings which were for the benefit of the general public. These were the grounds.

3497. Was the question mooted during the previous years?—I cannot recollect, but I think it was mooted for a long time.

3498. Was it ever put to a vote?—No, never, except in the case of Sir William Gilliland Johnston, there was a vote when the Queen came here.

3499. But why did they not vote a salary in 1872, 1873, 1874, 1875, or 1876 during which years some of the expenses were far heavier than before that?—The chief reason was that the general public disapproved of it, and it was in deference more or less to public sentiments, and not because of any conviction that they hadn't the power to do it, or that it was not a right thing to do under the circumstances.

3500. Was this salary not received by Alderman Lytle, Alderman M'Causland, and Councillor Frederick Harry Lewis?—Yes, it was.

3501. Had all these three persons been engaged in litigation with Mr. Rea?—Alderman Lewis was special respondent, and Alderman M'Causland was.

3502. Do you know of your own knowledge whether Noah Davis had actively interfered in the municipal elections?—I don't know that.

3503. Do you recollect whether at the time the twenty whigs were brought into the Council, as mentioned in the evidence before the select Committee on the Award Bill, it was with a view to their being instrumental in preventing the reimposition of the 1s. 6d. rate on premises above the value of £20?—I don't believe it, and I am perfectly satisfied that it is not true in fact.

3504. After this change in the political constitution of the Corporation, was there a meeting of the Council in committee to consider the rating question?—I don't recollect.

3505. Do you recollect that instead of the 1s. 6d. rate being reimposed, a resolution was passed unanimously by the Town Council in private that the 1s. 6d. rate should be doubled?—I don't, and I don't believe it.

3506. Do you know of any practice of charging to the general purposes rate what should be charged to the differential police rate?—I do not know that, and I believe that the rates are properly struck with a right intention according to the Act and duly applied.

3507. Mr. Lawson.—Have the Council relied on their want of funds to prevent improvements?—The Council have relied partly on the want of funds, but chiefly on account of the difficulties in the way of abating that nuisance. When the Sanitary Act of 1866 was passed, it gave the Corporation more powers, and the Corporation devoted their attention to abate that nuisance, and Mr. Montgomery's report was the result, and it will give you much more information than I can. That report was brought forward with an honest and sincere purpose to use every effort to abate that nuisance. In 1870 the Corporation applied for an Act, and they were compelled to withdraw it from pressure, and members of the Corporation—myself and others—had to pay the preliminary costs.

3508. Chairman.—What was the purport of that Act?—It was chiefly to deal with the Blackstaff and other nuisances. It was withdrawn.

3509. Was it thrown out upon Mr. Rea's opposition?—I believe it was withdrawn in consequence of pressure from without, urging that the sum of money required in dealing with matters of so great moment was too large, and should not be incurred, and would press too heavily on the ratepayers. The action that was taken in 1866 has been continued to the present day. One of the first things that was done was to consult the first engineer in London, and also Mr. Rawlinson, to assist Mr. Montgomery in dealing with a question of such magnitude. Every proposal that was brought forward in 1868, and re-reported upon in 1870 and 1878, has been kept constantly before the attention of the Corporation, and the carrying out of that scheme has involved a cost of about £20,000 incurred by the Corporation in carrying out those principles. I may mention that district drainage was one part of the scheme, and they resolved, when they could not get the powers they sought in the bill of 1870 to deal with such matters as the law enabled them to do, and go on with the outer drainage. The outer drainage involved an area of about 3,333 acres on the Antrim side, and the portion on the county Down side involved an area of 410 acres. The low level drainage which has not been touched, owing to the great expense likely to be connected with it, and the difficulties of its outflow, and other matters of that kind, has not been entered upon, nor has the intercepting high level sewer, but the whole works that have been going on from 1870 to the present time have been with a view to abate the Blackstaff nuisance, and to bring the whole system into one harmonious scheme with the drainage of Belfast, to put it into the most perfect form.

3510. The following extract of proceedings of Council in committee, 5th January, 1861, asked for by Mr. Rea, was then read:—

"Moved by Colonel Rollestony, seconded by Alderman Ewart—'That the Council approve of the proposition No. 1, that the present mode of raising money should be abolished by the proposed Bill, and that in lieu thereof, a uniform percentage rate not exceeding 2s. in the pound should be levied upon all tenements within the lighted and watched districts of the borough.' Carried unanimously."

3511. Chairman.—Do you remember that?—I recollect when that took place.

3512. Was that resolution confirmed at a public meeting of the Council?—I don't know, but I know it is well understood that every resolution in committee requires to be confirmed in public by the council.

3513. The following extract of meeting of Council in committee was next read:—

"5th January, 1864. Moved by Councillor Bell, seconded by Councillor Savage—'That instead of the proposition adopted by the Council on the 5th February, 1861, by which the rate that was to be submitted to the arbitrators, that a uniform 2s. rate should be levied on [illegible] of the present mode, the solicitor be instructed to submit to Mr. Conybeare, that inasmuch as circumstances render it impossible for the Council to obtain evidence before the arbitrators in favour of the amplified scale, they are prepared to satisfy the aforesaid [illegible] by conceding that the additional funds required for the purposes of Mr. Conybeare's award should be raised by an additional rate upon the present scale, but not on that proposed by Messrs. Bryson and Wyatt.'"

"Moved by Alderman Lindsay, seconded by Councillor Dalles, as an amendment: 'That in the absence of a general measure to organise the sewerage and [illegible] of the town, and the area to be assessed for sewerage purposes, the Council deem it expedient that the resolution of the 5th February, 1861, recommending the imposition of a uniform rate not exceeding 2s. in the pound, be rescinded, and that the solicitor, instead thereof, be authorised to propose to Mr. Conybeare, that the additional funds required for the purposes of Mr. Conybeare's award be raised by a separate and uniform poundage rate not exceeding 6d. in the pound.' The meeting broke up without either the resolution or amendment being put. James Lytle, mayor."

3514. Was that resolution of 1861 confirmed at the next public meeting of the Council?—I have no recollection.

3515. The Town-Solicitor having produced the minute book said—The only reference I find to that resolution at the public meeting in February, 1861, is this—

"The town clerk read the report of the Council in committee, 5th January.—Moved by Alderman Lindsay, seconded by Councillor Ferguson: That the report now read be referred for consideration to a special meeting of the Council to be held on Wednesday next at twelve o'clock."

3516. Is it true that instructions were sent to the town solicitor then in London to act on the authority of that resolution passed only in committee?—I don't know that, but I would say that whatever was done was communicated to the solicitor. The solicitor knew what took place.

3517. Do you know whether the passing of that resolution involved, as Mr. Rea suggests, a transfer of a quarter of a million of money from one class of ratepayers to another?—I don't know, but I am satisfied it never amounted to a tenth of the sum named. The differential rate was often discussed and continued, but the lower rate is exceedingly small in comparison with the higher rate on the amount of the valuation on which it is levied. It is not more than one-tenth of the valuation upon which the higher rate is levied.

3518. What would have been the result of that transfer to the various classes. I don't think it would have been very much. The small property valuation compared with the higher class I don't suppose is more than one-tenth.

3519. Would it not increase the taxation of the small householders?—Of course it would.

3520. And diminish the taxation of the richer people?—Well, of course it would to some extent.

3521. Have you any recollection of an affidavit being ordered to be lodged from the Corporation for the arbitrators in London as a reason why the 1s. 6d. rate should be made 2s.?—I have no recollection of it, but I have no doubt I could refresh my memory on the point. I have a distinct recollection of this, that during those proceedings it was incessantly urged that the Corporation was exclusively partisan, and of one class of politics, and it was so frequently urged that the special [illegible], the Conservative party, who were the great majority, had everything in their power, that by mutual consent and in order to meet exceptional circumstances, and not by any private arrange-

BELFAST. Jan. 4, 1877. — Mr. William Hellen.

[illegible] for any corrupt purpose, it was agreed that twenty gentlemen, Liberals in the strictest sense, most respectable gentlemen, should form, with twenty other members, the Corporation for the time being of Belfast. It was not with a corrupt view it was done, but to remove an oft-repeated objection that was made.

3522. Is it true, as alleged by Mr Rea, that that arrangement with regard to the return of the Liberals was carried out by Noah Davis, and the other officers of the Corporation, by the orders of the Corporation?—It was not carried out in that way, but it was carried out with the full consent and approval of the gentlemen—Liberals—the most distinguished and honourable men assenting and consenting to take the places of those retiring.

3523. From the time you became a member of the Corporation was there any arrangement made by you or other members of the Corporation with your knowledge, or to the best of your belief, that Noah Davis or any other officers should arrange the elections in the way referred to by Mr. Rea, or should arrange the elections at all?—There was not any such arrangement that I know of, and I believe no such arrangement was put into operation. I am perfectly satisfied that Noah Davis was never employed by the Corporation or by leading members of it to pack the Corporation in any way or form.

3524. You were a member of the Corporation then?—I was.

3525. Do you believe, from the part you took in the affairs at that time, that the arrangement was carried out through the instrumentality of the officials of the Corporation, and with the cognisance and approval of the Corporation?—No; it was not, as far as I know, with their connivance or approval, or at their instance.

3526. Did you, or any individual member of the Corporation, ever instruct Davis to have these returns arranged in this way?—I never did; nor am I aware that any of the officers of the Corporation were so employed by any member of the Corporation, and I believe the arrangement was come to at a public meeting that was held in Belfast, to which both parties were invited. I am satisfied that it was the result of public opinion, and that these gentlemen accepted office with a view to a settlement of the Chancery difficulties, of which the entire public were thoroughly sick and disgusted.

3527. Was Noah Davis then an officer of the Corporation?—No; I believe he was not. He was in the employment of the Conservative Society.

3528. What was the year in which that arrangement was made?—I think it was in 1855.

3529. Mr. Lawless.—Are you able to say how long they continued to be members of the Corporation?—I cannot say.

3530. Is it true that they resigned their seats soon after on the ground that the terms of the arrangement had not been carried out?—I don't remember that.

3531. Mr. Ewart.—Did they resign their seats?—Well, I think some of them did; but I understood that it was only a pro tem. arrangement with a view to a general settlement.

3532. Mr. Lawless.—Was it soon after that some of these twenty were resigned?—Well, it was possibly that year or soon after.

3533. Were there any of them put out in a contest?—I think not, sir.

3534. Did they all resign?—Oh no, sir. I was always considered to be one of the party. Some of them stayed in.

3535. Chairman (for Mr. Rea).—Is it true that it was when this party were out, this business of the Mayor's salary was first projected?—They were not all out.

3536. Was that compact existing in any form whatever when the vote was passed for the Mayor's salary?—I find a large number of Liberals still remaining in the year 1855—Mr. Charles Duffin, Mr. William Coates, Mr. Alexander Crawford, Sir Edward Coey, and some others.

3537. Mr. Ewart.—Was there any division on the question of the Mayor's salary when it was introduced?—I don't recollect. The minute book will tell that.

3538. Chairman (for Mr. Rea).—Were you one of the Mayors who received the £1,000?—I was, in 1866.

3539. Mr. Ewart.—Do you believe that Dr. Browne was given £800 a year for any improper motive?—I do not.

3540. Chairman (for Mr. Rea).—Do you know that the increase of the lower rates has very much deterred builders from building small houses for the artisans?—I don't know that, and I don't believe it.

3541. Are you aware that there is a project before the Corporation to build houses for artisans, that were formerly built by building speculators?—There is a proposition before the Council with a view to carry out the Artisans' Dwellings Act.

3542. Do you know that whenever the conduct of the rate collectors was impeached, it was always stated in their behalf that the collectors could not have done better, and that the disfranchisement of voters was attributed to the fault of the parties themselves?—I don't know.

3543. Are you aware of the fact that the rates are now so well collected that there are only fifteen or twenty disfranchised where formerly there were 800 or 1,000?—I believe they have been stimulated very much by the frequent committee to collect the rates, and that they make every effort.

3544. Were the Corporation as desirous from 1842 to 1865 to collect the rates as they have been since?—I believe they were.

3545. Were the rules for the collectors passed in 1865?—Yes.

3546. Were there any similar rules previous to 1865?—I am not sure that there were.

3547. Were there not any by-laws prescribing the duties of collectors before 1865?—I think they were enlarged and extended to suit the circumstances of the case.

3548. Were the rate collectors remiss in collecting the rates with the approval of the Corporation?—So far as I know, they were not. I was not a member of the finance committee.

Questions suggested by Mr. M'Erlean.

3549. Chairman.—Is the Corporation divided into two parties now?—It is not.

3550. Are all the officers of the Corporation members of the Conservative Society?—Not that I am aware of. I have never subscribed to that society, and I am sure other members of the Corporation, such as Mr. Hughes, Mr. Orr, and Mr. John Greenhill have never contributed one farthing.

3551. Is any money that is subscribed to the Conservative Society used to promote the election of members of the Corporation?—No, not that I know of.

Mr. J. S. W. De Courcy, borough cashier, was then re-examined.

3554. Chairman.—I want to ask you a few questions upon the evidence which you gave. You said you had never received any instructions from the Council, or any section of the Council, in reference to political matters. Do you adhere to that?—Yes, I still affirm that.

3555. Did you ever receive instructions to take part in political matters?—No.

3556. Have you ever, or has any official, to your knowledge, ever nominated any alderman or town councillor?—I have never done so, and I am not aware of any others having done so.

3557. Have you taken part as a member of the committee of St. Anne's Ward with reference to the election of Sir John Savage or Mr. Hamill?—No; I never was present at any committee meeting in reference to Sir John Savage's election, nor was I a member of St. Anne's Ward committee.

3558. Do you reside in St. Anne's Ward?—No, I reside in Cromac Ward.

3559. Have you ever taken any part in any committee meeting of any ward except the one you reside in?—Oh, yes; I have been present at the meetings of Dock Ward committee when resident in that part of the town.

3560. Have you canvassed for the return of members to the Town Council?—Yes.

3561. In any ward except that in which you are resident?—I have not canvassed in the ward in which I am resident, but I did in Dock Ward some years ago.

3562. In any other?—No, not in any other. I was resident in Dock Ward then, and have property in it.

3563. Since you ceased to be resident there, have you taken any part in municipal elections?—No.

3564. Did you, while you were an officer of the Corporation, take part in the elections for Dock Ward?—Yes, I did; but I was going on to say that my position did not contribute to my political influence.

3565. Did you ever, in conjunction with Mr. Noah Davis or any of the collectors, obtain lists of the wards for the purpose of facilitating a canvass of them?—The canvassing lists were prepared in the committees of the various organizations, whether Liberal or Conservative, and any citizen who wished to promote the candidature of any gentleman who was seeking a seat could obtain canvassing lists in those rooms.

3566. Were those lists made out by you or the collectors?—Certainly not.

3567. Or by any officials of the Corporation?—Certainly not.

3568. Did you, in your position as an official, obtain them?—No, certainly not.

3569. Have you ever collected money in any shape or form from members of the Corporation, or from any brother officials, for the purpose of promoting the interests of the candidates whom you favoured at the municipal elections?—Certainly not.

3570. Or in any way been a party to paying the expenses of those elections?—No, not in any form.

3571. Were you in court yesterday when Sir John Savage stated that Mr. Gaffikin was the gentleman from whom he heard the matters which he stated—viz., that you said you had been instrumental in promoting his return, and that you thought it ungrateful in him to oppose your increase of salary? Can you undertake to say whether that is the case?—I can undertake to say that at the time of the alleged conversation between Mr. Gaffikin and Sir John Savage, owing to a misapprehension on the part of Mr. Gaffikin that I was opposed to his election, he was not then on speaking terms with me, and the feeling of coldness between Mr. Gaffikin and myself was augmented by the fact that several scurrilous communications were published in the Whig newspaper——

3572. Well, we need not go into that. What I want to know is the fact whether you held any conversation with Mr. Gaffikin on the subject?—I did not in any way, directly or indirectly.

3573. Did you not speak to him with reference to the question of your salary or Sir John Savage's statement?—Never.

3574. Did you ever state to anybody that you returned Sir John Savage or caused him to be returned?—I now state most emphatically that I had no such conversation with Mr. Gaffikin or any other person.

3575. Or any other person?—No, nor have I ever used language capable of such interpretation. The whole thing is a fabrication.

3576. Have you ever directly or indirectly had it suggested to you to take, or have you taken, part in the municipal elections under suggestions or directions of any members of the Corporation?—Never.

3577. Have you been the instrument of any member or members of the Corporation in promoting the candidature of one Town Councillor over another?—Not in the slightest degree. I have far too much self respect to allow myself to be made a political tool of by any member of the Corporation.

3578. Have you canvassed individual members of the Council to vote for an increase of your salary?—Well, I have spoken to members of the Corporation on that subject.

3579. Have you in any way or at any time grounded those applications for increase of salary upon the basis that you rendered political services?—Never, and I would scorn to do so.

3580. Have you based your application on any other ground than the increased duties of your office?—Never.

3581. Mr. Lawless.—Was the Conservative society of which you are a member confined to any particular ward?—No, it was general.

3582. And, therefore, the exertions of the active members of it would naturally diverge into any ward?—Well, no; the operation of the organization is such that each ward has a committee, and the action of the members of committee would apply to the ward in which they were immediately situated.

3583. Were you on the committee for any ward?—I was a member of the committee of Dock Ward, and subsequently of Cromac Ward.

3584. When you were resident in Dock Ward were you a member of the committee?—Yes.

3585. Were the duties devolved to you as a member of the committee to be exercised within that ward?—Well, they were not in any way duties.

3586. Did you exercise political influence in your individual capacity only as a member of society and a citizen, or did you exercise whatever influence you could as a member of the committee for your ward?—I have stated that I exercised the privilege of a citizen, but I think it would be inaccurate to say that I exercised it in a political or partizan sense.

3587. Did you exercise it with reference to the return of members to the municipal body?—Yes; I have supported the candidature of gentlemen irrespective of political or religious feeling.

3588. Have you canvassed for some members of the Corporation as against others?—Yes.

3589. Do you say you did that only in your exercise of your privileges as a citizen?—Yes.

3590. Was it not well known that you were an officer of the Corporation?—Yes; but I conceive that that does not preclude the rights of citizenship.

3591. But you could not divest yourself of the fact of your being an officer?—Well, a man has two identities.

3592. But he generally carries both about with him?—Well, I never conceived that I was precluded from the exercise of my rights.

3593. This action was brought against you in November, 1874. I don't find in the report of the case that the receipt that was produced here, signed by Larmour, to Mr. William John Johnston, was produced?—It was produced in court, but the fact is not reported in the papers.

3394. Was not your defence that you hadn't contracted to pay him?—That is perfectly true; but this document was produced in court as collateral proof that the man was paid by the society.

3395. I cannot accept that statement; am I right in taking that report of the newspapers to be correct that Mr. Larmour's civil bill was dismissed without prejudice?—That is not my understanding of the case. It is reported in the *Ulster Examiner*.

3396. It is reported in the *Whig* that his Worship dismissed the case without prejudice, and that leave to the plaintiff in the case the right to bring another action if he pleases. That could not be the case if the receipt had been produced. That is, as I conceive, an interpretation of law.

3397. If it was not produced in answer to his demand there, why is it produced by you here?—It was produced in court, and the solicitor can prove it.

3398. Mr. Kernan.—I assure you that if this report in the papers be accepted as correct, any lawyer would say that the trial proceeded on the assumption that he brought the action against the wrong man; and I may further add that if the receipt had been produced at the trial it would have been received by the officer of the court.

3399. Mr. Lawless.—Was it known to the Corporation that you took a part in municipal elections?—I presume so; I have no reason to infer otherwise.

3400. Mr. Kernan.—Have you a doubt on the subject?—I have not the slightest doubt.

3401. Then why do you not say so? It is a curious answer to say, "I presume so," when the next moment you say you have not the slightest doubt of the fact.

3402. Mr. Lawless.—You stated on the day you were first examined that for the last two or three years you didn't take as active a part as formerly. Is that so? Yes; I stated the other day that for the last three years or so I had not been as constant an attendant at ward meetings as before, and that arose rather from a change of taste than from any abnegation of civil rights.

3403. It does, however, tally with the proceedings before the assistant barrister?—Well, the case took place at the time that I was interesting actively with my society.

3404. Chairman.—Do you mean that you ceased previous to or after the action?—I mean previous to.

3405. Mr. Kernan.—How long previous? When was the election of Councillors after which you ceased to take an active part?—I cannot recollect how long it is since.

3406. Mr. Lawless.—Are you able to say whether you took any part in the preparations for the election of November, 1874?—No; I believe not.

3407. Are you quite certain?—Well, I am almost morally certain that I did not.

3408. Mr. Kernan.—Did you in 1873?—I cannot charge my recollection.

3409. Chairman (handing newspaper).—Is that correct?—I presume so.

3410. Mr. Lawless.—Did you pay the costs of that journey before the chairman?—I did not; because the professional gentleman declined to accept a fee.

3411. Was the solicitor an officer of the Corporation?—No. It was Mr. M'Lean, the sessional crown solicitor.

3412. Is he the Mr. M'Lean who receives the salary from the Corporation?—No; certainly not; he is the father of that gentleman.

3413. Mr. Kernan.—Were you present at any ward meeting when there was more than one candidate nominated?—Very likely.

3414. Did you take part in voting for one candidate against another?—I cannot charge my recollection of having done so; but I am sure if I was present and if a vote arose or occasion for it, I would exercise my right, but I cannot charge my recollection.

3415. Did you ever nominate or support the nomination of a candidate yourself?—That I most positively deny.

3416. Do you recollect the occasion on which Mr. John Hamill was nominated?—Yes; I do.

3417. How many members were present at that meeting?—I could not say.

3418. Mr. Larmour said that there were five; was he right?—I cannot recollect; I think there were a considerable number present.

3419. Do you recollect the fact of a division taking place, some being for Mr. Hamill and some against him?—I believe I was not present at the time the division took place. The man who proposed Mr. Hamill was in court on Saturday last to give evidence.

3420. Were you present?—I was present; but not being a member of St. Anne's Ward Committee, I had no right to take part in the consideration of that question.

3421. Why were you present if you were not entitled to be there as a member of the committee?—I was there during the evening.

3422. Did you in your capacity see officers paid for their services in that society?—I don't apprehend your question.

3423. Do you not know that persons were employed to canvass by the society?—I know of no such case.

3424. What was the £67 paid to Larmour for?—He was an inspector.

3425. Have you ever used your influence to get inspectors paid?—Yes; the influence of a member of the committee like another.

3426. Have you been present when Larmour came in and gave returns of his canvassing?—I never recollect being present when he gave returns.

3427. Were you present when any other men gave them in?—Well, each ward had a separate committee, and he belonged to Anne's Ward, and I belonged to Dock Ward.

3428. How often did the committee of your own ward meet?—The meetings were only exceptional and occasional.

3429. Were you present when the canvassing lists were brought in from your own ward?—It was not customary to do so.

3430. It was stated that some town councillors knew that you were in the habit of interfering with elections. Is that so?—Yes.

3431. Do you recollect when Mr. Dinnen moved his resolution?—Perfectly well.

3432. Do you recollect that it was said then that it was not a fact that any of the officers interfered with the municipal elections, and that that was the reason it was not passed?—I was not present, but I think that was the ground on which it was decided to negative it.

3433. Mr. Lawless.—How can you tell when you were not present?—Well, from the newspaper reports.

3434. Mr. Kernan.—Is it a fact that your solicitor objected to a question before the Recorder as being impertinent?—The question was as to whether I had nominated candidates for the Town Council.

3435. Mr. M'Erlean asked this question before the chairman—"Have you, as a matter of fact, taken part in the nomination of members of the Town Council?" and the answer you gave was, "Not as an officer of the Corporation, but as a citizen I have"?—I am not disposed to accept the statement in the newspapers as correct.

3436. Is that a correct report?—Well, it conveys an incorrect impression.

3437. Did you swear that, or did you not?—I have no recollection of swearing it. If the question was put in this form—"Had I been present at the nomination," unquestionably I would say I was present, not in my official capacity, but as a citizen. If it implies that I had myself nominated, I would give that a decided negative.

3438. There can be no mistake as to the question put?—But there can be a question as to the accuracy of the report.

3439. Do you undertake to say that the report is untrue?—It is an exceedingly difficult thing at the lapse of three years to say whether a newspaper report of a trial is correct, and I would not feel myself bound to state whether it is an accurate report or not.

3440. I am not saying whether you are bound or not?—Well, I think from the hearing of that answer as you have read it, I never gave it, and therefore the report is, I think, inaccurate in that particular. It conveys a wrong sense altogether.

3441. The answer is "Not as an official, but as a citizen I have"?—Well, I have given my answer, and I cannot make it clearer.

3442. Chairman.—If you were asked whether you had yourself nominated or taken an active part in pro-

[illegible]
Mr. E. S. W. [illegible]

opting the nomination of any one, what would your answer be?—My answer would be a negative to that, because neither as an officer nor citizen did I do so.

3643. Then am I to understand that the extent of your interference has been voting and being present at the committee meetings, and canvassing in your particular ward?—Yes.

3644. Have you neither nominated nor taken an active part in nominating?—No; but I consider it perfectly lawful for me to do so, if I please.

3645. Was Larmour connected with your ward?—No.

3646. Did you interfere on his behalf or otherwise?—Allow me to explain. This man Larmour was an agent of the society which had various ramifications. It had committees for various wards, and he was agent for St. Anne's Ward, and I was member of committee for another ward, but the organization is all one. As a member of the committee and a member of the organization I advocated this man's payment as well as the others.

3647. Here is your letter, you say—"While you were an inspector for the Conservative Society I did all in my power to have your services recognised in the most liberal way"?—That is true.

3648. Then you did use your influence to get that man paid?—Yes; unquestionably.

3649. *Questions suggested by Mr. M'Erlean.*—Is that a copy of the rules of the Ulster Conservative Association?—I presume so.

3650. Do you know what has become of the books of that association?—No; I have not the slightest idea.

3651. CHAIRMAN (handing rules).—Have you ever seen that document before?—I don't recollect.

3652. MR. EXHAM.—Do you know James Connor, the inspector?—Yes.

3653. Was he an inspector for Dock Ward?—Yes.

3654. Were you on the committee when he was inspector?—Yes.

3655. Were there members of the Corporation on that committee?—I presume so.

3656. Look at this document now and see if there were?—Well this is the committee for 1869, and my memory is not so capacious as to recollect. I don't think any man living could recollect what was done seven years ago.

3657. CHAIRMAN.—Were there members of the Corporation on it seven years ago?—Yes; it appears so.

3658. MR. EXHAM.—The tenth rule of this society, the Ulster Conservative Registration Association, says—"The entire management of the parliamentary and municipal revision of the borough of Belfast, and all matters appertaining thereto, shall be left to the executive committee aforesaid, who shall be at liberty to pay the solicitor, the inspectors, and others casually employed by them, such salary or salaries as shall be stipulated by agreement." Do you know that rule?—I have no recollection of that rule. That society was not long in existence.

3659. How long was it in existence?—I think only for six or eight months, and I was not certain until I saw that document there now, that I was on the committee.

3660. And do you see that the seventh rule is—"The committee of each of the wards shall have the nomination of candidates for the offices of Town Councillors, Harbour Commissioners, Water Commissioners, and any other public body in the borough"?—That is a provision of all such organizations.

3661. Was there any other society that took its place afterwards of a similar character?—Oh, yes, there was.

3662. And does that continue still?—Well, there was another succeeded it, and there was another succeeded it again.

3663. All with the same object?—Yes.

3664. CHAIRMAN.—And the same rules?—Well, I am not aware, but party organizations have party rules.

3665. There is similar rule. "The committee of each of the wards shall have the nomination of candidates for the offices of Town Councillors, Harbour Commissioners, Water Commissioners, and any other public body in the borough." Now, what I want to know is whether the association that succeeded it had that same rule viz., that the nomination of candidates for the Corporation should be in the hands of the committee?—Well, I must admit that although a member of the Conservative organization, I am not conversant with the rules of it. I don't recollect whether there is a rule similar in character to that in the organizations after that.

3666. You said you were a member of committee for Dock Ward, and if so you must have taken an active part in the elections?—Well, in reply to the question put by Mr. Exham, I wanted to convey the idea that I was present at meetings where such nominations took place, but what I wanted to guard myself against was, that I had as an individual nominated any individual.

3667. But you went much further and said that you didn't take part in the nominations?—Well, I presume if you are present at a meeting in which a gentleman is nominated, in that sense, I would be a consenting party.

3668. MR. EXHAM.—Do you see that by the rule the nomination is adopted by a limited number, that is, the committee of each ward, who shall have the nomination of candidates for the offices of Town Councillors, Harbour Commissioners, Water Commissioners, and other public bodies, and then the allegation is that the whole society is pledged to the candidates selected by the committee?—Well, from my present recollection of the rules, now I believe they are not similar in character to that, and I believe that all candidates are to be submitted to a public meeting of the burgesses called by advertisement.

3669. MR. LAWSON.—By whom do you say the names are to be adopted?—By a meeting of the burgesses.

3670. By whom are they selected?—Well, it is competent for any ratepayer to propose a gentleman, and the party so proposed can be brought forward.

3671. You say that the names of persons who are first selected, are submitted for approval to the whole meeting. By whom are they really selected?—I have conveyed a wrong impression.

3672. I am afraid you have conveyed a good many wrong impressions?—Well, I'll decline to answer further questions if there are any influential observations of that kind made. They are very hurtful.

3673. I have given you every opportunity of explaining your answers?—Well, I don't mean to say that the candidates selected are selected by a certain coterie.

3674. CHAIRMAN.—What I want to understand is, whether or not you are a member of a committee which has such a rule as that?—Certainly not. Every gentleman who is nominated is nominated in a public meeting of ratepayers where every ratepayer has a right to be present.

3675. MR. EXHAM.—Recollect that you told me a little ago it was a meeting of the committee at which John Hamill was selected?—I am speaking as to the present.

3676. How can you speak of the present when you have told us you have not interfered for the last three years?—I speak of the constitution of the Conservative Association.

3677. I am requested to ask if you took the chair at any meeting of burgesses during the last year?—No; certainly not.

3678. Did you take the chair at a meeting in Cromac Ward in March last?—That might be; but not for municipal purposes.

3679. What was the object of the meeting?—Well, I cannot recollect at all.

3680. Do you mean to say that you took the chair at a meeting in Cromac Ward last year, and that you cannot recollect the object of it?—Well, the object of the meeting was twofold, and I think one of them was the enlargement of the committee—of adding names to the Conservative committee for the ward, and I believe it was an adjourned meeting, at which names of certain gentlemen came up, who were nominated as poor law guardians.

3681. Mr. LAWLESS.—Was that the general object? —Yes.

3682. CHAIRMAN.—I understand that this rule, or something like it, is a rule with the present Conservative Association, is it not?—My own impression is that the present rule is not so stringent as that.

3683. Is it, or is it not, the case, that although of course it is open to the public to go to the general meeting of the burgesses, certain names are brought forward as candidates for the Town Council or for municipal offices at a public meeting, which names have been previously selected by the committees?—That is not the course of procedure. They are not previously selected by the committee, for the names are submitted at a general meeting of burgesses.

3684. By whom?—By the ratepayers.

3685. But not by the committee?—No, sir.

3686. Then what is the meaning of the fact, that certain names are proposed and seconded in committee as candidates for the Town Council—you said you went away on one occasion before the voting took place?—Yes; I left before the voting took place, but I was not a ratepayer or burgess for St. Anne's Ward.

3687. But is not the inference to be derived from that, that the candidates are nominated at a committee meeting, as a preliminary to their being adopted by the ratepayers?—I understood that to be a meeting of the burgesses of St. Anne's Ward.

3688. Mr. REEVES.—Well, I understood that it was a meeting of the committee, and that you had no right to take part as you were not a burgess for the ward.

3689. CHAIRMAN.—Well now, before these ward meetings are called by public advertisement, is not there a private meeting at which it is arranged as to the candidates to be put forward?—Not that I am aware of.

3690. What was done at the meeting of which you were chairman? Did you speak?—Oh, yes.

3691. In favour of what?—I think I chiefly put the resolutions that came before us.

3692. What were the ward committees for? Were they to have no voice in the selection of candidates? —They are for controlling generally the organization so far as each ward is concerned.

3693. And not for selecting candidates?—No; certainly not. By the way, I made a statement the other day which I find by refreshing my recollection, was too general in its character. It was that no member of the Council had ever spoken to me with a view of influencing me in his favour, and I have to qualify that, by stating that Mr. Robert Carlisle called upon me in my office, and endeavoured to enlist my sympathies on behalf of his candidature for St. Anne's Ward. He adverted to the fact of the friendly feeling that he entertained to me as a member of the Council, and his disposition to see the officers well paid, and hoped that I would not oppose him in St. Anne's Ward. I told that person when he called upon me, that not being a burgess of Anne's Ward of course any influence I had would not lie in that way, and as a public officer I did not consider it right that I should mix myself up with a contest between himself and Sir John Savage; nor did I do so.

3694. Mr. REEVES.—I must say, I do not think Mr. Cobain has any right to speak of Mr. Carlisle as he has done, calling him that person.

3695. Mr. M'Erlean suggested a certain question, to show (he said) Lormour's veracity although contradicted.

3696. Mr. *Cobain*.—I wish to know if the evidence that is given here is of a voluntary character.

3697. CHAIRMAN.—Oh, certainly, you can decline to answer any question.—Well all I wish to say is this, that as one has been taken by cross-examination or by insults of conveying reflections on some of the most eminent citizens of Belfast, I'll decline to answer any question put outside the Commissioners.

3698. Oh, no, it is for the Commissioners to decide whether any suggested questions can be put.

3699. Mr. *Cobain*.—And it is for the witness to consider whether he shall answer or not.

3700. CHAIRMAN.—Yes, at his own risk.

3701. Mr. *Cobain*.—Well, I don't apprehend much risk.

3702. Mr. REEVES.—Were you ever a member of the Belfast Working Men's Conservative Association? —Yes, I was.

3703. As that is so, I will ask the question that Mr. M'Erlean desires me to ask. Do you see that second rule (handing copy of rules of above association)?—Yes.

3704. Was Lormour telling the truth when he said that the second rule was one of the rules of the association?—I don't recollect at all.

3705. Mr. LAWLESS.—Is that the rule of the Belfast Working Men's Conservative Registration Society—read it?—

"RULE 2nd.—That the association be composed of the Conservative electors of the borough of Belfast, whose object it will be to return to the Imperial Parliament men, who will honestly represent their Orange and Protestant principles; and likewise assist in the return to the various public Boards men who in matters of finance and local improvements, as well as politically, will truly represent their views."—

I don't recollect at all.

3706. Is that the rule of the Belfast Working Men's Conservative Registration Society?—I believe it is. And I should like the Commissioners to fully understand that I don't feel the slightest trepidation in making the avowal, that I was a member of the association. I was a member of the Conservative party. I am a member of the Conservative party, and I mean to be so. I have exercised my rights of citizenship, and I mean to do so. When I was appointed officer of the Corporation, I don't believe that any members of the Corporation knew what my political feelings were. I was a mere youth at the time. I believe that so far from my connexion with a political party having assisted me, it most unquestionably hindered me from bettering my position, and I state this emphatically, that the members of the Corporation from whom I politically differ were among those who most generously rewarded me. I have a number of witnesses to summon to corroborate what I have stated before you.

3707. The CHAIRMAN said the Commissioners did not consider it necessary to prolong that part of the inquiry any further, but they would take a note that an application had been made by Mr. Cobain to summon witnesses.

3708. Mr. *Robert Carlisle* having requested permission to reply to Mr. Cobain, said—The witness has said that at the time I was opposing Sir John Savage, for the aldermanship of St. Anne's Ward, I called upon him in his office and requested his influence on my behalf. I did call upon him, for I understood that he was canvassing against me, and giving his influence against me at the election. I cautioned him against doing so, and told him that I expected from him, that he would not interfere in the matter. That was the entire purport of the conversation. I was informed by a voter of the ward that he had done so.

3709. CHAIRMAN.—Did you ask him to support you because you were an advocate for paying the officers well?—No; and instead of that I had really voted against the rise of salary in the meantime.

3710. Or anything to that effect?—Nothing at all.

3711. Did you solicit his vote and support at the election?—No, I did not, for he was not in the ward at all.

3712. Mr. *Cobain*.—I give the statement the most unqualified contradiction.

3713. CHAIRMAN.—You need not say that. It is most improper.

3714. Mr. REEVES.—It would serve them if Mr. Cobain would listen to the whole evidence against him, and when it is over say—I give the most unqualified contradiction to everything that is said against me by everyone.

3715. Mr. *Carlisle*, referring to the resolution moved

by Mr. Dinnen in the Council about the officials not interfering in political matters, said the reason it was brought forward was a statement of Mr. Cobain attending in Dublin for the purpose of voting against Mr. Johnston, of Ballykilbeg, at the Grand Orange Lodge. And there was no doubt the finance committee gave him permission to go.

3716. Mr. Exham.—Do you mean to say that that was publicly mentioned in the Town Council as a reason for the resolution?—It was.

Mr. Charles Noah Davis examined.

3717. Chairman.—Are you one of the rate collectors of the Corporation?—Yes, since 1866.

3718. At the time that what is known as the Award Bill was before the committee of the House of Commons, did you, as collector, receive any instructions from the Corporation?—I was not a collector then, but I acted for the Conservative party as general secretary.

3719. Were you then agent for the Conservative party?—Well, I cannot say that I was agent. I carried on an extensive business in Castle-place, as a fur manufacturer. I also had a carpet business up to 1867, and a general drapery establishment in a small way.

3720. Was any arrangement come to in 1864 by which the constitution or political complexion of the Corporation was changed?—Yes.

3721. Was that arrangement carried out by your instrumentality?—Well, I did act for the Conservative party. It was my duty to call public meetings, and petitions were got up. The entire town was in disgust at the state of affairs and necessarily both Liberals and Conservatives were determined that such a state of things should not continue to exist in this country unit, and they tried to get a settlement through Parliament, and gentlemen were then nominated to go into the Town Council and accordingly that was carried out.

3722. Did you take an active part, under the instructions of the chief members of the Town Council in carrying out an arrangement by which the political complexion of the Corporation was to be changed?—To the best of my knowledge or belief I never had any communication with the Town Council on the subject.

3723. In what capacity did you act?—As an independent citizen.

3724. A member of the association?—Yes.

3725. Since you have been collector for the borough have you availed yourself of your position as rate collector to strike off or not return the names to the town clerk of persons who were qualified to vote?—I never was guilty of such an action in my life.

3726. Have you ever failed to return any persons on the burgess roll who paid their rates?—Never.

3727. Have you ever abstained from applying for rates to parties with a view of disfranchising them?—Never, and in proof of that if you have a tabular statement you will find that after checking off deaths, and miscellaneous parties who appear on the town clerk's lists that in eight years in this large and extensive ward—St. George's Ward—only fifty-one were disfranchised.

3728. Mr. Dinnen said this to us. "I may tell you that the rate collectors have in their own hands the returning of the different people who are entitled to be on the burgess roll, and I may tell you that one of the rate collectors was a notorious political agent before he was appointed and continues up to the present time, and he is also the Deputy Grand Master of an Orange Lodge." I asked who was that and he said it was Noah Davis; well now I want to know whether you continue since you were appointed rate collector to be a ward agent or a political agent?—Nothing of the kind. Mr. Dinnen was attorney for the Liberal party, and about as violent a politician as we have in Belfast, and he must have known by the construction of the burgess roll that no collector could put a name off or on, and he should know that in a legal point of view. I never did act in that way.

3729. Have you ever abstained from bringing forward the list of claims?—I have nothing whatever to do with that. It was merely a myth he was driving at.

3730. Have you ever received instructions directly or indirectly to make yourself active in these matters?—Never, sir.

3731. Mr. Exham.—I understand Mr. Larmour to say that in his own presence at the municipal revisions he saw you actively interfering in cases that were going on, and totally outside your duty. Is that so?—I say that it is utterly untrue, and I appeal to the town clerk if I ever interfered in any other way than when asked a question to return the answer in reference to the town lists. I might have been talking to some one sitting near me or giving a pass or something like that. When asked a question I answered it, but never interfered further.

3732. Have you ever taken part in the nomination of any candidates for the Town Council since you have been an officer of the Corporation?—Never, either directly or indirectly.

3733. Have you ever canvassed in any way?—I never have.

3734. Have you been a party to paying runners or street inspectors?—No.

3735. Have you been a member of the ward committee that Mr. Dinnen referred to?—No, I have not. I belong to George's Ward, and I have been a ratepayer in this town for thirty-three or thirty-four years, and generally on the burgess and Parliamentary rolls for George's Ward. I go in and out to the committee meetings for the ward when there is an advertisement calling one, and I merely take a seat and quietly sit down, and then walk out.

3736. Mr. Lawless.—Do you mean political meetings?—Yes, but they are called by advertisement.

3737. Chairman.—Have you ever been on a ward committee?—No.

3738. Mr. Exham.—Have you ever given out copies of the list of wards from your books?—Never in my life, and if I was going before my Maker, I never gave them directly or indirectly to any person.

3739. Mr. Lawless.—You stated the Council would discharge you if they thought you took part in canvassing?—I am quite sure they would.

3740. Were you engaged on one side or other in elections?—Oh, yes. I was engaged in political life for thirty-four years as a citizen in this town; and these parties who appeared here are all violent politicians.

3741. Did you take a part in political life before 1864?—Yes.

3742. Chairman.—Before 1864 were you a rate collector?—No. I'll explain that. I think in 1845 or 1846 for a short time I collected the borough rates, and then I gave it up, but even in that time I took no direct part in politics until the death of the late Mr. Bates.

3743. How long were you collector for the borough rates?—Two or three years.

3744. During that time were you collector of any other rate?—No, sir.

3745. Church rate or poor rate, or anything of that kind?—No.

3746. Mr. Lawless.—But for some time you were engaged as collector for the borough rate, and for some time before 1864 you did take part in municipal politics?—Yes; but not until after the death of the late Mr. Bates—about 1855 or 1856.

3747. You were appointed as collector in 1868?—No, sir. I was a candidate, and I was rejected two or three times, and I say that I owe my position——

3748. What was the year you were appointed?—About 1866; and I was saying that I owe my position chiefly to the Liberal members of the Council, who voted for me on that occasion—Mr. Charles Duffin and others.

Mr. Charles [illegible].

3749. As a matter of course, when they were appointing a person to such a position, the Council must have known what were the antecedents of the gentleman they were appointing?—Well, I have no doubt they did. They thought me competent for it, and if that is to be a barrier——

3750. Just answer this: Did they make it any condition then that you should give up your interference in municipal or Parliamentary politics?—Yes.

3751. How was that expressed?—There was a resolution passed by the Council, and I believe it was in existence many years ago, that no collector should take any part in politics.

3752. When was that resolution passed, for you are the first person mentioned in it?—I know it passed many years ago in the Town Council, and knowing that resolution I took no part——

3753. Was that resolution referred to by any members of the Council at the time you were appointed?—I don't think it was.

3754. At the time of your appointment were you aware of the existence of the resolution?—Yes.

3755. And aware that you acted on the spirit of it?—Decidedly.

3756. Mr. Exham.—It must have been after 1864, for such a thing does not appear to have been mentioned before the commission of the House of Commons.

3757. Mr. Lawless.—Have you anything to show as the date of that resolution?—I have not.

3758. Chairman.—Were you borough rate collector between 1847 and 1851?—Yes; I was for a short time; about then.

3759. Was that the time you heard of that resolution?—No, I don't think it was, sir.

3760. Have you ever seen the resolution, or was it hearsay?—Well, something runs in my mind that there was such a resolution.

3761. Mr. Exham.—Do you recollect was it after the allegations that were made against former rate collectors?—I believe it was, but the fact is I could not recollect everything that took place in the Council for twenty years——

3762. Chairman.—Mr. Black, could you find that resolution?

Mr. *Black*.—My attention was called by an ex-member of the Corporation to the fact that such a resolution was passed, and I directed the town clerk to search for it, and he reported that he could not find it; but I will make a further search.

3763. Mr. Exham.—Have you ever employed a deputy to collect any portion of your rates?—Never. I'll explain this. I serve all my own notices; I go out to collect the rates, and there may be a few exceptional times that I send out a person whom I employ to do office work, writing notices, and so, but I do my own work fearlessly, without favour, fear, or affection.

3764. Chairman.—Substantially you have collected yourself; but you won't say that you have not employed an assistant sometimes?—Oh, all the ratepayers know that I have done that.

3765. You don't say but there might be exceptional occasions where you did not collect yourself?—No; but I'll produce the blanks and the receipts from myself.

3766. Mr. Lawless.—Have you permitted a deputy to receive moneys instead of getting them into your own hands?—No; unless the party came into the office when I was absent.

3767. Mr. *Black*.—The Corporation are not aware of any deputies being employed.

3768. Chairman.—Do you, as a rule, always collect the rate personally yourself?—Yes.

3769. Mr. Exham.—You know that by the bylaw you cannot have a deputy?—Yes, sir; and I fully carried it out. There is one thing Mr. Lawless said; that was, that I compelled some one to serve a notice of objection on Charles H. Ward and Thomas Ward, and I give that an unqualified contradiction.

3770. Were you present when it was done?—No, sir.

Mr. JAMES GEORGE RANKIN examined.

3771. Chairman.—You are one of the rate collectors?—Yes.

3772. What ward do you collect for?—Dock Ward. I collected [illegible] for two years and I was transferred.

3773. How many years have you collected for Dock Ward?—Rather more than seven years.

3774. It has been stated here by a Mr. Stewart, that you don't collect your rates in person, but by deputy?—I keep an assistant, and I send him out with my receipts and he brings in the money.

3775. What is his name?—James Connor.

3776. Do you mean that your custom is not to collect the rates in person, but to fill in receipts and send them to the parties by this man Connor, who brings the money to you?—Yes, sir. I don't invariably collect rates myself.

3777. Do you or Connor collect?—We both collect, but he is the main party who collects outside my office.

3778. Is that with the consent of the Town Council or by yourself?—By my knowledge.

3779. Did you ever ask the permission of the Town Council for that?—No, sir.

3780. Mr. Exham.—Were you furnished with the bylaws of the Corporation?—Yes.

3781. Did you see by them that you were prevented from having a deputy to collect?—Yes, sir; but my only object was to get the rates in early.

3782. Don't you know that the Corporation won't allow a deputy?—I have no deputy; he is only an assistant, and signs no receipts.

3783. Chairman.—But it is in contravention of the bylaws?—Whatever I have done, I have done it on my own responsibility.

3784. But you were aware of it?—Quite aware of it.

3785. Mr. Exham.—Mr. Stewart said he paid your deputy for four years, and never paid you?—Well, there was a person named Bell, who lived in that house before Mr. Stewart; Mr. Bell paid his rates on the 9th August, 1872, and Mr. Stewart paid on the 14th July, 1873.

3786. Chairman.—Was that to yourself or your assistant?—I believe it was to my assistant; but I believe that Mr. Stewart during four years paid into my office; I believe he did.

3787. Mr. *Stewart*.—Never in my life. I was talking to Mr. Bell yesterday, and he says that during eight years he always paid to the assistant.

3788. Chairman.—Well, it is admitted. (To witness) —The great majority of the rates paid outside the office, you say, are paid to this Mr. Connor, on your receipt?—Yes, sir.

3789. Mr. Exham (reading rule)—"No deputy or assistant shall be employed for any other purpose than assisting in filling receipts, it being the intention of the Council that each collector should be a collector, and to personally collect the rates of the ward"?—Well, I am aware of that.

3790. Mr. Lawless.—Did Mr. Connor collect rates from any members of the Town Council?—I think he did. Mr. Connor, I may add, was in the office before I was appointed, and I took him over.

3791. Chairman.—In what capacity?—As assistant for Dock ward.

3792. Mr. Exham.—Do you lodge the rates collected every day yourself?—I have furnished to the Council bail for £2,000, and our money must be lodged every morning before eleven o'clock, and that is done.

3793. Do you do that yourself?—Certainly.

3794. Mr. Lawless.—Yourself or your assistant?—Myself.

3795. Mr. Exham.—One of the rules is that each collector shall report to the town clerk every Saturday all changes of occupancy he may have noticed during the week. If that is not done, the town clerk would have cognizance of the irregularity?—Well, that is carried out partly.

3796. CHAIRMAN.—But do you, according to the rules, report all changes in occupation every this day?—Well, I don't report the changes constantly.

3797. Mr. KERNAN.—Of your knowledge, is this Mr. Connor connected with any of these political societies in canvassing for the wards?—He is not.

3798. CHAIRMAN.—Have you ever abstained from collecting the rates either by yourself or this assistant for the purpose of disqualifying voters?—Never. During last year there were only seven parties disfranchised.

3799. Do you know whether James Connor, your assistant, is the James Connor, who in 1863, was an inspector for Dock ward for the Conservative committee?—I believe he was.

3800. Was he your assistant then?—He was.

3801. Then there must have been, at all events, one member of the Town Council knew of his being the inspector of that ward, because Alderman Alexander was then vice-chairman of the committee, and Mr. Coburn was also a member?—That may have been so. I don't know.

3802. Did you engage him or did you find him in the office?—I found him in the office when I was appointed.

3803. Mr. LAWLESS.—Did you ever hear of this rule that the collectors should take no part in elections?—I heard it was discussed at the Council, but nothing else.

3804. Were you ever furnished with any rule informing you that there was to be no interference with politics?—No, nothing of the sort.

3805. CHAIRMAN.—Were the Council aware that this Connor was your assistant?—Yes; I am sure they were, for he was in the office when I was appointed.

3806. Have you ever been reprimanded by any of the Council for permitting Connor to collect the rates?—No, never.

3807. Do you know whether it has been brought to their knowledge?—I never heard of any complaint.

Mr. CHARLES DUFFIN, J.P., examined.

3808. CHAIRMAN.—Were you a member of the Corporation?—Yes, five or six years ago.

3809. Are you a mill owner?—Yes, and I wish to contradict an allegation that I used my influence as a mill-owner with the Corporation whilst a member to prevent improvements to the state of the Blackstaff. Such a statement was made; and I want to show that so far from its being correct I did all I could to get the Blackstaff nuisance abated, and so far from wanting money compensation for the water being taken from us I said that we didn't want any compensation but a supply of water which they could easily give us from the Water Commissioners. We are at the lowest part of the Blackstaff, and we can erect sluices there and by that means dam up the river, and make the nuisance much worse than it is. We have a small weir across the river at our works—that is when we are working—but we can make it worse if we choose to do so. So far from that, we are still willing to give up our entire control over the river if we get a supply of water from some other source; and as to my influence with the Town Council, I don't think I would have much influence there.

3810. What I want to know is whether you, as a mill-owner and member of the Corporation, used your influence to prevent the Corporation taking steps against yourself and others to prevent your polluting the Blackstaff?—Certainly not. I never did. The Blackstaff would be as pure as the Lagan if the sewage was not sent into it.

3811. Do you increase the pollution by your mill?—Certainly the sewage of the mill goes into the Blackstaff; but that is not the cause of the spoiling of the water; it is the general sewage of the town going into it.

3812. When you say sewage, you mean the sewage of the mill?—Yes, from the workers. It goes into a tank first, and then the overflow goes into the river.

3813. Mr. KERNAN.—You get all the sewage as it comes from the others?—Yes.

3814. CHAIRMAN.—Do you use the Blackstaff water for condensing?—Yes.

3815. (By Mr. Carlisle).—Sir John Savage says that his mill is on the Pound Burn, which goes into the Blackstaff; Mr. Mulhol[illegible] said that his mill was on the Carr's Glen. Are not all these mills on the water which runs down and forms the Pound Burn, and are they not in reality the source of the pollution of the Blackstaff?—I don't know that.

3816. Mr. LAWLESS.—Are these mills near enough to go into it?—They are.

3817. Mr. Carlisle.—They are all on the main leading river, although it was stated by them that they are not.

3818. Mr. Duffin.—There is no person knows all about them better than Mr. Carlisle does.

3819. Mr. Black (Town Solicitor) next said:—An allegation was made by Mr. Culligan, that the Corporation had up to 1874 been wilfully violating certain rules of the Lord Lieutenant and Privy Council with reference to the graves. Well, sir, the cemetery was opened in 1869. Previous to its being opened the Council employed Mr. Joy of Bradford, who had a great experience in the laying out and management of cemeteries, and in framing rules for their guidance, and he instructed them how to do so. I am sure that in England you are perfectly aware it is the practice to open a grave a considerable depth for what is called public and proprietary ground. The remains of one person are interred in that ground, and then a certain quantity of earth is placed over the coffin. A cover is put upon the grave until perhaps the next day, or it may be that afternoon, when another body is brought in, and it is also placed in what appears to all intents and purposes a new grave. There is nothing to show that there are any remains previously buried there; and that goes on for two, or three, or four times, so that four or five bodies will be in the same place, but with a certain amount of earth between them.

3820. CHAIRMAN.—It is like a vault, except that it is not a vault?—Yes. Mr. Joy advised that system to be adopted, I suppose not being aware of the literal construction of the sixth rule of the Privy Council. However, in 1874, the attention of the Council was called to this, that it was a violation of the rule, and immediately I was instructed to confer with Mr. [illegible] and see if the rule bore such a construction, and he said it did, and immediately the practice which hitherto had prevailed was stopped altogether.

3821. And since that time only one body is buried in a grave?—Yes, sir; unless bodies of the members of the same family; and it never was with any idea to violate any rule.

3822. Mr. LAWLESS.—It was a plain violation of the rule?—I admit it; and when attention was drawn to it, it was at once stopped. Well, a matter was referred to about taking water from mill dams for watering the streets. I have the street inspector to show that no water has been used for that purpose for nine years. It might be inferred by the Commissioners that it was used.

3823. CHAIRMAN.—But is any water impregnated with sewage used for watering the streets?—Certainly not.

3824. (By Mr. M'Erlean).—Are you the solicitor for the Tramway Company?—I am not in any way.

3825. Or have you shares in it?—Not in any shape or form.

3826. Well, do you hold a farm convenient to the town, and do you receive at a certain price the manure from the Town Council?—Tenders were advertised for the sale of this slaughter-house manure. I put in the highest tender and it was accepted.

3827. Mr. LAWLESS.—And there was no undue favour?—Not the slightest.

This concluded the inquiry.

TRIM.—November 29, 1876.

(Before the Chairman, Mr. Cossety.)

Mr. John Reilly examined.

1. Mr. Cossety.—You are the clerk to the Town Commissioners here?—Yes.

2. How long have you been town clerk?—I acted for one month—April, 1872—before I was appointed, and then was appointed on the 6th May, 1872.

3. There are, I believe, nine Town Commissioners acting under the Town Improvement Act, the 17 & 18 Vic., chap. 103?—Yes; also Town Commissioners under the Act of 1854.

4. When did you adopt the Town Improvement Act in Trim?—Shortly after it became law.

5. In 1854?—I am not prepared to say just now, but it must have been shortly after that.

6. Is not Trim the county and assize town of Meath?—Yes.

7. And its population at the last census was 2,195?—Yes.

8. Which is a slight increase on the previous census, when I see it was 2,068?—Yes.

9. What is the area within the jurisdiction of the Town Commissioners—how many acres?—I can tell you from the rate-book, which I have at home.

10. Is not the Poor Law valuation £1,785?—Yes.

11. And the principal revenues which the Town Commissioners administer are derived from real property?—Yes, derived from landed property.

12. What is the acreage of that property?—The acreage of it is 119a. 3r. and 37p.—that is, Irish plantation measure.

13. That is, I see, exactly the quantity of land which was held by the old Corporation of Trim at the time the Commissioners of 1833 made their report?—Yes; but there are some lots not as yet in the possession of the Town Commissioners.

14. I see by their report that under the by-law of 3rd May, 1803, by which the Trim commons were divided, that they were divided into burgess' lots of from ten to twenty acres, and into freemen's lots of from four to ten acres?—Yes.

15. And that at the time they reported in 1833 the largest lot held by any one person was nineteen acres?—Yes; I believe that is right.

16. There were then, I find, fifteen burgess' lots and forty-seven freemen's lots, and each lot was held by the grantee for the term of his natural life?—Yes.

17. Held at the nominal rent of 1s. per year?—Yes, 1s. for the lot, in order to keep the reversion in the hands of the Town Commissioners.

18. Are any of these lives that existed in 1833 still running on?—Yes, some are still running on.

19. Persons holding under that by-law and living in 1833?—Yes, holding under the old grant.

20. How many of them are still living?—Some four or five of them. I know one man named Hughes in the town who is still living and in good health.

21. How many acres are respectively held by them under that tenure?—Something about from three to five acres.

22. They were, then, *freemen's* lots, not burgess' lots?—Yes; not burgess' lots.

23. Can you tell me whether, after the passing of the Act of 1840, this property was held by Commissioners appointed under the 9 Geo. IV., c. 82, or by a special board of Commissioners under the Act of 1840, called "The Municipal Commissioners"?—By the Commissioners appointed under 9 Geo. IV., c. 82. The number consisted of thirteen. They used to hold their sittings in this court.

24. And the said estate was to be applied by such Commissioners in aid of the rate and for the public benefit of the inhabitants?—Yes.

25. After the adoption of the Act of 1854 that property, by the 17th section of that Act, was transferred to and vested in the Commissioners under the new Act—the Act of 1854?—Yes.

26. [Chairman reads section of the Act relating to the transfer of the property to the Commissioners under the Act of 1854.]

27. How have these successive bodies of Commissioners dealt with the lots that have fallen in since the passing of the Act of 1840?—They have let them by a vote in the Council.

28. Have they let them by public auction?—Never to my knowledge; never on any occasion.

29. Have they never given any public notice, by advertisement or otherwise, of their intention to let them?—No public notice was ever given. There were no posters put up that I know of.

30. Have they ever let them to members of their own body?—Yes, they have.

31. Have they done so frequently?—Nearly every Commissioner got some.

32. Has this been the case ever since 1840, as the lives have fallen in?—As the lives fell in the parties who purchased the life interest of the grantee were preferred, and the lot was then valued by the Town Commissioners. Those persons who had purchased the life interest of the grantee then came in as the tenants of the Town Commissioners, and were accepted at the valuation placed on the land by the committee, consisting of the chairman and two Town Commissioners, which was appointed to value the land. They came to some agreement with the tenants, who generally accepted it.

33. Were they valued only by the Town Commissioners themselves, or by some qualified person?—Nearly all the lands until within the last three years were valued by themselves. In one case the land was valued by the Town Commissioners since I became town clerk, in the case of Mr. Carey, of Commonsland, Smith; but he will pay the rent Mr. Vaughan, the public valuator, will put on it.

34. You can produce, I suppose, the rental book?—The rental book is in the hands of the agent.

35. Is the agent Mr. Duignan?—Yes, Christopher Duignan.

36. How long has he received the rents?—Since the passing of the Act of 1840. The late town clerk was also appointed then. His name was Philip Reilly. He was somewhere about thirty-two years town clerk.

37. You succeeded him, I believe, in the office?—Yes.

38. Was he any relation of yours?—He was my father.

39. Had you, therefore, before you were town clerk, a considerable knowledge of the business of the Corporation?—Yes; I used to know a good deal about it.

40. You assisted your father, I suppose, in the performance of his duties to some extent?—Well, I was away for twenty-one years, but in the early part of my time I used to do so.

41. Have these lands in your judgment been let from time to time at their full value?—Well, I could not exactly say that they were let at their full value, because there was no competition for them.

42. Were the lands valued by the Town Commissioners when they were let to the Town Commissioners themselves?—Yes, they were, in every case, so far as my knowledge goes; there was a committee appointed to value the lands.

43. In the majority of cases do you say they were let to the Town Commissioners themselves?—There is no doubt about that.

44. Are there many Town Commissioners still holding land the property of the Corporation?—A good many of them are.

Trim. [illegible] Mr. John Reilly.

45. Has not a Town Commissioner resigned his office upon receiving a lease, or has he continued, nevertheless, to act as a Town Commissioner?—He has continued to act as a Town Commissioner; no resignation ever took place to my knowledge. (Witness hands in rental.)

46. You have the tenants' names I see on this rental, but not the quantities of land held by each?—We have the names of the tenants and the amount of rent due from each, and the arrears, but no quantities of land, nor is the rate per acre mentioned, so that it is of little or no value.

47. I gathered from the report of the late auditor that you were about to have a new map of the property made?—Mr. Finlay suggested the propriety of having a new map made—a map of the property with the rental showing all the particulars, and Mr. Collet, the present auditor, followed that up by even striking out the form in which he would wish it to be done—the form of rental to be attached to the map.

48. I see in his report of September, 1875—his last report but one—he says, "The Town Commissioners have ordered a survey and map of their property to be made, it will be soon completed and will be a complete record of this important part of their trust." He said that to the Local Government Board in 1875?—Yes.

49. Has that been done?—It is in progress now, and I waited on the civil engineer, Mr. Vaughan, who has it in hands, and he went over the lands. I was three or four days on the lands with him; but there are some little parts in the town that we did not know about, and I then waited on Colonel Wilkinson in the Phœnix Park, but he said that he had got no map of the town property. We have some holdings in the town, but we have no map showing what they are; they are not represented on the existing map. We derive rents from several houses in the town, but there are others which we should derive rents from and yet those rents are gathered by persons whom we know nothing about. In many cases I have the old counterpart leases of those places.

50. Then don't you know where those houses are?—We know where those plots of land and houses are, but Mr. Vaughan thought that Colonel Wilkinson had a map showing the frontage of the houses, and that it would be easy to make out the new map from it, but Colonel Wilkinson told me he had not such a map.

51. Have not Mr. Vaughan and you made now a complete survey of the town and the lands in the neighbourhood, which would enable you to make out the map?—North and south of the town he has done so, but we should make out a more searching one of the town.

52. You have, I understand then, identified that which lies outside the town, but not all the property which is inside the town?—No, not the tenements which are inside the town.

53. When you say that rents are received by persons you don't know anything about, do you mean that the rents are paid to other parties for these houses which ought to belong to the Commissioners?—Yes; to parties non-resident in the town, and the Town Commissioners do not even know them; they claim the property.

54. You mean, I suppose, that there is some property in the town which is in dispute, as to whether it is the property of the Town Commissioners or of other parties?—It is not exactly disputed; the Town Commissioners know well enough that they should hold it before the parties deriving the rent from the property should. For instance, that piece of land as you come from the railway, called the Crickmore, at present a man named Bell, a solicitor in Dublin, gets the rent of it.

55. What is his Christian name?—I do not know. There is another person named Donovan gets the rent from houses adjacent. They are all on one lot, burgess' lot or freeman's lot, I forget which, the portion of commons at the Athboy gate.

56. Is that one of the lots of which you say that the original holder is still living?—No; he is dead and gone long ago.

57. How is it that it has not fallen into the hands of the Town Commissioners, and that they have not let it?—It is a long time since the grantee died.

58. How long ago—before 1840 or after?—Very likely it was before 1840.

59. Surely your agent can tell that? You say he has been agent since 1840, and surely he can tell you whether the original grantee died before he became agent or subsequently?—Yes, he should.

60. How many acres are there in this lot?—It is not an acre. The two fields to the north of it belong to us. One is the possession of Arthur Darling.

61. Do the fields to the south of it belong to the Town Commissioners?—The road is to the south of it.

62. It is a tongue of land between the road and your land?—Yes, between the Athboy and Kells road.

63. Has any endeavour during all these years been made on the part of the Town Commissioners to establish their right to this land?—Not that I know of. Since 1840, whenever a freeman died, the Town Commissioners resumed possession of the land, except in one instance. There is a man named Malloy who holds a lot of commons, and he says it is his own estate. He entirely disputes the right of the Town Commissioners. They never took any action in the matter more than to speak about it. It is on our map of our property.

64. Is that another instance in which land has fallen in by the death of the original grantee, and to which the Town Commissioners have failed to establish their claim?—Yes; and they know they have a regular fair claim to it.

65. Who is the person deriving benefit from that land?—He is a farmer in the neighbourhood of the town. He knows the land belongs to the Town Commissioners.

66. Is he a relation of any of the Town Commissioners, or was he at the time the grant fell in?—I do not think that has any influence in the matter. He is brother-in-law to one of the Town Commissioners, but I must say I do not think it has any influence.

67. Have you ever suggested to them that it would be desirable to take some steps to establish their claim to the lands?—Yes, and there were some of the Town Commissioners who wished that the claim should be established. I understood they were going to get some legal opinion on the subject. Some of them were anxious to establish the claim; there are resolutions in the book about it.

68. Has it ever been put to the vote to know whether they should try to establish their claim?—It has been talked about over and over again in this individual case; as regards the others in the town there is only a misty opinion as to the property here and there through the town.

69. Can you show me a resolution about it on the minutes?—I think I can. It was talked about, but there was no regular resolution taken. The Town Commissioners knew the land should come into our hands. It is the very end of our land—the very extreme limit of our land. It was gone over by Mr. Vaughan when he was down here. He went over every inch of the land. It ended in a bit of talk. During my time no action was taken—that is since the year 1872.

70. Nor in your father's time?—No.

71. Will you kindly supply us with the minute relating to that afterwards?—Yes; on the 6th January, 1874, at the monthly meeting, the agent handed in a document, and here is a copy. "Lots of commons outstanding by reason of the life existing." "James Walker"—he is alive; "William Carey"—he is alive; "Henry Parsons"—he is dead; "Samuel Allen"—dead; "Edward Parsons"—doubtful; I think he is living in Dublin; "William Parsons"—alive; "John Hughes"—alive; "Richard Malloy"—overholding; that is the person I speak about.

Trim. Nov. 10, 1876. Mr. John Reilly.

72. Have those persons whom you say are dead died since?—Henry Parsons died since, and we got the land; Samuel Allen was dead, I think, when the line was handed in, but we did not get the lands at the time. Just at that time there was an examination made of the lot that Samuel Allen holds, and it was let to these persons on July 6, '74, as follows:—"John Neville, 10a. 0r. 10p., at 27s. 6d. per acre (that is Irish measure), yearly value £14 0s. 6d.; Patrick Gillick, 3a. 3r. 35p., at 27s. 6d. per acre, yearly value £4 1s. 3d., and Patrick Gannon, 2r. 21p. at 30s. per acre, yearly value £1 6s. 6d.; on the 10th March, '74, Christopher M'Keon, part of William Curry's lot, 1a. 0r. 31p. at 50s., yearly value £2 16s. 6d.; and there was a portion of William Curry's lot let to James Plunkett, 3a. 2r. 11p., at 40s., yearly value £5 16s. 6d.; and there was a small piece of land, with a house on it (16 perches it contained), let to Ellen Fagan at 60s., yearly value 6s.

73. Is not Mr. Plunkett one of the Town Commissioners?—Yes.

74. Were any of these parties to whom these lands were sublet Town Commissioners at the time?—Christopher M'Keon was a Town Commissioner, and had been frequently Chairman of the Town Commissioners.

75. Was he so at the time?—Not then, but he had been previously.

76. Mr Plunkett—was he then a Town Commissioner, and is he so still?—Yes.

77. Was Neville a Town Commissioner?—No; he was a farmer. He held under Mr. Allen; it was let to him. He had the preference because he held under the previous grant.

78. You have given us the rate at which these lots were let, can you give me the value for that property (the poor law valuation)?—Yes.

79. Who valued this property of Allen's and Curry's?—Here is the certificate by Mr. Vaughan—

"[illegible], 18th December, 1872.

"Dear Sir,—I beg to hand you the valuation of lands referred to in your letter of the 3rd. The quantities were taken from the Ordnance Survey.—I am, dear Sir, faithfully yours, Edward Vaughan." "I have made a careful examination of the value of the buildings, the property of the Town Commissioners of Trim, in the county of Meath, and value the lands as here set forth."

80. And are they let at that valuation?—Yes; the letting took place on the 10th March, 1874. The first letting was moved by Patrick Malone and seconded by Richard Davis.

81. What I want to know is this—was there any public notice given that these lands which had so fallen in would be let on that 10th March, 1874?—No.

82. Therefore there were no tenders from persons outside the Commissioners' room?—None; the Town Commissioners gave the lands to the parties holding from the old freemen whose life interests they had purchased. They gave the preference to the persons in possession.

83. To the sub-lessees of the original grantees?—Exactly. I am not aware that they ever posted up bills to say there would be a letting, here or there. I do not see any notice of it in the books.

84. And failing a sub-lessee of the original grantee, to whom did they give the preference?—I do not know of such an instance. Generally the persons managed to get into possession of the lands because they knew the Town Commissioners would give them leases; they gave good value to get in.

85. We already got from you that many of these lands are now held by the Town Commissioners themselves. Have they been often let to Town Commissioners as sub-lessees of the original grantees?—In some cases they were.

86. And in some they were not?—Yes.

87. Was Mr. Plunkett a sub-lessee?—Yes. He held from William Curry.

88. And the gentleman whom you say was formerly a Town Commissioner had he been a sub-lessee of an original grantee?—I understand, and I can see from the book, that there was a Town Commissioner Neville Preston Newman, who obtained several lots of common lands, and who parted with two lots to M'Keon for a valuable consideration. I see Mr. Newman's name on several leases, and there is no transfer recorded on our books, and that creates great difficulty in finding out who the persons are that are actually in possession. I know several instances of persons paying rent and there is no mention of them on the lease, and no transfer executed on the lease to them with the sanction of the Town Commissioners; so that if you take up a lease you cannot tell who is in possession. The counterpart tells you nothing whatever about it. There is only one case in which there is such a thing, and that is in the case of Henry Parsons, the former town clerk under the old Corporation. He executed a transfer of somewhere about six acres of land (his life interest in it) to Mr. Michael Allen for a consideration of £40, and that is the only case in which it was done.

89. Was that prior to 1840?—In 1842.

90. And that is the only transfer you find?—Yes.

91. Are there many of these holdings now held by other parties who are paying the rent for them but to whom no fresh lease was granted by the Town Commissioners, and no transfer?—Yes. When I take up a lease now I do not know who is in possession of the land.

92. Whose duty was it to see that fresh leases were granted, or that transfers were made?—It should be the duty of the agent to keep the property together.

93. I presume it would be. Has he or anyone been asked by you or by your father to furnish you with a proper account of these transfers?—Here is an order made on the 7th September, 1876:—

"That the agent, Christopher Dungan, furnish from the rental a list of the names of the present occupiers of the several holdings in the town property, with the names of the original occupiers of such holdings, from the date of the establishment of the Commission (in 1855). That said list be delivered to the town clerk, and used in the preparation of the new rental and map of the town property in which Mr. Edward Vaughan is at present engaged."

94. Has that order been complied with?—No; and here is the next minute on the subject:—

"October 12, 1876.

"At the monthly meeting the agent not having furnished to the town clerk the names of the tenants, as per order at meeting of the last monthly meeting, the town clerk is now directed to visit the tenants on the property, and to ascertain from them the names of former parties or dates of transfer since the establishment of the present Commission."

95. Since 1854?—Yes, and then at the last meeting, on the 9th November, 1876:—

"The foregoing minutes were read by the town clerk, and on the chairman asking if there was any objection to the signing of the minutes, the agent stated that he knew nothing about the order to furnish the names of the occupiers of the several holdings of the town property and so forth, for the purpose of making a correct rental, and that he objected to the signing of the minutes. The chairman stated that any objection to the signing of the minutes could not be [illegible] by the [illegible] made by a Town Commissioner. Whereupon Town Commissioner Malone said he would have no objection to the signing of the minutes, as Mr. Vaughan [illegible] the town clerk if Mr. Vaughan had surveyed the town property with a chain. The town clerk stated that Mr. Vaughan took his quantities from the Ordnance Survey, the standard survey of Ireland, and that he had personally answered Mr. Malone's question. Commissioner Malone then said he would make a motion to the effect that the agent be not called upon to give information with regard to the tenants, as mentioned in the list of the persons at present in occupation where transfers were made. He was reminded by the chairman that he should first give notice of motion to rescind the order made at the meeting on the 7th September last, and with which the agent should have complied, as the matter deeply concerned the interest of the town property. The chairman remarked that if the tenants were brought here this evening to pay their rents, the Town Commissioners would be no longer in ignorance of who their tenants were, and of the extent of their several holdings. Commissioner Gibbons remarked that he was now a good time acting as Commissioner, and would be glad to be well acquainted with the rental, but at present he knew very little about it, and had no source of information. Commissioner Gregory expressed himself similarly, and Commissioner Malone having stated that the town clerk should have furnished a copy of the order in question to the agent, was [illegible] by Commissioner [illegible] that the agent was present at the meeting when the said order was made, and was bound in the discharge of his duty to take a note of such an order, and to furnish the information sought. After some still further discussion, Commissioner [illegible] handed in

TRIM.
[illegible]
Mr. [illegible] Kelly.

[illegible] of motion to the chairman, who requested him to [illegible] his [illegible] of [illegible] to be [illegible]. Commissioner [illegible] then said that the chairman was [illegible] of [illegible], and having [illegible] up his [illegible] of [illegible], said that he (Commissioner [illegible]) no longer had [illegible] as the Commissioner, and that he might as well put [illegible], as he was to that as any."

96. That was at your very last meeting?—Yes, the minutes were then signed by the chairman, and I have to remark, that when I came here many of the Commissioners were very willing to do their duty straight off, but the others were inclined not to do business, but to wrangle and retard the business of the town at the Board whether it was about business or not; and there was often a great deal of disputing as to whether the minutes would be signed or not. However, they were always signed, and I am ready to swear as to the accuracy of them. It is on record that several Commissioners said, that no Commissioner ought to be afraid of his words being recorded.

97. Have the minutes drawn up by you been all signed by the chairman?—They were all signed by the chairman.

98. At the next meeting?—Yes.

99. I see that the total acreage is 176a. 3r. 37p.?—Yes.

100. Will you tell me what is the annual rent derived from it?—I see there was brought into the account at the last audit £537 0s. 2½d.—Yes.

101. But it does not follow that that was the annual rental?—There were some arrears paid. About £560 would be the average. The exact half year's rental in 1873, of which I have a copy, was £319 0s. 11d.; that is for the half year ending 25th March, 1873. I have no copy since.

102. How is that?—Because it is quite useless to have a rental without the quantities. I have no acreage.

103. Have you ever applied to the agent, or been directed by the Town Commissioners to apply for the quantities of those lands?—The matter was talked about over and over again. I know of one case in which a tenant called in to know how much land he had, and they could not tell him. It was then stated that it would be well to get the quantity of land held by each tenant, but there is neither the yearly value per acre, nor the number of acres, and therefore the rental is no use. At that date (25th March, 1873), there was £90 0s. 0d. outstanding arrears.

104. Doubling the half year's rental you have given as at that date would bring, would it not, the annual rent to £638 18s. 2d.?—And it would be a little over that now, because since then we got in a couple of lots of commons.

105. Lots which you had not [illegible] before?—Which we had not in our possession before.

106. By decree?—Yes; two or three lots which would come up to £30 or £40 more. It would be close to £670 now.

107. Looking at the character of the land around Trim, is that not a very small rental for 150 acres to produce?—It is a very small rental.

108. Is this grazing land generally?—Yes, generally grazing land.

109. What is the average value of grazing land about Trim?—From £4 to £4 10s., or £4 12s. 6d. I know that to be paid by parties who take eighty or ninety acres. They pay from £4 to £4 10s. or £4 12s. 6d.

110. Is the land of the Town Commissioners equally good with that land?—In a good many places it is quite as good. Some of the first land in the county Meath is held by the Town Commissioners.

111. And you do not get quite 80s. an acre?—Not quite 30s.

112. I have a lease here before me which was granted on the 7th September, 1868, between the Town Commissioners of Trim, under the 17th and 18th Vic., to Thomas Fox, of Doggstown, farmer, by which two lots are let to him, making altogether 22a. 2r. 21p. for a term of thirty-one years, at the yearly rent of £27 15s. Do you know that land?—I do.

113. Where is that land?—In the immediate neighbourhood.

114. What is it worth?—It ought to be worth 50s.

115. No more?—About 50s. Anyone in the town would give 50s. for it that required land.

116. But you see it is let only for a fraction more than 22s.?—Yes.

117. When was that let?—In 1868.

118. Four years before you were town clerk?—Yes.

119. Do you know how that was let?—I understand that Thomas Fox, who was in possession of the land, was in America.

120. Was this land which had fallen in from one of the old grants?—Yes, some of it; a very peculiar letting that was. There was a person named Taylor got from the present Town Commissioners, in the year 1849, a portion of it—say fourteen or fifteen acres, and nineteen years of that lease had expired, and there was no consideration given to the Town Commissioners for the renewal.

121. A lease for how long?—Thirty-one years.

122. At what rent, do you know?—I have the lease in the town hall. I have not got it here, but I can tell you.

123. Nineteen years of that lease had then expired?—Yes, and there was a portion of a lot of commons in the possession of Henry Parsons containing 5a. 3r. 31p.

124. Those two lots together make up the twenty-one acres, which are the subject of Fox's lease?—Yes. Nineteen years of the lease to Taylor had expired, and there was a new lease made then, by joining the two lots together, and by their taking away nineteen years' rights that the townspeople had acquired in Taylor's lease.

125. How was it that Taylor surrendered to Thomas Fox?—He did so for a consideration.

126. What consideration?—I do not know. Very likely he would get money from him to emigrate.

127. When was Parsons' lease granted?—It was granted by the old Corporation, and Parsons sold (this is the lease I mentioned on which a transfer was executed), in the year 1847, his life interest to Michael Allen.

128. Parsons, then, had been one of the old grantees?—Yes.

129. At the nominal rent of 1s. a year?—I think the consideration in that case was about 3s. In 1843 he executed a transfer, and then sold his life interest to Michael Allen, and he was a relative of Thomas Fox. Allen gave £60 to Parsons for his life interest in the lease, and not liking to rest contented with same, surrendered to the Town Commissioners lest he might be disturbed on the Commissioners resuming after Parsons' demise.

130. Was that surrender in 1843?—Yes, in 1843; and since then after the Town Commissioners accepted him as tenant; and that is the only instance in which a life interest was surrendered to the Town Commissioners.

131. Did not the Commissioners, in consideration of the surrender, grant him a fresh lease?—Yes.

132. For how long?—I cannot say whether they granted him a fresh lease or merely secured him in possession.

133. He paid the rent up to this for the lease being granted?—Yes. Allen was a long time dead before the grant of that lease.

134. Thomas Fox was in America at the time?—Yes.

135. Who represented him when he was in America?—The agent of the Town Commissioners was managing the property of Thomas Fox at the time. You will see his name on that lease, and he acts by power of attorney.

136. Do you know on whose application this lease was granted to Thomas Fox?—I cannot tell you.

137. You do not know where Taylor was when he surrendered his lease?—I do not know. I heard that

Taylor emigrated to the colonies—to Australia or somewhere.

138. Was Thomas Fox in any way connected with the Town Commissioners?—Not that I know of. I do not think he was.

139. Nor had he been holding under them as sub-lessee of any of those places?—He was living on the property.

140. I thought he went to America?—He had only recently gone to America before 1868.

141. For some time previously, then, to 1868 he had been in occupation of that property?—Yes.

142. How many leases have been granted by the Town Commissioners since you have been town clerk?—I think there might be something about five or six.

143. During the last four years?—Yes.

144. Have these all been made to persons who were in possession as sub-lessees of the original grantees?—Yes.

145. Have any of those been Town Commissioners themselves?—No, I think not, with the exception of Mr Plunkett.

146. That we already had?—Yes.

147. Have there been no other leases granted to Town Commissioners within the last four years?—Not to Town Commissioners.

148. Can you tell me for what periods those five or six leases were granted?—For thirty-one years.

149. All for thirty-one years?—Yes; and where a lease is promised to be made it is understood to be for thirty-one years.

150. Have they been let at a high rate, or about the same rate as this lease before me to Mr. Thomas Fox?—Something about from 30s. to 40s.

151. The land is let for about 25s. per acre?—That is an exceptionally low case.

152. Previous to the time you became town clerk, the practice, you told us, was for some of the Town Commissioners to value the land themselves?—Yes.

153. Since then Mr. Vaughan has valued it?—Yes.

154. I think you said in every case but one?—Yes. There is a man called John Moore who is to get a lease of the holding of which he was in possession for a certain time back at the valuation to be placed on the same by Mr. Vaughan, when he goes to inspect the land on a final survey. I may observe that some of the Town Commissioners thought it a very invidious thing to go and value the lands themselves. Some of them entertained an objection to go and examine the lands.

155. But in no case has the land been put up by public auction?—In no case.

156. Nor were tenders invited?—In no case.

157. Can you tell me what lands are now held by Town Commissioners? Some of the Town Commissioners now hold lands, do they not, the property of the Town Commissioners?—Yes; I can give you the names.

158. Mr. Plunkett we know of. Does he hold anything of the Town Commissioners' besides those two acres that we heard of?—Yes.

159. What other property of the Town Commissioners' besides that which was let in 1871?—The house he lives in belongs to the Town Commissioners.

160. Do you know what rent he pays?—I could not tell you; I am not acquainted with the rental.

161. Is there any other gentleman?—There is Mr. Kennedy. He holds some lots of Commons. He is a Town Commissioner. Mr. Blake holds some Commons. Mr. Gibbons is a tenant. Mr. Gibbons holds the land which was occupied by Thomas Fox.

162. I am speaking of holding directly from the Town Commissioners?—He does not hold directly from the Town Commissioners.

163. Is it Patrick Gibbons himself or is it his brother holds the lands?—I could not say. They trade under the name of "Gibbons Brothers." I am not aware of any other Town Commissioners, but there are parties in the town who were Town Commissioners, and who, when they were Town Commissioners, obtained lands. The Town Commissioners appointed after the Act of 1840 all got a piece of land. Their names were in the counterpart leases, but they are nearly all dead.

164. The lands generally went to their assignees?—Yes.

165. Can you tell me whether or not any of the Town Commissioners sublet lands granted to them by their own body for higher rents than they have been paying to the Town Commissioners?—No; I do not think so. I do not think the Town Commissioners ever sublet the lands, but they sold their interest in them.

166. That is about the same thing. They sold their interest, and did they obtain considerable sums of money?—Yes.

167. We heard just now of one man who got £60?—Yes, exactly.

168. Has any instance of that occurred since the Town Commissioners of 1854 were appointed, do you know?—I am not prepared to say.

169. You cannot say?—No.

170. Does the agent hold any lands?—He holds two lots of the Commons lands.

171. When were those granted to him?—A good long time ago. He has two lots, and there was some dispute about a lot of Commons, and he and the party who disputed were brought before the board, and the minutes state that the matter was arranged neither to the satisfaction of Christopher Duignan nor the other person; but Mr. Duignan retained possession of the lot of Commons claimed by Phelim Curry, to whom, I suppose, he had lent some money. It is remarked particularly in the minutes that neither party was satisfied, but that Mr. Duignan retained possession of the land.

172. You cannot tell me the quantity of land?—I cannot tell you.

173. There was a map in 1783?—Yes.

174. Which was referred to by the Commissioners of 1835? That map you still have?—Yes. It is in the possession of the surveyor, who is preparing the new map, and it will be of great service to him, as it contains the whole quantity.

175. That map shows a total acreage of 479a. 3r. 37p.?—Yes, exactly. It contains the quantity of land set to each tenant, and so on. It is a very good map. Judge Flanagan said he never saw a better map in his life.

176. Have you the tracing of that map?—Yes. (Witness produces tracing.)

177. The tracing does not set out the quantities?—No, only the numbers—the very page that there is on the map.

178. I see that the land is all surrounding the town?—Yes, and all the public roads are made through the Commons lands.

179. There was a lot which was long in dispute, was there not?—Yes; there was a very extensive law suit about it. One of the Town Commissioners informed me that the transactions arising out of that were of great expense to the Town Commissioners. Chief Baron Pigot, who heard the case, had a large number of the books copied, and the expense was very great.

180. How did that get into dispute?—It belonged to a freeman, and he went out of the country, and this was taken possession of by Mr. Christopher Duignan for some debt, as he stated to the Town Commissioners, that he owed to him.

181. There is a small piece of land here with something written on it, and it is marked "claim nine, first division," did you make a claim of that land on behalf of the Town Commissioners?—Yes, and by their order.

182. And did you establish your claim?—Yes; and it is now in our possession.

183. Was that heard before Judge Flanagan?—Yes.

184. How came there to be any dispute about that land?—The Town Commissioners could not take possession of that land so long as John Allen was alive

(the party entitled to the life interest—the old grantee under the old corporation), and when the tenant in possession of the adjacent land (which belonged to the Leslie family) found that it would square out his holding comfortably, he destroyed the fence.

185. Whilst Allen's consent?—Allen was then away out of the country.

186. And who was occupying the adjacent land?—Henry was occupying the adjacent land as the tenant of Leslie.

187. And who was occupying the land which had been granted to Allen?—That land was occupied by Mr. Duignan.

188. What Mr. Duignan was that?—The agent of the Town Commissioners.

189. Was he holding it on behalf of the Town Commissioners, or as lessee under Allen?—For his own benefit. As I understand it, Allen owed money to him, and he took possession of the land, and afterwards parted with it to Mr. Hipwell for a consideration, and the Town Commissioners made a lease to Mr. Hipwell, omitting this portion which I subsequently recovered.

190. I want to know was it while Duignan was holding the land for Allen that Mr. Leslie's tenant obliterated the fences?—That I cannot say, but all the townspeople knew that the land belonged to the Town Commissioners, and Judge Flanagan stated that it was an attempt by Mr. Leslie's tenant to filch the land from the Town Commissioners.

191. Are not the lands to which you referred at the commencement of your evidence as being held by a man named Malloy who refused to pay rent for it in defiance of the Town Commissioners, lot 23 on the map, at the extremity of the estate?—Yes.

192. How much might there be of it?—I might say about seven or eight acres—Mr. Vaughan can say how much, for we were on the land together.

193. The Town Commissioners were put you say to great expense to recover this lot which Duignan took possession of?—Yes.

194. How much was the expense of recovering that small lot which was obtained before Judge Flanagan?—There was no expense. I made the application; I told the judge that the Town Commissioners' property was mortgaged, and that they could not pay expenses, and he said it was quite right for the Town Commissioners to send their officer to make the application under the circumstances.

195. And did he make an order upon your application without your employing solicitor or counsel?—Yes; he said it was quite right to send a person there to save the expense.

196. Why did they not do it in the same way with regard to lot 23?—They could not do that. This property was up for sale in the Landed Estates Court, and that is the reason it was so easy to do it.

197. Is there any other land on this map which is in dispute at present except the lot 23, or of which you are not receiving the rent?—None, except houses in the town, and we must have a close inspection of these houses. Mr. Vaughan said he would have a very close inspection of the house property. There is another instance. There is a Mr. Thompson living near the town here, and I understand he has tenements in Brownstown, and I am not sure that there is not a dispute about a field for which he gives receipts, and for which we are not receiving any rent. That is to be ascertained when Mr. Vaughan comes down.

198. What are the other receipts besides those from land to which the Town Commissioners are entitled. I see casual tolls set down at £11 4s. 8d.; have you a market here?—Yes, we have a market here; fine market sheds and every convenience.

199. Are there tolls paid for that market?—We have no tolls in the market. These tolls are only for weighing.

200. You are, I believe, the weighmaster, and you have a market, but have no market tolls?—No, we have not; the market is free.

201. The tolls for weighing are, I suppose, all collected by you as weighmaster at the Town Commissioners' weighing machine?—Yes; they have the cranes for corn and butter.

202. Then besides the £11 4s. 8d. casual tolls do you not get £3 3s. 1d. for weighing corn, and £1 18s. 6½d. for weighing butter at the crane?—Yes.

203. The next item is for dog tax?—Yes, £4 18s 4d. Mr. Wingfield sends the amount into the bank direct to the credit of the Town Commissioners. Then there are the petty sessions fines. I get no fine; I simply get the treasurer's account. The auditor remarked at the last audit that we were not now getting the previous amount of fines. The fines at our own court were £5 11s. 3d.

204. These are fines for drunkenness?—Yes. These are all the extra items of receipts we have.

205. What was that surcharge of £4 13s. for?—It was made on the account of the sewer contractor, and was a payment made to Mr. Davis.

206. Over the amount of his contract?—Yes.

207. Eight pounds two shillings was a payment made to Mr. James Fawkett, being law expenses incurred by him for the Town Commissioners in reference to a surcharge by the previous auditor, Mr. Finlay, of the sum of £28 to Messrs. Malone and Brennan. This was law expenses incurred in resisting that surcharge?—Yes.

208. Has that surcharge been paid?—Yes.

209. Although Mr. Finlay was not aware of it at the time he gave evidence before the select committee, Have not all the surcharges made by Mr. Finlay at his last audit, and the surcharges made by Mr. Collet at his audit, been now paid?—Yes, they are now all paid.

210. I see there is building stone from Quarry-bank which produces £3 5s.?—Yes. The Quarry-bank is finished, so that there is no more to come from that source. The Town Commissioners had a quarry, and they found that it did not pay, and these sums that appear in this and the previous audit are sums that remained outstanding for stones. The Town Commissioners ceased to work the quarry because it did not pay.

211. Was this £1 16s. 6d., "drainage of houses," a repayment from parties for work done for them?—Yes, for work we have done in connecting houses in the town with the main sewers. We have very good drains in the town. There are three good drains, which are the main arteries of the town; they are 13-inch pipes.

212. Were they made by the Town Commissioners prior to the Act of 1874—the Public Health Act—which transferred the sanitary duties to the board of guardians?—Yes, they were.

213. I see that your receipts for the last year, as audited on the 14th November, 1876, were £1,[illegible] 14s. 8d.?—Yes.

214. And your expenditure for the same period was £1,049 11s. 10¾d.?—Yes.

215. Leaving a balance in the treasurer's hands of £37 14s. 2d.

216. In the agent's hands one farthing, and in the town clerk's hands £14 6s. 8½d.?—Yes.

217. Do you generally have a current balance in your hands?—No; sometimes you will see I have to advance money.

218. Do you pay all wages?—Yes, and I pay all the accounts. They are very small payments; they are inscribed on the back of the cheques, and countersigned by three Town Commissioners.

219. I see that the cheques are made payable to you for small payments?—Yes.

220. And on the counterfoil the names of the parties to whom they are payable are mentioned on the back?—Yes.

221. In larger payments the cheques are, I suppose, made payable to the parties themselves?—Yes.

222. Do you give a bond?—Yes. I give a bond for £300; it is lodged with the treasurer in the Ulster Bank.

223. The Ulster Bank is your treasurer?—Yes.

224. Does Mr. Duignan give a bond?—Yes.

225. Is that lodged in the same place?—I do not know.

226. Do you make out all the accounts for the Town Commissioners?—Yes; all except the rental.

227. What is your salary?—£20.

228. How much have you as town clerk?—It is altogether. I am town clerk and weighmaster and gas manager, and I have £50 a year in money, with apartments in the town-hall and fire and light.

229. I see there is a town sergeant. What does he get?—10s. a week and a suit of clothes annually.

230. Is he what is called town inspector in other places?—Yes.

231. Is he the person who has the charge of the streets?—Yes; he has to look after the ordinary business of the town. The scavenging is very well done, and everything is in good order.

232. Prior to the passing of the Public Health Act what did you do in the way of sanitary work?—We did all the work that we had power to do—kept the streets and the crossings clean, put down gratings, kept the watercourses and drains clean, removed nuisances, and watered the streets of the town occasionally, and until Mr. Collet at the last audit struck out the expense of keeping the pumps in order, we always supplied water to the inhabitants.

233. How many pumps are there?—Seven public pumps.

234. In this last account there is, I see, a charge of £9 as per contract for keeping the pumps in order?—Yes.

235. And that was disallowed by Mr. Collet?—Yes.

236. He told you, I suppose, that all the powers and duties were, by the Act of 1874, transferred to the board of guardians as the sanitary authority for the district?—Yes.

237. Do you still water the streets?—Yes. We have a watering cart. He told me that everything connected with the surface we could do without any fear of being surcharged. At the first meeting of the Town Commissioners he said it would be well for them to communicate with the board of guardians.

238. Have you done anything since?—I don't know of anything since.

239. He was here, I believe, so lately only as the 16th of this month?—That is so.

240. The next charge is £4 4s. 0d. for keeping the clock in order?—Yes.

241. Is that an annual charge?—Yes; there is thirteen guineas in that—we pay £4 a year.

242. The town sergeant you say only gets 10s. a week?—Yes.

243. But I see you paid £76 8s. 6d. for scavenging last year?—Yes.

244. Have you two regular scavengers besides the town sergeant?—Yes.

245. What do you pay them?—One of them 11s. a week and the other 8s. And we also had additional scavengers last year. Our roads are very soft in the winter time. The Town Commissioners think it well to keep the town in a good healthy state, and they put on extra men, but all the work for the future will be done by the board of guardians with regard to the sewerage, and the pumps will be also looked after by them.

246. I see the agent's fees are 1s. in the pound on the landed property?—Yes; £23 17s. he got.

247. And on the building ground accounts 1s. in the pound—he got 8s. for that?—Yes.

248. And there are agent's fees on a portion of the gas rents?—He was receiving a portion of the gas rents, but the rents are now collected by me.

249. He received 1s. in the pound on these?—Yes; it was £4 7s. 6d.

250. He gets 1s. in the pound, it seems, on everything that passes through his hands?—Yes; there was a surcharge about the lodgment of some money, and 18s. was charged in the account on the money refunded because Mr. Duignan lodged it; the charge of 18s. being 1s. in the pound for lodging that money, which ought to have been lodged by the parties themselves. He was obliged to refund that amount by the auditor. It has been refunded.

251. Do you get 1s. in the pound on the collection of the gas rents?—I get none whatever. It is my duty to do it free of all charges. The town clerk from the beginning of the gasworks made out the accounts and collected the rents.

252. How came Mr. Duignan to get this?—Some persons among the Town Commissioners wished to give him the collection of it.

253. In the previous account there was a much larger sum—£15 17s. 3d.?—Yes; there were several resolutions, and at last it had to be given up, and the collection was transferred to me.

254. £7 13s. 1d. He got 7s. 6d. on the collection of that amount that should have been paid direct without any fee. Did you give him any authority to collect it?—That 7s. 6d. was the percentage. It should have been paid to me without any fee.

255. So that on the gas rents which you should have collected he got £15 17s. 3d.?—Yes.

256. Did not the auditor surcharge him with that amount?—No, because the matter was in dispute. Some of the Town Commissioners wanted him to collect the rents, and some thought that the town clerk should collect them as formerly. It was for a collection two years ago.

257. The percentage on this £37 8s 6d. is on a collection made by him more than two years ago?—Yes, the auditor did not disallow it on the ground that some of the Commissioners had been favourable to his collecting them at that time. The only rents we have to pay ourselves are for the town hall and the gasworks.

258. I see election expenses one guinea. I suppose that is for the election of Town Commissioners?—Yes.

259. A regular annual charge?—Yes.

260. £4 1s. 9d. for a quitrent; that is on the lands?—Yes; the inland revenue make that charge upon us every year.

261. Poor rates, £20 1s. 0½d.?—Yes, they are poor rates paid on the Town Commissioners' property.

262. Income tax, £4 13s. 11d.?—Yes.

263. The next item is the interest on the loan of £2,400, at 4½ per cent., £108 15s. What is that loan?—It was money borrowed on the security of the rents for the purpose of building the market house and of putting up market sheds, building the gasworks, laying public service-pipes, erecting lamps, and so forth.

264. When was that loan contracted?—Some time about the year 1858. It was by the old Town Commissioners, and the interest is paid half-yearly.

265. Was not the original loan more than £2,400?—It was £2,800 originally, and it has been reduced by the sale of some lands to the railway company for £400.

266. When was that do you know?—In 1860.

267. Were the particulars of this large item of £27 11s. 3d. for general expenses all submitted to the auditor? Was he satisfied with them all?—Yes.

268. The principal item was, I see, connected with the drainage works, £26 17s.?—Yes.

269. The only thing that I have not yet noticed, and which appears on both sides of your account, is the gas rental and the gas expenditure?—Yes.

270. I see in this year's account you got £370 18s. 10d. gas rents brought into the account, and £17 16s. on two other items, sale of tar and lime, and so on?—Yes; we do not sell the coke now, we always want it ourselves.

271. On the other side the expenses of the gasworks were, stokers' wages, £77 18s. [illegible]d.?—Yes; we pay one stoker 15s. a week for seven nights, and the other stoker 14s. a week for seven days, and we pay 2s. 6d. a week to one of the scavengers for lighting the lamps.

Tuam.
[illegible]
Mr. John Kelly.

Trim.
Dec. [illegible], 187[illegible].
Mr. John Reilly.

and putting them out, and for taking care of the lamps. The lamps are lighted from the 1st of October in one year till the 30th of April in the next year, with the exception of three or four nights before full moon, and the same time after the full moon, when we do not require to have them lit. The lamps are lighted till about half-past ten o'clock at night, which is sufficient for the people in the town.

272. How many lamps have you?—We have thirty-four lamps, and we got six more recently.

273. Your expenditure for coal in this account was £231 3s. 1d.?—Yes; and we had on hands very close on sixty tons of coal at the close of the year, and we had not any on hands at the end of the previous year.

274. What are you paying for coal now?—23s. 6d. a ton for coals delivered, but these coals cost us 23s. 3d. at the railway station, and 1s. 3d. a ton for cartage and delivery.

275. You had sixty tons on hand at the close of the year?—Yes; such a thing never occurred before—we got a large supply.

276. I see here "Repairs at the gasworks, meters, lamps, &c., £103 3s. 7d."?—Yes.

277. The expense of new retorts and repairs?—This was an exceptional year. It had not been so much for three or four years.

278. One year's rent for the gasworks £11 8s.?—£12 is the yearly rent of the gasworks, and 12s. is deducted for poor rate. We light the police barrack and the town hall free of charge, but of course when exhibitions come to the town hall they pay for the gas themselves.

279. Your expenditure this year was £533 1s. 6d., and your receipts were only £397 14s. 10½d.?—Yes; that with our stock of coal, and the cost of lighting the town will more than balance the expenditure.

280. The stock of coals we may take at sixty tons of coals at 25s. per ton, that would be £75?—Yes.

281. And the cost of lighting. I want to see what you light the town for?—The cost would be about £3 per lamp.

282. For thirty-four lamps?—Yes.

283. Then assuming that the lamps are lit free, and that they cost you £102, that with £75 for your stock of coal in hand, and £397 14s. 10½d., your receipts would make a total of £574 14s. 10½d., leaving, with an expenditure of £533 1s. 6d. a balance in your favour of £41 13s. 4½d., an assumed profit on the year's working of the gasworks?—Yes.

284. What is the price of gas?—The price for the running quarter is 6s. 8d. per 1,000 cubic feet. These last two years we charged 8s. 4d., for the auditor said the gasworks had not being paying since the rise in the price of coal.

285. In consequence of the rise in the price of coal you charged 8s. 4d.?—Yes.

286. In this year's account how much is it?—In this year's account it is 8s. 4d.; it is only for this current quarter that it is 6s. 8d.

287. I see by the auditor's report of the two last years, that you worked your gasworks from 1873 to 1874, at a loss of £101 6s. 10d. after allowing for the lighting of the public lamps; and from 1874 to 1876, at a loss of £19 6s. 10½d., so that you have been gradually bettering your position?—Yes.

288. Am I right in saying that all these coals were got in the last year?—They were got in last year.

289. And there were no coals in hands on the preceding year?—There were none; I have the record of that here.

290. For the first time, then, you this year work the gas concern at a profit?—Yes.

291. You never, I believe, have made any rate in Trim?—There was never a municipal rate made in Trim. The property was sufficient for all purposes; the Town Commissioners felt their way as the rental was increasing, and lately they did a good deal for the town. We have attended to the footpaths, although the county surveyor says it is the duty of the road contractor to have them kept in order, still we must do it because we cannot have the people scrambling about in the streets. We made some very good footways.

292. What fairs are there in the town?—Fairs are held on the 5th May, 1st October, 16th November, and the 27th March. The October fair is a very large one; the fairs are held on the Fair-green.

293. Is that Fair-green the property of the Town Commissioners?—Yes; and is at present let to a tenant.

294. What size is it?—Two or three acres. The infantry barrack is on the green, and the Government rent the site.

295. At what rent?—About 1s. in the year.

296. And at what is the Fair-green let?—It is let to a tenant at £7 a year.

297. Let, I suppose, for grazing purposes?—Yes; and for exhibitions that come to the town, such, for instance, as a circus.

298. And the reservation that you have is for the fairs?—Yes; fairs are held also monthly for the sale of small stock, and these are held in the streets.

299. The only fairs held by the Town Commissioners there are the four fairs which you mentioned, and you do not levy any tolls at them, and I suppose the Commissioners have no patent?—No.

300. Is a fair held in the streets on the first Saturday of every month?—Yes.

301. Has it never been suggested to hold these fairs for young and small stock on the Fair-green instead of in the streets?—No; there is no objection to having them on the streets.

302. Do they not leave the streets in a very filthy state?—The filth has to be cleared up immediately after the fair.

303. Are they not complained of as being a nuisance?—No, never.

304. Do not you think they are a nuisance?—No, I do not.

305. I suppose the people who would like to have them on the streets are publicans?—Well, there is more than publicans—all the trades-people would like it.

306. I suppose every grocer in the town has a licence?—Yes, they have, and some of the people in the town sell everything.

307. I have got a list here in which Mr. Plunkett is described as a merchant—is he also a publican?—That is a portion of his business, but only a small portion of it. He is extensively in the hardware and timber trade. He is the most extensive merchant we have in the town.

308. Do all who are put down here as grocers have retail spirit licenses?—Yes, every grocer has a spirit license.

309. Up to the year 1874, in fact to a still more recent period, you made all the sewerage in the town?—Yes.

310. You say you made three good main sewers?—Yes.

311. Do they serve the principal streets of the town?—Yes.

312. Are there connecting drains from the houses to these sewers?—No; very few as yet. It does not do to do much of that work in the winter time.

313. Since the passing of the Act of 1874 has the sanitary authority taken any steps to improve the sanitary condition of the town?—No, indeed. As I told you before, there was a necessity to make sewers, and they noticed the Town Commissioners to make it. Under the Public Health Act they summoned them before a bench of magistrates to make the sewer (one in particular that was very necessary, that was a great nuisance in the district), and the magistrates displayed great ignorance of the Public Health Act—

314. You say that the magistrates did not appear to have any knowledge of the Public Health Act?—None; and they declined to make any order.

315. Is the condition of Trim, in a sanitary point of view, tolerably good, with the exception of the

Trim. Jan. [illegible]

Mr. John Reilly.

...houses of connexion between the houses and the main sewer?—Yes, it is very healthy and very clean; but they particularly want good houses in place of thatched cottages, of which there are a good many in the town.

316. With the exception of what belongs to the Town Commissioners, is the town the property of one landlord, or is it in the hands of a good many owners?—It is in the hands of many owners, unfortunately, and in the hands of a good many who never see the town or take any interest in it.

317. Are there a good many dilapidated houses?—Yes, a good many dilapidated houses. The landlord in one case, will not do anything. He would prefer that the houses tumbled about the heads of the tenants in order to get them out.

318. Is this an absentee landlord who, you say, would prefer that his houses should fall into utter disrepair, and that the people should leave them?—Yes; that is a fact. There are other people holding property in Trim who never saw the town at all. There is one very good landlord, Mr. Thompson, who has some cottages in very good order.

319. He keeps his property, you say, in very good condition?—Yes.

320. Do the Town Commissioners generally keep their houses in good condition?—Yes; they generally have very tidy houses.

321. I mean the town property, not the houses they live in?—Oh, I do not know anything about that.

Mr. Patrick Malone.

Mr. Patrick Malone examined.

322. CHAIRMAN.—You are a Town Commissioner?—Yes, and a civil engineer.

323. Your name was mentioned by the town clerk as objecting to the signing of the minutes, as you thought that Mr. Vaughan should furnish the map without the names of the people being in it?—It is not stated properly—with the names and the acreage and the value.

324. What was your objection to the signing of the minutes?—Because Mr. Duignan did not get the order in writing from the town clerk that was made on the face of the books.

325. Was Mr. Duignan not present at the meeting when that order was made?—He said he did not mind hearing anything about it. I objected to ask Mr. Vaughan to put on the face of the map anything more than the tenants' names, and the acreage and the annual value. Mr. Reilly wished that he should put the names of the men who had it up to 1840, when it came into the hands of the Town Commissioners from the old Corporation.

326. What part of the resolution did you object to?—I took it to mean that Mr. Vaughan was to put not only the names of tenants, but the names of everyone who had held the land. I was for only putting on the name of the present tenant; but if he said that I wanted him not to put the acreage on it, he is mistaken.

327. What you mean is that you wanted only the names of the existing tenants?—That is all.

328. Did you wish the acreage to be on it?—Yes. I am a Town Commissioner since 1834, except for two years, and it was always the case that as the old members died there was a motion brought in by the agent, and there was an order made to get that surveyed by the local surveyor here, and valued by three Town Commissioners, and I never knew a lot to come into the hands of the Town Commissioners without it being done. It is all on the face of the books.

329. Do you not know that in that rental book kept by Mr. Duignan there is no entry of the lots held by the different tenants showing the acreage—it is on the minute book, but there is no summary of it.

330. You do not want the back tenants' names entered?—No.

331. Is it correct that, on being told by the chairman of the Town Commissioners that you could give a notice of motion, you prepared a notice of motion, and then, in consequence of something that fell from the chairman, who requested you to date it, you said the chairman was full of crotchets, and tore up your notice of motion, and said you had no business there, and might as well not attend in the future?—I did not say that I would not attend in the future. I attended when hardly anyone else would attend. I have attended as the fifth Town Commissioner to enable them to have the meeting.

332. Did you tear up your notice of motion?—Yes; he handed it back to me in a pettish way to date it, and he said that it was not a notice of motion, that it was a positive resolution. It is nearly eighteen months since the map was ordered, and he was to be ordered to furnish it at once.

333. Why do you object to entering the names of the back tenants?—I object to giving a regular history on the face of the map.

334. Did you object to the minute being signed because Mr. Duignan said that he had received no written order from the town clerk?—Yes.

335. Do you not know whether Mr. Duignan was present when the original resolution was passed?—No; I do not know.

336. Is there any other point that you wish to draw attention to in Mr. Reilly's evidence?—He told you there were no connexions between the houses and the main pipe, but there are twenty-five houses connected with the twelve-inch pipes.

337. I understood him to say that very few were connected with the main sewer?—He said none. Those houses were connected, and the parties were charged for the making of the connexions.

338. Is any money still due to the town commissioners for connexions made with the main drains?—Yes, through the neglect of Mr. Reilly in not collecting it.

339. It would seem that from £20 to £30 must be still due in that way to the town commissioners?—Yes. I wish to add that I suggested at one time that the fairs should be transferred to the green, and held the same as the other fairs.

340. Do you think it would be desirable that the monthly fairs should be transferred to the fair green?—Yes; I thought at the time that the green should be the place for the new fairs.

341. Did you give any notice of motion with regard to the transfer of the fairs?—No; nothing was done except what passed in conversation.

342. Your opinion is that it would be desirable to do so?—My idea was that when they grew large enough they should be transferred.

343. Do you consider that the present fairs held in the streets are a nuisance in the streets?—They are always very dirty on Sunday after the fair.

344. Are not the streets cleaned up by the Sunday?—There is an attempt made to clean them, but a very bad smell comes from it.

345. The streets, in your opinion, are not in a fit state on the following Sunday?—No; but at the same time I know that the people generally wish to have the monthly fairs held in the streets.

346. Can you give me any information with reference to Molloy's lot to which the town clerk referred?—I am connected with the town commissioners for a long time. In 1844, after the town commissioners were established, we were nine or ten years fighting with the old Corporation—trying to get hold of the property in some way or other. The lots were not standing in, and it was a long time before we got one lot. I made one valuation in 1844 after the establishment of the town commissioners. Previous to that, Molloy had

possession of a lot from the old Corporation, and we made efforts at the time to trace out from the old Corporation any point that would enable us to take proceedings against him, and get the lot. Mr. Fay, who was our solicitor at the time, came here and went over the books, trying if we could in any way establish a claim against this Molloy's lot. We could not do so, however, and the claim was dropped. Here is Mr. Fay's note (handing in the solicitor's notes to show that the town commissioners made every effort to establish a claim). We got opinions on the subject at a subsequent period.

347. In what year was that?—In 1867 or 1868.

348. In 1836 the commissioners made their report—the commissioners employed to report on the state of the Corporations in Ireland—and they reported that Trim stood in a peculiar position; that the Corporation of Trim held all the property that they had in the year 1700; and they complimented the town commissioners of Trim on not having lost any of their property. The object of this (the solicitor's books), you say, is to show that the town commissioners tried to trace the connexion with this lot?—Yes; to show that they did not neglect it.

349. You are a surveyor and civil engineer, and you valued the town in 1844?—Yes.

350. Did you value the town commissioners' property?—The town only—the houses. The old town commissioners objected to the preliminary proceedings that the inhabitants took to establish the town commissioners under the 9th Geo. IV.

351. Living in the town have you a pretty good idea of the value of property in the town?—Yes.

352. How much is the land worth per acre?—There was hardly a lot valued since I was a town commissioner that I was not one of the three who were sent out to value it. They are all let at a fair value.

353. You say you were one of the Commissioners generally who valued the land?—Yes, generally, because I was a valuator.

354. Is the land of the Town Commissioners let at anything like its fair value as the land goes?—It is let at a fair reasonable value to the tenants.

355. If that land was let by public tender, would it not let at a higher rent?—It would now on account of the improvements that the tenants made on it.

356. Take the lots let in 1866 to Thomas Fox, what are they worth?—At the present time or at the time they were let? One-half of that land was a lake in my memory. After it dropped into the hands of the old Corporation he sold his interest in it.

357. How much did he get for his interest?—I do not know. The Town Commissioners then spent money on draining the place; the bulk of it was covered with water in winter, it was dry in summer.

358. Very good land might be covered with water at a certain season of the year?—The one-half of the land was like the bottom of a lake that you would dry.

359. What would you give for it?—I would not give a shilling more than was given for it at the time it was first let.

360. How much in 1868? What was it worth eight years ago?—It was worth about thirty shillings an acre at that time. There was a lease for twelve years given.

361. Did you not let it at twenty-one shillings per acre?—Mr. Ball was our counsel when the attempt was made to take the whole of the property from us, and he advised us to get in all outstanding lots. He told us to get hold of Parsons' lot, and we gave him payment for surrendering Parsons' lot to us.

362. If the land was worth more then when the lease was granted, would it not be much better that Taylor's lease should have been suffered to expire instead of granting a fresh lease, which resulted in there being nineteen years more to run against the Corporation at a rent below its real value?—It would be bad for the reason that I have given. I induced Mr. Fox to come in and surrender it, and that was allowed him for his interest in one lease. We got £100 we would not be entitled to at all for this eleven years.

363. That life was not running against you?—It was.

364. He had surrendered his right absolutely for £40?—He sold it to another person and not to us.

365. *Town Clerk*.—That Parsons surrendered to another.

366. *Witness*.—Mr. Reilly is not stating the fact. We had a lawsuit about that. He said, "I'll pay you no rent for it," and we lost £400 contending for that. Judge Ball was our leading counsel, and he said, "There are nine or ten lots out, and you should go and get round the people who have them. Try to make terms with them or you may lose it altogether."

367. You say you were acting under Judge Ball's advice?—Yes; Mr. Reilly knows nothing about it.

368. We will refer to the records of the Corporation, and see which is true. What I understand is this, that Parsons actually came and surrendered his lease to the Town Commissioners?—He had no lease.

369. Fox came in and surrendered his lease?—We got nearly £100 for that that we were not entitled to, and we allowed him for that.

370. Did you value the land sold to the railway company?—I acted on the part of the Town Commissioners.

371. How much was sold to the railway company?—I think about four acres and some perches.

372. And what did they give you per acre for it?—I valued it, and Sir John M'Neill came down and made arrangements and settled with the tenants.

(End of first day.)

December 5, 1876.

[illegible]

382. Were you not the person who moved that they should be reduced?—I think so.

383. Why did you do so?—I thought that the competition put up the lands, that were let at that time, too high, and I proposed the reduction.

384. Was it in 1836 that those lands were let to those people?—Yes; those were the only lots let by competition.

385. And they were reduced afterwards?—Yes.

386. Can you tell me what they were reduced to?—They were reduced by 10s. an acre.

387. Can you give me the amount of the rental and the valuation?—The rental is £665 13s. 6d., and the valuation is £464 10s.

388. Were you the valuator for the railway when you made your award?—No, not for a long time afterwards.

389. After you had valued on behalf of the Town Commissioners did the railway company ask you to become valuator for them?—Yes. A long time subsequently.

390. You got £300 for the lands sold to the railway company—how much of that £300 did you give to the tenants as compensation?—Not a shilling. They agreed to take a reduction of the rent as a compensation for the loss of the land.

391. You sold 5a. 3r. 30p. for £300, and you lost, I believe, about £8 on the rent?—Yes, and I think it was a very good bargain. We sold it very high.

392. How much land did King give up?—1a. 0r. 12p.

393. And what rent did he pay for his land?—27s. an acre.

394. Did you take half an acre from Patrick Kennedy? How much did he pay per acre? How many acres did he hold?—About seven acres.

395. And what rent was paid for that land of which the railway took half an acre?—Beyond £2.

396. Something over £2 an acre?—Yes.

397. How much did Bryan Watson give up?—The portion for the road, 3a. 10p. The railway ran diagonally through the boundary of this holding. He would be entitled to £11 or £12 for his interest in the land.

398. You reduced the rent, did you not, by £1 8s. 7d.?—Yes; some of the tenants said we were not reducing them enough, and there were some alterations made at the time.

399. You say that you have been a Town Commissioner, with very little exception, since 1831?—Yes.

400. And during that time you say you never knew any land falling in to the Town Commissioners being let to Town Commissioners?—No lands falling in.

401. Do you remember the lot on the Hallowed falling about twenty years ago which I believe is the very lot we were speaking about as let to Mr. Kennedy?—I remember that his interest in it expired and that he was treated like all tenants in competition.

402. Do you remember that lot?—I do.

403. Was there a Mrs. King who offered £3 10s. an acre for it?—No.

404. Was there no offer made for it to the Town Commissioners?—No; because the Town Commissioners hold the principle that they would not disturb any person in possession.

405. Had not she priority either as the widow of the previous tenant or as sub-lessee?—I am not aware that she had. We treated Mr. Kennedy like any one else.

406. What was it let to Mr. Kennedy for?—Something over £2 an acre.

407. And I understand that Mrs. King, who, under your general rule had priority, made an offer of £3 10s. an acre, and it was let to Mr. Kennedy when he was a Town Commissioner?—I am not aware of it.

408. Do you remember a Town Commissioner named Neagan?—Yes; in my early days.

409. Twenty years ago?—It is thirty years.

410. He was a Town Commissioner, and did he not get a lot?—I heard he got a lot.

411. Did he not sell it within a week afterwards?—I heard that, but I am not aware of it myself. He was put out of the Commissioners. He was hooted out of the town altogether. He was tampering with the property.

412. You say Brennan had lands?—Yes; he got one of those lots by public competition.

413. Did not he get part of Chambers' lot?—We gave them to the highest bidder.

414. And he became a Commissioner at the next election, and still continued to hold the land?—Yes.

415. And got his rent reduced?—Yes; there was no opposition at the time to the reduction of the rent. There was a cry got up in the town that they should not have lands, and he gave up his to another man.

416. What did he get for it?—I do not know; the land was too high and what he got must have been very small.

417. Mr. Plunkett had lands?—Yes; he got lands by marrying a Mrs. Fynn.

418. Did not he get a part of that other lot that belonged to a man named Curry, and also the house he lives in?—That is under a lease for ever or some lease that we do not understand.

419. He was not one of the original grantees?—He purchased it.

420. He pays, I see, £3 17s. 11½d. for the land, and 6s. 1½d. for his house?—Yes; that is an old grant.

421. Is the original grantee alive?—I presume he is. He pays rent for the house to another party, but he only pays that headrent for the landlord.

422. Is the original grantee alive?—It is a lease for ever; all the old grants were for ever.

423. No indeed they were leases for life?—No; you are under a mistake about that.

424. They were so granted under the by-law of 1705, to which I referred the other day. The lands were granted at the nominal rent of 1s. a year and for the term of the grantee's natural life?—That is not true of all the Corporation property, but only of the Commons in 1820, and it was merely to make £10 voters of them; the houses granted were all leases for ever.

425. I should like to see the lease of that house for which Mr. Plunkett pays 6s. 1½d. a year, and the value of it. What is it rated at?

426. Town Clerk.—This is the list of voters for the past year, and Mr. Plunkett is rated at £19—£17 and £2.

427. Which is the £17 for?—The houses, and £2 for the land.

428. Is the house and garden included in that 6s. 1½d.?—I cannot tell you.

429. Mr. Christopher Duignan.—It is.

430. Chairman.—I want to know how it is this house has not fallen in?

431. Mr. Malone.—Because there was a lease for ever.

432. Did not Mr. M'Keon, who was a Town Commissioner, get lands?—Not when he was a Town Commissioner, nor during my time. He was proposed for lands, and Mr. Sheridan moved that no Town Commissioner should get lands.

433. But had he not town land?—He did not get it from the Town Commissioners.

434. At least you will not deny that Mr. M'Keon and others continued to be Town Commissioners after they got lands which were vested in the Town Commissioners?—I cannot deny that.

435. Neagan's lease is lost—there is no doubt about that?—That was the most corrupt man we had in the town, and we put him out. The public spirit of the town got up, and he was chased away out of it.

436. Was not Dowling's lease granted in 1809?—Yes.

437. He had a lease of 2a. 2r. 25p. for thirty-one years from March, 1818?—Yes.

438. Town Clerk.—He was a Town Commissioner. His name appears here. Hugh Duignan was chairman then.

Tuam. Dec. 5, 1876. Mr. Patrick Malone.

439. CHAIRMAN.—What were Donovan's lots?

Mr. *Malone.*—They were set up for public competition.

440. In your time?—Yes.

441. What do you mean by public competition?—Handbills were circulated and tenders taken in. Donovan was the man who got the lot.

442. Part of Samuel Allen's lot?—Yes.

443. Is Donovan the tenant now?—Yes.

444. In each case that you let the lands by public competition did you not reduce the rents shortly afterwards?—Not shortly afterwards. A good landlord would do so, and we wished to be a good landlord.

445. Were not Chambers' lands set at £3 5s. an acre?—Yes.

446. But they were reduced to £2 5s. an acre?—To about £2 10s. an acre.

447. *Town Clerk.*—Donovan's land was let in January, 1861. This is his proposal, dated 14th January, 1861:—"I, Patrick Donovan, propose to give £3 15s. per acre for that lot of the North Commons lately held by Samuel Allen, deceased."

448. CHAIRMAN.—There was, I see, another man who offered to give £4?

449. Mr. *Malone.*—The lease was granted in 1864. He offered £3 15s. One other person offered £4, but he was ineligible, because he got land previously. There were other tenders—one at £3 10s. per acre, one at £3 5s., and another at £3 7s. 6d.

450. *Henry Duignan.*—I offered to give £3 15s. for the land. It was worth above that then, and I would give it now.

451. CHAIRMAN.—When were the rents reduced?

Mr. *Christopher Duignan.*—In 1870.

452. Upon the only occasions in which the land was let by so-called public competition — when Chambers' land was let and this lot of Samuel Allen's—in both cases I find the rent was reduced afterwards?

Mr. *Malone.*—Yes.

453. CHAIRMAN.—One of the tenants, Mr. Brennan, parted, I am told, with his lot for £40. Was not that his share of Chambers' lot?

Town Clerk.—Yes. When he sold it it was understood that the rent should be reduced.

454. Did Mr. Brennan assign his interest in that land?—The counterpart lease is in the name of Mr. Brennan, and there is no assignment executed on the counterpart lease.

455. There was no assignment, you said, executed except in one case—the case of the late town clerk?—Yes; that was all.

456. When did Chambers' lot fall in?—In 1858.

457. When were they reduced?—In June, 1870.

458. Do you not now refer to another lot—to Donovan's lot—which had been Allen's lot, or were they all reduced at the same time?—I will just read you the minutes of June, 1870:—

"At the adjourned monthly meeting of the Town Commissioners the former minutes were read by the town clerk and signed by the chairman. Business done.—It was moved by Mr. Malone, and seconded by Mr. Atkinson, and—'That the rents of Messrs. Luke Moore's, Benjamin Allen, Richard Burke, and Michael Kelly's lots be reduced 10s. per acre, and the rent of Patrick Donovan's at 15s. per acre.' There is an amendment to that resolution to reduce the rents—It was moved by Mr. M'Keon, and seconded by Mr. Lennard—'That the rents continue still as they are until the reply from the Lords of the Treasury be received.'"

It would appear from that that a memorandum was sent to the Lords of the Treasury to see if they should do so.

"On a division the amendment was lost, and the original resolution was carried by a majority of two votes—four to two. For the motion—Messrs. Raymond Brennan, Patrick Malone, George Atkinson, and Richard Burke. Against the motion—Christopher M'Keon and Nicholas Lennard."

459. Is that the only occasion on which rents were reduced?—Yes.

460. And the only two cases in which lands were let by competition were those lots?—Yes.

461. One on the death of Samuel Allen and another on the death of Chambers?—Yes.

Mr. Bernard Brennan.

Mr. BERNARD BRENNAN examined.

462. CHAIRMAN.—You had one of those lots of Chambers'?—Yes; but I got that lot before I was a Town Commissioner at all.

463. In 1858?—Yes; I was not a Commissioner at the time.

464. But did you hold it after you were a Town Commissioner?—I did.

465. And did you then part with your interest in it to Mr. Kelly?—Yes.

466. And is it true, as has been said, that you got £40 for surrendering your interest in it?—That is totally false; decidedly false.

467. Did you get anything for it?—At the time we got those lands we were obliged to pay each year's rent in advance. I held it for three or four years, and Mr. Kelly came to me and I said to him, "I am getting tired of this land, I have not time to attend to it, do you pay me the year's rent that I pay in advance, and step into my shoes." I never got another farthing.

468. How many acres had you?—Four acres and three quarters or so—nearly five acres.

469. At £3 an acre, so that it would be about £15?—Yes; I paid that before I went into possession of it at all.

470. £14 9s. 6d. it would be?—Yes; that was all I got.

471. You had 4a. 3r. 18p., and got you say £14 9s. 6d. for giving it up?—Yes.

472. When did you give it up to Mr. Kelly?—I had it three or four years; I gave it up about 1862.

473. Was there any understanding between you that you were to try and get the rent reduced?—No such thing. It was never mentioned. There was some reduction some time afterwards.

474. At that time did nothing pass between you about reducing the rent?—No understanding at all between us except, "Pay me the year's rent which I paid in advance, and have the farm; I am better by it."

Mr. Patrick Malone.

Mr. PATRICK MALONE recalled.

475. CHAIRMAN.—You say that while you were chairman you recovered lands which people were overholding?—Yes; there was a seven years' notice served in 1863 to throw the onus on the parties in possession to prove that the persons who went to America were still alive. We could not prove that they were dead. We recovered the lands then. We had a good lawsuit.

476. Yes; that was referred to before as costing a good deal of money, and that was given as the reason why you would not contest the possession of this Molloy's lot?—Yes, because it cost so much. In one way or other we recovered the whole of that rental, which was nearly lost like Molloy's lot.

477. Have you got that opinion of the Lord Chancellor which was referred to?

478. *Town Clerk.*—No; nor that opinion of counsel which was referred to. Neither of them are in the minutes.

479. CHAIRMAN.—£240 is Griffith's valuation, I see, and you get £265 12s. 6d.?—Yes.

480. *Town Clerk.*—I am asked to read this resolution:—

"[illegible], 18[illegible].—Moved by Mr. [illegible] and seconded by Mr. Davis. Resolved—In order to save this body from even the suspicion of partiality or corruption, no town commissioners in future be considered eligible to be proposed for any tenancy to a lot of [illegible] at the [illegible] of the town commissioners.

"Amendment proposed by Mr. Wilmore and seconded by Mr. Leonard. Resolved—That Mr. [illegible]'s motion is out of place."

The amendment was carried by a majority of one vote.

Town, Jan. 4, 1876. Mr. Francis Ridson.

Mr. James Plunkett examined.

Mr. James Plunkett.

481. Chairman.—You are a merchant in the town, and one of the town commissioners?—Yes.

482. You are one of the gentlemen, I think, who got part of the land that was held by a man named Curry?—Yes.

483. Did you get 4a. 2r. 13p. of Curry's land?—No, about two acres one rood. I got it by Vaughan's valuation.

484. Very recently—while you were a town commissioner?—Yes, on 19th December, 1873.

485. You paid, did you not, 15s. an acre?—Yes.

486. Was that valued by Mr. Vaughan?—Yes.

487. You also hold a house?—Yes.

488. How do you hold that house?—There is a lease of it. It is in Chancery at present.

489. You pay £11 5s. 4d. rent. To whom do you pay it?—Mr. E. John Wharton.

490. Did you buy the interest in the house you live in from Mr. Mulvany?—No; from Mr. M'Cormac.

491. Who did he hold from?—From Mr. Wharton.

492. Who did Wharton hold from; how is he entitled to that house?—I do not know.

493. Do you pay 12s. 2d. head rent to the town commissioners?—Yes.

494. How is it that the lease has not fallen in?—I cannot tell you.

495. Do you know nothing about it?—No. I have a lease for ninety-nine years.

496. From whom?—From Mulvany. I am the representative of Mulvany. He has a lease for ninety-nine years.

497. Had Mulvany a lease for ninety-nine years from Wharton, and did MacCormac get Mulvany's lease?—Yes.

498. Have you got the lease?—Yes.

499. For ninety-nine years?—Yes.

500. Can I see that lease?—Yes.

501. How is it that it did not revert to the Town Commissioners?—I cannot tell you.

502. You hold two lots of land, one at £1 17s. 11½d. half yearly—that would be £3 15s. 10d. a year?—Yes.

503. Which is that?—That is the first lot.

504. For the other you pay, I see, £2 18s. 3½d. half yearly, which would be £5 16s. 6d. for the whole year?—Yes.

Mr. Thomas Kennedy examined.

Mr. Thomas Kennedy.

505. Chairman.—You hold more than one lot?—Yes.

506. You hold two lots?—Yes.

507. Were these granted to you or to your father?—One was granted to my father.

508. Was your father a Town Commissioner at that time?—Yes, he was.

509. Who was the other lot granted to?—William Burnell.

510. He was the man whose lot fell in, he having gone to America?—Yes; he sold his interest to me.

511. For what?—For a consideration that I gave him—a sum of money.

512. What sum of money?—Well, I suppose I gave him—he had land from me and from the Town Commissioners, and I paid him for about twelve acres that he gave to me; afterwards I returned all his land except two acres, and although I gave him £200 for twelve acres, I charged him no tenant-right.

513. You gave him £200 for the common lands?—No.

514. You hold one lot from your father, and, you say, another from William Burnell?—Yes.

515. Who did Burnell get that land from—was it let to him by the Town Commissioners?—Yes.

516. Were you then a Town Commissioner?—Yes.

517. Can you tell me when it was—was it about '64?—About that time.

518. How many acres did Burnell hold from the Town Commissioners?—He held about five acres; there is three acres to other tenants who pay him rents.

519. How much did you get from Burnell?—Three or four acres only.

520. You paid £12 for one lot and £14 0s. 11d. for another?—Yes.

521. Which is your father's lot?—The £14 one.

522. How much did you give Burnell?—£200 I gave him to surrender the lease.

523. How many acres did you get for this £12 a year?—Four or five acres; there are two other tenants who paid rent for one and half acres.

524. I want to know the quantity for which you paid £200, and for which you pay the Town Commissioners rent?—4a. 2r. 16p., and two other tenants were tenants of Burnell.

525. Is 4a. 2r. 16p. the whole of it?—Yes.

526. Which you purchased Burnell's interest in, he having got a lease from the Town Commissioners?—Yes.

527. You gave Burnell £200, and he surrendered his interest in that lot which he had from the Town Commissioners, and that outstanding lease which he had from you?—Yes.

528. How much of that £200 did you consider you were giving for the Town Commissioners' land?—A portion of it.

529. I want to know how much of it?—I suppose I gave £150 for Burnell's interest in the Corporation land.

530. With regard to the lot which you had from your father, how many acres is in that?—There is six and a half acres.

531. Then it would be nearly £2 5s. an acre?—Yes.

532. That your father got when he was a Town Commissioner?—Yes.

533. Was he a tenant of the land before he got a lease of it?—Yes; he held under James Taylor.

534. Was there a person named Mrs. King, who also held under James Taylor?—Not that I am aware of; she held under my father.

535. Your father held under Taylor, who was the original grantee, and you say Mrs. King held under your father?—Not the same land.

536. Some other land?—Yes.

537. Adjoining land?—A good distance from it—near to the town.

538. Did Mrs. King make an offer to the Town Commissioners?—I was not a Town Commissioner at the time.

539. Did you hear that she did?—I heard something about it.

540. Do you know how much she offered for it?—No.

541. Did you hear that she made an offer for it?—Yes.

542. Do you keep the land in your own hands, or do you sublet it?—I have that lot sublet to Burrell at the same rent.

543. At the same rent that you pay to the Town Commissioners?—Yes. It was so bad that I could not keep it.

544. Was there any arrangement to that effect between you?—No, none at the time that he sold the interest to me.

545. Is that all the land you hold from the Town Commissioners?—Yes.

546. Do you hold some surrounding land of about the same value as that which you hold from the Town Commissioners?—The land I hold from the Earl of *Essex* is very nearly twice as good. I hold land much better than the Corporation land at 31s. an acre.

547. How near is Lord Essex's land to Trim?—All surrounding the town.

548. And so is the Corporation land, is it not?—No, it is at a considerable distance.

549. What you hold is not a considerable distance from the town?—It is. The Corporation lands are inferior lands; they are not good pasture lands.

550. When you got the land—you or your father—for which you pay £3 1s. per acre, was it put up to public competition or not?—I am not aware.

551. You have heard that Mrs. King made an offer?—Yes.

552. And a higher offer than your father?—I do not know. I heard she made an offer, and at the time she did so it was disposed of to another, and entered on the books.

553. Have you not heard that she made a higher offer? I have not.

Mr. Christopher Patrick Duncan examined.

554. Chairman.—You are the agent of the Trim Town Commissioners?—Yes.

555. And have been, I believe, since 1843?—Yes. In 1847 I received the first rent. I was appointed treasurer in 1843.

556. Are you treasurer as well as agent?—I was at that time, when there was no bank.

557. Since that time have you received all the rents of the Corporation?—Yes.

558. Have you got a list of all the tenants?—Yes.

559. Besides this one which you handed me the other day have you got a list from the commencement? —Yes, when they came in.

560. In the year 1843 was there a list of the tenants handed to you?—There was only one tenant. John King was the first man who paid me money for land. He paid one and a half year's rent in 1844. That was the first lot that dropped into the new Town Commissioners.

561. Had that lease been granted to King, or was it granted after you became agent?—I do not know the date when it was granted.

562. Was it granted whilst you were agent?—Yes.

563. In 1843?—Yes. Some of the lands were let to the then Corporation members at the nominal rent of 1s. in order to give them power to vote.

564. The bulk of the Corporation lands were let at the time you came into office?—There was only one lot not let.

565. The Corporation lands, in round figures, are about 150 acres?—Yes.

566. Who were they held by when you became agent?—They were let out to the old Corporation, who paid no rent.

567. To members of the old Corporation?—Yes.

568. Freemen and burgesses?—Yes.

569. And they paid 1s. a year for each of their holdings?—Some did, and some did not.

570. Did you ever receive any of these shillings?—Yes; from some of them.

571. I do not see any shillings entered here. Did any of them ever pay their 1s. a year?—Some of them paid it to me afterwards.

572. Not at that time?—No; not for a long time afterwards.

573. Did not the old Corporation get at that time even the benefit of this 1s. a year?—Yes.

574. You never got any of them until 1845, and you were appointed in 1843?—I got one in 1844.

575. How many lots was the property divided into in 1843?—I cannot tell you.

576. You kept no record of it?—No.

577. Had you no record whatever of how the property was distributed?—No.

578. You never had?—Never had.

579. The first lease you say that fell in was King's? —On the death of a man named Francis Taylor the bargain lot fell in.

580. Was that let to King in September, 1843?—Yes.

581. Did he pay you rent on the 25th March, 1844?—Yes.

582. And he then paid you £36. Would that be three half years' rent?—Yes.

583. Did you ever see the lease? Did he not hold from 1843 till 1849 before the lease was made?—Yes.

584. Was John King a Town Commissioner?—Never; he did not live in the town.

585. Richard Flood. Was his an old tenancy?—No.

586. Have you got a list anywhere showing the quantity of land held by each tenant?—No, only this one. We have a record of it on the minute book.

587. You have no such book?—No.

588. Nor any means of making such a book?—No means of making such a book.

589. You have been agent for thirty-three years, and have got a great number of corporate lands let since then?—Yes.

590. How many of the old lots are still outstanding? —I think there are five.

591. Under old grants?—Yes.

592. With those exceptions, have they not all fallen in during that time?—Yes.

593. Surely it would be your duty to enter on the rental not only the names of the tenants but also the number of acres held by each?—They were all put in the minute book. I never saw any form of rental book but that.

594. You have not got it at all events?—I have not got it.

595. Do you remember the order being made by the Town Commissioners—I think last September—that you should furnish the town clerk with the names of the tenants from the commencement of each letting?—A thing that I could not do. The only thing I could do would be to refer him to the rental as I had it myself.

596. You could at least have put down the names of all the tenants?—Sure they are all here.

597. The names of all the tenants in succession. You were there when the order was made?—I told them I could not do it.

598. You heard that resolution (the town clerk having read the resolution ordering the list of names to be supplied)?—Yes. I could not do it.

599. Did you tell them that?—I did.

600. Who was chairman then?—Dr. O'Reilly. I gave this rental to the town clerk to write out, and he had the names on the minute book by which he could check it.

601. Did you move an objection to the signing of the minutes?—I did.

602. What was the ground of your objection?—That I would not make out the return from the commencement of these lettings, which was ordered at the meeting before.

Trim.

Mr. C. P. Duignan.

603. Did you say that you said so at the preceding meeting?—Yes; that I could not do it; that I would give the rental as I had it.

604. What was the date of the original grant of the land of which Mr. Ball, the solicitor in Dublin, receives the rent, and of which another person receives the rent of the adjacent cottage? Mr. Ball in Dublin, I understand, receives the rent of certain lands, and a Mr. Donovan receives the rent of an adjacent cottage?—He is Councillor Donovan.

605. Who was the original grantee of those lands? —I cannot tell that.

606. Surely you can tell that. You keep a rental book, and the original grantee was bound to pay you a shilling a year?—I never got a shilling.

607. You are paid to look after those things?—I am paid to get the rent as soon as the tenants are declared.

608. How do they hold?—They hold in some way that I could never find out.

609. Do you believe that the lands belong to the Corporation?—I am sure they do.

610. Why do you not try to get the land?—I never knew who held it.

611. Has no application been made to Mr. Ball, in Dublin?—No.

612. Do you not consider it part of your duty, as agent to find out what land belongs to the Corporation, and what rent you ought to receive for it?—Certainly.

613. If you find that land belonging to the Town Commissioners is held by parties who do not pay rent to the Town Commissioners for it, it is your duty to look after it?—Surely.

614. What other land is there besides this of which Ball and Donovan receive the rent, and Molloy's lot for which the Town Commissioners are not paid rent? —There are no other lands that I know of.

615. Those are the only ones?—Yes. Molloy's is over-holding.

Dr. Francis John O'Reilly, J.P.

Dr. Francis John O'Reilly, J.P., examined.

616. Chairman.—Were you present as chairman of the town commissioners when the resolution of 7th September was passed? Do you remember that resolution being passed?—Yes.

617. Did the agent then state to the town commissioners that it was impossible for him to furnish the information?—I do not remember. I have no recollection of it. I do not know whether he made that explanation or not.

618. Have you any information to give us with regard to the sanitary work in the town?—There has a great deal been done. You will see the number of reports that the sub-sanitary officer made to me, and I have acted on those reports always. I think I could say for the town of Trim that it is better off in that respect than most towns in Ireland. Most of the houses are creditable to the people.

619. You are the sanitary officer to the board of guardians as well as chairman of the town commissioners? Have you reported nuisances to the board of guardians as the sanitary authority for Trim?—Perhaps in 150 cases.

620. And has action been taken in all those cases? —Yes.

621. Have there been any connections made with main sewers?—In as many as could be made.

622. Have they called upon the people to make them?—Yes.

623. And have they acted upon such notice?—They have not; they were brought before the petty sessions and the magistrates refused to act upon it. One gentleman was summoned and he refused to attend before the magistrates and no order was made in that case. The board of guardians have done all in their power, and it rests with the magistrates.

Mr. C. P. Duignan.

Mr. Christopher P. Duignan recalled.

624. Chairman.—Can you give me a list of the outstanding lots of which parties had grants for lives before 1840, and the Poor Law Valuation of each?—James Walker holds a lot of four acres—Poor Law Valuation, £5 10s.; William Carey, £5 10s.; Edward Parsons, £5 10s.; William Parsons, £5; and John Hughes, £5 15s.

625. Are those original grants by the old Corporation?—Yes.

626. Were those all freeman's or burgess's lots?—All freeman's lots.

627. Do you know how many acres those comprise? —Edward Parsons' lot is about four acres, and the others are from three to four acres generally.

628. You may say about twenty acres outstanding on those five lots?—Yes.

629. Why are no transfers indorsed on the leases—are they not prepared by you?—No; by the solicitor in Dublin. There is no clause in the lease to prevent them from selling out.

630. Why do you not keep a record of whatever transfers are granted?—I do. I was ordered by the present town commissioners to put the names as I have them here.

631. Why do you not identify the lots on your own rental-book?—I have them.

632. Is it not on the face of your rental?—But I have it.

633. If you had that, there would be no excuse for saying you could not give the information which was asked?—It is recorded on the minute-book.

634. Why is it not down with every lot? You know of course the name of the new tenant and the name of the old grantee?—Since 1866 I did that but not before that time.

635. I want to know something about Mr. Thomas Fox. This lease to him is signed by you as Fox's agent?—Yes.

636. How is it that you acted as agent for Fox and agent for the town commissioners?—Yes; I was agent for both. Before he went away he gave me power of attorney and gave up his land to pay the rent until he came back. He was in debt when he went away. He held a good deal of land about the town. I did not keep the dates of his coming and going. I paid up all his rents—the rents of the corporation lands, and the rents of the manor lands that he held, paying upwards of £100 a year for them. He then wrote to his cousin, the Rev. Father Allen, and I was instructed to settle with Father Allen the same as if I was settling with himself.

637. What I understand is this, that when Fox went to America he owed money. Did he owe you money?—He owed me the rent of the Commissioners' lands only as agent.

638. He owed you no private debt?—No.

639. He asked you to hold and farm this land, and pay the rent for him?—Yes.

640. For your own benefit or for his?—For his benefit.

641. Suppose there was a profit out of the land, who got the money?—He did. I sent him money occasionally.

642. How much did he hold when he went to America?—About eighteen acres of the Corporation lands.

Tuam.
Jan. 8, 1877.
Mr. C. P. Duignan.

643. Any besides the fourteen acres?—He held fourteen acres and some he got from Parsons.

644. He did not hold that direct from the Corporation?—Yes then.

645. Do you say then all he there held was fourteen acres?—He was after giving up Parsons' lot, and making an agreement to have the leases put into one.

646. Did he make an agreement to get a lease of Taylor's?—Yes.

647. Was Taylor dead then?—Taylor went to America a long time before him.

648. There was a lot of 4a. 3r. 21p. under Parsons?—Yes.

649. And 14a. 3r. under Allen?—From Taylor; he got it from Taylor.

650. Taylor was the man who held from the Town Commissioners?—Yes; after his father's death.

651. And had not nineteen years of his—Taylor's—lease expired?—I cannot say the exact number of years.

652. He had a lease for thirty-one years?—Yes.

653. And had Parsons a lease for thirty-one years?—A lease for his life.

654. Yes; he was one of the old grantees?—Yes.

655. In what year did this man Fox go to America?—I have not got the date of it here.

656. How long was he gone when you got this lease from him?—Two or three years.

657. Were you doing business for him those two or three years?—Yes.

658. Was it by his directions that you applied to the Town Commissioners for this lease?—Yes; the agreement to give him the lease was made before he went away.

659. When?—As soon as he wished to prepare it.

660. When did Henry Parsons die?—In 1874.

661. Parsons was not dead when this lease was granted in 1846?—No; he came in and surrendered it; forty shillings an acre, I think, he gave for Parsons' land; Henry Parsons died on the 21st October, 1874; Fox bought from Parsons, and he came in then and surrendered his lease to the Town Commissioners; Fox surrendered Parsons' lease to the Town Commissioners, and he was paying rent from the year 1863, and so there was thirteen years' rent paid to the Town Commissioners that they had not any right to unless Fox surrendered to them.

662. Allen paid Parsons £60 for his lease in 1842, did he not, and he then gave up the lease to Fox. Was Allen Fox's uncle?—Yes.

663. From 1842 to 1863 I want to know who paid the rent to the Town Commissioners for the lease that was surrendered by Allen?—No rent was paid by anyone.

664. How much of that time was Fox holding from Allen?—I cannot tell you how long that was. It was after the uncle's death that Mrs. Allen gave it to her nephew.

665. And you applied to the Town Commissioners for this lease in 1863?—Mr. Fox before he went away made application to the Town Commissioners, and surrendered his lease, and the lease was to be granted to him.

666. How was it that it stood over till 1863?—I cannot say how that was. It was on the books that he was to get the lease.

667. Did you go to the town commissioners and ask for this lease to be granted?—I did.

668. In 1863?—Yes.

669. Have you continued to hold this land ever since for Fox?—Oh, not at all.

670. Who holds it now?—I got a letter from America, and before Mr. Fox died there——

671. Is he dead?—Yes.

672. When did he die?—About three years ago.

673. Up to the time of his death did you hold it?—After I gave it up to his cousin, Father Allen, he died in America. I held it till about 1872. I farmed it for him, and paid the rents to the town commissioners and to the Rev. Father Allen, and paid the debt he was in when he went away.

674. Did he pay you a commission?—Yes; he paid me £40 a year.

675. Was there any dispute between you and Phœbe Carry about some land?—Between her son and I.

676. What was it?—There was a lease made to her of a small portion of land—1a. 1r. 11p.—which is immediately outside the town. She sold a small plot of land to another party for £10, and she went to that party to sell a second lot. She came to me on the 4th May, 1842, and told me she was after being offered £10 by a certain party in town (who is dead since), but that she would have to give up possession of it at the time, and she did not wish to do that, as she had two cows. I then gave her £10, leaving her in possession as long as she lived; and if she lived after me, she was to make the best hand she could of it. I was not to go in until after her death, and I gave her £10 for her interest in the lease.

677. Was it a lease for thirty-one years?—Yes.

678. What was the date of her lease?—20th September, 1841. She was the widow of the town sergeant.

679. She got the lease in 1841?—Yes.

680. You gave her £10 for the reversion of her interest?—Yes.

681. What age was she then?—She lived up to sixty-five.

682. Did you tell the town commissioners?—No, nothing about it till her death, and I went in and took possession then.

683. Was there any dispute that was brought before the board between you and Phœbe Carry about the matter?—No. It was about the land; she was dead then.

684. It was between her son and you?—Yes. I claimed the land under this agreement, and there was another party who was to give them money, and the son or son-in-law went in and wanted to put me out of possession.

685. What was the decision of the town commissioners?—For me to pay the rent and hold the land.

686. And you hold it since?—I do.

687. You hold two lots?—Yes.

688. From whom did you get the other one?—It consisted of five acres, Irish plantation measure, on lease of thirty-one years, at £7 10s. a year. I laid out £73 7s. 6d. on that £7 10s. lot before I got anything from it; and on the other (Phœbe Carry's lot) I laid out £40 besides the amount I paid her for it.

689. That is not an answer to my question, and you know it. There was some land let to a man named John Allen; how did you get possession of that lot?—He owed me £20 when he went away, and he gave the lease up to me for the £20.

690. Did he give you an assignment of his interest?—He had no interest.

691. Was it not a freeman's lot?—But he was going away.

692. How many acres is there in that lot?—I suppose there is about four or five acres.

693. Is that man still living?—I never heard anything of him since he left the country.

694. Did Allen get a grant of that lot for his life?—I could not say.

695. Do you know whether he is living or not?—I am sure he is not. I never heard of him since.

696. Have you ever paid any rent for it?—I have.

697. How much?—£3 a year.

698. Who did you pay that to?—The town commissioners.

699. Did you get a lease of it?—I did.

700. From whom?—From the town commissioners. I think I got a lease, but I am not sure.

701. *Town Clerk.*—Mr. Higwell got the lease, Mr. Duignan did not.

702. CHAIRMAN.—Allen paid no rent?

703. *Mr. Duignan.*—No.

704. Who holds it now?—Mr. *Higwell.*

Tralee, Dec. 4, 1876. — Mr. C. F. [illegible]

705. How much did Mr. Hipwell give you for it?—£30.

706. How long did you hold it after Allen went away before you sold it?—I think I had it somewhere about three years.

707. Is that the land from which Henry removed the fence?—Yes, a portion of it.

708. Who gave him power to remove the fence?—Sixty or eighty years ago it was removed by Mr. Chambers. He held Henry's farm.

709. Was the fence gone before you got the land from Allen?—It was.

710. Did Henry occupy the land that was afterwards recovered by Judge Flanagan's order?—Hipwell has it.

711. Did not Judge Flanagan make an order that it belonged to the town commissioners?—Yes.

712. Was there not some lawsuit before Chief Baron Pigot?—Yes, as to land that was conferred on a man named Robert Francis.

713. Did you not get possession of that land?—Yes. I got possession of it after the row being about it.

714. When was that?—I could not tell you in what year.

715. Who occupies that land now?—Mr Hanbury got it at £6 a year after the second trial. It was tried before Judge Monahan, and a compromise was come to, and Hanbury, who was then in occupation, was allowed by arrangement to remain in as tenant to the commissioners at a rent of £6 a year on a new lease for thirty-one years from 29th September, 1862.

716. How was it that you collected gas rents?—In May, 1872, the present town clerk was ordered to read the meters and give me the readings, and I was to collect the rents at five per cent.

717. Have you got that order?—It is on the books.

718. One man collects it for nothing, and you would collect it at five per cent.?—When I was collector every collection that I lodged I gave the name of the man who paid it. Now no one knows what is to be collected.

719. At all events this year the gasworks is a paying concern, the audited account shows it?—We wanted to have one person to read the meters and one to collect the gas rents. The land I had from Allen was leased in 1868 to Hipwell at a rent of £6 a year. It consists of five acres three roods, Irish plantation measure; that was the only lease the town commissioners made of that land.

720. No lease was granted to you?—No.

721. How many years did you hold it?—I could not have held it more than two or three years, because I had to go through Mr. Hipwell's land that he held in perpetuity to it.

722. Did you pay any rent for it during those years?—I could not swear that I did unless I had my books here.

JANUARY 11, 1877.

(Before the Chairman, Mr. [illegible].)

Mr. Terence [illegible] examined.

Jan. 11, 1877. — Mr. [illegible] examined.

723. CHAIRMAN. You wish to be examined, and you are, I believe, the postmaster of Tralee?—Yes; I am the postmaster of the town of Tralee, and I object on principle to the letting of the corporation lands by public auction, because the demand is excessive and the supply limited.

724. You have been a town commissioner?—Yes.

725. For how many years?—I was connected with the Town Commissioners for about twenty-five years as auditor of the Commissioners and as chairman.

726. Were you the auditor before the appointment of a Government auditor?—Yes.

727. For how many years were you a Town Commissioner?—I could not say exactly.

728. When were you a Town Commissioner last?—Five years ago.

729. You say you were at one time chairman of the Town Commissioners?—Yes; I was chairman twice—for two years consecutively.

730. Were you a member of the Town Commissioners between the years 1840 and 1854?—No; nor for a long time after.

731. You were not a member of that body until after the passing and the adoption of the Towns Improvement Act of 1854?

732. I understand you to say in this document you have laid before me that you have some practical experience of the value of the town lands?—Yes, I have.

733. How—in what way?—As having myself held part of them.

734. What land did you hold?—I held part of the North Commons—part of Captain Mosley's land.

735. How much did you hold?—Ten acres.

736. What rent did you pay for that ten acres?—I paid the trustees 27s 6d. per acre.

737. In what years did you hold the land?—In 1838, 1839, and 1840. Captain Mosley died in 1845 or 1846.

738. You gave up the land, then, before his death?—I gave it up in 1840.

739. Was that land partly pasture and partly arable land?—Yes.

740. Did you sublet any portion of it?—No; I did not.

741. Were you a yearly tenant?—Yes.

742. And was it re-let every year?—No, every seven years.

743. Did you bid for the land again in 1840?—Yes, I bade for it every year.

744. When Captain Mosley died his land in the North Commons, which you say was about twenty Irish acres, fell in, and, of course, the Town Commissioners took possession of the land and re-let it?—Yes.

745. How did they let it?—I think in four or five lots.

746. On leases for thirty-one years?—Yes.

747. Was it the same class of land as the rest of the North Commons that you got?—Yes, the lot that I got was a very fair sample—a lot by which you could estimate the value of the whole of them.

748. Was the land re-let immediately after his death?—Yes.

749. To whom was it re-let?—To Matthew Colwell by William Colwell, £4. 1s. 3½d., from January 1st, 1860, for a term of thirty-one years.

750. Was he a Commissioner?—*Town Clerk*.—He was.

751. CHAIRMAN (to witness).—Were you a Commissioner at the time?—No; I knew it was let by competition. It was agreed to divide the lot into five parts—four lots of about four acres each, and the balance. It was subsequently agreed that a committee should retire to value the lots, and to select the names of the tenants. There were twenty-two applicants for the lands. The committee retired to value them, and announced that the highest offer was 10s., and the lowest 34s. per acre.

752. Did the committee value the lots, on that basis, and at the next meeting were the names of the persons selected out of the twenty-two applicants read out to the Town Commissioners?—Yes.

753. Can you tell me whether any of those persons selected were Town Commissioners, and then present and voting?—David O'Leary was present as a commissioner at that meeting, James Keary was also present as a commissioner; Richard Neville was a poor farmer.

754. Had he not some kind of a claim?—Yes; he was a tenant who occupied under Captain Mosley. Bryan Wallace was present as a commissioner.

755. In fact all of those who got lots except Neville?—Yes.

756. Did O'Leary get 3a. 2r. 0p., at £7 1s. 3d.?—Yes.

757. And Kenny, 2a. 2r. 3p., at £6 11s. 3d.?—Yes.
758. Neville, 3a. 2r. 35p., at £7 5s. 9d.?—Yes.
759. Watters, 3a. 2r. 6p., at £7 1s. 6d.?—Yes.
760. And Colwell, 4a. 1r. 35p., at £5 16s. 9d.?—Yes.

761. You say these lands were a fair sample of the North Commons?—I do.

762. For which you for what you held had paid at the rate of 27s. 6d. per acre?—Yes.

763. At the time they were let do you think they were worth more or less than they were let for to these people?—I think it was an excessive rent at the time. In fact, I may say the parties who took these lands had no other lands; they did not take the lands for the purpose of making any profit out of them.

764. You say you object to let land by competition?—I do; I have always objected to it.

765. What is your reason for objecting to it?—Because the demand is excessive, and the supply limited.

766. With regard to the reduction of rent—this is only the third instance which we have had of there having been any reduction for corporate lands. On the two previous occasions we heard of parties who then [illegible] lands surrendering their interests, and of an abatement then being made?—Yes, I remember that. The only case that I remember is Brennan's case. He was here before you; and he, in the most positive manner, contradicted the statements made by the town clerk. With regard to the cause of the rent reduction, we know the value of the land was much depreciated by the potato blight, and if the commissioners had taken this into consideration at the time they would not be regarded as landlords. I say they would have been justified in making the reduction.

Mr. Thomas Kennedy recalled.

767. Chairman.—Was this 8a. 2r. for which you pay £12 a year, let to your father originally, or to you?—There were seven acres let to my father at £3 1s. per acre.

768. Irish or English measure?—Irish. I pay £12 a year for this 8a. 2r.

769. You say that seven acres were let originally to your father whilst he was a Town Commissioner?—Yes.

770. And you hold it by succession from him?—Yes.

771. He had a thirty-one years' lease of it?—Yes.

772. Did you get the additional land which you hold while you were a town commissioner?—No; I got it from Mr. William Burnell. I was not a town commissioner at the time.

773. That is the 8a. 2r. for which you now pay £12 a year?—Yes.

774. Is that lot of the same value as that you had from your father?—No; it was let to William Burnell and he got a thirty-one years' lease.

775. How did you get it?—He gave it to me.

776. He surrendered it to you?—Yes.

777. When?—I do not know exactly. I think about ten years ago.

778. What did you give him for his interest in it?—I think about £150.

Mr. John Neary examined.

779. Chairman.—Have you any complaints to make about not getting some land to which you thought you were entitled?—No.

780. What is your complaint? Is it that you do not get a chance of bidding for any of the Corporation lands when let to others—because you do not hear about their being vacant?—Just so; and many another as well as myself in the town.

781. You would wish, I suppose, that the Corporation lands should be put up to public auction?—Yes.

782. You want some notice to be given, in fact, whenever such land is to be let?—Yes.

Mr. Patrick Donovan examined.

783. Chairman.—Your name was mentioned to us the last time I was here as holding land from the Corporation?—Yes.

784. How long have you held land from the Commissioners?—I think about six years; I do not know exactly.

785. Is it part of Samuel Allen's lot?—It is.

786. I believe there were a good many people tendered for the land when you got it?—Yes.

787. It is one of the lots that were said to have been put up to public competition?—Yes.

788. How was it put up to public competition? Was it by advertisement in the newspapers or by handbills?—By handbills.

789. You have held the land ever since?—Yes.

790. You were not a Town Commissioner, I believe?—No, I was not.

791. Nor a relation of any of the Commissioners?—No.

792. What rent do you now pay per acre?—£3 per acre.

793. Was it not let to you in January, 1864, at £3 15s. per acre?—I do not know exactly. Mr. Malone and three Commissioners came down and saw it before I got it.

794. Why was it reduced?—Because it was all a lake. The three Commissioners went down and valued it.

795. It was six years after you got it, I believe, that it was reduced?—Yes. For three years I had no crops in it. The river got choked, and the land got all flooded over.

796. Do you know that another man offered £4 an acre for that land?—Yes.

797. And why did you get it?—Because he had land; he had land of his own.

798. Did the handbills by which it was advertised say the lands should not be let to any person who had land already?—Yes.

799. Would you like to let it to anyone else now?—I would give it up.

800. Have you ever been offered any money for it?—No; I keep a dairy, and it is useful for getting a lot of manure from it.

801. Were you in court the last day I was here, when a ratepayer named Henry Deignan said he would willingly give £3 15s. an acre for it now?—No.

Mr. Plunkett recalled.

802. Chairman.—I want to know something more about the circumstances under which you hold the lands and house which were before referred to. You are rated, I see, at £17 for houses and gardens, and you appear only to pay 8s. 1½d.?—No; I pay £11 2s. 6d.

803. You are not the tenant of the Corporation for the houses?—No; I am the tenant of Wharton. The property is in Chancery. I pay the head rent for Wharton.

804. I understand all the old grants were leases for lives, but Mr. Malone told us that the grant to Wharton is a lease for ever?—I cannot tell you what it is for. I recollect that some years ago the Corporation

Trim. Jan. 15, 1877. Mr. Plunket.

put the matter into the hands of Mr. Ford to try the risk, and he said that he could make nothing out of it.

805. CHAIRMAN (to Mr. *Christopher Duignan*).—Who was the original grantee?—I cannot tell you that.

806. That is one of the faults I have to find with you—that you are not acquainted with matters of that sort. You were appointed agent in 1813?—Yes.

807. You knew, of course, it was your duty as agent to get a list of all town property, and to ascertain who were the parties holding grants for lives?—At the time the late town clerk was here, he had a list of all that. What happened to it I do not know.

808. Was Wharton the person whom O'Leary held under?—Mr. *Plunket*—Yes.

809. And you do not know of anyone else?—No.

810. Did Mulvany get a lease for ninety-nine years from Wharton?—Yes.

811. Have you ever seen it?—No.

812. And did Macnamara then get Mulvany's lease?—Yes.

813. Is he living now?—No.

814. How did it get into Wharton's hands?—I cannot tell you.

815. You hold from Macnamara?—Yes; I bought the interest in the lease. I heard from Macnamara that Mulvany had a ninety-nine years' lease.

816. Who was that lease from? Was it from the Town Commissioners?—No; from Macnamara.

817. Mulvany got Macnamara's lease?—Yes.

818. And you had it from Mulvany?—Yes.

819. For £75?—Yes.

820. That is the house you live in?—Yes.

821. What is the date of your lease?—I cannot tell you.

822. Have you got the lease?—Yes.

823. Will you be kind enough to fetch it for me to see?—I will try to find it.

Mr. DUIGNAN recalled. Mr. Duignan.

824. CHAIRMAN.—Have you ever seen this lease to Mr. Westby Percival?—I did.

825. It is a lease of two houses in Trim the property of the Corporation?—Yes.

826. To Westby Percival?—Yes.

827. On lives renewable?—Yes.

828. And I see the present Duke of Leinster is one of those lives?—Yes.

829. And the only surviving life?—Yes.

830. Who occupies those houses?—A man named Lake in one of them, and a man named Dalton in the other.

831. Did you ever hold these houses?—No; I held Dalton's house for a while.

832. Did not your brother hold one, and you the other?—He is the immediate landlord of Dalton.

833. And are you the immediate landlord of the other?—No.

834. How did your brother get possession of this house?—He bought the lease from Mr. Ralph Tew.

835. And have you dealt with these two houses in any way since Westby Percival's death?—Yes; I received the rent up to within the last five years. I think there is five years' rent due now. There is another portion of Percival's property—a portion of the Newtown lands, about thirteen acres that belonged to Mr. Percival. These houses in the town also belonged to him. Young Mr. Percival went away, and raised money on the property.

836. You know perfectly well I am only inquiring about the property of the commissioners and that we have nothing to do here with his own land?—No.

837. Do you say that Lord Dunsany is now the landlord of these two houses?—He is the man who receives the rent from the sub-tenants.

838. How did he get them?—He purchased them from the man (an attorney in Dublin) who advanced the money to Mr. Percival.

839. Is he the son of the Mr. Percival who died, and to whom the original lease was granted?—Yes.

840. And is he now abroad?—Yes.

841. He has disappeared?—Yes.

842. And you say Lord Dunsany purchased his interest in these houses from the solicitor who advanced the money to Mr. Percival?—Yes.

843. Did Percival ever come in and surrender his lease to the commissioners?—Never.

844. What do you say is Lord Dunsany's right?—He has the counterpart of this lease.

845. Has the question of Lord Dunsany's right ever been raised?—He came in to pay me the money, and I was told not to receive any money from him until those things were settled. I went to the solicitor of the town commissioners and he told me I should not refuse the money.

846. Did you not suggest that Lord Dunsany should be accepted as the assignee of Westby Percival?—I did not suggest it to the commissioners.

847. Did you ever see any transfer or assignment to Lord Dunsany, or was any such ever produced to the commissioners?—Not produced that I heard of.

848. Did not the commissioners, therefore, pass a resolution to re-enter upon the buildings for the benefit of the ratepayers?—Not that I heard of.

849. Have you, on behalf of the commissioners, taken any steps to re-enter or claim possession?—I received an order from the commissioners to do so.

850. Have you done so, and if not, why not?—No answer.

851. When were you first told, and by whom, not to accept rent from Lord Dunsany or his agent for those premises?—By the commissioners at their meeting; I don't know the exact date.

852. Did you ever receive any money from Lord Dunsany or his agent?—No; because I would not be allowed to receive it.

853. Who was the last person that you received rent from for this place?—Mr. Vincent; the lease was made to Westby Percival who died. No one came in to surrender the lease. His son raised money on property, which included these houses, from a Mr. Vincent. Vincent paid head-rent for the houses after young Westby Percival disappeared. Lord Dunsany bought Westby Percival's interest in these houses from Mrs. Vincent. The last person whom I received rent from was Mr. Vincent, which was about six years ago. Lord Dunsany offered to pay the rent to me, but I was told not to receive any rent from him until the matter was settled.

854. What interest had you or your brother in these houses?—A man named Tew paid £4 1s. 6d. a year to Mr. Percival. My brother gave somewhere about £80 to Mr. Tew for one of the houses.

855. Has he since paid rent for it?—He has paid rent ever since to Mr. Vincent, and paid rent last year to Lord Dunsany.

856. What rent did he pay to Mr. Vincent and Lord Dunsany?—He paid the same rent.

857. Have you an interest in either of these houses?—I have no interest in them myself, and had nothing to say to them except to get the rent.

858. What rent did you receive last year from Vincent?—It is a lease in perpetuity.

859. In whose name were the proceedings taken to eject Dalton?—In my brother's name—in Hugh Duignan's name.

860. On whose authority?—His own. He set the house to Dalton who owed him six years' rent. It was only yesterday he was decreed for the six years' rent, and he is not able to pay it, let alone six years' rent. He is to get £5 for giving up possession in the month of November, in addition to not paying the amount of the decree. My brother bought from Tew, and he held from Westby Percival, and he now pays rent to Lord Dunsany.

861. Your brother has got a judgment in the

court against Dalton?—Yes; he has got a decree for possession.

862. Is your bond for £400?—Yes.

863. And is it lodged in the Ulster Bank?—Yes.

864. It is a bond with two sureties for £200 each?—Yes.

865. When was the last bond executed?—About five years ago. I want to get a new man in one case.

866. Why; is one of them dead?—No.

867. Is he insolvent?—Yes.

868. And you have not yet got a new one?—No.

869. [The Chairman here stated that Mr. Vaughan, the valuer in Dublin, who had been employed by the Town Commissioners, and whom he had requested to attend here to give evidence both at the last adjourned inquiry and to-day, had sent an excuse on both occasions that he was too unwell to attend. He had, however, called at the Local Government Commissioners' Office at the Four Courts after the last adjournment on the 7th December, and had then made a statement relative to his valuation of the property of the Town Commissioners, of the substance of which the Chairman had had a note taken, which he would read to the Commissioners and ratepayers then present, as it had not been made in open court; and he considered it only fair that it should be read there before it was attached to the other notes of the evidence taken on this inquiry. It would, he said, be satisfactory to Mr. Malone to find that Mr. Vaughan considered the land which Mr. Malone had valued for the Commissioners to the railway company, and respecting which some question had arisen, realized its full value.]

Mr. Vaughan's statement was then read by the Chairman, and was as follows:—

"Edward Vaughan, of 18 Rutland-square, Dublin, stated that he had been called in by the Town Commissioners with reference to making a valuation of their property. He had supplied an estimate for such valuation, but the estimate did not include a map of the estate. The valuation is not yet completed, though Mr. Vaughan states that he has surveyed the property for his own information. No definite or written instructions were received by Mr. Vaughan for the drawing out of a map, although it was several times mentioned in a casual way that the Commissioners would require one. Had the valuation been completed, Mr. Vaughan would have given with it a copy of the Ordnance Map, but he would not construct a new one without receiving extra payment for doing so. Possibly the Town Commissioners may have [illegible] from [illegible] on this point, as one of their number, Mr. Malone, being a surveyor and valuer himself, evidently [illegible] to [illegible] of the work. Thomas Kennedy, a Town Commissioner, [illegible] a piece of land, consisting of eight and a half Irish acres, which would be equivalent to about 13a. 3r. 20p. English measure. This land is valued on the Poor Law valuation at £[illegible] a year, or [illegible] per acre. In Mr Vaughan's opinion this was worth fifty [illegible] per acre. Kennedy pays £[illegible] a year rent for this land. In addition to this, Thomas Kennedy holds another piece of land of about seven Irish acres, or 11a. 1r. 18p. English, which is rated at [illegible] per acre. Mr. Vaughan's valuation for this is [illegible] per acre. As a general rule, Mr. Vaughan's valuation of the corporate property is about 60 or 70 per cent. above that of the Poor Law valuation; but such a disparity (as in the case of Thomas Kennedy) between the rent received by the Town Commissioners and Mr. Vaughan's valuation does not in other instances exist. The property along the [illegible] is estimated as follows by Mr. Vaughan:—

L. Moore, valued at	. . . .	[illegible] per acre.
P. Allen,	. . . .	60s. 0d. „
M. Kelly,	. . . .	40s. 0d. „
E. Brogan,	. . . .	47s. 6d. „

"The Corporation, for the [illegible] mentioned tenants, in Mr. Vaughan's opinion, are in receipt of nearly full value. For example, M. Kelly holds 4a. 3r. 12p. Irish measure, or 7a. 3r. 37p. English, for which he pays £17 17s. 6d. a year. Mr. Vaughan's valuation for this was £19 a year. Mr Vaughan considers that the land sold to the railway company for £[illegible] realized about its value. Mr. Vaughan's private opinion is that the transactions of the Town Commissioners during the last four or five years have been straightforward, as the public are not brought to bear on them, but previous to that 'it was a different thing altogether.'"

WICKLOW.—November 11, 1876.

(Before Mr. Cotton, Chairman, and Mr. Exham, Q.C.)

A certificate was read to the effect that Mr. Halpin, the town clerk, was unable to attend owing to illness.

Mr. John Chapman examined.

1. Chairman.—You are the agent and collector of rents of the Town Commissioners?—I am.

2. How long have you been so?—Nearly six years.

3. The Town Commissioners are incorporated under the 9th George IV. cap. 82?—Yes.

4. Has the Towns Improvement Act ever been adopted here?—Never.

5. All the revenues of the Town Commissioners of Wicklow are derived from real property?—Yes, except the dog tax and a few other receipts.

6. Have they ever struck any rates?—No.

7. Have you got a book showing what the real property of the Commissioners consists of?—Yes (a book and printed rental handed in).

8. According to the printed rental of 1874 I see the rents were £1,313 3s. 1d., and this year's rental is £1,235 4s. 6d., which is correct?—Both are correct, it varies for every year, for there is always some small letting or place falling in.

9. How did that difference arise?—I think it was caused by the reduction of rent of a couple of holdings on the Murrough.

10. Point out those two holdings?—Those of James A. Travers, Northquay. They were £30 a year and reduced to £15, that is the rent now.

11. Has the rental been an increasing one during your agency, or a decreasing?—An increasing.

12. But there are cases in which the rent has been reduced?—About three or four cases.

13. You remember the property held by Colonel Gun Cuninghame?—Yes.

14. In the year 1874 that property fell in?—Yes.

15. What had his rent been? £3 1[illegible]s. 10½d.?—Yes.

16. It became vested in the Commissioners in 1874?—Yes.

17. What did they do with it?—They let it to the tenants in occupation.

18. Did they let it to the highest bidder?—No.

19. Or by auction?—No.

20. Or by public tender?—There were advertisements put in the newspapers to the effect that the property was to be let.

21. Have you got the advertisement?—I have not, but the town clerk has.

22. You say that advertisements were put in to announce that the property was to be let?—Yes.

23. What tenders were sent in in consequence of that advertisement?—I don't think there were any tenders except two or three.

24. Mr. Nolan (Chairman of the Town Commissioners).—I think you are labouring under a mistake, because there were other tenders sent in. The occupying tenants all sent in tenders.

25. Chairman.—Did the occupying tenants all send in tenders?—Yes. All Colonel G. Cuninghame's tenants sent in tenders.

26. Did outsiders—those who were not tenants also send in tenders?—Yes; those are the two or three persons I referred to.

27. Was any of the property let to any but the tenants who had holdings under Colonel Gun Cuninghame?—No.

28. Was it all reset to old tenants?—Yes.

29. Where was the property situate?—In different parts of the Main-street and town.

30. Were there tenders for higher amounts sent in by others?—Only two or three, I think.

31. Did they tender to pay a higher amount than the tenants had paid?—Yes.

32. What did Cuninghame's tenants pay in the gross? Have I it right here, £167 12s.?—Yes.

33. Is it true that the aggregate of Griffith's valuation of this property amounted to £300 10s. 2d.?—I believe that to be correct.

34. Was the property paid to each of the tenants?—Yes.

35. Were all these tenants continued in their holdings?—They were.

36. What did the following tenants pay, and what do they now pay—Henry M'Phail?—£5 a year, and now £1 1s. 10d.

37. William M'Phail?—£5 a year, and now £3 4s. 4d.

38. P. Fox?—£8; and Miss Hamilton, his successor, now pays £3 6s. 9d.

39. Are all the new lettings on the property of Colonel Cuninghame on leases for seventy-five years instead of yearly tenancies?—Yes.

40. Dr. O. Haydn?—£5 14s., and 15s. for a yard, now £3 12s., and £1 10s. for the yard.

41. Is he any relation to the Town Clerk?—No.

42. Joseph Fitzgerald?—£7, and now £2 12s. 6d.

43. J. Heppenstal?—£22, and his widow now pays £3.

44. J. Sullivan?—£14, and now £3.

45. J. Byrne?—£17 12s.; and his son-in-law, Robert Caldwell, now pays £7 10s. 6d.

46. John Wisdom?—£6 10s., and now £3.

47. George Newman?—£6 10s., and now £3.

48. George Smith?—£13, and now £5 4s. 6d.

49. William Williams?—He paid £4 a year, and it was let to a man named Maguire who is no connection to Williams, but he had been a tenant of that house before Williams took it, and had been for years, and his father before him.

50. How much does Maguire pay now?—£1 12s. 6d.

51. T. Ellis paid £6, and now £1 5s., and the representatives of Dunn?—£20, and now £5 15s. 6d.

52. Mr. J. Chapman?—£30, and now £15.

53. Is that yourself?—It is; but I wish to mention that I did not get the whole of the plot that I had held from Colonel Gun Cuninghame.

54. Who got the other portion of it?—There were four back houses that I gave up to the commissioners to accommodate the adjoining tenants with a row.

55. What did they let them for?—They did not put any rent on them separately, for they gave them as a row to the front houses that were to be built. These houses were behind the front houses.

56. Were they given to them for nothing?—They were.

57. And although these front houses had been reduced in rent, these others were thrown in?—They were.

58. Who were the persons holding them?—They are now held by a Mrs. Dunne.

59. Has her rent been reduced from £20 a year to £5 15s. 6d., and was she supposed to get four cottages at the back thrown in besides, which would be equivalent to £15 a year more?—Yes.

60. Then in fact not more than £15 a year is received by the Town Commissioners for what you paid £30 a year?—Not more; I told you that I gave up a portion of my former holding.

61. Mr. Ennis.—Let us see those leases—your own lease for instance will show what reality there is in the transaction. In fact I want to see all the leases with the advertisements relative to the letting of this property; any tenders sent in by parties offering themselves as tenants; and all the books in reference to the transaction. It was stated that they would be procured if possible from the Town Clerk's house, where it was stated they were.

62. Chairman.—What was Griffith's valuation of the property that you yourself held under Colonel Gun Cuninghame?—I cannot tell exactly.

63. Mr. Ennis.—I can; for it is here set down at £40 (reading from a document produced).

64. Chairman.—That is the 1874 rental. Is that the valuation of the premises for which you pay £15 a year now?—No; that is the valuation of all I held, including the four back houses.

Wicklow.
Jan. 12, 1876.
Mr. John Chapman.

65. Including that portion the use of which was given to Miss Dunne?—Yes.

66. What was the area given to her?—Four back houses, each about 16 feet square, two stories high, and with a yard of about 3 feet behind some of them.

67. Then these houses were 64 feet in frontage, and 18 feet in depth?—Yes, including the 3 feet of yard.

68. Mr. Ennis.—Were you also a tenant of Colonel Gun Cuninghame for these houses?—Yes.

69. What did you let these four houses for?—I had them let at 1s. 6d. a week each.

70. Chairman.—That will nearly make up the £15 reduction?—Yes.

71. Are all these houses pulled down now?—Not yet; but the building is going on in front, and they will be all pulled down.

72. And are they thrown into Miss Dunne's holding?—Yes.

73. Without saying anything?—Yes.

74. Who is Miss Dunne—is she connected with the Town Commissioners in any way?—No.

75. Neither the present nor the past?—Her father was a Town Commissioner about twenty years ago.

76. How many Commissioners are there amongst those whose names we have gone through?—There was not one at the time the leases were made.

77. Is Mrs. Heppenstal connected with any of them?—No.

78. The reduction in her case seems to be greatest of all, £22 to £3; were they asked to make it?—Not that I know of.

79. What was the value of the property she got?—I don't know.

80. Can you give me any idea why Mrs. Heppenstal pays now only £3 a year on a lease for what she formerly paid £22 as a yearly tenant?—No, I have no idea of it, but she covenanted to lay out £300 on it.

81. If it was put up to public competition what do you think it would have brought? What would you have given for it yourself?—I don't know, but she has since laid out a good deal of money on it, and improved it. When she got it, it was nothing but a tumbled down old house.

82. Mr. Ennis.—Was she a yearly tenant then?—Yes.

83. And did she pay £22 a year for a tumbled down old house?—Yes.

84. Chairman.—Is Mr. J. Sullivan a connexion of any of the Town Commissioners?—No; he got his holding in a different way.

85. How is that?—A man of the name of Healy had the place before him and built the house on it; he died and his widow got into bad circumstances, and was ejected. J. Sullivan then took it from Colonel Gun Cuninghame.

86. At £14 a year?—Yes.

87. But that does not explain how he had it reduced to £3 a year?—The widow put in a tender at the expiration of the old lease on the ground that the house had been built by her husband, and that she had lost it by becoming hard up, and that she expected that the Commissioners would take her claims into their consideration.

88. Do you know what she tendered?—I don't think she named any amount, but she claimed the house as having been built by her husband, and that the Commissioners should give it to her. She and Sullivan then agreed on terms that he would give her a sum of money; and the Commissioners then gave it to Sullivan at the rent they would have given it to her for.

89. How much did he give her?—£75.

90. So that Sullivan paid the old tenant who had put in a claim for it £75 in order to induce her to withdraw that claim?—Yes, otherwise he would not have got it.

WICKLOW.
Jan. 15, 1876.
Mr. John Chapman.

91. Mr. EXHAM.—Do you mean to say that Colonel Gun Cuninghame got £13 a year for this property as a ground rent, for you say that Keedy built the house that was on it, and they must therefore have paid the £13 a year for the ground rent?—I will explain that. Mr. Keedy was a builder, and he had a house on the ground at that rent, but it was falling down, and Colonel Gun Cuninghame would not allow anything for repairing it. Keedy then threw it down, and rebuilt it nearly all new, but it was on the faith of getting it at the ground rent when the lease would be out.

92. On whose faith?—He did it believing he would get it from the Commissioners.

93. What right had he to believe it?—I don't know.

94. CHAIRMAN.—Who is Mr. Caldwell who now holds for £7 10s. 6d. a year the property held by Byrne for £17 13s. a year?—He is a stamp distributor and excise officer.

95. Is he a member of the Town Council?—No, but he was at one time.

96. At that time he was, at the time the place was coming out of lease; but not at the time of the reletting, because it could not be let to him when a Town Commissioner.

97. You say it could not be let to him while he was a Town Commissioner. Did he resign for the purpose of getting this property let to him?—Well, not that.

98. Mr. Fedow (the Chairman of the Town Commissioners).—The custom house authorities required him to resign.

99. Witness.—I heard that there were complaints sent in about his being a custom house officer and a Town Commissioner at the same time, and that the authorities required that he should resign, and he did so at the time.

100. CHAIRMAN.—And he happened at the time to get this property at the reduced rent?—Yes.

101. Who were the Town Commissioners who did resign, and who had property relet to them?—William M'Phail, Henry M'Phail, Dr. George Halpin, and Mr. Caldwell.

102. Were those all?—Those were all.

103. Mr. EXHAM.—All I can say is that Mr. Caldwell's name appears on the town clerk's books as Commissioner on 25th March, 1874.

104. CHAIRMAN.—You say that two of them were reelected, was it at the next election?—Yes.

105. Who were they?—William M'Phail and Dr. George Halpin.

106. And Henry M'Phail and Caldwell were not?—They were not.

107. Mr Exham has drawn my attention to the fact that Henry M'Phail, William M'Phail, and Dr. Halpin were present and acted at the meeting in April at the time when these leases were granted.

[Mr. EXHAM read the minutes of the meeting of Commissioners held in the town hall, Wicklow, on the 6th April, 1874, at which Henry M'Phail, William M'Phail, Dr. Halpin, Robert Caldwell, and John Chapman were present. There were sixteen present at the meeting in the morning, and it was adjourned by resolution until seven o'clock the same evening, when there were twenty present, including the above.]

108. CHAIRMAN (to Witness).—You were not a Town Commissioner?—No, my name is put down there as agent.

[Mr. EXHAM then read the resolution of the 6th April, 1874, as to the granting of leases to Henry M'Phail, William M'Phail, Dr. Halpin, and Robert Caldwell, who were Commissioners then present, and to Mr. Chapman and other tenants.]

[Mr. Gaden (Town Commissioner) said that the whole of the proceedings of that day were rescinded as the Commissioners found out that they were illegal.]

The CHAIRMAN directed the following note to be taken as a summary from the minute-book:—

"At a meeting, at which Henry M'Phail, William M'Phail, Dr. Halpin, and Robert Caldwell were present, held on the 6th April, 1874, it was arranged that they should each have leases of their premises for seventy-five years, also that these resolutions were not then acted upon in consequence of legal advice obtained to the effect that it was illegal to grant leases to any sitting Commissioner. The case was submitted to counsel, and his opinion was that it was illegal to grant leases to sitting Commissioners."

109. Do you know, as a matter of fact that these or similar resolutions to these were afterwards acted upon?—Yes.

110. CHAIRMAN (after referring further to the minute-book) directed the following note also to be made:—

"On the 18th of May, 1874, the assignments of Henry M'Phail, William M'Phail, and Dr. Halpin having been executed at a previous meeting, leases for seventy-five years were granted unanimously upon the terms agreed upon on the 6th April, 1874, to each of those parties, and on the 18th May a similar lease was granted to Mr. Robert Caldwell, he having also previously resigned."

(To Witness).—I find that the total amount now received out of the property is £67 5s. 6d. per annum, whereas Colonel Gun Cuninghame had it let to nearly the same persons as his tenants at £167 12s. yearly?—Yes.

111. So that there is a loss of £100 a year?—Yes, but it might be right to inform you that in all these cases houses were either to be built, or old houses had been thrown down and newly built, or new houses had been recently built. And, moreover, the tenants had paid Colonel Gun Cuninghame a much larger rent on yearly lettings on the faith or expectation that when his own lease fell in, they would get their holdings from the Commissioners upon something like a ground rent. That was the clear understanding between the tenants of the property for thirty years, and the Commissioners. And as a lease was considered safe and its granting never doubted or questioned, the tenants built their houses feeling as certain of getting the lease as if they had it in their pockets.

112. But I am told there was only one new house built upon the property?—That is not the case. I built four new houses.

113. Mr. EXHAM.—Did you rebuild the old ones, or build them new from the foundation?—I built three small ones and one large one where there never was a house before.

114. That was while you were Colonel Gun Cuninghame's tenant?—Yes. I built them on the faith that the Town Commissioners would not take advantage of my expenditure at the expiration of the lease.

115. CHAIRMAN.—Do you mean to say you built these houses upon any direct promises from any of the Commissioners. If so name them?—No; but on the general understanding that existed between the tenants on the Corporation property and the Commissioners.

116. Mr. Gaden.—There is a resolution on the books to that effect.

117. If there is let it be produced. With whom do you say there was that understanding?—I don't think that there was any resolution to that effect, but it was believed and understood, and acted upon in all cases, that when the lease fell in new leases would be given to the under tenants.

118. Do you mean to say that these houses were built and this understanding acted upon without any assurance from the Commissioners or any person representing them that leases would be granted on the terms before stated?—I do.

119. Then if you had no assurance or understanding of the kind from the Commissioners or anyone acting for them, why do you say that the houses were built on the faith that a new lease would be given at nearly a ground rent?—I do not know, except that I always took it for granted.

120. Do you mean to say that there was an impression or understanding on your mind, and that of the other tenants, that you were to get the ground for which you were paying Colonel Gun Cuninghame rent as a yearly tenant at a reduced rent upon lease?—Certainly, at a reduced rent; but not in that way or shape, but at a fair rent—at a ground rent for those parties who had built the same as if they were going to build, and for those parties who were going to build for the first time at a ground rent.

WICKLOW Dec. 11, 1884.

Mr. John Chapman.

121. But you were paying Colonel Gun Cuninghame £20 a year before you built these houses?—Yes, I lived on it and I built on it.

122. Then you paid him a ground rent in fact, and built four houses?—I did. I built on the open space feeling certain that the Commissioners would not take advantage of my toil when the old lease would expire, and that I would get the plot on the same terms as if I was only going to build them.

123. You might think you would not have any increased rent upon it after your outlay, but then you got it for half the sum you paid for it before you built at all?—But then I was getting nearly £14 a year for what I was giving up, which would bring it up and make it more than the rent I am paying the Commissioners.

124. In what year did you become the tenant of Colonel Gun Cuninghame at £20 a year ground rent?—About thirty or forty years ago.

125. Did you pay him £20 a year ever since?—Yes.

126. What houses did you build on it?—The house I live in, and I covenanted with the Commissioners to rebuild it, and I did rebuild it at a greater expense than if I were building a new one. I have built more than I covenanted to build, and I will build more.

127. What sum did you covenant by the lease to expend?—There was no covenant to expend money, but I laid out some hundreds of pounds.

128. Mr. Smyth (to the Chairman).—Would you kindly ask him if it is not a fact that he let one of the small houses in the front street for £20 a year, and that the man who took it rebuilt the house himself or slated it?

Witness.—It is not.

129. CHAIRMAN.—Have you underlet any portion of the property for which you are paying £15 a year?—Yes, a portion of the front.

130. What do you get for it?—£20 a year; it is part of what I built.

131. Was it since 1874 or prior?—It was part of the house I built before Colonel Gun Cuninghame's lease fell in; but then I covenanted in the lease to raise the house to the height of the house I live in, and I have done that at my own expense.

132. Have you got £20 a year for it?—Yes.

133. Have you sublet any other portion of that for which you pay £15 a year?—I have.

134. What part?—The part adjoining that.

135. For how much?—£10 a year.

136. Is there any building on it?—I raised it, put a new roof on it, put in new windows, and repaired it generally.

137. Was it built before 1874?—Yes.

138. And you repaired it since?—Yes.

139. Have you let that for £10 a year?—Yes.

140. Any other portion let?—No.

141. So that you are paid £30 a year for a portion of what you pay the Commissioners £15 a year, and have your own house to live in besides?—Yes.

142. What is the rateable value of the part of the house that you live in?—£14 a year.

143. Have you any other property under this seventy-five years' lease at the £15 a year?—Yes; there is another new house not yet finished.

144. Have you made up your mind as to what you will ask for that?—No; I have not.

145. What is the valuation of the £20 house?—£16.

146. And that of the £10 letting?—It is part of the other house I live in, and I set it to the man next door to extend his premises, and give him more space.

147. Can you give me the valuation of that which is not let, and of that which is not built on?—The old house was valued at £8 10s., and I raised it to the height of the house I live in. I built another addition in the rere at large as the front and raised the front to the height of the house I live in. That I have not finished or let yet.

148. Is there any other property comprised in the lease of the Commissioners to you?—None.

149. Were there not some houses that were to be pulled down?—There are some on the lower road that are set to weekly tenants, but I was bound in the lease not to set them any more; they are to be used for stores to the front houses.

150. That is another part that you have not mentioned?—That is connected with the house.

151. Are those parts of the property for which you paid the £20 a year?—Yes; part of them is let with the front house that I let at £20 a year. My tenant gets one of the houses which is on a line straight down from his house.

152. Part of this is connected with the house that you let in the front?—Part of it is gone with the house that is let, and part of it will go with the house that I am building, the other small portion is an appurtenance to my own house.

153. Mr. Kirrah.—It was therefore inaccurate for you to say that they were to be pulled down?—I gave them for the use of the dwelling-houses in front.

154. You had them let previously at 1s. 6d. a week each?—Yes.

155. It was covenanted that they were not to be let as dwellings, and they were not?—Yes.

156. How long is it since you had those houses let at 1s. 6d. a week each?—Up to the end of Cuninghame's lease.

157. CHAIRMAN.—But why was it that you were not to let them for dwelling-houses?—The agreement was that they should be allowed to be as outhouses for the front premises.

158. But what was the reason of that?—Because there was no rere to those in front.

159. Were they in a dilapidated condition?—No.

160. Why was it that the Commissioners objected to their being used any longer as dwelling-houses?—Because there was no rere to them, and they wished them for accommodation of the houses in the front street, and every one along the line was bound to do that.

(The Commissioners then adjourned for the purpose of looking at the house property referred to.)

On resuming Witness produced some leases.

161. Mr. Kirrah.—What leases are these?—The old ones that were made thirty or forty years ago; I went down and brought up my own old lease.

162. The CHAIRMAN said they had viewed the premises and that they were satisfied from their condition, the Commissioners had made a very proper stipulation with Mr. Chapman, that he should not use those back premises any longer as dwelling-houses.

163. CHAIRMAN.—What was the rental in 1873?—£1,109 10s. 11d.

164. Does that include the rental from the Murrough?—It does.

165. Is that a large tract of land by the seashore, which includes the railway station? What rent do the Corporation get for it?—1s. a foot frontage ground rent for all that is let there.

166. What do they get for the herbage?—Nothing.

167. It looks very good pasturage for sheep?—There is very little grass grown on it, and the Commissioners have often considered whether they would let it for grazing purposes or not; but they determined to keep it for the public as a promenade. They would not get more than £8 or £10 a year for it for grazing, and they would not forfeit the promenade for that. The militia also use it as a training ground, and it is of as much value to the people of Wicklow as the Phœnix-park is to the citizens of Dublin.

168. I see that Mr. Francis Wakefield, of the Marine Hotel, has a fifty-nine years' lease at £8 15s. 6d. and another lease at £5 5s., that is £13 1s. 6d., while Griffith's valuation of the property is £83 10s. How do you reconcile that?—The rents are original ground rents; and Griffith's valuation includes the buildings on it.

169. Was it not let in March, 1858, at £10 16s. 6d., and ten years afterwards reduced to the present rent, £3 16s. 6d. How was that?—He applied for a reduction of the rent. It had then been turned into an hotel instead of a school, which it had originally been. I know that he gave such an explanation to the Commissioners as satisfied them that they ought to reduce the rent.

170. Who is Mr. William John Nolan?—He is dead.

171. But his representatives hold under a lease made in 1869 to William John Nolan for seventy-five years, at a rent of £15 13s., and it is valued at £45 10s.?—Yes; that property is in the main street, near my own.

172. Was that a building lease?—There were old stores there, but he built a new store on the ground to the rere of that block.

173. Mr. Byrne.—But at the time of the lease the valuation was three times more than the rent, so the buildings must have been there to make it valuable to that extent?—Yes.

174. Did Nolan hold from year to year before he got the lease?—I think he held from Lord Powerscourt before his lordship's lease fell in. I think that there was some property fell in from Lord Powerscourt in 1859.

175. Chairman.—I scarcely find a case in which Griffith's valuation is not three times the rent paid to the Commissioners?—Yes, in nearly every case the rent is for the ground merely, and the valuation is of the houses after they were built.

176. William Donagh, his place is valued at five times his rent?—That must have been the ground rent, and the valuation must have been for the buildings.

177. In 1867 a lease was granted to Mrs. Parker of house property, which was let at £3 a year, and valued at £30 a year. Explain why that lease was made?—It was originally an old preaching house, and the tenant afterwards threw that down and built another house.

178. I want to know how he got this house in that way?—That is the valuation of the present house—the one he built.

179. Mr. Gates said that the building had been held by the Methodist minister, at a rent of 2s. 6d. a year; that it had since been pulled down and a new house built in its stead, and that it was on that new house the valuation had been made by Griffith.

180. Mr. Byrne.—But take the whole thing, I find that Griffith's valuation of the property in 1873 was £1,098 11s. 10d., and that was let by the Commissioners at £1,108 19s. 11d. the same year?—Yes.

181. Did Griffith's value represent the value of Colonel Cunningham's property at the time the lease fell in with the buildings as they then stood?—Yes.

182. Therefore at that time the existing buildings were there, which with the value of the ground represented the valuation of £300 13s. 8d., whether they were out of repair or not, and the Commissioners let them at £67 5s. 6d. a year. Is that not the fact?—It is, but then the great bulk of those buildings had been built by the tenants.

183. Chairman.—I see the exact figures of Griffith's valuation for the Cunningham lot on the 25th March, 1871, in which year the lands were relet, amounting to £384, and in every case, except two or three, the land and buildings thereon were let at a seventy-five years' lease. Is that not so?—Yes, it is.

184. Mr. Byrne.—The extraordinary part of it is this: that in the few yearly tenancy cases they are let up to Griffith's valuation in every instance.

Mr. Francis Wakefield examined.

185. Chairman.—I see that the rent of a lease of the Marine Hotel on the Murrough, which belongs to you, was reduced by £4 a year in 1868, ten years after the lease was granted?—That was because they had included in the lease some bits of land unnecessary for an hotel. The building was originally built for schools. A company was got up, and turned it into an hotel. These bits of land were entirely useless to it as an hotel. I lost and advanced over £2,800 to the company which came to grief, and I had a new lease made to me, being of course quite ready to give it up if I got my money back. I found when I came first to pay the rent that the old lease included a bit of land from front to back which was no use to me, and that I was also paying for other land, which would have been against the interests of the Commissioners to give me. I was determined to try the matter with them, and I proposed to give those bits up, and to have the ground measured straight up and down, instead of across the Murrough; they then consented to make the abatement in the rent and keep the ground, and the new lease was made.

186. Have you surrendered the part you say was useless?—Yes.

187. In 1873 you had not surrendered it?—I think I had.

188. When did you take it?—About seven or eight years ago.

189. Were you a Town Commissioner when the rent was reduced?—Yes.

190. Has the reduced rent been paid ever since?—Oh, yes it has been surrendered. It went right across the Murrough.

191. Are you a tenant for any other property under the Commissioners?—Yes I am tenant for two yards, they are in fact a house and stable.

192. Have you not a lease for seventy-five years at £7 5s. a year made in 1846, of ground which Griffith valued at £15? At the time you got the lease were the buildings on it, that are on it now?—I have the lease but I built one house and a cottage there, which let for £14 or £13 a year. The house and cottage used to let for £32, and they now let for £23. The field I hold at over Griffith's valuation.

193. That you hold as a yearly tenant?—Yes.

Mr. Chapman's examination resumed.

194. Byrne.—You made a remark Mr. Chairman that all the yearly tenancies were up to the valuation or above it and that all the leases were under it; the reason of that is that in the case of the yearly tenancies there was nothing to be laid out upon them. While in that of the lease tenancies there was something to be built and money to be spent upon them.

195. Chairman.—"John Byrne, two cottages in Bath-street, valued at £30 a year." Were those two cottages put up by Byrne?—Byrne got that ground at 1s. per foot it was mere gravel ground.

196. What are the two cottages which he put up and are valued at £30 a year let at?—About £30 a year.

197. Mr. Byrne.—The time that the lease was made to that man he got the ground and nothing else?—Yes.

198. That is what the Act of Parliament contemplated.

199. Chairman.—"John Oat (by Mrs. Owens), 23rd of March, 1866, ground on which fifteen slated houses are built, rent 5s. 3d. a year, Griffith's valuation is £16 10s. a year." Did she build these houses or were the houses there when she got the lease?—Every house on it she built.

200. Didn't you make any stipulation as to the class of houses that should be built? She must have built a very bad class of houses when fifteen slated cottages are only valued at £16 10s. a year, including ground rent?—They are a very bad class.

201. Well, it is not good management to let land on building leases for seventy-five years if the parties are not bound to put up a better class of house than that?—The whole of that end of the town was then nothing but old thatched cabins, and the Commissioners thought it good management to let it to people to build cottages at 6d. a foot.

202. But here, Mrs. Owens paid 5s. 3d. a year for ground upon which she put up fifteen cottages; that ground must have been let at 1d. or ½d. per foot?—I don't know; I think that rent is only for a front cottage.

203. Surely it is not in the interest of the town to encourage buildings of this kind?—No, and it is not done now.

204. The Commissioners are in this dilemma, that they have let on lease for seventy-five years, a plot of ground for 5s. 3d. a year, on which fifteen houses are built, which are valued at £18 10s.; and are described to us as being injurious to the public health and to that of the occupiers. If there were a building Act in this town that could not have been allowed?—(In reference to an old plan.) I find that the lease was granted by the old Corporation in 1841, and that it was a printer's mistake to insert "1850."

205. Mr. Exham.—What is the valuation of the ground which Mr. Newbold holds in the Main street?—Two dwelling houses and yards at £20 and £16.

206. What is the rent?—£1 10s. per year.

207. That cannot be the one I mean?

Witness.—Look at "Abraham Newbold—dwelling-house, Main-street, lease seventy-five years, at £1 10s. a year."

208. Mr. Exham.—That is not it; this is a lease of the 7th of March, 1870?—Yes, that is the same.

209. It is not the same; the rent in this lease is £3 a year?—It is so.

210. Has the rent been reduced from £3 to £1 10s. per annum?—Yes, that is correct.

211. I think you will find it anything but correct. On what grounds has it been reduced?—I don't know on what ground.

212. Now listen to this, and let me know what justification there is for it. (Mr. Exham reads a lease of March, 1874, giving Mr. Newbold the premises comprised in the lease of 1870 at the rent of £3 a year, from the 24th of March, 1874, for seventy-five years, at the reduced rent of £1 10s. a year.) Now will you tell me on what grounds was that lease given to him, then having a rent of £3 10s. for the same premises?—The tenant applied to the Commissioners to have the rent reduced, and they agreed to do so, and I collected the new rent accordingly.

213. Mr. *Galen.*—You will find it all in the books.

214. Mr. Exham.—Perhaps it is, but I want you to tell me what legal authority you have for dealing with the property of the public in this way?

Mr. *Galen.*—We did it by a resolution. The property is vested in us, and we can deal with it as we think right.

215. Mr. Exham (to Mr. Chapman).—Is Mr. Newbold a solvent man?—Yes.

216. Do you mean to say that it is only worth £1 10s. a year?—That is only for the ground. Newbold built every stick and stone on it. He built on the front first, and he built on the rere; and if you were to see the place he was about to build upon, you would say that it would not have been worth 2s. a foot.

217. Chairman.—Did he build the house in conformity with the requirements of the lease?—He did, and he built another in the rere; and in consideration of that the rent was reduced from £3 to £1 10s.

218. Mr. Exham.—No, what was demised to him at £3 a year was the then existing dwelling-house, and what he covenanted to build were some privies, and that no building should be made on the premises without the consent of the Commissioners, &c.?—That is the lease of 1870, and it commences from the year 1864.

219. Chairman.—But what was the consideration that induced the Commissioners to cancel the lease of 1870 at £3 a year, and give him a new lease in 1874 at 30s. a year?—I don't know, unless it was that he applied to have the rent reduced as being too high, and they reduced it for him accordingly.

220. Is that a common case here?—No, I never heard of a similar case before.

221. Was the lease of 1870 surrendered?—I do not believe it was.

222. Mr. Exham.—There is a resolution of the 6th of August, 1874—"Proposed by Mr. Hayden, and resolved, that Mr. Newbold having surrendered his lease a new lease be made out for him for seventy-five years from 25th March, 1874, at £1 10s. a year reserved rent." No reasons are given why the old lease was surrendered, and in point of fact the statement is incorrect. Can you tell us anything about the passing of this resolution?—I cannot.

223. You have given him a reduction of rent by about one-half, and no reasons are assigned for it. Can you give any, why that was done?—I cannot.

224. I see here a lease was granted to John Hayden, of a plot of ground for building on, Kevin Terrace Road, from the 25th of March, 1853, for seventy-five years, at £6 10s. a year, with a covenant to build within a limited time, and I also see a marginal note by you—"Mrs. Meagher's rent reduced to £3 a year." Did he build on it?—No.

225. Did he sublet it to Mrs. Meagher?—I understand he assigned his lease to the nuns, and Mrs. Meagher is the superioress of the nuns.

226. Do you say that he assigned his lease to her, and that the Commissioners afterwards reduced the rent to her to £3?—Yes; but the lease is not surrendered, nor has a new one been granted.

227. But you say a new lease is about to be made?—Yes.

228. Has the consent of the Treasury been obtained for any of these leases?—Not for the building leases for seventy-five years. The consent of the Treasury is not necessary unless for a lease for ever, or for a longer period than the Act of Parliament allows. In some cases we applied to the Treasury, and they consented to our granting long leases.

229. For how long a period is it proposed to grant a lease to Mrs. Meagher?—I think that they intended to memorial the Treasury to give Mrs. Meagher a lease for ever, as the establishment is intended for educational purposes.

230. Are you receiving the reduced rent from Mrs. Meagher, although the old lease is the only one in force?—The lease has not been surrendered as yet, nor the new lease made, but I have been instructed to receive, and have received the new rent.

231. Do you mean that you have been receiving £3 instead of £6 10s.?—Yes.

232. Who instructed you to receive the reduced rent?—The Commissioners at their meeting. I hesitated to receive it, waiting until the lease would be perfected, and then the Commissioners passed the resolution authorizing me to receive it, and I have received the £3 a year for two years.

233. Mr. *Barkhill* (Solicitor to the Commissioners).—Do you recollect my telling you not to receive any rent from those parties; we feared you might create a tenancy from year to year, by which the Commissioners would be bound?—I cannot recollect.

234. Chairman.—Do you recollect going to Mr. Barkhill's office with Mr. Hayden to consult him as to the form of receipt which should be given to Mr. Hayden?—I don't recollect that; I recollect often speaking to him about it.

235. Do you recollect Mr. Barkhill giving you any caution about the rent which you were to receive from Mr. Hayden or his assignees?—Well, I don't recollect; he may have told me; we had a great many conversations about that and other things.

236. Did he caution you not to receive any reduced rent or any rent at all from the nuns?—I don't recollect.

Wicklow.
[illegible]
Mr. John
[illegible]

Wednesday, Jan. 12, 1876.

Mr. John Chapman.

237. Had you any conversation with him relative to it?—Several times.

238. What was the effect of the conversation? What did you go to Mr. Barkin to consult him about?—I think that the chief conversation that I had with Mr. Barkin was when he had Mr. Hayden under or about to serve him with an ejectment for non-fulfilment of the covenant to build in his lease.

239. You knew that there was an intention to serve an ejectment upon Hayden for non-fulfilment of that covenant?—Yes.

240. When did you cease to receive rent from Mr. Hayden himself?—He paid rent up to March, 1874, and then the application was made to the Commissioners to have the rent reduced, and the lease transferred to the nuns.

241. Has he been a Commissioner for some time, and was he chairman of the Commissioners in 1875?—Yes.

242. Did you then receive instructions from Mr. Hayden or from the Commissioners to receive the rent from the nuns instead of Hayden, and to receive the reduced rent?—I did, from the Commissioners.

243. Had you any conversation with Mr. Barkin after that?—No; I think it is two years ago.

244. Was it in the board-room you got the instructions?—Yes, from the Commissioners. I was present when the resolution was passed.

245. Was Mr. Hayden a Commissioner at the time?—Yes.

246. Was he chairman at the time?—No.

247. Listen to this:—"Proposed by Mr. Hayden and seconded by Mr. Smith, and resolved, that a lease of the land be given for ever to Eliza Meagher," &c. on behalf of the nuns, &c. Another resolution proposed by Mr. Hayden, seconded by Mr. Hamilton, was read, and it was resolved that a memorial be sent to the Lords of the Treasury asking their sanction to the granting of a lease in perpetuity to Ellen Meagher. Is that the property in question?—Yes.

248. And the Commissioner who makes that proposal is at the same time threatened with an action of ejectment for non-fulfilment of the covenants contained in his own lease?—Yes, when Mr. Hayden would be applied to by me for his own rent, he has asked me had I got the rent from the nuns, and I said not; and he has told me that if I would go and apply for it I would get it. I did not apply to them till the resolution was passed.

249. Why did you not apply to them before?—I told him that I was waiting till matters were arranged.

250. But you say that you received for two years £3 a year rent instead of £8 10s. Did you receive that from Mrs. Meagher on behalf of the nuns, or from whom?—From Mrs. Meagher.

251. Did you receive the rent from Mrs. Meagher?—I did.

252. Had you not been cautioned not to receive any rent from the nuns by the solicitor, Mr. Barkin?—I don't recollect. He may have mentioned it to me if he says he did. I thought myself I would wait until the new lease was made, and I hesitated to call to take the rent.

253. Didn't you know that the new lease had never been sent forward to the Treasury?—I did; but then the Commissioners passed the resolution.

254. When Hayden told you that you had nothing to do but go and ask for the rent, did you go and ask for it?—I did not. It was in consequence of that resolution that you read that I first received the rent.

255. Did you know that the old lease was surrendered?—I know that it was not.

256. In what form did you pass the receipt: to whom did you pass it?—I gave the receipt in name of John Hayden, the lessee, per Mrs. Meagher, and Mrs. Meagher asked me why I did not give it in her own name, and I told her that I would not do that until she got the new lease.

257. Mr. Kernan.—I advise the Commissioners very strongly not to take any surrender of this lease from Mr. Hayden, or make a new one without proper advice. After to-day they cannot say they were not properly warned as to what they should do, and should not do.

258. Chairman.—Can you tell us in how many instances since you have been agent have the rents been reduced, exclusive of the ones on the Cunningham property?—In very few, besides Travers's, Newbold's, Wakefield's, and the nuns, for Hayden's plot. There were a few cabins which were set at 2s. 6d. per month, and I suggested to the Commissioners to reduce them to 6d. per month, and let the parties repair them, and they agreed.

259. On the 4th May, 1846, Griffith's valuation of the property was £1,168 11s., and your total rental amounted to £1,243 7s. 11d.?—Yes.

260. The total acreage of the property is 18a. 2r. 7p.?—Yes.

261. Were you a Town Commissioner before being agent?—Yes.

262. How long?—Twenty-seven years.

263. During those twenty-seven years, were the rents reduced in many cases of existing leases—I don't mean where old leases fell in—were existing leases ever cancelled, and fresh leases granted at reduced rents?—I don't remember any case.

264. How many cases have occurred since you were appointed agent?—I don't know of any except those that have been before you.

265. You know that of Newbold's, which is an accomplished fact, and of Hayden's, which is not an accomplished fact; do you know of any others?—I do not, except the others I have also mentioned.

266. Has any old lease of considerable property fallen in during the last half-dozen years, except that of Colonel Otho Cuninghame?—Except that of Lord Meath.

267. When did that old lease of Lord Meath's fall in?—About eight years ago.

268. That was before you were agent, and while you were a Commissioner?—Yes.

269. Did Lord Meath hold much ground, and what did he pay for it?—£7 13s. 6d. half-yearly.

270. Did you let that for an increase of £250 a year?—Yes.

271. And is that all land, and all let in yearly lettings?—Yes; with the understanding that all lands wanted for building will be given up when called upon.

272. That is the portion to which I referred some time ago—land which seemed to be let above Griffith's valuation?—Yes.

273. And is that the only large property that has fallen in during the last ten years?—Yes; but there has been some small property.

274. Do you know what Lord Meath let that property for?—I don't know exactly; but I am sure the Commissioners get a great deal more for it than he got.

275. With regard to any of the other properties which have fallen in, do the Commissioners get more or less rents than the original lessees were getting for them from their under-tenants?—I don't know, except some yards on the Murrough, and I don't know what the tenants were previously paying for them. I know that the head-rents the Commissioners were getting for them were very small, and I think it was represented to me by the tenants that they were paying less now than to the original lessees.

276. You think that they were paying more before than they are now?—I do.

277. What were the cases on the Murrough in which the tenants now pay less to the Commissioners than they paid their previous landlord?—I think there are two cases; two yards of Travers's which were reduced to £7 10s.

278. Mr. Kernan.—Do you know Mr. Fitzgerald, who has got one of the leases?—Yes.

279. How many houses did he build on the ground since he got the lease?—I am not aware. I don't think he built any.

280. Don't you know that he covenanted by his

been now produced to build three houses within three years from 1874; and that the rent was to be 6d. per foot frontage in consideration of his building. Has he built them?—He has not.

281. CHAIRMAN.—Is it your business to see that the tenants who get their leases carry out their contracts?—No.

282. Whose business is it?—I think it is the clerk's.

283. Have you been receiving the 6d. per foot frontage rent from him ever since?—Yes.

284. Have you reported that the covenants in his lease have not been performed?—No; I have not.

285. In 1874, was a lease to be made to Mrs. Keely of her late husband's house?—Yes.

286. Mr. KEENAN.—Can you explain this resolution (reads resolution of 19th May, 1874, and also of 22nd May, 1874.) With respect to the premises leased to J. Sullivan, upon what principle was his tender offering to pay £5 a year rent, and to pay £75 to Mrs. Keely not accepted, and the tender offering to pay £3 a year, and a smaller sum of £75 was accepted?—As well as I can recollect when the rent was fixed at £3 a year, he was to give a lease same. I think £30.

287. No. Here are the resolutions (reads resolution) of 19th May, 1874:—"Resolved that John Sullivan get his premises in the Main-street, at £5 a year and to pay Mrs. Keely £75." Then it was subsequently resolved on 22nd May, 1874, to rescind the resolution of the 19th of May, relative to the amount of rent, and reduce it to £3 a year, but he was still to pay the same sum to Mrs. Keely. Can you explain why the rent was reduced from £5 to £3?—I cannot.

288. The allegation is that the Commissioners give the lettings to the old tenants; John Sullivan was not an old tenant. Why then did they give it to him?—I don't believe they agreed to give it to him until he agreed to give the £75 to her.

289. CHAIRMAN.—The impression on your mind was that Sullivan at first offered to take the house for £5 a year, and to pay £50 to Mrs. Keely; and that the Commissioners afterwards agreed to reduce the rent to £3 a year, he paying Mrs. Keely £75. If that were so, in order to get Mrs. Keely £25 more, the ratepayers would lose £2 a year for seventy-five years. Is that not so?—They would have given it to Mrs. Keely for £3 a year, if Sullivan had not agreed to give the £75 to Mrs. Keely.

290. Mr. KEENAN.—Don't you see now that is a wrong impression for he was to pay her £75 under both resolutions?—Yes.

291. CHAIRMAN.—Do you receive any other moneys but the rents?—No.

292. What are the rent days?—The 25th March and the 29th September. There are some monthly rents. The great bulk of the rents is paid in March and September.

293. What is about the amount of your average outstanding arrears of rent?—I could tell what it was by looking at the account as it stood on the 31st of last December. My accounts are made up to that date for audit.

294. Then tell me what it was at that time to begin with?—(Books handed to witness.) On the 31st December, 1875, there was £1,576 1s. 6d. for the year's rent and previous arrears outstanding. There was collected £1,171 5s. 2d.; bad debts £1 14s. 6d., and £103 3s. 10d., arrears to be collected, carried forward to the next account.

295. Does £100 represent the average of arrears outstanding from year to year?—Yes.

296. Are the rents paid in by you to the treasurer?—Yes. There was a list of arrears brought before the Commissioners and it was resolved to consider it; but nothing has been done since.

297. Two half years' rent have accrued due since?—Yes. At the end of each year about £400 is what would be outstanding.

298. Cannot you collect them closer than that?—Well, a good many tenants hold on and pay one year within another; others have only a hanging gale.

299. How much of the arrears of £103 3s. 10d. do you think cannot be collected?—About £100. Some of it is sixteen years due, and has been regularly brought forward. I have given a list to have steps taken for their recovery, or to strike them off altogether.

300. Did you produce a list of uncollectable arrears to the Commissioners, and ask them to strike them off?—I did, and asked them to strike them off altogether or to take steps to enforce them, and one of them is a letting to the Courtown Mining Company, in respect of which there is £40 due. I also showed the list to Mr. Finlay, the auditor.

301. Are any of the Commissioners in arrear for their rents?—There are, but not in those that I have put down as really irrecoverable.

302. How much do those who are in arrear owe?—Some of them owe a couple of hanging gales.

303. Or more?—I don't think any of them owe more than three half years.

304. Why don't you make them pay?—I have applied to them frequently, but they won't pay me.

305. When you get this money, to whom do you pay it?—At once into the treasurer, the National Bank.

306. Mr. Finlay says in his first audit report of 1873 that you kept large balances in your hands, that he objected to the manner in which the funds were dealt with, and that he had recommended you to alter the system?—I wish to explain how that occurred. I was directed to pay the interest on the mortgages first, and then lodge the balance in the Bank. I used to lodge the money for that purpose in my own name; but that would be only a day or two previous to the interest on the mortgages coming due, and then I would give a cheque for the amount. I used to give a cheque on the 11th January for a half-year's interest on the mortgages; but on the 30th December there appeared to be so much in my hands, and I used to keep it to pay the interest I had. Mr. Finlay himself said I should lodge all my receipts to the credit of the Commissioners, and that they should give a cheque for the interest on the mortgages.

307. Have you adopted that course since?—Yes.

308. Is there any resolution limiting the amount you can hold in your hands?—None.

309. As a matter of fact, what is the largest amount you do hold in hand?—I don't keep any in hand; I lodge all I get in by the end of each month.

310. But I see you had £17 13s. in your hands, the Town Clerk had £63 14s. 2d., and the Treasurer £619 2s. 2d.; how comes the Town Clerk to have so large a balance in hand?—I don't know.

311. What money does he receive? Do you pay him any money?—No. The £17 13s. I had in hand I lodged at the end of the month, but I don't know how the Town Clerk could have £63 14s. 2d. in his hands.

312. All you know is you don't pay him any money?—No.

313. How much do you receive on the half-yearly rent days?—I generally receive on those days about £250, but I pay it in the next morning. After the usual rent-days I pay in the next morning to get rid of it at once.

314. For how much do you give security?—£1,000.

315. With two sureties?—Yes.

316. Are the sureties living?—Yes.

317. What is the date of the bond?—At the time of my appointment, 1870.

318. Who has the bond?—The Commissioners or the town clerk have the bond.

319. On what mortgages do you pay interest?—On £12,000, which was borrowed in the year 1864 to lend to the Harbour Commissioners.

320. Is that the only mortgage on the estate?—There is another mortgage of £100. It is due to Mr. Goodison; that was taken over from the old corporation.

321. What was the amount paid on it?—I don't

Wexford, Feb. 11, 1877.

Mr. John Chapman.

know. It was some few pounds. I never had anything to say to it, and I don't know what was paid on it.

322. Have the Harbour Commissioners paid the interest of that £12,000?—No; the Town Commissioners borrowed the money on the security of their property, and they lent it to the Harbour Commissioners on the security of the tolls; but the tolls have never been collected under the Harbour Act. They did not get the desired depth of water, and consequently could not enforce the tolls.

323. Mr. Finlay, in his evidence before the Committee of the House of Commons, drew attention to it—that the first thing the Commissioners had to pay was £340 interest on the mortgage debt. Who are the mortgagees?—The trustees of Mr. T. C. Lawrence.

324. Is that the first charge—or do you know of any others that you pay interest on out of your receipts?—I know nothing of any other mortgagees. I never paid interest on any of them.

325. Do you hold any other office besides that of agent under the Commissioners?—None.

326. What commission do you get?—Five per cent. on my actual receipts.

327. Mr. Exham.—I have been handed the opinion upon the case submitted by Mr. Barkin to Mr. Gibson with reference to the bringing of the action against Mr. Hayden for breach of the covenants in his lease, and it is stated in the case that Mr. Hayden had sold his interest under the lease to the same. Is that a fact?—I have heard that it was so.

328. How much did he get for it?—I never heard the sum he got, but I believe from hearsay that he sold his interest.

329. Did you hear that before the resolution was put on the books to give the same a new lease?—Yes. Before his lease was cancelled.

330. Before the Commissioners directed you to take the reduced rent, did you hear that he sold his lease?—Yes; but I did not hear what he got for it.

331. But if he sold his interest he must have got money or money's worth for it?—I don't know as to that.

332. Chairman.—You said you refused to collect the rent until you were directed by the Commissioners to do so at the reduced rate, and that before the resolution to that effect was passed, you heard that Mr. Hayden had sold his interest?—Certainly I did.

333. Who paid for the leases to the different tenants?—Each owner paid for his new lease.

334. Now let us go through your expenditure. "New works and repairs including £30, flagging of the footway, £114 8s. 4d."?—Yes.

335. Cleansing and watering the town, £18 10s. 6d.?—Quite right.

336. Cost of water supply, including cost of reservoir for the new waterworks, £348 10s.?—Quite right.

337. Has that reservoir been handed over to the Board of Guardians?—It has.

338. Have they repaid you for it?—No. It will take £200 to complete the work, and they will strike a rate for that amount.

339. I see that £148 3s. 1d. was paid for lighting the public lamps in 1875?—It would be more now.

340. Rent and taxes, £13 5s. 3½d. What is that? Is it head-rent?—Head-rent in some cases. We have to pay half the poor-rate and the ground rent.

341. Interest on bonds and mortgages, £343 11s. 6d.?—Yes.

342. Transferrer for interest advanced, £3 1s. 7d.?—That was charged by the National Bank, who acted as treasurer.

343. I cannot understand your ever being overdrawn?—That interest is charged when the Commissioners overdraw.

344. Then they do overdraw?—Yes.

345. You told me that the town clerk's salary was £50; I see that he only gets £40?—That was a mistake on my part. I thought it was £50 a year.

346. And the town sergeant £34?—Yes.

347. Agent's fees per centage, £48 11s.?—Yes.

348. I see you pay in respect of salaries £138 11s.?—Yes.

349. Printing, advertising and stationery, £79 13s.?—Quite right.

350. Postage and receipt stamps, £1 8s. 1d.?—Yes.

351. Law expenses, £4 1s.?—That is right.

352. You began, I see, with a balance in your favour of £603 11s. 4d., and you end with a balance of £480 6s. 0d.?—Quite right.

353. The town clerk had in hand £48 13s. 6½d., you had £19 0s. 6½d., and the treasurer £303 13s. 1d.?—Yes.

354. Does the town clerk give any security?—I don't know; he was town clerk long before I became connected with the Commissioners.

355. How many Commissioners have you?—Twenty and the chairman.

356. How many rated occupiers are there?—In 1874 there were 313 burgesses.

Mr. John Nolan examined.

357. Chairman.—You are chairman of the Town Commissioners?—Yes.

358. How long have you been so?—Since last August.

359. Is this the first year in which you are chairman?—I was so before for two years.

360. How long have you been a Commissioner?—Since 1856.

361. What officers do you pay besides your agent, Mr. Chapman?—The town clerk and the town sergeant—that is all.

362. Had you not a sanitary inspector at £20 a year?—That was before the Sanitary Act of 1874.

363. What do you pay the town clerk?—£40 a year.

364. And what the town sergeant?—14s. a week.

365. What are the duties of the town sergeant?—He has to mind, clean out, and clean the town hall, to look after the corporate property, and see that there are no trespassers. He has to attend the fairs which are held here on the last Tuesday of every month for the purpose of keeping order, and seeing the cattle kept in their proper places.

366. Has he anything to do with the cleansing of the streets?—No.

367. Whom do you employ to do that?—In some cases they are cleansed by the road contractor, but lately the Commissioners have found it necessary to try and keep them even partially clean.

368. Are the streets repaired by the Grand Jury contractor?—Yes.

369. To clean the footways is the duty of the Commissioners?—Yes.

370. Does the contractor clean the alleys and lanes?—No; it was let by contract, but it was found that it did not answer. Both the watering and cleansing of the streets was very badly done, and we found it necessary to employ men to do the work under the direction of the town sergeant, who is now responsible for the work to us.

371. Does he employ them?—He does, under the direction of the town clerk.

372. Is anybody employed to do it regularly?—No, only periodically and partially.

373. And not to your satisfaction?—Oh, no; not at all.

374. How often are fairs held here?—On the last Tuesday in every month, with the exception of the horse and cattle fair, which is held on the 15th of August.

375. Where are they held?—The cattle fairs are held on the fair green, and the horse fair on the Murragh.

376. Do you receive any tolls from those fairs?—No

377. Were they not levied here once?—No, not in my recollection.

378. Mr. *Chapman*.—I wish to say that they were never levied in my recollection. It was not considered that it would be the Commissioners' interest to levy tolls if they wished to get up the fairs. And in order to get them established they looked upon it as best to offer inducements to owners of stock and buyers to attend fairs here, and they have now established some of the best fairs in the county.

379. CHAIRMAN.—But you don't make any profit by them?—No. When they were getting them up they put up placards, and advertised them in all parts of England and Ireland.

380. CHAIRMAN (to Mr. *Nolan*).—Do you keep the animals off the streets?—Well, I cannot say that. The pig fair is generally held in the street opposite this.

381. Is the town sergeant active in cleaning after them?—He is not expected to handle a brush; but he looks after the labourers.

382. Is the fairgreen the property of the Commissioners?—Yes.

383. Have you any market?—No; we have no regular market. We have very good shops; the market-square is opposite this, but it is not used generally.

384. One of the gentlemen, when we were below viewing the premises we went to look at, said that you wanted a public market badly; do you think that?—I don't think we do. There are so many good shops that I don't think a market is necessary.

385. Mr. *Chapman*.—The Commissioners tried to have a market; they tried to induce parties to come here and sell their goods, and failed. All we could do was to prevent parties selling in the streets, but we could not make them come up here. We fitted up this place with scales, weights, and everything necessary, but we could not get them to come up here.

386. CHAIRMAN (to Mr. *Nolan*).—I understand that Mr. Wakefield applied to Lord Fitzwilliam for a piece of ground for a fairgreen?—Yes; but there were many people thought we wanted other things more.

387. What else do you want more?—Water. We are about to get some very good water. We spent £300 in making a very large tank, but it has not been used up to this. There have been great discussions at the Rathdown Union as to whether a water supply ought to be carried out on a large scale or by this tank scheme.

388. Are the Poor Law Guardians of that union the sanitary authority?—Yes.

389. What is the population here?—I think it is but little under 4,000.

390. I see in 1871 that there is a certain sum of money expended on engineers, &c., were all these expenses incurred with reference to the water tank?—Yes.

391. What is your annual payment for Grand Jury cess?—I am not prepared to answer that.

392. You have got an income of from £1,200 to £1,300 a year from rents and certain small sums besides?—Yes.

393. "Railway company in lieu of surplus water, £10"—what is that?—The railway company laid a water pipe to convey water to their station through a portion of the corporate property, and for that accommodation we charged them £10 a year.

394. You get some small sums from the dog-tax?—Yes; £6 or £7.

395. Do you get anything from the sale of manure?—Scarcely anything. We have none to sell; because the streets are never swept. It is all left lying there.

396. I see you got only £3 last year; is that as much as you generally get?—Yes.

397. These, with a few trifling items, are the whole of your receipts?—Yes.

398. Why do you not get the police fines?—I cannot answer about the fines. We do not get any.

399. Why do you not apply to the Castle about them?—We will do so.

400. After paying £346 for interest on the mortgage have you not still got a surplus income of over £600 a year?—Yes.

401. How is that spent, besides paying the salaries you mentioned?—We supplement the county work, and flag portions of the town.

402. What are the poor rates and county cess?—The poor rate was 1s. 6d. in the £1 last year, and the county cess was 10d. in the £1 for each half year.

403. Mr. EVANS.—Do they keep all the roads in repair?—They ought, but they would not flag the town unless they got something more. It is only within the last few years that we had a surplus at all.

404. But you have got a very considerable surplus now?—Yes, and we hope to increase it. It is only very recently that we have had any money to do anything with.

405. CHAIRMAN.—How is the town lighted?—With very good gas, at 7s. 6d. a thousand cubic feet. We have a very good company.

406. How many lamps are there?—I cannot tell exactly; but I think sixty-nine.

407. Do you pay by the lamp?—Yes, about £2 10s. per lamp all round.

408. I see that up to the 1st April, 1873, you paid £130 5s. for the lamps?—Yes; but we pay more now, as we have increased the number, and sometimes before when coals were dearer we paid more.

409. How many public pumps have you?—We have some.

410. Maintained by the Commissioners?—Yes.

411. How many?—Two pumps and four fountains.

412. Is the water good?—Generally good.

413. Has it been analysed?—Yes.

414. By whom?—Professor Cameron and Professor Reynolds. It was found better than from most pumps. I drink it myself.

415. Do the guardians carry out the Sanitary Act properly since 1874?—We have not had experience enough yet.

416. Has there been much improvement within the last year?—I think it is in a satisfactory way towards improvement. Dr. Halpin, the sanitary officer, will be able to answer that question. In some cases I think that more might be done.

417. I see by the report in the last audit that Mr. Finlay, made some surcharges against you and Mr. Oakes, as well as other gentlemen?—Yes, very unfairly. He surcharged us with the sum of £10 each for our expenses in going to London in reference to our opposing a bill promoted by the Dublin, Wicklow, and Wexford Railway Company, and which seriously injured us.

418. Mr. Finlay says that he disallowed £3 17s. for the loan of a screen, which was put up here as a polling booth?—Yes.

419. Did the Town Clerk lend the screen?—Yes; he sent it up from his own house to the room here for the purpose of fixing up a polling booth.

420. What would be the worth of it if it was new?—Mr. Halpin, the town clerk, valued it at £10. I don't think he would get many to give him £3 for it.

421. Did he take it back to his house as soon as the election was over?—Yes, but he offered to lend it again.

422. At the same price?—Yes.

423. He also disallowed £3 for the services of Mr. Oakes, one of the Commissioners, at the election?—Yes.

424. What was Mr. Oakes paid that fee for?—I don't know, except for attending at the election.

425. How many hours was the screen here?—The greater part of three days. It had to be put up the day before the election, and was removed the day after.

426. Mr. Finlay also calls attention to the fact that the cheques that were drawn for £10 each by the Town Clerk, and handed by him to Mr. Oakes and Mr. Nolan, were signed by himself, but were not passed or signed at any meeting of the Commissioners, and that he therefore surcharged each of you with that

WICKLOW. Jan. 11, 1875.

Mr. John Nolan.

[illegible]. Jan. 12, 1876.

Mr. John [illegible].

[illegible]. Was that so?—Yes. We had not twelve hours to prepare to go off to London.

427. You wanted the money first?—We could not go to London without money. It was a little irregular because there was no time to call a meeting.

428. Then, in point of fact, the cheques were not signed at any meeting of the Commissioners?—Yes; and we had to bring the cheques to two other Commissioners at their own houses to be signed. It was on a Saturday, and we had to be in London by Monday morning.

429. I am glad to see that he says the rents were collected in a most satisfactory manner by Mr. Chapman. He takes here this case of Abraham Newbold's, and he tells us more about it than we knew before; that the plot of ground is not only valued at £7, but that he paid £2 a year for it to Lord Fitzwilliam; that it was subsequently reduced to £4, and that now it is £1 10s. a year. Is that so?—Yes. I made several suggestions as to the old leases being revalued, with a view of calculating the new rent with which they ought to be charged, but the Commissioners let them as you have heard.

Dr. George [illegible].

Dr. George [illegible] examined.

430. CHAIRMAN.—I understood you to say that you pay a little more rent now than you did to Colonel Gun Cuninghame?—I only paid Colonel Gun Cuninghame £3 1s. a year on my original lease from him.

431. How does it appear in the schedule of the rents paid to Colonel Cuninghame that you paid him £3 15s.?—It is so stated; but I was badly treated in the matter. I had a lease from him which expired twelve or fourteen years before Colonel Gun Cuninghame's [illegible] expired. When it dropped, I went to him and said:—"I am about to build a new house, and I will pay you now in order that I may be able to go before the Commissioners in obtaining a new lease." He said, after some conversation, that if I would pay him more he would give me a new lease. The rent was then fixed at £3 15s.; but as soon as I paid him a gale or two he refused to give me any lease.

432. What was the term of your old lease?—Sixty-five years, or three lives.

433. Mr. Gedes (through the Chairman.)—Did you not commence to build on the faith of a resolution passed by the Commissioners, that they would give you a lease?—I appeared before the Commissioners, and they told me that I would be safe in building, and that I would get the premises at a ground rent when Cuninghame's lease fell in.

434. Which of the Commissioners told you this, and when?—I cannot say now.

435. CHAIRMAN.—You pay them £3 15s., the same as you lately paid Colonel Cuninghame, and you pay £1 10s. a year for the yard, instead of 15s. a year, which you paid him?—Yes; and I laid out about £800 on the same property.

436. I can quite understand that; and this was what you wanted to explain?—Yes; I cannot say that I consider I got any bargain by the plot, it is such an expensive place to build upon. Another member of my family took out a lease from Earl Fitzwilliam with double as large a frontage in a square plot, and he got it at £2 12s. a year for ninety-nine years, from Lord Fitzwilliam.

437. I understand that you are the sanitary officer for the Board of Guardians?—I am.

438. What is the sanitary condition of this place?—It is very much improved; but it could be more improved.

439. Is the water good?—It is not a bad drinking water.

440. Is the drinking water good?—It is; but sometimes it [illegible] deal.

441. Is it fouled by sewage?—No, I don't know any place where sewage gets into the pumps or wells. We hope soon, now to have the water from the new reservoir. Dr. Cameron gave it as his opinion that it was the best water he had analysed in Ireland.

442. Is there much difficulty in supplying the poor people with water now?—In summer there is a scarcity of water. Most of the pumps were dry last summer, and they had to get the water from the river.

443. Is there any portion of the water supplied from the river?—There is. When the fountains and pumps run dry the inhabitants are very much dependent on the river. It is very much fouled by cattle going in and drinking about the place where people have to get water, and there are two tributaries there [illegible]; but that water is not used for drinking purposes—only for washing.

444. Have the guardians commenced the contract for the waterworks yet?—Nothing has been done by the guardians since they became the sanitary authority. Before the Sanitary Act of 1874 passed, we had more facility for carrying on the sanitary work than we have now. At that time the sub-sanitary officer had liberty to go about with a book in his pocket, and take down the names of parties, and issue summonses where he found a nuisance, but now he has to fill in a form and send it to the sanitary authority at Rathdrum, and await their reply before he can issue a summons.

445. Do you think the sanitary condition of the town would be improved if it were under the Commissioners, instead of the Board of Guardians?—No; I don't mean to say that, but I will explain what I do mean. In every district like this there is a dispensary committee, and I think it would be better to have the authority centred in the dispensary committee, who would be able to attend at once to applications, and who know the locality and the people, instead of having the sanitary work for the whole union discharged by the Board of Guardians of Rathdrum. I think that wherever there is a dispensary committee they should be the sanitary committee under the Board of Guardians, and have the power to act immediately, and in certain cases to order summonses, where the people did not comply with their orders. At present it is only after two or three meetings of the Guardians that an order is made to abate the nuisance, and before a summons can be issued for the petty sessions several weeks will have elapsed, and the nuisance is all this time continuing, and there is no means of remedying it.

446. We have been told that there is a great scarcity of privies and ash-pits in houses here?—There is; but the great want of all is yard accommodation, and that induced the Commissioners to throw in the small houses at the back of some of the front houses for yard accommodation.

447. Were any steps taken by the Commissioners before the Act of 1874 to remedy the sanitary defects you have been speaking of?—There were. The present sub-sanitary officer under the Board of Guardians was in the pay of the Commissioners as their nuisance inspector, and they did all that could be done at that time.

448. Were any privies or ash-pits then erected at their instance?—No; in some of the late leases covenants are put in to that effect. There are some of the houses without back entrances, and the people have to take out the contents of the privies and ash-pits through the houses by the front doors.

Mr. Robert [illegible].

Mr. Robert [illegible] examined.

449. Mr. [illegible].—You have been acting as solicitor to the Town Commissioners?—At times only. I prepared most of their leases.

450. Did you prepare all the leases in 1874, after Colonel Gun Cuninghame's lease had expired?—Yes.

451. Were you aware that these leases were granted at a less rent than the tenants had been paying to him?—No; I knew nothing at all about the original rents. I drew the leases from the resolutions and the maps—the resolution being signed by the town clerk as to the terms of the lease, the description of the premises, &c.

452. You knew nothing as to what passed at the meeting of the Commissioners?—I did not.

453. Had you known it, would you have advised them to execute the leases and to let the property without having publicly advertised it?—I considered that the resolutions that were given to me must have been considered by the Commissioners in accordance with the opinions of Mr. Gibson and Mr. Hemphill, which I obtained for and submitted to them.

454. What was the effect of those opinions?—Mr. Hemphill advised that they were trustees of the property, and had no right to grant any new lease without having the proposed new lettings duly advertised and put up for public competition. I read that opinion over for and left it with them.

455. Did you advise them to follow counsel's opinion?—Certainly, and cautioned them against acting in opposition to it.

456. Did they consult you afterwards as to their acting against counsel's opinion?—Certainly not. The next I heard of it was being ordered to prepare leases in conformity with the resolutions.

457. Were you ever consulted about their cancelling any lease that had been granted, and granting a fresh lease of the same premises at a lower rent?—I recollect being consulted on only one occasion and I told the Commissioners that they had no power to cancel a lease once made. I told them that when once they had executed a lease it was their duty to enforce the payment of the rent and performance of the covenants in it, until it was legally put an end to, and that they should not attempt to cancel it, and I cautioned them that they had no power to give a new lease when an existing one was in force.

458. Were you, after you gave them the opinions at all consulted about these matters until you were employed to have these leases drawn?—No.

459. What instructions did you receive from them?—To prepare leases for seventy-five years according to the resolutions.

460. Were the cases laid by you before counsel, on behalf of the Commissioners, and upon their verbal instructions as to the points on which they wished for counsel's advice?—Yes, certainly.

461. It is stated in the case submitted by you to counsel, that Mr. Hayden sold the property to the tenant about three years ago?—That statement was made to me by Mr. Halpin, the town clerk. We had a good deal of consultation about it in the first instance, for there was a question as to whether there was a breach of covenant in not building, for which I believed an ejectment could then have been maintained. I recollect a long conversation on that subject, and in the cases submitted to Mr. John Gibson, and afterwards to Mr. Edward Gibson, you will find it stated that the town clerk informed me that Mr. Hayden had sold his interest to the tenant. I recollect afterwards having a conversation with Mr. Chapman. At the time I was bringing an ejectment, and I cautioned Mr. Chapman relative to not receiving rents from the tenants, fearing that a tenancy from year to year might be created.

462. CHAIRMAN.—Do you know whether they ever put any of the property that fell in, up for public competition or public tender?—All I can tell you is this that I told them I considered they would not only be personally responsible, but that it would be an act of injustice to grant leases without doing so; and there was a day appointed by resolution upon which the public were invited to send in tenders.

463. MR. EXHAM.—By the opinions of both these gentlemen, the Commissioners had fair warning that they were acting illegally in the way in which they were granting these leases.

464. CHAIRMAN.—Do you know anything of the circumstances under which the £12,000 was advanced to the Harbour Commissioners?—I ought to know something about that, inasmuch as there is £260 of taxed costs owing to me in connexion with that transaction. I recollect Mr. Chapman and some others coming to me, and I consented to give them a memorandum that I would forego my claim until the harbour was completed; for I would have done anything for the improvement of the town. But I may ask shall we ever see the harbour completed? And one thing I want to know is, have we any Harbour Commissioners? If ever there were Harbour Commissioners, there are none now. There is a gentleman who was at one time chairman of the harbour board, and he, with the secretary, receive the tonnage paid to them by the vessels coming into the harbour, but they have no more right to do so than any person in this room.

465. Was the whole of this £12,000 advanced to the Harbour Commissioners for improving the harbour?—Yes.

466. And how was it expended?—A great deal of it was spent upon the case of Killeen against the Harbour Commissioners, which occupied thirty-two days at trial in the Court of Exchequer before the late Chief Baron Pigot, and for which I paid something about £1,000 in fees. That suit went against the Commissioners, and Killeen got out of his contract and compelled the Commissioners to pay him without his performing it at all.

467. What security had the Commissioners from the Harbour Commissioners for this loan?—They have a mortgage for the first loan—a mortgage executed by the Harbour Commissioners to the Town Commissioners for £12,000, which was secured upon the tolls. It was thought that when the harbour was improved there would be a large income from tolls; but it is not half what was expected; and there is no prospect of any improvement until the harbour is improved. What is got now can do more than pay the interest, &c. on the last loan that was got from the Public Works Loan Commissioners. We had all to forego our claims before the Loan Commissioners would advance the money, £6,000; but after it was expended, no good resulted from the expenditure.

468. Is there anybody to check the accounts of these Harbour Commissioners?—They should furnish the accounts to the clerk of the peace of the county.

469. Is there no one to check the accounts, and see how they spend that money? Is there any auditor?—Their late chairman is the auditor; but there is not any board, legal or illegal now.

470. As far as you can judge, is there any chance of the Commissioners getting back either capital or interest from the Harbour Commissioners?—Not until the harbour is completed.

471. If the harbour were completed, would it be a paying concern?—No doubt it would pay all off in a few years. There is a feeling amongst certain classes in the town that their trade would be very much injured if the harbour were deepened and improved. They wish to keep the trade to the small class of vessels which they own.

me see those documents, but he said he could not until Monday—the day the audit began. I brought the matter before Mr. Finlay, who censured Mr. Halpin for not having complied with the Act of Parliament. There is another matter I wish to speak of. It is with reference to the water question. It is at present before the Local Government Board and the Board of Guardians; but there are many who consider the money we are laying out for the supply of water is altogether too small for the town. There is no provision for flushing of the sewers, nor for supplying the Murragh, with its 600 inhabitants and eighty houses, no provision for flushing the main sewers, or washing out privies or ashpits, where the liquid matter is allowed to sink into the ground and create a miasma in our dwelling-houses. The proposed supply would not be more than 80,000 gallons in any one day—merely a supply for drinking and household purposes; but not for the other purposes I mentioned. There is no provision made here for getting rid of the contents of the cesspools; and in many cases there are no privies, the houses being built back to back, in a way that would be really disgraceful to an African village. I wrote to the Board of Guardians, but they took no notice of my letter, and since then I have been in communication with the Local Government Board, and have expressed to them the same opinions very much more strongly. They have at present my letter under consideration. I see by the last meeting of the Guardians that the Local Government Board have called upon them to supply them with the specifications and estimate for the water supply.

February 10, 1877.

(Before Mr. Commissioner Exham, Q.C.)

Mr. Robert Halpin examined.

174. Mr. Exham.—You are secretary to the Town Commissioners, I believe?—I am.

175. Show me the minute book of the proceedings of the Town Commissioners for the year 1874. (Minute book produced.)

176. Mr. Exham reads—"Meeting held on the 2nd March, 1874. Fifteen Commissioners present, amongst whom were Mr. Henry M'Phail, and Mr. Robert Coldwell. 'Resolved—That the secretary and agent take possession of the buildings out of lease on the 25th March next, and that the parties be put in as caretakers at one penny a week until the plans are arranged.'" To what property had that resolution reference?—To the houses and premises in Gen. Cuningham's lease, which was to expire on the 25th March, 1874, and also as to a holding of Mrs. Galatia, in the Main-street (not in Gen. Cuningham's lease), but which was to be out of lease on that day.

177. You had a memorial presented to the Lords of the Treasury with regard to giving you leasing powers?—Yes, the resolution is as follows:—"Resolved—That the draft memorial to the Treasury for an extension of leasing powers be adopted." That was intended to be generally applied—not confined to Gen. Cuningham's property alone, but for all other properties.

178. Did the Treasury grant the prayer of your memorial?—No; we got an answer to say that each case would be considered upon its own merits, that they could not give a general order.

179. When the lease fell in on the 25th March was possession taken up from all the tenants, and were they all put in as caretakers?—They were, with the exception of two sub-tenants, and the landlord got possession of the houses, and gave them up. That was Mr. Coldwell who got possession from his under tenants himself and he then gave us possession, and we put them into the two houses.

180. It was stated on the last occasion that the Commissioners set here that there was a public advertisement inviting tenders for these several premises, and that tenders were received for all of them?—Yes.

181. Mr. Exham reads:—

"The next meeting was held on the 6th April, 1874. There were sixteen Commissioners present, amongst whom were Mr. Henry M'Phail, Dr. Halpin, and Mr. Robert Coldwell. Twenty-two applications for premises were received, amongst others, from Mr. Chapman, Mr William M'Phail, Dr. Halpin, Mr. Henry M'Phail, and Mr. Robert Coldwell. The following tenders, amongst others, were given in and read—Tender dated the 2nd of March, 1874, from Mr. John Chapman, in the following terms:—'Gentlemen, I beg to apply to become your tenant for my holding, viz., the house I live in, and those lately built by me in the Main-street and on the Quay upon such terms as you may consider right. There are three houses on the Quay also held by me, which I have not in my ..., but I am not applying for them. I am only applying for what I live in and what I built.

'Your obedient servant,

'John Chapman.'

'Tender of Mistr Dinney of the 25th March, 1874.

'Gentlemen,—As the lease of my premises here will expire on the 25th March, and you are to become the future landlords of my holding in the Main-street, Wicklow, I trust, to ... that position ... from a public body, and the ... I have ... ... Corporation of Wicklow; and my ... house with a ... on the quay ... as all ... of the Main-street have expired or expired from the 25th March, 1874.'

'Application from Mrs. Hartshell.

'Wicklow, 2nd March, 1874.

'To the Chairman and Commissioners of Wicklow.

'Gentlemen,—I beg leave to apply to become your tenant for my house and premises, as my term from Lieutenant-Colonel Cuningham will expire on the 25th instant. I am willing to pay such rent as you consider fair, and trust it will be your pleasure to give me the benefit, and [illegible] the ... on the town property, etc., giving the tenant to possession the preference.

'I remain your obedient servant,

'Julia Hartshell.'

'Mr Galbraith's Proposal.

'27th February, 1874.

'Gentlemen,—As Colonel Cuningham's interest in the premises I hold under him will terminate on the 25th March next, I suppose to become your tenant, under lease from that date. Previous to the late Mr. Byrne getting possession of the dwelling-house from the late Mr Kealy, he paid him £105 for his interest therein, and has since laid out a good deal on house and premises. In the rere, a stable, barn, and cow-house have been built, and in front, under the Hall, two dwelling-houses, one of which was subsequently burnt, and had to be restored. It is my intention to raise the walls of the dwelling-house, put on a new roof, new floors, windows, &c., which will cost at least £200. I now beg to remind the Commissioners that in conjunction with Mr Byrne, we have built twenty-three substantial dwelling-houses on your property, considerably enhancing the value of same. Seventeen of those have been built within the past seven years. I therefore consider I may fairly claim a lease of the premises applied for, viz., the dwelling-house and premises, and the two houses under the Hall, which I built about twenty-three years since, upon such just and reasonable terms as you Board may determine.'

Margaret Flynn sent in an application for the same premises in the following terms:—

"28th February, 1874.

"Gentlemen,—The house and premises so held by my late husband for many years, under the late Mr. James Byrne, and by me, since his death, I have fallen into the hands of the Commissioners on the 25th March next. I beg to offer myself as tenant for them upon such terms as may be considered fair and reasonable. My husband expended a money and labour a considerable sum in keeping the premises in repair, the building, which I hope the Commissioners will take into their consideration, as our late landlord promised nothing towards the expenditure.

"I am, gentlemen, your obedient servant,

"Margaret Flynn."

182. Mr. Exham to Mr. *Halpin*.—Do you happen to know what rent she paid Mr. Coldwell as sub-tenant?—I could not say with certainty. No lease was made to her.

Mr. Exham reads:—

"Application of Mr. Henry M'Phail.

"Gentlemen,—I beg to apply to you for a lease of my holding in the Main-street, Wicklow, comprising the dwelling-house, outoffices, and small yard or passage, to the South-quay. I also request you will give a small portion of the yard adjoining that of Dr. Halpin on the opposite side, as communication with a house in the street is so very badly wanted.

"Your obedient servant,

"Henry M'Phail."

'Tender of Mr. William M'Phail.

'Mr. William M'Phail applied for a lease of his houses which he occupied in the Main street, on fair and reasonable terms; and he would also thank them to give him some additional rear accommodation.'

"[illegible]

"7th March, 1874.

"May I ask of you to ascertain from the Town Commissioners whether they will grant to me [illegible] a renewal of the lease [illegible]."

483. Mr. [illegible] to Mr. *Halpin*.—Did you give any reply or state whether it would be renewed upon any terms?—I did not give him any written answer, but I gave a verbal one to him, saying that the Town Commissioners would not entertain any application from him.

484. Were all those tenders read at the existing meeting?—They were.

485. Was the meeting adjourned?—Yes; until seven o'clock in the evening.

486. Who were present then?—There were then sixteen Commissioners present, including Messrs. Henry and William M'Phail, Mr. Caldwell, and Dr. Halpin, and also Mr. Chapman, and it was then

"Resolved—That Joseph Smith get a seventy-five years' lease of his premises in the Main street, from the 25th March, 1874, at [illegible] per foot frontage. [illegible]

"Resolved—That William M'Phail get a seventy-five years' lease of his premises in the Main street, from the 25th of March, 1874, at [illegible] per foot frontage. Mr. M'Phail to raise the wall and build in conformity with the adjoining houses.

"Resolved—That Henry M'Phail get a seventy-five years' lease of his premises in the Main street, from the 25th March, 1874, at [illegible] per foot frontage. Mr. M'Phail to raise the wall and build in conformity with the adjoining houses.

"Resolved—That Dr. Halpin get a seventy-five years' lease of his premises in the Main street, from the 25th March, 1874, at [illegible] per foot frontage.

"Resolved—That Miss [illegible] get a seventy-five years' lease of her premises at [illegible] per foot frontage, [illegible] 25th March, 1874, in accordance with all the building regulations [illegible]

"Resolved—That John Chapman get a seventy-five years' lease of his building, at a rent of [illegible] per foot frontage, from 25th March, 1874, [illegible] adjoining houses; [illegible]"

The meeting was then adjourned until the next day the 7th April, when there were eighteen Commissioners present (and Mr. Chapman), amongst whom were Messrs. Henry and William M'Phail, Dr. Halpin, and Mr. Caldwell, and it was—

"Resolved—That Robert Caldwell get a lease for seventy-five years' of his premises in the [illegible] from the 25th March, 1874, at [illegible] per foot frontage.

"[illegible]

"Resolved—That the meeting adjourn until the next day."

487. Who was present on the 8th April, 1874?—Twenty Commissioners, amongst them Messrs. Henry and William M'Phail, Mr. Caldwell, and Dr. Halpin, and it was

"Resolved—That Miss [illegible] get [illegible] compensation for giving up her house and premises [illegible]

"Another resolution was passed giving Thomas Fitzgerald a lease at [illegible] per foot frontage. It was also

"Resolved—That Mrs. [illegible] get the two houses in [illegible] at [illegible] per foot frontage, at lease for seventy-five years from the 25th March, 1874, [illegible]

"Resolved—That the meeting adjourn until the following evening at seven o'clock."

Next evening at seven o'clock the adjourned meeting was held. Twenty Commissioners present, amongst whom were Messrs. Henry and William M'Phail, Dr. Halpin, and Mr. Caldwell, and it was—

"Resolved—That Robert Caldwell get a seventy-five years' lease of his two houses under the Hall, from the 25th March, 1874, at [illegible] per foot frontage.

"Resolved—That Dr. Halpin get his yard on [illegible] at yearly tenant at the yearly rent of £1 [illegible] from 25th March, 1874.

"Resolved—That the meeting do adjourn until the following evening at seven o'clock."

488. What is the next entry?—

"Meeting of the 10th April, 1874, held. Eighteen Commissioners present, including Messrs. Henry and William M'Phail, Dr. Halpin, and Mr. Caldwell, and it was adjourned until the 13th April when there were present, sixteen Commissioners, including Messrs. Henry and William M'Phail, Mr. Caldwell, and Dr. Halpin, and it was

"Resolved—That the houses in the rear of Mr. [illegible] and Mrs. [illegible] plot, now used as dwelling houses, shall be no longer used as such, [illegible]"

WICKLOW. Feb. 23, 1875.

Mr. Robert Halpin.

489. Mr. *Chapman*.—Those are the premises where I had the small houses let at 1s. 6d. a week.

490. Mr. [illegible] reads from book—

"The next meeting is held on the 14th April. Present, fifteen Commissioners, including Messrs. Henry and William M'Phail, Mr. Caldwell, and Dr. Halpin, and the record of these gentlemen being present as Commissioners, is signed by Mr. John Oakes, as chairman."

The next meeting is held on the 15th April. There were sixteen Commissioners present, including Mr. Henry M'Phail and Mr. Caldwell; Mr. William M'Phail and Dr. Halpin were not present.

"Resolved—That, having consulted with Mr. [illegible] Mr. [illegible] draw up a full case and get the opinion of Mr. [illegible] The minutes signed by Mr. Oakes as chairman."

491. To Mr. *Halpin*.—What was the next thing done?—Nothing was done from that until the 23rd April when there was a committee meeting of the whole body held at which there were five present, Mr. Henry M'Phail and Mr. Robert Caldwell and three others. Mr. [illegible] attended professionally, and read Mr. Hemphill's opinion, and it was

"Resolved—That, having heard the case and opinion read, a special meeting of the Town Commissioners be called to lay the same before them."

492. What is the next entry?—27th April, 1874:—

"A special meeting of the Town Commissioners was held this evening to receive counsel's opinion as to the case submitted to him. There were fifteen Commissioners present. Mr. [illegible] attended professionally. Messrs. Henry and William M'Phail were both present. Dr. Halpin was not, and it was

"Resolved—That Mr. [illegible] be requested to attend the meeting of the Commissioners, and,

"Resolved—That this meeting do adjourn until to-morrow evening at seven o'clock, to reconsider the leases made during the last fourteen days.

"(Signed) JOHN OAKES, Chairman."

493. What is the next?—28th April, 1874.

"An adjourned meeting of the Commissioners held this evening. Twelve Commissioners present. Mr. [illegible] attended professionally. Proposed by John [illegible], and seconded by W. J. [illegible]—

"'Resolved—That John Oakes act as chairman for the residue of the year.'

"Resignations were read from Henry M'Phail, William M'Phail, Robert Caldwell, and Dr. Halpin resigning their seats as Commissioners. The [illegible] were proposed. Mr. Caldwell's resignation, which is marked 'read' by the town clerk is in these terms—

"'Wicklow, Saturday, 25th April, 1874.

"'DEAR SIR,—Having heard counsel's opinion read last night I beg to tender my resignation as a Town Commissioner, and at the same time to inform you that it is not my intention to act as a Commissioner further.

"'I am, dear sir, yours truly,

"'ROBERT CALDWELL.

"'To the Chairman of the Town Commissioners, Wicklow.'"

"Resolved—That this meeting do adjourn till Monday the 11th May next. That an advertisement be inserted in the local papers to the effect that the Commissioners will on that occasion consider tenders for the amount of rent which the tenderers propose to give for the different buildings lately come into their possession owing to the lease of Colonel Cunninghame having expired on the 25th March, 1874.

"(Signed) JOHN OAKES, Chairman."

494. Was this ever inserted, and where is it?—On Saturday the 9th May the advertisement was inserted in the public newspaper, as follows—

"Town Hall, Wicklow,
"April 30, 1874.

"The Town Commissioners of Wicklow will, at their adjourned meeting to be held on Monday, the 11th day of May, 1874, at [illegible] o'clock, [illegible], at the Town Hall, receive sealed tenders stating the amount of rent that each person proposes to give for the different buildings lately come into the possession of the Commissioners by the lease to Colonel Cunninghame having expired on the 25th of March last.

"Tenders to be lodged with the secretary at or before ten o'clock a.m., on the 11th day of May, 1874, and marked on the outside, '*Tender for premises*.'

"By order, [illegible], Secretary."

495. Were the vacancies filled up, and when?—On the 6th May it was resolved that John Kelly Twomey be elected a Town Commissioner in place of Dr. Halpin, who had resigned. On the 11th May it was resolved that Dr. Taylor, Thomas Smith, Joseph Collins, and Dr. L'Estrange be elected Commissioners in place of Robert Caldwell, Henry M'Phail, William M'Phail, and John D. Smith who had resigned. The meeting then adjourned to the 15th May.

496. What took place at that meeting?—There were fifteen Commissioners present, and it was

"Resolved—That Henry M'Phail's tender for premises in the Main-street, at [illegible] per foot frontage be accepted, the premises to have rere [illegible] to [illegible], term seventy-five years' lease from [illegible] of March, 1874.

"Resolved—That William M'Phail's tender for premises in the [illegible] Main-street, at [illegible] per foot frontage be accepted, the premises to have [illegible] to [illegible]. Term seventy-five years' lease from 25th March, 1874.

"Resolved—That Dr. Halpin's tender for premises in the Main-street be accepted, at [illegible] per foot frontage, the premises to have [illegible]. Term seventy-five years' lease from 25th of March, 1874."

497. Mr. Exham.—Will you show me those tenders [Produces William M'Phail's tender, as follows]:—

"I propose to take a lease of my house and premises in the Main-street of [illegible], containing in front twenty-[illegible] feet eight inches, at the yearly rent of [illegible] per foot frontage. I have expended on my house the sum of £[illegible] on buildings. I also propose to pay £[illegible] for [illegible] feet frontage of the [illegible] premises, [illegible] for the accommodation of my dwelling-house."

Mr. Halpin.—The latter part of his tender was refused.

498. Mr. Exham.—Have you got Mr. Henry M'Phail's second tender?—Mr. Halpin.—I have not got it, and according to my recollection Mr. Henry M'Phail did not send in a second tender, but stated that he would let his first tender stand for the second.

499. Mr. Henry M'Phail.—I am under the impression that I did send in a second tender in the same terms as the first.

500. Mr. Exham.—Let me see Dr. Halpin's second tender. [Dr. Halpin's second tender was produced.]

"Gentlemen,—I propose to pay you for the plot on which my house and out-offices are built, the sum already named by the [illegible] of your Board, that is at the rate of [illegible] per foot. I also propose to pay, and accept of the terms named for my yard, that is £1 10s. per year."

501. Mr. H. M'Phail.—I also proposed to pay £1 10s. a year for a yard, but I was refused it.

502. Mr. Exham.—At the same meeting resolutions were adopted for accepting Miss Hamilton's, Mary Ann Dunne's, and Mr. Chapman's tenders, subject to the resolutions of the 6th April, 1874. A tender was given in by Margaret Flynn, of the 11th May, 1874, for the house which she held for the last twenty-three years, proposing to pay £3 a year for it; and if the Corporation required any alteration in the improvements of her house, she was willing to do anything they might suggest, and hoped if that were so, a reduction might be made in her rent as was usual in such cases. She had paid £4 a year previously for it. (To Mr. Halpin).—Was that read at the meeting?—It was.

503. Was it complied with?—No.

504. Who got it?—Mr. Caldwell.

505. At what rent?—£3 3s. a year.

506. Mr. Exham.—A tender was received from J. Whelan, proposing to become their tenant for the house and premises in his possession on the Mall, for which he had paid rent for forty years. What rent did he pay?—He had paid £4, and he got it at £3.

507. A tender was also read from George Lawson, proposing to become tenant of his premises at the rate of rent they had already decided upon, or he would comply with whatever regulations they might make. What rent did he pay?—He paid £4 [illegible] before, and he got it for £3. These last two were yearly tenancies, and the parties were bound to keep them in repair.

508. On the 19th May a meeting was held, at which there were fourteen Commissioners present, when it was resolved—"That Robert Caldwell's tender and proposal for premises in the Main-street, and for two houses under the Mall be accepted, viz.:—for premises in Main-street £3 3s. per annum, and for the two houses under the Mall £3 3s. per annum; the premises in Main-street to have rere to High-street, in which Mr. Caldwell lately built two houses." The result of all this is, that in May, 1874, you gave nearly all these persons leases according to the resolutions of the 6th April, 1874. On the 22nd May, it was resolved—"That John Sullivan get his premises in the Main-street, at £3 per annum, and to pay Mrs. Keely £[illegible] now, £[illegible] in six months, and £[illegible] in twelve months."

509. Mr. H. M'Phail.—I wish to call your attention to the fact that the best building plots on Earl Fitzgibbon's estate can be had for 2s. 6d. per foot frontage. I also desire to mention that the Corporation have allowed their property to be taken from them. I refer to what are called the Burgess Plots.

510. Mr. Exham.—How have they allowed property to go out of their hands?

511. Mr. M'Phail.—I cannot tell you how, but that they have done so is the fact. When there was a petition, some five or six years ago, to sell one of the Burgess Plots in the Landed Estates Court, the Commissioners never attempted to interfere, but allowed the thing to be done.

512. Mr. Exham.—How is that?

Mr. Halpin.—We had no title to it at all; we examined all the books, and we could not find any trace of it.

513. Mr. Chapman.—We made every inquiry we possibly could, and we could not trace it out as being corporate property. It belonged to Lord Ranelagh.

514. Mr. Halpin.—The way the matter stands is this:—There are isolated plots scattered here and there between the corporate property, and which may have belonged to us two hundred years ago, but we have searched the books one hundred and sixty years back and we can find no trace by which we could establish a right to them, or show that they had ever been ours.

515. Mr. Exham (at the request of Mr. [illegible]).—Who is the tenant of these Burgess Plots at present?

Mr. Chapman.—I am.

516. Mr. Exham.—From whom do you hold them?

Mr. Chapman.—Colonel Cunninghame. He holds various plots in the town.

517. Mr. Exham.—There is one other matter which we are particularly desirous of having fully explained, it was very late in the day on the last occasion when it was introduced, and it was not sufficiently sifted, I mean the loan to the Harbour Commissioners.

518. Mr. H. M'Phail.—There is no such body as a harbour board at all.

519. Mr. Exham.—This is a very important matter, and it is the principal thing that brought me down. Who received the dues?

520. Mr. H. M'Phail.—That is the very thing we want to know.

521. Mr. Halpin.—I can give you every information on the subject.

522. Mr. Exham.—Very well; then we shall examine you with reference to the Harbour Board.

523. Mr. Halpin then stated.—I am the secretary to the Harbour Commissioners. I now produce a list of mortgages and other debts, amounting in the year 1874 to £36,994 13s. 8d.

DEBTS DUE OF HARBOUR OF WICKLOW.

	£ s. d.	£ s. d.	£ s. d.	£ s. d.
Mortgage due Town Commissioners,		8,000 0 0		
Interest on same, at 4 per cent., to 6th December, 1875,		6,[illegible] 0 0		
			14,[illegible] 0 0	
Mortgage due Town Commissioners,		4,000 0 0		
Interest on same, at 4 per cent., to 10th November, 1875,		2,[illegible] 0 0		
			6,[illegible] 0 0	
				21,[illegible] 0 0
Mortgage due London Loan Commissioners,		1,000 0 0		
Interest on same to 11th November, 1875,	[illegible] 0 [illegible]			
By cash paid,	[illegible] 0 [illegible]			
		[illegible] 0 0		
			1,[illegible] 0 0	
Mortgage due London Loan Commissioners,		2,000 0 0		
Interest on same to 6th November, 1875,	2,[illegible] [illegible] [illegible]			
By cash paid,	[illegible] [illegible] [illegible]			
		[illegible] 0 0		
			3,[illegible] 0 0	
				4,[illegible] 0 0
Amount due Robert Halpin from 18[illegible] to 18[illegible],		-		[illegible] 0 0
Amount due Robert Barklie, [illegible],		-	[illegible] 16 7	
Less amount paid by Harbour Commissioners,		-	[illegible] 0 0	
				[illegible] 16 7
Amount due the following Harbour Commissioners, advanced personally for Harbour purposes:—				
John Pursin,		-	[illegible] 16 0	
William Kelso,		-	[illegible] 11 0	
William Kelso, junior,		-	[illegible] 11 0	
James Kelso,		-	[illegible] 16 0	
John Edwards,		-	[illegible] [illegible] 0	
John [illegible],		-	[illegible] [illegible] 0	
Thomas [illegible],		-	[illegible] [illegible] 0	
Edward [illegible],		-	[illegible] 11 [illegible]	
John [illegible],		-	[illegible] 11 0	
Joseph [illegible],		-	[illegible] 14 0	
Thomas Gregory,		-	[illegible] 14 0	
				[illegible] 0 1
				[illegible] 18 [illegible]

There is a mortgage debt due from 1851 to the Town Commissioners of £13,000, and interest. That £13,000 was borrowed on the corporate estate, with the consent of the Treasury to lend to the then Harbour Commissioners. They lent it to them in 1854, and took a mortgage on the tolls in expectancy when the works would be finished, as provided by the 5th and 6th Vic., c. 111. In 1854, Mr. Brett, the county surveyor was our engineer, and we advertised for contracts. (I have been secretary to the Harbour Commissioners from the commencement to the present), and made a contract for £8,500 for completing the works to an extent sufficient to entitle us to the tolls. These tolls were estimated at £1,500, which was ample to pay the loan and interest if the work had been done. The contractor went on slowly and badly, and not at all in accordance with the specifications, the result of which was that an action had to be taken against him for breach of contract, and there was a long and protracted trial. Killeen, of Malahide, was the name of the contractor. The trial lasted in the Court of Exchequer upwards of thirty-one days, and we spent over £1,000 upon it. Afterwards we had a Chancery suit which cost upwards of £1,600 more. This suit was brought by Killeen against the Commissioners personally. The £13,000 was all gone, and he sued them individually, and made them personally liable, and they paid money out of their own pockets amounting to £1,400; then another £6,000 was got from the Government for the harbour, but no good results followed, and the harbour is still in a defective state.

524. Mr. KEEnAN.—Is there a Harbour Board now?—No.

525. How long is it since there was a Board?—Since 1872 there has been no Board. The harbour is now in the hands of the Government mortgagees, the Public Works Loan Commissioners. The tolls and dues are received by me, and accounted for to the Government on foot of the £6,000 loan.

526. Are the dues regulated by an Act of Parliament?—They are not. We had a decision in the Queen's Bench which laid down that the dues which are received are fair and legitimate, and lawful for tonnage and quayage, but there are no tolls under the Harbour Act, as the harbour was never sufficiently deepened to entitle us to collect them. We merely charge for tonnage and quayage—in fact for the use and occupation of the property.

527. They say you never completed the harbour, and therefore you cannot get the dues?—Just so.

528. Mr. *Chapman*.—The clause in the Act said there should be a certain depth over the outer bar before tolls could be levied. That depth has not been attained.

529. Mr. *Halpin*.—We cannot levy the tolls under the Harbour Act, because the harbour has never been deepened to the required depth.

530. Mr. KEEnAN.—Is there any great anxiety here to deepen the harbour?—There would be if we had the means.

531. You say there has been no Board since 1872?—Yes.

532. Was there any gentleman sitting on the last Board who had never taken the oath?

Mr. *Halpin*.—Not one. They were all duly qualified, and took their declarations. The tonnage and quayage dues are received by me as their secretary. The accounts are furnished annually to the Loan Fund Commissioners, who are the mortgagees of the estate, and who have a prior claim to the Town Commissioners.

533. Mr. KEEnAN.—Was priority given to the Government Loan over yours?—There was. They would not lend the £6,000 otherwise until the Town Commissioners had foregone their claim.

534. Who audits the accounts?—Mr. Wakefield, the late chairman.

535. What right has Mr. Wakefield to audit them?—As the trustee of the mortgagees.

536. Mr. *M'Phail*.—Mr. Halpin is Mr. Wakefield's agent.

537. Mr. KEEnAN.—Who is Mr. Wakefield, and by what authority does he audit the accounts?—He was the last chairman of the board, and he is trustee for the mortgagees.

538. By what authority do you now receive these dues?—Under an Act of Parliament.

539. Who authorises you under the Act?—The mortgagees.

[illegible]

540. Have you any letter of authority?—I have not. Mr. Wakefield is the trustee, and he is acting for the mortgagees.

541. Who authorises Mr. Wakefield to examine the accounts?—The Public Works Loan Commissioners who lent the money. He has authority from them to examine the accounts.

542. Did you ever see any document from them authorising him to do so?—I did.

543. If you take an action against any person for these tolls what authority can you show for doing so. Have you any power of attorney or written authority?—The Loan Commissioners have the power.

544. Do you say that you are in possession as agent for them?—Yes.

545. Were you appointed by them?—I was.

546. By letter?—Not by letter; verbally.

547. Tell me the name of the person who appointed you?—Why the secretary, Mr. Walbank; he told Mr. Wakefield.

548. Did you hear him?—I did not.

549. Then in point of fact, you are collecting them by the authority of Mr Wakefield?—I am collecting them by the authority of the Loan Fund Commissioners.

550. You never got verbal or written authority from them?—I was with them in London, and got authority.

551. Give me the name of the person who authorised you to receive these tolls on behalf of the Loan Fund Commissioners?—Mr. Barnes their solicitor, gave me authority to collect these fees.

552. Have you a power of attorney from him?—I have not.

553. When did he give you this authority?—In London in 1871.

554. Are you receiving the tolls ever since, and does Mr. Wakefield audit the accounts?—Yes.

555. And what do you do with the money?—I send it to the mortgagees.

556. What commission is allowed you for collecting the dues?—Ten per cent. I had £30 in hands in December, 1876. Since then £60 has been laid out on the new quay wall.

557. Who authorised you to expend this money?—I have the Commissioners' instructions to keep the quays in perfect repair.

558. Have you a harbour master?—We have.

559. What salary does he receive?—£20 a year.

560. Who enters into the contracts for repairing the walls?—I do.

561. Does the harbour master receive the tolls?—Some of them and hands them to me.

562. Do you charge ten per cent. on what he receives?—I do.

563. Then it appears to me as if you and the harbour master were just doing what you like between you. Have you any verbal or written directions since, you saw that gentleman in London, with regard to the way you were to manage the harbour affairs?—(No answer).

564. I shall take care to put on our notes the way this matter is being managed by your acting as is alleged here?—I don't care what people do, for there is nothing to be made by it.

565. Mr. *Cobden*.—Will you ask who Mr. Wakefield has his authority from?

566. Mr. Exham.—You may make your mind easy as all about it can be found out, but I cannot pursue the inquiry any further. (To Mr. *Hodgkin*).—Who looks after the harbour now?—I do and have done so for the last twenty-five years. The Loan Fund Commissioners are in possession of the harbour as mortgagees and I am acting as their agent with their authority.

This closed the inquiry.

APPENDIX—PART II.

APPENDIX No. 1.

[The following document was accidentally omitted from the Appendix to the Waterford Report in Part I.]

1875.—Report of the Board of Trade.—Waterford Improvement Bill.

By this Bill the Corporation of Waterford seek to obtain various powers in connexion with their borough, and among these certain powers with respect to certain dues which appear to have been known as water bailiff's fees.

Clauses 75 to 79 of the Bill are as follows:—

74. The Corporation may, if they think fit, and upon such terms as may be mutually agreed upon, appoint the Harbour Commissioners to collect the water bailiff's fees, and to account for them to the Corporation.

75. From and after the passing of this Act, the fees, dues, or charges taken or considered to be taken within the Port of Waterford by the water bailiff, or his deputy or deputies duly authorised in that behalf, shall be estimated, levied, and taken in British currency, and shall be the fees, dues, or charges following and none other (that is to say):—

One penny per ton upon all vessels discharging or taking cargo of whatsoever kind within the Port of Waterford.

76. The Corporation and the water bailiff shall have, with respect to the collection and recovery of the fees continued or authorised by this Act, and with respect to the vessels and persons liable to the payment thereof, similar powers of recovery, removal, control, levy, distress and sale, to the powers conferred on the Corporation and water bailiff respectively, or either of them by the Police Act, or upon the Harbour Commissioners in respect of dues leviable by them under the Act 9th and 10th Vict., c. 291.

77. Unless or until the Corporation shall otherwise determine, the water bailiff's fees, as and when received by the water bailiff or his deputy or deputies, shall be payable and paid by him or them to the treasurer, or shall be otherwise accounted for to the Corporation in accordance with the provisions in that behalf of the Municipal Corporation Acts, and shall be carried to the borough fund.

78. The Corporation may from time to time, as and when they think fit, make and give effect to arrangements or agreements with the Harbour Commissioners as to the collecting of the fees, dues, or charges known as the water bailiff's fees, or any part or parts thereof, and as to the application thereof.

79. Nothing in the foregoing sections or in the Act contained shall affect or alter the anchorage dues levied by the Corporation within the port.

The following is an extract from the Report of the Royal Commission of Inquiry into Local Charges upon Shipping (presented to Parliament in 1853):—

Description of Dues and Charges Levied by the Municipal Corporation of Waterford.

1. Tonnage Dues:

One penny, late Irish currency, per ton of registered tonnage.

2. Anchorage Dues:

Vessels not exceeding 100 tons register, 2s. 6d. late Irish currency, equal to 2s. 3d. present currency. Vessels exceeding 100 tons register, 5s. late, equal to 4s. 6d. present currency.

In addition, vessels, principally colliers, requiring beams and scales, pay 2s. 6d. (4s. late currency) for use of the set.

All foreign ships pay double.

In the case of steamers plying between Waterford and New Ross and Dungarvan, the foregoing charges have been commuted for a yearly payment of £20 for each steamer.

Gross amount of tonnage and anchorage dues levied in 1852, £350 19s. 10d.

The Municipal Corporation of Waterford have been, from very remote times, possessed of the office of water bailiff, and as appurtenant to it were entitled to levy a considerable number of ancient dues and fees. They have not, of late years, enforced the payment of any other dues than those above mentioned.

By an arrangement made with the Harbour Commissioners, these dues are collected by them and applied, in the first instance, to defraying the expense of a quay and river police, of lighting the quays, and some other matters closely connected with the harbour, the surplus, if any, forming part of the Waterford borough fund.

The expenses thus defrayed by the Harbour Commissioners nearly absorb the whole revenue derived from these dues; the amount that went to the borough fund (out of which is paid the water bailiff's salary of £75 a year) in 1852 was £40.

The dues are claimed within that part of the river Suir which is within the borough of Waterford, and they are in practice levied throughout.

No differential dues were charged on foreign vessels in 1852.

The Waterford Steamship Company have addressed to the Board of Trade a memorial which is printed in the Appendix.

These dues do not appear to have, at any time, received the sanction of the Legislature, and having regard to the fact that they are a tax upon shipping, the Board of Trade would suggest that the dues should not be legalised until provision can be made for their application to shipping purposes.

This would be in accordance with the principle, generally adopted in modern legislation, of authorising taxation on shipping or on goods carried in ships only where the taxes levied are to be applied to shipping purposes.

T. H. Farrer.

Board of Trade, April, 1875.

Appendix.—Representation from the Waterford Steamship Company.

In the year 1849 a memorial was sent to the Board of Trade applying for their interference relative to an impost on shipping trading to the port, termed water bailiff's fees, levied by order of the Town Council under, as they alleged, authority of a charter of King John, confirmed by various other Royal charters. To that memorial the Town Council replied through the town clerk, and in their reply gave a schedule of fees settled in 1660, and which schedule contained an item of 1d. per ton on goods landed, in return for which the water bailiffs were to furnish planks and stages. This they state to be the water bailiff's fees, which are now levied on the ships and not on the goods, although where that change took place, or by whose authority it was made, they now profess themselves unable to state.

The result of that memorial and reply, and of the negotiations consequent thereon, was an agreement between the Town Council and the Harbour Commissioners that three-fourths of the fees should be at the disposal of the Harbour Commissioners for shipping purposes, and the remaining one-fourth be paid over to the Town Council for the general advantage of the borough.

In order to promote harmony between the two great co-operative bodies of the town, your memorialists did not object to this arrangement, although they then thought, and still consider, that dues paid by shipping should be at the disposal and under the sole control of the harbour authorities. In the Bill now being promoted, called the Waterford Improvement Bill, however an attempt is made to obtain powers to levy these dues, to apply them solely to borough purposes, should it so please the Town Council, and by embodying them with the borough fund, to make them liable to the debts of the Corporation. In Waterford there are no dues levied upon goods for harbour purposes, and your memorialists therefore respectfully submit that shipowners have thereby an additional claim that the dues paid by shipping should be applied solely to their use, and be under the control of the harbour authorities. Your memorialists do not object to paying the dues if so applied, and they therefore respectfully ask that the Board of Trade will intervene on their behalf, and either insist upon all sections relative to imposts on shipping being expunged from the Bill; or its being so framed as will place these dues at the disposal of, and under the control of the existing harbour authorities, for your memorialists would object to the Town Council being permitted to receive and expend those even although on shipping, as it would in fact create two governing bodies with concurrent jurisdiction; all the clauses relating to imposts on shipping should be expunged from the Bill, or if power to levy these be taken, they shall be under the control of the proper harbour authorities, to be expended solely for the benefit of shipping.

In which case your memorialists do not make any objection to their imposition, as they consider that the income so levied is required for the improvement of the port, and for furnishing accommodation to the shipping frequenting it.

For the Waterford Steamship Company, Limited.

WILL. MALCOMSON, Chairman.

Waterford, 8 March, 1878.

APPENDIX No. 2.

BOROUGH OF BELFAST.

LIST OF OFFICERS AND SALARIES.

	£	s.	d.
J. H. Otway, Q.C., Recorder,	[illegible]	0	0
Alex. Caldwell, Recorder's Crier,	10	0	0
W. C. Cunningham, Clerk of Peace,	[illegible]	0	0
Dr Hodges, Borough Analyst,	100	0	0
Samuel Black, Town Clerk,	[illegible]	0	0
A. W. Oakman, Town Clerk's Assistant,	170	0	0
Do. Registrar of Cemetery,	[illegible]	0	0
J. J. Montgomery, Borough Surveyor,	[illegible]	0	0
J. C. Bretland, Assistant Surveyor,	[illegible]	0	0
John Whitehead, Do. Do.	[illegible]	0	0
James McCoy, Surveyor of Sewerage,	[illegible]	0	0
James Moore, Clerk (Surveyor's Office),	[illegible]	0	0
R. McC. Weeks, Accountant,	[illegible]	0	0
W. [illegible], Accountant's Assistant,	[illegible]	0	0
R. [illegible], Do.	[illegible]	0	0
E. S. W. De Cobain, Coroner,	[illegible]	0	0
George Kelly, Superintendent Fire Brigade,	[illegible]	0	0
James [illegible], Street Inspector,	[illegible]	0	0
J. M'[illegible], Do.	[illegible]	0	0
John Charley, Petty Sessions Attorney,	[illegible]	0	0
A. O'Rorke, Jun., Do.	[illegible]	0	0
A. Woods, Clerk of Markets,	[illegible]	0	0
W. Cowan, Assistant Do.	[illegible]	0	0
William Davey, Inspector of Provisions,	[illegible]	0	0
Samuel Browne, M.D., Consulting Sanitary Officer,	[illegible]	0	0
C. Boyd, Executive Sanitary Officer,	[illegible]	0	0
George M'Cann, Superintendent of Cemetery,	[illegible]	0	0
Thomas Dickson, Parks Superintendent,	[illegible]	0	0
Thomas [illegible], Car Inspector,	[illegible]	0	0
D. Hall, Do.	[illegible]	0	0
J. G. [illegible], Deputy Superintendent Fire Brigade,	[illegible]	0	0
J. W. [illegible], Apprentice,	[illegible]	0	0
H. C. M'Cormick, Do.	[illegible]	0	0
W. G. [illegible], Do.	[illegible]	0	0
Robert Moore, Do.	[illegible]	0	0
J. [illegible], Sergeant at Mace,	[illegible]	0	0
W. [illegible], Do.	[illegible]	[illegible]	0
J. Johnston, Hall Keeper, &c.,	[illegible]	0	0
J. [illegible], Hall Porter,	[illegible]	12	0
Alex. Kerr, Chairman,	[illegible]	[illegible]	0
John Stewart, Caretaker (Coroner's Court),	[illegible]	0	0
Fire Brigade Firemen,	[illegible]	0	0
R. F. Dill, M.D., Borough Coroner,	Paid by Fees.		
Total,	£[illegible]	19	0

APPENDIX No. 3.

BOROUGH of BELFAST CORPORATION GAS ACCOUNTS, for the Year ending 30th June, 1878.

ABSTRACT of the ACCOUNTS of the BELFAST CORPORATION GAS WORKS for the Year ended the 30th June, 1878, showing the Receipts and Expenditure under the several heads during that period.

No. 1.—CAPITAL ACCOUNT.

RECEIPTS.

	£	s.	d.
To Loans on Mortgage,	[illegible]	0	0
" Perpetual Annuities,	9,[illegible]	15	11
" Purchase-money of the [illegible] Property,	150	0	0
	£[illegible]	15	11

EXPENDITURE.

	£	s.	d.
By Expenditure to June 30th, 1877,	[illegible]	5	0
ADDITIONAL OUTLAY.			
By Cost of Conveyance of Works, Mortgage Stamps, &c., and Commission on Loans,	[illegible]	[illegible]	[illegible]
" New Buildings, Machinery, and Extension of Works, including Quay Wall, Experimental Works, and Square Sett Paving,	[illegible]	[illegible]	[illegible]
" New Mains,	[illegible]	[illegible]	[illegible]
" New Services,	[illegible]	10	[illegible]
" New Meters,	[illegible]	[illegible]	[illegible]
	£[illegible]	[illegible]	[illegible]
" Balance,	[illegible]	[illegible]	[illegible]
	£[illegible]	[illegible]	[illegible]

App. No. 6. Belfast Corporation Gas Accounts.

No. 2.—Revenue Account.

Receipts.

	£ s. d.	£ s. d.	£ s. d.
To Sale of Gas,		7[illegible] 15 8	
Less Discount,	4,7[illegible] 1 8		
" Bad Debts,	[illegible] 9 2		
		[illegible] 11 4	
			7[illegible] 7 4
" Public Lighting, and under Agreements,			[illegible] 9 3
" Rental of Meters,		4,11[illegible] 11 6	
Less Discount,	4 9 11		
" Bad Debts,	17 0 8		
		[illegible] 10 7	
			[illegible] 0 11
" Residual Products— Sales of Coke and Breeze, less Labour, &c.,		1[illegible] 17 11	
[illegible]		[illegible] 0 9	
			[illegible] 13 8
" Sales of Tar,			[illegible] 7 4
" " Ammoniacal Liquor,			479 16 6
" Rents,			65 7 8
" Gas Rents recovered (formerly written off as bad),			7 8 6
			£[illegible] 19 0

Expenditure.

	£ s. d.
By Coals, including Dues, Cartage, Unloading, and all expenses of depositing same on Works,	[illegible] 6 11
" Purification and Scrubbing, including Labour, £[illegible] &c.,	1,[illegible] 8 9
" Salaries of Engineers and Assistants,	[illegible] 15 2
" Wages (Carbonizing),	[illegible] 5 3
" Repairs and Maintenance of Works and Plant (including renewal of Retorts, Holders, Apparatus, Tools, Materials, and Labour,	[illegible] 6 6
" Residual Products used in Carbonization and for Engines,	[illegible] 0 8
By Distribution of Gas—	
Salaries of Chief Inspector, Inspectors, and Clerks in Department,	[illegible] 18 0
Repairs, Maintenance, and Renewal of Mains and Service Pipes, including Materials, Laying and Paving, and Labour,	[illegible] 8 4
Repairing, Renewing, and Refixing Meters,	1,[illegible] 0 11
By Public Lamps—Lighting and Repairs,	[illegible] 6 6
" Rents, Rates, and Taxes—	
Rents,	1[illegible] 0 0
Rates and Taxes,	[illegible] 13 0
By Salaries of Cashier, Accountant and Clerks, Office-keepers, and Messengers,	1,[illegible] 15 10
" Salaries of Collectors,	[illegible] 0 0
" Stationery and Printing,	1[illegible] 6 7
" General Establishment Charges and Incidental Expenses,	818 11 5
" Audit Fees,	[illegible] 0 0
" Law Charges,	44[illegible] 12 11
	47[illegible] 15 [illegible]
By Balance carried to Net Revenue Account,	[illegible] 3 4
	£[illegible] 19 0

I certify the foregoing to be a true abstract of the Receipts and Expenditure of the Revenue Account of the Belfast Corporation Gas Works for the year ended the 30th June, 1876.

Dated this [illegible] day of September, 1876.

R. [illegible], Auditor.

No. 3.—Profit and Loss Account.

Net Revenue.

Dr.	£ s. d.	Cr.	£ s. d.	£ s. d.
To Balance from last year's Account,	13,[illegible] 1 5	By Interest on Purchase Money and Loans for the year ending June 30th, 1876 (less Bank Interest, £[illegible])		[illegible] 18 1
" Revenue Account,	[illegible] 3 4	By Balance—consisting of Balance from last year's Account,	[illegible] 1 5	
		Net Profit on Year's Working,	[illegible] 8 2	
				[illegible] 10 7
	£[illegible]			£[illegible]

I certify the foregoing to be a true abstract of the Profit and Loss Account of the Belfast Corporation Gas Works for the year ended the 30th June, 1876.

Dated this [illegible] day of September, 1876.

R. [illegible], Auditor.

No. 4.—Balance Sheet.

Dr.	£ s. d.	Cr.	£ s. d.	£ s. d.
To Balance from Revenue Account,	[illegible] 10 7	By Cash at Bankers,		[illegible] 15 0
" Capital Account,	[illegible] 9 5	" Value of Stocks in hand,		[illegible] 4 11
To Sundry Accounts due for Interest to June 30th, Legal Costs, &c.,	[illegible] 9 6	" Accounts due for Gas,	[illegible] 7 9	
		" Accounts due for Meter Rent,	[illegible] 18 8	
				[illegible] 6 5
		" Sundry Accounts for Coke, Tar, &c.,		1,[illegible] 15 11
		" Sundry Accounts for Service Pipes,		[illegible] 0 5
		" Sundries—consisting of Council Lamp Account (£[illegible] &c.), Highway Lamp Account (£[illegible]), &c.,		[illegible] 0 5
		" Half-year's Taxes unexpired carried forward,		1,[illegible] 16 6
	£[illegible] 15 5			£[illegible] 18 6

APPENDIX No. 4.

Borough of Belfast.

Statement, prepared by H. M'C. Woods, showing the Total Amounts Borrowed by the Corporation under the powers of their several Local Acts, Amounts paid off, and the Balances now due, exclusive of Gas Loans.

		Amounts borrowed.	Paid off.	Now due.
		£ s. d.	£ s. d.	£ s. d.
On Police Rate—Acts 1845 and 1846:—				
Primary Mortgages,		[illegible]	[illegible]	[illegible]
Amend Act, 1850(?):—				
Secondary Mortgages,		[illegible]	[illegible]	[illegible]
Loan, England—purchase money,		[illegible]	[illegible]	
Total on Police Rate,		[illegible]	[illegible]	[illegible]
On General Purposes Rate—Act 1878(?):—				
For one-third cost of Antrim Road District Sewers,		[illegible]	[illegible]	[illegible]
For one-third cost of Ravenscroft(?) Road District Sewers,		[illegible]	[illegible]	[illegible]
Paid,	[illegible]			
Less Interest on Principal to 1st November, 1878,	[illegible]			
Paid off,	[illegible]			
For one-third cost of Windsor District Sewers. On account of £3,000 to be borrowed,		[illegible]	—	[illegible]
For Permanent Paving of Streets,		[illegible]	[illegible]	[illegible]
Total on General Purposes Rate,		[illegible]	[illegible]	[illegible]
On District Sewers Rates—Acts 1865 and 1868(?):—				
On Cromac and Oldpark Road District Sewers Rate,		[illegible]	[illegible]	[illegible]
On Antrim Road District Sewers Rate,		[illegible]	[illegible]	[illegible]
On Ravenscroft(?) Road District Sewers Rate,		[illegible]	[illegible]	[illegible]
Paid,	[illegible]			
Less Principal and Interest to 1st November, 1878,	[illegible]			
Paid off,	[illegible]			
On Windsor District Sewers Rate, on account of £3,000 to be borrowed,		[illegible]	—	[illegible]
Under Public Parks Act, 1869(?):—				
On Borough and Parks Rate,		4,000 0 0	—	4,000 0 0
On Cemetery and Burial Rate Act, 1856(?):—				
For Purchase and Completion of Cemetery,		[illegible]	[illegible]	[illegible]
Total of all Moneys Borrowed, Paid off, and now Due,		[illegible]	[illegible]	[illegible]

18th December, 1878.

APPENDIX No. 5.

ABSTRACT of the ACCOUNTS of the TOWN COUNCIL for the Year ended the 31st December, 1875, showing the Receipts and Expenditure under the several heads during that period.

POLICE FUND.

RECEIPTS. Source of Receipt.		£	s.	d.	EXPENDITURE. Source of Expenditure.	£	s.	d.
Balance in hand 1st January, 1875,		2,431	16	7	Police Rate—refunded,	[illegible]	15	10
Police Rent, including Bounty from Government in lieu of Rate,		34,[illegible]	1	5	Commission to Collectors,	465	6	5
Markets,		9,[illegible]	7	5	Markets,	2,807	17	5
Weights and Measures Adjusting Account,		155	15	8	Weights and Measures Adjusting Account,	71	16	4
Slaughter House,		[illegible]	5	8	Slaughter House,	348	14	8
Fees—Ferry Steamers, &c.,		5,[illegible]	16	8	Fees, Stamps on Committals, &c.,	166	17	5
Licenses,		[illegible]	5	6	Car Inspectors,	163	10	6
Rent Account,		60	5	9	Rent Account,	18	10	5
Fire Account,		253	14	6	Fire Account,	1,[illegible]	17	2
Income-tax,		44	5	11	Interest on Mortgages,	6,318	15	8
Lighting Account,		34	9	6	Income-tax,	34	19	9
Interest,		165	18	4	Lighting Account,	7,[illegible]	13	6
Law Costs,		6	18	6	Advertising, Printing, and Stationery,	119	1	1
Burial Ground,		1	6	6	Law Costs,	1,194	6	9
Horse Account,		88	15	8	Sanitary Account,	81	5	6
Miscellaneous,		49	8	7	Horse Account,	771	9	6
Street Improvements,		86	17	8	Salaries,	876	10	9
Treasurer—overdrawn per Bank Pass Book,	2,069 17 8				Superannuations,	[illegible]	9	4
Cheques Issued—No. 5, 55, 56, [illegible]—unpaid at Bank,	65 14 1				Miscellaneous,	848	10	6
		2,0[illegible]	11	6	Constabulary,	16,160	15	11
					Slaughter House (erection of),	48	18	7
					Market Improvements,	2,091	8	10
					Street Improvements,	5,[illegible]	9	2
					Municipal Buildings,	1,071	18	0
					Sinking Funds Account,	6,[illegible]	10	9
					Balance in hands of Cashier,	4	4	6
		£[illegible]	19	6		£[illegible]	19	8

Signed only for Balance due to the Belfast Banking Company, on Police Fund Account, say Two Thousand and Two Pounds, Seventeen Shillings, and Eight Pence sterling.

A. JOHNS, Treasurer.
R. [illegible], Auditor.

BOROUGH FUND.

RECEIPTS.

			£ s. d.
Balance in hands of Treasurer, 31st August, 1875,			5,[illegible] 15 10
Borough Rate—			
Amount of outstanding Rate on 31st August, 1875,	£2,[illegible] 8 4		
Amount of Assessment, 1st January, 1875, as per Schedule 4,	5,[illegible] 10 6		
	7,[illegible] 19 10		
Amount collected within the period of this Account— Arrears, £[illegible] 11 5; Rate, 3,411 8 5	£5,[illegible] 0 4		
Irrecoverable Struck off, [illegible] 14 7			[illegible] 0 0
	5,[illegible] 13 8		
Amount of Rate uncollected, 31st August, 1875,	2,[illegible] 4 7		
Miscellaneous—			
S. Wangfield, esq., Dog Licenses, 1875,	[illegible] 17 7		
J. [illegible], esq., for Carpenter [illegible], Pawnbrokers' Certificates, Burgess Lists, &c.,	17 15 6		
Constable Campbell, fees on resignation of office,	13 10 0		
			944 6 7
Amount from Treasurer on Bank Account,			140 17 6
PUBLIC PARKS ACCOUNT.			
Ormeau Park—			
From Sale of Timber, £[illegible] 1s. 6d.; Garden Produce, £[illegible] 11s. 6d.,		[illegible] 15 0	
John Browne, one year's rent of [illegible] Land, to 1st August, 1875,	£35 0 0		
A. Taggart, balance of Rent for Grazing of Surplus Ground, Cleaning of Park, and Rent of Lodge, to 1st Nov., 1875,	65 0 0		
Same, on account Grazing of Surplus Ground, Cleaning of Park, and Rent of Lodge, to 1st November, 1875,	77 10 0		
		177 10 0	
Falls Park—		[illegible] 5 7	
[illegible] Dunlop, for Grazing,		[illegible] 0 0	
			[illegible] 6 [illegible]

EXPENDITURE.

			£ s. d.
Borough Rate—			
Refunded,			7 6 1
Schedule 5—			
Salaries and Allowances to Officers,	£2,[illegible] 0 6		
Commission to Collectors of Rate,	1[illegible] 9 6		
			[illegible] 9 0
Schedule 1—			
Deputy Assessor at Elections,	[illegible] 10 0		
Attendance at Revision,	5 7 0		
Advertising and Printing,	[illegible] 4 1		
Burgess and Tax Lists,	60 17 6		
Rent of Premises for Elections, and fitting up Polling Booths,	[illegible] 5 0		
Rate Books for making out Burgess Lists,	22 10 6		
			[illegible] 15 5
Contingent Expenses—			
Books, Stationery, Advertising and Printing,	[illegible] 0 11		
Miscellaneous,	411 2 5		
Weights and Measures,	5 16 0		
			[illegible] 5 4
Public Parks Account, as per Schedule,			2,[illegible] 10 4
Sanitary Account, as per Schedule,			720 7 9
Balance in hands of Treasurer, as per Bank Passbook,	4,[illegible] 12 6		
Cash,	11 17 9		
			4,[illegible] 10 3

App. No. 1.

Abstract of the Accounts of the Borough of Belfast.

General Purposes Fund.

Receipts.

Nature of Receipt.	£ s. d.	Amount. £ s. d.
Cash in hands of Cashier, 1st January, 1875,	[illegible] 0 10	
Cash in hands of Treasurer on Malicious Injuries Account,	[illegible] 12 7	
		[illegible] 12 11
General Purposes Rate,		[illegible]
Special Rate,		[illegible]
Interest,		[illegible] 14 [illegible]
Commissioners of Public Works—Loans,		[illegible]
Income Tax,		[illegible]
[illegible]		1,415 0 0
Miscellaneous,		[illegible]
[illegible] Account—Materials charged to sundry works,	[illegible] 9 11	
Less amount as per contra,	[illegible] 6 5	
		[illegible] 0 [illegible]
[illegible] Account—Sundry persons for making [illegible], &c.		7 [illegible] 6
Scavenging—For manure and [illegible]		2,[illegible] 14 [illegible]
[illegible]		[illegible] 17 7
Special Works—Sundry persons for [illegible]		[illegible] 4 11
Extended Works—Sundry persons for making [illegible]		[illegible]
[illegible]		[illegible]
[illegible] Works from Owners of Property,		[illegible]
[illegible] and Old Park Roads District Drainage, [illegible] Rate,		[illegible] 13 7
[illegible] Road District Drainage: Personal Accounts—Sundry owners of property, their proportion of cost of sewers,	[illegible] 1	
[illegible] Rate,	[illegible] 9 10	
		[illegible]
[illegible] Road District Drainage: Personal Accounts—Sundry owners of property, their proportion of cost of sewers,	[illegible]	
[illegible] Rate,	[illegible]	
Commissioners of Public Works—Loans,	[illegible] 0 0	
Miscellaneous,	[illegible] 17 1	
		[illegible] 13 4
Treasurer, overdrawn, as per Bank Pass Book,	[illegible] 13 11	
Cheques No. [illegible] not yet presented to Bank,	76 4 7	
		[illegible]
		[illegible]

Expenditure.

Nature of Expenditure.	£ s. d.	Amount. £ s. d.
Balance due to Treasurer, 1st January, 1875,		[illegible]
General Purposes Rate refunded,		[illegible]
Commission to Collectors on General Purposes Rate,		[illegible]
Ditto ditto Special Rate,		[illegible]
Special Rate refunded,		[illegible]
Malicious Injuries,		[illegible]
Interest,		[illegible]
Law costs,		[illegible]
County Antrim General Purposes Account,		[illegible]
County Down General Purposes Account,		[illegible]
Constabulary,		[illegible]
Salaries,		[illegible]
Advertising, Printing, and Stationery,		[illegible]
Renewal of Mortgages,		[illegible]
Mortgage Accounts paid off,		[illegible]
Commissioners of Public Works,		[illegible]
Income Tax,		[illegible]
[illegible] refunded,		[illegible]
[illegible]		[illegible]
Stores and Accounts—Materials purchased,	[illegible] 6 5	
[illegible] Account,		[illegible]
Scavenging,		[illegible]
Repairs of Streets,		[illegible]
Special Works,		[illegible]
Extended Works,		[illegible]
Permanent Paving,		[illegible]
[illegible] Works—Expended on Works,		[illegible]
[illegible] and Old Park Roads District Drainage:		
Commission to Collector of Rate,	[illegible]	
Interest on Mortgages,	[illegible]	
Mortgage paid off,	[illegible] 0 0	
		[illegible] 14 4
[illegible] Road District Drainage:		
Commission to Collector of Rate,	[illegible] 1 0	
Interest on Mortgages,	[illegible]	
Loans paid off,	[illegible] 0 0	
[illegible]—Balance of his Contract,	[illegible] 0 0	
		[illegible] 0 0
[illegible] Road District Drainage:		
[illegible] on Sewers,	[illegible] 10 1	
[illegible] on Account,	[illegible] 1 10	
[illegible] supplied to Contractor,	[illegible]	
Commissioners of Public Works,	[illegible]	
[illegible], on, preliminary Mortgages,	[illegible]	
Commission to Collector of Rate,	[illegible] 7 4	
		[illegible] 17 7
Treasurer—Malicious Injuries Account,		[illegible] 7 11
Cash in hands of Cashier,		[illegible] 0 0
		[illegible]

Signed only for Balance due to the Belfast Banking Company, on General Purposes Fund Account, say £4,[illegible] 19s. 11d.; and for Balance due by the Belfast Banking Company on Malicious Injuries Account, say £[illegible] 7s. 11d. sterling.

(Signed), A. Jones, Treasurer.
R. [illegible], Auditor.

Burial Fund.

Receipts.

	£ s. d.	£ s. d.	£ s. d.
Balance in hands of Treasurer, 31st August, 1874,	[illegible] 1		
Cash,	[illegible] 15 0		
			1,[illegible] 1 1
Burial Fees—			
Amount of Rate outstanding 31st August, 1874,	[illegible] 0 10		
Amount of Rate struck 1st January, 1875,	[illegible] 13 [illegible]		
	[illegible] 13 0		
Amount [illegible] collected within the period of this Account,	2,[illegible] 11 5		2,271 11 5
Irrecoverable Rate struck off,	74 13 7		
		[illegible] 0	
Amount uncollected 31st August, 1875,	[illegible] 0 0		
Rent Account—			
From [illegible], half year's Rent of [illegible] to 1st January, 1875,			[illegible] 0 0
[illegible] of Vaults,			[illegible] 0 0
From Treasurer—Interest on Bank Account,			11 14 0
,, Sundry persons—[illegible] of [illegible] Ground,			1,107 [illegible]
Fees for opening of Graves, &c.,			[illegible] 0 0
[illegible] Ground, [illegible] Receipts, Sale of Hay, Grass, and Flowering of Graves, [illegible] of Parish Ground,			[illegible] 0 10
Commissioners of [illegible] from Sundry persons on balance paid,			4 6 7
			[illegible]

Expenditure.

	£ s. d.	£ s. d.
Commission to collectors,		[illegible] 1 10
[illegible] Account and [illegible]		[illegible]
Interest on Mortgages, due 5th October, 1874,	[illegible] 0 0	
Interest on Mortgages, due 5th April, 1875,	[illegible] 4 7	
		[illegible]
Advertising, Printing, and Stationery,		[illegible]
[illegible] of Vaults, Stock, Wages, &c.,		[illegible]
[illegible] and Roads,		[illegible]
[illegible], Tiles, and Wages,		[illegible]
[illegible] Wages,		[illegible]
Salaries,		[illegible]
Miscellaneous, Water Piping, Plumbers' Work, Auditing of Burial Fund Accounts for 1874, Postage, Receipts, &c.,		[illegible] 15 4
Taxes—Half year's County Cess on Burying Ground, Poor-rate,		15 17 6
Building for the temporary reception of the Dead, on account of Contract,		[illegible] 0 0
Amount transferred for Payment of Loans,		2,[illegible]
Paid Commissioners of Income Tax,		[illegible] 10
Balance due by Treasurer, as per Bank Pass Book,		1,211 19 9
		[illegible]

Signed only for Balance due by the Belfast Banking Company, say £1,211 19s. 9d. sterling.

A. Jones, Treasurer.
R. [illegible], Auditor.

8th November, 1875.

APPENDIX No. 6.

App. No. 6.

Contributions to County Antrim Grand Jury from 1865 to 1875, inclusive.

Contributions to County Antrim Grand Jury.

	£	s.	d.		£	s.	d.		£	s.	d.
The Year 1866,	[illegible]	[illegible]	[illegible]	The Year 1870,	[illegible]	[illegible]	[illegible]	The Year 1873,	[illegible]	0	[illegible]
" 1867,	[illegible]	[illegible]	[illegible]	" 1871,	[illegible]	[illegible]	[illegible]	" 1874,	[illegible]	0	[illegible]
" 1868,	[illegible]	[illegible]	[illegible]	" 1872,	[illegible]	[illegible]	[illegible]	" 1875,	[illegible]	[illegible]	[illegible]
" 1869,	[illegible]	[illegible]	[illegible]								

APPENDIX No. 7.

App. No. 7.

Statement of Dr. Samuel Browne, Consulting Sanitary Officer, Belfast.

Statement of Dr. Browne, Consulting Sanitary Officer, Belfast.

I am intimately acquainted with the sanitary condition of Belfast. I commenced the practice of my profession here in 1842. In 1848, along with the late Dr. Malcolm, I instituted an inquiry into the sanitary state of the town, and in union with a number of other gentlemen, formed a sanitary committee to watch over the health of the inhabitants.

The Town Council took the matter up, and, through its police committee, carried out the various important suggestions that were made to them in 1848 and 1850; and again in 1853–54 I was appointed medical officer of health, under the Council. In 1854, when the suit in Chancery was instituted against the Corporation, I resigned my office, and in doing so strongly recommended the Town Council to carry out the operations of the several Acts then in existence for promoting the public health. These recommendations the Corporation partially observed by having some sanitary inspectors employed in inspecting and removing nuisances. In 1845 I became a member of the Corporation, and in 1861, on my motion, a sanitary committee of the Council was appointed to superintend and regulate all sanitary operations. Of that committee I was a member and the present mayor was chairman. We had an inspector and five sub-inspectors of nuisances, being one for each ward of the borough, and there cannot be any question that the committee and their officers did a large amount of work and effected a considerable amount of good.

In December, 1874, the Public Health Act of that year was put in operation in this borough, and the staff of officers was remodelled under the sanction of the Local Government Board.

A consulting sanitary officer, an executive sanitary officer, and nine sanitary officers and six sub-sanitary officers were duly appointed.

As consulting sanitary officer I attend my office at the Town Hall every day to advise and co-operate with the executive and sub-sanitary officers. I also attend all meetings of the sanitary committee, and every week make a report on the public health. I also attend the meetings of the Town Council when required. I draw up monthly the portion of the sanitary report which relates to the amount of zymotic diseases and the mortality from these complaints; and at the end of every quarter I give a report on the health of the town.

As consulting sanitary officer I have charge also of carrying out the Adulteration of Food and Drugs Act, and have for the present the services of the market inspector, who gives a portion of his time to obtaining samples of food and drugs for analysis. I have suggested a better arrangement for the services of such an officer, and I hope soon to have the work more efficiently performed as the committee have the matter under consideration.

The Artizans' and Labourers' Dwellings Act has recently been put in action here, and a scheme, on my representation, has been prepared affecting one of the worst localities in the borough. When it is seen how this scheme will work, other unhealthy localities will be reported on; and then, in a short time, it is hoped that great improvements will be effected.

The Act for the regulation and inspection of bakehouses is carefully observed, and the inspection of graveyards, school-houses, and slaughter-houses, is regularly carried out, with a close and prompt attention to the abatement of every nuisance reported on by our several sanitary officers or by any ratepayer.

The executive sanitary officer has drawn up a statement of his duties and work, and also of the sub-sanitary officers, which is handed in. The sanitary officers report on any nuisances they may observe, and daily make a return to the consulting sanitary officer of any infectious diseases newly entered on their books.

Having thus far defined my duties, I may be permitted to say that the sanitary committee and Town Council are ever desirous of carrying my views and attending to my suggestions. In my department everything works harmoniously and pretty satisfactorily.

In any future legislature, I would respectfully suggest a change in the names designating the several officials in towns, viz.:—

Consulting Sanitary Officer, either "The Medical Officer of Health," or "Superintendent Medical Officer of Health."

Executive Sanitary Officer, "Head Sanitary Inspector."

Sanitary Officer, "District Medical Officer of Health."

Sub-sanitary Officers, "Inspectors of Nuisances."

I think this would be more in accordance with the duties these officers perform, and would be better understood by the public.

Samuel Browne,
Consulting Sanitary Officer.

The sanitary staff have had the following works executed by the owners of property from 1st January, 1876, till 1st December, 1876:—

- 4716 Houses and [illegible] were inspected for sanitary regulations.
- [illegible] Houses provided with backyards and necessary accommodation.
- [illegible] Feet of pipe drain laid connecting house drains with sewers.
- [illegible] House drains improved.
- [illegible] Privies and ashpits opened, and [illegible] private.
- [illegible] Water-closets erected, and [illegible] repaired.
- [illegible] House drains cleansed.
- [illegible] [illegible] put in house drains.
- [illegible] Yards [illegible], and [illegible] repaired.
- [illegible] Walls [illegible] to prevent [illegible] from adjoining premises.
- [illegible] [illegible] cleansed.
- [illegible] Houses provided with water-spouts.
- [illegible] [illegible] and [illegible] of [illegible] removed.
- [illegible] Roofs repaired.
- [illegible] Houses closed up which were unfit for habitation.
- [illegible] Chimneys [illegible].
- [illegible] Cesspools cleansed.
- [illegible] Open and offensive drains cleansed.
- [illegible] Houses whitewashed.
- [illegible] Open [illegible] closed up.
- [illegible] Privies and ashpits [illegible].
- [illegible] [illegible] fumigated and whitewashed where contagious disease occurred.

APPENDIX No. 8.

JOINT REPORT of the SANITARY and TOWN IMPROVEMENT COMMITTEES to be presented to the COUNCIL.

Your committees have conferred with the consulting sanitary officer as to the desirability of putting the Artisans' Dwellings Act into force in the district between Hercules-street and Smithfield, referred to them by resolution of the Council.

Annexed to this report is copy of one from the consulting sanitary officer on the subject, which is based upon a division of the district into three portions, in which the Act might with advantage be applied.

An official representation has also been made by him, under the provisions of the Act, as to the houses in district No. 1, as shown on the map.

Your committees have reason to believe that an improvement scheme for same can be carried out at a comparatively moderate cost, viz., under £10,000. And they recommend the Council to declare the district referred to an unhealthy area, and to authorise your committees to have a scheme for its improvement prepared and to be submitted to the Council for confirmation.

Such scheme will effect a great improvement in a populous district of the town, and enable the Council to try the working of the Act on a comparatively small scale, before entering upon more extensive changes.

JOHN BROWNE, Chairman.

Dated 20th September, 1878.

APPENDIX to the foregoing REPORT.

To the SANITARY and IMPROVEMENT COMMITTEES.

Town Hall, Belfast,
19th September, 1878.

GENTLEMEN,—I herewith beg to submit a copy of the representation I am about to make through you to the Town Council, and which refers to the unhealthy area which comprises Smithfield-court, Smithfield-place, Ritchie's-place, Hudson's-court and entry.

I am also prepared to make a representation to the Town Council of the areas bounded by the rear of Hercules-street, West side, rear of Berry-street, Smithfield, East side, and Torrens'-row, within which areas there are several streets in a bad sanitary condition from narrowness, want of light, and ventilation, and many houses unfit for human habitation from their sanitary defects, and which come within the provisions of the "Artisans' and Labourers' Dwellings Improvement Act," while there may be several dwellings interspersed among them which are in a better state; hence there will be greater difficulty and expense in the reconstruction and rearrangement of these areas than of that on which I have prepared my representation to the Town Council.

I have the honour to be, Gentlemen,

Your obedient Servant,

SAM. BROWNE, L.R.Q.C.P.I., &c.,
Consulting Sanitary Officer.

Sanitary Department, Town Hall,
19th September, 1878.

To the TOWN COUNCIL of the Borough of Belfast.

GENTLEMEN,—Having carefully examined the houses in Smithfield-court, Smithfield-place, Ritchie's-place, Hudson's-court and Hudson's-entry, I beg to report that they are unfit for human habitation, and that diseases indicating a generally low condition of health have from time to time been prevalent in the area comprising these courts, entries, and streets, and that such prevalence may reasonably be attributed to the closeness, narrowness, and bad arrangement of the streets, and to the want of air, light, and ventilation, or proper conveniences for the houses within said area.

And I further represent that the evils connected with the houses, courts, entries, and streets, and the sanitary defects of said area cannot be effectually remedied otherwise than by an improvement scheme for the rearrangement and reconstruction of the streets and houses contained therein.

I have the honour to be, Gentlemen,

Your obedient Servant,

SAM. BROWNE, L.R.Q.C.P.I., &c.,
Consulting Sanitary Officer.

APPENDIX to REPRESENTATION to be submitted to the TOWN COUNCIL on the unhealthy area comprising Smithfield-court, Smithfield-place, Ritchie's-place, Hudson's-court and entry.

This area has 86 houses, inhabited by the labouring class, and has a population of 378 individuals, among whom there have occurred in the five years ending December, 1878, 230 cases of sickness and 46 registered deaths. These figures show a ratio of sickness of 19 per cent per annum and a death-rate of 34 per thousand, while the average death-rate of the entire borough for the same period was 27·27.

APPENDIX No. 9.

REPORT by Mr. MONTGOMERY, BOROUGH SURVEYOR, on 13th February, 1878, embracing a summary of his Original Report in 1846, upon the Drainage of Belfast.

I have carefully reconsidered the whole question of the Drainage of Belfast, and I am not able to suggest any material improvement in the scheme which I designed in the year 1846, and which is clearly described in the accompanying report and plan published in that year.

This scheme was afterwards referred to an engineer of the highest authority in matters of this kind, Sir J. W. Bazalgette, C.B., who reported his general approval of it, and I advise that his services be still retained in conjunction with mine.

That project embraced three great objects, viz.:—

I. The removal of all sewage and other impurities from the River Lagan and the other streams which flow through the town, by means of intercepting sewers discharging below the Twin Islands.

II. The utilization of the collected sewage by irrigation, or such other means as might ultimately be proved to be successful; thus preventing the pollution of the shores of the Lough, and injury to the Harbour and Docks.

App. No. 9. — Report by Mr. Montgomery.

III. The impounding of the storm waters of the Forth[illegible] Burn and Blackstaff, in regulating reservoirs constructed in the higher portions of their courses—e.g., in the Forth River Valley—so as to abate the occasional flooding of certain streets, and to economise the water for the millowners and the public.

Division No. I.—The first object was to be attained by forming three great intercepting sewers—two on the County Antrim side of the Borough, and one on the County Down side.

The greater portion of the Borough, on the Antrim side, lies sufficiently high to be drained by gravitation, and to effect this a *High Level Sewer* was to be constructed through the Plains, by Lower Crescent, the Workhouse, Clifton[illegible]-road, Millfield, North Queen-street, or York-street, to the North end of Twin Island West, discharging, for the time, into the deep water and strong current there.

The other portion of the Antrim side of the Borough, not being drainable by gravitation, was to be drained by a *Low Level Sewer*, from Lisburn[illegible]-road, by Basin-lane, Cromac-street, Corporation-street, to the Pumping Station near the New Docks, where the sewage would be raised by steam pumps into the High Level Sewer.

The Down side would be drained by an Intercepting Sewer commencing ultimately near Rosetta, and continued by Ormeau-road, Lagan Village, Short Strand, through the Harbour Commissioners' lands, to the deep water of the Old Channel, at Twin Island East.

The cost of these three sewers, and the works in connection with them, would amount now to £200,000.

Division No. II.—The cost of utilizing the sewage cannot be estimated until some decision be arrived at as regards its disposal.

Division No. III.—The cost of the regulating reservoirs may be taken at £100,000.

I do not think that the carrying out of any one or two of the three great divisions, viz.:—the Intercepting Sewers, the Utilization, and the Regulating Reservoirs—would give entire satisfaction; and I must say here—that, in my judgment, the disposal of the sewage is the first thing to be considered. Suppose all these sewers were in operation, and all the sewage of Belfast were discharged at the entrance of the New Channel, it might be found anything but satisfactory. The alternative of conveying the sewage for miles down the Lough—as was once suggested—is hardly a question for the present time. Recent attempts at utilizing the sewage of large towns have been somewhat disappointing. Glasgow is now making another effort to find out what can be done.

The flooding of certain parts of Belfast arises from several causes—e.g., in some streets, from the great flow of sewage during excessive rain-fall, in sewers which happen to be then closed by the pressure of the tide against the valves of the sewers.

In other streets, extraordinary tides rise through the sewers which have no valves, and which cannot have valves, owing to the sewers being the outlets of streams.

Again, some streets drain directly into the Blackstaff and Forth[illegible] rivers, and during great floods the river water forces its way through their sewers, on to the low streets adjacent.

There is no doubt that if the beds of these streams were lowered, and the submerged weirs and obstructions, erected by millowners and others, were removed, the flooding could be greatly diminished. Of late years the flooding has been much abated by lowering the bed, where allowed by the mill-owners, and by constructing four overflow culverts where sanctioned by them.

The streams will never be in a satisfactory state, so long as they contain weirs, and that manufacturers foul them with refuse or warm and impure water.

It must be borne in mind that all these questions are exercising the powers of the ablest thinkers of the day. Nearly every great town has its drainage difficulty; and no town situated like Belfast has yet made an approximation to the solution of the problem. Legislation has long been promised in aid of local efforts, but if something must be done in anticipation, let it be something least likely to be affected by future enactments and further experience.

The High Level Sewer would be the work of most general use, as an instalment, and the least costly, if the co-operation of the Harbour Board could be secured. It would materially assist in keeping down the flooding in the lower parts of the town—as at Corporation-street, Dock-street, &c. It would also tend in some way about the vicinity of North-street, Smithfield, &c., which was frequently flooded until of late years, and where there has been great difficulty in keeping the flooding down. It is quite true that, in consequence of the various sewers, overflows, and other works, executed by the Town Council, the flooding is very much less than it was years ago, but still, the town grows so fast, that all such contrivances may not be able to cope with the ever-increasing volume of sewage. This High Level Sewer would cost about £80,000, and a rate of 2d. in the pound would fully defray this expense.

J. J. Montgomery.

13th *February*, 1875.

APPENDIX No. 10.

App. No. 10. — Report of the Improvement Committee.

Appendix to the Report of the Improvement Committee, December 29th, 1875.

Review of the Principal Work of the Borough Surveyor's Department during the year 1875.

The most important work executed during the year was the drainage of the chief part of the county Down side of the borough. The cost of the system of drainage just completed there was about £23,000, and the length about 19,524 feet. This makes the third drainage district recently completed, and the whole cost expended on the three districts was about £40,000.

The permanent paving of Corporation-street, Garmoyle-street, part of Victoria-street, and Townhall-street, has been completed, at a cost of nearly £13,600.

The macadam roads have been maintained in fair condition at a cost less than usual, in consequence of the permanent paving recently executed. Next year the saving will be more apparent. The paved highways have also been regularly repaired.

The total length of streets and roads maintained and repaired by surveyor's department is ninety-one miles, of which forty-three miles are macadam.

A weighbridge has been erected at Rosetta school-house, which has reduced the cost of material.

A large number of men have been employed in preventing flooding from the Blackstaff and other streams, by keeping the courses clear. This work, together with the four large overflow sewers, has proved most successful in preventing the streams flooding the town recently, when so many other towns were inundated.

The public sewers have been properly maintained and cleansed, and several have been reconstructed.

A large number of new doorways, channels, &c., have been formed and flagged in the principal roads and streets, e.g.:—Donegall[illegible]-street, Clifton-street, Cliftonville-road, Donegall-street, Donegall-quay, Lombard-street, Townhall-street, Wilson's-court, North-street, Great Victoria-street, New Lodge-road, Crumlin-road, Ormeau-road, Antrim-road, Lisburn[illegible]-street, Grosvenor-road, Whitla-street, Cromac-street, Great

App. No. 10.

Report of the Improvement Committee.

Patrick-street, Bedford-street, Donegall-square, south, Adelaide-street, Clifford-street, North Queen-street, Albert-bridge-road, Logan Village-road, Short-strand, Church-lane, Dublin-road, Little May-street, Donegall Pass, Friar's-bush road, Shankill-road, and Logan Bank-road.

Crossings have been formed on Lisburn-road, Crumlin-road, Durham-street, Logan Village-road, Whitla-street, and Newtownards-road.

Several new cartdrafts have been, and are being, formed.

The bridges in Great Victoria-street and North Howard-street have been considerably improved and widened.

Number of streets sewered and paved at cost of owners under the direction of the borough surveyor,	70
Number of houses and buildings of which plans were approved,	1,269

STREET IMPROVEMENTS.

Considerable portions of ground having been obtained for widening the following streets, the works have been carried out, viz.:—

Old Lodge-road and Peter's-hill—a very important improvement is nearly completed here, the old buildings being removed and the avenue very much widened, under the Provisional Order recently obtained; the outlay on this work will be about £8,000, a considerable portion of which will be repayable. Great Victoria-street, at and near the bridge; New Lodge-road, Grosvenor-road, Ormeau-road, North-street, Antrim-road, Donegall-street, Logan Village-road, Short-strand, Church-lane, Dublin-road, North Queen-street, Little May-street, Donegall-quay, and Bedford-street.

The following works have been completed, or are in progress on the Corporate property, viz.:—

Grain market, new buildings and paving, at a cost of £1,000. New slaughter-house for sheep. Quay improvements. Flax and pork markets, new buildings. Gasworks, new quay and gasholder manager's house. Mortuary chapel in borough cemetery. New yard and buildings for scavenging department. Heating and ventilating borough courts, cells, &c., and sundry improvements at municipal buildings. Ormeau Park skating pond. Falls Park, removal and alteration of buildings and other works.

The markets and corporate property have been kept in repair.

Seats have been erected along the chief suburban roads.

Plans have been prepared for improving the lighting of the principal thoroughfares, and the work is proceeding.

There are also a great many works and duties of a miscellaneous character, which it is not necessary to refer to.

J. J. Montgomery.

29th December, 1875.

App. No. 11.

Correspondence between Dr. Dorrian, Roman Catholic Bishop of Belfast, and the Town Clerk.

APPENDIX No. 11.

Copy of Correspondence between Dr. Dorrian, Roman Catholic Bishop of Belfast, and the Town Clerk, and material portions of the Resolutions of the Cemetery Committee thereon, extracted from the Report of the said Committee to the Town Council, dated 1st April, 1869.

Belfast, January 20, 1869.

Dear Sir,—You may recollect that I applied to you some time ago for information as to the power which the Roman Catholic bishop will have over the ground in the new cemetery intended for the burial of members of his flock.

A bishop is not at liberty by the rules of his church to consecrate any such ground unless the right to protect it from desecration is secured to him.

As this matter deeply affects the interests of my people, I write again to respectfully solicit some information as to your earliest convenience, and I beg to remain,

Dear sir, very truly yours,

✠ P. Dorrian.

James Guthrie, esq.

Resolved—That the printed rules as approved by the council, be forwarded to the Rev. Dr. Dorrian, and that his attention be called to the 20th section of the Act 19 & 20 Vic., chap. 98, and that he be requested to furnish to this committee what addition he proposes to have made to these rules, so as to give the right to prevent the desecration which he appears to apprehend.

Brooklyn House, Hollywood,
February 16, 1869.

My Dear Sir,—On receipt of your letter of 2nd inst., enclosing a copy of the Rules for the Regulation of the Cemetery, and also a resolution of the Cemetery Committee, I have set about making inquiries to enable me to supply the information your committee have asked of me in that communication.

In reference to the Act of Parliament to which my attention was called (20th sec. of 19 & 20 Vic., cap. 98), I beg to say that I was aware that this section, with some other things embodied in it, gives to the bishop the right to consecrate certain ground for the interment of certain persons. But I drew the attention of the committee to the fact that a bishop cannot consecrate such ground unless he shall be also able legally to forbid its being used for the interment of those to whom the Church refuses Christian burial, and other things of a like nature.

This is not a question of controversy or of personal opinion, but of the liberty to be interpreted as conferred by the Act on every religious denomination, and I am anxious to come to an understanding with your committee, so that no doubt may be hereafter raised when, perhaps, it might be too late for both your committee and for the Catholics concerned.

Then, in reference to the addition—that is the right I seek to protect the ground from desecration if it shall be consecrated—I only seek such arrangement as has been made elsewhere under similar circumstances in England and Ireland.

I shall give but two examples. In Liverpool the portion of the cemetery set apart for Catholics has been consecrated by the bishop, he having first received the security to which I refer under the sign and seal of the Home Secretary, with payment also of a small fee to the clergyman for each service. In Limerick, in Ireland, the Corporation have leased to the parish priests of the city the burying ground, at a rent of £20 per year, and the Corporation pay £30 a year to the clergymen who perform the service at the funerals of the poor.

The Corporation have also made known their perfect willingness to do the same to the Protestant or any other religious denomination, should ground be required by them.

Now either of the above arrangements affords the security which I am bound by the rules of our Church to have in regard to any ground I should at any time consecrate for the above purpose, and I hope that your committee will make some such reasonable arrangement about the Belfast Cemetery.

There are some other points, but they are of minor importance, and can be easily postponed.

I have the honour to remain, my dear sir,

Your faithful servant,

✠ P. Dorrian.

James Guthrie, esq., Town Clerk.

Resolved.—That in reply to the letter of Dr. Dorrian, the Town Clerk be instructed to write that the rules for the regulation of the cemetery have already been approved of by the council, and that the committee, having considered his suggestions, regret they cannot comply with same.

Your committee ask for authority to employ counsel to represent them before the Privy Council on the hearing of the above memorial, and that the Mayor and a deputation from this committee should also attend.

Report of the Cemetery Committee presented to the Council on the 19th day of July, 1869.

A deputation from your committee, acting under the instructions given by the council, attended by counsel before the Privy Council on 23rd June, at the hearing of the memorial presented to the Lord Lieutenant, praying that an order might be made that the public portions of the Shankill and Friars' Bush burying grounds should be absolutely closed against future interments. It was further sought to have future interments in the proprietary portions of those grounds, and also in the Old Poor House burial ground regulated by the Orders of the Privy Council made in the year 1866.

The council are aware that in the year 1867, when Dr. Keen held a preliminary inquiry into the condition of the existing burial grounds and the proposed allocation of the new cemetery, much discussion took place as to the portion to be allotted for the use of the Roman Catholics. It was hoped that the concessions then made, and the construction of the walk from separating the Catholic and Protestant portions of the ground at an expense of £480, would have removed all grounds of complaint on the part of Bishop Dorrian, and that there would be no further controversy on the subject. But at the beginning of the present year a correspondence took place with the bishop, which has been duly reported to the council, in which he claimed as a condition precedent to the consecration of the Roman Catholic ground, that he should be invested with the right to inhibit the interment there of any person who, in his judgment, was not entitled to be interred in consecrated grounds. Your committee were of opinion that they had no right to invest Bishop Dorrian with any such authority, and the council confirmed their decision.

At the hearing before the Privy Council the Corporation were represented by Mr. Macdonogh, Mr. May, and Mr. Andrews; Mr. Butt and Mr. Harvey appeared for Bishop Dorrian.

Mr. Macdonogh stated to the Privy Council the ground upon which the Corporation asked to have an order made pursuant to the prayer of the memorial. Mr. Butt, on the part of Bishop Dorrian, objected to the closing of Friar's Bush until arrangements were made to give the bishop such control over the Roman Catholic portion of the new cemetery as would induce him to consecrate it according to the usages of the Roman Catholic Church, or, in case no such agreement could be come to, until time had been given to enable the Catholics to provide a cemetery of their own. Counsel for the Corporation submitted that by the plan which had been sanctioned by the Lord Lieutenant a fair proportion of the ground had been allotted for the use of the Roman Catholics, and that as the governing body having the control and the responsibility of the management of the cemetery the Corporation could not legally confer any such power or authority upon the bishop of any church. Although the members of the Privy Council who were present appeared to acquiesce in this view, and to be quite satisfied as to the propriety of closing the present public grounds, they granted an adjournment to give the parties an opportunity of coming to an agreement.

App. No. 11

Correspondence between Dr. Dorrian, Roman Catholic Bishop of Belfast, and the Town Clerk.

On the 28th of June the following rules were submitted to your committee as carrying out Bishop Dorrian's views:—

Rules proposed to the Town Council as conditions to be annexed to the allotment of a portion of the Burial-ground as a place of Roman Catholic Interment, and to be at all times hereafter observed in relation to same:—

I.—The portion of ground allotted shall at all times hereafter be and continue to be dedicated as a Roman Catholic burying-ground, and no part of it shall be ever applied to, or used for any purpose inconsistent with such dedication.

II.—For the better and more effectually securing of the above, no portion of the ground so allotted shall ever be used for any purpose unless with the consent and approbation of the person for the time being exercising functions of Roman Catholic bishop in the place where such burial-ground is situated, and no interments shall take place within the limits of the ground so allotted except upon a certificate from such bishop, or such person as he may from time to time appoint; and all grants of rights of burial made by the burial board within the grounds so allotted shall be made subject to the above conditions.

III.—There shall be at all times appointed a sufficient number of gravediggers and other necessary attendants for the care of the ground so allotted to Roman Catholics; and no person shall be so appointed except with the approbation of such bishop.

IV.—Out of the funds received by the burial board for interments on this portion of the burial-ground shall be allotted the remuneration of a Roman Catholic clergyman attending the burials therein; and the burial board shall also provide a suitable and sufficient chapel within the limits of such allotted ground for the celebration of the rights of burial according to the rules and usage of the Roman Catholic Church.

V.—That no soil shall be carted off or removed outside the consecrated portion of said grounds without the consent in writing of said bishop for the time being.

Accompanying these rules a copy was sent of an opinion given by Mr. Butt to the effect that the Court of Queen's Bench would grant a writ of mandamus to compel the Corporation to "make all such arrangements as according to the rules of the Church are conditions precedent to consecration;" and that the rules which he had settled carried out the conditions which the bishop regarded as essential rules and principles of his Church.

Your committee felt bound to decline voluntarily to adopt these rules, and upon consultation with counsel they were advised that they had acted rightly in doing so. Upon the further hearing before the Privy Council Mr. Butt submitted that time ought to be allowed before the order for closing Friar's Bush takes effect, to enable Bishop Dorrian either to memorial the Lord Lieutenant, or to apply to the Court of Queen's Bench for a mandamus. After some discussion the Privy Council fixed the 30th of November next as the date from which their order is to take effect with respect to the public portion of Friar's Bush; and the 1st of August with respect to the other grounds, including the proprietary portion of Friar's Bush.

[Here follows a copy of the order in the matter of the closing of the Belfast burial-grounds.]

Your committee did not wish to enter into any controversy with Bishop Dorrian as to the propriety of the claim so put forward on his behalf; they endea-

App. No. 11.

Correspondence between the Rev. Roman Catholic Bishop of Belfast, and the Town Clerk.

vanned to be guided throughout by the plain meaning of the Act of Parliament as interpreted by their legal advisers. The Corporation as the burial board are bound to retain, and are responsible for the management, direction, and control of the cemetery, and are to make rules and regulations for that purpose. It is obvious that unless expressly authorized to do so the burial board cannot divest themselves of this authority, or delegate to the Roman Catholic bishop the power which he seeks for; and further, that to apply any portion of the fees reserved for investment in the public cemetery in payment of a Roman Catholic priest for performing service would be a clear misapplication of the fund.

App. No. 12.

The Belfast Banking Company to the Corporation of Belfast.

APPENDIX No. 12.

The Belfast Banking Company to the Corporation of Belfast.—Conveyance.

This Indenture, made the 16th day of November, 1875, between the Belfast Banking Company (hereinafter called the Company) of the one part, and the Mayor, Aldermen, and Burgesses of the borough of Belfast (hereinafter called the Corporation) of the other part. Whereas, by the 30th section of the Belfast Borough Act, 1865, the Corporation were empowered, with the consent, in writing, of the owners and lessees of the lands adjoining to a certain foot passage running at the rear of the Belfast Bank, between Donegall-street and North-street, in the said borough of Belfast, to close and stop up such passage, and to convey the same in exchange for another passage or for other land of equal value, to be used either for enabling the Corporation to widen the adjoining street or for the formation of another public passage in lieu of the one so closed; and whereas, by an agreement bearing date the 31st day of March, 1875, and made between the Corporation of the one part and the Company of the other part, it was agreed, amongst other things, that the Corporation would, for the consideration therein mentioned, forthwith pass a resolution to close and stop up the said passage, and would, when required, convey to the Company the ground or soil of such passage. And that in consideration of the closing and stoppage of the said passage and of the agreement for the conveyance to them of the ground thereof, the Company would convey, by way of exchange to the Corporation, for the use of the public, and to widen a portion of North-street aforesaid a strip of ground eight feet six inches in width, being the front portion of the Company's premises in North-street aforesaid, then or lately in the occupation of Greenhill Brothers, and would also procure Patrick M'Guinness to convey to the Corporation the strip of ground fronting the building erected by him in North-street aforesaid and coloured yellow on the plan endorsed on said agreement in order that the same might be dedicated to the public use as part of the said street. And whereas the Corporation, with the consent of the Company, who then were, and still are, the owners and lessees of the lands adjoining said foot passage on the 1st day of April, 1875, duly passed a resolution to close and stop up the said passage; and whereas, by indenture bearing equal date herewith and made between the said Patrick M'Guinness of the first part, the Company of the second part, and the Corporation of the third part, the said Patrick M'Guinness, at the request and by direction of the Company, and in consideration of £300 paid to him by them, did grant unto the Corporation and their successors the said strip of ground situate on the east side of North-street, in the town of Belfast aforesaid fronting the building lately erected by him. To hold unto the Corporation and their successors for ever as part of the street called North-street; and whereas, the Corporation are satisfied that the said two strips of ground respectively conveyed to the Corporation by the said hereinbefore recited indenture of equal date herewith, and by these presents are of equal or superior value to the said foot passage; and whereas, the Corporation have required the Company, pursuant to the said hereinbefore recited agreement to convey to the Corporation said strip of ground in front of the premises of the Company in North-street aforesaid. Now, this Indenture witnesseth that for further effectuating the said agreement of the 31st day of March, 1875, on the part of the Company and in consideration of the premises, they, the Company, do, by these presents, grant unto the Corporation and their successors all that the said strip of ground, eight feet six inches in width, being the front portion of the Company's premises in North-street aforesaid, lately in the possession of Messrs. Greenhill Brothers, and coloured pink upon the map or plan hereupon endorsed and which said premises are situate in the borough of Belfast, in the barony of Upper Belfast, and county of Antrim. To hold unto the Corporation and their successors, to the use of the Corporation and their successors henceforth for ever as part of the street called North-street; and the Company do hereby for themselves their successors and assigns covenant with the Corporation and their successors that notwithstanding any matter or thing by them done, omitted, or knowingly suffered, they, the Company, now have power to grant the said premises hereinbefore expressed to be hereby granted unto the Corporation and their successors in manner aforesaid free from encumbrances, and that all the said premises shall be quietly entered into, held, and enjoyed by the Corporation and their successors in manner aforesaid without any interruption by the Company or any person claiming through, or in trust, for them, and further, that the Company and every person having or claiming any estate, right, title, or interest in or to the said premises through or in trust for them will at all times hereafter at the cost of the Corporation, their successors, or assigns, execute and do every such assurance and thing for the further or more perfectly assuring all or any of said premises to the use of the Corporation, their successors and assigns as by them shall be reasonably required. In witness whereof, the Company have hereunto affixed their common seal, and the Corporation have hereunto affixed their corporate seal the day and year first herein written.

Present when the common seal of the Belfast Banking Company was hereunto affixed, Hugh [illegible], Belfast Bank, Belfast. Alex. [illegible], Belfast Bank, Belfast.	Directors present when the seal of the Company was affixed, (Seal.) E. H. Clarke. A. Jones.

APPENDIX No. 13.

STATEMENT prepared by MR. BLACK to show particulars of TAXATION, and how applied.

App. No. 13. — Mr Black's Statement of Taxation.

—	[illegible]	[illegible]	[illegible]	[illegible]
				£ s. d.
[illegible]	[illegible]	[illegible]	[illegible]	[illegible]
[illegible]	[illegible]	[illegible]	[illegible]	[illegible]
[illegible]	[illegible]	—	[illegible]	[illegible]
[illegible]	[illegible]	—	[illegible]	[illegible]
[illegible]	[illegible]	[illegible]	[illegible]	[illegible]

—	[illegible]	[illegible]	[illegible]	[illegible]
[illegible]	[illegible]	[illegible]	[illegible]	[illegible]
[illegible]	[illegible]	[illegible]	—	[illegible]
[illegible]	[illegible]	—	—	[illegible]
[illegible]	[illegible]	—	—	[illegible]
[illegible]	[illegible]	—	—	[illegible]

APPENDIX No. 14.

ILLUSTRATIONS of DISCREPANCIES between RATED and LETTING VALUE of HOUSE PROPERTY under Griffith's Valuation of 1860.

App. No. 14. — Discrepancies between the Rated and Letting Value of House Property.

[illegible]	[illegible]	[illegible]	[illegible]	[illegible]	[illegible]	[illegible]	[illegible]
	£ s. d.	£ s. d.			£ s. d.	£ s. d.	
1	[illegible]	[illegible]	Let on Lease.	[illegible]	[illegible]	[illegible]	
[illegible]	[illegible]	[illegible]	Do.	[illegible]	[illegible]	[illegible]	Let on Lease.
[illegible]	[illegible]	[illegible]		[illegible]	[illegible]	[illegible]	
[illegible]	[illegible]	[illegible]		[illegible]	[illegible]	[illegible]	
[illegible]	[illegible]	[illegible]	Do.	[illegible]	[illegible]	[illegible]	
[illegible]	[illegible]	[illegible]		[illegible]	[illegible]	[illegible]	
[illegible]	[illegible]	[illegible]		[illegible]	[illegible]	[illegible]	
[illegible]	[illegible]	[illegible]		[illegible]	[illegible]	[illegible]	
[illegible]	[illegible]	[illegible]	Do.	[illegible]	[illegible]	[illegible]	
[illegible]	[illegible]	[illegible]	Do.	[illegible]	[illegible]	[illegible]	
[illegible]	[illegible]	[illegible]	Do.	[illegible]	[illegible]	[illegible]	
[illegible]	[illegible]	[illegible]	Do. and large fine paid.	[illegible]	[illegible]	[illegible]	
[illegible]	[illegible]	[illegible]		[illegible]	[illegible]	[illegible]	
[illegible]	[illegible]	[illegible]		[illegible]	[illegible]	[illegible]	
14	[illegible]	[illegible]		[illegible]	[illegible]	[illegible]	

APPENDIX No. 15.

EXTRACT from the OPINION of GEORGE A. C. MAY, Esq., Q.C., as to the Blackstaff and Forced Burn.

With respect to the other question of the nuisance occasioned by the pollution of the streams.

Sufficient powers are given by the Act of 1850 (so far as concerns the Forced Burn), and by the Sanitary Acts, but under the circumstances of this case, I do not think these powers would be found available. These streams appear by general consent to have been converted into public sewers. The sewers constructed by the Town Council run into them, and it is stated that in fact no other means exist of discharging the sewage of part of the town. It would be very difficult to treat individuals as guilty of a nuisance, because they use these watercourses as sewers; and with respect to the return of heated water to the streams, probably that of itself would not constitute a nuisance, but the waters being polluted are rendered additionally offensive by being heated. However, if it could be shown that the return of heated water to the river increased the nuisance materially, I think that might constitute a public nuisance, and be capable of being remedied either by indictment or otherwise. But such an act as this does not seem to be a nuisance within the meaning of the Sanitary Acts. Upon the whole, such a case as the present seems to fall within the [illegible] section of the Nuisances Removal Act, 1855. The only effectual remedy would be that suggested in the case, the construction of an intercepting sewer. But this is a means would be attended with very considerable expense.

Upon the whole I fear the Town Council will find it very difficult, if not impossible, by legal proceedings directed against individuals, to enforce any abatement of the existing evils. They are the result of a long continued state of facts connived at by the public, and it would be very difficult to induce a jury to find a verdict against any particular individual.

I fear that the only relief to be hoped for is from particular legislation on the subject.

GEORGE A. C. MAY.

APPENDIX No. 16.

LIST of the MEMBERS of COUNCIL, for the year 1876, and their Professions or Occupations, with Amounts of their Valuations.

Aldermen. Name.	Profession or Business.	Valuation. £	s.
James Combe,	Linen Manufacturer,	*2,884	1[illegible]
Sir John Savage,	Do.	1,149	10
William Ewart(?),	Wholesale Grocer,	438	1[illegible]
Edward Hughes,	Flour Merchant and Baker,	893	0
John Preston,	Flax Merchant,	1,347	0
Henry Whitla,	Apothecary,	250	0
Sir Edward Bing,	Knight,	144	0
Edward F. Cowan,	Wholesale Wine and Spirit Merchant,	192	0
Thomas G. Lindsay,	Warehouseman,	1,440	0
James A. Alexander,	M.D.,	30	0
Councillors.			
Samuel Lowther,	Ship Owner and Merchant,	138	0
William Harvey,	Contractor,	64	0
Robert Kelly,	Solicitor,	89	0
George H. Gow,	Goldsmith,	115	10
R. K. Thompson,	Linen Merchant,	130	0
Daniel Dixon,	Ship Owner and Timber Merchant,	691	0
James Henry,	Builder,	254	0
Robert Thompson,	Linen Merchant,	*2,380	0
John Corath(?),	Flour Merchant,	58	0

Councillors. Name.	Profession or Business.	Valuation. £	s.
John Bowden(?),	Gentleman,	138	0
Robert Stewart,	Linen Merchant,	160	0
James H. Haslett,	Druggist,	130	0
W. Q. Ewart,	Linen Manufacturer and Merchant,	3,807	10
W. H. Brabazon(?),	Commander,	165	0
John Gordon(?),	Flax Merchant,	330	0
James Adams,	Baker,	[illegible]	0
John Greenhill,	Grain Merchant,	143	0
David Carlisle(?),	Wholesale Grocer and Spirit Merchant,	[illegible]	0
John Hamill(?),	Gentleman (since dead),	725	0
James A. Henderson,	Newspaper Proprietor,	143	0
John Rogers,	Wine Merchant,	[illegible]	[illegible]
John Browne,	Timber Merchant,	[illegible]	0
Thomas Coffield(?),	Linen Merchant,	173	0
George C. Hughes(?),	Commission Merchant,	[illegible]	0
James Pinion(?),	Provision Merchant,	[illegible]	10
James Jenkins(?),	Gentleman,	[illegible]	0
R. D. [illegible],	Solicitor,	147	0
William Gregg,	Iron Merchant,	[illegible]	0
James Hart(?),	Textile Manufacturer,	64	0
Thomas H. Browne(?),	Timber Merchant,	[illegible]	0
		£21,[illegible]	15

Every Member gives an average of £[illegible] [illegible]s. [illegible]d. each.

* Limited Liability Company.

APPENDIX No. 17.

NAMES of TOWN COMMISSIONERS for TRIM for the year 1876, with their Qualifications and Occupations.

Name and Occupation	£	s.	d.
John Francis O'Reilly, Chairman, Doctor of Medicine,	[illegible]	0	0
John Bresnan(?), Baker,	15	0	0
James Blake(?), Grazier and Cattle Exporter,	15	0	0
John Gregory, Grocer and Spirit Merchant,	15	0	0
Patrick [illegible], Grocer and Spirit Dealer,	15	0	0

Name and Occupation	£	s.	d.		£	s.	d.
Thomas Kennedy, Miller and Grazier,	50	0	0	and	15	10	0
Hercules L'Estrange(?), Sub-Sheriff and Attorney-at-Law,	50	0	0	"	[illegible]	[illegible]	0
Patrick Nolan(?), Civil Engineer,	50	0	0	"	[illegible]	0	0
James Plunkett, Hardware and Spirit Merchant,	17	0	0	"	[illegible]	0	0

APPENDIX No. 18.

App. No. 18. Accounts of the Town Commissioners, Trim, 1876.

TRIM.

Towns Improvement (Ireland) Act, 1854. Number of Commissioners, 9. Number of Burgesses, 84. Population in 1871, 2,198. Acreage within Municipal Boundary, 184a. 2r. 15p. Rateable value of Buildings and Lands, £3,006 15s. No rates levied.

Abstract of the Accounts of the Town Commissioners of Trim for the Year ended the 30th April, 1876, showing the Receipts and Expenditure under the several heads during that period.

Receipts.	£ s. d.	£ s. d.	Expenditure.	£ s. d.	£ s. d.	£ s. d.
To Rents of property of Town Commissioners,		[illegible]	By Balance due to Treasurer at commencement of the year,			[illegible]
Gas rents collected,	[illegible]		Salary of Town Clerk and Weighmaster,		[illegible]	
Sales of gas works,	[illegible]	[illegible]	Cleansing, including salary of Town Surveyor,		[illegible]	
General tolls,	[illegible]		Clothing for Town Surveyor,		[illegible]	
Market ...	[illegible]		Gas Works—			
...	[illegible]	[illegible]	Meters,	[illegible]		
Fines at Petty Sessions,	[illegible]		Coals,	[illegible]		
... Town Court,	[illegible]	[illegible]	Repairs, ... &c.,	[illegible]		
Dog tax,		[illegible]	Rent,	[illegible]	[illegible]	
Building rents,		[illegible]	Agent's fees for—			
Hire of ...		[illegible]	Rents of property,	[illegible]		
Hire of Assembly Room,		[illegible]	Gas rents,	[illegible]		
Lodgment to credit of ... under Auditor's surcharge,		[illegible]	Building rents,	[illegible]	[illegible]	
Miscellaneous receipts,		[illegible]	Rent and taxes—			
			Rent of Town Hall,	[illegible]		
			Courthouse,	[illegible]		
			... and County Cess,	[illegible]		
			Insurance,	[illegible]	[illegible]	
			General expenses, including printing, stationery, and sundry works,		[illegible]	
			Town clerk,		[illegible]	
			Election expenses,		[illegible]	
			Interest on loan of £3,000, less income tax,		[illegible]	
			Interest on overdrafts,		[illegible]	
			Expenditure for pumps, ... by Auditor,		[illegible]	
			Total expenditure,			[illegible]
						[illegible]
			Balance in hands of Treasurer at close of year,		[illegible]	
			Balance in hands of Town Clerk at close of year,		[illegible]	[illegible]
		[illegible]				[illegible]

I certify the foregoing to be a true abstract of the Receipts and Expenditure of the Town Commissioners of Trim for the year ended the 30th April, 1876.

Thomas Colley, Local Government Auditor.

Dated this 16th day of November, 1876.

APPENDIX No. 19.

TRIM.

List of Lands or Tenements, the Property of the Town Commissioners, of which Leases have fallen in since 1840; Names of Parties to whom re-let; the Rents and Terms for which Leases made, and the Rateable Value on each, by Griffith's Valuation, stating if any of the Parties to whom Leases made were, at the time, or shortly before, or since, Members or Officers of the Municipal Body, or in any instance nearly related to such Member or Officer.

Denomination of Lands and Tenements of which Leases have fallen in since 1840.	Names of Persons to whom re-let on Lease.	Rent, per Annum.	Term of Lease, and whether ... by the ... of the Tenancy.	... Valuation.	Whether ... Members of, or nearly related to Officers of Town Commissioners.	Whether let at public auction or by Town Commissioners, ...
		£ s. d.		£ s. d.		
Buildings at ...	Allen, Richard,	[illegible]	Lives of the Queen (Vic.), Prince Albert, and the Prince of Wales, or ...	[illegible]	None.	Not.
Plot of Ground in High-street.	Allenson, George,	[illegible]	Lives of ...	[illegible]	None.	Not.
... Lands, ...	Allen, Benjamin,	[illegible]	For 31 years from the ...	[illegible]	None.	Not.
... Lands, ... and Corporation Land, North.	Allen, John,	[illegible]	For 31 years from ... Sept., 18..	[illegible]	None.	None.

LIST of LANDS or TENEMENTS, the Property of the Town Commissioners, of which Leases have fallen in since 1840; Names of Parties to whom re-let; the Rents and Terms for which Leases made, and the Rateable Value on each, by Griffith's Valuation, stating if any of the Parties to whom Leases made were, at the time, or shortly before, or since, Members or Officers of the Municipal Body, or in any instance nearly related to such Member or Officer—*continued*.

[illegible]	[illegible]	Rents, per Annum.	[illegible]	[illegible]	[illegible]	[illegible]
		£ s. d.		£ s. d.		
Common Lands, South,	[illegible]	[illegible]	For [illegible] years from [illegible] March, [illegible].	[illegible]	No.	No.
Common Lands, [illegible]	[illegible]	[illegible]	For [illegible] years from [illegible] Sept., [illegible].	[illegible]	Town Commissioner.	[illegible]
Corporation Lands, [illegible]	[illegible]	[illegible]	For [illegible] years from [illegible] Sept., [illegible].	[illegible]	No.	No.
Common Lands, North,	[illegible]	[illegible]	For [illegible] years from [illegible] Sept., [illegible].	[illegible]	No.	No.
Ditto,	[illegible]	[illegible]	For [illegible] years from [illegible] March, [illegible].	[illegible]	No.	No.
Ditto,	[illegible]	[illegible]	For [illegible] years from [illegible] Sept., [illegible].	[illegible]	No.	No.
Ditto,	[illegible]	[illegible]	For [illegible] years from [illegible] Sept., [illegible].	[illegible]	No.	No.
Common Lands, South,	[illegible]	[illegible]	For [illegible] years from [illegible] March, [illegible].	[illegible]	No.	No.
Corporation Lands, [illegible]	[illegible]	[illegible]	For [illegible] years from [illegible] Sept., [illegible].	[illegible]	No.	No.
Common Lands, South,	[illegible]	[illegible]	For [illegible] years from [illegible] March, [illegible].	[illegible]	No.	No.
Commons, [illegible] Division, [illegible]	[illegible]	[illegible]	For [illegible] years from [illegible] Sept., [illegible].	[illegible]	No.	No.
Corporation Land, North, [illegible]	[illegible]	[illegible]	For [illegible] years from [illegible] March, [illegible].	[illegible]	No.	No.
Corporation Land, North, [illegible]	[illegible]	[illegible]	For [illegible] years from [illegible] March, [illegible].	[illegible]	No.	No.
Corporation Land, North,	[illegible]	[illegible]	For [illegible] years from [illegible] March, [illegible].	[illegible]	Town Commissioner.	No.
Ditto,	Ditto,	[illegible]	For [illegible] years from [illegible] Sept., [illegible].	[illegible]	[illegible]	[illegible]
Commons, [illegible] Division,	[illegible]	[illegible]	For [illegible] years from [illegible] Sept., [illegible].	[illegible]	No.	[illegible]
Ditto,	[illegible]	[illegible]	For [illegible] years from [illegible] March, [illegible].	[illegible]	No.	No.
Common Lands, North,	[illegible]	[illegible]	For [illegible] years from [illegible] [illegible].	[illegible]	Town Commissioner.	[illegible]
[illegible]	[illegible]	[illegible]	For [illegible] renewable for ever.	[illegible]	No.	No.
[illegible]	[illegible]	[illegible]	For lives, renewable for ever.	[illegible]	No.	[illegible]
Commons, [illegible] Division,	[illegible]	[illegible]	For [illegible] years from [illegible] Sept., [illegible].	[illegible]	No.	No.
Ditto,	[illegible]	[illegible]	For [illegible] years from [illegible] March, [illegible].	[illegible]	No.	No.
Common Lands, North,	[illegible]	[illegible]	For [illegible] years from [illegible] March, [illegible].	[illegible]	Town Commissioner.	[illegible]
Common Lands, South,	[illegible]	[illegible]	For [illegible] years from [illegible] March, [illegible].	[illegible]	[illegible]	No.
Common Lands, North,	[illegible]	[illegible]	For [illegible] years from [illegible] Sept., [illegible].	[illegible]	No.	[illegible]
Ditto,	[illegible]	[illegible]	For [illegible] years from [illegible] March, [illegible].	[illegible]	No.	[illegible]
Common Lands, South,	[illegible]	[illegible]	For [illegible] years from [illegible] March, [illegible].	[illegible]	No.	No.
Common Lands, North,	[illegible]	[illegible]	For [illegible] years from [illegible] [illegible].	[illegible]	No.	No.
Common Lands, South,	[illegible]	[illegible]	For [illegible] years from [illegible] March, [illegible].	[illegible]	Town Commissioner.	[illegible]
Common Lands, South [illegible]	[illegible]	[illegible]	For [illegible] years from [illegible] March, [illegible].	[illegible]	No.	[illegible]
Common Lands, South,	[illegible]	[illegible]	For [illegible] years from [illegible] March, [illegible].	[illegible]	No.	[illegible]
Ditto,	[illegible]	[illegible]	For [illegible] years from [illegible] Sept., [illegible].	[illegible]	No.	No.
[illegible]	[illegible]	[illegible]	For lives renewable for ever.	[illegible]	No.	No.
[illegible]	[illegible]	[illegible]	For lives renewable for ever.	[illegible]	No.	No.
Common Lands, North,	[illegible]	[illegible]	For [illegible] years from [illegible] March, [illegible].	[illegible]	Town Commissioner.	[illegible]
[illegible]	[illegible]	[illegible]	For lives renewable for ever.	[illegible]	Town Commissioner.	[illegible]
Common Lands, South,	[illegible]	[illegible]	For [illegible] years from [illegible] Sept., [illegible].	[illegible]	No.	[illegible]
Ditto,	[illegible]	[illegible]	For [illegible] years from [illegible] March, [illegible].	[illegible]	No.	No.
Common Lands, North,	[illegible]	[illegible]	For [illegible] years from [illegible] March, [illegible].	[illegible]	No.	No.
Ditto,	[illegible]	[illegible]	For [illegible] years from [illegible] March, [illegible].	[illegible]	No.	No.
Ditto,	[illegible]	[illegible]	For [illegible] years from [illegible] March, [illegible].	[illegible]	Town Commissioner.	No.
Common Lands, South,	[illegible]	[illegible]	For [illegible] years from [illegible] September, [illegible].	[illegible]	No.	No.

List of Lands or Tenements, the Property of the Town Commissioners, of which Leases have fallen in since 1840; Names of Parties to whom re-let; the Rents and Terms for which Leases made, and the Rateable Value on each, by Griffith's Valuation, stating if any of the Parties to whom Leases made were, at the time, or shortly before, or since, Members or Officers of the Municipal Body, or in any instance nearly related to such Member or Officer—*continued*.

[illegible]	[illegible]	Rent, per Annum.	[illegible]	Poor Rate Valuation.	Whether Town Commissioners, or [illegible]	[illegible]
		£ s. d.		£ s. d.		
Common Lands, [illegible]	[illegible], Luke,	17 [illegible] [illegible]	For [illegible] years from [illegible] September, [illegible]	[illegible] [illegible] [illegible]	[illegible]	[illegible]
Common Lands, South,	[illegible]	[illegible]	For [illegible] years from [illegible] September, [illegible]	[illegible]	Town Commissioner.	[illegible]
Common Lands, North,	Ditto,	[illegible]	For [illegible] years from [illegible] March, [illegible]	13 [illegible] [illegible]	Town Commissioner.	[illegible]
Common Lands, [illegible]	National Education Commissioners.	[illegible]	For [illegible] years from [illegible] March, [illegible]	Exempt.	[illegible]	[illegible]
Common Lands, North,	[illegible], Bridget,	[illegible] 17 [illegible]	For [illegible] years from [illegible] September, [illegible]	[illegible]	[illegible]	[illegible]
Common Lands, South,	[illegible]	[illegible]	For [illegible] years from [illegible] September, [illegible]	[illegible]	[illegible]	[illegible]
Ditto,	O'Connell, Rev. John,	17 [illegible] [illegible]	For [illegible] years from [illegible] March, [illegible]	11 [illegible] [illegible]	Town Commissioner.	[illegible]
Common Lands, [illegible]	[illegible], John,	[illegible]	For [illegible] years from [illegible]	[illegible]	[illegible]	[illegible]
Ditto,	[illegible]	[illegible]	For [illegible] years from [illegible] March, [illegible]	[illegible]	Town Commissioner.	[illegible]
Ditto,	Kennedy, [illegible]	[illegible]	For [illegible] years from [illegible] March, [illegible]	[illegible]	Town Commissioner.	[illegible]
Common Lands, [illegible]	Kennedy, Thomas, and [illegible]	[illegible]	For [illegible] years from [illegible] Sept., [illegible]	[illegible]	Town Commissioner [illegible]	[illegible]
Ditto,	King, [illegible]	[illegible]	For [illegible] years from [illegible] March, [illegible]	[illegible]	[illegible] Commissioner [illegible] Kennedy.	
Ditto,	King, John,	[illegible]	For [illegible] years from [illegible] March, [illegible]	[illegible]	[illegible]	[illegible]
Ditto,	[illegible]	[illegible]	For [illegible] years from [illegible] Sept., [illegible]	[illegible]	[illegible]	[illegible]
[illegible]	[illegible]	[illegible]	For [illegible]	[illegible]	[illegible]	[illegible]
Common Lands, North,	[illegible]	[illegible]	For [illegible] years from Sept. [illegible]	7 [illegible] [illegible]	[illegible]	[illegible]
Ditto,	[illegible]	[illegible]	For [illegible] years from [illegible] March, [illegible]	7 [illegible] [illegible]	[illegible]	[illegible]
Ditto,	[illegible]	[illegible]	For [illegible] years from [illegible] Sept., [illegible]	[illegible]	[illegible]	[illegible]
Common Lands, South,	[illegible], Philip,	[illegible] 17 [illegible]	For [illegible] years from [illegible]	17 [illegible] [illegible]	[illegible]	[illegible]
Common Lands, [illegible]	[illegible]	[illegible]	For [illegible] years from [illegible] Sept., [illegible]	[illegible]	[illegible]	[illegible]
Common Lands, South,	Ditto,	7 1 [illegible]	For [illegible] years from [illegible] March, [illegible]	[illegible]	[illegible]	[illegible]
Ditto,	Ditto,	[illegible]	For [illegible] years from [illegible] Sept., [illegible]	[illegible]	[illegible]	[illegible]
Common Lands, North,	[illegible]	[illegible]	For [illegible] years from [illegible] March, [illegible]	[illegible]	[illegible]	[illegible]
Common Lands, South,	[illegible]	[illegible]	For [illegible] years from [illegible] March, [illegible]	[illegible]	[illegible]	[illegible]
Common Lands, North,	[illegible]	[illegible]	For [illegible] years from [illegible]	[illegible]	[illegible]	[illegible]
Ditto,	[illegible]	[illegible]	For [illegible] years from [illegible] March, [illegible]	[illegible]	Town Commissioner.	[illegible]
Ditto,	[illegible]	[illegible]	For [illegible] years from [illegible] Sept., [illegible]	[illegible]	[illegible]	[illegible]

APPENDIX No. 20.

App. No. 20.

Names of Commissioners of Wicklow.

Names of Commissioners of Wicklow.

John [illegible], Chairman,	Gentleman.	Joseph [illegible],	[illegible] and Wine Merchant.
George Wynne,	Secretary Grand Jury and County Treasurer.	[illegible]	[illegible]
John [illegible]	[illegible], Wicklow.	[illegible]	Draper.
[illegible]	Medical Doctor.	Thomas [illegible],	Draper.
John Kelly [illegible],	[illegible], Co. Wicklow.	[illegible]	Draper.
[illegible]	[illegible]	William [illegible],	[illegible] and Stationer.
Joseph O'Connell,	Coal Merchant.	John [illegible],	[illegible]
William [illegible],	Baker.	John [illegible],	[illegible]
Joseph [illegible],	[illegible], Ironmonger.	Thomas [illegible],	Wine and Spirit Merchant.
Michael M'Cabe,	[illegible]	James [illegible],	Coal Merchant.
		Henry [illegible],	[illegible]

APPENDIX No. 91.

WICKLOW.

9th Geo. IV., cap. 82. Number of Commissioners, 21. Number of Burgesses, 115. Population in 1871, 3,164. Acreage within Municipal Boundary not ascertainable. Rateable value of Lands and Buildings, £4,000. No Rates have ever been levied except a 6d. rate in 1836.

Abstract of the Accounts of the Receipts and Expenditure of the Town Commissioners of Wicklow for the Year ended the 31st December, 1875.

Receipts.

	£	s.	d.	£	s.	d.
To Balances at end of previous year:—						
In Treasurer's hands,	479	8	2			
In Town Clerk's hands,	65	16	9			
In Agent's hands,	17	13	6½			
				563	11	4½
" Railway Company, in lieu of supply of Surplus Water,				10	0	0
" Rents of Corporation Property,				1,171	3	11
" Dog License Duty,				6	17	7
" Interest from Treasurer,				9	15	1
				£1,791	1	9

Expenditure.

	£	s.	d.	£	s.	d.
By New Works and Repairs, including £20 to County Wicklow Grand Jury towards ... and £97 ... for repairs of Town Hall and widening lane,				811	4	4½
" Cleansing and Watering the Town,				15	10	6
" Water Supply,				212	10	6
" Lighting:—Gas Company for Lighting Public Lamps,				153	1	1
" Rent and Taxes,				71	8	3½
" Interest:						
On Mortgage and Bond,	£342	11	6			
To Gas Company on Capital expended in erecting Lamp Posts,	9	0	0			
Treasurer on Advances,	2	1	7			
				353	13	1
" Salaries and Agent's Fees:—						
Town Clerk,	50	0	0			
Town Sergeant,	21	0	0			
Agent's Fees,	56	11	0			
				127	11	0
" Printing, Advertisements, and Stationery,				27	13	6
" Postage and Receipt Stamps,				1	6	4
" Law Expenses,				4	4	0
" Disallowed by Auditor,				20	3	0
				1,330	16	4
" Balances at end of year:—						
In Treasurer's hands,	429	19	3			
In Agent's hands,	18	0	8½			
In Town Clerk's hands,	12	13	4½			
				460	4	7
				£1,791	1	9

I certify that the foregoing is a true abstract of the Accounts of the Town Commissioners of Wicklow for the year ended 31st December, 1875.

Dated 20th October, 1876.

George W. Finlay, Auditor.

www.ingramcontent.com/pod-product-compliance
Lightning Source LLC
Chambersburg PA
CBHW021845230426
43669CB00008B/1090
* 9 7 8 3 7 4 1 1 0 4 5 5 8 *